Preparing for the

REGENTS EXAMINATION

ALGEBRA 2

and

TRIGONOMETRY

Ann Davidian
Mathematics Department Chair
General Douglas MacArthur High School
Levittown, New York

Christine T. Healy
Teacher of Mathematics, Retired
Bethpage High School
Bethpage, New York

AMSCO

AMSCO SCHOOL PUBLICATIONS, INC.
315 Hudson Street, New York, N.Y. 10013

Dedication

To John, Michael, and Liza—thanks so much for all of your love and support.

To Rosemary Kaste and Dr. Michael Totoro—in appreciation for your encouragement and mathematical assistance.

For Savannah, Kathleen, Maria, T.J., Ryan, and all the students who will use this book. Good luck on your Regents!

Reviewers

Steven J. Balasiano
Assistant Principal,
    Supervision Mathematics
Canarsie High School
Brooklyn, NY

Debbie Calvino
Mathematics Supervisor,
    Grades 7–12
Valley Central High School
Montgomery, NY

Sal Sutera
Teacher of Mathematics
New Utrecht High School
Brooklyn, NY

Text Design by Monotype, LLC
Cover Design by Meghan J. Shupe
Composition and art by Progressive Information Technologies
Cover Photo Jupiter Images/Image Ideas

Please visit our Web site at:
   www.amscopub.com

Regents Examination included: 6/10 and 8/10

Additional Practice Examinations can be found at
Amsco's eLearning site: *amscoelearning.com*.

When ordering this book, please specify either **R 238 W** or
PREPARING FOR THE REGENTS EXAMINATION: ALGEBRA 2
AND TRIGONOMETRY

ISBN 978-1-56765-705-0

NYC Item: 56765-705-9

Printed in the United States of America

6 7 8 9 10   14 13 12 11 10

Contents

Chapter 3: Real Numbers and Radicals

Chapter 4: Relations and Functions

Chapter 5: Quadratic Functions and Complex Numbers

Chapter 6: Sequences and Series

Chapter 7: Exponential Functions

Chapter 8: Logarithmic Functions

Chapter 16: Probability

Assessment

Cumulative Reviews

Algebra 2 and Trigonometry Regents Examinations

Sources

Index

Getting Started

About This Book

Welcome to *Preparing for the Regents Examination Algebra 2 and Trigonometry*, written for you, the student. In recent years, New York State has changed the Regents Examinations in many subject areas. Mathematics A and B Regents Examinations are being replaced with a three-year three Regents Examination series for high school mathematics. The third examination is the Algebra 2 and Trigonometry Regents. This book is designed to help you review the necessary mathematics to meet the performance standards outlined for the Algebra 2 and Trigonometry Regents in the 2005 Performance Indicators listed in the New York State Core Curriculum. We hope that, in this review book, we have offered you a sufficient number of explanations and problems to fully acquaint you with the format and type of questions you can expect to see on the Algebra 2 and Trigonometry Examination.

Preparing for the Regents Examination Algebra 2 and Trigonometry contains topic reviews with Model Problems, Practice, Chapter Reviews, and Cumulative Reviews to help you study. The problems in these sections incorporate both content and problem-solving situations that are similar to those found in the Core Curriculum and on the Regents Examinations. The book also contains three practice tests to assist you in preparing for your Regents Examination. In addition, *Preparing for the Regents Examination Algebra 2 and Trigonometry* also contains what we call FYI, For Your Information, sections before Chapter Reviews to introduce you to the mechanics of your TI-83+/TI-84+ calculator. Some of the questions on the Algebra 2 and Trigonometry Regents can be solved more easily if you are comfortable performing operations on the calculator, not only to solve problems but also to check those you are required to solve showing all your work.

How to Use This Book

- **Read** the material that is presented. This book was written for you to read.
- **Do the Model Problems.** Don't just read them. Use paper and pencil to work the problems out. When you are finished, see how your solution and your

answer compare with the method shown in the book. Remember, there are often alternative ways to solve many of these problems, but you should arrive at the same answer.

- **Do the Practice Problems and the Chapter Reviews.** Sometimes it is helpful to work with a friend. Remember, mathematics is not a spectator sport—you learn by doing.
- **Use the Cumulative Reviews** to refresh your memory on many topics. You can either do each Cumulative Review as you finish the chapter, or save them all until you have finished the book. Since the Regents Examination is cumulative, you must constantly review concepts that were previously covered.
- **Do the Regents Examination** that is provided in the back of the book. Answering these questions will give you a good idea of how you may perform on your examination.
- **Start NOW!** Do not wait until the last minute, hoping to cram all of the information into your head. Learning mathematics takes time! Many concepts are built from concepts previously learned and you cannot comprehend all of this at once.

Test-Taking Strategies

General Strategies

- <u>Become familiar with the directions and format of the test ahead of time.</u> The Algebra 2 and Trigonometry Regents Examination has four parts with a total of 39 questions. You must answer *all* of the questions. There are 27 multiple-choice questions and 12 questions where you must show your work. For each of the 12 open-ended questions, you must show the steps you used to solve the problem, including formulas, diagrams, graphs, charts, and so forth, where appropriate.
- <u>Be aware of how the test is scored.</u> Part I consists of 27 multiple-choice questions, worth two points each. There is no partial credit and you must answer every one of them. Part II contains eight questions worth two points each. Part III contains three questions worth four points each. Part IV contains one question worth six points. For Parts II, III, and IV, you *must* show your work and answer all of the questions in each part. A correct numerical answer without the appropriate work will receive only one point. The entire test is worth 88 points. The test is then scaled to produce a numerical grade equivalent to the score out of 100 points.
- <u>Pace yourself.</u> You have three hours to answer 39 questions. Do not race to answer every question immediately. On the other hand, do not linger over any problem too long. Keep in mind that you will need more time to complete Parts II, III, and IV, since you will have to show your work.
- <u>Practice, Practice, Practice.</u> The more you practice, the more comfortable you will be with the material.
- <u>Write in the test booklet.</u> Scrap paper is not permitted for any part of the Regents Examination. You must use the blank spaces in the booklet as your scrap paper. A sheet of *scrap* graph paper is provided at the end of the booklet. Be aware that any work done on the graph paper will *not* be scored.
- <u>Keep track of your place on the answer sheet.</u> A separate answer sheet is provided for Part I. If you find yourself bogged down on a problem, skip it and come back to it later. Make a note in the margin of the test booklet so that you

can locate the skipped problem easily. Be careful when you skip a problem. Be sure to leave the answer line blank that corresponds to the question you skipped. In fact, many students prefer to do all of the Part I questions and then check them before entering any answers on the answer sheet.

Specific Strategies

- <u>Do not assume that your answer is correct just because it appears among the choices.</u> The wrong choices usually represent common student errors. After you find an answer, always reread the problem to make sure you have chosen the answer to the question that is asked, not the question you have in your mind.
- <u>Familiarize yourself with the formula sheet</u> included in your Regents. When you get your examination booklet, detach the page and keep it on your desk for easy reference.
- <u>Do not leave any blanks on the multiple-choice questions (Part I).</u> There is no penalty for guessing on this test.
- <u>Be certain to show all work on the open-ended questions (Parts II, III, and IV).</u> Even if you are not completely sure of your answer, you will receive partial credit for appropriate, correct mathematics shown.
- <u>Do not round values too soon!</u> If you find an answer to the first part of a question using your calculator and realize you will need it for another part of the question, be sure to store the number in your calculator and then recall it for further use. Remember that you must use, until the very last step of the problem, all of the decimal places found on your calculator for any necessary calculations. Then you should round your answer to the specified decimal place.
- <u>Make a sketch and label it</u> to assist you in your solution, if a question contains information about a geometric figure or you need to visualize what the question is asking.

If you follow these strategies, you will become comfortable with the material and will do your best work on the test. Good luck! We hope our book will help you to ace the exam!

Ann Davidian & Christine T. Healy

The Integers

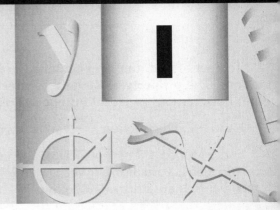

1.1 Reviewing Real Numbers

The first numbers most of us learn are the **counting numbers**: 1, 2, 3, ... (The three dots indicate that the numbers continue forever.) Another name for counting numbers is **natural numbers**. If we include zero, we get the set of **whole numbers**. The whole numbers are 0, 1, 2, 3, ...

By extending the set of whole numbers to include negative numbers, we have the set of **integers**. The integers are . . . , −3, −2, −1, 0, 1, 2, 3, ... Notice the . . . to the right of 3 and to the left of −3. This indicates that the set of integers continues forever in both directions.

To include the numbers between integers, we must define the set of rational numbers. A **rational number** is a number that can be expressed as a ratio in the form $\frac{a}{b}$, where a and b are both integers, and $b \neq 0$.

Note that the set of rational numbers also includes the set of integers, since every integer a can be expressed as $\frac{a}{1}$.

If a number is not rational, it is said to be irrational. An irrational number is a number that cannot be expressed in the form $\frac{a}{b}$, where a and b are both integers, and $b \neq 0$. Instead, an **irrational number** is a nonrepeating, nonterminating decimal. Examples of irrational numbers include π, $\sqrt{2}$, 0.12112211122211112222. . . . These numbers, when expressed in decimal form, never end, and never repeat. (Note: Although we often use $\frac{22}{7}$ as an approximation for π, it is only an approximation since π is an irrational number.)

A calculator can be used to find the approximate rational value of many irrational numbers.

Enter: $\sqrt{3}$
Display: 1.732050808

The value of this number can be rounded to the nearest thousandth to produce $\sqrt{3} \approx 1.732$. However, when asked for an exact answer, it would be $\sqrt{3}$.

The set of **real numbers** is the union of the set of rational numbers and the set of irrational numbers. Every real number can be associated with a point on the number line and every point on the number line can be associated with a real number. On the number line, numbers increase from left to right.

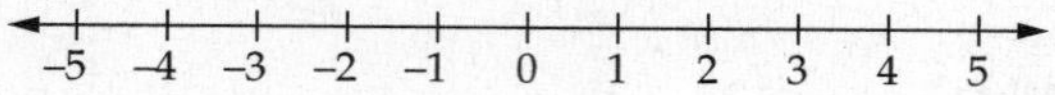

The set of real numbers contains more points than are illustrated in the figure above. The **property of density** assures us that there is always another real number between any two real numbers. For example, the number -1.34 lies between -1 and -2. The fraction $\dfrac{19}{4}$ can be rewritten as 4.75, which we know lies between 4 and 5. Since $\sqrt{7} \approx 2.645751311$, it lies between 2 and 3. We know that $\pi \approx 3.141592654$, so it lies between 3 and 4. The positions of these numbers on the number line are illustrated below.

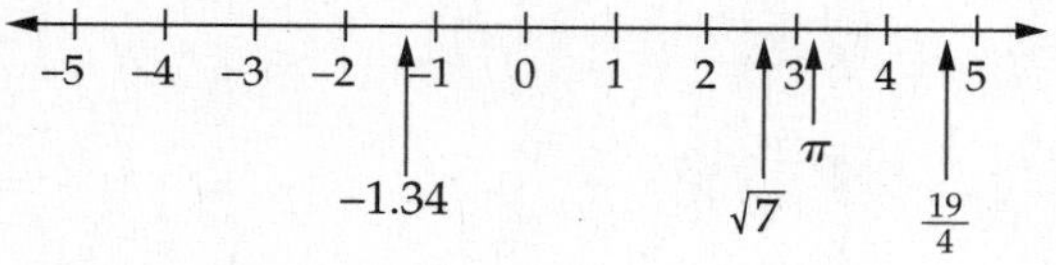

MODEL PROBLEM

Match each value with the letter on the number line that shows its position.

$\sqrt{10}, -\dfrac{4}{9}, \sqrt{2}, -\sqrt{15}, 4.6, -\dfrac{9}{5}, \sqrt{22}$

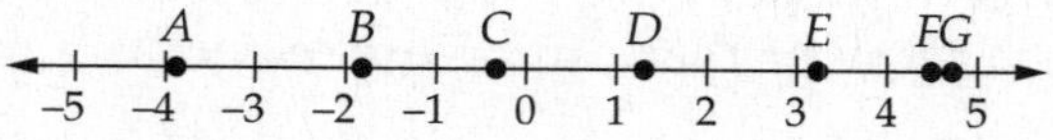

SOLUTION

The easiest way to determine the placement of each of these values on the number line is to express them as decimals.

Use a calculator to approximate each value.

$\sqrt{10} \approx 3.16227766$ This point lies between 3 and 4 and matches point E.

$-\dfrac{4}{9} = -0.44444444\ldots$ This point lies between 0 and -1 and matches point C.

$\sqrt{2} \approx 1.1414213562$ This point lies between 1 and 2 and matches point D.

$-\sqrt{15} \approx -3.872983346$ This point lies between -3 and -4 and matches point A.

4.6   This point lies between 4 and 5. Since there are two points indicated between 4 and 5, we'll have to wait to see which of the two points represents this value.

$-\dfrac{9}{5} = -1.8$ This point lies between -1 and -2 and matches point B.

$\sqrt{22} \approx 4.69041576$ This number is greater than 4.6 so 4.6 matches point F and $\sqrt{22}$ matches point G.

Answer: $A = -\sqrt{15}, B = -\dfrac{9}{5}, C = -\dfrac{4}{9}, D = \sqrt{2}, E = \sqrt{10}, F = 4.6,$ and $G = \sqrt{22}$

 Practice

Exercises 1–8: Which of the following numbers are rational and which are irrational? Justify your answer.

1 -0.5

2 $0.45454545\ldots$

3 $\sqrt{25}$

4 $\sqrt{35}$

5 0

6 $0.12112111211112\ldots$

7 π

8 $\sqrt{\dfrac{1}{2}}$

Exercises 9–15: State whether the statement is true or false and why.

9   All rational numbers are real numbers.

10   All real numbers are rational numbers.

11   All counting numbers are whole numbers.

12   All whole numbers are counting numbers.

13   A number can be both rational and irrational.

14   A number can be both real and irrational.

15   The set of whole numbers is the same as the set of natural numbers.

Exercises 16–19: Name two integers between which each number lies.

16 π

17 $\sqrt{2}$

18 $\sqrt{\dfrac{1}{2}}$

19 $\sqrt{101}$

Exercises 20–25: Arrange each of the following sets of numbers in order from least to greatest. (If two numbers are equal to each other, state that they are equal.)

20 $1.4, 4.4, 0.444$

21 $\sqrt{5}, 2\sqrt{2}, \dfrac{\sqrt{8}}{2}$

22 $\dfrac{7}{3}, \sqrt{7}, \sqrt{\dfrac{7}{3}}$

23 $\dfrac{1}{2}, \sqrt{\dfrac{1}{2}}, \dfrac{1}{\sqrt{2}}$

24 $\pi, \dfrac{22}{7}, 3.14$

25 $\dfrac{1}{3}, \dfrac{3}{10}, 0.33333$

1.2 Writing and Solving Equations and Inequalities

Equations

An **equation** is defined as a mathematical statement of equality. Each of these equations has only one solution.

$$5x + 3 = 18 \qquad 12 - 2x = x - 9 \qquad 4(x - 4) = x + 2(x - 5)$$

To solve these equations, we use inverse operations to relocate the terms so the variables are on one side of the equal sign and constants on the other.

$5x + 3 = 18$ Since the 3 is being added, we use the inverse operation,
$\quad -3 \quad -3$ subtraction, to relocate it.

$\quad 5x = 15$ Since 5 is multiplying the variable, we divide both sides by 5.

$\quad \div 5 \quad \div 5$

$\qquad x = 3$ The solution to this equation is 3.

In the next equation, there are variables and constants on both sides, so we need to relocate the terms. Remember, it does not matter whether you move variables to the left and constants to the right or vice versa; your solution will be the same.

$12 - 2x = x - 9$ Since the $2x$ is negative, we add $2x$ to each side of the equation.

$\quad 12 = 3x - 9$ Now we perform another inverse operation, adding 9 to each side.

$\quad 21 = 3x$ Next we perform the inverse of multiplication; we divide by 3.

$\quad 7 = x$ The solution to this equation is 7.

The solution of the last equation requires the distributive property as well as inverse operations.

$4(x - 4) = x + 2(x - 5)$ First, multiply each expression in parentheses by the constant in front of it. On the left, multiply each term in the parentheses by 4. On the right, each term in the parentheses is multiplied by 2.

$4x - 16 = x + 2x - 10$ Combine like terms.

$4x - 16 = 3x - 10$ Since the 16 is negative, use the inverse operation; add 16 to each side of the equation.

$\quad 4x = 3x + 6$ Now subtract $3x$ from each side of the equation.

$\quad x = 6$ The solution to this equation is 6.

Sometimes you will be asked to write an equation that describes a particular situation. It is helpful to think of this as a translation from English into algebra. Just as in a foreign language, there is a specific vocabulary with which you must be familiar in order to translate accurately. In algebra, certain words and phrases will always refer to specific operations, as indicated in the table on the next page. Note that the variable n replaces the phrase "a number."

English Phrase	Operation	Algebra
Four **more than** a number	Addition	$4 + n$
Five **greater than** a number	Addition	$5 + n$
A number **increased by 14**	Addition	$n + 14$
A number **exceeded by 2**	Addition	$n + 2$
Twelve **decreased by a number**	Subtraction	$12 - n$
Ten **less than** a number	Subtraction	$n - 10$
One **smaller than** a number	Subtraction	$n - 1$
The difference between a number and four	Subtraction	$n - 4$
The product of a number and seven	Multiplication	$7n$
Three **times** a number	Multiplication	$3n$
Twice a number	Multiplication	$2n$
One-half **of** a number	Multiplication	$\frac{1}{2}n$
A number **divided by** six	Division	$\frac{n}{6}$

The expressions in the table above include only some of the many key words that indicate mathematical operations. See how many more you can think of for each of the four operations.

Inequalities

An **inequality** is a mathematical statement that indicates that two quantities are related but not equal. One may be greater than ($>$) the other, greater than or equal to the other ($\geq$), less than the other ($<$), or less than or equal to the other ($\leq$). The procedure for writing the inequality is the same as that for equations, but we use a different symbol and rather than just one solution, we can have an infinite number of solutions.

MODEL PROBLEMS

Translate the given information into an equation or inequality and solve.

1   Ariel loves to go to baseball games. This season she has already attended 23 New York Ducks games. If Ariel attended nine more weekend games than weekday games, how many weekday games did she attend?

SOLUTION

Let g = the number of weekday games

$9 + g$ = the number of weekend games

$g + 9 + g = 23$ Combine like terms.

$2g + 9 = 23$ Use an inverse operation to eliminate the 9.

$2g = 14$ Use an inverse operation to eliminate the 2.

$g = 7$

To check:

Replace the g in your initial expressions with 7.

7 = weekday games

$9 + 7 = 16$ = weekend games

Since $7 + 16 = 23$, the solution checks.

Answer: Ariel attended 16 weekend games and 7 weekday games.

2   Last year Matthias's uncle worked for the Ducks. Therefore, Matthias attended more home Ducks games than Paco. In fact, Matthias went to one more than twice the home games Paco did. If the two of them attended a total of at least fifty-eight home games, how many home games might Paco and Matthias actually have attended last year?

SOLUTION

Let h = home games Paco attended

$1 + 2h$ = home games Matthias attended

$h + 1 + 2h \geq 58$ Combine like terms.

$3h + 1 \geq 58$ Use an inverse operation to eliminate the 1.

$3h \geq 57$ Use an inverse operation to eliminate the 3.

$h \geq 19$

$1 + 2h \geq 39$

Answer: Last season, Paco attended 19 or more home games and Matthias attended at least 39 home games.

3   Last Halloween, the local Teens' Club had a party for the sixth graders. There were c students in costume and $2c$ less than twenty-four students not in costume. If there were more than eighteen students present, what is the greatest possible number of students who were not in costume?

SOLUTION

Let c = students in costume

$24 - 2c$ = students not in costume

$24 - 2c + c > 18$

$24 - c > 18$

$-c > -6$

$c < 6$

Note: When solving an inequality, multiplying or dividing by a negative number changes the direction of the inequality.

Answer: The greatest possible value of c is 5.

 **Practice**

Exercises 1–10: Solve the following equations and inequalities.

1 $14 - 5x = 2x$

2 $3x + 7 = 43 - x$

3 $8x + 4 = 2x + 28$

4 $6x - 6 = 2(x + 13)$

5 $5x - 11 = 2(x + 5)$

6 $4(x + 4) = x + 2(x + 11)$

7 $3x + 1 \geq x - 7$

8 $4(2x + 3) \leq x - 2$

9 $3x - 7 < 2 - (2x + 6)$

10 $14 + 3(x + 2) > 3 - 2(x + 9)$

Exercises 11–18: Translate the following situations into algebraic equations or inequalities and solve.

11 Eight more than twice a number is equivalent to three times the number.

12 Three times a number increased by eight is five less than twice the number plus seventeen.

13 Seven increased by four less than twice a number is twelve more than the number.

14 The difference between five times a number and eleven is greater than or equal to three times the number decreased by one.

15 Mr. Morales often buys books for his children. The number of books he bought in February exceeded the number of books he bought in January by three. In March he bought 4 more than twice the number of books he bought in January. In April he bought twice as many books as he bought in January and February combined, but in May the number of books he bought was only half the number of books he purchased in March. In June, his shopping produced two fewer than the books he bought in March. If Mr. Morales bought a total of 50 books between January and June, how many did he purchase each month?

16 Iris earns $8.90 an hour as a lifeguard at the Pierce County Country Club. She also receives d dollars a day meal credit when she works six or more hours. Last week, she worked five hours Monday and Tuesday, six hours Wednesday and Friday, and eight hours on Saturday. Find the value of d if her net pay was $313.50.

17 Kelly volunteered to help at the Special Olympics at the Nassau County Aquatic Center. She was put in charge of a souvenir booth that sold calendars, beach towels, and swimsuits to help support the Special Olympics. The calendars sold for $10 each, the towels for $15, and the swimsuits for $24. Kelly sold twice as many calendars as swimsuits, and sixteen more towels than swimsuits. If she sold 452 items,

a how many items were swimsuits, towels, and calendars?
b how much money did Kelly collect (tax was already included in the price)?

18 Colby told his twin sister Carlyn that he could sell more magazine subscriptions for the senior class than she could. Colby sold eight more than twice what their friend Paolo sold and Carlyn sold two more than three times the number Paolo sold. If the three of them sold a total of forty-six subscriptions, was Colby right? How many did each of the seniors sell?

1.3 Absolute Value Equations and Inequalities

Absolute Value Equations

The absolute value of a number n is the distance from n to the origin. The symbol for the absolute value of n is $|n|$. Thus, $|5| = 5$ and $|-5| = 5$ since the distance from both positive 5 to 0 and negative 5 to 0 is 5. Algebraically, $|n| = \begin{cases} n \text{ if } n \geq 0 \\ -n \text{ if } n < 0 \end{cases}$

MODEL PROBLEMS

1 Solve for x: $|x| = 8$

SOLUTION

We must think about what number(s) are at a distance of 8 units from the origin. Since both 8 and -8 are 8 units from the origin, the solution is $x = 8$ or $x = -8$.

Answer: $x = 8, x = -8$

2 Solve for x: $|x + 2| = 9$

SOLUTION

We know that $x + 2$ must equal 9 or -9. Therefore, we set up two equations:

$$x + 2 = 9 \qquad x + 2 = -9$$
$$x = 7 \qquad x = -11$$

We must now check that the solutions to our equations work in the original equation.

Check:
$$|x + 2| = 9 \qquad\qquad |x + 2| = 9$$
$$|7 + 2| \stackrel{?}{=} 9 \qquad\qquad |-11 + 2| \stackrel{?}{=} 9$$
$$|9| \stackrel{?}{=} 9 \qquad\qquad |-9| \stackrel{?}{=} 9$$
$$9 = 9 ✔ \qquad\qquad 9 = 9 ✔$$

Answer: $\{7, -11\}$

3 Find the solution set: $|2a - 4| = 10$

SOLUTION

$$2a - 4 = 10 \qquad 2a - 4 = -10$$
$$2a = 14 \qquad\quad 2a = -6$$
$$a = 7 \qquad\qquad a = -3$$

Check:

$\|2a - 4\| = 10$	$\|2a - 4\| = 10$
$\|2(7) - 4\| \stackrel{?}{=} 10$	$\|2(-3) - 4\| \stackrel{?}{=} 10$
$\|14 - 4\| \stackrel{?}{=} 10$	$\|-6 - 4\| \stackrel{?}{=} 10$
$\|10\| \stackrel{?}{=} 10$	$\|-10\| \stackrel{?}{=} 10$
$10 = 10$ ✔	$10 = 10$ ✔

Answer: $\{-3, 7\}$

4   Solve: $\|5n - 4\| + 18 = 8$

SOLUTION

First, isolate the absolute value:

$\|5n - 4\| = -10$

Answer: { } The solution set is empty.

5   Solve: $\|x + 6\| - 18 = 2x$

SOLUTION

$\|x + 6\| - 18 = 2x$

First, isolate the absolute value: $\|x + 6\| = 2x + 18$

Then create two separate equations and solve:

$x + 6 = 2x + 18$	$x + 6 = -2x - 18$
$6 = x + 18$	$6 = -3x - 18$
$x = -12$	$-3x = 24$
	$x = -8$

Check in the original equation:

$\|x + 6\| - 18 = 2x$	$\|x + 6\| - 18 = 2x$
$\|-12 + 6\| - 18 \stackrel{?}{=} 2(-12)$	$\|-8 + 6\| - 18 \stackrel{?}{=} 2(-8)$
$\|-6\| - 18 \stackrel{?}{=} -24$	$\|-2\| - 18 \stackrel{?}{=} -16$
$6 - 18 \stackrel{?}{=} -24$	$2 - 18 \stackrel{?}{=} -16$
$-12 \neq -24$ Doesn't check	$-16 = -16$ ✔

Answer: The solution set is $\{-8\}$, which can be shown on a number line.

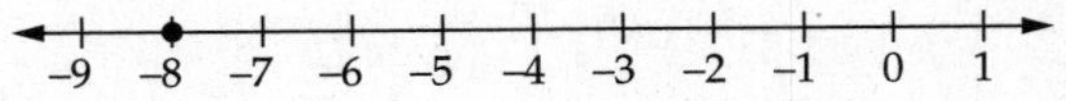

> **Note:** There is no number whose absolute value is negative.

 **Practice**

Exercises 1–6: Solve each equation and check the answer.

1 $|3x - 6| = 12$

2 $|2y + 5| = 11$

3 $5 + |8 - 4z| = 13$

4 $|5n - 10| - 4 = 11$

5 $|c - 6| = 2c - 3$

6 $|4r + 5| + 3r = 10$

Exercises 7–12: Select the numeral preceding the choice that best completes the statement or answers the question.

7 What is the solution set of $|4n + 8| = 16$?

   (1) $\{-6\}$ (3) $\{-6, 2\}$
   (2) $\{2\}$ (4) $\{\ \}$

8 What is the solution set of $|2 - y| = 3$?

   (1) $\{-5, -1\}$ (3) $\{-1, 5\}$
   (2) $\{-5, 1\}$ (4) $\{1, 5\}$

9 Solve for x: $|2x - 6| - x = 3$

   (1) $x = 1, x = 9$
   (2) $x = -9, x = -1$
   (3) $x = 1$
   (4) $x = -9$

10 Which equation has no solution?

   (1) $|2x - 3| - 4 = 7$
   (2) $|2x + 3| - 4x = 7$
   (3) $|4 - x| = 5$
   (4) $|4 - x| + 10 = 4$

11 Which equation represents the numbers whose distance from 7 is 6 units?

   (1) $x - 7 = 6$ (3) $x - 6 = 7$
   (2) $|x - 7| = 6$ (4) $|x - 6| = 7$

12 The solution set to which equation is $\{-4, 12\}$?

   (1) $\left|\dfrac{3}{2}x - 6\right| = 12$

   (2) $\left|\dfrac{2}{3}x - 6\right| = 12$

   (3) $\left|\dfrac{3}{2}x + 6\right| = 6$

   (4) $\left|\dfrac{2}{3}x + 6\right| = 12$

13 The distance from a number, x, to the number 10 is seven units on the number line.

   a Write an equation involving absolute value that could be used to express this information.
   b Solve the above equation to find possible value(s) for x.

14 The distance from a point P to the origin is 5 more than twice the value of P.

   a Write an equation involving absolute value that could be used to express this information.
   b Solve the above equation to find possible value(s) for P.

15 The average age of a student in Claudine's math class is 16 years old. However, the difference between Claudine's age, a, and the average age of 16 is half a year.

   a Write an equation involving absolute value that could be used to express this information.
   b Solve the above equation to find a.

Absolute Value Inequalities

In solving absolute value inequalities we must consider the range of numbers that will fulfill our requirements. To find the solution for $|x| = 5$, we must remember that the solution set is $x = 5$ and $x = -5$. Given $|x| < 5$, we must also consider both 5 and -5. We would want all values of x between these two numbers: $-5 < x < 5$. Given $|x| > 5$, we must again consider both 5 and -5. However, in this case we need the numbers whose absolute values are greater than 5. Thus, our solution set is $x > 5$ or $x < -5$.

MODEL PROBLEMS

Solve:

   a $|x + 3| < 5$

   b $|5x - 2| \geq 18$

SOLUTION

   a $|x + 3| < 5$

     We consider the two cases:

     $x + 3 < 5 \qquad x + 3 > -5$

     and solve:

       $x < 2 \qquad\quad x > -8$

     Putting the two solutions together, we obtain: $-8 < x < 2$.

     We can actually do all of this work at once.

     $|x + 3| < 5$

     When we consider the two cases:

     $x + 3 < 5 \qquad x + 3 > -5$

     we are looking for values of x *between* -5 and 5.

     Therefore,

     $-5 < x + 3 < 5$

     Subtract 3 from each of the three parts of the inequality to find the range of values for x.

Answer: $-8 < x < 2$

On a number line the solution would look like this:

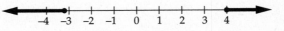

   b $|5x - 2| \geq 18$

     Set up the two inequalities and solve.

     $5x - 2 \geq 18 \qquad 5x - 2 \leq -18$

       $5x \geq 20 \qquad\quad 5x \leq -16$

        $x \geq 4 \qquad\quad\;\; x \leq -3.2$

Answer: The solution set is $\{x : x \leq -3.2 \text{ or } x \geq 4\}$.

The graph is as follows:

Exercises 1–7: Solve the absolute value inequality.

1 $|2a| + 4 \leq 24$

2 $|3x - 6| > 21$

3 $|5d + 2| \leq 22$

4 $\left|\dfrac{x + 4}{3}\right| \geq 5$

5 $\left|\dfrac{n}{2} - 4\right| > 3$

6 $|7y| - 2 < 12$

7 $|3m - 6| + 4 \geq 22$

Exercises 8–13: Select the numeral preceding the choice that best answers the question.

8 Which is the graph of the solution set of $|10x - 20| \geq 30$?

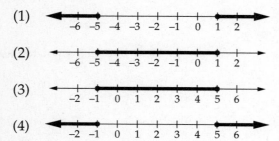

(1)

(2)

(3)

(4)

9 Which inequality has the solution set represented by the graph below?

(1) $|4x - 2| - 6 \leq 8$
(2) $|4x + 2| - 6 \leq 8$
(3) $|4x - 2| + 6 \leq 8$
(4) $|4x + 2| + 6 \leq 8$

10 What is the solution set of $|8x - 4| > 20$?

(1) $\{x : x < -2 \text{ or } x > 3\}$
(2) $\{x : x < -3 \text{ or } x > 2\}$
(3) $\{x : -2 < x < 3\}$
(4) $\{x : -3 < x < 2\}$

11 What is the solution set of $|6x - 3| < 21$?

(1) $\{x : x < -4 \text{ or } x > 3\}$
(2) $\{x : x < -3 \text{ or } x > 4\}$
(3) $\{x : -4 < x < 3\}$
(4) $\{x : -3 < x < 4\}$

12 At Jennifer's sweet sixteen party, all of her friends were within 6 months of her age. Using a to represent the age of Jennifer's friends in years, which inequality would represent this statement?

(1) $a - 16 \leq 6$ (3) $|a - 16| \leq 6$
(2) $a - 16 \leq 0.5$ (4) $|a - 16| \leq 0.5$

13 The average IQ for people of all ages is said to be approximately 100. If most people's IQ falls within 15 points of the average, which inequality would represent this statement? (Use I to represent a person's IQ.)

(1) $I - 15 \leq 100$ (3) $|I - 100| \leq 15$
(2) $I - 100 \leq 15$ (4) $|I - 100| \geq 15$

14 Normal body temperature is 98.6°F.

a If a person is considered unhealthy if his or her body temperature differs from 98.6°F by 1.4° or more, express this as an absolute value inequality.

b Solve the absolute value inequality to determine what body temperatures would be considered unhealthy.

15 Con Sistent is an excellent baseball player. His batting average always falls within .010 points of .500.

a Write an absolute value inequality that will express this fact.

b Solve the absolute value inequality to determine the range of Con's batting average.

16 When an oven is set to 350°, the temperature varies slightly from this setting. When the temperature varies by more than 7°, the oven will turn on (or off) until it reaches 350° again.

a Write an absolute value inequality that will express this fact.

b Solve the absolute value inequality to determine when the oven will turn on or off.

1.4 Adding and Subtracting Polynomials

A **polynomial** is an algebraic expression consisting of one or more monomials being combined through addition or subtraction.

Examples: $5a^2 + 3b$ $-2x^2 + 3xy - y^2$ $4c^4 + 2c^3 + 5c^2$ $-7x^2y^3z - 2$

The **degree of a polynomial** is the largest sum of the exponents of the variables in one term.

Examples:

$5a^2 + 3b$	Degree: 2
$-2x^2 + 3xy - y^2$	Degree: 2
$4c^4 + 2c^3 + 5c^2$	Degree: 4
$-7x^2y^3z - 2$	Degree: 6

When adding or subtracting polynomials, we combine the coefficients of like terms but keep the exponents unchanged.

MODEL PROBLEMS

1 Add: $(4x^3 - 2x^2 + 7x - 5) + (-2x^3 + x^2 - 4x - 3)$

SOLUTION

Since there are four terms in each expression, we can rewrite the problem to show like terms written as follows:

$(4 + (-2))x^3 + ((-2) + 1)x^2 + (7 + (-4))x + (-5 + (-3))$

or rewrite the two polynomials vertically, aligning the like terms:

$$\begin{array}{r} 4x^3 - 2x^2 + 7x - 5 \\ -2x^3 + x^2 - 4x - 3 \\ \hline \end{array}$$

Either way, combine the coefficients of the like terms.

Answer: $2x^3 - x^2 + 3x - 8$

2 Simplify: $6x^a - 7y^b + 4x^a + y^b$

SOLUTION

Combine like terms.

$6x^a + 4x^a - 7y^b + y^b$

Answer: $10x^a - 6y^b$

Although the exponents in this problem are variables, they are treated the same way as numerical exponents. Like terms are combined and exponents are unchanged.

3 Subtract: $6x^4y + 2x^2y^3 - 4xy^4$
$\qquad\qquad\quad 2x^4y + 5x^2y^3 + 7xy^4$

SOLUTION

Remember, to subtract in algebra, we change all the signs of the subtrahend, and then combine like terms. The new problem can be written as: $(6 + (-2))x^4y + (2 + (-5))x^2y^3 + (-4 + (-7))xy^4$

or $6x^4y + 2x^2y^3 - 4xy^4$
$\quad -2x^4y - 5x^2y^3 - 7xy^4$

Combine like terms.

Answer: $4x^4y - 3x^2y^3 - 11xy^4$

4 Find the degree of the polynomial that results after performing the following:

$(-6a^3 + 5a^2b + ab^2 - 4b^3) + (2a^3 - 3a^2b + 3ab^2 - b^3)$

SOLUTION

Again, think of the problem as though it had been written as

$(-6 + 2)a^3 + (5 + (-3))a^2b + (1 + 3)ab^2 + (-4 + (-1))b^3$

or

$-6a^3 + 5a^2b + \ ab^2 - 4b^3$
$\ \ 2a^3 - 3a^2b + 3ab^2 - \ b^3$

Combine like terms to get the polynomial: $-4a^3 + 2a^2b + 4ab^2 - 5b^3$

Find the sum of the exponents in each term of the polynomial:

$-4a^3 + 2a^2b + 4ab^2 - 5b^3$

The degree of each term is 3.

Answer: This is a third-degree polynomial or a polynomial of degree 3.

 Practice

Exercises 1–7: Perform the indicated operations and state the degree of the polynomial that results after performing those operations.

1 Add: $3x^4 - 2x^3 + 2x^2 - 5x - 4$
$\qquad\quad -4x^4 + \ x^3 + 3x^2 + 7x + 9$

2 Subtract: $c^5d^2 - 2c^4d^3 + 14c^3d^4$
$\qquad\qquad\quad 2c^5d^2 + 3c^4d^3 - 11c^3d^4$

3 Add: $3c^4 - 4c^3 + 2c - 11$
$\qquad\quad -4c^4 + 3c^3 + 3c + 14$

4 Subtract: $-7w^2 + 5w + 2$
$\qquad\qquad\quad 2w^2 - 4w - 2$

5 $(4x^4 + 3x^3 - 2x + 1) + (5 - 2x^2 + 5x^3 - x^4) - (6x^2 + 2x - 3)$

6 $(7y^2 + 3xy - 2x^2) - (3x^2 + 4xy - y^2) + (x^2 - 8y^2)$

7 From the sum of $(3a^2b^2 - 4a^2b + 5ab^2)$ and $(2a^2b^2 + 6a^2b - 3ab^2)$, subtract the polynomial $(-2a^2b^2 + 4a^2b - ab^2)$.

Exercises 8–15: Select the numeral preceding the choice that best answers the question.

8 Melody downloaded $4x^2 + 3x + 8$ songs to her MP3 player yesterday. Previously she had downloaded $12x^2 - 8x + 17$. If she deleted $2x^2 - x + 4$ songs, how many are on her MP3 player now?

(1) $18x^2 - 6x + 29$
(2) $14x^2 - 4x + 21$
(3) $6x^2 - 6x + 13$
(4) $14x^2 - 6x + 29$

9 Which would result in a polynomial of the second degree?

(1) $\begin{aligned} 8x^3 - 2x^2 + 3x - 7 \\ + 5x^3 + 2x^2 \quad\quad\ + 4 \end{aligned}$

(2) $\begin{aligned} 3c^4 - 5c^2 + 10 \\ -(-3c^4 + 3c^2 - 3) \end{aligned}$

(3) $\begin{aligned} 3c^4 - 5c^2 + 10 \\ +(-3c^4 + 3c^2 - 3) \end{aligned}$

(4) $\begin{aligned} 8x^3 - 2x^2 + 3x - 7 \\ - 5x^3 + 2x^2 \quad\quad\ + 4 \end{aligned}$

10 Michael spent $2x^2 - 6x + 10$ dollars at the sports store. He gave the cashier $5x^2 + x - 12$ dollars. Which expression represents the amount of change Michael received?

(1) $7x^2 - 5x - 2$ (3) $3x^2 - 7x + 22$
(2) $3x^2 - 5x - 2$ (4) $3x^2 + 7x - 22$

11 Avaril, Tiffany, and Nadia collected soda cans to recycle for a school project. Avaril collected $12c^2 + c - 4$ cans, Tiffany collected $8c^2 - 5c + 3$ cans, and Nadia brought in $7c^2 - 11c + 13$ cans. Which expression represents the total number of cans recycled by these girls?

(1) $27c^2 - 15c + 12$
(2) $19c^2 - 16c + 20$
(3) $27c^2 + 15c - 12$
(4) $27c^2 - 16c + 20$

12 Tyler, Bhavya, and Mac participated in the run for a cure fund-raising event. The three boys collected a total of $13a^2 - 16ab + 8b^2$ dollars in pledges. If Tyler brought in $4a^2 + 2ab - 3b^2$ dollars and Bhavya got $5a^2 - 4ab + 3b^2$ dollars, how much money did Mac raise?

(1) $9a^2 - 2ab$
(2) $a^2 - 6ab + 6b^2$
(3) $4a^2 - 14ab + 8b^2$
(4) $4a^2 - 18ab + 8b^2$

13 Jamison decided to compete in the Teen Summer Triathlon. He had to run $5c^2 - 4c - 4$ kilometers, swim $3c^2 + 7c + 4$ kilometers, and bike $6c^2 - 8c + 2$ kilometers. What was the total distance he had to complete to finish the event?

(1) $14c^2 - 5c + 2$
(2) $2c^2 - 11c + 2$
(3) $14c^2 - 17c + 10$
(4) $14c^2 + 17c - 2$

14 Sagar, Alex, and Jarrett shared a lawn and pool service job this summer. Sagar cut $4x + 10$ lawns each week; Alex took care of $x^2 - 2x - 5$ lawns, and Jarrett cleaned $2x^2 - 7x + 8$ pools a week. If each boy worked at a different house, how many homes in the neighborhood employed the boys?

(1) $3x^2 - 5x + 13$
(2) $3x^2 - 13x + 13$
(3) $x^2 - 5x + 23$
(4) $3x^2 - 13x + 23$

15 At camp, Savannah likes getting mail from her friends and family. The first week she got $2m - 4$ letters; the second week, $5m - 8$ letters; the third week, $3m - 6$ notes and cards; the fourth week, $12 - 2m$; the fifth week, $7m + 3$ pieces of mail; and during the last week at camp she got $8 - 3m$ pieces. During her time at camp, how many cards, letters, and packages did Savannah receive in total?

(1) $23m + 41$ (3) $23m + 5$
(2) $12m + 5$ (4) $12m - 5$

1.5 Multiplying Polynomials

When multiplying algebraic terms, multiply the coefficients of like terms, and remember *to add* their exponents!

The distributive property is used when multiplying a polynomial by a monomial.

MODEL PROBLEMS

1 Multiply $4x^2z(2x^3 - 3x^2z + xz^2 - 3z^3)$.

SOLUTION

Use the distributive property.

$4x^2z \cdot 2x^3 + 4x^2z \cdot (-3x^2z) + 4x^2z \cdot xz^2 + 4x^2z \cdot (-3z^3)$

Answer: $8x^5z - 12x^4z^2 + 4x^3z^3 - 12x^2z^4$

The distributive property may also be used to multiply two binomials. Each term in the first parentheses is distributed over each term in the second parentheses.

2 Multiply $(7c - 2)(5c + 8)$.

SOLUTION

$7c(5c + 8) - 2(5c + 8)$

$(7c)(5c) + (7c)(8) + (-2)(5c) + (-2)(8)$

$35c^2 + 56c - 10c - 16$ Now combine like terms.

Answer: $35c^2 + 46c - 16$

3 Multiply: $(5a^c + 4)(3a^{2c} - 2)$

SOLUTION

Notice that in this problem, the exponents are variables, but we follow the standard procedure of adding the exponents of like terms.

$(5a^c)(3a^{2c}) + (5a^c)(-2) + (4)(3a^{2c}) + (4)(-2)$

After multiplying, the solution is $15a^{3c} - 10a^c + 12a^{2c} - 8$.

Write the solution in standard form for your answer.

Answer: $15a^{3c} + 12a^{2c} - 10a^c - 8$

4 Multiply: $(2x - 5)(3x^2 + x - 4)$

SOLUTION

We may also use the distributive property to multiply a binomial and a trinomial.

$2x(3x^2 + x - 4) - 5(3x^2 + x - 4)$

Multiply.

$(2x \cdot 3x^2) + (2x \cdot x) + (2x \cdot (-4)) + (-5 \cdot 3x^2) + (-5 \cdot x) + (-5 \cdot -4)$

$6x^3 + 2x^2 - 8x - 15x^2 - 5x + 20$

Combine like terms.

Answer: $6x^3 - 13x^2 - 13x + 20$

5 Multiply $(2d^2 - 3cd + c^2)(3d^3 - 3c^2d^2 + c^3)$.

SOLUTION

Use the distributive property to multiply all terms.

$(2d^2 \bullet 3d^3) + (2d^2 \bullet (-3c^2d^2)) + (2d^2 \bullet c^3) + (-3cd \bullet 3d^3) + (-3cd \bullet -(3c^2d^2))$
$+ (-3cd \bullet c^3) + (c^2 \bullet 3d^3) + (c^2 \bullet (-3c^2d^2)) + (c^2 \bullet c^3)$

Answer: $6d^5 - 6c^2d^4 + 2c^3d^2 - 9cd^4 + 9c^3d^3 - 3c^4d + 3c^2d^3 - 3c^4d^2 + c^5$

 **Practice**

> **Note:** No matter how large the polynomial, we always multiply each term in the first polynomial by each term in the second polynomial.

Exercises 1–12: Perform the indicated multiplication in each problem below and combine like terms if possible.

1 $(6x^2)(3x^3 - 2x^2 + x - 1)$

2 $(m^2 - 4)(m^2 + 4)$

3 $(3a^2b^3)(4a^3b - 3a^2b^2 + 5ab^3)$

4 $(5cd + 3)(2c^2d^2 - 1)$

5 $(5c - 4)(2c + 5)$

6 $(6z + 5)^2$

7 $(7y + 2)(7y - 2)$

8 $(2p + 3)(p^2 - p + 2)$

9 $(4x^2 - 1)(2x + 1)$

10 $(7 - 3y)(2 - 5y + 2y^2)$

11 $(8c^a - 3)(2c^a + 3)$

12 $(-2h^2 - 3kh + 2k^2)(3h^2 - 2hk - k^2)$

Exercises 13–18: Perform all indicated operations and write the answer in simplest terms.

13 $(4j + 5)^2 - (3j - 4)^2$

14 $(2x)(2 - x) + (3x + 1)(x - 4)$

15 $2m^2n(3mn^2 - n) + 3m^2n^2(2mn - 1)$

16 $5m^b(2m^b - 3) - (4m^b + 1)(2m^b - 7)$

17 $(2y - 3)(y^2 - 4y + 5) - y(15 - 11y)$

18 $(7x + 6)(2x + 3) - (5x - 2)(2x - 9)$

Exercises 19 and 20: Find the area of each figure in terms of x.

19

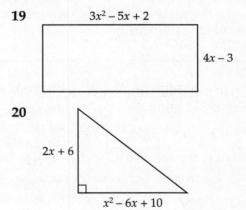

20

Exercises 21 and 22: Select the numeral preceding the choice that best answers the question.

21 If Amelia Grace worked $(2h + 5)$ hours last week and earned $(h - 2)$ dollars per hour, which represents the total amount she earned?

(1) $2h^2 - h + 10$ (3) $2h^2 + 9h - 10$
(2) $2h^2 + h - 10$ (4) $h + 3$

22 Tyrone scored an average of $(7p + 2)$ points per game for the Wildcats. If he played in $(p^2 + 4p - 5)$ games last season, which represents the total number of points he scored for the team?

(1) $p^2 + 11p - 3$
(2) $7p^3 + 26p^2 - 27p - 10$
(3) $7p^3 + 30p^2 - 27p - 10$
(4) $7p^3 + 30p^2 - 43p - 10$

1.6 Factoring

When we factor a number, we break it down into the two or more numbers whose product is that number. For example:

$$24 = 4 \bullet 6 \qquad\qquad 50 = 5 \bullet 10 \qquad\qquad 84 = 7 \bullet 12$$
$$ = 2 \bullet 2 \bullet 2 \bullet 3 \qquad = 5 \bullet 5 \bullet 2 \qquad\quad = 7 \bullet 3 \bullet 2 \bullet 2$$
$$ = 2^3 \bullet 3 \qquad\qquad\quad = 5^2 \bullet 2 \qquad\qquad = 7 \bullet 3 \bullet 2^2$$

Numbers may be initially factored in more than one way. For example, 24 also equals 3 times 8, 50 equals 2 times 25, and 84 equals 4 times 21. When we factor algebraic expressions, we do the same thing: break them down into smaller parts which, when multiplied, produce that algebraic expression.

$$6x + 12 \qquad 15x^2 - 5x \qquad 9a^2 + 18 \qquad 21 - 7c$$
$$6(x + 2) \qquad 5x(3x - 1) \qquad 9(a^2 + 2) \qquad 7(3 - c)$$

Some common forms of algebraic factoring are Greatest Common Factor, Difference of Two Perfect Squares, and Trinomial Factoring. Study the table below to familiarize yourself with the Greatest Common Factor and Difference of Two Perfect Squares methods of factoring.

Type of Factoring	Example	Factoring Rules	Solution
Greatest Common Factor	$4x^2 - 12x^3 + 6x^4$	Divide out the greatest possible monomial term; put the quotient in parentheses.	$2x^2(2 - 6x + 3x^2)$
Difference of Two Perfect Squares	$9m^2 - 25$	Take the square root of each term; put each one in parentheses, one with a + sign and one with a − sign.	$(3m + 5)(3m - 5)$

Given a trinomial in $ax^2 + bx + c$ form where $a \neq 0$, there are two cases to consider before factoring. These are outlined below.

Trinomials When $a = 1$

- Since $a = 1$, the factors of the first term ax^2 are x and x.
- Find the factors of the last term c to be p and q such that $p \cdot q = c$.
- Make certain that $xq + xp = bx$ since $ax^2 + bx + c = (x + p)(x + q)$.

For example, consider the trinomial $x^2 + 8x + 15$.

$ax^2 = x^2$	Since $a = 1$, each of the two factors must be x.
$c = 15$	p could equal 15 and q could equal 1, or p could equal 5 and q could equal 3.
$b = 8x$	If $p = 15$ and $q = 1$, then $1x \cdot 1 + 1x \cdot 15 = 16x$. Hence, $p = 5$ and $q = 3$ since $1x \cdot 3 + 1x \cdot 5 = 8x$.

The solution is $(x + 5)(x + 3)$.

In short, factor the first term, then find the numbers whose product is the last term and whose sum is the middle term.

Factor: $x^2 - 5x - 24$

$ax^2 = x^2$	Since $a = 1$, each of the two factors must be x.
$c = -24$	p could equal 2 and q could equal -12, p could equal 4 and q could equal -6, p could equal 3 and q could equal -8, or p could equal 1 and q could equal -24.
$bx = -5x$	If $p = 2$ and $q = -12$, then $bx = 1x \cdot 2 + x \cdot -12 = -10x$.
	If $p = 4$ and $q = -6$, then $bx = 1x \cdot 4 + 1x \cdot -6 = -2x$.
	If $p = 3$ and $q = -8$, then $bx = 1x \cdot 3 + 1x \cdot -8 = -5x$.

Therefore, $p = 3$ and $q = -8$. The solution is $(x + 3)(x - 8)$.

> Note: Since b, the sum of the products of the inside and outside terms, is negative in this example, the larger numbers in the possible factor pairs have been given the negative sign.

Trinomials When $a \neq 1$

Sometimes the value of a in a trinomial is not 1. In these cases, you must take care in factoring the ax^2 term as well as the c term. Given a trinomial in $ax^2 + bx + c$ form where $a \neq 0$ and $a \neq 1$, we do the following:

- Find the factors of the first term ax^2 to be mx and nx such that $m \cdot n = a$. In these problems, $m \cdot n \neq 1$.
- Find the factors of the last term c to be p and q such that $p \cdot q = c$.
- Make certain that $mxq + nxp = bx$.

MODEL PROBLEMS

1 Factor $16a^2b + 8ab - 24ab^2$.

SOLUTION

Use the Greatest Common Factor or GCF. The GCF of all the terms in this polynomial is $8ab$.

Answer: $16a^2b + 8ab - 24ab^2 = 8ab(2a + 1 - 3b)$

2 Factor $5c^3 - 25c^2 + 10c$.

SOLUTION

Use the GCF. The GCF of all the terms in this polynomial is $5c$.

Answer: $5c^3 - 25c^2 + 10c = 5c(c^2 - 5c + 2)$

3 Factor $49 - 4a^2$.

SOLUTION

49 and $4a^2$ are both perfect squares. Use the Difference of Squares model to factor the binomial.

$\sqrt{49} = 7 \qquad \sqrt{4a^2} = 2a$

Answer: $49 - 4a^2 = (7 - 2a)(7 + 2a)$

4 Factor $\dfrac{1}{9}x^2 - 25$.

SOLUTION

$\dfrac{1}{9}x^2$ and 25 are both perfect squares. Use the Difference of Squares model to factor the binomial.

$\sqrt{\dfrac{1}{9}x^2} = \dfrac{1}{3}x \qquad \sqrt{25} = 5$

Answer: $\dfrac{1}{9}x^2 - 25 = \left(\dfrac{1}{3}x + 5\right)\left(\dfrac{1}{3}x - 5\right)$

5 Factor $3x^2 - 4x - 4$.

SOLUTION

$ax^2 = 3x^2$ Since 3 is prime, mx and px can equal only $3x$ and x. So we know this part of the answer: $(3x \quad)(x \quad)$.

$c = -4$ The factors of -4 are -1 and 4, or ± 2 and ∓ 2, or 4 and -1. However, until we determine the effect of multiplying these terms by each other, we cannot be certain of our answer.

$(3x - 1)(x + 4)$	$(3x - 2)(x + 2)$	$(3x + 2)(x - 2)$	$(3x + 4)(x - 1)$
Inside product: $-x$	Inside product: $-2x$	Inside product: $2x$	Inside product: $4x$
Outside product: $12x$	Outside product: $6x$	Outside product: $-6x$	Outside product: $-3x$
Combined: $11x$	Combined: $4x$	Combined: $-4x$	Combined: x

Based on combining the products of the outside and inside terms, the correct solution to this factoring problem is $(3x + 2)(x - 2)$.

Answer: $(3x + 2)(x - 2)$

Practice these types of factoring in the following exercises. In all cases, factor completely so the answer has no common factors left.

Factor each of the following expressions.

1 $x^2 - 7x + 10$

2 $x^2 + x - 20$

3 $c^2 + 8c + 12$

4 $y^2 - 16x - 36$

5 $a^2 - 11a + 30$

6 $x^2 + 2x - 35$

7 $p^2 + 7x - 30$

8 $m^2 + 3m - 54$

9 $x^2 - 5x - 14$

10 $4z^2 - 81$

11 $2x^3 - 6x^4 + 4x^5$

12 $9c^4d - 21c^3d^2 + 6c^2d^3$

13 $4x^2 - x - 5$

14 $36y^2 - \dfrac{25}{49}z^2$

15 $18 - 7a - a^2$

16 $4p^3 - 64p$

17 $2x^2 - 16x + 30$

18 $d^2 - 2d - 48$

19 $m^{y+2} - 25m^y$

20 $3a^2 - 10a + 3$

21 $y^{2a} - y^a - 6$

22 $8c^2 - 13c + 5$

23 $7a^2 + 11a - 6$

24 $4n^2 - 12x + 9$

1.7 Solving Quadratic Equations with Integral Roots

Quadratic equations are equations that may be expressed in the form $ax^2 + bx + c = 0$ where $a \neq 0$, and a, b, and c are constants. These are examples of quadratic equations:

$$3x^2 - 4x + 1 = 0$$

$$10x - 21 = x^2$$

$$x^2 - 4 = 3x$$

When solving quadratic equations by factoring:

- Set the equation equal to zero.
- Factor.
- Set each factor equal to zero.
- Solve each resulting equation for x.

To factor a trinomial, remember these rules:

- If $a = 1$, the factors of the first term and the factors of the last term combine to produce the middle term, which is the sum of the outer and inner products.
- When $a \neq 1$, you must take extra care to consider the sum of the outer and inner products to find the correct combination of factors.
- If the sign of the last term in the trinomial is positive, both factors take the same sign as the middle term of the trinomial.

- If the sign of the last term in the trinomial is negative, there is one positive factor and one negative factor. If $a = 1$, the larger of the two factors takes the sign of the middle term of the trinomial.
- Once the trinomial is factored, set each factor equal to zero and solve.

The table below gives some sample quadratic expressions, the first and last terms that must be factored to form the middle term, and the factored form of the quadratic.

Quadratic Expression	First Term	Last Term	Factored Form
$x^2 + 4x - 5$	x^2	-5	$(x + 5)(x - 1)$
$x^2 - 3x - 10$	x^2	-10	$(x + 2)(x - 5)$
$x^2 + 7x + 12$	x^2	12	$(x + 3)(x + 4)$
$2x^2 - 7x + 3$	$2x^2$	3	$(2x - 1)(x - 3)$
$3x^2 + 5x - 2$	$3x^2$	-2	$(3x - 1)(x + 2)$

After you have factored the left side of the equation $3x^2 + 5x - 2 = 0$, you have two binomials: $(3x - 1)$ and $(x + 2)$. Since their product is zero, at least one of the binomials must equal zero. Therefore, set each individual factor equal to zero and solve for its variable.

$$3x - 1 = 0 \qquad x + 2 = 0$$
$$3x = 1 \qquad\qquad x = -2$$
$$x = \frac{1}{3}$$

Check both answers by substituting them into the original equation.

$$3x^2 + 5x - 2 = 0$$

$$3\left(\frac{1}{3}\right)^2 + 5\left(\frac{1}{3}\right) - 2 \stackrel{?}{=} 0 \qquad\qquad 3(-2)^2 + 5(-2) - 2 \stackrel{?}{=} 0$$

$$3\left(\frac{1}{9}\right) + \frac{5}{3} - 2 \stackrel{?}{=} 0 \qquad\qquad 3(4) - 10 - 2 \stackrel{?}{=} 0$$

$$\frac{1}{3} + \frac{5}{3} - \frac{6}{3} \stackrel{?}{=} 0 \qquad\qquad 12 - 10 - 2 \stackrel{?}{=} 0$$

$$\frac{6}{3} - \frac{6}{3} \stackrel{?}{=} 0 \qquad\qquad 2 - 2 \stackrel{?}{=} 0$$

$$0 = 0 \checkmark \qquad\qquad 0 = 0 \checkmark$$

Since both solutions check, they are both valid.

MODEL PROBLEMS

1 Solve for x: $4x - 5 = \dfrac{6}{x}$, $x \neq 0$

SOLUTION

Multiply by the LCM to eliminate the fraction. $\qquad\qquad 4x^2 - 5x = 6$

Set the equation equal to zero. $\qquad\qquad\qquad\quad 4x^2 - 5x - 6 = 0$

Factor. $\qquad\qquad\qquad\qquad\qquad\qquad\qquad (4x + 3)(x - 2) = 0$

Set each factor equal to zero. $\qquad\qquad\quad 4x + 3 = 0 \qquad\quad x - 2 = 0$

Solve for x. $\qquad\qquad\qquad\qquad\qquad\qquad\quad x = -\dfrac{3}{4} \qquad\qquad x = 2$

Check each solution in the original equation.

$$4x - 5 = \frac{6}{x}$$

$$4\left(-\frac{3}{4}\right) - 5 \overset{?}{=} \frac{6}{-\dfrac{3}{4}} \qquad\qquad 4(2) - 5 \overset{?}{=} \frac{6}{2}$$

$$\qquad\qquad\qquad\qquad\qquad\qquad\quad 8 - 5 \overset{?}{=} 3$$

$$-3 - 5 \overset{?}{=} -\frac{24}{3} \qquad\qquad\qquad 3 = 3 ✔$$

$$-8 = -8 ✔$$

Since both solutions check, they are both valid.

Answer: $x = -\dfrac{3}{4}, x = 2$

2 Solve for all values of x: $\sqrt{4x + 1} - 1 = x$

SOLUTION

Isolate the radical by adding 1 to each side of the equation. $\sqrt{4x + 1} = x + 1$

Square each side of the equation. $\qquad\qquad\qquad \left(\sqrt{4x + 1}\right)^2 = (x + 1)^2$

$$4x + 1 = x^2 + 2x + 1$$

Set the equation equal to zero. $\qquad\qquad\qquad\qquad\qquad 0 = x^2 - 2x$

$$0 = x(x - 2)$$

Solve the resulting equation. $\qquad\qquad\qquad\qquad x = 0 \qquad\qquad x - 2 = 0$

$$x = 2$$

Be sure to check that your solution works in the original equation.

$$\sqrt{4(0) + 1} - 1 \overset{?}{=} 0 \qquad\qquad \sqrt{4(2) + 1} - 1 \overset{?}{=} 2$$

$$\sqrt{1} - 1 \overset{?}{=} 0 \qquad\qquad\qquad \sqrt{9} - 1 \overset{?}{=} 2$$

$$0 = 0 ✔ \qquad\qquad\qquad\quad 3 - 1 = 2$$

$$2 = 2 ✔ \quad \text{Both solutions check.}$$

Answer: $x = 0, x = 2$

Solve each equation for x and check the solutions.

1 $2x^2 + 8 = 8x$

2 $x^2 - 2x = 48$

3 $x^2 - 2x + 12 = 3x + 36$

4 $x^2 - 14 = 5x$

5 $4x^2 - 36 = 0$

6 $x + 3 = \dfrac{28}{x}$

7 $7 - 4x = 3x^2$

8 $2x^2 - x = 15$

9 $\dfrac{8x^2}{3} = 2x + 3$

10 $2x - 3 = \dfrac{20}{x}$

11 $3x^2 = 3x + 18$

12 $2x^2 + 1 = \dfrac{11x}{3}$

13 $5x^2 = 8x + 4$

14 $x^2 - 4x + 2 = x - x^2$

15 $8x^2 - 32 = 0$

16 $2x - 1 = \dfrac{15}{x}$

17 $3x^2 - 20x = 32$

18 $4x^2 = 7x + 36$

19 $5x^2 = 2(7x + 12)$

20 $3x - 13 = \dfrac{10}{x}$

21 $\sqrt{x + 5} + 1 = x$

22 $2\sqrt{3x - 2} = x + 2$

23 $\sqrt{2x - 1} = x - 8$

24 $x + 3 = 2\sqrt{4x - 3}$

1.8 Quadratic Inequalities

We have spent some time working on quadratic equations. Now let's look at quadratic inequalities. Given: $y = x^2 - x - 6$. By graphing the function, we can see that when $y = 0$, $x = 3$ or $x = -2$. Thus, we say that $x = 3$ and $x = -2$ are the *zeros* or *roots* of the function.

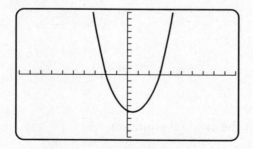

To solve the inequality $x^2 - x - 6 < 0$ graphically, look at which x-values produce negative y-values (that is, values of $y < 0$). We can see this occurs when $-2 < x < 3$. Now find the solution of $x^2 - x - 6 < 0$ algebraically. Our inequality translates into finding x-values that will make the quadratic negative (i.e., less than zero). The next question is how to solve this inequality.

First, factor the inequality: $(x - 3)(x + 2) < 0$. Now, we know that $(x - 3)(x + 2) = 0$ when $x = 3$ or $x = -2$. We can put this information on a number line:

Think of the number line as divided into three regions: $x < -2$, $-2 < x < 3$, and $x > 3$ (i.e., numbers to the left of 2, between 2 and 3, and to the right of 3). Choose a number in each of these regions. For example, in the region $x < -2$, you might choose -5. Substitute this number into the inequality $(-5 - 3)(-5 + 2) < 0$ to determine whether your answer is positive or negative. We obtain $(-8)(-3)$ which gives us $+24$. It is not important what the actual *value* of your answer is. All that matters is the *sign* of your answer.

By choosing a number in the region $-2 < x < 3$, we get $(-)(+) = -$. In the region $x > 3$, we get $(+)(+) = +$. We can put all of this information on our number line:

Since we are looking for values of x that will produce a negative answer, we choose the interval in which our values are negative, that is, $-2 < x < 3$.

If we had wanted values of x such that $x^2 - x - 6 > 0$, we could have proceeded in a similar manner. Graphically, we would look for x-values that would produce positive y-values (that is, values of $y > 0$). We can see that our solution is: $x < -2$ or $x > 3$.

Algebraically, we must solve $x^2 - x - 6 > 0$. Looking at the number line above, we are interested in obtaining x values that will make the inequality positive (greater than 0). So we choose $x < -2$ or $x > 3$.

MODEL PROBLEM

Given: $x^2 - 2x - 20 > 4$

  a Find the solution set.

  b Graph the solution set on a number line.

SOLUTION

  a First, we must subtract 4 from each side:

$$x^2 - 2x - 20 > 4$$

$$x^2 - 2x - 24 > 0$$

To solve this inequality algebraically:

Factor:

$$(x - 6)(x + 4) > 0$$

Plot the zeros on a number line:

Choose a value for x in each region and substitute this value for x in the inequality. Determine whether the answer you obtain is positive or negative, and mark this on your number line, as shown below.

Since we want to solve $x^2 - 2x - 24 > 0$, we are looking for positive x-values (values of $x > 0$). Thus, our solution is $x < -4$ or $x > 6$.

To solve the inequality graphically, graph $y = x^2 - 2x - 24$ as shown below.

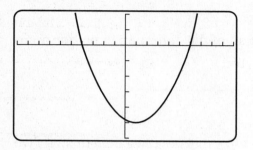

Since we are solving $x^2 - 2x - 24 > 0$, we are looking for positive y values ($y > 0$). This occurs when $x < -4$ or $x > 6$.

Answer: $x < -4$ or $x > 6$

Note: If we were asked to solve $x^2 - 2x - 24 \geq 0$, we would use solid dots for -4 and 6.

b To graph the solution set, we shade in the region less than -4 and also the region greater than 6.

✏️ **Practice**

Exercises 1–10: Write the solution set for the inequality and graph the solution set.

1 $x^2 - x - 56 > 0$

2 $x^2 - 9 \geq 0$

3 $x^2 - 3x - 3 < 7$

4 $x^2 + 3x \geq -2x - 4$

5 $2x^2 + 7x + 3 > 0$

6 $x^2 \leq -4x + 12$

7 $3x^2 \geq -4x - 1$

8 $4x^2 < 9$

9 $x^2 + 32 > 12x$

10 $x^2 - 4x \leq x$

Exercises 11–16: Select the numeral preceding the choice that best completes the statement or answers the question.

11 The solution set of $x^2 - 3x > 18$ is

(1) $\{x: -3 < x < 6\}$
(2) $\{x: x < -3 \text{ or } x > 6\}$
(3) $\{x: -6 < x < 3\}$
(4) $\{x: x < -6 \text{ or } x > 3\}$

12 The solution set of $x^2 - 36 \leq 0$ is

(1) $\{x: x \leq -6 \text{ or } x \geq 6\}$
(2) $\{x: -3 \leq x \leq 6\}$
(3) $\{x: x \leq -3 \text{ or } x \geq 6\}$
(4) $\{x: -6 \leq x \leq 6\}$

13 The graph below is the solution for which inequality?

(1) $x^2 - 4x - 21 \geq 0$
(2) $x^2 - 4x - 21 \leq 0$
(3) $x^2 + 4x - 21 \leq 0$
(4) $x^2 + 4x - 21 \geq 0$

14 Which graph is the solution set of $x^2 \leq 3x$?

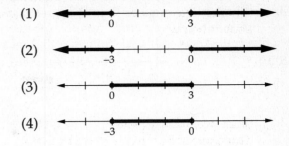

15 The graph of the solution set of $x^2 - 4x - 6 > 2x + 10$ is:

(1)
(2)
(3)
(4)

16 What is the solution set of $x^2 + x - 2 < 12x - 32$?

(1) $\{x: x < -6 \text{ or } x > 5\}$
(2) $\{x: x < 5 \text{ or } x > 6\}$
(3) $\{x: -6 < x < -5\}$
(4) $\{x: 5 < x < 6\}$

→ FYI

You can use your calculator to solve many of the equations presented in this chapter. For example, let's take the equation $|3x + 1| = 5$.

To solve this equation graphically, we put $|3x + 1|$ into Y_1 and 5 into Y_2 in the [Y=] and see where the two graphs intersect.

Press [Y=] and enter the information as shown below.

```
Plot1  Plot2  Plot3
\Y1▪abs(3X+1)
\Y2▪5
\Y3=■
\Y4=
\Y5=
\Y6=
\Y7=
```

To obtain the abs(, you can go into Catalog by pressing (2nd) (0) and selecting the first entry. Alternatively, you can go to the (MATH) menu, right arrow across to NUM, and select the first entry. Once the information is entered, graph the equations in the standard viewing window, which is Xmin = −10, Xmax = 10 and Ymin = −10, Ymax = 10 or [−10, 10] × [−10, 10].

(ZOOM) (6) was used to produce the standard window shown in this screen.

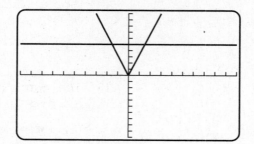

To find the two points of intersection (whose *x*-coordinates are the two solutions of our equation), we will use the CALC feature of the calculator.

Select (2nd) (TRACE) to get the screen shown below.

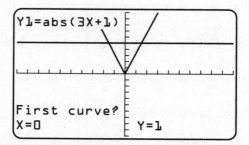

Select 5:intersect. Since there are only two curves, when you are asked for the First curve and the Second Curve, simply press (ENTER).

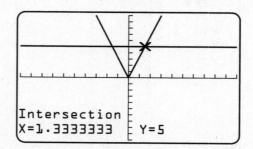

Next, you will be asked for a guess. Move your cursor closer to one of the intersection points and then press (ENTER). If you move your cursor closer to the right point, you should get the screen shown below.

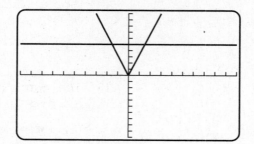

We can see that the left side of our equation, $|3x + 1|$, is equal to the right side of our equation when $x = 1.3333333$. You may recognize this as the fraction $\frac{4}{3}$. If you would like the calculator to convert the decimal to a fraction, press (2nd) (MODE) to return to the home screen. Press (X,T,θ,n) and then (ENTER). The calculator will show what value is stored as x (in this case x was 1.3333333).

Now, press (MATH) (1). This will convert the decimal 1.3333333 to the fraction $\frac{4}{3}$. The screen below illustrates what was done.

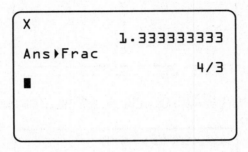

```
X
             1.333333333
Ans▶Frac
                     4/3
■
```

We can find the other solution to the equation by following the same procedure as outlined above, except selecting the left intersection point. This will give us the value of $x = -2$.

Let's solve the same equation algebraically:

$$|3x + 1| = 5$$

$$3x + 1 = 5 \qquad\qquad 3x + 1 = -5$$

$$3x = 4 \qquad\qquad\quad 3x = -6$$

$$x = \frac{4}{3} \qquad\qquad\quad x = -2$$

The graphing calculator also has a Solver feature. To begin the process, select (MATH) (0).

```
MATH NUM CPX PRB
4↑3√(
5:×√
6:fMin(
7:fMax(
8:nDeriv(
9:fnInt(
0:Solver...
```

You should get the screen shown below.

```
EQUATION SOLVER
eqn:0=■
```

If you do not get this screen, you already have an equation entered into your Solver. Press [▲] to return to the Solver screen and clear whatever equation is there. Because the Equation Solver requires the equation to equal zero, we have to transform our equation by moving all the terms to the right. Type the information as shown below.

```
EQUATION SOLVER
eqn:0=abs(3X+1)-
5█
```

Once the information is entered, press (ENTER) or [▼] to get the screen as shown.

```
abs(3X+1)-5=0
X=-1█
bound={-1E99,1...
```

Your x may have a different value from the one shown above. The x-coordinate shown corresponds to the x-coordinate last used in your graph. You may change this by simply typing in a value you would like to try. Type in -1 as a guess for the x-coordinate. Press (ALPHA) (ENTER) to solve the equation. You will then get the information shown below.

```
abs(3X+1)-5=0
▪X=-2█
 bound={-1E99,1...
▪left-rt=0
```

Notice that we obtain only one answer, the answer closest to -1.

Be aware that Solver can be unreliable and will sometimes fail to find a solution that exists.

Go back to some of the equations in this chapter. Try solving them graphically, or by using the Solver feature of your calculator.

Note: When you are entering equations involving fractions, be sure to use parentheses to group the whole numerator and the whole denominator. For example, the fraction $\dfrac{x + 1}{x + 2}$ must be entered as $(x + 1)/(x + 2)$.

CHAPTER REVIEW

Exercises 1–10: Perform the indicated operations and simplify.

1 $(x - 4)(x + 5)$

2 $3(a^2 - 6a + 2) - (a - 6)$

3 $(3c^2 - 2c + 1) + (c^2 - 4c + 7)$

4 $(2w - 3y)(w + 5y)$

5 $(2x + 3)(x^2 - 4x + 2)$

6 $(3a + b)^2$

7 $2a^2b(3a^2 - 4a + b)$

8 $5(x + y)^2 - 3x(x - 2y)$

9 $ab(2a - b) - b(3b - 4)$

10 $(r - s)(r^2 + 3rs - s^2)$

Exercises 11–18: Solve for x.

11 $|9 - 2x| = 5$

12 $|x| + 3 = 4$

13 $|3 + x| \le 5$

14 $x^2 - 3x = x + 12$

15 $3x^2 + 8x - 10 = x^2 + 7x + 5$

16 $x^2 + x - 56 > 0$

17 $x^2 - 5x \le 24$

18 $x^2 - 6x \ge x$

Exercises 19–23: Factor completely.

19 $3a^2 - 27$

20 $b^2 + 13b + 12$

21 $3x^2 - 6x - 9$

22 $2x^2 - 5x - 12$

23 $9c^2d^2 - 16$

Exercises 24–35: Select the numeral preceding the choice that best completes the statement or answers the question.

24 Which number is rational?

(1) 0.121122111222 . . .
(2) 0.33333 . . .
(3) $\sqrt{3}$
(4) $\sqrt{26}$

25 The length of a rectangle is two feet greater than its width. If the area of the rectangle is 24 square feet, what is its length?

(1) 7 feet   (3) 5 feet
(2) 6 feet   (4) 4 feet

26 The expression $(2x^2 + 5x - 6) - (5x^2 - 6x + 1)$ is equivalent to

(1) $-3x^2 - x - 5$
(2) $-3x^2 + 11x - 7$
(3) $7x^2 - x - 5$
(4) $7x^2 - x - 7$

27 When $3a^2 + 6a - 4$ is subtracted from $2a^2 + 7a$, the difference is

(1) $a^2 - a - 4$
(2) $a^2 - a + 4$
(3) $-a^2 + a + 4$
(4) $-a^2 + 13a - 4$

28 Which expression has the *greatest* value?

(1) -3.14
(2) $-\sqrt{10}$
(3) $-\pi$
(4) $-\dfrac{22}{7}$

29 What is the solution set of the equation $x^2 - 7x = -6$?

(1) $\{-3, -2\}$
(2) $\{3, -2\}$
(3) $\{-1, 6\}$
(4) $\{1, 6\}$

30 What is the length of a side of a square whose perimeter and area have the same numerical value?

(1) 1   (3) 3
(2) 2   (4) 4

31 What is the solution set of the inequality $x^2 - 2x - 40 \geq 8$?

(1) $\{x : x \leq -6 \text{ or } x \geq 8\}$
(2) $\{x : -6 \leq x \leq 8\}$
(3) $\{x : x \leq -8 \text{ or } x \geq 6\}$
(4) $\{x : -8 \leq x \leq 6\}$

32 What is the solution set of the inequality $|12 - 3x| \geq 21$?

(1) $\{x : -3 \leq x \leq 11\}$
(2) $\{x : x \leq -3 \text{ or } x \geq 11\}$
(3) $\{x : -11 \leq x \leq 3\}$
(4) $\{x : x \leq -11 \text{ or } x \geq 3\}$

33 What is the solution set of the inequality $x^2 + 5x < 3x$?

(1) $\{x : x < -2 \text{ or } x > 0\}$
(2) $\{x : -2 < x < 0\}$
(3) $\{x : x < 0 \text{ or } x > 2\}$
(4) $\{x : 0 < x < 2\}$

34 The graph below is the solution set for which inequality?

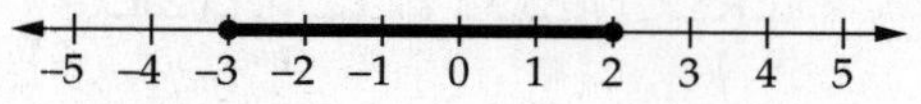

(1) $x^2 + x \leq 6$
(2) $x^2 + x \geq 6$
(3) $x^2 - 5x \leq 6$
(4) $x^2 - 5x \geq 6$

35 A manufacturer produces metal rods 10 cm long. A rod can differ from the perfect 10-cm length by 0.001 cm and still be acceptable. Which equation could be used to represent this?

(1) $|x + 10| \leq 0.001$
(2) $|x - 10| \leq 0.001$
(3) $|10 + 0.001| \leq x$
(4) $|x - 0.001| \leq 10$

The Rational Numbers

2.1 Simplifying Rational Expressions

As you recall, a **rational number** is a number in the form $\frac{a}{b}$, where a and b are both integers, and $b \neq 0$. Similarly, a **rational expression** is a fraction in the form $\frac{P_1}{P_2}$ where P_1 and P_2 are both polynomials and $P_2 \neq 0$. Examples of rational expressions include $\frac{x}{6}$, $\frac{3}{x}$, $\frac{11}{x-2}$, and $\frac{a-3}{a^2-7a-9}$.

Just as a rational number is undefined if its denominator is zero, a rational expression is said to be **undefined** if its denominator is zero.

Have you ever wondered why division by zero is said to be undefined?

Look at these examples:

$$\frac{24}{4} = 6 \text{ because } 4(6) = 24$$

$$\frac{18}{9} = 2 \text{ because } 9(2) = 18$$

$$\frac{0}{5} = 0 \text{ because } 5(0) = 0$$

BUT:

What can we do with $\frac{3}{0}$? This division has no solution because there is no number that you could multiply by 0 to get 3.

Thus, we say that $\frac{3}{0}$ is undefined.

For what value(s) of x is the fraction undefined?

1 $\dfrac{5}{x}$

SOLUTION

A fraction is undefined when the denominator is equal to zero. To solve each problem, set the denominator equal to zero and solve for x.

$\dfrac{5}{x}$

Answer: $x = 0$

2 $\dfrac{11}{x - 7}$

SOLUTION

$\dfrac{11}{x - 7}$

$x - 7 = 0$

Answer: $x = 7$

3 $\dfrac{x - 2}{x^2 - 9}$

SOLUTION

$\dfrac{x - 2}{x^2 - 9}$

$$x^2 - 9 = 0$$

$$(x + 3)(x - 3) = 0$$

$x + 3 = 0 \text{ or } x - 3 = 0$

Answer: $x = -3 \text{ or } x = 3$

4 $\dfrac{x^2 - x - 12}{x^2 - 7x + 10}$

SOLUTION

$\dfrac{x^2 - x - 12}{x^2 - 7x + 10}$

$$x^2 - 7x + 10 = 0$$

$$(x - 5)(x - 2) = 0$$

$x - 5 = 0 \text{ or } x - 2 = 0$

Answer: $x = 5 \text{ or } x = 2$

A rational expression is said to be in **simplest form** or **reduced to lowest terms** if its numerator and denominator do not have any common factor other than 1 or -1. To reduce a rational expression to lowest terms (or express a rational expression in simplest form), factor both the numerator and denominator and divide each of them by their greatest common factor. This is very similar to reducing rational numbers to lowest terms. When a rational expression is reduced, it is understood that the equivalent form of the expression equals the original expression only for those values for which the original fraction is defined.

MODEL PROBLEMS

Express each rational expression in simplest form.

1 $\dfrac{16x^4y^3z^6}{24x^3yz^{10}}$

SOLUTION

To reduce this fraction to lowest terms, divide the numerator and denominator by their greatest common factor (GCF). We will treat each numeric or variable factor shared by the numerator and denominator separately.

The GCF of 16 and 24 is 8, so divide the numerator and denominator by 8.

The GCF of x^4 and x^3 is x^3, so divide the numerator and denominator by x^3.

The GCF of y^3 and y is y, so divide the numerator and denominator by y.

The GCF of z^6 and z^{10} is z^6, so divide the numerator and denominator by z^6.

Thus, $\dfrac{16x^4y^3z^6}{24x^3yz^{10}} = \dfrac{2xy^2}{3z^4}$, $(x \neq 0, y \neq 0, z \neq 0)$.

Answer: $\dfrac{2xy^2}{3z^4}$, $(x \neq 0, y \neq 0, z \neq 0)$

2 $\dfrac{x^2 - 25}{x^2 - 5x}$

SOLUTION

First, factor the numerator and denominator:

$\dfrac{x^2 - 25}{x^2 - 5x} = \dfrac{(x + 5)(x - 5)}{x(x - 5)}$

Since the $(x - 5)$ is common to both the numerator and denominator, divide both the numerator and denominator by $(x - 5)$.

Thus, $\dfrac{x^2 - 25}{x^2 - 5x} = \dfrac{(x + 5)\cancel{(x - 5)}}{x\cancel{(x - 5)}} = \dfrac{x + 5}{x}$, $(x \neq 0, 5)$.

Answer: $\dfrac{x + 5}{x}$, $(x \neq 0, 5)$

> **Note:** You can reduce fractions only by dividing numerator and denominator by their greatest common factor. You *cannot* cancel addends. Thus, you cannot cancel the x's in the rational expression $\dfrac{x + 5}{x}$.
>
> It is already in simplest form.

3 $\dfrac{6x + 18}{x^2 + x - 6}$

SOLUTION

Factor the numerator and denominator and divide both by their GCF, as follows:

$$\frac{6x + 18}{x^2 + x - 6} = \frac{6(x + 3)}{(x + 3)(x - 2)} = \frac{6}{x - 2}, (x \neq 2, -3)$$

Answer: $\dfrac{6}{x - 2}, (x \neq 2, -3)$

4 $\dfrac{24 - 6x}{x^2 - 7x + 12}$

SOLUTION

Factor the numerator and denominator:

$$\frac{24 - 6x}{x^2 - 7x + 12} = \frac{6(4 - x)}{(x - 4)(x - 3)} = \frac{-6(x - 4)}{(x - 4)(x - 3)} = \frac{-6}{x - 3}, (x \neq 3, 4)$$

Answer: $-\dfrac{6}{x - 3}, (x \neq 3, 4)$

> **Note:** We have $(4 - x)$ in the numerator and $(x - 4)$ in the denominator. If we factor out -1, we can rewrite $(4 - x)$ as $-(x - 4)$.

One way to check if your reduced fraction is equivalent to the original fraction is to graph both fractions and see if the two graphs appear to be identical. For example, enter the original fraction given above, $\dfrac{24 - 6x}{x^2 - 7x + 12}$ into Y_1 and the reduced fraction, $\dfrac{-6}{x - 3}$ into Y_2, as shown in the figure below. Be sure to put parentheses around the numerator and denominator of each fraction!

```
Plot1 Plot2 Plot3
\Y1=(24-6X)/(X²-
7X+12)
\Y2=(-6)/(X-3)
\Y3=■
\Y4=
\Y5=
\Y6=
```

Now, graph both equations. The window shown in the figure on the next page is the standard viewing window, which has Xmin = −10, Xmax = 10, Ymin = −10, and Ymax = 10. (You can obtain this window by selecting (ZOOM) (6) on your calculator.)

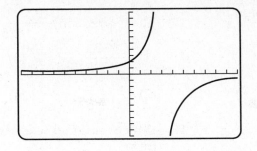

You will notice that you cannot see the second graph at all. That is because the second fraction is equivalent to the first. To be sure that the second fraction is being drawn, you can return to the [Y=] screen and move your cursor over to the \ to the left of Y_2. Continue to hit [ENTER] until you get the ball with the tail, as shown in the figure below.

```
 Plot1 Plot2 Plot3
\Y1=(24-6X)/(X²-
7X+12)
⁰Y2=(⁻6)/(X-3)
\Y3=
\Y4=
\Y5=
\Y6=
```

Now, when you graph the two equations you'll be able to see the second graph being drawn.

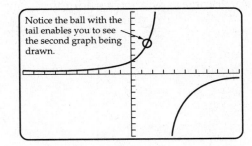

Notice the ball with the tail enables you to see the second graph being drawn.

Practice

Exercises 1–6: Find the value(s) of x for which the fraction is undefined.

1 $\dfrac{23}{6x}$

2 $\dfrac{12}{x-2}$

3 $\dfrac{4}{x^2-5x}$

4 $\dfrac{x-2}{x+9}$

5 $\dfrac{x^2-25}{x^2+6x+8}$

6 $\dfrac{6x-12}{3x+15}$

Exercises 7–15: Reduce the rational expression to lowest terms.

7 $\dfrac{21a^3bc^6}{28a^2b^4c^6}$

8 $\dfrac{8x^3y^7z^{10}}{4x^2y^6}$

9 $\dfrac{5x}{10x^2 + 20x}$

10 $\dfrac{6 - 2x}{x - 3}$

11 $\dfrac{x - 5}{x^2 - 25}$

12 $\dfrac{x^2 - 2x - 24}{x^2 - 16}$

13 $\dfrac{x^2 + 8x + 15}{x^2 + 3x}$

14 $\dfrac{y^4 - 16}{y - 2}$

15 $\dfrac{7x - x^2}{x^2 - 10x + 21}$

Exercises 16–20: Select the numeral preceding the choice that best completes the statement or answers the question.

16 Which expression is defined for all real numbers?

(1) $\dfrac{x + 3}{x^2}$ (3) $\dfrac{5}{(x + 2)^2}$

(2) $\dfrac{4}{(x - 2)^2}$ (4) $\dfrac{7}{x^2 + 3}$

17 The expression $\dfrac{10 - 2x}{x^2 - 25}$ is equivalent to

(1) $\dfrac{-2}{x + 5}$ (3) $\dfrac{-2}{5 - x}$

(2) $\dfrac{-2}{x - 5}$ (4) $\dfrac{2}{5 + x}$

18 Which rational expression is in simplest form?

(1) $\dfrac{x^2 + 4x}{4x}$ (3) $\dfrac{x^2 + 4x}{x}$

(2) $\dfrac{x^2 + 4x}{4}$ (4) None of them

19 For what value(s) of x is the rational expression $\dfrac{x - 4}{x^2 - 6x}$ undefined?

(1) $x = 0, x = 4, x = 6$
(2) $x = 4$
(3) $x = 6$
(4) $x = 0, x = 6$

20 Which expression is equivalent to $\dfrac{x^3 - 16x}{x^3 + 12x^2 + 32x}$?

(1) $\dfrac{-1}{2}$ (3) $\dfrac{x + 4}{x + 8}$

(2) $\dfrac{x - 4}{x + 8}$ (4) $\dfrac{x(x - 4)}{x + 8}$

2.2 Multiplying and Dividing Rational Expressions

Multiplying two rational expressions is similar to multiplying two rational numbers.

- Factor the numerators and denominators.
- Divide the numerators and denominators by all common factors.
- Multiply remaining factors in the numerators and remaining factors in the denominators.

> Note: You can only "cancel" factors in a numerator with factors in a denominator. You cannot "cancel" factors in two numerators or two denominators.

MODEL PROBLEM

1 Multiply and express the product in simplest form.

a $\dfrac{3x^4}{25y^2} \cdot \dfrac{35y}{9x^3}$

b $\dfrac{x^2 - 25}{2x + 10} \cdot \dfrac{4x + 12}{x^2 - 2x - 15}$

c $\dfrac{x^2 - 6x}{6 - x} \cdot \dfrac{8 + 2x}{x^2 + 4x}$

SOLUTION

a $\dfrac{3x^4}{25y^2} \cdot \dfrac{35y}{9x^3}$

Since we have monomials in both numerators and denominators, there is no factoring to be done. We can simply divide 3 into 3 and into 9, divide 5 into 25 and 35, divide y into y and y^2, and divide x^3 into x^3 and x^4.

Thus, we get: $\dfrac{3x^4}{25y^2} \cdot \dfrac{35y}{9x^3} = \dfrac{\cancel{3}\overset{1}{}\cancel{x^4}\overset{x}{}}{\cancel{25}\underset{5}{}\cancel{y^2}\underset{y}{}} \cdot \dfrac{\cancel{35}\overset{7}{}\cancel{y}\overset{1}{}}{\cancel{9}\underset{3}{}\cancel{x^3}\underset{1}{}} = \dfrac{x}{5y} \cdot \dfrac{7}{3} = \dfrac{7x}{15y} \ (x \neq 0, y \neq 0)$

Answer: $\dfrac{7x}{15y}, (x \neq 0, y \neq 0)$

b $\dfrac{x^2 - 25}{2x + 10} \cdot \dfrac{4x + 12}{x^2 - 2x - 15}$

Factor the numerators and denominators and "cancel" like factors.

$\dfrac{x^2 - 25}{2x + 10} \cdot \dfrac{4x + 12}{x^2 - 2x - 15} = \dfrac{(x + 5)\cancel{(x - 5)}}{2\cancel{(x + 5)}} \cdot \dfrac{\overset{2}{\cancel{4}}(x + 3)}{(x - 5)\cancel{(x + 3)}} = \dfrac{2}{1} = 2 \ (x \neq -5, -3, 5)$

Answer: $2, (x \neq -5, -3, 5)$

c $\dfrac{x^2 - 6x}{6 - x} \cdot \dfrac{8 + 2x}{x^2 + 4x}$

Factor the numerators and denominators and "cancel" like factors.

$\dfrac{x^2 - 6x}{6 - x} \cdot \dfrac{8 + 2x}{x^2 + 4x} = \dfrac{x(x - 6)}{6 - x} \cdot \dfrac{2(4 + x)}{x(x + 4)}$

$= \dfrac{-1\cancel{x}\cancel{(6 - x)}}{\cancel{6 - x}} \cdot \dfrac{2\cancel{(4 + x)}}{\cancel{x}\cancel{(x + 4)}} = \dfrac{-2}{1} = -2 \ \ (x \neq 0, -4, 6)$

Answer: $-2, (x \neq 0, -4, 6)$

> **Note:** Since addition is a commutative operation, $(x + 4) = (4 + x)$. Since subtraction is not commutative, $(x - 6) \neq (6 - x)$. However, if we factor out -1, we can see that $(x - 6) = -1(6 - x)$.

Dividing two rational expressions is similar to dividing two rational numbers. Multiply the dividend by the *reciprocal* of the divisor and then follow the rules for multiplication. In other words, leave the first expression alone and invert the second expression. Then multiply them together. For example:

$$3x^3y^2 \div 6xy = 3x^3y^2 \bullet \frac{1}{6xy}$$

$$= \frac{\overset{x^2 \ y}{\cancel{3x^3y^2}}}{\underset{2}{\cancel{6xy}}} = \frac{x^2y}{2} \ (x \neq 0, y \neq 0)$$

📖 MODEL PROBLEM

2   Divide and express the quotient in simplest terms.

a $\dfrac{4a^2b^3}{25ab} \div \dfrac{8ab^3}{35a^2b^4}$

b $\dfrac{x^2 - 64}{x^2 + 8x} \div \dfrac{8x - 64}{4x + 4}$

SOLUTION

a $\dfrac{4a^2b^3}{25ab} \div \dfrac{8ab^3}{35a^2b^4}$

First, multiply the first fraction by the reciprocal of the second fraction:

$$\frac{4a^2b^3}{25ab} \div \frac{8ab^3}{35a^2b^4} = \frac{4a^2b^3}{25ab} \bullet \frac{35a^2b^4}{8ab^3}$$

Now, follow the rules for multiplication by dividing numerators and denominators by common factors.

$$\frac{4a^2b^3}{25ab} \div \frac{8ab^3}{35a^2b^4} = \frac{\cancel{4a^2b^3}}{\underset{5}{\cancel{25ab}}} \bullet \frac{\overset{7}{\cancel{35a^2b^4}}}{\underset{2}{\cancel{8ab^3}}} = \frac{a^2b^3}{5} \bullet \frac{7}{2} = \frac{7a^2b^3}{10} \ (a \neq 0, b \neq 0)$$

Answer: $\dfrac{7a^2b^3}{10}, (a \neq 0, b \neq 0)$

Note: Any number that makes a denominator zero must be excluded.

b $\dfrac{x^2 - 64}{x^2 + 8x} \div \dfrac{8x - 64}{4x + 4}$

First, multiply the first fraction by the reciprocal of the second fraction.

$$\frac{x^2 - 64}{x^2 + 8x} \div \frac{8x - 64}{4x + 4} = \frac{x^2 - 64}{x^2 + 8x} \bullet \frac{4x + 4}{8x - 64}$$

Now, factor the numerators and denominators and follow the rules for multiplication by dividing numerators and denominators by common factors.

$$\frac{x^2 - 64}{x^2 + 8x} \div \frac{8x - 64}{4x + 4} = \frac{x^2 - 64}{x^2 + 8x} \bullet \frac{4x + 4}{8x - 64} = \frac{(x + 8)\cancel{(x - 8)}}{x\cancel{(x + 8)}} \bullet \frac{\cancel{4}(x + 1)}{\underset{2}{\cancel{8}\cancel{(x - 8)}}} = \frac{x + 1}{2x} \ (x \neq 0, -1, -8, 8)$$

Answer: $\dfrac{x + 1}{2x}, (x \neq 0, -1, -8, 8)$

Exercises 1–18: Perform the indicated operation. Reduce your answer to lowest terms.

1 $\dfrac{4a^3b}{6b^2c^5} \cdot \dfrac{8abc^5}{24ac^3}$

2 $\dfrac{15x^4y^5}{25xyz} \div \dfrac{10x^3y^2}{30xz}$

3 $\dfrac{x^2 - 4}{6x} \div \dfrac{x + 2}{3x - 6}$

4 $\dfrac{6x + 6y}{12xy} \cdot \dfrac{24x^2}{x^2 + xy}$

5 $\dfrac{a^2 - 9}{9 - 3a} \div \dfrac{a^2 + 5a + 6}{6a + 12}$

6 $\dfrac{7x}{7x + 7} \cdot \dfrac{x^2 - 1}{x^2 - x}$

7 $\dfrac{a^2 - ab}{a^2 - b^2} \cdot \dfrac{3a + 3b}{6a^2}$

8 $\dfrac{x^2 - x - 12}{4x + 12} \div \dfrac{x^2 - 2x - 8}{6x + 12}$

9 $\dfrac{18 - 6a}{a^2 - 9a + 18} \div \dfrac{4a}{2a - 12}$

10 $\dfrac{a^3 - 4a}{a^2 - 7a + 10} \cdot \dfrac{a^2 - 8a + 15}{a^2 + 5a + 6}$

11 $\dfrac{4w^2 - 1}{2w^2 + 3w - 2} \cdot \dfrac{4w + 8}{4w + 2}$

12 $\dfrac{64 - d^2}{8d + 64} \div \dfrac{4d - 32}{16d}$

13 $\dfrac{3x^2 - x - 2}{6x + 4} \div \dfrac{x^2 - 1}{4x + 4}$

14 $\dfrac{y^2 - y - 12}{y^2 + y - 20} \cdot \dfrac{y^2 + 11y + 30}{y^3 + 9y^2 + 18y}$

15 $\dfrac{7 - z}{z^3 - 49z} \cdot \dfrac{z^2 + 10z + 21}{3 + z}$

16 $(2x + 6) \cdot \dfrac{x - 3}{x^2 - 9}$

17 $(5x + 20) \div \dfrac{x^2 - 16}{3x - 12}$

18 $\dfrac{x^2 - 36}{3x - 18} \div (x^2 - 2x - 48)$

Exercises 19–23: Select the numeral preceding the choice that best completes the statement.

19 The product of $\dfrac{x^2 - 9}{3 - x}$ and $\dfrac{4x + 16}{x^2 + 7x + 12}$ is

(1) -4 (3) 1
(2) -1 (4) 4

20 The quotient $\dfrac{x^2 + 4x + 3}{6x + 6} \div \dfrac{x^2 + 3x}{6x} = 1$ for all values of x where

(1) $x \neq -1$
(2) $x \neq 0$
(3) $x \neq -1$ or $x \neq 0$
(4) $x \neq -3$ or $x \neq -1$ or $x \neq 0$

21 If the length of a rectangle is equal to $\dfrac{x + 1}{x + 2}$ and the area of the rectangle is $\dfrac{4x + 4}{2x + 4}$, the width of the rectangle is

(1) 1 (3) $\dfrac{x + 2}{x + 1}$
(2) 2 (4) 4

22 If the length of a rectangle is $\dfrac{3x + 3}{4x^2 - 4}$ and the width of the rectangle is $\dfrac{8x - 8}{6}$, the area of the rectangle is

(1) 1 (3) $\dfrac{x + 1}{x - 1}$
(2) 2 (4) 4

23 If the length of a rectangular solid is x, the width is $\dfrac{x + 1}{x + 2}$, and the height is $\dfrac{3x + 6}{x^2 + x}$, the volume is

(1) 1 (3) 3
(2) 2 (4) 4

2.3 Adding and Subtracting Rational Expressions

Expressions with the Same Denominator

Adding and subtracting rational expressions is similar to adding and subtracting rational numbers. First, make sure that the denominators are the same, then keep the denominator, and simply add (or subtract) the numerators.

MODEL PROBLEM

1   Perform the indicated operation. Reduce your answers to lowest terms.

   a $\dfrac{3}{2a} + \dfrac{5}{2a}$

   b $\dfrac{2x}{x-1} - \dfrac{2}{x-1}$

   c $\dfrac{x^2}{4x+12} - \dfrac{9}{4x+12}$

   d $\dfrac{y^2+2y}{y^2+7y+12} + \dfrac{3y+4}{y^2+7y+12}$

   e $\dfrac{z^2+5z}{z^2+8z} - \dfrac{2z+40}{z^2+8z}$

SOLUTION

In each of the above cases, both rational expressions have the same denominator. So all we need to do is keep the denominator and add (or subtract) the numerators.

   a $\dfrac{3}{2a} + \dfrac{5}{2a}$

We will keep the common denominator and rewrite the two rational expressions as one fraction.

$$\frac{3}{2a} + \frac{5}{2a} = \frac{3+5}{2a}$$

Now, add the two terms in the numerator:

$$\frac{3}{2a} + \frac{5}{2a} = \frac{3+5}{2a} = \frac{8}{2a}$$

This fraction can be reduced. Divide the numerator and denominator by 2:

$$\frac{3}{2a} + \frac{5}{2a} = \frac{3+5}{2a} = \frac{8}{2a} = \frac{4}{a} \quad (a \neq 0)$$

Answer: $\dfrac{4}{a}, (a \neq 0)$

b $\dfrac{2x}{x-1} - \dfrac{2}{x-1}$

We will keep the common denominator and rewrite the two rational expressions as one fraction.

$$\frac{2x}{x-1} - \frac{2}{x-1} = \frac{2x-2}{x-1}$$

The numerator of our new fraction can be factored, and the fraction can then be reduced:

$$\frac{2x}{x-1} - \frac{2}{x-1} = \frac{2x-2}{x-1} = \frac{2\cancel{(x-1)}}{\cancel{x-1}} = 2 \quad (x \neq 1)$$

Answer: $2,\ (x \neq 1)$

c $\dfrac{x^2}{4x+12} - \dfrac{9}{4x+12}$

Once again, the denominators are the same. Keep the common denominator, subtract the numerators, factor, and reduce.

$$\frac{x^2}{4x+12} - \frac{9}{4x+12} = \frac{x^2-9}{4x+12} = \frac{(x+3)(x-3)}{4(x+3)} = \frac{x-3}{4} \quad (x \neq -3)$$

Answer: $\dfrac{x-3}{4},\ (x \neq -3)$

d $\dfrac{y^2+2y}{y^2+7y+12} + \dfrac{3y+4}{y^2+7y+12}$

Keep the common denominator, rewrite the rational expressions as one fraction, combine like terms, factor, and reduce.

$$\frac{y^2+2y}{y^2+7y+12} + \frac{3y+4}{y^2+7y+12} = \frac{y^2+2y+3y+4}{y^2+7y+12} = \frac{y^2+5y+4}{y^2+7y+12}$$

$$= \frac{(y+4)(y+1)}{(y+3)(y+4)} = \frac{y+1}{y+3} \quad (y \neq -3,\ -4)$$

Answer: $\dfrac{y+1}{y+3},\ (y \neq -3,\ -4)$

e $\dfrac{z^2+5z}{z^2+8z} - \dfrac{2z+40}{z^2+8z}$

We have to be *very* careful when we are subtracting rational expressions. Remember when we subtract, we are adding the additive inverse of the second rational expression. Be sure to change *all* of the signs in the numerator of the fraction immediately following the subtraction sign!

$$\frac{z^2+5z}{z^2+8z} - \frac{2z+40}{z^2+8z} = \frac{z^2+5z-(2z+40)}{z^2+8z} = \frac{z^2+5z-2z-40}{z^2+8z} = \frac{z^2+3z-40}{z^2+8z}$$

$$= \frac{(z+8)(z-5)}{z(z+8)} = \frac{z-5}{z} \quad (z \neq 0,\ -8)$$

Answer: $\dfrac{z-5}{z},\ (z \neq 0,\ -8)$

Remember: When you are adding (or subtracting) rational expressions that have a common denominator:

- Keep the denominator the same.
- Rewrite the expressions as one fraction.
- Combine like terms.
- Factor.
- Reduce.

Practice

Perform the indicated operation. Express your answer in simplest form.

1 $\dfrac{4}{3a} + \dfrac{5}{3a}$

2 $\dfrac{5x}{x-2} - \dfrac{10}{x-2}$

3 $\dfrac{6x}{11} + \dfrac{5x}{11}$

4 $\dfrac{4x}{x^2 - 2x} - \dfrac{8}{x^2 - 2x}$

5 $\dfrac{3x+5}{x^2 - 5x - 24} + \dfrac{4}{x^2 - 5x - 24}$

6 $\dfrac{2y^2 + 2y}{y^2 - y - 56} - \dfrac{y^2 + 35}{y^2 - y - 56}$

7 $\dfrac{z^2}{z^2 - z} - \dfrac{3z - 2}{z^2 - z}$

8 $\dfrac{3}{a^2 - a - 6} - \dfrac{a}{a^2 - a - 6}$

9 $\dfrac{b^2 + 2b}{2b + 10} + \dfrac{4b + 5}{2b + 10}$

10 $\dfrac{n^3 - n^2 - 2n}{2n^2 - 4n} + \dfrac{n^3 + n^2 - 6n}{2n^2 - 4n}$

Expressions with Different Denominators

Adding (or subtracting) rational expressions that have different denominators is similar to adding (or subtracting) rational numbers with different denominators. Rewrite each fraction as an equivalent fraction with a common denominator, then keep the common denominator and add (or subtract) the numerators.

MODEL PROBLEMS

2 Perform the indicated operation. Express your answer in simplest form.

a $\dfrac{a}{3} + \dfrac{3a}{2}$

b $\dfrac{7}{3b} - \dfrac{5}{b}$

c $\dfrac{2x}{x-4} + \dfrac{8}{4-x}$

d $\dfrac{x}{x-3} - \dfrac{18}{x^2 - 9}$

e $\dfrac{3}{x+1} - \dfrac{2}{x}$

f $\dfrac{1}{x^2+3x+2} + \dfrac{2}{x^2-1}$

SOLUTION

a $\dfrac{a}{3} + \dfrac{3a}{2}$

First, we must find a common denominator. Since 3 and 2 are each factors of 6, our common denominator is 6. We multiply the numerator and denominator of the first fraction by 2 and the numerator and denominator of the second fraction by 3.

$$\dfrac{a}{3} + \dfrac{3a}{2} = \dfrac{a}{3} \bullet \dfrac{2}{2} + \dfrac{3a}{2} \bullet \dfrac{3}{3} = \dfrac{2a}{6} + \dfrac{9a}{6}$$

Once again, rewrite the expressions as one fraction and combine like terms.

$$\dfrac{2a}{6} + \dfrac{9a}{6} = \dfrac{2a+9a}{6} = \dfrac{11a}{6}$$

Answer: $\dfrac{11a}{6}$

b $\dfrac{7}{3b} - \dfrac{5}{b}$

The common denominator is $3b$. The first fraction is fine. We must multiply the numerator and denominator of the second fraction by 3. Then, rewrite the two expressions as one fraction and combine like terms.

$$\dfrac{7}{3b} - \dfrac{5}{b} = \dfrac{7}{3b} - \dfrac{5}{b} \bullet \dfrac{3}{3} = \dfrac{7}{3b} - \dfrac{15}{3b} = \dfrac{7-15}{3b} = \dfrac{-8}{3b} \quad (b \neq 0)$$

Answer: $\dfrac{-8}{3b}, \ (b \neq 0)$

c $\dfrac{2x}{x-4} + \dfrac{8}{4-x}$

Notice that the denominator of the second fraction is the additive inverse of the denominator of the first fraction. We can rewrite $(4-x)$ as $-(x-4)$. Since $\dfrac{8}{-(x-4)} = -\dfrac{8}{x-4}$, and adding a negative is the same as subtracting a positive, we can replace the addition sign between the two fractions with a subtraction sign. Then, rewrite as one fraction, factor the numerator, and reduce the fraction.

$$\dfrac{2x}{x-4} + \dfrac{8}{4-x} = \dfrac{2x}{x-4} + \dfrac{8}{-(x-4)} = \dfrac{2x}{x-4} + \left(-\dfrac{8}{(x-4)}\right) = \dfrac{2x}{x-4} - \dfrac{8}{x-4}$$

$$= \dfrac{2x-8}{x-4} = \dfrac{2\cancel{(x-4)}}{\cancel{x-4}} = 2 \quad (x \neq 4)$$

Answer: $2, \ (x \neq 4)$

d $\dfrac{x}{x-3} - \dfrac{18}{x^2-9}$

Before we can begin, we must factor the denominator of the second expression.

$$\frac{x}{x-3} - \frac{18}{x^2-9} = \frac{x}{x-3} - \frac{18}{(x+3)(x-3)}$$

Now, we can see that our common denominator is $(x+3)(x-3)$.

Multiply the numerator and denominator of the first expression by $(x+3)$, rewrite as one fraction, factor, and reduce.

$$\frac{x}{x-3} - \frac{18}{x^2-9} = \frac{x}{x-3} - \frac{18}{(x+3)(x-3)}$$

$$= \frac{x}{x-3} \cdot \frac{x+3}{x+3} - \frac{18}{(x+3)(x-3)}$$

$$= \frac{x(x+3) - 18}{(x+3)(x-3)}$$

$$= \frac{x^2 + 3x - 18}{(x+3)(x-3)}$$

$$= \frac{(x+6)\cancel{(x-3)}}{(x+3)\cancel{(x-3)}}$$

$$= \frac{x+6}{x+3} \quad (x \neq 3, -3)$$

Answer: $\dfrac{x+6}{x+3}, (x \neq 3, -3)$

e $\dfrac{3}{x+1} - \dfrac{2}{x}$

To get a common denominator, we have to find the least common multiple of $x + 1$ and x. Since they have no common factors, the least common multiple is $x(x+1)$. We multiply the numerator and denominator of the first fraction by x, and the numerator and denominator of the second fraction by $x + 1$.

$$\frac{3}{x+1} - \frac{2}{x} = \frac{3}{x+1} \cdot \frac{x}{x} - \frac{2}{x} \cdot \frac{x+1}{x+1}$$

$$= \frac{3x - 2(x+1)}{x(x+1)} \qquad \text{Rewrite the two expressions as one fraction.}$$

$$= \frac{3x - 2x - 2}{x(x+1)} \qquad \text{Be certain to distribute the } -2.$$

$$= \frac{x-2}{x(x+1)} \qquad (x \neq 0, -1)$$

Answer: $\dfrac{x-2}{x(x+1)}, (x \neq 0, -1)$

> **Note:** We can get a common denominator only by multiplying.

f $\dfrac{1}{x^2 + 3x + 2} + \dfrac{2}{x^2 - 1}$

To begin, factor the denominators of both expressions.

$$\frac{1}{x^2 + 3x + 2} + \frac{2}{x^2 - 1} = \frac{1}{(x + 2)(x + 1)} + \frac{2}{(x + 1)(x - 1)}$$

Our common denominator is $(x + 2)(x + 1)(x - 1)$.

Multiply the numerator and denominator of the first expression by $x - 1$.

Multiply the numerator and denominator of the second expression by $x + 2$.

$$\frac{1}{x^2 + 3x + 2} + \frac{2}{x^2 - 1} = \frac{1}{(x + 2)(x + 1)} + \frac{2}{(x + 1)(x - 1)}$$

$$= \frac{1}{(x + 2)(x + 1)} \bullet \frac{x - 1}{x - 1} + \frac{2}{(x + 1)(x - 1)} \bullet \frac{x + 2}{x + 2}$$

$$= \frac{1(x - 1) + 2(x + 2)}{(x + 2)(x + 1)(x - 1)} \qquad \text{Rewrite as one fraction.}$$

$$= \frac{x - 1 + 2x + 4}{(x + 2)(x + 1)(x - 1)} \qquad \text{Distribute the 2.}$$

$$= \frac{3x + 3}{(x + 2)(x + 1)(x - 1)} \qquad \text{Combine like terms.}$$

$$= \frac{3\cancel{(x + 1)}}{(x + 2)\cancel{(x + 1)}(x - 1)} \qquad \text{Factor and reduce.}$$

$$= \frac{3}{(x + 2)(x - 1)} \qquad (x \neq -2, -1, 1)$$

Answer: $\dfrac{3}{(x + 2)(x - 1)}, (x \neq -2, -1, 1)$

3 Transform the mixed expression $a - 2 + \dfrac{5}{a}$ into a rational expression.

SOLUTION

Just as there are mixed numbers such as $2\dfrac{1}{3}$, there are mixed expressions such as $2x + \dfrac{1}{x}$.

A mixed expression can be written as a rational expression.

$$a - 2 + \frac{5}{a}$$

We can think of this problem as three separate rational expressions, two of which have denominators of 1:

$$a - 2 + \frac{5}{a} = \frac{a}{1} - \frac{2}{1} + \frac{5}{a}$$

The common denominator is a. Multiply the numerator and denominator of the first two fractions by a, and follow the procedure for adding and subtracting rational expressions.

$$a - 2 + \frac{5}{a} = \frac{a}{1} - \frac{2}{1} + \frac{5}{a}$$

$$= \frac{a}{1} \cdot \frac{a}{a} - \frac{2}{1} \cdot \frac{a}{a} + \frac{5}{a}$$

$$= \frac{a^2 - 2a + 5}{a} \quad (a \neq 0)$$

Answer: $\dfrac{a^2 - 2a + 5}{a}, \ (a \neq 0)$

 Practice

Exercises 1–15: Perform the indicated operation. Express your answer in simplest form.

1 $\dfrac{2x}{7} - \dfrac{x}{3}$

2 $\dfrac{4}{5x} + \dfrac{2}{x}$

3 $\dfrac{3}{x^2} - \dfrac{2}{x}$

4 $\dfrac{5}{a^2} - \dfrac{3}{2a}$

5 $\dfrac{3c}{c - 5} + \dfrac{15}{5 - c}$

6 $\dfrac{x}{x^2 - 16} + \dfrac{4}{x - 4}$

7 $\dfrac{5}{2x + 6} - \dfrac{2}{5x + 15}$

8 $\dfrac{2}{x^2 - 1} + \dfrac{3}{x^2 - x}$

9 $\dfrac{6}{x} - \dfrac{6}{x + 2}$

10 $\dfrac{y + 2}{y^2 - y - 2} + \dfrac{1}{3y + 3}$

11 $\dfrac{6}{x^2 + 4x + 3} + \dfrac{3}{x^2 + 7x + 12}$

12 $\dfrac{3}{x^2 + 5x - 14} - \dfrac{2}{x^2 + 8x + 7}$

13 $\dfrac{x}{x^2 + 9x + 18} - \dfrac{3}{x^2 + 3x}$

14 $\dfrac{x + 2}{x^2 + 7x + 12} + \dfrac{2}{x + 4} + \dfrac{1}{x + 3}$

15 $\dfrac{x - 3}{x^2 - 1} + \dfrac{3}{x - 1} - \dfrac{4}{2x + 2}$

Exercises 16–18: Transform the mixed expression into a rational expression.

16 $n + \dfrac{n}{3}$

17 $a + 2 + \dfrac{a}{5}$

18 $r + 2 + \dfrac{3}{r}$

Exercises 19–22: Select the numeral preceding the expression that best completes the statement or answers the question.

19 To find the sum of $\dfrac{x + 2}{x}$ and $\dfrac{x}{x + 3}$, the common denominator is

(1) x (3) $x^2 + 3x$

(2) $x + 3$ (4) $x^2 + 2x$

20 On the first day of her hike into the mountains, Courtney walked one-third of the distance to base camp. The next day, she walked one-fourth of the distance to base camp. If the distance to base camp is m miles, what is the total number of miles that Courtney has walked?

(1) $\dfrac{1}{7}m$ (3) $\dfrac{5}{12}m$

(2) $\dfrac{2}{7}m$ (4) $\dfrac{7}{12}m$

21 If the length of a rectangle is $\dfrac{x+1}{x}$ and its width is $\dfrac{x+2}{2}$, which expression represents the perimeter of the rectangle?

(1) $\dfrac{x^2+4x+2}{x}$ (3) $\dfrac{x^2+4x+2}{2x}$

(2) $\dfrac{x^2+4x+2}{2}$ (4) $\dfrac{x^2+8x+4}{2x}$

22 Mrs. Rose has p papers to mark. She marks $\dfrac{2}{5}$ of them before supper, and $\dfrac{1}{3}$ of them after supper. Which expression represents the number of papers that Mrs. Rose has left to mark?

(1) $\dfrac{2}{15}p$ (3) $\dfrac{11}{15}p$

(2) $\dfrac{4}{15}p$ (4) $\dfrac{3}{8}p$

2.4 Ratio and Proportion

A **ratio** is a relationship between two quantities, expressed as the quotient of one quantity divided by the other. The ratio of two numbers, a and b, where $b \neq 0$, is the number $\dfrac{a}{b}$, which can also be written in the form $a:b$.

A ratio can be simplified by dividing each term by the same nonzero number. A ratio is in **simplest form** when the terms of the ratio are integers that have no common factor other than 1 or -1. For example, $4:8 = \dfrac{4}{4}:\dfrac{8}{4} = 1:2$. In general, for $x \neq 0$, $ax:bx = a:b$

An equivalent ratio can also be written by multiplying each term of the ratio by the same nonzero number. For example, $2:3 = 2(5):3(5) = 10:15$. In general, for $x \neq 0$, $a:b = ax:bx$.

You have come across many ratios in your studies of mathematics. For example, in Section 1.1, we defined a rational number as a number in the form $\dfrac{a}{b}$, where a and b are both integers, and $b \neq 0$. Thus, a rational number is a number that can be expressed as the ratio of two integers.

A **rate** is a fixed ratio between two quantities. A rate can express how long it takes to do something, such as traveling a certain distance. If you drove 50 miles in one hour, you drove at a rate of 50 mph. The rate is the ratio of the number of miles driven to the amount of time spent driving $\left(\dfrac{50 \text{ miles}}{1 \text{ hour}}\right)$. As of 2008, if your rate of pay was the minimum wage, you would be paid $7.15 per hour. This rate is the ratio of the amount of money received to the time worked $\left(\dfrac{\$7.15}{1 \text{ hour}}\right)$.

A **proportion** is an equation that states that two ratios are equal. A proportion is written as $\dfrac{a}{b} = \dfrac{c}{d}$ or $a:b = c:d$, where $b \neq 0$ and $d \neq 0$. The first and fourth terms, a and d, are called the **extremes** of the proportion. The second and third terms, b and c, are called the **means** of the proportion. In a proportion, the product of the means is equal to the product of the extremes.

MODEL PROBLEMS

1 Determine whether or not each statement represents a true proportion.

a $\dfrac{3}{4} = \dfrac{9}{12}$ **b** $\dfrac{2}{3} = \dfrac{4}{9}$

c $8:5 = 4:3$ **d** $20:30 = 4:6$

SOLUTION

To solve this problem, check if the product of the means is equal to the product of the extremes.

a $\dfrac{3}{4} \overset{?}{=} \dfrac{9}{12}$ **b** $\dfrac{2}{3} \overset{?}{=} \dfrac{4}{9}$

$4(9) \overset{?}{=} 3(12)$ $3(4) \overset{?}{=} 2(9)$

$36 = 36$ $12 \neq 18$

$\dfrac{3}{4} = \dfrac{9}{12}$ $\dfrac{2}{3} \neq \dfrac{4}{9}$

c $8:5 \overset{?}{=} 4:3$ **d** $20:30 \overset{?}{=} 4:6$

$5(4) \overset{?}{=} 8(3)$ $30(4) \overset{?}{=} 20(6)$

$20 \neq 24$ $120 = 120$

$8:5 \neq 4:3$ $20:30 = 4:6$

Answers: **a** true   **b** false   **c** false   **d** true

2 Solve for x in each of the following proportions.

a $\dfrac{4}{7} = \dfrac{x}{x + 6}$

b $\dfrac{x + 1}{4} = \dfrac{4x + 1}{12}$

SOLUTION

Remember, the product of the means is equal to the product of the extremes.

a $\dfrac{4}{7} = \dfrac{x}{x + 6}$

$4(x + 6) = 7x$

$4x + 24 = 7x$

$24 = 3x$

$x = 8$

Check:

$\dfrac{4}{7} = \dfrac{x}{x + 6}$

$\dfrac{4}{7} = \dfrac{8}{8 + 6}$

$\dfrac{4}{7} = \dfrac{8}{14}$

$\dfrac{4}{7} = \dfrac{4}{7}$ ✔

b $\dfrac{x + 1}{4} = \dfrac{4x + 1}{12}$

$12(x + 1) = 4(4x + 1)$

$12x + 12 = 16x + 4$

$8 = 4x$

$x = 2$

Check:

$\dfrac{x + 1}{4} = \dfrac{4x + 1}{12}$

$\dfrac{2 + 1}{4} = \dfrac{4(2) + 1}{12}$

$\dfrac{3}{4} = \dfrac{8 + 1}{12}$

$\dfrac{3}{4} = \dfrac{9}{12}$

$\dfrac{3}{4} = \dfrac{3}{4}$ ✔

3 On July 4, 2008, one U.S. dollar was worth 0.6318 euros. On that day, Michael and Liza were in Paris, and their dinner cost 76 euros. How much was that in U.S. dollars?

SOLUTION

Use the conversion rate of one U.S. dollar to 0.6318 euros to set up a proportion.

$\dfrac{1 \text{ dollar}}{0.6318 \text{ euros}} = \dfrac{x \text{ dollars}}{76 \text{ euros}}$

$76 = 0.6318x$

$x = 120.2912314$

Answer: The dinner cost \$120.29.

4 The number of cell phone subscribers in the United States increased from 340,213 in 1985 to 253,000,000 in 2007. What was the percent of increase?

SOLUTION

The word *percent* comes from the Latin *per centum*, meaning "by the hundred." Since a percent is a ratio of a number to 100, you can use the proportion $\dfrac{\text{part}}{\text{whole}} = \dfrac{\text{percent}}{100}$ to solve problems involving percent.

The number of cell phone subscribers increased from 340,213 to 253,000,000. This is an increase of 252,659,787 users. To determine the percent increase, we will set up a proportion.

$$\frac{\text{part}}{\text{whole}} = \frac{\text{percent}}{100} \quad \text{or} \quad \frac{\text{change in value}}{\text{original value}} = \frac{\text{percent}}{100}$$

$$\frac{252{,}659{,}787}{340{,}213} = \frac{p}{100}$$

$$p = 74{,}265.17711$$

Answer: This is an increase of approximately 74,265.2%.

5 In Gotham High School, the ratio of girls to boys is 3:2. If there are 500 students in the high school, how many boys are there?

SOLUTION

The ratio of girls to boys is 3:2. Thus, the number of girls : the number of boys = $3:2 = 3x:2x$.
Therefore,

the number of girls = $3x$

the number of boys = $2x$

and

$$3x + 2x = 500$$

$$5x = 500$$

$$x = 100$$

Answer: There are $2x = 2(100) = 200$ boys.

Practice

Exercises 1–4: Determine whether or not each statement represents a true proportion.

1 $\dfrac{4}{8} = \dfrac{3}{6}$

2 $\dfrac{5}{7} = \dfrac{25}{49}$

3 $4:3 = 5:4$

4 $3:9 = 2:6$

Exercises 5–12: Solve each proportion.

5 $\dfrac{4}{5} = \dfrac{x}{25}$

6 $\dfrac{6}{9} = \dfrac{10}{y}$

7 $\dfrac{7}{10} = \dfrac{z+4}{2z}$

8 $\dfrac{1}{x} = \dfrac{x}{4}$

9 $\dfrac{y}{y-1} = \dfrac{12}{9}$

10 $\dfrac{12}{3z} = \dfrac{8}{z+5}$

11 $\dfrac{x}{8} = \dfrac{1}{x+2}$

12 $\dfrac{x-3}{x} = \dfrac{5}{x+4}$

Exercises 13–21: Select the numeral preceding the choice that best completes the statement or answers the question.

13 Which ratio is *not* equivalent to the other three?

(1) 3:5 (3) 9:25
(2) 6:10 (4) 15:25

14 Which proportion is *not* equivalent to the other three?

(1) $\dfrac{x}{3} = \dfrac{4}{x+1}$ (3) $\dfrac{x}{x+1} = \dfrac{4}{3}$

(2) $\dfrac{x}{4} = \dfrac{3}{x+1}$ (4) $\dfrac{3}{x} = \dfrac{x+1}{4}$

15 Solve the proportion $3:x = 9:27$ for x.

(1) $x = 1$ (3) $x = 3$
(2) $x = 9$ (4) $x = 27$

16 If there are 5,280 feet in one mile, approximately how many miles are there in 20,000 feet?

(1) 3.677 (3) 4.013
(2) 3.788 (4) 10,560

17 At Eastvale College, the ratio of girls to boys is 2:3. If there are 500 more boys than girls, how many girls attend Eastvale College?

(1) 500 (3) 1,500
(2) 1,000 (4) 2,500

18 A recipe calls for 2 cups of flour and $\dfrac{1}{2}$ cup of sugar. Instead of putting in 2 cups of flour, Marie mistakenly put in 2 cups of sugar. How many cups of flour must she use to keep the proportions correct?

(1) $\dfrac{1}{2}$ (3) 4
(2) 2 (4) 8

19 If $\dfrac{x}{3} = \dfrac{a}{b}$, $b \neq 0$, then x is equal to

(1) $\dfrac{a}{3b}$ (3) $\dfrac{3a}{b}$

(2) $\dfrac{3b}{a}$ (4) $\dfrac{3}{ab}$

20 On a map, $\dfrac{1}{2}$ inch represents 5 miles. On the map, the distance from Melville to Newburgh measures 4 inches. Approximately how many miles is it from Melville to Newburgh?

(1) 10 (3) 40
(2) 20 (4) 80

21 The ratio of the width of a rectangular picture to its length is 5:7. If the perimeter of the picture is 48 inches, how long is the picture?

(1) 5 inches (3) 10 inches
(2) 7 inches (4) 14 inches

22 One inch is equal to 2.54 centimeters. Lauren bought a skirt with a length of 56 centimeters. What is the length in inches?

23 The maximum slope for wheelchair ramps should be 1 inch of rise to every 12 inches of length. Johnny is building a wheelchair ramp to provide access to his new home. If the doorway is about 20 inches high, how long must the ramp be to provide safe access to the doorway?

24 In a poll, only 25% of Americans approved of the way the president was handling his job. The results were based on 1,100 telephone interviews with a nationwide random sample of adults 18 years and older. How many of these people approved of the way the president was handling his job?

25 Joey's hybrid car is estimated to average 32 miles per gallon of gasoline. If Joey drives from Huntington Station to Buffalo, a distance of approximately 435 miles, how many gallons of gasoline should he expect to use?

26 The ratio of adult tickets to child tickets sold for a school play was 1:2. If a total of 1,200 tickets were sold, how many were adult tickets?

27 The Fibonacci sequence is a sequence of numbers, 1, 1, 2, 3, 5, 8, 13, 21, . . . , in which each term is found by adding the two previous terms. For example, the third term is the sum of the first and second terms, and the fourth term is the sum of the second and third terms. As you extend the sequence, the ratio of each term to the one before it approaches the golden ratio.

a What are the next five numbers in the Fibonacci sequence?

b Compute the ratio of each term from part **a** to the one before it to three decimal places.

c The ratio of each successive pair of numbers in the Fibonacci sequence approximates the golden ratio, represented by the Greek letter phi (ϕ), which is equal to $\dfrac{1 + \sqrt{5}}{2}$. Compare this to your approximations in part **b**.

2.5 Complex Rational Expressions

A complex fraction is a fraction that contains other fractions. Examples of complex fractions are

$$\dfrac{\frac{5}{6}}{\frac{2}{3}}, \quad \dfrac{2\frac{1}{2}}{5}, \text{ and } \dfrac{4}{1\frac{1}{3}}.$$

A complex rational expression is a rational expression that contains other rational expressions. Examples of complex rational expressions are

$$\dfrac{\frac{2}{3x}}{\frac{1}{x}}, \quad \dfrac{x - \frac{1}{x}}{x + 1}, \text{ and } \dfrac{x + 2}{1 + \frac{5}{x} + \frac{6}{x^2}}.$$

The procedure for simplifying a complex fraction or a complex rational expression is basically the same. There are two methods that are commonly used. We will demonstrate both methods. Use the method that looks more familiar to you. (If neither method looks familiar, chose the method that looks easier to you.)

📐 MODEL PROBLEM

1 Simplify each complex fraction.

a $\dfrac{\frac{5}{6}}{\frac{2}{3}}$

b $\dfrac{2\frac{1}{2}}{5}$

c $\dfrac{4}{1\frac{1}{3}}$

SOLUTION

We will demonstrate both methods for part **a** and then use one method for part **b** and the other method for part **c**.

a $\dfrac{\frac{5}{6}}{\frac{2}{3}}$

Method 1

Look at the complex fraction as a division problem. You are being asked to divide $\dfrac{5}{6}$ by $\dfrac{2}{3}$. Therefore, we can rewrite the complex fraction as a division problem and utilize the rules for division.

$$\frac{\frac{5}{6}}{\frac{2}{3}} = \frac{5}{6} \div \frac{2}{3} = \frac{5}{\cancel{6}_2} \bullet \frac{\cancel{3}}{2} = \frac{5}{4}$$

Remember: Rewrite the complex fraction as a division problem. Follow the rules for division

Method 2

Multiply the entire complex fraction by the least common denominator of all of the denominators in the complex fraction. In this case, the common denominator of $\dfrac{5}{6}$ and $\dfrac{2}{3}$ is 6, so we multiply both $\dfrac{5}{6}$ and $\dfrac{2}{3}$ by 6.

$$\frac{\frac{5}{6}}{\frac{2}{3}} = \frac{\frac{5}{6}}{\frac{2}{3}} \bullet \frac{6}{6} = \frac{\frac{5}{\cancel{6}} \bullet \cancel{6}}{\frac{2}{\cancel{3}} \bullet \cancel{6}_2} = \frac{5}{4}$$

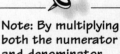

Note: By multiplying both the numerator and denominator of the complex fraction by 6, we are actually multiplying the fraction by $\dfrac{6}{6} = 1$.

Answer: $\dfrac{5}{4}$

b $\dfrac{2\frac{1}{2}}{5}$

We will use Method 1 to simplify this complex fraction. First, rewrite $2\dfrac{1}{2}$ as the improper fraction $\dfrac{5}{2}$, then rewrite the entire expression as a division problem and follow the rules for division.

$$\frac{2\frac{1}{2}}{5} = \frac{\frac{5}{2}}{5} = \frac{5}{2} \div \frac{5}{1} = \frac{\cancel{5}}{2} \bullet \frac{1}{\cancel{5}} = \frac{1}{2}$$

Note: Before beginning our division, we got a single fraction in the numerator and a single fraction in the denominator.

Answer: $\dfrac{1}{2}$

c $\dfrac{4}{1\frac{1}{3}}$

We will use Method 2 to simplify this complex fraction. First rewrite $1\frac{1}{3}$ as an improper fraction. We must now find the least common denominator of $\dfrac{4}{1}$ and $\dfrac{4}{3}$, which is 3. We then multiply numerator and denominator by 3, and simplify.

$$\dfrac{4}{1\frac{1}{3}} = \dfrac{\frac{4}{1}}{\frac{4}{3}} = \dfrac{\frac{4}{1}}{\frac{4}{3}} \cdot \dfrac{3}{3} = \dfrac{\frac{4}{1} \cdot 3}{\frac{4}{\cancel{3}} \cdot \cancel{3}} = \dfrac{12}{4} = 3$$

Answer: 3

Now let's look at complex rational expressions. We will use the same methods for simplifying these.

MODEL PROBLEM

2 Express each rational expression in simplest form.

a $\dfrac{\frac{2}{3x}}{\frac{1}{x}}$

b $\dfrac{x - \frac{1}{x}}{x + 1}$

c $\dfrac{x + 2}{1 + \frac{5}{x} + \frac{6}{x^2}}$

SOLUTION

We will demonstrate both methods for part **a** and then use one method for part **b** and the other method for part **c**.

a $\dfrac{\dfrac{2}{3x}}{\dfrac{1}{x}}$

Method 1

Look at the complex rational expression as a division problem—it is asking you to divide $\dfrac{2}{3x}$ by $\dfrac{1}{x}$.

We can rewrite the complex fraction as a division problem and utilize the rules for division.

$$\frac{\dfrac{2}{3x}}{\dfrac{1}{x}} = \frac{2}{3x} \div \frac{1}{x} = \frac{2}{3\cancel{x}} \cdot \frac{\cancel{x}}{1} = \frac{2}{3}$$

Method 2

Multiply the entire complex fraction by the least common denominator of all of the denominators in the complex fraction. In this case, the common denominator of $\dfrac{2}{3x}$ and $\dfrac{1}{x}$ is $3x$, so we multiply both $\dfrac{2}{3x}$ and $\dfrac{1}{x}$ by $3x$.

$$\frac{\dfrac{2}{3x}}{\dfrac{1}{x}} = \frac{\dfrac{2}{3x}}{\dfrac{1}{x}} \cdot \frac{3x}{3x} = \frac{\dfrac{2}{3\cancel{x}} \cdot 3\cancel{x}}{\dfrac{1}{\cancel{x}} \cdot 3\cancel{x}} = \frac{2}{3}$$

Answer: $\dfrac{2}{3}, (x \neq 0)$

b $\dfrac{x - \dfrac{1}{x}}{x + 1}$

We will use Method 1 to simplify this complex rational expression. First, rewrite the numerator and denominator each as a single fraction. Then rewrite the entire problem as a division problem and follow the rules for division.

$$\frac{x - \dfrac{1}{x}}{x + 1} = \frac{\dfrac{x}{1} - \dfrac{1}{x}}{x + 1} = \frac{\dfrac{x^2 - 1}{x}}{\dfrac{x + 1}{1}} = \frac{x^2 - 1}{x} \div \frac{x + 1}{1} = \frac{x^2 - 1}{x} \cdot \frac{1}{x + 1}$$

$$= \frac{(x + 1)(x - 1)}{x} \cdot \frac{1}{x + 1} = \frac{x - 1}{x}$$

Answer: $\dfrac{x - 1}{x}, (x \neq 0, -1)$

c $\dfrac{x + 2}{1 + \dfrac{5}{x} + \dfrac{6}{x^2}}$

We will use Method 2 to simplify this complex rational expression. We must find the least common denominator of $x + 2$, 1, $\dfrac{5}{x}$, and $\dfrac{6}{x^2}$, which is x^2. Multiply each term in the numerator and denominator by x^2, and simplify.

$$\dfrac{x + 2}{1 + \dfrac{5}{x} + \dfrac{6}{x^2}} = \dfrac{x + 2}{1 + \dfrac{5}{x} + \dfrac{6}{x^2}} \bullet \dfrac{x^2}{x^2} = \dfrac{x^2(x + 2)}{x^2(1) + \cancel{x^2}\left(\dfrac{5}{\cancel{x}}\right) + \cancel{x^2}\left(\dfrac{6}{\cancel{x^2}}\right)}$$

$$= \dfrac{x^2(x + 2)}{x^2 + 5x + 6} = \dfrac{x^2\cancel{(x + 2)}}{\cancel{(x + 2)}(x + 3)} = \dfrac{x^2}{x + 3} \quad (x \neq 0, -2, -3)$$

Answer: $\dfrac{x^2}{x + 3}, (x \neq 0, -2, -3)$

Practice

Exercises 1–18: Express each complex fraction or complex rational expression in simplest form.

1 $\dfrac{\dfrac{4}{5}}{\dfrac{2}{5}}$

2 $\dfrac{\dfrac{5}{9x}}{\dfrac{2}{3x}}$

3 $\dfrac{\dfrac{6}{7}}{14}$

4 $\dfrac{\dfrac{3}{7}}{2\dfrac{1}{3}}$

5 $\dfrac{1 + \dfrac{1}{a}}{3a}$

6 $\dfrac{\dfrac{2}{3} + \dfrac{5}{9a}}{\dfrac{7}{18a}}$

7 $\dfrac{2a + 2b}{\dfrac{2}{a} + \dfrac{2}{b}}$

8 $\dfrac{\dfrac{1}{3} + \dfrac{3}{w}}{\dfrac{6}{w}}$

9 $\dfrac{\dfrac{1}{x} + \dfrac{1}{y}}{\dfrac{1}{x} - \dfrac{1}{y}}$

10 $\dfrac{\dfrac{2n}{3} + \dfrac{3}{2n}}{\dfrac{4n}{9} + \dfrac{1}{n}}$

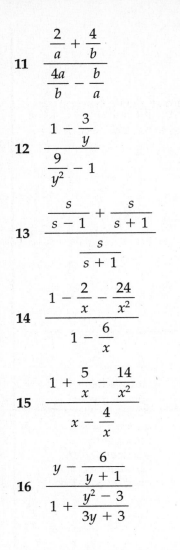

11 $\dfrac{\dfrac{2}{a}+\dfrac{4}{b}}{\dfrac{4a}{b}-\dfrac{b}{a}}$

12 $\dfrac{1-\dfrac{3}{y}}{\dfrac{9}{y^2}-1}$

13 $\dfrac{\dfrac{s}{s-1}+\dfrac{s}{s+1}}{\dfrac{s}{s+1}}$

14 $\dfrac{1-\dfrac{2}{x}-\dfrac{24}{x^2}}{1-\dfrac{6}{x}}$

15 $\dfrac{1+\dfrac{5}{x}-\dfrac{14}{x^2}}{x-\dfrac{4}{x}}$

16 $\dfrac{y-\dfrac{6}{y+1}}{1+\dfrac{y^2-3}{3y+3}}$

Exercises 17 and 18: Select the numeral preceding the choice that best completes the statement.

17 In electronics, when two resistors, R_1 and R_2, are connected in parallel, their combined resistance is given by the formula $\dfrac{1}{\dfrac{1}{R_1}+\dfrac{1}{R_2}}$.

When simplified, this complex rational expression is equivalent to

(1) $R_1 + R_2$ (3) $\dfrac{R_1 + R_2}{R_1 R_2}$

(2) $R_1 R_2$ (4) $\dfrac{R_1 R_2}{R_1 + R_2}$

18 In physics, the formula for the focal length of a mirror is $\dfrac{1}{\dfrac{1}{s}+\dfrac{1}{s'}}$. This complex rational expression can be simplified to

(1) $s \bullet s'$ (3) $\dfrac{s \bullet s'}{s + s'}$

(2) $s + s'$ (4) $\dfrac{s + s'}{s \bullet s'}$

2.6 Solving Rational Equations

To solve an equation containing fractions or rational expressions, multiply both sides of the equation by the least common denominator of all fractions and rational expressions that appear in the equation. Then, solve the resulting equation.

MODEL PROBLEM

1 Solve for x and check.

a $\dfrac{2}{3}+\dfrac{4}{x}=\dfrac{5}{6}$

b $\dfrac{10}{x^2}+\dfrac{3}{x}=1$

SOLUTION

a $\dfrac{2}{3} + \dfrac{4}{x} = \dfrac{5}{6}$

First find the least common denominator of $\dfrac{2}{3}$, $\dfrac{4}{x}$, and $\dfrac{5}{6}$, which is $6x$, and multiply both sides of the equation by $6x$. Then solve the resulting equation.

$$\frac{2}{3} + \frac{4}{x} = \frac{5}{6}$$

$$6x \cdot \left(\frac{2}{3} + \frac{4}{x}\right) = \left(\frac{5}{6}\right) \cdot 6x$$

$$\overset{2}{\cancel{6}}x \cdot \frac{2}{\cancel{3}} + 6\cancel{x} \cdot \frac{4}{\cancel{x}} = \frac{5}{\cancel{6}} \cdot \cancel{6}x$$

$$4x + 24 = 5x$$

$$x = 24$$

Check:

To check our answer, substitute 24 for x in the original equation.

$$\frac{2}{3} + \frac{4}{x} = \frac{5}{6}$$

$$\frac{2}{3} + \frac{4}{24} \overset{?}{=} \frac{5}{6}$$

$$\frac{2}{3} + \frac{1}{6} \overset{?}{=} \frac{5}{6}$$

$$\frac{4}{6} + \frac{1}{6} \overset{?}{=} \frac{5}{6}$$

$$\frac{5}{6} = \frac{5}{6} \checkmark$$

Answer: $x = 24$

> **Note:** When checking your solution, ALWAYS go back and substitute the solution for the variable into the original equation.

b $\dfrac{10}{x^2} + \dfrac{3}{x} = 1$

First find the least common denominator of x^2, x, and 1, which is x^2. Multiply both sides of the equation by x^2 and solve the resulting equation.

$$\frac{10}{x^2} + \frac{3}{x} = 1$$

$$x^2 \cdot \left(\frac{10}{x^2} + \frac{3}{x}\right) = x^2 \cdot (1)$$

$$\cancel{x^2} \cdot \frac{10}{\cancel{x^2}} + \overset{x}{\cancel{x^2}} \cdot \frac{3}{\cancel{x}} = x^2 \cdot 1$$

$$10 + 3x = x^2$$

We have a quadratic equation. Set it equal to zero, factor, and solve.

$$x^2 - 3x - 10 = 0$$

$$(x - 5)(x + 2) = 0$$

$$x - 5 = 0 \qquad\qquad x + 2 = 0$$

$$x = 5 \qquad\qquad\qquad x = -2$$

Check:

$$x = 5 \qquad\qquad\qquad\qquad x = -2$$

$$\frac{10}{x^2} + \frac{3}{x} = 1 \qquad\qquad \frac{10}{x^2} + \frac{3}{x} = 1$$

$$\frac{10}{5^2} + \frac{3}{5} \stackrel{?}{=} 1 \qquad\qquad \frac{10}{(-2)^2} + \frac{3}{-2} \stackrel{?}{=} 1$$

$$\frac{10}{25} + \frac{3}{5} \stackrel{?}{=} 1 \qquad\qquad \frac{10}{4} - \frac{3}{2} \stackrel{?}{=} 1$$

$$\frac{2}{5} + \frac{3}{5} \stackrel{?}{=} 1 \qquad\qquad \frac{5}{2} - \frac{3}{2} \stackrel{?}{=} 1$$

$$1 = 1\ ✔ \qquad\qquad\qquad 1 = 1\ ✔$$

Answer: $x = 5, -2$

When you multiply both sides of the equation by the least common denominator, the derived equation may not be equivalent to the original equation. The following example will demonstrate this.

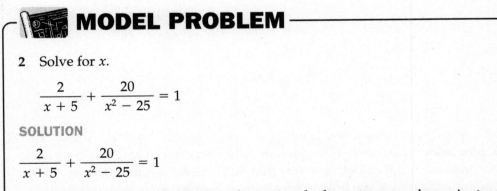 **MODEL PROBLEM**

2 Solve for x.

$$\frac{2}{x + 5} + \frac{20}{x^2 - 25} = 1$$

SOLUTION

$$\frac{2}{x + 5} + \frac{20}{x^2 - 25} = 1$$

Factor the second denominator to determine the least common denominator, multiply both sides of the equation by the common denominator, and solve the resulting equation.

$$\frac{2}{x + 5} + \frac{20}{(x + 5)(x - 5)} = 1$$

The least common denominator is $(x + 5)(x - 5)$.

$$(x + 5)(x - 5) \cdot \left(\frac{2}{x + 5} + \frac{20}{(x + 5)(x - 5)} \right) = 1 \cdot (x + 5)(x - 5)$$

$$\cancel{(x + 5)}(x - 5) \cdot \frac{2}{\cancel{x + 5}} + \cancel{(x + 5)(x - 5)} \frac{20}{\cancel{(x + 5)(x - 5)}} = 1 \cdot (x + 5)(x - 5)$$

$$2(x - 5) + 20 = (x + 5)(x - 5)$$

$$2x - 10 + 20 = x^2 - 25$$

$$2x + 10 = x^2 - 25$$

$$x^2 - 2x - 35 = 0$$

$$(x - 7)(x + 5) = 0$$

$$x - 7 = 0 \qquad x + 5 = 0$$

$$x = 7 \qquad x = -5$$

Although the question did not specifically require a check, we MUST check our answers. As you will see, both answers may not check.

Check:

$$\frac{2}{x + 5} + \frac{20}{x^2 - 25} = 1 \qquad\qquad \frac{2}{x + 5} + \frac{20}{x^2 - 25} = 1$$

$$x = 7 \qquad\qquad\qquad x = -5$$

$$\frac{2}{7 + 5} + \frac{20}{7^2 - 25} \overset{?}{=} 1 \qquad\qquad \frac{2}{-5 + 5} + \frac{20}{(-5)^2 - 25} \overset{?}{=} 1$$

$$\frac{2}{12} + \frac{20}{49 - 25} \overset{?}{=} 1 \qquad\qquad \frac{2}{0} + \frac{20}{0} \neq 1$$

Division by 0 is undefined. Thus, the statement here is meaningless, and $x = -5$ is not a root.

$$\frac{1}{6} + \frac{20}{24} \overset{?}{=} 1$$

$$\frac{1}{6} + \frac{5}{6} \overset{?}{=} 1$$

$$1 = 1 \ \checkmark$$

Answer: $x = 7$

Remember: Always check your answers in the *original* equation. In this example, if we had checked our answers in an equation other than the original, both answers may have checked. Although $x = -5$ is a root of the derived equation, it is *not* a root of the original equation. It is called an **extraneous root**.

We can also solve rational equations graphically. To demonstrate this technique, we will use the equation from Model Problem 2.

MODEL PROBLEM

3 Solve for x.

$$\frac{2}{x+5} + \frac{20}{x^2 - 25} = 1$$

Enter the left side of the equation in Y_1 and the right side of the equation in Y_2. Be sure to put parentheses around the denominators of the fractions!

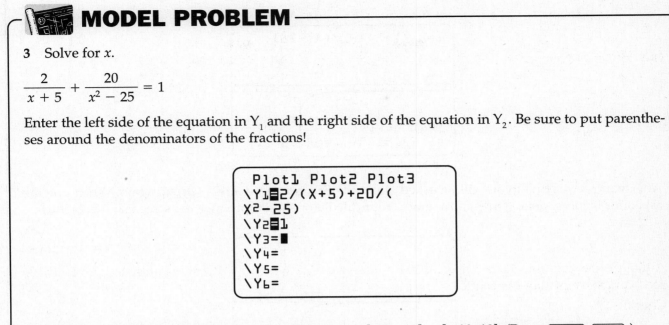

Graph the equations in the standard viewing window $[-10, 10] \times [-10, 10]$. (Press **ZOOM** **6**.)

Notice that there is one point of intersection. To determine the coordinates of this point (whose x-coordinate is the solution of our equation), we will use the CALC feature of the calculator. Select **2nd** **TRACE** to get the window shown below.

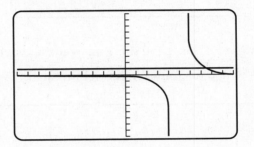

Select 5:intersect.

When you are asked about the First curve, your cursor will be near the origin. This portion of the curve does not intersect the line $y = 1$. You must move your cursor until it is near the intersection point, as illustrated in the screen shown below.

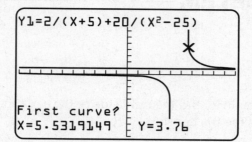

After you press (ENTER) you will be asked about the Second curve. Press (ENTER) again. When you are asked for a guess, press (ENTER) once more. Your calculator should produce the screen shown below.

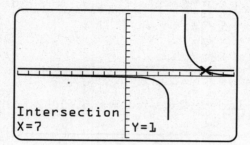

The solution to our equation is $x = 7$. This is the same answer that we obtained algebraically.

Note: The extraneous root -5, which we found in Model Problem 2, is clearly *not* an answer.

Practice

Exercises 1–15: Solve each equation.

1 $\dfrac{3}{a} + \dfrac{5}{2a} = \dfrac{1}{2}$

2 $\dfrac{4}{r} + \dfrac{9 - 4r}{3r} = \dfrac{r}{3}$

3 $\dfrac{1}{6x} + \dfrac{8}{x} = \dfrac{x}{6}$

4 $4 + \dfrac{b}{b + 5} = \dfrac{30}{b + 5}$

5 $1 + \dfrac{2}{x} = \dfrac{3}{x^2}$

6 $3 + \dfrac{a}{a - 6} = \dfrac{6}{a - 6}$

7 $\dfrac{1}{4} + \dfrac{2}{a + 3} = \dfrac{3}{8}$

8 $\dfrac{2}{y + 3} + \dfrac{4}{y} = \dfrac{6}{2y + 6}$

9 $\dfrac{5}{a + 3} - \dfrac{3}{a + 4} = \dfrac{21}{a^2 + 7a + 12}$

10 $2 + \dfrac{4}{x + 2} = \dfrac{6x - 4}{x^2 - 4}$

11 $\dfrac{y}{y - 4} + \dfrac{2}{y + 1} = \dfrac{y - 5}{y^2 - 3y - 4}$

12 $\dfrac{x + 1}{x + 2} - \dfrac{2}{x} = \dfrac{-4}{x^2 + 2x}$

13 $\dfrac{1}{2} + \dfrac{2}{z - 2} = \dfrac{5}{z - 1}$

14 $\dfrac{4n + 3}{n - 6} + \dfrac{n - 4}{6 - n} = \dfrac{44}{2n - 12}$

15 $\dfrac{2b}{5 + b} - \dfrac{1}{5 - b} = \dfrac{10}{b^2 - 25}$

16 What fraction, when added to its reciprocal, is equal to $\dfrac{13}{6}$?

17 The denominator of a fraction is one more than the numerator. If 2 were added to both the numerator and the denominator, the new fraction would equal $\dfrac{4}{5}$. Find the original fraction.

18 Arif estimates that it will take him 8 hours to type his term paper. If he could convince his girlfriend Natisha to bring over her laptop computer and help him with the typing, the two of them could type the paper in 5 hours.

  a What portion of the term paper could Arif type in 1 hour?

  b What portion of the term paper could Arif type in 5 hours?

  c If it takes Natisha n hours to type the paper alone, what portion of the paper could she type in 1 hour? In 5 hours?

  d Arif and Natisha have decided to work together. Write an equation that could be used to estimate the time it would take Arif and Natisha to type the paper if they worked together.

  e Solve the equation from part **d** to find how long it would take Natisha to type the paper if she worked alone.

19 Janine's old printer took 10 minutes to print her assignment. She bought a new printer that printed the same assignment in 5 minutes. She has decided to network the two printers so that they can share the work and print even faster.

  a If t represents the time it would take to print the assignment if the two printers start and stop printing at the same time, what portion of the assignment would her old printer complete?

  b What portion of the assignment would her new printer complete?

  c Determine how long it would take to print the assignment if the two printers were sharing the job.

20 Stan is opening a home repair business. He estimates that it will cost him $300 to buy his equipment, and $20 a week to rent storage space for his equipment.

  a If w represents the number of weeks that Stan is in business, represent the total cost to Stan when he is in business for w weeks.

  b What is the average cost per week that Stan is in business?

  c Stan wants to determine the number of weeks he will have to stay in business for the average cost per week to equal $50. Write an equation to represent this and solve the equation.

Exercises 21–24: Select the numeral preceding the choice that best answers the question.

21 What is the solution set of the equation $\dfrac{x}{x + 3} + \dfrac{2}{x + 1} = \dfrac{6}{x^2 + 4x + 3}$?

  (1) $\{-3\}$ (3) $\{-3, 0\}$

  (2) $\{0\}$ (4) $\{\ \}$

22 While driving to Syracuse, Jennifer and Evan drove 50 mph for x hours and 60 mph for y hours. What is their average rate of speed, in miles per hour, for the whole trip?

  (1) 55 (3) $\dfrac{50x + 60y}{110}$

  (2) $\dfrac{110}{50x + 60y}$ (4) $\dfrac{50x + 60y}{x + y}$

23 What is the solution set of the equation $\dfrac{w}{w - 4} - \dfrac{1}{w + 3} = \dfrac{28}{w^2 - w - 12}$?

  (1) $\{\ \}$ (3) $\{-6\}$

  (2) $\{4, -6\}$ (4) $\{4\}$

24 Wanda's Widget Company manufactures widgets. It costs Wanda $1,000 per month for her fixed costs, plus $10 to produce each widget. If Wanda produces w widgets each month, what is the average cost per widget?

  (1) $\dfrac{1,000 + 10w}{w}$ (3) $\dfrac{1,000 + 10w}{10}$

  (2) $\dfrac{1,000w + 10}{w}$ (4) $\dfrac{1,000w + 10}{1,000}$

2.7 Solving Rational Inequalities

Solving a rational inequality is similar to solving a rational equation, except special care must be taken when multiplying or dividing the inequality by a negative number.

MODEL PROBLEMS

1 Solve: $\dfrac{x}{2} < 6$

SOLUTION

To solve this inequality, we multiply both sides of the inequality by 2, giving us:

$x < 12$

Answer: $x < 12$

2 Solve $\dfrac{x}{-2} < 6$.

SOLUTION

To solve this inequality, we multiply both sides of the inequality by -2 and change the direction of the inequality sign, giving us:

$x > -12$

Answer: $x > -12$

> **Note:** When we multiply or divide an inequality by a negative number, we must reverse the direction of the inequality.

When multiplying or dividing an inequality by a variable, we must be careful to consider what happens when the variable is positive, and what happens when the variable is negative.

MODEL PROBLEM

3 Solve $\dfrac{2}{x} < 6$.

SOLUTION

Since we are working with an inequality, we must consider the two cases of whether x is positive or negative.

If $x > 0$, then $\dfrac{2}{x} < 6$.

When we multiply by a positive value of x, we get

$$\frac{2}{x} \cdot x < 6 \cdot x$$

$$2 < 6x$$

$$\frac{1}{3} < x$$

We can rewrite this as $x > \frac{1}{3}$.

We now have $x > 0$ and $x > \frac{1}{3}$. Thus, $x > \frac{1}{3}$.

Now consider the second case. If $x < 0$,

$$\frac{2}{x} < 6$$

When we multiply by a negative value of x, we have to reverse the direction of the inequality.

$$\frac{2}{x} \cdot x > 6 \cdot x$$

$$2 > 6x$$

$$\frac{1}{3} > x$$

We can rewrite this as $x < \frac{1}{3}$.

We now have $x < 0$ and $x < \frac{1}{3}$. Thus, $x < 0$.

The solution of this inequality is $\left\{x : x < 0 \text{ or } x > \frac{1}{3}\right\}$.

ALTERNATIVE SOLUTION

We can also solve this inequality by identifying the critical x-values and utilizing them to divide a number line into appropriate intervals to see which intervals satisfy the inequality.

Solve $\frac{2}{x} < 6$.

- Solve the corresponding equality for x.

$$\frac{2}{x} = 6$$

$$6x = 2$$

$$x = \frac{1}{3}$$

- Determine the value(s) of x for which the equation is undefined. A fraction is undefined when its denominator equals zero. In this case, the fraction is undefined when $x = 0$.

- Use the two values of x to partition the number line into three intervals.

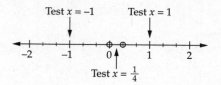

In the first interval, we consider values $x < 0$. In the second interval, we consider values $0 < x < \dfrac{1}{3}$.

In the third interval, we consider values $x > \dfrac{1}{3}$.

- Test an x-value in each interval to see if it satisfies the original inequality. If it does, every x-value in the interval will satisfy the inequality. If it does not, no x-value in the interval will satisfy the inequality.

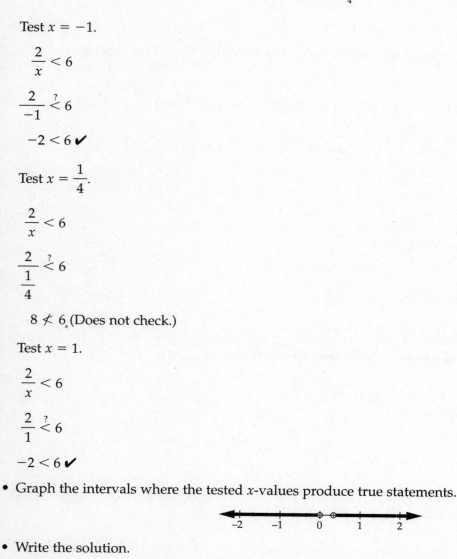

Test $x = -1$.

$$\frac{2}{x} < 6$$

$$\frac{2}{-1} \overset{?}{<} 6$$

$$-2 < 6 \ \checkmark$$

Test $x = \dfrac{1}{4}$.

$$\frac{2}{x} < 6$$

$$\frac{2}{\frac{1}{4}} \overset{?}{<} 6$$

$$8 \not< 6 \ \text{(Does not check.)}$$

Test $x = 1$.

$$\frac{2}{x} < 6$$

$$\frac{2}{1} \overset{?}{<} 6$$

$$-2 < 6 \ \checkmark$$

- Graph the intervals where the tested x-values produce true statements.

- Write the solution.

Answer: $\left\{ x : x < 0 \text{ or } x > \dfrac{1}{3} \right\}$

To summarize this method of solving a rational inequality:

- Solve the corresponding equality for x.
- Determine the value(s) of x for which the equation is undefined.
- Use the above values of x to partition the number line into the appropriate intervals.
- Test an x-value in each interval to see if it satisfies the original inequality. If it does, every x-value in the interval will satisfy the inequality. If it does not, no x-value in the interval will satisfy the inequality.
- Graph the intervals where the tested x-values produce true statements.
- Write the solution.

We can also solve this inequality graphically, following a similar procedure to the one outlined above.

MODEL PROBLEM

4 Solve $\dfrac{2}{x} < 6$.

SOLUTION

Enter the left side of the inequality in Y_1 and the right side of the inequality in Y_2.

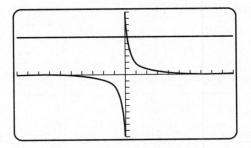

Graph the equations in the standard viewing window, $[-10, 10] \times [-10, 10]$. (Press **ZOOM** **6**.)

Notice that there is one point of intersection. To determine the coordinates of this point, we will use the CALC feature of the calculator. Select **2nd** **TRACE** and choose 5:intersect.

When you are asked for the First curve, you will not be able to see a cursor, since the fraction $\dfrac{2}{x}$ is undefined when $x = 0$. You must move your cursor until you can see it on the graph of $y = \dfrac{2}{x}$, as illustrated in the screen shown on the next page.

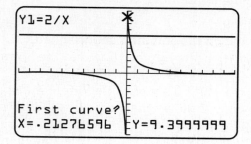

After you press (ENTER), you will be asked for the Second curve. Press (ENTER) again. When you are asked for a Guess, press (ENTER) once more. Your calculator should produce the screen shown below.

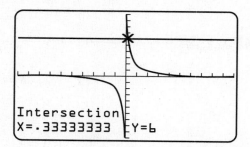

The solution to our equation is $x = 0.33333333$.

You may recognize this as the fraction $\frac{1}{3}$. If you would like the calculator to convert the decimal to a fraction, press (2nd) (MODE), which will return you to the home screen. Press (X,T,θ,n) and then (ENTER). The calculator will show you what value is stored as x (in this case x was 0.33333333). Now press (MATH) and select option 1:Frac. This will convert the decimal 0.33333333 to the fraction $\frac{1}{3}$. The screen shown below illustrates this.

```
X
                    .3333333333
Ans▶Frac
                            1/3
```

We have determined that when $x = \frac{1}{3}, \frac{2}{x} = 6$. However, we want to solve the inequality $\frac{2}{x} < 6$. By looking at the graph above, we can see that when $x > \frac{1}{3}, \frac{2}{x} < 6$. The fraction $\frac{2}{x}$ is undefined when $x = 0$. When $0 < x < \frac{1}{3}, \frac{2}{x} > 6$. When $x < 0, \frac{2}{x} < 6$. Thus, the solution of our inequality is $\left\{x : x < 0 \text{ or } x > \frac{1}{3}\right\}$. This is the same answer that we obtained algebraically.

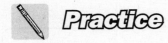

Exercises 1–15: Solve each of the following inequalities.

1 $\dfrac{a}{2} - \dfrac{5}{2} \leq 2$

2 $\dfrac{n-2}{n+4} > 3$

3 $\dfrac{5}{s} + \dfrac{1}{6} > \dfrac{2}{3} + \dfrac{4}{s}$

4 $\dfrac{12}{x-1} > 3$

5 $5 < \dfrac{1}{2y+9} + 4$

6 $\dfrac{g-11}{g+5} - 2 < 7$

7 $\dfrac{7}{r} - \dfrac{3}{2} \geq \dfrac{1}{4}$

8 $\dfrac{1}{4v} + \dfrac{3}{4} < \dfrac{7}{v}$

9 $\dfrac{5}{z} - \dfrac{2}{3} \leq \dfrac{1}{3z}$

10 $\dfrac{3d+2}{d+4} \geq 1$

11 $\dfrac{5k-2}{k+5} < 2$

12 $\dfrac{5}{q+4} \geq \dfrac{4}{q+2}$

13 $y - \dfrac{12}{y} \leq 1$

14 $\dfrac{3}{w-1} + \dfrac{4}{w} \geq \dfrac{5}{w-1}$

15 $\dfrac{x^2 + 6x - 12}{x+2} < 3$

16 Joey is thinking of changing his cellular phone company. With his present phone company, the average cost per minute is $0.05 (after taking into account the monthly charge). CellsRUs has a plan for $25 per month plus $0.03 per minute.

a If n is the number of minutes Joey spends on the phone per month, what is the total cost for Joey per month if he switches to CellsRUs?

b Including the monthly charge, represent the average cost per minute if Joey signs on with CellsRUs.

c How many minutes does Joey have to use per month for CellsRUs to be the better deal?

17 In electronics, when two resistors, R_1 and R_2, are connected in parallel, their total resistance, R, is given by the formula $R = \dfrac{R_1 R_2}{R_1 + R_2}$. One resistor has a resistance of 2 ohms. Find the resistance of the other resistor if the total resistance must be greater than 1.5 ohms.

18 Dante is planning to drive from Poughkeepsie to Yellowstone National Park. On the first day, he expects to drive at a rate of 50 mph in the morning. After lunch, he hopes to drive at 60 mph for a distance of 100 miles greater than he drove in the morning. If he does not want to drive for more than 9 hours, what is the most distance that he can cover on the first day?

**FYI**

Your calculator can determine whether a given statement of equality or inequality is true or false. Using *Boolean algebra,* the calculator will display a 1 if a statement is true and a 0 if a statement is false. The symbols for equality and inequality are found in the TEST menu. (Press **2nd** **MATH**.)

Enter this into your calculator: $3 < 4$. Notice that your calculator prints a 1, indicating that this statement is true.

Now enter $3 < 2$ into your calculator. This time the calculator prints a 0, indicating that this statement is false. This is illustrated in the figure below.

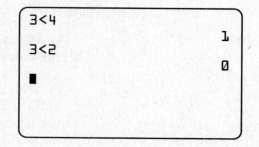

We can use this feature to check our solution to a rational inequality.

Let's look at the inequality $\dfrac{3x + 1}{x + 2} > 2$.

We will first solve the inequality algebraically, utilizing the second method of solving a rational inequality as outlined in Section 2.7. Then we will check our solution using Boolean algebra.

- Solve the corresponding equality for x.

$$\frac{3x + 1}{x + 2} = 2$$

$$3x + 1 = 2x + 4$$

$$x = 3$$

- Determine the value(s) of x for which the equation is undefined.

A fraction is undefined when its denominator equals zero. In this case, the fraction is undefined when $x = -2$.

- Use the two values of x to partition the number line into three intervals.

In the first interval, we consider $x < -2$. In the second interval, we consider $-2 < x < 3$. In the third interval, we consider $x > 3$.

- Test an x-value in each interval to see if it satisfies the original inequality. If it does, every x-value in the interval will satisfy the inequality. If it does not, no x-value in the interval will satisfy the inequality.

Test $x = -3$ Test $x = 4$

Test $x = 0$

Test $x = -3$.

$$\frac{3x + 1}{x + 2} > 2$$

$$\frac{3(-3) + 1}{-3 + 2} \stackrel{?}{>} 2$$

$$\frac{-8}{-1} \stackrel{?}{>} 2$$

$$8 > 2 \; \checkmark$$

Test $x = 0$.

$$\frac{3x + 1}{x + 2} > 2$$

$$\frac{3(0) + 1}{0 + 2} \stackrel{?}{>} 2$$

$$\frac{1}{2} \not> 2 \text{ (Does not check)}$$

Test $x = 4$.

$$\frac{3x + 1}{x + 2} > 2$$

$$\frac{3(4) + 1}{4 + 2} \stackrel{?}{>} 2$$

$$\frac{13}{6} > 2 \; \checkmark$$

- Graph the intervals where the tested x-values produce true statements.

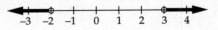

- Write the solution.

Answer: $\{x : x < -2 \text{ or } x > 3\}$

To check our solution to the inequality, we enter this inequality in the Y= menu as shown below.

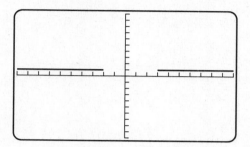

```
 Plot1 Plot2 Plot3
\Y1⊟(3X+1)/(X+2)
>2
\Y2=█
\Y3=
\Y4=
\Y5=
\Y6=
```

We could graph the inequality in the standard viewing window $[-10, 10] \times [-10, 10]$. (Press ZOOM 6 .) As you can see from the screen shown below, this does not appear to be very helpful.

However, in Boolean algebra, a value of 1 indicates that a statement is true, and a value of 0 indicates that a statement is false.

Press TRACE and move your cursor left and right as shown below.

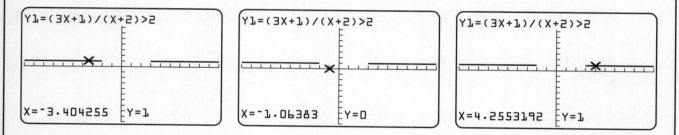

Notice for values of $x < -2$, $y = 1$. For x-values $-2 < x < 3$, $y = 0$. For values of $x > 3$, $y = 1$. This indicates that for $x < -2$ or $x > 3$, the statement is true. For x-values $-2 < x < 3$, the statement is false. Thus, our solution is correct.

If we turn off the axes, it is easier to see what is going on. Press 2nd ZOOM to access the Format menu, and turn off the axes.

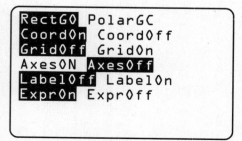

```
RectGO PolarGC
CoordOn CoordOff
GridOff GridOn
AxesON AxesOff
LabelOff LabelOn
ExprOn ExprOff
```

Now, when you press (GRAPH), you can see what's happening.

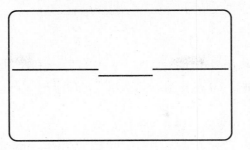

We can also Zoom Decimal. (Press (ZOOM) (4).) Now, when you press (TRACE), the cursor moves in increments of one-tenth of a unit.

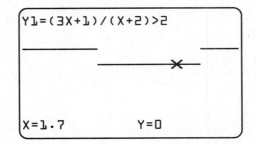

Thus, we can see that the solution to our inequality is $\{x : x < -2 \text{ or } x > 3\}$.

CHAPTER REVIEW

Exercises 1–16: Select the numeral preceding the choice that best completes the statement or answers the question.

1 For what value(s) of x is the rational expression $\dfrac{x - 4}{x^2 - 6x}$ undefined?

  (1) $x = 0, x = 4, x = 6$
  (2) $x = 4$
  (3) $x = 6$
  (4) $x = 0, x = 6$

2 Which fraction is in simplest terms?

  (1) $\dfrac{x^2 + 2x - 3}{x - 1}$ (3) $\dfrac{x}{x^2 - x}$

  (2) $\dfrac{x^2 - 4}{3x + 6}$ (4) $\dfrac{x + 1}{x^2 + 1}$

3 The expression $\dfrac{10 - 2x}{x^2 - 25}$ is equivalent to which of the following?

  (1) $\dfrac{-2}{x + 5}$ (3) $\dfrac{-2}{5 - x}$

  (2) $\dfrac{-2}{x - 5}$ (4) $\dfrac{2}{5 + x}$

4 Which is equivalent to $\dfrac{x^3 - 16x}{x^3 + 12x^2 + 32x}$?

  (1) $\dfrac{-1}{2}$ (3) $\dfrac{x + 4}{x + 8}$

  (2) $\dfrac{x - 4}{x + 8}$ (4) $\dfrac{x(x - 4)}{x + 8}$

5 The product of $\dfrac{x^2 - 9}{x + 3}$ and $\dfrac{4x + 16}{x^2 + x - 12}$ is

(1) -4 (3) 1
(2) -1 (4) 4

6. If the length of a rectangular garden is represented by $\dfrac{x^2 + 2x}{x^2 + 2x - 15}$ and the width is represented by $\dfrac{2x - 6}{2x + 4}$, which expression represents the garden's area?

(1) x (3) $\dfrac{x^2 + 2x}{2(x + 5)}$

(2) $x + 5$ (4) $\dfrac{x}{x + 5}$

7 The expression $\dfrac{a}{a - b} + \dfrac{b}{b - a}$ is equivalent to

(1) 1 (3) $\dfrac{ab}{a - b}$

(2) -1 (4) $\dfrac{a + b}{a^2 - b^2}$

8 Mr. DeStefano created a parallelogram-shaped garden in his backyard. If the base of the garden is represented as $\dfrac{a^2 - 36}{a^2 - 7a + 6}$ and the height of the garden is represented as $\dfrac{6a - 6}{a^2 + 4a - 12}$, which represents the area of the garden?

(1) 6 (3) $\dfrac{6}{a - 2}$

(2) $\dfrac{a}{a - 1}$ (4) $\dfrac{3}{a}$

9 When combined into a single fraction, $\dfrac{3}{x + 2} - \dfrac{2}{x - 2}$ becomes

(1) $\dfrac{1}{x - 2}$ (3) $\dfrac{x - 10}{x^2 - 4}$

(2) $\dfrac{5}{x + 2}$ (4) $\dfrac{x - 4}{x^2 - 4}$

10 In simplest form, the expression $\dfrac{\dfrac{x^2}{16} - 1}{\dfrac{x}{8} - \dfrac{1}{2}}$ equals

(1) $\dfrac{x + 4}{4} \cdot \dfrac{x - 4}{2}$ (3) $\dfrac{x + 8}{2}$

(2) $\dfrac{x + 4}{2}$ (4) $\dfrac{x - 4}{2}$

11 In simplest form, the expression $\dfrac{\dfrac{1 - 2c}{4c}}{c - \dfrac{1}{4c}}$ equals

(1) $\dfrac{2}{2c - 1}$ (3) $-\dfrac{1}{2c + 1}$

(2) $\dfrac{1}{2c + 1}$ (4) $-\dfrac{1}{c}$

12 When simplified, the complex fraction $\dfrac{1 + \dfrac{1}{x}}{\dfrac{1}{x} - 1}$, $x \neq 0$, is equivalent to

(1) 1 (3) $\dfrac{1}{1 - x}$

(2) $\dfrac{x + 1}{1 - x}$ (4) -1

13 The solution set for the equation $\dfrac{m - 2}{m} = \dfrac{4}{m^2 - 2m}$ is

(1) $\{\ \}$ (3) $\{0, 4\}$
(2) $\{-2, 2\}$ (4) $\{4\}$

14 Which of the following is the solution set for $\dfrac{y - 1}{y + 2} = \dfrac{1}{y - 4} + \dfrac{1}{y + 2}$?

(1) $\{1\}$ (3) $\{6\}$
(2) $\{1, 6\}$ (4) $\{\ \}$

15 Mr. and Mrs. James are having their home remodeled. If the floor plans use a scale of 1 cm to 18 in. and the family room on the diagram measures 8 cm by 14 cm, what are the actual dimensions of the family room *in feet*?

(1) 12 by 21   (3) 14 by 21
(2) 18 by 14   (4) 144 by 252

16 The ratio of boys to girls in the math club is 7 to 4. If there are 12 girls in the club, how many members are there in the club?

(1) 11   (3) 33
(2) 16   (4) 44

Exercises 17–22: Perform all indicated operations and simplify your answer, where possible.

17 $\dfrac{c^3 - 9c}{2c^2 + 7c + 3} \cdot \dfrac{4c^2 - 1}{5c - 15}$

18 $\dfrac{a^2 + 2a - 8}{a^2 + 3a - 4} \cdot \dfrac{3a^2 + 3a}{3a - 6}$

19 $\dfrac{4y^2 - y - 18}{8y - 18} \div \dfrac{y^2 - 4}{2y^2 - 5y + 2}$

20 $\dfrac{3y^2 + 11y + 10}{5y^2 + 11y + 2} \div \dfrac{3y^2 - y - 10}{1 - 25y^2}$

21 $\dfrac{x}{x^2 - 9} + \dfrac{2}{2x - 6} - \dfrac{2}{x + 3}$

22 $\dfrac{x^2 + 6}{x^2 - x} - \dfrac{8 - x}{x^2 - x}$

Exercises 23 and 24: Solve for x.

23 $\dfrac{7x + 1}{6x} = \dfrac{4x + 2}{6x - 4}$

24 $\dfrac{x - 4}{x - 1} + \dfrac{2}{x - 2} = \dfrac{2x + 1}{(x - 1)(x - 2)}$

Exercises 25 and 26: Solve for x and sketch the solution set on the number line.

25 $\dfrac{3x + 2}{x - 1} > x - 2$

26 $\dfrac{2}{x - 2} + \dfrac{x}{x + 2} \leq 2$

CHAPTER 3

Real Numbers and Radicals

3.1 Real Numbers and Absolute Value

In Section 1.2, we explored solving absolute value equations and inequalities, but now we want to look at the solutions using graphic displays on number lines. Since the solution set to any inequality includes an infinite number of solutions, the number line graph is a good way to show answers.

MODEL PROBLEMS

1 Solve and graph on a number line:

   a $|2n - 5| \leq 7$

   b $\left|6 - \dfrac{n}{3}\right| - 3 > 4$

SOLUTION

   a $|2n - 5| \leq 7$

We must consider both the case in which the expression within the absolute value bars is less than or equal to 7 and the case in which the expression inside the absolute value bars is greater than or equal to -7.

$$2n - 5 \leq 7 \qquad 2n - 5 \geq -7$$
$$2n \leq 12 \qquad\quad 2n \geq -2$$
$$n \leq 6 \qquad\qquad n \geq -1$$

In this type of problem, the solution is the intersection of the two solutions: $-1 \leq n \leq 6$.

Answer: $-1 \leq n \leq 6$

Note: You can check your answer by choosing a value in the interval and substituting it into the original inequality. If it is a solution, you should get a true statement

When we graph this on a number line, our answer includes all the values from −1 to 6, including −1 and 6. Hence, the circles at those values are filled in as below.

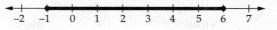

b $\left|6 - \dfrac{n}{3}\right| - 3 > 4$:

First isolate the absolute value. $\left|6 - \dfrac{n}{3}\right| > 7$

Now, set up the two inequalities and solve.

$6 - \dfrac{n}{3} > 7$ $6 - \dfrac{n}{3} < -7$

$-\dfrac{n}{3} > 1$ $-\dfrac{n}{3} < -13$

$n < -3$ $n > 39$

Remember: Reverse the inequality sign when you multiply by a negative number.

In this case, the solution is the union of the two solutions, that is, all numbers less than −3 as well as all numbers greater than 39.

Answer: $\{n : n < -3 \quad or \quad n > 39\}$

The graph of this solution is

2   The "average" twenty-five-year-old female in the United States measures 5 feet 4 inches tall.

   a   If most twenty-five-year-old women measure within 2 inches of this height, use an absolute value inequality to express this fact. (Hint: Convert 5 feet 4 inches to inches.)

   b   Determine the range of heights that satisfy this inequality. Express your answer in feet and inches.

   c   Graph the solution on a number line, using inches as your unit of measure.

SOLUTION

   a   First, do the conversion. Since there are 12 inches to 1 foot, 5′ = 12(5) = 60″. Thus, 5′ 4″ = 60″ + 4″ + 64″. The average twenty-five-year-old female is 64 inches tall.

Let h represent the height of the twenty-five-year-old women. The difference between the women's heights and the average height falls within two inches.

Answer: $|h - 64| \leq 2$

   b   We must consider the two cases, $h - 64 \leq 2$ and $h - 64 \geq -2$.

Set up the compound inequality and solve:

$-2 \leq h - 64 \leq 2$

$62 \leq h \leq 66$

We can see that most twenty-five-year-old women are between 62" and 66" tall. To convert to feet and inches, we divide each of these numbers by 12, to obtain an answer of between 5'2" and 5'6" tall.

Answer: The range of heights is 5 feet 2 inches to 5 feet 6 inches.

c   Graphed on a number line, the solution looks like this:

Practice

Exercises 1–10: Solve the absolute-value inequality and graph the solution set.

1 $|7x - 5| > 16$

2 $\left|\dfrac{1}{2}x + 3\right| \leq 7$

3 $\left|2 - \dfrac{x}{3}\right| \geq x + 4$

4 $\left|\dfrac{2}{3}x + 6\right| \leq 5$

5 $\left|\dfrac{4c - 3}{6}\right| > 2$

6 $|x - 1| - 3 < 2$

7 $|3c| \leq 2c + 6$

8 $|2x + 1| \geq 6 - x$

9 $\left|\dfrac{7 - n}{2}\right| - 8 < 1$

10 $13 + |5y + 2| > 33 - y$

Exercises 11–16: Select the numeral preceding the choice that best answers the question.

11 Which is the graph of the solution set of the inequality $|6 - 2x| < 8$?

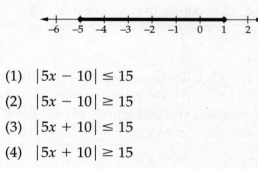

12 Which inequality has the solution set represented by the graph below?

(1) $|5x - 10| \leq 15$

(2) $|5x - 10| \geq 15$

(3) $|5x + 10| \leq 15$

(4) $|5x + 10| \geq 15$

13 The Westin Town Library allows students to borrow no more than 3 reference works overnight during times when school is in session. Which graph below indicates that policy?

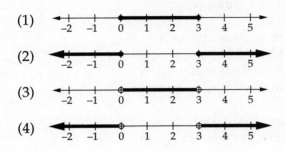

(1)

(2)

(3)

(4)

14 The solution set of $|12 - 3a| + 2 < 4 + a$ is which of the following?

(1) $\left\{-7 < a < -\dfrac{5}{2}\right\}$

(2) $\left\{-7 < a < \dfrac{5}{2}\right\}$

(3) $\left\{-\dfrac{5}{2} < a < 7\right\}$

(4) $\left\{\dfrac{5}{2} < a < 7\right\}$

15 Crimsen Elementary School has a policy in which the average class size is 24 students. All classes must be within 3 students of that average. If S represents the number of students in the class, which inequality shows this policy?

(1) $|S - 24| \le 3$

(2) $|S - 24| \ge 3$

(3) $|S + 3| \le 24$

(4) $|3 + 24| \le S$

16 The quality control department of Penelope's Parisian Petits Fours allows only a 0.4-ounce discrepancy in weight in their one pound (16 ounce) box. If w represents the weight of a box of these treats, which inequality expresses this standard?

(1) $|1 - 0.4| \le w$

(2) $|w - 16| \le 0.4$

(3) $|w + 0.4| \ge 16$

(4) $|16 - w| \ge 0.4$

17 On Friday nights, the average number of patrons at Saratoga's Dance Club is 132. The attendance varies by no more than 26 people.

a Use D to represent the number of people in the club and write an absolute value inequality to express this situation.

b Solve the absolute value inequality.

c If the Fire Marshall has stated that the occupancy of the club by more than 160 people is illegal, is the club within the law?

18 This year the winner of the hot dog eating contest at the Greenville Fair ate 23 hot dogs. In past years, the contest winner has been within 6 hot dogs of this year's number.

a Use H to represent the number of hot dogs eaten and write an absolute value inequality to express this situation.

b Solve the absolute value inequality to determine the range of the winning numbers of hot dogs.

c Graph the solution on a number line.

19 The United States has won an average of 37 gold medals in each of the Olympics held between 1988 and 2008. At all the games, United States athletes earned within 8 medals of this average.

a Use M to represent the number of gold medals won by the United States and write an absolute value inequality to express this situation.

b Solve the absolute value inequality to find the range of the number of gold medals.

c Graph the solution on a number line.

20 Mom's Diner sells an average of 14 fried chicken and mashed potato dinners each night, but they have sold as many as 20 and as few as 8 of these meals.

a Express this discrepancy as an absolute value inequality, using C to represent the number of chicken dinners sold.

b Solve the absolute value inequality.

3.2 Simplifying Radicals

A radical sign $\left(\sqrt{}\right)$ is used to indicate square root of a number, one of two equal factors of a number. Thus, $\sqrt{9} = \pm 3$. The positive root, in this case 3, is called the **principal square root**. When talking about the square root of a number, we generally mean the principal square root.

When seeking a root other than a square root, we must include the **index**, a number written within the hook of the radical, which indicates how many equal factors we are seeking, or the number roots. Hence, $\sqrt[3]{8}$ asks for three equal factors of 8 and is called the **cube root**. The symbol $\sqrt[4]{81}$ means you must find four equal factors of 81, or the fourth root.

Any radical sign without an index is understood to mean square root.

When the number under the radical, known as the **radicand**, is a perfect square, we remove the radical sign and keep one of the equal factors.

The following are some of the square roots that you should already know:

$$\sqrt{4} = 2 \qquad \sqrt{9} = 3 \qquad \sqrt{16} = 4 \qquad \sqrt{25} = 5 \qquad \sqrt{36} = 6$$
$$\sqrt{49} = 7 \qquad \sqrt{64} = 8 \qquad \sqrt{81} = 9 \qquad \sqrt{100} = 10 \qquad \sqrt{121} = 11$$

When the radicand is *not* a perfect square, it needs to be simplified. To do this, factor the number under the radical sign into two factors, one of which is a perfect square and one of which is not. Take the square root of the square factor and leave the remaining factor under the radical sign.

MODEL PROBLEMS

1 Simplify: $\sqrt{24}$

SOLUTION

24 can be factored into 2×12, 3×8, or 4×6, but the only pair of factors that includes a perfect square is 4 and 6.

$\sqrt{24} = \sqrt{4} \cdot \sqrt{6}$

Since $\sqrt{4} = 2$, we replace $\sqrt{4}$ with 2.

Answer: $2\sqrt{6}$

2 Simplify $\dfrac{1}{3}\sqrt{18}$.

SOLUTION

If there is a coefficient multiplying the radical, we must simplify the radicand first and then perform the multiplication.

First, we consider the possible factors of 18: 2 and 9, 3 and 6. Since the only perfect square factor is 9, we use the factors 2 and 9.

$\dfrac{1}{3}\sqrt{18} = \dfrac{1}{3}\sqrt{9} \cdot \sqrt{2}$ We know $\sqrt{9} = 3$, so we replace $\sqrt{9}$ with 3.

$\qquad\quad = \dfrac{1}{3} \cdot 3 \cdot \sqrt{2}$ Multiply $\dfrac{1}{3} \cdot 3$ but leave the radical untouched.

Answer: $1\sqrt{2}$ or $\sqrt{2}$

3 Simplify $\sqrt{\dfrac{4x^2}{3y}}$.

SOLUTION

When simplifying a fractional radicand, consider the fraction as two separate radicals, one in the numerator and one in the denominator.

$$\sqrt{\dfrac{4x^2}{3y}} = \dfrac{\sqrt{4x^2}}{\sqrt{3y}} \qquad \text{Simplify the numerator and denominator, if possible.}$$

$$= \dfrac{2x}{\sqrt{3y}}$$

We need to eliminate the radical in the denominator by making it a perfect square, but to do so, we must multiply both the numerator and denominator by the same radical. This is called **rationalizing the denominator**.

$$= \dfrac{2x}{\sqrt{3y}} \cdot \dfrac{\sqrt{3y}}{\sqrt{3y}} \qquad \textit{Note:} \text{ The term used as a multiplier should always equal 1.}$$

$$= \dfrac{2x\sqrt{3y}}{\sqrt{9y^2}}$$

Answer: $\dfrac{2x\sqrt{3y}}{3y}$

4 Simplify $2a\sqrt{\dfrac{5}{8a^6}}$.

SOLUTION

Here we have a fractional radicand with a coefficient. First, create two separate radicals.

$$2a\sqrt{\dfrac{5}{8a^6}} = 2a \cdot \dfrac{\sqrt{5}}{\sqrt{8a^6}}$$

$$= 2a \cdot \dfrac{\sqrt{5}}{\sqrt{4a^6} \cdot \sqrt{2}} \qquad \text{Simplify if possible.}$$

$$= 2a \cdot \dfrac{\sqrt{5}}{2a^3\sqrt{2}} \qquad \text{Cancel the coefficients.}$$

$$= \dfrac{\sqrt{5}}{a^2\sqrt{2}} \qquad \text{Rationalize the denominator.}$$

$$= \dfrac{\sqrt{5}}{a^2\sqrt{2}} \cdot \dfrac{\sqrt{2}}{\sqrt{2}}$$

$$= \dfrac{\sqrt{10}}{2a^2} \qquad \textit{Note:} \text{ Since } \sqrt{2} \cdot \sqrt{2} = \sqrt{4} = 2, \text{ we can go immediately to that step.}$$

Answer: $\dfrac{\sqrt{10}}{2a^2}, (a \neq 0)$

Exercises 1–10: Simplify the expression.

1 $\sqrt{12}$

2 $\sqrt{54}$

3 $5\sqrt{50x^6}$

4 $\frac{1}{2}\sqrt{80}$

5 $\frac{2}{3}\sqrt{63}$

6 $-2\sqrt{48a^4b^9}$

7 $8\sqrt{\frac{1}{2}}$

8 $4\sqrt{\frac{2}{8}}$

9 $-\sqrt{27n^3}$

10 $\frac{3}{5}\sqrt{75}$

11 $\sqrt[3]{128}$

12 $\frac{1}{2}\sqrt[5]{32}$

Exercises 13–18: Select the numeral preceding the choice that best answers the question.

13 The expression $\sqrt{96}$ can be rewritten as $a\sqrt{b}$ where a and b are integers. Which represents a?

   (1) 16   (3) 6
   (2) 12   (4) 4

14 Which expression is equivalent to $-\frac{3}{8}\sqrt{72}$?

   (1) -9 (3) $-\frac{9}{4}\sqrt{2}$

   (2) $-\frac{3}{4}\sqrt{2}$ (4) $-3\sqrt{9}$

15 Which is *not* equal to $\sqrt{200y^{16}}$?

   (1) $10y^8\sqrt{2}$ (3) $5y^8\sqrt{8}$
   (2) $8y^4\sqrt{5}$ (4) $2y^8\sqrt{50}$

16 Simplify $8\sqrt{\frac{3}{8}}$.

   (1) $\frac{1}{3}$ (3) $6\sqrt{2}$

   (2) $2\sqrt{6}$ (4) $\sqrt{3}$ ·

17 The area of a square is 120 square inches. In simplest radical form, what is the length of one side?

   (1) $\sqrt{120}$ (3) $\frac{1}{2}\sqrt{240}$

   (2) $2\sqrt{30}$ (4) $15\sqrt{8}$

18 If $5x^2\sqrt[3]{2} = \sqrt[3]{a}$, which of the following equals a?

   (1) $10x^5$
   (2) $50x^6$
   (3) $250x^5$
   (4) $250x^6$

3.3 Adding and Subtracting Radicals

When working with all numerical expressions, we can add and subtract only like terms. To add and subtract radicals, both the index and radicand must be the same. That is, we cannot add a cube root and a square root, such as $\sqrt[3]{10} + 2\sqrt{5}$. We also cannot add $\sqrt{12}$ and $\sqrt{75}$ until the radicands have been simplified.

📖 MODEL PROBLEMS

1 Add $\sqrt{12} + \sqrt{75}$.

SOLUTION

First simplify each of the radicands.

$\sqrt{12} + \sqrt{75} = \sqrt{4} \cdot \sqrt{3} + \sqrt{25} \cdot \sqrt{3}$

$\qquad\qquad = 2\sqrt{3} + 5\sqrt{3}$ Combine the coefficients of the like radicands.

Answer: $7\sqrt{3}$

2 Simplify: $\dfrac{2a}{3}\sqrt{27x^3} + \dfrac{1}{2a}\sqrt{48a^4x^3} - x\sqrt{147a^2x}$

SOLUTION

Follow the order of operations. First simplify the radicands, multiply each by its coefficient, then combine like terms. Always simplify the smallest radicand first so you may get a hint as to how to factor the larger radicands. In this example, once you find that $\sqrt{3x}$ is a common factor of $\sqrt{27x^3}$ and $\sqrt{48a^4x^3}$, you can test that as a factor of $\sqrt{147a^2x}$.

$\dfrac{2a}{3}\sqrt{27x^3} + \dfrac{1}{2a}\sqrt{48a^4x^3} - x\sqrt{147a^2x} = \dfrac{2a}{3}\sqrt{9x^2} \cdot \sqrt{3x} + \dfrac{1}{2a}\sqrt{16a^4x^2} \cdot \sqrt{3x} - x\sqrt{49a^2} \cdot \sqrt{3x}$

$\qquad\qquad\qquad\qquad\qquad\qquad = \dfrac{2a}{3} \cdot 3x \cdot \sqrt{3x} + \dfrac{1}{2a} \cdot 4a^2x \cdot \sqrt{3x} - x \cdot 7a \cdot \sqrt{3x}$

$\qquad\qquad\qquad\qquad\qquad\qquad = 2ax\sqrt{3x} + 2ax\sqrt{3x} - 7ax\sqrt{3x}$

Answer: $-3ax\sqrt{3x},\ (a \neq 0)$

3 Simplify $6\sqrt{\dfrac{1}{2}} - \sqrt{18}$.

SOLUTION

Simplify each radical expression and rationalize the denominator.

$6\sqrt{\dfrac{1}{2}} - \sqrt{18} = 6 \cdot \dfrac{\sqrt{1}}{\sqrt{2}} \cdot \dfrac{\sqrt{2}}{\sqrt{2}} - \sqrt{9} \cdot \sqrt{2}$

$\qquad\qquad\qquad = 6 \cdot \dfrac{\sqrt{2}}{2} - 3\sqrt{2}$

$\qquad\qquad\qquad = 3\sqrt{2} - 3\sqrt{2}$

Answer: 0

4 Solve and check: $3x - \sqrt{80} = \sqrt{20}$

SOLUTION

$3x - \sqrt{80} = \sqrt{20}$ First group all radicals on one side of the equals sign.

$3x = \sqrt{20} + \sqrt{80}$ Simplify the radicals.

$3x = \sqrt{4} \cdot \sqrt{5} + \sqrt{16} \cdot \sqrt{5}$

$3x = 2\sqrt{5} + 4\sqrt{5}$ Combine like terms.

$3x = 6\sqrt{5}$ Divide by 3.

Check: $3x - \sqrt{80} = \sqrt{20}$

$3(2\sqrt{5}) - \sqrt{16} \cdot \sqrt{5} \overset{?}{=} \sqrt{4} \cdot \sqrt{5}$

$6\sqrt{5} - 4\sqrt{5} \overset{?}{=} 2\sqrt{5}$

$2\sqrt{5} = 2\sqrt{5}$ ✔

Answer: $x = 2\sqrt{5}$

Practice

Exercises 1–8: Simplify.

1 $2\sqrt{28p^2} + \sqrt{63p^2} - 3\sqrt{112p^2}$

2 $3\sqrt{96} - 4\sqrt{\dfrac{2}{3}} + \sqrt{24}$

3 $\dfrac{2}{5}\sqrt{125} - 3\sqrt{20} + 2\sqrt{45}$

4 $5\sqrt{27} - 3\sqrt{75} + \dfrac{1}{2}\sqrt{48}$

5 $\dfrac{3}{7}\sqrt{98} + 6\sqrt{50} - 5\sqrt{32}$

6 $\dfrac{3}{5}\sqrt{75a^4b^6c} - \dfrac{1}{2}\sqrt{192a^4b^6c}$

7 $\dfrac{3}{2}\sqrt{24} - 2\sqrt{54} + \sqrt{6}$

8 $\dfrac{1}{2}\sqrt{72} + 3\sqrt{18} - \sqrt{32}$

Exercises 9–14: Select the numeral preceding the choice that best completes the statement.

9   In simplest form, $5\sqrt{12} + 7\sqrt{108}$ equals

(1) $12\sqrt{2}$ (3) $2\sqrt{13}$
(2) $52\sqrt{3}$ (4) $2\sqrt{26}$

10   The sides of a triangle measure $3\sqrt{12}$, $\sqrt{27}$, and $2\sqrt{48}$. The perimeter of this triangle is

(1) $6\sqrt{87}$ (3) $17\sqrt{3}$
(2) $13\sqrt{3}$ (4) $42\sqrt{3}$

11   The sides of a triangle measure $3\sqrt[3]{24}$, $\sqrt[3]{27}$ and $2\sqrt[3]{81}$. The perimeter of this triangle is

(1) $12\sqrt[3]{3} + 3$ (3) $6\sqrt[3]{3} + 3$
(2) $\sqrt[3]{3} + 3$ (4) $12\sqrt[3]{3}$

12   The value of x in the equation $2x + \sqrt{150} = \sqrt{294}$ is

(1) $2\sqrt{344}$ (3) 12
(2) $2\sqrt{6}$ (4) $\sqrt{6}$

13   In the equation $\sqrt{300} - 5x = \sqrt{75}$, the value of x is

(1) $\sqrt{3}$ (3) $-5\sqrt{3}$
(2) $5\sqrt{3}$ (4) 15

14   The solution to $2x + \sqrt{108} = \sqrt{147}$ is

(1) $x = \dfrac{13}{2}\sqrt{3}$ (3) $x = \dfrac{3}{2}\sqrt{3}$
(2) $x = \sqrt{3}$ (4) $x = \dfrac{1}{2}\sqrt{3}$

3.4 Multiplying Radicals

From our work with real numbers, we know that $a \cdot b = ab$. In a similar manner, we know that $\sqrt{a} \cdot \sqrt{b} = \sqrt{a \cdot b} = \sqrt{ab}$. We can multiply radicals only if they have the same index. That is, the terms must both be square roots or cube roots. As long as the roots are the same, we can multiply the radicands and then simplify, if possible. You will find that in some cases, radicals that could not be simplified before multiplication produce a product that can be simplified.

MODEL PROBLEMS

1 Multiply: $\left(\sqrt{6}\right)\left(\sqrt{3}\right)$

SOLUTION

$$\left(\sqrt{6}\right)\left(\sqrt{3}\right) = \sqrt{18}$$
$$= \sqrt{9} \cdot \sqrt{2}$$

Answer: $3\sqrt{2}$

2 Multiply: $\left(\sqrt{7}\right)\left(\sqrt{2}\right)$

SOLUTION

$$\left(\sqrt{7}\right)\left(\sqrt{2}\right) = \sqrt{14} \qquad \text{This cannot be simplified further.}$$

Answer: $\sqrt{14}$

3 Multiply: $\dfrac{5}{6}\left(\sqrt{6}\right) \cdot \left(\dfrac{3}{5}\sqrt{15}\right)$

SOLUTION

If coefficients are present, multiply the coefficients and then multiply the radicals separately.

$$\dfrac{5}{6}\left(\sqrt{6}\right) \cdot \left(\dfrac{3}{5}\sqrt{15}\right) = \dfrac{5}{6} \cdot \dfrac{3}{5} \cdot \sqrt{6} \cdot \sqrt{15}$$
$$= \dfrac{1}{2}\sqrt{90}$$
$$= \dfrac{1}{2}\sqrt{9} \cdot \sqrt{10}$$
$$= \dfrac{1}{2} \cdot 3\sqrt{10}$$

Answer: $\dfrac{3}{2}\sqrt{10}$

4 Multiply: $\left(\dfrac{2y^2z}{3}\sqrt{15w}\right)\left(\dfrac{6}{z}\sqrt{3w^3x^2}\right)$

SOLUTION

$$
\begin{aligned}
\left(\dfrac{2y^2z}{3}\sqrt{15w}\right)\left(\dfrac{6}{z}\sqrt{3w^3x^2}\right) &= \dfrac{2y^2z}{3} \bullet \dfrac{6}{z} \bullet \sqrt{15w} \bullet \sqrt{3w^3x^2} \\
&= 4y^2\sqrt{45w^4x^2} \\
&= 4y^2\sqrt{9w^4x^2} \bullet \sqrt{5} \\
&= 4y^2 \bullet 3w^2x\sqrt{5}
\end{aligned}
$$

Answer: $12w^2xy^2\sqrt{5},\ (z \neq 0)$

In some cases, we need to use the distributive property to multiply. When multiplying a polynomial by a monomial, remember to distribute the monomial over every term of the other expression. When multiplying a polynomial by a binomial, you must distribute every term of the binomial over every term of the other expression.

MODEL PROBLEMS

5 Multiply $\sqrt{2}\left(2\sqrt{2} + 3\sqrt{6}\right)$.

SOLUTION

$$
\begin{aligned}
\sqrt{2}\left(2\sqrt{2} + 3\sqrt{6}\right) &= \left(\sqrt{2} \bullet 2\sqrt{2}\right) + \left(\sqrt{2} \bullet 3\sqrt{6}\right) \\
&= 2\sqrt{4} + 3\sqrt{12} \\
&= 2 \bullet 2 + 3 \bullet \sqrt{4}\sqrt{3} \\
&= 4 + 3 \bullet 2\sqrt{3}
\end{aligned}
$$

Answer: $4 + 6\sqrt{3}$

You'll notice that sometimes when multiplying by a radical fraction, the fraction disappears through the multiplication.

6 Multiply $\sqrt{\dfrac{1}{2}}\left(3\sqrt{32} - 5\sqrt{8}\right)$.

SOLUTION

$$
\begin{aligned}
\sqrt{\dfrac{1}{2}}\left(3\sqrt{32} - 5\sqrt{8}\right) &= 3\sqrt{32} \bullet \sqrt{\dfrac{1}{2}} - 5\sqrt{8} \bullet \sqrt{\dfrac{1}{2}} \\
&= 3 \bullet \sqrt{16} \bullet \sqrt{2} \bullet \dfrac{\sqrt{1}}{\sqrt{2}} - 5 \bullet \sqrt{4} \bullet \sqrt{2} \bullet \dfrac{\sqrt{1}}{\sqrt{2}} \\
&= 3\sqrt{16} - 5\sqrt{4} \\
&= 3 \bullet 4 - 5 \bullet 2 \\
&= 12 - 10
\end{aligned}
$$

Answer: 2

7 Multiply $(2 - \sqrt{3})(4 + 3\sqrt{3})$.

SOLUTION

$$(2 - \sqrt{3})(4 + 3\sqrt{3}) = (2 \bullet 4) + (2 \bullet 3\sqrt{3}) + (-\sqrt{3} \bullet 4) + (-\sqrt{3} \bullet 3\sqrt{3})$$
$$= 8 + 6\sqrt{3} - 4\sqrt{3} - 3\sqrt{9}$$
$$= 8 + 2\sqrt{3} - 3 \bullet 3$$
$$= 8 + 2\sqrt{3} - 9$$

Answer: $-1 + 2\sqrt{3}$

8 Multiply $(1 + \sqrt{7mn})(1 - \sqrt{7mn})$.

SOLUTION

In this example, we are multiplying the sum and difference of terms, so two of the terms in the multiplication will cancel each other.

$$(1 + \sqrt{7mn})(1 - \sqrt{7mn}) = 1 - \sqrt{7mn} + \sqrt{7mn} - \sqrt{49m^2n^2}$$
$$= 1 - 7mn$$

Answer: $1 - 7mn$

 **Practice**

Exercises 1–11: Simplify.

1 $2\sqrt{5x}\left(3\sqrt{8x} + \dfrac{1}{2}\sqrt{5x}\right)$

2 $3\sqrt{2}(\sqrt{6} - 4\sqrt{18})$

3 $(1 - \sqrt{6})(3 + 2\sqrt{6})$

4 $5\sqrt{2}(4\sqrt{8} - \sqrt{32})$

5 $(4 - 2\sqrt{3})(4 + 2\sqrt{3})$

6 $(2 + \sqrt{5})(1 - 3\sqrt{5})$

7 $(4 - \sqrt{2})^2$

8 $(7 - 2\sqrt{5})(7 + 2\sqrt{5})$

9 $(5 - \sqrt[3]{16})(4 + 2\sqrt[3]{108})$

10 $\sqrt{\dfrac{1}{3}}(4\sqrt{12} - 3\sqrt{27} + 5\sqrt{48})$

11 $(2 - 3\sqrt{6})^2$

Exercises 12–14: Select the numeral preceding the choice that best completes the statement or answers the question.

12 The product of $(6\sqrt{5})$ and $\left(\dfrac{3}{2}\sqrt{10}\right)$ is

(1) $12\sqrt{50}$ (3) $45\sqrt{2}$

(2) $\sqrt{600}$ (4) $120\sqrt{5}$

13 Which example produces a product of 18?

(1) $(3 + \sqrt{6})(5 + 2\sqrt{6})$

(2) $(3 - 2\sqrt{5})^2$

(3) $(4 - 2\sqrt{3})(4 + 2\sqrt{3})$

(4) $(6 + 3\sqrt{2})(6 - 3\sqrt{2})$

14 The length of a rectangle is represented by the expression $6 + 2\sqrt{12}$. The width of the rectangle is represented by $3 + 4\sqrt{3}$. Which expression represents the area of the rectangle?

(1) $66 + 36\sqrt{3}$ (3) $18 + 16\sqrt{3}$

(2) $9 + 8\sqrt{3}$ (4) $32 + 3\sqrt{36}$

3.5 Dividing by Radicals

Monomial Divisors

Just as in multiplication, when you divide by radicals, the radicands do not have to be the same as long as the indexes are the same. Remember that you may divide a square root by another square root, or a cube root by another cube root. If the divisor is a monomial and the numerator is evenly divisible by it, simply divide the terms and then simplify the answer, if possible.

MODEL PROBLEM

1 Perform the following divisions.

a $\dfrac{\sqrt{24}}{\sqrt{2}}$

b $\dfrac{6\sqrt{40}}{4\sqrt{5}}$

c $\dfrac{\frac{1}{3}\sqrt{54}}{\sqrt{3}}$

SOLUTION

a $\dfrac{\sqrt{24}}{\sqrt{2}} = \sqrt{\dfrac{24}{2}} = \sqrt{12} = 2\sqrt{3}$

b $\dfrac{6\sqrt{40}}{4\sqrt{5}} = \dfrac{6}{4} \bullet \sqrt{\dfrac{40}{5}} = \dfrac{3\sqrt{8}}{2} = \dfrac{3 \bullet 2\sqrt{2}}{2} = 3\sqrt{2}$

c $\dfrac{\frac{1}{3}\sqrt{54}}{\sqrt{3}} = \dfrac{1}{3} \bullet \sqrt{\dfrac{54}{3}} = \dfrac{1}{3}\sqrt{18} = \dfrac{1}{3} \bullet 3\sqrt{2} = \sqrt{2}$

If a numerator is not evenly divisible by the denominator, we must eliminate the radical denominator by rationalizing the denominator. With monomial denominators, we usually do this by multiplying the radical by itself, although sometimes a smaller number may be used to create a perfect square. This approach is shown in part **c** of Model Problem 2.

2 Rationalize the denominators of the following expressions.

a $\dfrac{\sqrt{7}}{\sqrt{2}}$

b $\dfrac{1 + \sqrt{5}}{\sqrt{3}}$

c $\dfrac{2 - \sqrt{6}}{\sqrt{12}}$

SOLUTION

a $\dfrac{\sqrt{7}}{\sqrt{2}}$

In this example, the quotient will not be an integer, so we cannot simply divide. Instead, we rationalize $\sqrt{2}$ by multiplying the entire fraction by 1 in the form of $\dfrac{\sqrt{2}}{\sqrt{2}}$.

$$\dfrac{\sqrt{7}}{\sqrt{2}} = \dfrac{\sqrt{7}}{\sqrt{2}} \bullet \dfrac{\sqrt{2}}{\sqrt{2}} = \dfrac{\sqrt{14}}{\sqrt{4}} = \dfrac{\sqrt{14}}{2}$$

Since $\sqrt{14}$ and 2 do not have the same index, we cannot divide any further.

Answer: $\dfrac{\sqrt{14}}{2}$

b $\dfrac{1 + \sqrt{5}}{\sqrt{3}}$

Here we must multiply the numerator and denominator by $\sqrt{3}$, distributing the $\sqrt{3}$ over the binomial in the numerator.

$$\dfrac{1 + \sqrt{5}}{\sqrt{3}} = \dfrac{1 + \sqrt{5}}{\sqrt{3}} \bullet \dfrac{\sqrt{3}}{\sqrt{3}} = \dfrac{\sqrt{3}\left(1 + \sqrt{5}\right)}{\sqrt{9}} = \dfrac{\sqrt{3} + \sqrt{15}}{3}$$

Since $\sqrt{3}$ and $\sqrt{15}$ are not like terms, we cannot combine them.

Answer: $\dfrac{\sqrt{3} + \sqrt{15}}{3}$

c $\dfrac{2 - \sqrt{6}}{\sqrt{12}}$

Since $\sqrt{12} \bullet \sqrt{3} = \sqrt{36}$, which is a perfect square root, we do not need to multiply by $\dfrac{\sqrt{12}}{\sqrt{12}}$ to rationalize this denominator. Doing so will, as you will see below, create extra work. Instead, we can save time and multiply the whole fraction by $\dfrac{\sqrt{3}}{\sqrt{3}}$ to rationalize the denominator.

$$\frac{2 - \sqrt{6}}{\sqrt{12}} \cdot \frac{\sqrt{3}}{\sqrt{3}} = \frac{\sqrt{3}\left(2 - \sqrt{6}\right)}{\sqrt{36}}$$

$$= \frac{2\sqrt{3} - \sqrt{18}}{6}$$

$$= \frac{2\sqrt{3} - 3\sqrt{2}}{6}$$

$$\frac{2 - \sqrt{6}}{\sqrt{12}} \cdot \frac{\sqrt{12}}{\sqrt{12}} = \frac{\sqrt{12}\left(2 - \sqrt{6}\right)}{\sqrt{144}}$$

$$= \frac{2\sqrt{12} - \sqrt{72}}{12}$$

$$= \frac{2 \cdot 2\sqrt{3} - 6\sqrt{2}}{12}$$

$$= \frac{2\left(2\sqrt{3} - 3\sqrt{2}\right)}{12}$$

$$= \frac{2\sqrt{3} - 3\sqrt{2}}{6}$$

Answer: $\dfrac{2\sqrt{3} - 3\sqrt{2}}{6}$

Binomial Divisors

If the divisor is a binomial containing a radical, a different method must be used to rationalize it. We do this by multiplying the entire fraction by 1 in the form of the **conjugate** of the divisor. A conjugate of a binomial contains the same two terms but the inverse operation. For example, $3 + \sqrt{2}$ and $3 - \sqrt{2}$ are conjugates. Think about what happens when we multiply $(x + 3)(x - 3)$: the middle terms cancel out and we have a binomial answer. The same thing happens when we multiply radical conjugates and the middle terms that cancel are the radicals.

$$\left(3 + \sqrt{2}\right)\left(3 - \sqrt{2}\right) = 9 - 3\sqrt{2} + 3\sqrt{2} - \sqrt{4}$$

$$= 9 - 2$$

$$= 7$$

Therefore, to rationalize binomial denominators that contain radicals, always multiply by the conjugate of the denominator.

MODEL PROBLEMS

3 Simplify: $\dfrac{7}{4 - \sqrt{6}}$

SOLUTION

$$\frac{7}{4 - \sqrt{6}} \cdot \frac{4 + \sqrt{6}}{4 + \sqrt{6}} = \frac{7\left(4 + \sqrt{6}\right)}{16 + 4\sqrt{6} - 4\sqrt{6} - \sqrt{36}}$$

$$= \frac{28 + 7\sqrt{6}}{16 - 6}$$

$$= \frac{28 + 7\sqrt{6}}{10}$$

Answer: $\dfrac{28 + 7\sqrt{6}}{10}$

4 Simplify: $\dfrac{14p}{3 + \sqrt{2}}$

SOLUTION

$$\frac{14p}{3 + \sqrt{2}} \bullet \frac{3 - \sqrt{2}}{3 - \sqrt{2}} = \frac{14p\left(3 - \sqrt{2}\right)}{9 - 3\sqrt{2} + 3\sqrt{2} - \sqrt{4}}$$

$$= \frac{14p\left(3 - \sqrt{2}\right)}{7}$$

$$= \frac{2p\left(3 - \sqrt{2}\right)}{1}$$

$$= 6p - 2p\sqrt{2}$$

Answer: $6p - 2p\sqrt{2}$

Notice that in this example, it was possible to reduce the resulting fraction.

 **Practice**

Exercises 1–15: Rationalize the denominator and write each example in simplest terms.

1 $\dfrac{3\sqrt{32}}{6\sqrt{8}}$

2 $\dfrac{2\sqrt{150a}}{\sqrt{6a}}$

3 $\dfrac{\dfrac{1}{2}\sqrt[3]{54}}{\dfrac{1}{4}\sqrt[3]{16}}$

4 $\dfrac{8\sqrt{3}}{\sqrt{12}}$

5 $\dfrac{15\sqrt{20}}{2\sqrt{5}}$

6 $6\sqrt{80} \div 2\sqrt{10}$

7 $9\sqrt{96} \div 3\sqrt{12}$

8 $\dfrac{8\sqrt{32} + 12\sqrt{18}}{4\sqrt{2}}$

9 $\dfrac{12\sqrt{45} - 6\sqrt{20}}{6\sqrt{5}}$

10 $\dfrac{6}{4 + \sqrt{7}}$

11 $\dfrac{7}{6 + \sqrt{15}}$

12 $\dfrac{9}{2 - \sqrt{3}}$

13 $\dfrac{2 - \sqrt{5}}{4 + \sqrt{2}}$

14 $\dfrac{1 + 2\sqrt{5}}{5 + \sqrt{5}}$

15 $\dfrac{7 + \sqrt{2}}{3 - \sqrt{6}}$

Exercises 16–20: Choose the numeral preceding the choice that best completes the statement.

16 Simplify $4\sqrt{\dfrac{3}{8}}$.

(1) $\sqrt{3}$ (3) $6\sqrt{2}$

(2) $\sqrt{6}$ (4) $\dfrac{1}{3}$

17 $\dfrac{16\sqrt{125}}{8\sqrt{5}}$ is equivalent to

(1) $\dfrac{\sqrt{5}}{2}$ (3) 10

(2) 5 (4) 50

18 When simplified, $\dfrac{15\sqrt[3]{48} - 5\sqrt[3]{6}}{5\sqrt[3]{6}}$ is equal to

(1) 10 (3) 5

(2) 7 (4) 4

19 When the denominator of $\dfrac{3 + \sqrt{5}}{3 - \sqrt{5}}$ is rationalized, the resulting answer is

(1) $\dfrac{3 + \sqrt{5}}{4}$ (3) $\dfrac{14 - 6\sqrt{5}}{14}$

(2) $\dfrac{7 + 3\sqrt{5}}{2}$ (4) $\dfrac{14 + 6\sqrt{5}}{14}$

20 The expression $\dfrac{12}{4 - \sqrt{10}}$ is equivalent to

(1) $4 + \sqrt{10}$ (3) $8 - 2\sqrt{10}$

(2) 2 (4) $8 + 2\sqrt{10}$

3.6 Solving Radical Equations

A **radical equation** is an equation in which the variable is contained under a radical. To solve a radical equation, first isolate the radical. Then, if the radical is a square root, square both sides; if the radical is a cube root, cube both sides; and so on. After you solve the resultant equation, be sure to check that your solution works in the original equation.

📖 MODEL PROBLEMS

1 Solve for x: $\sqrt{3x + 6} - 2 = 7$

SOLUTION

$$\sqrt{3x + 6} - 2 = 7$$

$$\sqrt{3x + 6} = 9$$

$$\left(\sqrt{3x + 6}\right)^2 = 9^2$$

$$3x + 6 = 81$$

$$3x = 75$$

$$x = 25$$

Now, we must check our solution in the original equation:

$$\sqrt{3x + 6} - 2 = 7$$

$$\sqrt{3(25) + 6} - 2 \stackrel{?}{=} 7$$

$$\sqrt{81} - 2 \stackrel{?}{=} 7$$

$$7 = 7 \checkmark$$

Answer: $x = 25$

2 Solve for x: $2\sqrt{2x - 6} + 8 = 4$

SOLUTION

$$2\sqrt{2x - 6} + 8 = 4$$

$$2\sqrt{2x - 6} = -4$$

$$\sqrt{2x - 6} = -2$$

$$\left(\sqrt{2x - 6}\right)^2 = (-2)^2$$

$$2x - 6 = 4$$

$$2x = 10$$

$$x = 5$$

Check:

$$2\sqrt{2x - 6} + 8 = 4$$

$$2\sqrt{2(5) - 6} + 8 \stackrel{?}{=} 4$$

$$2\sqrt{4} + 8 \stackrel{?}{=} 4$$

$$4 + 8 \stackrel{?}{=} 4$$

$$12 \neq 4$$

Since we get a false statement when we check, this equation has no solution. We could have predicted this result when we saw the negative value on the right side of the radical equation.

Answer: { }

3 Solve for x: $\sqrt[5]{3x - 1} = 2$

SOLUTION

$$\sqrt[5]{3x - 1} = 2$$

$$\left(\sqrt[5]{3x - 1}\right)^5 = 2^5$$

$$3x - 1 = 32$$

$$3x = 33$$

$$x = 11$$

Check:

$$\sqrt[5]{3x - 1} = 2$$

$$\sqrt[5]{3(11) - 1} \stackrel{?}{=} 2$$

$$\sqrt[5]{32} \stackrel{?}{=} 2$$

$$2 = 2 ✔$$

Answer: $x = 11$

4 Solve for a: $2\sqrt{4a - 6} = 6\sqrt{a - 4}$

SOLUTION

First, isolate one of the radicals by dividing both sides of the equation by 2:

$$\sqrt{4a - 6} = 3\sqrt{a - 4}$$

Now, square both sides:

$$\left(\sqrt{4a - 6}\right)^2 = \left(3\sqrt{a - 4}\right)^2$$

$$4a - 6 = 9(a - 4)$$

$$4a - 6 = 9a - 36$$

$$30 = 5a$$

$$a = 6$$

Check:

$$2\sqrt{4a - 6} = 6\sqrt{a - 4}$$

$$2\sqrt{4(6) - 6} \stackrel{?}{=} 6\sqrt{6 - 4}$$

$$2\sqrt{18} \stackrel{?}{=} 6\sqrt{2}$$

$$2\sqrt{9}\sqrt{2} \stackrel{?}{=} 6\sqrt{2}$$

$$6\sqrt{2} = 6\sqrt{2} ✔$$

Answer: $a = 6$

Practice

Exercises 1–15: Solve.

1 $\sqrt{x - 4} = 6$

2 $\sqrt{3x + 7} = 5$

3 $\sqrt[4]{2x - 5} = 3$

4 $\sqrt{5x - 1} + 4 = 12$

5 $3\sqrt{x - 9} = 21$

6 $\sqrt{6x - 2} = \sqrt{3x + 10}$

7 $5\sqrt{4x - 8} + 2 = 12$

8 $3\sqrt{5a - 1} + 12 = 6$

9 $4\sqrt{6b + 1} - 5 = 15$

10 $\sqrt[3]{4x + 1} = 5$

11 $\frac{2}{3}\sqrt{9x + 27} = 6$

12 $5\sqrt{5a + 6} = 10\sqrt{3a - 2}$

13 $3\sqrt{2x + 6} + 22 = 4$

14 $4\sqrt{5a + 16} = 24$

15 $x = -2 + \sqrt{3x + 16}$

Exercises 16–20: Select the numeral preceding the choice that best completes the statement or answers the question.

16 Which equation has the empty set as its solution?

(1) $3\sqrt{2x - 5} = -6$
(2) $2 + \sqrt{2x - 1} = 5$
(3) $\sqrt{3x + 3} = 6$
(4) $3\sqrt{4x - 7} = 15$

17 The solution to $4 + \sqrt{6x - 2} = 8$ is

(1) 1   (3) 3
(2) 2   (4) { }

18 The solution to $x = 1 + \sqrt{x + 5}$ is

(1) $\{-1, 4\}$ (3) $\{-1\}$
(2) $\{-4, 1\}$ (4) $\{4\}$

19 If $\sqrt{2x - 1} + 2 = 5$, then x is equal to

(1) 1   (3) 5
(2) 2   (4) 4

20 Given the equation $x + 4 = 2 + \sqrt{6x + 16}$, what is the first step in finding its solution?

(1) Square both sides of the equation.
(2) Find the square root of $6x + 16$.
(3) Subtract 2 from each side.
(4) Make one side of the equation equal zero.

CHAPTER REVIEW

Exercises 1–15: Select the numeral preceding the choice that best completes the statement or answers the question.

1 What is the solution set for the equation $|2x - 4| + 3 = 5$?

(1) $\{1\}$ (3) $\{3\}$
(2) $\{1, 3\}$ (4) $\{\pm 3\}$

2 The sum of $\sqrt{27c^3}$ and $\sqrt{12c^3}$ is

(1) $6\sqrt{2c^3}$ (3) $3c\sqrt{13c}$
(2) $5c\sqrt{3c}$ (4) $c\sqrt{39c}$

3 If $n > 0$, then $\sqrt{36n^2 + 64n^2}$ equals

(1) $10\sqrt{n}$ (3) $10n$
(2) $n\sqrt{10}$ (4) $14n$

4 Which is the graph of the solution to $|12 - 3x| \geq 30$?

(1) ![number line with open circles at -6 and 14, shaded outside]
(2) ![number line with closed dots at -6 and 14, shaded between]
(3) ![number line with closed dot at -14, shaded left]
(4) ![number line with closed dots at -6 and 14, shaded outside]

5 When $\sqrt{48}$ is expressed in simplest $p\sqrt{r}$ form, what is the value of p?

(1) 1   (3) 3
(2) 2   (4) 4

6 In simplest form, the expression $\dfrac{18\sqrt[3]{32y^7}}{6\sqrt[3]{4y}}$ is equivalent to

(1) $3\sqrt[3]{2y}$ (3) $6y^2$
(2) $6\sqrt[3]{y}$ (4) $12y^3$

7 Which is *not* in the solution set of $\left|\dfrac{3x - 12}{4}\right| \leq 6$?

(1) 12   (3) -4
(2) 2   (4) -6

8 Which expression is equivalent to $\dfrac{3 + \sqrt{5}}{3 - \sqrt{5}}$?

(1) -7 (3) $\dfrac{7 + 3\sqrt{5}}{2}$
(2) -1 (4) $-\left(7 + 3\sqrt{5}\right)$

9 When Dr. Leroi Mathman, an eccentric scientist, was asked how long it takes him to get to work, he said, "Depending on traffic, $|x - 30| \le 10$." How would a nonmathematician describe the length of the trip?

(1) from 10 to 30 minutes
(2) 10 minutes less than 30 minutes
(3) 40 minutes
(4) from 20 to 40 minutes

10 The solution set of the equation $\sqrt{2x + 48} = x$ is

(1) $\{-6\}$ (3) $\{-6, 8\}$
(2) $\{8\}$ (4) $\{\ \}$

11 Which expression represents the sum of $\dfrac{2}{\sqrt{3}}$ and $\dfrac{3}{\sqrt{2}}$?

(1) 1 (3) $\dfrac{2\sqrt{3} + 3\sqrt{2}}{6}$

(2) $\dfrac{5}{\sqrt{5}}$ (4) $\dfrac{4\sqrt{3} + 9\sqrt{2}}{6}$

12 The expression $\dfrac{8}{2 + \sqrt{6}}$ is equivalent to

(1) $4\sqrt{6} - 8$ (3) $\dfrac{8 - 4\sqrt{6}}{5}$

(2) $2\sqrt{3} - 2$ (4) $\dfrac{8 + 4\sqrt{6}}{5}$

13 The expression $\sqrt{27x^6y^9}$ is equivalent to

(1) $3x^2y^4\sqrt{3y}$ (3) $3y\sqrt{9x^6y^8}$
(2) $y^3\sqrt{27x^6}$ (4) $3y^3\sqrt{3x^6}$

14 What is the product of $\left(2 - \sqrt{7}\right)$ and its conjugate?

(1) -5 (3) 3
(2) -3 (4) 5

15 The bottling machine at JJ's Juice Company is set to reject any bottles that do not contain within $\dfrac{1}{4}$ ounce of the amount of juice that appears on the label. If the label states that the bottle contains 12 ounces, which inequality represents the number of ounces in an acceptable bottle of juice? (Let a represent the amount of juice in the bottle.)

(1) $|a - 12| \le \dfrac{1}{4}$ (3) $|a - 12| \ge \dfrac{1}{4}$

(2) $|a + 12| \le \dfrac{1}{4}$ (4) $|a + 12| \ge \dfrac{1}{4}$

Exercises 16–25: Simplify each expression, rationalizing any denominators that contain radicals.

16 $3\sqrt{96}$

17 $3\sqrt{75} - 4\sqrt{300}$

18 $\left(2 - 5\sqrt{3}\right)\left(7 + 2\sqrt{3}\right)$

19 $\dfrac{4}{2 + \sqrt{3}}$

20 $\dfrac{3 - 4\sqrt{5}}{2 + \sqrt{5}}$

21 $2\sqrt{3}\left(\sqrt{18} - \sqrt{6}\right)$

22 $4\sqrt{\dfrac{9}{16}}$

23 $\sqrt{\dfrac{2}{3}} + \sqrt{24}$

24 $\dfrac{3}{2}\sqrt{128x^6} - \dfrac{2}{3}\sqrt{18x^6}$

25 $\sqrt{\dfrac{1}{2}} - \sqrt{\dfrac{1}{3}}$

Exercises 26–30: Solve for x.

26 $|3x - 6| = 15$

27 $\sqrt{5x - 4} = 8$

28 $x = \sqrt{4x + 32}$

29 $|4x - 7| \le 13$

30 $|2x + 1| > 9$

Relations and Functions

4.1 Relations and Functions

Relations

In mathematics, a **relation** is a set of **ordered pairs**. A relation can consist of numbers or other items, and may be represented as a list, table, or graph. The following are examples of relations.

Relation A: {(February, 2), (April, 4), (June, 6), (August, 8), (November, 11)}

Relation B: {(1991, 28), (1996, 29), (1997, 28), (2000, 29), (2003, 28)}

Relation C: {(Joachim, 64), (Israel, 67), (Tomei, 56), (Marsha, 68), (David, 63)}

Relation D: {(4, 13), (−2, 7), (5, 14), (−8, 1), (−4, 5)}

Relation E:

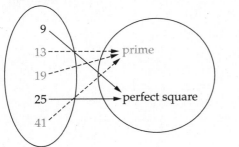

Relation F:

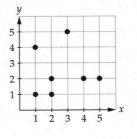

Relation G:

x	y
1	−5
2	−3
2	−1
−4	1
−4	3

Relation H:

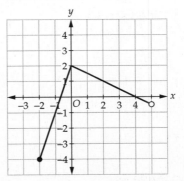

The **domain** of a relation is the set of first, or independent, elements. The **range** of a relation is the set of second, or dependent, elements. The domains and ranges of the relations above are listed in the table below. Notice that the numbers of elements in a domain and range are not necessarily equal since an element appearing twice in a domain or range is listed only once.

Relation	Domain	Range
A	{February, April, June, August, November}	{2, 4, 6, 8, 11}
B	{1991, 1996, 1997, 2000, 2003}	{28, 29}
C	{Joachim, Israel, Tomei, Marsha, David}	{64, 67, 56, 68, 63}
D	{4, −2, 5, −8, −4}	{13, 7, 14, 1, 5}
E	{9, 13, 19, 25, 41}	{prime, perfect square}
F	{1, 2, 3, 4, 5}	{1, 2, 4, 5}
G	{1, 2, −4}	{−5, −3, −1, 1, 3}
H	{$x : -2 \leq x < 5$}	{$y : -4 \leq y \leq 2$}

In some relations, there is a rule or method to the relationship that may be discovered and used to find other elements, or ordered pairs, of the relation. For example, the rule in relation A is that each element of the range is the number of the month on the calendar. Another element of that relation would be (July, 7). In relation D, the elements in the range are nine more than their corresponding elements in the domain. Another element of relation D would be (0, 9). In relation H, because the graph is continuous, all points, integer and noninteger, have to be included in the domain and range so it is necessary to use different notation.

 **Practice**

Exercises 1–6: State the domain and range of each relation. Find the rule that defines the relation, if possible.

1 {(Albany, New York), (Bismarck, North Dakota), (Juneau, Alaska)}

2 {(1, January), (4, July), (11, November), (25, December)}

3 {(*The Dark Knight*, Christian Bale), (*Legally Blonde*, Reese Witherspoon), (*Mr. and Mrs. Smith*, Angelina Jolie), (*Pirates of the Caribbean*, Johnny Depp), (*The Bourne Identity*, Matt Damon), (*Titanic*, Leonardo DiCaprio)}

4 {(3, 9), (−2, 4), (4, 16), (−1, 1), (−3, 9), (5, 25)}

5 {(−10, 4), (−8, 3), (−4, 1), (−2, 0), (0, −1)}

6 {(2, 1), (4, 5), (5, 7), (7, 11), (9, 15)}

Exercises 7–10: State the relationship as a set of ordered pairs and then state the domain and range for each relation.

7

8

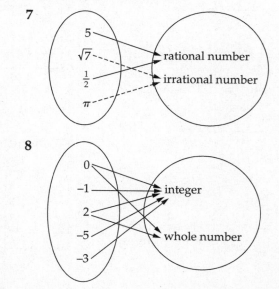

9

1st element	2nd element
–6	–5
–1	5
4	15
9	25

10

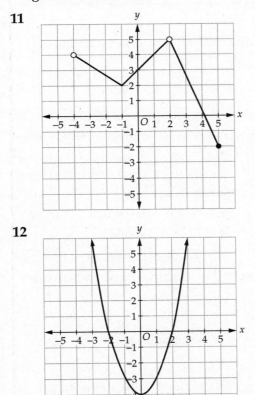

Exercises 11–15: Each graph shows a relation on a set of coordinate axes. State the domain and range of each relation.

11

12

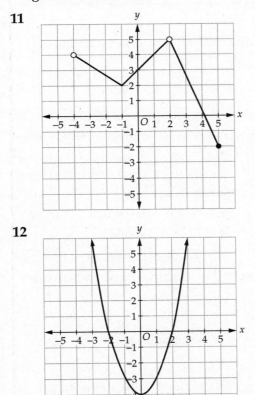

13

14

15

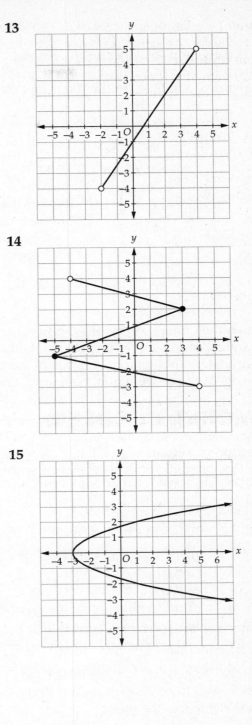

Functions

A **function** is a relation in which each element of the domain corresponds to a unique element in the range. That is, every independent variable is paired with only one dependent variable. In the diagram below, Relation *A* is not a function but Relation *B* is.

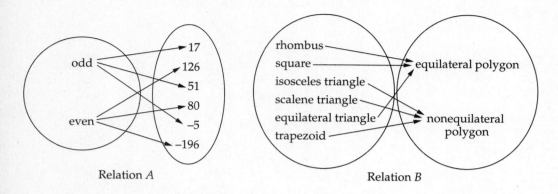

Relation *A*   Relation *B*

In relation *A*, the domain entry of even number corresponds to more than one value in the range, so it is not a function. In relation *B*, each figure in the domain is either an equilateral polygon or it is not. None of the polygons can correspond to both elements of the range. Thus, each input corresponds to only one output.

MODEL PROBLEM

List the domain and range of each relation below and explain why the relation is or is not a function.

a *A*: {(purple, lilac), (yellow, daffodil), (pink, carnation), (purple, tulip)}

b *B*: {(−7, 3), (−3, 8), (−1, 10), (4, 3)}

c *C*: {(4, 2), (9, −3), (25, 5), (16, −4), (9, 3)}

d *D*: {(1, 13), (5, 10), (9, −7), (13, −4), (17, −1)}

SOLUTION

a Domain of *A*: {purple, yellow, pink} Range of *A*: {lilac, daffodil, carnation, tulip}

A is *not* a function because purple corresponds to both tulip and lilac. Each element of the domain must have one and only one corresponding element in the range for the relation to be a function.

b Domain of *B*: {−7, −3, −1, 4} Range of *B*: {3, 8, 10}

B is a function even though 3 repeats in the range, since each element of the domain corresponds to one and only one element in the range.

c Domain of *C*: {4, 9, 25, 16} Range of *C*: {2, −3, 5, −4, 3}

C is *not* a function because 9 in the domain corresponds to both 3 and −3 in the range.

d Domain of *D*: {1, 5, 9, 13, 17} Range of *D*: {13, 10, −7, −4, −1}

D is a function because each value of the domain corresponds to one and only one value in the range.

Vertical-Line Test

Consider a relation represented as a graph on a set of coordinate axes. If a value in the domain corresponds to more than one value in the range, the graph shows those two or more values of the range lying directly above or below one another. Thus, we can draw a vertical line to see if the graph of any relation represents a function. The **vertical-line test** tells us that if a vertical line drawn at any position over the domain of the graph intersects the graph more than once, the graph does *not* represent a function. In other words, if any *x*-value corresponds to more than one *y*-value, the graph does not represent a function.

Consider the following graphs.

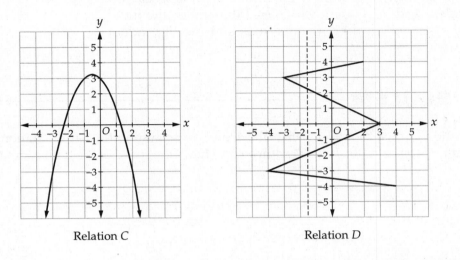

Relation *C*   Relation *D*

For relation *C*, a vertical line drawn anywhere on the graph of the parabola will touch the parabola only once, which means that each *x*-value corresponds to only one *y*-value. Therefore, relation *C* is a function. On the other hand, a vertical line on the graph of relation *D* at $x = -1.6$ intersects the graph four times, which means that there are four different *y*-values that correspond to the *x*-value of -1.6. Therefore, relation *D* is not a function.

A function is **onto** if every element in the range is the image of at least one element in the domain. If there are elements in the range that do not correspond to any elements in the domain, the function is not onto.

MODEL PROBLEM

Determine whether each of the following functions is onto.

a   **b**   **c**   **d**

SOLUTION

Functions **b** and **c** are onto since each element in the range is the image of at least one element in the domain.

Functions **a** and **d** are not onto. In function **a**, 17 is not the image of any element of the domain. In function **d**, 3 is not the image of any element of the domain.

Answers: **a** not onto   **b** onto   **c** onto   **d** not onto

Applications of Functions

There are many situations in everyday life that can be represented as graphs in which one variable is a function of the other. For example, distance may be a function of time, salary might be a function of years of experience, or number of items sold might be a function of the cost to produce each item.

For some of these functions, you may not be able to write an algebraic equation. However, it is often possible to sketch a graph of the situation as long as you clearly identify the independent and dependent variables. (Remember, the independent variable is usually assigned to the horizontal axis and the dependent variable is on the vertical axis.)

MODEL PROBLEM

A New York subway train slows down as it approaches the 42nd Street Station, stops at the station for two minutes, and then continues on its route. Which graph below shows the speed of the train compared to the time elapsed?

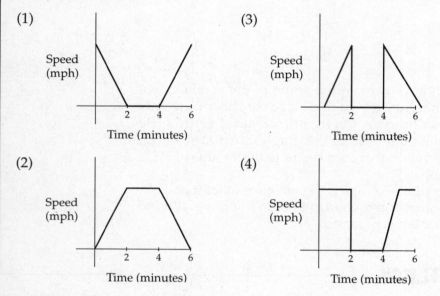

(1)

(3)

(2)

(4)

SOLUTION

Look carefully at each graph to determine what events are represented there.

Choice 1: The train's speed gradually decreases to zero over a two-minute period, remains at zero for two minutes, and then increases again to its original speed.

Choice 2: The train's speed increases from zero to an unspecified speed, continues at that speed for two minutes, and then decreases back to zero.

Choice 3: The train's speed increases from zero to an unspecified speed, drops instantly to zero, remains at zero for two minutes, instantly increases back to the earlier speed, and then gradually decreases to zero.

Choice 4: The train travels at a constant speed for two minutes, the speed decreases instantly to zero, remains at zero for two minutes, increases quickly to its previous speed, and then remains at that speed.

The answer is choice 1, since it most realistically represents the given situation.

Answer: (1)

Practice

Exercises 1–15: Determine if each relation is or is not a function. Explain your reasoning.

1

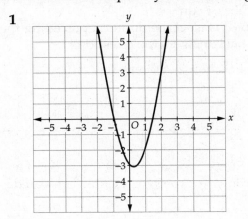

2

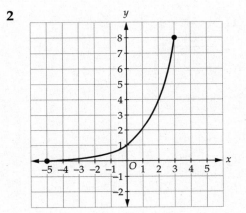

3

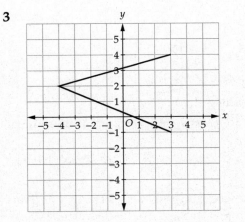

4

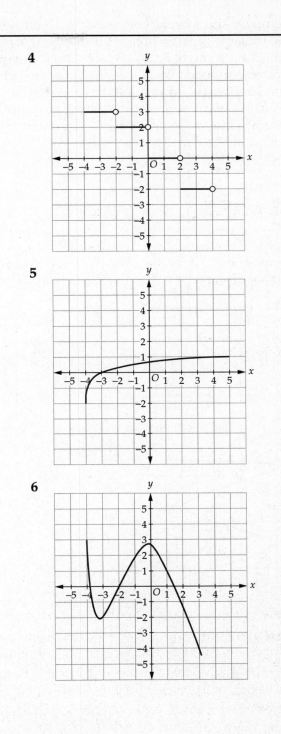

5

6

7

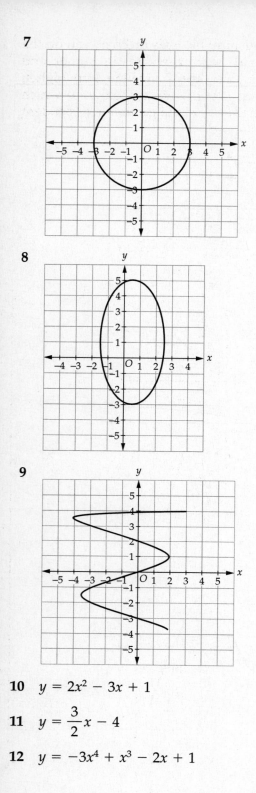

8

9

10 $y = 2x^2 - 3x + 1$

11 $y = \dfrac{3}{2}x - 4$

12 $y = -3x^4 + x^3 - 2x + 1$

13 Relation *A*: $\{(4, -1), (7, -3), (10, -5), (13, -7)\}$

14 Relation *B*: $\{(\text{January, Aquarius}), (\text{April, Aries}), (\text{May, Gemini}), (\text{August, Leo})\}$

15 Relation *C*: $\{(-2, 8), (0, 5), (3, -1), (0, 7), (-2, 10)\}$

Exercises 16–19: Select the numeral preceding the choice that best answers the question.

16 Which function is *not* onto?

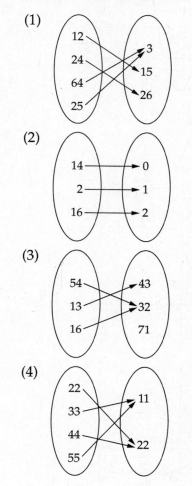

17 Abdul left for school and walked casually until he realized he'd forgotten his calculator. He turned and hurried home, got the calculator, and then ran to school so he wouldn't be late for class. Which graph depicts the situation in which distance from home is a function of time elapsed?

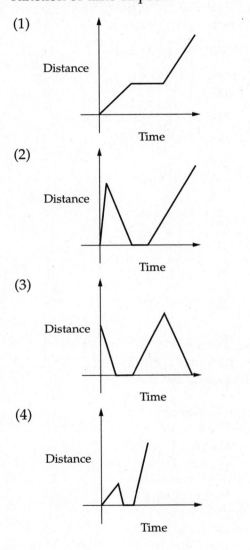

18 Josef is pushing his little brother Ivan on the swings and Ivan wants to go higher and higher. If Josef keeps pushing him higher, which graph represents a function in which Ivan's height above the ground is dependent on time elapsed?

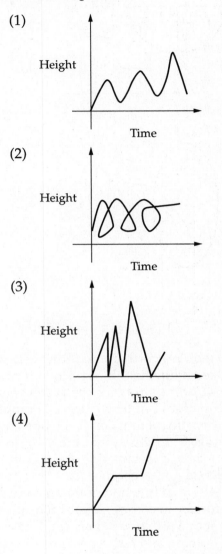

19 Hollis had money in her savings account. She spent some money on new clothes, then worked a part-time job and saved her salary until she had to pay her car insurance. Which graph shows her savings as a function time?

(1)

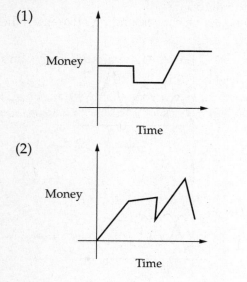

(2)

(3)

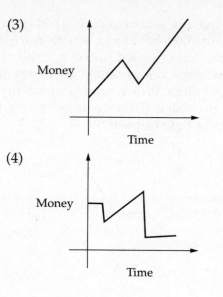

(4)

4.2 The Algebra of Functions

Function notation is shorthand to indicate that the relation or equation being discussed is indeed a function. If a rule of a function states that "each element of the range is one greater than twice the corresponding element of the domain," then the rule (or equation) can be written in a number of ways.

One way of writing a function is the one you have seen throughout algebra, the equation. $y = 2x + 1$ tells us that the y-value is one more than twice the x-value. This equation clearly assigns one element in the range, y, to each element in the domain, x, creating a function.

Another method of function notation names the function, indicates the variable inside parentheses, and then defines the rule of the function. In this format, the same rule as above is expressed as $f(x) = 2x + 1$. In this case, x represents the elements in the domain and $f(x)$ represents the corresponding elements in the range. Note that $f(x)$ does *not* mean f times x. The notation $f(x)$ indicates the value of *the function* at x. An ordered pair belonging to the solution set of this function could be represented as $(x, f(x))$ rather than (x, y).

The function may also be written as $x \xrightarrow{f} 2x + 1$. This states that *under the function f*, each element of the domain becomes twice itself plus one.

MODEL PROBLEMS

1 If $f(x) = 3x - 4$, evaluate $f(5)$.

SOLUTION

In this case, x represents the element in the domain and $f(x)$ represents the corresponding element in the range.

We are evaluating the quantity "three times the domain element minus four." We substitute 5 for x and find that $f(5) = 3(5) - 4 = 11$.

To check our answer, we can look at the graph of the original function. We can see that the point $(5, 11)$ is on the graph of the line $y = 3x - 4$, as shown below. Since the value we found for $f(x)$ corresponds to the function value for the given x on the graph, we know that our answer is correct.

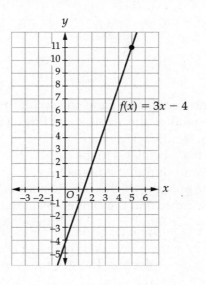

To test this idea using the same function, $f(x) = 3x - 4$, evaluate $f(1)$.

$f(x) = 3x - 4$	Write the rule for the function.
$f(1) = 3(1) - 4$	Substitute for the variable and simplify.
$f(1) = 3 - 4$	
$f(1) = -1$	This means that when $x = 1$, $y = -1$.

Notice that the coordinate point $(1, -1)$ appears on the graph of this function.

Answer: $f(5) = 11$

2 If the function $h(x)$ is represented by the mapping below, find

   a $h(-3)$
   b $h(1)$
   c $h(3)$
   d   the value of x if $h(x) = 5$

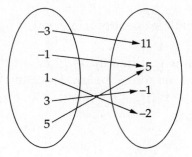

SOLUTION

   a   Since the first set of numbers represents the domain and the second the range, we look in the first set to find the element -3 and then follow the arrow to find the corresponding value in the range. We see that $h(-3)$ maps to 11, so $h(-3) = 11$.

   b   As above, we look in the first set for 1 and see that it maps to -2.

   c   As above, we look in the domain for 3 and find that it maps to -1.

   d   In this example, we are given the value of $h(x)$, which is an element in the range, so we look in the second set to find 5 and work backward to find the element(s) in the domain that correspond to 5. There are two values in the domain, -1 and 5, for which the statement $h(x) = 5$ would be true. There are two solutions, $x = -1$ and $x = 5$.

Answers: **a** $h(-3) = 11$ **b** $h(1) = -2$ **c** $h(3) = -1$ **d** $x = -1$ and $x = 5$

We can perform arithmetic operations with functions in a manner similar to the way we perform arithmetic operations with numbers. We can add, subtract, multiply, or divide functions, as shown below.

📖 MODEL PROBLEM

If $f(x)$ is defined as $f(x) = x + 2$ and $g(x)$ is defined as $g(x) = x^2 - 4$, find

   a $f(x) + g(x)$
   b $f(x) - g(x)$
   c $f(x) \bullet g(x)$
   d $\dfrac{g(x)}{f(x)}$

SOLUTION

These operations are performed by the same rules as they are in arithmetic or algebra.

   a   To add functions, combine like terms:

$$f(x) + g(x) = (x + 2) + (x^2 - 4)$$
$$= x^2 + x - 2$$

b To subtract functions, negate the second function and then follow the rules for addition:

$$f(x) - g(x) = (x + 2) - (x^2 - 4)$$
$$= x + 2 - x^2 + 4$$
$$= -x^2 + x + 6$$

c To multiply functions, use the distributive property to multiply the polynomials:

$$f(x) \bullet g(x) = (x + 2)(x^2 - 4)$$
$$= x^3 + 2x^2 - 4x - 8$$

d To divide functions, factor each and reduce if possible:

$$\frac{g(x)}{f(x)} = \frac{x^2 - 4}{x + 2}$$
$$= \frac{(x + 2)(x - 2)}{x + 2}$$
$$= x - 2$$

Answers: **a** $x^2 + x - 2$ **b** $-x^2 + x + 6$ **c** $x^3 + 2x^2 - 4x - 8$ **d** $x - 2$

 **Practice**

1 If a function $f(x)$ is defined as $f(x) = x^2 + x - 2$, evaluate

   a $f(3)$

   b $f\left(\dfrac{1}{2}\right)$

   c $f(-1)$

2 A function $g(x)$ is defined as $g(x) = 3 - 5x - 2x^2$. Find the value of

   a $g(-2)$
   b $g(1.4)$
   c $g(5)$

3 Given $f(x) = 4 - \dfrac{1}{2}x$, find x such that $f(x) = 1$.

4 Given $g(x) = x^2 - 3x - 1$, find x such that $g(x) = 3$.

5 If the function $h(x)$ is defined as $h(x) = x^3 - x^2 + 1$, find

   a $h(-2)$
   b $h(2.5)$

   c $h\left(-\dfrac{1}{2}\right)$

   d x such that $h(x) = 1$

6 Given $f(t) = t + 3$ and $g(t) = 2t + 6$, find
   a $f(t) + g(t)$
   b $5f(t)$

   c $\dfrac{g(t)}{2}$

   d $\dfrac{g(t)}{f(t)}$

   e $f(t) \bullet g(t)$

Exercises 7–15: Use the graph of the function $f(x)$ shown below.

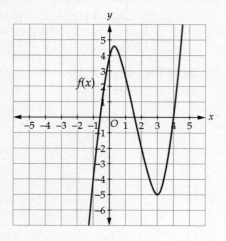

7 Find $f(2)$.

8 Find $f(-1)$.

9 Find $f(4)$.

10 Find $f(3.5)$.

11 Find $2f(0)$.

12 Find $f(2) \cdot f(3)$.

13 Find $f(0) + f(1)$.

14 For how many values of x does $f(x) = -2$?

15 If $f(x) = -5$, find all possible values of x.

Exercises 16–21: The rule that defines the function $g(x)$ is given. Find

   a $g(1)$
   b $g(-2)$

16 $g(x) = 12 - 3x$

17 $g(x) = x^2 - 4$

18 $g(x) = \dfrac{2x + 1}{x}$

19 $g(x) = 5$

20 $g(x) = -\dfrac{3}{4}x + 7$

21 $g(x) = 2x^2 - 5x + 3$

Exercises 22–28: Select the numeral preceding the choice that best completes the statement or answers the question.

22 Given the function $f(x) = 2x^4 - 3x^3 + x - 7$, the point $(2, f(2))$ appears on the graph of $f(x)$. The value of $f(2)$ is

(1) −13   (3) 3
(2) 2   (4) 227

23 If $x \xrightarrow{g} 3 - 2x$, which point appears on the graph of this function?

(1) $(1, -2)$ (3) $(-1, 2)$
(2) $(2, -1)$ (4) $(-2, 1)$

24 If $s(t) = 3t$ and $r(t) = t^2$, $s(2) + r(-4) =$

(1) −10   (3) 14
(2) −2   (4) 22

25 If $f(x) = -x^2$ and $g(x) = \sqrt{x - 4}$, then $f(-3) - 2g(8) =$

(1) 1   (3) −17
(2) 5   (4) −13

Exercises 26–28: Use the diagram below.

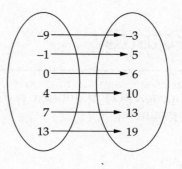

26 If $f(x) = 13$, what is the corresponding element in the domain?

(1) 19   (3) 0
(2) 7   (4) −3

27 The statement $f(-1) = 5$ implies which of the following to be true?

(1) 5 is in the domain and −1 is in the range.
(2) The point $(-1, 5)$ would appear on the graph of this function.
(3) The point $(5, -1)$ would appear on the graph of this function.
(4) Both −1 and 5 are elements in the range of this function.

28 Given the partial mapping of the domain and range of the function $f(x)$ in the diagram on page 112, which of the following might represent the rule of the function $f(x)$?

(1) $f(x) = 3x - 9$
(2) $f(x) = 1 - 2x$
(3) $f(x) = x$
(4) $f(x) = x + 6$

29 Given $f(x) = x^2$.

a Does $f(1 + 4) = f(1) + f(4)$? Explain.
b In general, for a and b, does $f(a + b) = f(a) + f(b)$? Explain your answer.
c Are there any values of a and b such that $f(a + b) = f(a) + f(b)$? How did you arrive at your answer?

30 Each year, Mrs. Santiago keeps track of the number of girls and boys in her class. If $g(y)$ represents the number of girls Mrs. Santiago has in year y, and $b(y)$ represents the number of boys she has in year y, explain what is meant by each of the following:

a $g(2007) = 10$
b $g(2008) = b(2008) + 5$
c $b(y) = 2g(y)$
d $t(y) = g(y) + b(y)$

31 Let $m(w)$ represent the number of gallons of milk the Longarzo family buys in w weeks and $i(w)$ represent the number of gallons of ice cream they buy in w weeks. Explain what is meant by each of the following:

a $m(3) = 7$
b $i(3) = m(3)$
c $m(2) + i(2) = 8$
d $m(w) = 3i(w)$
e $m(w) - i(w) = 2$

4.3 Domain and Range

In many cases, the domain and range of a function are the set of all real numbers $\mathbb{R}$, such as in the case of a linear function. The diagrams below represent a few functions whose domain and range are the real numbers.

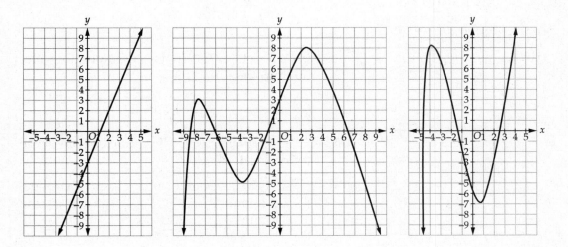

There are other functions that have limited domains. For example, the function $f(x) = \dfrac{x + 3}{x^2 - 4}$ is not defined when $x = \pm 2$. Therefore, we say the domain is all real numbers except ± 2. We can write this as: $\{x : x \neq -2, 2\}$ or $\{x : x \neq \pm 2\}$. A graph of this function is shown below.

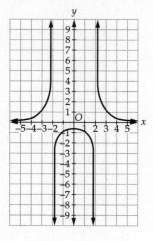

Notice that while the graph approaches the x-values of $+2$ and -2 from both the right and the left, it never actually reaches those values.

Another type of function whose domain must be limited is a radical function, such as $g(x) = \sqrt{x - 6}$. Since there is no real number that is the square root of a negative number, this function can be defined only in the real number system if we input values of x that are greater than or equal to 6. Looking at the graph below, we see that the domain is restricted to values of x such that $x \geq 6$. We can write this as $\{x : x \geq 6\}$.

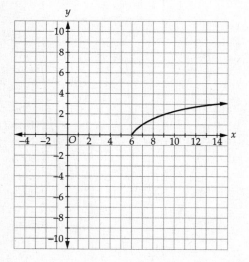

Some helpful hints for finding domain and range are summarized in the table below.

Type of Function	Example of Function	Domain	Range	Comments
Linear function	$y = 2x - 1$	All real numbers	All real numbers	Lines in the form $y = mx + b$, where $m \neq 0$, extend infinitely.
Quadratic function	$y = x^2 - 4$	All real numbers	$\{y : y \geq -4\}$	If a parabola opens upward, its range has a minimum value at the vertex, but the range increases without limit in a positive direction.
	$y = -2x^2 + 4x + 5$	All real numbers	$\{y : y \leq 7\}$	If a parabola opens downward, its range has a maximum value at the vertex, but the range grows without limit in a negative direction.
Rational function	$y = \dfrac{3}{x + 5}$	$\{x : x \neq -5\}$	$\{y : y \neq 0\}$	A fraction is undefined when its denominator is zero. Since the numerator of this fraction is 3, the fraction can never equal zero.
Functions with radicals	$y = \sqrt{10 - x}$	$\{x : x \leq 10\}$	$\{y : y \geq 0\}$	The number under the radical cannot be negative. Set the radicand greater than or equal to zero and solve to find the domain.
	$y = \dfrac{1}{\sqrt{x + 8}}$	$\{x : x > -8\}$	$\{y : y > 0\}$	The rules for both fractions and radicals apply here. When a radical appears in the denominator of a fraction, set the radicand greater than zero (instead of greater than or equal to zero) and solve to find the domain.

MODEL PROBLEMS

1   Find the domain of $f(x) = \dfrac{3x + 1}{x^2 + 3x - 4}$.

SOLUTION

To find the domain, set the denominator equal to zero and solve to find the values that are not included in the domain. The domain will be all real numbers *except* those values for which $x^2 + 3x - 4 = 0$.

$x^2 + 3x - 4 = 0$

$(x + 4)(x - 1) = 0$

$\qquad\qquad x = -4, x = 1$

Answer: $\{x : x \neq -4, 1\}$

2   Find the domain of $g(x) = \dfrac{7x}{\sqrt{5 - 2x}}$.

SOLUTION

Since there is a radical in the denominator, the radicand cannot equal zero. To find the domain, we set the radicand greater than zero and solve.

$5 - 2x > 0$

$\quad -2x > -5$

$\qquad x < \dfrac{5}{2}$

Answer: $\left\{ x : x < \dfrac{5}{2} \right\}$

> **Note:** When dividing an inequality by a negative number, reverse the direction of the inequality.

3   Find the domain of $h(x) = \sqrt{2x - 4}$.

SOLUTION

To find the domain, set the radicand greater than or equal to zero and solve.

$2x - 4 \geq 0$

$\quad 2x \geq 4$

$\quad x \geq 2$

Answer: $\{x : x \geq 2\}$

4   Determine the domain and range of $g(x) = x^2 - 8x + 15$.

SOLUTION

The domain of a quadratic function is all real numbers. To find its range, find the vertex. We use the equation $x = -\dfrac{b}{2a}$ to determine the axis of symmetry. In this case, $-\dfrac{b}{2a} = \dfrac{-(-8)}{2(1)} = 4$.

Substitute 4 into the quadratic equation to find the y-value at the vertex point.

$$g(4) = 4^2 - 8(4) + 15$$
$$= 16 - 32 + 15 = -1$$

Thus, the vertex of the parabola is $(4, -1)$. Since the parabola opens upward, the range of the function is $y \geq -1$.

You could also use a calculator to graph the function and determine the coordinates of its vertex.

Answer: domain: all real numbers   range: $\{y : y \geq -1\}$

5 Determine the domain and range of $f(x) = \dfrac{2}{3}x + 10$.

Since this is a linear function in the form $y = mx + b$, $m \neq 0$, the domain and range are the set of all real numbers.

Answer: domain: $\mathbb{R}$ range: $\mathbb{R}$

6 Determine the domain and range of $h(x) = \sqrt{3x + 9}$.

SOLUTION

To find the domain, set the radicand greater than or equal to zero and solve.

$$3x + 9 \geq 0$$
$$3x \geq -9$$
$$x \geq -3$$

The range is the set of all nonnegative numbers, $y \geq 0$.

Answer: domain: $\{x : x \geq -3\}$ range: $\{y : y \geq 0\}$

7 If the function $f(x)$ is defined as $f(x) = 4x - 7$ with a domain such that $-2 \leq x \leq 7$, find

   a   the range
   b   the least element in the range

SOLUTION

   a   We see that $f(x)$ is a linear function with a positive slope. This tells us that the function is increasing from left to right. To find the range of such a function when given a domain, substitute the least and greatest elements of the domain in the function and find the boundaries of the range. In this case,

$$f(-2) = 4(-2) - 7 = -15 \quad \text{and} \quad f(7) = 4(7) - 7 = 21$$

Therefore, the range for $f(x)$ is $-15 \leq y \leq 21$.

   b   The least element in the range is -15.

Answers: **a** $\{y : -15 \leq y \leq 21\}$ **b** -15 is the least element in the range.

8 If the function $g(x)$ is defined as $g(x) = x^2 - 5x - 14$ with a domain such that $-1 \leq x \leq 7$, find

    a the smallest element in the range
    b the range as determined by the given domain

SOLUTION

    a $g(x)$ is a quadratic function. To find its range, find the vertex point. We use the equation $x = -\dfrac{b}{2a}$ to determine the axis of symmetry. In this case,

$$x = -\frac{b}{2a} = \frac{-(-5)}{2(1)} = \frac{5}{2} \text{ or } 2.5$$

Substitute $\dfrac{5}{2}$ into the quadratic equation to find the y-value at the vertex point.

$$y = g(2.5) = 2.5^2 - 5(2.5) - 14$$
$$= -\frac{81}{4} \text{ or } -20.25$$

Thus, the vertex of the parabola is $(2.5, -20.25)$. Since the parabola opens upward, the least y-value of this function is -20.25.

You could also use your calculator to graph the function and determine the coordinates of its minimum point.

Answer: -20.25

    b To find the range determined by the given domain, substitute the least and greatest values of the given domain into the original function for x.

$g(-1) = (-1)^2 - 5(-1) - 14$ $g(7) = 7^2 - 5(7) - 14$

$g(-1) = -8$ $g(7) = 0$

Since we know from part **a** that the least value of the range is -20.25, we choose the greater value now as the other boundary of the range.

Answer: $\{y : -20.25 \leq y \leq 0\}$

> **Note:** The least element in the range does *not* always correspond to the least element of the domain.

Model Problems 9–11: Approximate the domain and range of each graph.

9

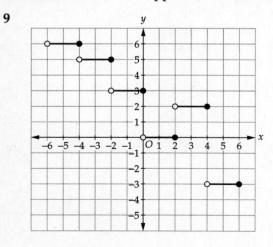

SOLUTION

Find the points farthest to the left and right to determine the domain, and then find the highest and lowest points to determine the range.

This graph shows what is called a "step function." The y-values are not continuous but appear to jump in steplike movements. The range, therefore, is not a continuous set of values but a limited set of integers: $\{6, 5, 3, 2, 0, -3\}$. The domain, despite the open points on the left ends of the line segments, is a continuous set of numbers between -6 and 6, because the closed points include the omitted values on the next line segment.

Answer: domain: $\{x : -6 < x \le 6\}$ range: $\{-3, 0, 2, 3, 5, 6\}$

10

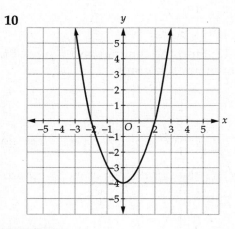

SOLUTION

The vertex of this parabola appears to be the point $(0, -4)$. This is a minimum, so the range will be all y-values greater than or equal to -4. The arrows at each end of the parabola indicate that it continues to widen, so the domain is understood to be all real numbers.

Answer: domain: all real numbers   range: $\{y : y \ge -4\}$

11

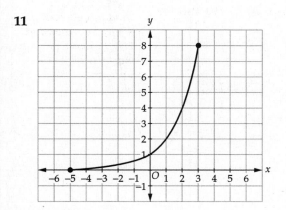

SOLUTION

Since this graph has points at both ends instead of arrows, it is understood not to continue past the boundaries of these points.

Answer: domain: $\{x : -5 \le x \le 3\}$ range: $\{y : 0 \le y \le 8\}$

Exercises 1–8: Select the numeral preceding the choice that best completes the statement or answers the question.

1 Given the function $f(x) = x^2 - 6x - 7$ with a domain of $-2 \leq x \leq 8$, the smallest value in the range is

(1) 9   (3) -16
(2) -7 (4) -31

2 Which function has a limited domain?

(1) $y = 5x - 1$ (3) $y = \dfrac{2x + 5}{x - 6}$
(2) $y = x^2 - 9$ (4) $y = 4$

3 If $g(x)$ is defined as $g(x) = -2x^3 + 5x^2 + 4x - 3$ and the domain is $-3 \leq x \leq 5$, the greatest element in the range is

(1) 189   (3) 25
(2) 84   (4) 9

4 What is the domain of the function $h(x)$, defined as $h(x) = \dfrac{x + 4}{x^2 - 5x}$?

(1) $\{x : x \neq -4\}$ (3) $\{x : x \neq -5, 0\}$
(2) $\{x : x \neq 0, 5\}$ (4) $\{x : x \neq -5, -4, 0\}$

5 What is the domain of the function $y = \sqrt{3x + 12}$?

(1) $x \geq 4$ (3) $x \geq -12$
(2) $x \geq -4$ (4) $x \geq 0$

6 What is the range of the relation $f(x) = 3x^2 - 5x$ if the domain is $\{0, 1, 2\}$?

(1) $\{0, 1, 2\}$ (3) $\{-1, -2, 0\}$
(2) $\{-2, 0, 2\}$ (4) $y \geq 0$

7 Which value is *not* in the domain of the function $f(x) = \dfrac{5 - x}{\sqrt{2x^2 - 8}}$?

(1) -3 (3) 3
(2) -2 (4) 5

8 Which function does *not* have a domain of all real numbers?

(1) $y = \dfrac{1}{2}x - 3$
(2) $f(x) = x^3 - 4x^2 + 7$
(3) $y = \dfrac{x + 3}{5}$
(4) $y = \dfrac{4}{x - 2}$

Exercises 9–12: Find the domain and range of the function shown in each graph.

9

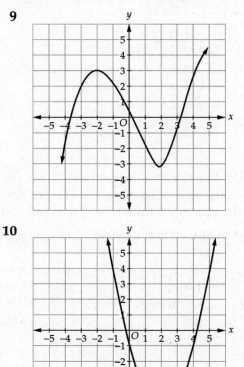

10

11

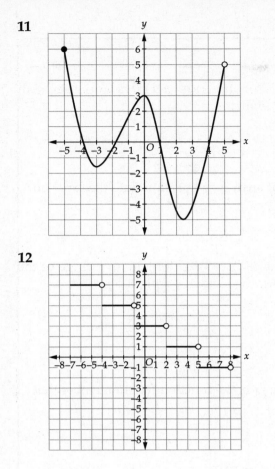

12

Exercises 13–15: Find the domain for each function.

13 $g(x) = \dfrac{x^2 + 2x + 1}{3x^2 - 12}$

14 $f(x) = \dfrac{2x - 4}{\sqrt{3x + 9}}$

15 $h(x) = \dfrac{x - 3}{\sqrt{x^2 + 1}}$

Exercises 16–21: Find the domain and range for each function.

16 $y = 16 - x^2$

17 $f(x) = \dfrac{2}{3}x + 1$

18 $y = x^2 + 6x + 9$

19 $g(x) = \sqrt{9 - x^2}$

20 $h(x) = -x^2 + 3$

21 $y = x^3 - 2x^2 - 1$

4.4 Composition of Functions

In Section 4.2 we discussed the four operations of adding, subtracting, multiplying, and dividing functions. We will now introduce a fifth operation called **composition**. In composition of functions, the result obtained from performing the operation of one function is then used as the domain value in a second function. Compositions may be indicated by one set of parentheses within another, such as $f(g(x))$, or by using a small open circle as the notation: $(f \circ g)(x)$. Both notations are read as "f of g of x," "f following g of x," or "f composition g of x." To perform a composition, it is important to remember that just as we always begin operations inside the parentheses, we complete the function inside the innermost parentheses (or on the right) first.

Note: Always perform compositions from right to left.

MODEL PROBLEM

If $f(x)$ is defined as $f(x) = x + 2$ and $g(x)$ is defined as $g(x) = x^2 - 4$, find

    a $f(g(3))$

    b $(g \circ f)(3)$

    c $(f \circ f)(5)$

SOLUTION

    a   The notation $f(g(3))$ means we must find $g(3)$ and use that answer as our input into the function f. Since $g(x) = x^2 - 4$, we replace x with 3 and evaluate.

$g(x) = x^2 - 4$

$g(3) = 3^2 - 4 = 5$

Next, we evaluate $f(5)$.

$f(x) = x + 2$

$f(5) = 5 + 2 = 7$

Answer: $f(g(3)) = 7$

    b   To evaluate $(g \circ f)(3)$, we first find $f(3)$ by substituting 3 for x in the function $f(x)$. Remember that $(g \circ f)(3)$ can be written $g(f(3))$.

$f(x) = x + 2$

$f(3) = 3 + 2 = 5$

Next, we evaluate $g(5)$.

$g(x) = x^2 - 4$

$g(5) = 5^2 - 4 = 21$

Answer: $(g \circ f)(3) = 21$

    c   To evaluate $(f \circ f)(5)$, we first find $f(5)$.

$f(x) = x + 2$

$f(5) = 5 + 2 = 7$

Next, we evaluate $f(7)$.

$f(7) = 7 + 2 = 9$

Answer: $(f \circ f)(5) = 9$

Sometimes we are asked to find the **rule of a (composite) function**. The rule of a composite function is defined as the single function that will perform the same operation as the composition, but in one step. To find the rule of a composite function, we replace the x in the outer function with the innermost function.

MODEL PROBLEMS

1 If $f(x)$ is defined as $f(x) = x + 2$ and $g(x)$ is defined as $g(x) = x^2 - 4$, find the rule of

    a $g(f(x))$

    b $f(g(x))$

SOLUTION

    a   Finding $g(f(x))$ is equivalent to finding $g(x + 2)$, so we simply replace each x in $g(x)$ with $(x + 2)$.

$$g(f(x)) = g(x + 2)$$
$$= (x + 2)^2 - 4$$
$$= x^2 + 4x + 4 - 4$$
$$= x^2 + 4x$$

Answer: The rule of $g(f(x))$ is $x^2 + 4x$.

    b   Finding $f(g(x))$ is equivalent to finding $f(x^2 - 4)$, so we simply replace each x in $f(x)$ with $x^2 - 4$.

$$f(g(x)) = f(x^2 - 4)$$
$$= x^2 - 4 + 2$$
$$= x^2 - 2$$

Answer: The rule of $f(g(x))$ is $x^2 - 2$.

> **Note:** Notice that composition is not a commutative operation. You cannot assume that $(g \circ f)(x)$ is the same as $(f \circ g)(x)$.

2 If $h(x) = 3x + 2$ and $f(x) = \dfrac{x - 2}{3}$, find

    a $(f \circ h)(x)$

    b $(h \circ f)(x)$

What unusual results do you find?

SOLUTION

    a $(f \circ h)(x) = f(3x + 2)$

$$= \frac{(3x + 2) - 2}{3} = \frac{3x}{3} = x$$

Answer: $(f \circ h)(x) = x$

    b $(h \circ f)(x) = h\left(\dfrac{x - 2}{3}\right)$

$$= 3\left(\frac{x - 2}{3}\right) + 2$$
$$= x - 2 + 2$$
$$= x$$

Answer: $(h \circ f)(x) = x$

In this case, $(f \circ h)(x) = (h \circ f)(x)$.

It is unusual for the commutative property to apply to composition of functions, yet in Model Problem 2 on page 123, $(h \circ f)(x) = (f \circ h)(x)$. We will discuss cases like this in greater detail in the next section.

The graphs of functions can also be used to find compositions. Consider the graphs of $g(x)$ and $j(x)$ shown in the model problem below.

MODEL PROBLEM

Using the graphs of $g(x)$ and $j(x)$ below, evaluate the following compositions.

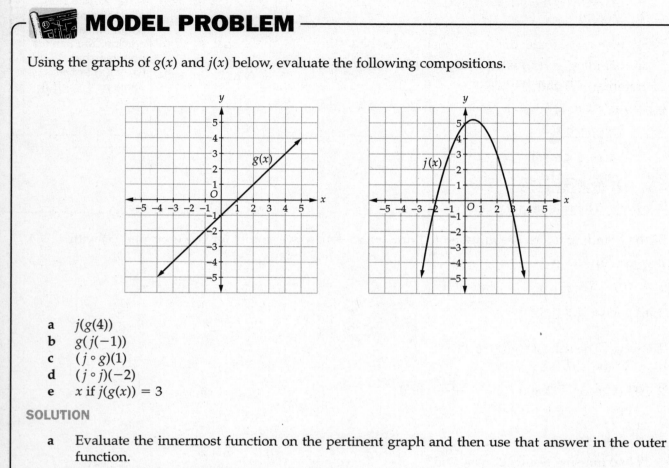

a $j(g(4))$
b $g(j(-1))$
c $(j \circ g)(1)$
d $(j \circ j)(-2)$
e x if $j(g(x)) = 3$

SOLUTION

a Evaluate the innermost function on the pertinent graph and then use that answer in the outer function.

By examining the function labeled $g(x)$, we find $g(4) = 3$.
Next, we find $j(3)$ on the graph of $j(x)$ and discover that $j(3) = -1$.
Thus, $j(g(4)) = j(3) = -1$.

b By examining the graph of $j(x)$, we find $j(-1) = 3$.
Then, evaluate $g(3)$ on the $g(x)$ graph to find that $g(3) = 2$.
Thus, $g(j(-1)) = g(3) = 2$.

c Remember, $(j \circ g)(1) = j(g(1))$. When we look at the graph of $g(x)$, we find $g(1) = 0$.
We then look at the graph of $j(x)$, and learn that $j(0) = 5$.
Thus, $(j \circ g)(1) = j(0) = 5$.

d On the graph of $j(x)$, $j(-2) = -1$.

To complete the composition, substitute -1 into the same function to find $j(-1) = 3$.

Thus, $(j \circ j)(-2) = j(-1) = 3$.

e Given the y-value after a composition, work backward to determine the original x-value(s).
First, find the x-values on the graph of the $j(x)$ function for which $j(x) = 3$.

The two x-values that correspond to $j(x) = 3$ are $x = -1$ and $x = 2$.

Next, look at the graph of $g(x)$ and determine the x-values that make $g(x) = -1$ and $g(x) = 2$.

We see that $g(x) = -1$ when $x = 0$ and $g(x) = 2$ when $x = 3$.

Therefore, $x = 0$ and $x = 3$.

Answers: **a** $j(g(4)) = -1$ **b** $g(j(-1)) = 2$ **c** $(j \circ g)(1) = 5$ **d** $(j \circ j)(-2) = 3$ **e** $x = 0, x = 3$

Practice

Exercises 1–14: Use the functions

$f(x) = 2 - 5x$ $g(x) = x^2 - 16$

$h(x) = \sqrt{x + 16}$ $j(x) = x^2 - 3x - 4$

to find each of the following:

1 $g(x) + j(x)$

2 $f(x) \cdot g(x)$

3 $j(x) - g(x)$

4 $\dfrac{g(x)}{j(x)}$

5 $(h \circ j)(4)$

6 $g(f(2))$

7 $f(g(2))$

8 $f(j(-3))$

9 $j(f(-3))$

10 $(g \circ h)(-7)$

11 $(h \circ j)(-7)$

12 $g(h(x))$

13 $(h \circ j)(x)$

14 $(f \circ g)(x)$

Exercises 15–20: Using the functions whose graphs are shown below, select the numeral preceding the choice that best completes the statement or answers the question.

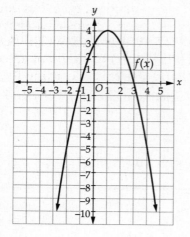

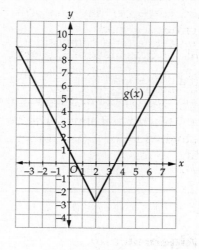

15 The composition $(g \circ f)(2)$ is

(1) −3
(2) −1
(3) 3
(4) not visible on graph

16 The composition $(f \circ g)(0)$ is equivalent to which composition?

(1) $(g \circ f)(0)$
(2) $(f \circ g)(3)$
(3) $(f \circ f)(1)$
(4) $(f \circ g)(4)$

17 The composition $(f \circ g)(-1)$ is

(1) 1   (3) −1
(2) 0   (4) 4

18 For which values of x does $(f \circ g)(x) = 3$?

(1) {0, 2, 4, 8}
(2) {−1, 5, 7, 9}
(3) {−0.5, 0.5, 3.5, 4.5}
(4) {−1.5, 0, 1.5, 2.5}

19 Which is false with respect to functions $f(x)$ and $g(x)$?

(1) $(f \circ g)(1) = 0$
(2) $(g \circ f)(1) = 1$
(3) $(f \circ g)\left(\dfrac{1}{2}\right) = 3$
(4) $(f \circ g)(2) = -1$

20 The composition $(f \circ g)(4.5)$ equals

(1) 1   (3) 3
(2) 2   (4) { }

21 A store has a 20% discount on prom dresses. Juanita plans to buy a prom dress and would like to write a function to determine the cost of the dress.

a If the tax rate is 8.25%, write an equation for $t(x)$, the cost of an item including the tax.

b Write an equation for $c(x)$, the cost of a prom dress after the 20% discount.

c Use a composition of functions to express the cost of the dress after the discount and the tax.

d Use your answer to part **c** to determine the total cost of a dress that was originally $300.

22 Frankie is going to spend a semester in Italy. He plans to arrive a few days early and spend some time touring the area. He can find a hotel for 60 euros per day and will spend 30 euros per day for food.

  a If Frankie will be traveling for d days, write a function, $f(d)$, that will model the cost of his hotel and meals for d days.

  b Frankie found a book describing how he can stay in Italy for $95 per day. Write a function, $b(d)$, that will model the cost for d days according to this book.

  c To compare the two functions, Frankie must convert euros to dollars. If 1 euro is approximately equal to $1.3849, write a function, $c(x)$, that could be used to convert x euros to dollars.

  d Write a composite function, $c(f(d))$, that will enable Frankie to convert the cost of his stay according to the model in part **a**.

  e If Frankie stays in Italy for 5 days, compare the cost according to the two models.

4.5 Inverse Functions

Finding Inverses Algebraically

In Section 4.1, we defined a function as a relationship in which each element of the domain corresponds to exactly one element in the range. Functions are said to be **one-to-one** when each element of the domain has a unique value in the range, and vice versa.

For a one-to-one function $f(x)$, if we interchange the domain and range of the original function, we obtain a new function called $f^{-1}(x)$, read "f-inverse." Hence, the **inverse** of a one-to-one function is a function in which the domain and range of the original function have been exchanged.

Consider function A: $\{(3, 11), (2, 7), (1, 3), (0, -1)\}$. The domain of A is $\{3, 2, 1, 0\}$, and its range is $\{11, 7, 3, -1\}$. The inverse of A, written A^{-1}, has points $\{(11, 3), (7, 2), (3, 1), (-1, 0)\}$. The domain of A^{-1} is $\{11, 7, 3, -1\}$ and its range is $\{3, 2, 1, 0\}$. Since each element in the domain has a unique value in the range, and vice versa, this is a one-to-one function.

To find the inverse of a function algebraically, we interchange the domain and range. In working with a function defined by an equation, we exchange x and y, the symbols for the domain and range, and then isolate the new independent variable.

> **Note: Be careful.** $f^{-1}(x)$ is <u>not</u> the reciprocal of $f(x)$. It represents the <u>inverse</u> of the function $f(x)$.

MODEL PROBLEMS

1 Find $f^{-1}(x)$, the inverse of $f(x)$, if $f(x) = \dfrac{2}{3}x + 4$.

SOLUTION

If $y = f(x)$, the given equation can be written as:

$$y = \frac{2}{3}x + 4.$$

Rewrite the equation, interchanging x and y:

$$x = \frac{2}{3}y + 4.$$

Isolate y:

$$x - 4 = \frac{2}{3}y$$

Muliply both sides of the equation by $\frac{3}{2}$: $\quad \frac{3}{2}(x - 4) = y$

Simplify and substitute the $f^{-1}(x)$ notation for y: $\quad \frac{3}{2}x - 6 = f^{-1}(x)$

Answer: The inverse of the original function is $f^{-1}(x) = \frac{3}{2}x - 6$.

2 Find $g^{-1}(x)$ if $g(x) = \sqrt[3]{2x - 1}$.

SOLUTION

Rewrite the equation using x and y: $\qquad\qquad y = \sqrt[3]{2x - 1}$

Interchange the domain and range: $\qquad\quad x = \sqrt[3]{2y - 1}$

Cube both sides: $\qquad\qquad\qquad\qquad\qquad x^3 = 2y - 1$

Perform inverse operations to isolate y: $\quad x^3 + 1 = 2y$

$$\frac{x^3 + 1}{2} = y$$

Rewrite in function notation.

Answer: $\quad g^{-1}(x) = \dfrac{x^3 + 1}{2}$

3 Given the function $g(x) = 2x^2 - 1$ with $x \geq 0$, find each of the following:

a $\quad g^{-1}(x)$
b $\quad (g \circ g^{-1})(x)$
c $\quad (g^{-1} \circ g)(x)$
d $\quad$ What is unusual about the answers in parts **b** and **c**? What could they suggest? (You may want to look back at Model Problem 2 in Section 4.4.)

SOLUTION

a $\qquad\qquad y = 2x^2 - 1$

$\qquad\qquad\quad x = 2y^2 - 1$

$\qquad\qquad x + 1 = 2y^2$

$\qquad\qquad \dfrac{x + 1}{2} = y^2$

$\qquad\qquad \sqrt{\dfrac{x + 1}{2}} = y$

$\qquad\qquad \sqrt{\dfrac{x + 1}{2}} = g^{-1}(x)$

b $(g \circ g^{-1})(x) = g\left(\sqrt{\dfrac{x+1}{2}}\right)$

$\qquad\qquad\quad = 2\left(\sqrt{\dfrac{x+1}{2}}\right)^2 - 1$

$\qquad\qquad\quad = 2 \cdot \dfrac{x+1}{2} - 1$

$\qquad\qquad\quad = x + 1 - 1$

$\quad (g \circ g^{-1})(x) = x$

c $(g^{-1} \circ g)(x) = g^{-1}(2x^2 - 1)$

$\qquad\qquad\quad = \sqrt{\dfrac{(2x^2 - 1) + 1}{2}}$

$\qquad\qquad\quad = \sqrt{\dfrac{2x^2}{2}}$

$\qquad\qquad\quad = \sqrt{x^2}$

$\quad (g^{-1} \circ g)(x) = x$

> **Note:** While it is true that $\sqrt{x^2} = |x|$, in this case $x \geq 0$, so only nonnegative x-values are valid.

d The composition of the function of the inverse and the composition of the inverse of the function both yielded answers of x.

For any function, if $(f \circ g)(x) = (g \circ f)(x) = x$, then $f(x)$ and $g(x)$ are inverses of one another. This means that $(f \circ f^{-1})(x) = (f^{-1} \circ f)(x) = x$. (The function $f(x) = x$ is called the **identity function**.)

Finding Inverses Graphically

To find the inverse of a function algebraically, we interchange the domain and the range. We do the same when graphing. You may recall from your geometry course that the point (x, y) maps to (y, x) when reflected in the line $y = x$. So, to find an inverse graphically, reflect the graph of the function in the line $y = x$.

MODEL PROBLEM

Sketch the function $f(x) = 2x + 4$ and, on the same set of axes, sketch its inverse.

SOLUTION

The function $f(x) = 2x + 4$ has a y-intercept of $(0, 4)$ and a slope of 2. Therefore, we begin at the point $(0, 4)$ and move up 2 units and to the right 1 unit to find each successive point. We could also begin at the point $(0, 4)$ and move down 2 units and to the left 1 unit to plot additional points to help sketch the original function. To sketch the inverse, reflect the points in the line $y = x$ and sketch the inverse function.

For example,

Original $\longrightarrow$ Inverse

$(-4, -4) \longrightarrow (-4, -4)$

$(-3, -2) \longrightarrow (-2, -3)$

$(-2, 0) \longrightarrow (0, -2)$

$(0, 4) \longrightarrow (4, 0)$

$(1, 6) \longrightarrow (6, 1)$

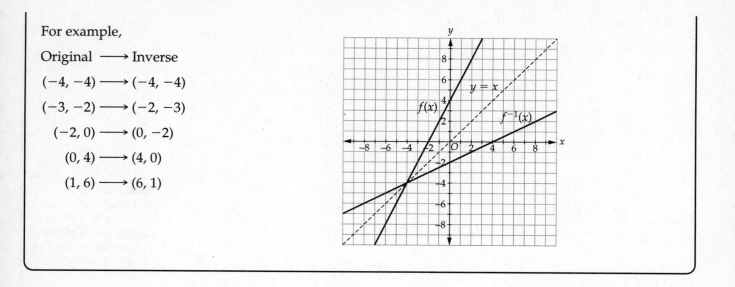

We know from Section 4.1 that to determine whether a graph represents a function, we can use the vertical-line test. The vertical-line test says that if a vertical line drawn at any position over the domain of the graph intersects the graph more than once, the graph does *not* represent a function. In other words, if any x-value corresponds to more than one y-value, the graph does not represent a function.

To determine if a function's inverse will also be a function, we can use the **horizontal-line test**. A function passes the horizontal-line test when any horizontal line drawn intersects the graph of the function at most once. Since the domain of the original function becomes the range of its inverse, no y-value can be repeated if a function is to have an inverse.

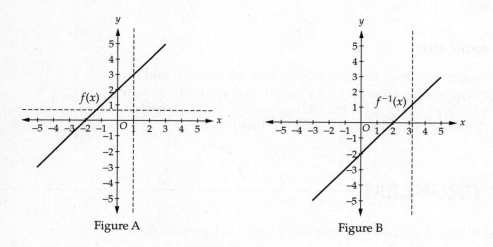

Figure A   Figure B

Notice that the graph of $f(x)$, defined as $f(x) = x + 2$, and its inverse, $f^{-1}(x)$, are functions. We can be certain of this because $f(x)$ passes both the vertical- and horizontal-line tests (Figure A). When we graph $f^{-1}(x)$, as shown in Figure B, it passes the vertical-line test.

If a function passes the vertical- and horizontal-line tests, the function is one-to-one since each element of the domain has a unique value in the range, and vice versa. We can say that a function is one-to-one if and only if no horizontal line intersects the graph of the function more than once.

Now consider the graph below.

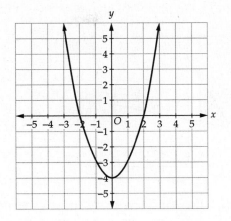

This graph will pass the vertical-line test but fail the horizontal-line test, so it is not a one-to-one function. It does not have an inverse.

MODEL PROBLEM

If $f(x) = 3x + 9$, find the equation of its inverse, $f^{-1}(x)$.

SOLUTION

Find the inverse algebraically as we've done before.

Interchange the domain and range: $\qquad x = 3y + 9$

Perform inverse operations to isolate y: $\qquad x - 9 = 3y$

$$\frac{x}{3} - 3 = y$$

Answer: $f^{-1}(x) = \dfrac{x}{3} - 3$

To check this, enter your original function in Y_1 and enter what you found to be the inverse in Y_2. Now, go to the DRAW menu (2nd   PRGM) and select 8:DrawInv.

```
DRAW POINTS STO
3↑Horizontal
4:Vertical
5:Tangent(
6:DrawF
7:Shade(
8:DrawInv
9↓Circle(
```

Press ENTER. This transfers the command to the home screen where the calculator waits for you to tell it which function you want the inverse of. Press VARS ► ENTER, and then choose 1:Y_1 to tell the calculator you want the inverse of Y_1. Now press ENTER.

The calculator will graph $f(x)$, your answer for $f^{-1}(x)$, and the calculator's drawing of $f^{-1}(x)$.

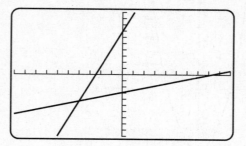

You should see only two graphs on the screen, since the drawing of the inverse should be the same as the graph of your inverse function. If a third graph appears, then your definition of the inverse is incorrect.

Note: The Draw menu produces a "drawing," not a graph. Neither the trace function nor any of the CALCULATE operations will work on a drawing. To erase the drawing, you must go to the Draw menu and choose 1: ClrDraw.

Be careful: since this is a Draw command, the calculator will draw the inverses of functions even if they are not one-to-one.

As stated earlier, a function has an inverse only if it is a one-to-one function, that is, if each element of the domain has one and only one corresponding element in the range. Therefore, it is necessary with some functions to *restrict the domain* in order to eliminate double values in the range.

For example, consider the function $y = x^2$. If the domain were unrestricted, the function would not have an inverse because the function fails the horizontal-line test and the new relation fails the vertical-line test, as shown below.

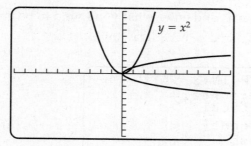

If we restrict the domain of $y = x^2$ to $x \geq 0$ to limit the elements in the domain, the function does have an inverse, as shown below.

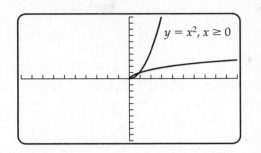

Restricting the domain is often necessary with quadratic and trigonometric functions, as you will see later in this course.

Practice

Exercises 1–4: Find the inverse of each function.

1 A: {(8, 5), (6, 8), (4, 11), (2, 14)}

2 B: {(–2, 3), (–5, 5), (–8, 7), (–11, 9)}

3 C: {(*, &), ($, %), (@, +), (#, !)}

4 D: {(2, 9), (4, –5), (13, 8), (–1, –10)}

5 If E = {(*Aladdin*, Jasmine)}, {(*Beauty and the Beast*, Belle)}, {(*Little Mermaid*, Ariel)}, {(*Sleeping Beauty*, Aurora)}, what is E^{-1}(Belle)?

Exercises 6–11: Find the inverse of each function and write it in simplified form.

6 $y = 4x + 7$

7 $y + 3x = -1$

8 $f(x) = \dfrac{2}{5}x - 6$

9 $f(x) = \sqrt[3]{x - 4}$

10 $g(x) = 3x^3 - 6$

11 $y - \dfrac{2}{3} = 4x$

Exercises 12–20: Select the numeral preceding the choice that best completes the statement or answers the question.

12 If $g(x) = 3x + 1$, then $g^{-1}(4)$ equals

(1) 1

(2) $\dfrac{1}{4}$

(3) $\dfrac{1}{13}$

(4) 12

13 For which pair of functions does $(f \circ g)(x) = (g \circ f)(x)$?

(1) $f(x) = 2x, g(x) = 2 - x$

(2) $f(x) = x^3, g(x) = \sqrt[3]{x}$

(3) $f(x) = 1 - x, g(x) = x - 1$

(4) $f(x) = 4x + 1, g(x) = x - 4$

14 If the function $j(x)$ is defined by $j(x) = \sqrt{x - 4}$ for $x \geq 4$, which represents $j^{-1}(x)$?

(1) $\sqrt{4 + x}$

(2) $\dfrac{1}{\sqrt{x - 4}}$

(3) $x^2 + 4$

(4) $4 - x^2$

15 If $h(x) = \frac{1}{2}x - 3$ and $j(x) = 2x - 1$, the solution to $j(h^{-1}(-3))$ is

(1) 0

(2) $-\dfrac{1}{3}$

(3) -1

(4) -10

16 If $f(x) = \sqrt{\dfrac{2}{3}x - 1}$, then $f^{-1}(9)$ is

(1) $\sqrt{5}$

(2) $\sqrt{7}$

(3) 120

(4) 123

17 If $h(x) = 2 - \dfrac{x}{2}$, find $(h \circ h^{-1})(2)$.

(1) x

(2) 2

(3) $\dfrac{1}{2}$

(4) 0

18 Which relation is a one-to-one function?

(1) $\{(x, y), (x, z), (x, a)\}$
(2) $\{(x, y), (y, z), (z, y)\}$
(3) $\{(x, z), (y, z), (a, y)\}$
(4) $\{(x, y), (y, z), (z, a)\}$

19 If $f(x) = 10 - 2x$, which represents $f^{-1}(x)$?

(1) $f^{-1}(x) = 2x + 10$

(2) $f^{-1}(x) = \dfrac{1}{2}x - 5$

(3) $f^{-1}(x) = 2x - 10$

(4) $f^{-1}(x) = -\dfrac{1}{2}x + 5$

20 If $g(x) = \sqrt[3]{2x + 3}$, $g^{-1}(2)$ equals

(1) $-\dfrac{1}{2}$

(2) $\sqrt[3]{7}$

(3) $\dfrac{5}{2}$

(4) $\dfrac{11}{2}$

4.6 Transformations of Linear, Absolute Value, and Polynomial Functions

Linear Functions

A linear function is a function whose graph is a line. Let's look at the function $y = x$. We can create a table by filling in the corresponding y-values for some x-values. We can then graph the function.

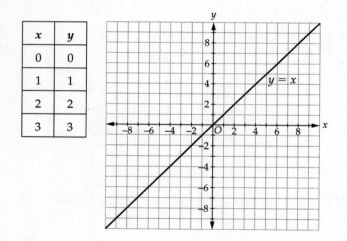

Notice that this linear function and all other linear functions are one-to-one and onto.

We will now perform several transformations on the function $y = x$.

The table and graph below illustrate the results when we add or subtract a constant from the original function.

x	$y = x$	$y = x + 3$	$y = x - 5$
0	0	3	-5
1	1	4	-4
2	2	5	-3
3	3	6	-2

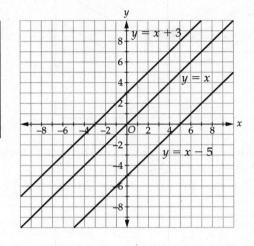

Notice that adding 3 to the function shifts it 3 units up, while subtracting 5 from the function shifts it 5 units down.

In general, the graph of $f(x) + a$ is the graph of $f(x)$ moved up a units when a is positive and moved down a units when a is negative.

Absolute Value Functions

Let's look at another familiar function, $y = |x|$.

To graph this function in your calculator, go to your (Y=) screen and press (MATH) (▶) (ENTER) to produce the screen shown below.

```
Plot1  Plot2  Plot3
\Y1▉abs(█
\Y2=
\Y3=
\Y4=
\Y5=
\Y6=
\Y7=
```

Enter (X,T,θ,n) ( )) and then press (GRAPH). The graph below is viewed on a standard viewing window ((ZOOM) (6)).

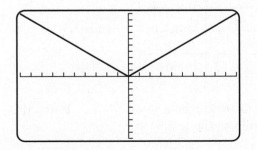

Now look at the graphs of $y = |x| + 3$ and $y = |x| - 5$ in the same viewing window.

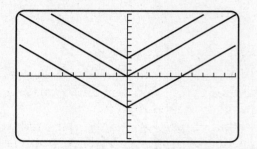

Once again we notice that adding 3 to the function shifts it 3 units up, while subtracting 5 from the function shifts it 5 units down.

Let's see what happens when we graph $y = |x + 3|$ and $y = |x - 5|$.

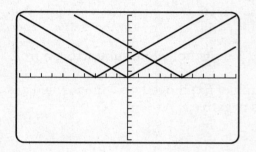

The graphs above show us that $y = |x + 3|$ shifts the graph 3 units left, while the function $y = |x - 5|$ shifts the graph 5 units right.

Looking at a table may help us to understand why the graph shifts as it does.

x	$y = |x|$	$y = |x + 3|$	$y = |x - 5|$
−5	5	2	10
−4	4	1	9
−3	3	0	8
−2	2	1	7
−1	1	2	6
0	0	3	5
1	1	4	4
2	2	5	3
3	3	6	2
4	4	7	1
5	5	8	0

In the function $y = |x + 3|$, an x-value of -3 produces a y-value of 0. Thus, this function shifts the graph of $y = |x|$ three units to the left.

Similarly, in the function $y = |x - 5|$, an x-value of 5 produces a y-value of 0. Thus, this function shifts the graph of $y = |x|$ five units to the right.

In general, the graph of $f(x + a)$ is the graph of $f(x)$ moved a units to the left when a is positive and a units to the right when a is negative.

Polynomial Functions

A **polynomial function of degree n** is a function of the form $y = a_n x^n + a_{n-1} x^{n-1} + \cdots + a_0$, $a_n \neq 0$. Each term is the product of a constant and a variable raised to a whole-number power. (You can think of the last term as $a_0 x^0$.)

The simplest polynomial function is a function of the form $y = c$, where c is a constant. For example, $y = 2$ is a constant function of degree zero whose graph is a horizontal line. A linear function is a polynomial function of degree one.

Quadratic Functions

A **quadratic function** is a polynomial function of degree 2 whose graph is called a **parabola**. The general form of a quadratic function is $y = ax^2 + bx + c$, $a \neq 0$. When a is positive, the parabola opens upward and has a minimum value. When a is negative, the parabola opens downward and has a maximum value. Yet even if we ignore the sign of a, the coefficient a also alters the shape of the parabola, as indicated in the diagrams below.

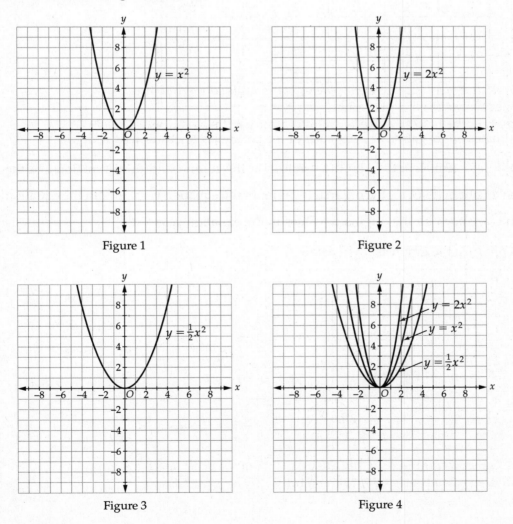

Figure 1

Figure 2

Figure 3

Figure 4

In Figure 1 on page 137, $a = 1$ while in Figure 2, $a = 2$ and in Figure 3, $a = \frac{1}{2}$. The fourth figure combines the graphs of all three functions so you can see the differences in the shape of the particular parabolas.

MODEL PROBLEM

Graph the equations $y_1 = -x^2$, $y_2 = -2x^2$, and $y_3 = -\frac{1}{2}x^2$ on the same set of axes.

Discuss the similarities and differences in the appearance of these parabolas.

SOLUTION

When calculated, the coordinates of the points for each equation are the following:

$y_1 = -x^2$		$y_2 = -2x^2$		$y_3 = -\frac{1}{2}x^2$	
x	y	x	y	x	y
-3	-9	-3	-18	-3	-4.5
-2	-4	-2	-8	-2	-2
-1	-1	-1	-2	-1	-0.5
0	0	0	0	0	0
1	-1	1	-2	1	-0.5
2	-4	2	-8	2	-2
3	-9	3	-18	3	-4.5

Since all of the y-coordinates are negative or zero, each of the parabolas opens downward.

Notice the effect of the coefficients 2 and $\frac{1}{2}$ on the y-values in the second and third functions. In the function $y_2 = -2x^2$, the y-values are twice the original y-values in the equation $y_1 = -x^2$. In the equation $y_3 = -\frac{1}{2}x^2$, the y-values are one half the original y-values in the equation $y_1 = -x^2$.

These tables of values produce the graphs shown below.

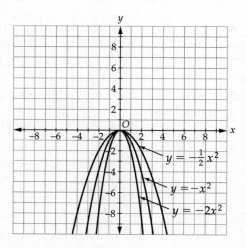

As is seen in the graphs on page 138, the larger the absolute value of a, the more steeply the parabola rises or falls and the narrower it appears. The smaller the absolute value of a, the less steeply the parabola rises or falls and the wider it appears, with a flatter appearance at the vertex. In these three examples, the turning point or vertex of the parabola remains the same, as does the axis of symmetry, $x = 0$.

MODEL PROBLEM

Graph the parabolas $y_1 = x^2$, $y_2 = (x - 4)^2$, and $y_3 = x^2 - 4$ on the same set of axes.

What similarities and differences occur in the axes of symmetry, the vertices, and the shapes of the parabolas?

SOLUTION

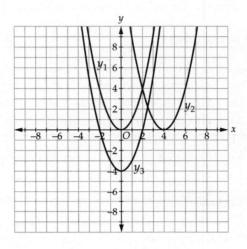

As seen in the diagram above, the shape of all of three parabolas is the same, since the coefficient of the x^2 term is the same for all of them. We see that y_2 is the original parabola shifted 4 units to the right while y_3 is the original parabola shifted 4 units down. Both y_1 and y_3 have an axis of symmetry of $x = 0$, while the axis of symmetry of y_2 is $x = 4$. All three parabolas have different vertices: y_1 has a vertex at $(0, 0)$, y_2 has a vertex at $(4, 0)$, while y_3 has a vertex at $(0, -4)$.

The **zeros** of a quadratic function are the values of x for which $y = 0$. A quadratic function can have at most two zeros. Looking at the parabolas from the previous example, we see that y_1 and y_2 each have one zero, while y_3 has two zeros. The zero for y_1 is $x = 0$, the zero for y_2 is $x = 4$, and the zeros for y_3 are $x = 2$ and $x = -2$.

To find the zeros of a function algebraically, set the function equal to zero and solve.

MODEL PROBLEM

Find the zeros of the functions $y_1 = x^2$, $y_2 = (x - 4)^2$, and $y_3 = x^2 - 4$.

SOLUTION

To find the zeros, set each function equal to zero and solve:

$$y_1 = x^2 \qquad\qquad y_2 = (x - 4)^2 \qquad\qquad\qquad y_3 = x^2 - 4$$

$$x^2 = 0 \qquad\quad (x - 4)^2 = 0 \qquad\qquad\qquad x^2 - 4 = 0$$

$$x = 0 \qquad\qquad x - 4 = 0 \qquad\qquad (x - 2)(x + 2) = 0$$

$$x = 4 \qquad\qquad\qquad x = 2, \quad x = -2$$

Answer: $x = 0$; $x = 4$; $x = 2$, $x = -2$

Higher-Degree Polynomial Functions

As you have seen in the quadratic functions shown above, a second-degree polynomial function (quadratic function) has at most two zeros and one turning point. A third-degree polynomial function (cubic function) has at most three zeros and two turning points. A fourth-degree polynomial function (quartic function) has at most four zeros and three turning points. In general, a polynomial function of degree n has at most n zeros and $n - 1$ turning points.

MODEL PROBLEMS

1 Find the zeros and y-intercept of the function $y = (x - 2)(x + 2)(x + 4)$.

SOLUTION

To find the zeros of the function, set the function equal to zero and solve for x.

$$y = (x - 2)(x + 2)(x + 4)$$

$$(x - 2)(x + 2)(x + 4) = 0$$

$$x = 2, x = -2, x = -4$$

We can also look at the graph of the function to find its zeros.

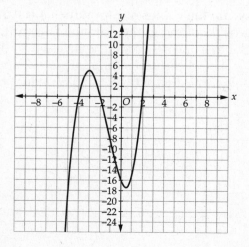

Looking at the graph, we see that the zeros occur when $x = 2$, $x = -2$, $x = -4$.

To find the y-intercept, we set $x = 0$ and solve for y.

$$y = (x - 2)(x + 2)(x + 4)$$
$$= (0 - 2)(0 + 2)(0 + 4)$$
$$= (-2)(2)(4)$$
$$= -16$$

The y-intercept can also be seen on the graph.

Answer: Zeros are $x = 2$, $x = -2$, $x = -4$; y-intercept $y = -16$.

2 Find the zeros of the function $f(x) = x^3 - 5x^2 - 6x$.

SOLUTION

We can find the zeros of this function by setting the function equal to zero and solving for x.

$$f(x) = x^3 - 5x^2 - 6x$$
$$x^3 - 5x^2 - 6x = 0$$
$$x(x^2 - 5x - 6) = 0$$
$$x(x - 6)(x + 1) = 0$$
$$x = 0, x = 6, x = -1$$

Alternatively, we can use the calculator to find the zeros.

Graph the function $f(x) = x^3 - 5x^2 - 6x$, as shown below.

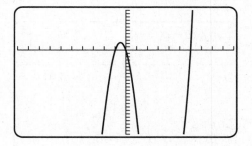

The function is graphed in a viewing window with Xmin = -10, Xmax = 10, Ymin = -15, and Ymax = 10. Looking at the graph, it appears that there are zeros at $x = -1$, $x = 0$, and $x = 6$, but it is difficult to be sure. We can check to see if these are the zeros by substituting each value into the original equation and checking. However, we can also use the calculator to find the zeros.

Press (2nd) (TRACE) to get the screen below.

```
CALCULATE
1:value
2:zero
3:minimum
4:maximum
5:intersect
6:dy/dx
7:∫f(x)dx
```

Choose 2: zero and get the following screen:

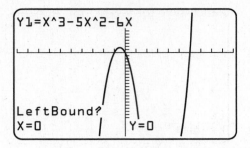

You are asked first to go to the left of one of the zeros. We'll find the negative zero first, so move your cursor to the left of the zero. Alternatively, you can just enter an x-value that you know is to the left of the zero. From the graph, it is clear that -4 is to the left of the zero, so we enter -4.

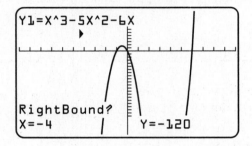

Next, either enter an x-value that is to the right of the zero, or move your cursor to a position that is to the right of the zero. We entered 0 for x.

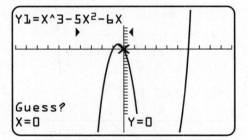

Finally, you are asked to guess. Make sure that the zero you are seeking is located between the two arrows at the top of the graph.

Since there are three zeros, and two of them are between the two arrows, move your cursor near the zero you are trying to find (or enter an x-value for the guess). This time, we moved the cursor near the negative zero, as shown below.

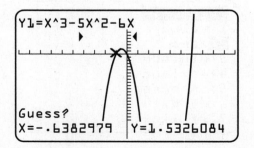

Press (ENTER).

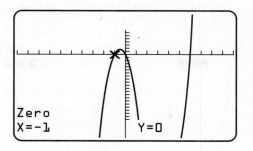

As you can see, $x = -1$ is one of the zeros of the function. Repeat the process to find the other two zeros.

 Practice

Exercises 1–10: Select the numeral preceding the choice that best completes the statement or answers the question.

1 What is the vertex of the parabola $y = x^2 + 3$?

(1) $(0, 3)$ (3) $(3, 0)$
(2) $(0, -3)$ (4) $(-3, 0)$

2 What is the vertex of the parabola $y = (x + 3)^2$?

(1) $(0, 3)$ (3) $(3, 0)$
(2) $(0, -3)$ (4) $(-3, 0)$

3 The function $f(x) = |x - 10|$ is a shift of $f(x) = |x|$

(1) 10 units up
(2) 10 units down
(3) 10 units to the right
(4) 10 units to the left

4 Which is a zero of the function $g(x) = (x + 3)(x - 4)(x + 2)$?

(1) -4 (3) 3
(2) 2   (4) 4

5 Which is *not* a zero of the function $h(x) = x^3 - 7x^2 + 7x + 15$?

(1) -1 (3) 3
(2) 0   (4) 5

6 The function $f(x) = |x + 5| - 3$ is a shift of $f(x) = |x|$

(1) 5 units up and 3 units to the right
(2) 5 units down and 3 units to the left
(3) 5 units to the right and 3 units up
(4) 5 units to the left and 3 units down

7 The function $f(x) = (x - 2)^2 + 1$ is a shift of $f(x) = x^2$

(1) 2 units up and 1 unit to the left
(2) 2 units down and 1 unit to the right
(3) 2 units to the right and 1 unit up
(4) 2 units to the left and 1 unit down

8 What is the vertex of the parabola $y = (x - 1)^2 + 5$?

(1) $(1, 5)$ (3) $(-1, 5)$
(2) $(1, -5)$ (4) $(-1, -5)$

9 Which could be the equation of the function graphed below?

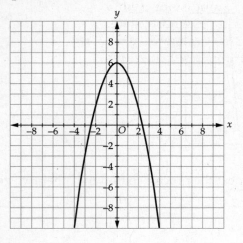

(1) $y = -x^2 + 6$ (3) $y = -(x^2 + 6)$
(2) $y = -x^2 - 6$ (4) $y = -(x^2 - 6)$

10 Which could be the equation of the function graphed below?

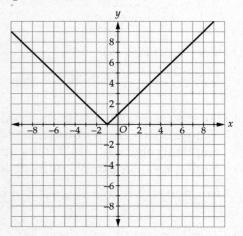

(1) $y = |x| + 1$ (3) $y = |x + 1|$
(2) $y = |x| - 1$ (4) $y = |x - 1|$

11 **a** Graph the function $y = x(x - 3)(x - 1)(x + 2)$ and determine its zeros.
   b What is the degree of this polynomial function?

12 **a** Graph the function $f(x) = x^3 + 2x^2 - 3x - 5$.

   b How many zeros does this function have?
   c Between what two consecutive integers does each of the zeros lie?
   d Find the zeros, to the nearest hundredth.

13 **a** Graph the function $g(x) = x^4 - 3x^3 - 2x^2 + 3x + 5$.

   b How many zeros does this function have?
   c Between what two consecutive integers does each of the zeros lie?
   d Find the zeros to the *nearest hundredth*.

Exercises 14–20: Graph each pair of equations on the same set of axes. Discuss their similarities and differences.

14 $y_1 = x^2$
   $y_2 = (x + 3)^2$
   $y_3 = x^2 + 3$

15 $y_1 = x^2$
   $y_2 = (x - 3)^2$
   $y_3 = (x - 3)^2 + 2$

16 $y_1 = (x - 1)^2$
   $y_2 = 4(x - 1)^2$
   $y_3 = \dfrac{1}{2}(x - 1)^2$

17 $y_1 = |x|$
   $y_2 = |x - 3|$
   $y_3 = |x + 2| - 3$

18 $y_1 = |x - 1|$
   $y_2 = 4|x - 1|$
   $y_3 = \dfrac{1}{2}|x - 1|$

19 $y_1 = x^3$
   $y_2 = (x + 3)^3$
   $y_3 = x^3 - 2$

20 $y_1 = x^4$
   $y_2 = 3(x - 1)^3$
   $y_3 = \dfrac{1}{2}x^3 - 2$

4.7 Circles

As you know from geometry, a **circle** is the locus of points equidistant from a given point, known as the center. The standard equation of a circle whose center is at the point (h, k) is $(x - h)^2 + (y - k)^2 = r^2$, where r represents the length of the radius. If the center of the circle is at the origin, the equation can be written $x^2 + y^2 = r^2$.

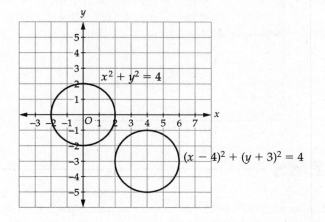

The equation $x^2 + y^2 = 4$ represents a circle with its center at $(0, 0)$ and a radius of length 2. Every point on the circle is 2 units away from the origin, the center of the circle.

The equation $(x - 4)^2 + (y + 3)^2 = 4$ represents a circle with a center at $(4, -3)$ and a radius of length 2. Every point on the circle is 2 units away from the center $(4, -3)$. This circle is the same size as the circle $x^2 + y^2 = 4$, but its center is at $(4, -3)$.

Notice that neither of the circles drawn above is a function because each x-value corresponds to two y values. (Circles fail the vertical-line test.) Since the TI-83+/84+ calculator graphs functions only from the $\boxed{\text{Y=}}$ menu, using the calculator to graph circles is a bit tricky. It can be done, however, with a little algebraic manipulation.

To graph the circles $x^2 + y^2 = 4$ and $(x - 4)^2 + (y + 3)^2 = 4$:

- First, solve the equations for y by isolating the y in each expression.

$$y^2 = 4 - x^2 \qquad\qquad (y + 3)^2 = 4 - (x - 4)^2$$

- Now, take the square root of each side of the equations.

$$y = \pm\sqrt{4 - x^2} \qquad\qquad y + 3 = \pm\sqrt{4 - (x - 4)^2}$$

- Once again, isolate the y if necessary.

$$y = -3 \pm \sqrt{4 - (x - 4)^2}$$

We now have two different functions for each equation to enter as Y_1, Y_2, Y_3, and Y_4 on the calculator. Each of the equations is a semicircle that will appear to be a circle when joined with its partner if your window is set properly.

In the standard graphing window of your calculator, the size of the intervals on the x-axis are *not* drawn the same size as the intervals on the y-axis. Thus, on the left-hand graph in which Xmin = −4, Xmax = 8, Ymin = −8, and Ymax = 4, the circles look elliptical. However, if we press ⬤ZOOM and choose 5:ZSquare, the intervals appear equally sized and our circles look round. This is shown on the right-hand graph.

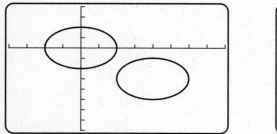 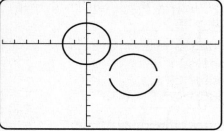

MODEL PROBLEMS

Model Problems 1–3: Determine the center and radius of each circle whose equation is below.

1 $x^2 + y^2 = 10$

Answer: center: (0, 0); radius = $\sqrt{10}$

2 $(x + 3)^2 + y^2 = 9$

Answer: center: (−3, 0); radius = 3

3 $(x − 1)^2 + (y + 4)^2 = 16$

Answer: center: (1, −4); radius = 4

4 Which point is *not* on the circle $x^2 + y^2 = 25$?

   (1) (5, 0)   (2) (3, 4)   (3) (−5, 5)   (4) (−3, 4)

SOLUTION

(−5, 5) is not on the circle because if you substitute the coordinates into the equation, you find that $x^2 + y^2 = 50$, not 25.

Answer: (3)

Practice

Exercises 1–10: Select the numeral preceding the choice that best completes the sentence or answers the question.

1 The center of the circle $(x − 4)^2 + (y + 2)^2 = 9$ is

   (1) (4, −3)   (3) (−4, 2)
   (2) (4, 2)   (4) (4, −2)

2 Which circle has a center of (1, 0) and a radius of length 4?

   (1) $x^2 + y^2 = 4^2$
   (2) $(x + 1)^2 + y^2 = 4^2$
   (3) $(x − 1)^2 + y^2 = 4^2$
   (4) $x^2 + y^2 = 4$

3 Which point is *not* on the circle $(x - 4)^2 + (y - 3)^2 = 25$?

   (1) $(8, 6)$
   (2) $(-1, 3)$
   (3) $(0, 0)$
   (4) $(-4, -3)$

4 The graph of the equation $(x - 2)^2 + (y + 3)^2 = 16$ is a circle with

   (1) center $(2, -3)$, radius 4
   (2) center $(2, -3)$, radius 16
   (3) center $(-2, 3)$, radius 4
   (4) center $(-2, 3)$, radius 16

5 Which is the equation of the circle shown below?

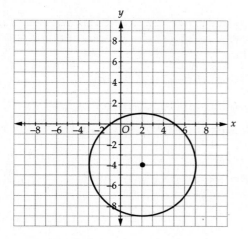

   (1) $(x + 2)^2 + (y - 4)^2 = 5$
   (2) $(x + 2)^2 + (y - 4)^2 = 25$
   (3) $(x - 2)^2 + (y + 4)^2 = 5$
   (4) $(x - 2)^2 + (y + 4)^2 = 25$

6 Which is a graph of the circle whose equation is $(x + 3)^2 + (y + 2)^2 = 4$?

   (1)

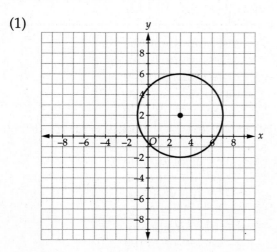

(2)

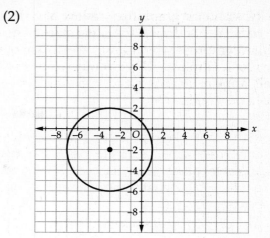

(3)

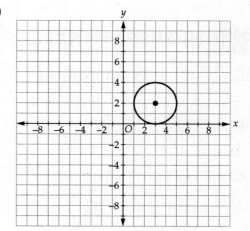

(4)

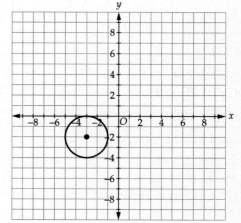

7 Which circle lies entirely in the fourth quadrant?

(1) $(x - 4)^2 + (y + 6)^2 = 5$
(2) $(x - 4)^2 + (y + 6)^2 = 5^2$
(3) $(x + 4)^2 + (y - 6)^2 = 5$
(4) $(x + 4)^2 + (y + 6)^2 = 5^2$

8 Jenfryda is playing with a Frisbee whose diameter is 12 inches. If she tosses it onto a coordinate plane, and its center falls on the point $(-2, 1)$, what is the equation of the Frisbee?

(1) $x^2 + y^2 = 36$
(2) $(x - 2)^2 + (y - 1)^2 = 36$
(3) $(x + 2)^2 + (y - 1)^2 = 36$
(4) $(x - 2)^2 + (y + 1)^2 = 36$

9 Harmony and Melodie were blowing bubbles when one of them landed on Derek's mathematics homework and burst on the graph paper. The bubble formed a perfect circle on the coordinate grid with a center at $(6, -5)$ and a radius of 4.5. Which represents the equation of the bubble's circle?

(1) $(x - 6)^2 + (y + 5)^2 = 4.5$
(2) $x^2 + y^2 = 4.5^2$
(3) $(x + 6)^2 + (y - 5)^2 = 20.25$
(4) $(x - 6)^2 + (y + 5)^2 = 20.25$

10 A hot coffee mug stained Mrs. Hilton's coffee table. If the equation of the circle left by the coffee mug is $(x - 1)^2 + (y + 4)^2 = 7.84$, what is the diameter of the mug?

(1) 7.84   (3) 2.8
(2) 5.6   (4) 1.4

Exercises 11–15: Find the center and the length of the radius of each circle.

11 $(x + 7)^2 + y^2 = 29.16$

12 $x^2 + (y - 3)^2 = 13.69$

13 $(x + 2)^2 + \left(y + \dfrac{1}{2}\right)^2 = 16$

14 $(x - 5)^2 + (y + 2)^2 = 23.04$

15 $(x + 1.5)^2 + (y - 3.6)^2 = 10$

Exercises 16–20: Write an equation for the circle with the given conditions.

16 Center at $(-1, -5)$, radius of 8

17 Center at $(0, 3)$, diameter of 2

18 Center at $(-2, 0)$, radius of 1.2

19 Diameter with endpoints $(2, 6)$ and $(6, 10)$

20 Diameter with endpoints $(-7, -3)$ and $(3, 5)$

4.8 Direct and Inverse Variation

A group of 50 students from New York City would like to go to Playland Amusement Park in Rye. The cost of taking a train would be $18 round-trip for each of them. However, if they charter a bus for 50 people, the cost would be only $15 for each of them.

Although these two scenarios seem similar, they are quite different mathematically. In the first case, the price per person is a constant $18, regardless of the number of people taking the train. If n represents the number of people going on the trip, and C represents the total cost of the trip, we can write the equation $C = 18n$. In this case, the price per person remains constant. As the number of people going on the trip increases, the total cost increases. This is an example of a **direct variation**.

In the second case, the price per person depends upon the number of people taking the bus. The constant in this case is the cost of the bus. If 50 people take the bus, they will pay $15 each. Thus, the bus company will receive $750. If fewer students take the bus, the bus company will still charge $750 for the bus. Therefore, each student will have to pay more for the trip. If n represents the number of people going on the trip and P represents the price per person, we can write the equation $P = \dfrac{750}{n}$. In this case, total cost remains constant. As the number of people going on the trip increases, the price per person decreases. This is an example of an **inverse variation**.

Direct Variation

Another common example of direct variation is the relationship between the price of an item and its total cost, including tax. If the sales tax rate is 8%, the total cost, C, of an item costing d dollars can be represented by the equation $C = 1.08d$. Notice that this is a linear function. We can also see that as d increases, C increases and as d decreases, C decreases.

In general, a quantity Q is directly proportional, or varies directly, to a quantity t if $Q = kt$, where k is the **constant of proportionality**. As we can see by its form, this function is a linear function.

> Note: The constant of proportionality is also referred to as the <u>constant of variation</u>.

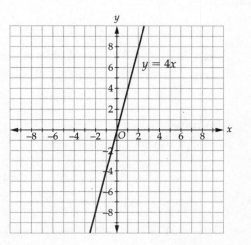 **MODEL PROBLEMS**

1   If y varies directly as x and $y = 12$ when $x = 3$:

    a   Find the constant of proportionality for y in terms of x, and use this value to express y as a function of x.

    b   Graph the linear function.

SOLUTION

    a   Since y varies directly as x, we know that $y = kx$.

$$y = kx$$

$$12 = 3k$$

$$k = 4$$

We replace k with 4 and get $y = 4x$.

Answer: $k = 4, y = 4x$

    b   We know that the linear function passes through the origin and has a slope of 4. The equation is shown below.

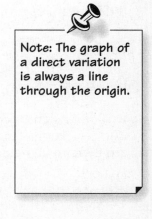

> Note: The graph of a direct variation is always a line through the origin.

2 Driving along I-95 at a constant rate, Edgar drove 165 miles in 3 hours. If he continued to travel at the same rate, how long would it take him to travel another 143 miles?

SOLUTION

At a constant speed, the distance a car travels is proportional to the time spent traveling. This is expressed by the formula distance = rate · time, $d = rt$. If Edgar travels for 3 hours and drives 165 miles, we have $165 = 3r$. Solving for r, we see that Edgar is traveling at a rate of $\dfrac{165}{3} = 55$ miles per hour. This is the constant of proportionality. Thus, $d = 55t$.

To determine the time for him to travel another 143 miles, we can substitute 143 for d in the equation above and solve for t.

$d = 55t$

$143 = 55t$

$t = 2.6$

Answer: 2.6 hours

Practice

Exercises 1–9: Select the numeral preceding the choice that best answers the question.

1 If r varies directly as s and $r = 5$ when $s = 7$, what is r when $s = 21$?

(1) 0.714   (3) 15

(2) 1.4   (4) 29.4

2 If p varies directly as w and $p = 12$ when $w = 15$, what is the constant of variation?

(1) 0.75   (3) 1.5

(2) 0.8   (4) 3

3 Which expresses a direct variation, where k is the constant of proportionality?

(1) $xy = k$ (3) $\dfrac{k}{y} = x$

(2) $x + y = k$ (4) $\dfrac{x}{y} = k$

4 If 10 potato chips contain approximately 105 calories, approximately how many calories are there in 25 potato chips?

(1) 42   (3) 238

(2) 210   (4) 263

5 Manuel worked for 13 hours and received $74.75. At the same rate of pay, how much would he earn for working 17 hours?

(1) $295.65   (3) $97.75

(2) $102   (4) $93.55

6 In the following table, a varies directly as b. What value of a does the question mark represent?

a	12	19.2	?
b	5	8	12

(1) 5   (3) 29.3

(2) 28.8   (4) 31.2

7 What is the y-intercept of the graph of a function that represents a direct variation?

(1) 1

(2) 0

(3) $\dfrac{y}{x}$

(4) It cannot be determined.

8 If y varies directly as x, what is the slope of the graph of the function that represents this variation?

(1) 1

(2) x

(3) $\dfrac{y}{x}$

(4) It cannot be determined.

9 Which graph illustrates a direct variation?

(1)

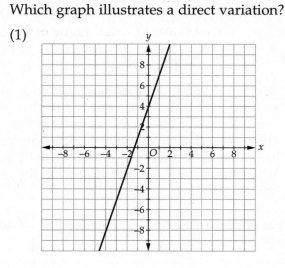

(2)

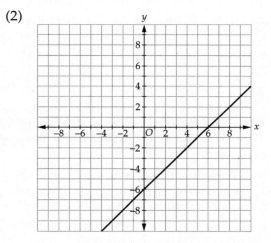

(3)

(4)

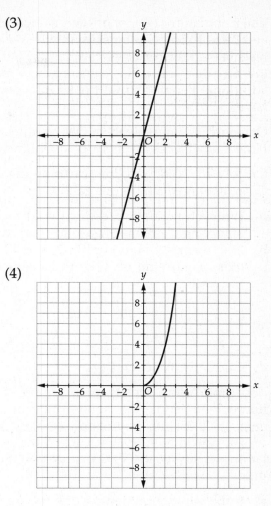

Exercises 10–13: Determine whether or not the table shows a direct variation between the two variables. If there is a direct variation, write the formula for the linear function that expresses this relationship.

10

C	2	4	6	8
D	2.4	4.8	7.2	9.6

11

G	2	4	6	8
H	5	7	9	11

12

K	2	5	7	8
M	7.2	18	25.2	28.8

13

W	2	4	5	8
V	4	16	25	64

14 The population, $P(t)$, of a town is increasing at a rate of 250 people per year, where t represents the number of years since 2007. If the town's rate of growth is constant, how many additional people should the town expect to have in 2010?

15 One inch is equivalent to 2.54 centimeters. How many inches are there in 30 centimeters?

16 On July 14, 2008, gasoline prices on the East Coast averaged $4.074 per gallon.

  a Write a function expressing the cost, $C(g)$, of buying g gallons of gasoline on July 14.

  b Find the cost of buying 10, 15, and 20 gallons of gasoline on July 14 to complete the table.

g	10	15	20
$C(g)$			

  c Graph the function $C(g)$.

17 The population density of a region is the number of people per square mile of land area. In 2005, the population of New York was approximately 19,254,630 and the population density was 407.82 people per square mile.

  a If the population density of New York increases to 415.36 people per square mile, what would the state population be? (Assume the land area is constant.)

  b If you know the area of a city such as Albany or Rochester, do you think using the state's population density will give a good estimate of the city's population? Explain why or why not.

18 When doctors prescribe medication, the amount is sometimes determined by a patient's weight. This is often true for children's medications. Since many drug handbooks use weight in kilograms, doctors have to convert from pounds to kilograms to determine the correct dosage.

  a If an 88-pound child's weight is equivalent to 40 kilograms, write a formula to express weight in kilograms, w, as a function of weight in pounds, p.

  b Use your answer from part **a** to determine the weight, in kilograms, of a 22-pound child.

  c If the child in part **b** is given a dosage of 3 mg/kg per day, what is his daily dosage?

  d Write the equation representing the dosage of this drug, d, for a child who weighs p pounds.

19 **a** Is every direct variation a linear function? Why?

  b Is every linear function a direct variation? Why?

  c If your answer to either part **a** or **b** is no, provide a counterexample to explain your answer.

20 Collect several cylinders and obtain a measuring tape to answer the following question. You may use a can, a cup, a bottle, etc. Use the measuring tape to find the diameter and the circumference of the base of each cylinder. Record the information in the table below.

Type of Cylinder	Diameter	Circumference	Ratio

  a In the last column, record the ratio of the circumference to the diameter. What number does this ratio seem to approximate?

  b What formula have you used that expresses the circumference of a circle proportional to its diameter?

  c If a circle has a diameter of 40 inches, what is its circumference?

Inverse Variation

If you have ever sat at a lunch table with pizza and some hungry people, you are familiar with inverse variation. If you have agreed to evenly divide up the number of slices for each person, as the number of people eating the pizza increases, the number of slices available for you decreases. The number of slices of pizza you get to eat varies inversely with the number of people sharing the pie. If there are a total of 24 pieces of pie, and p represents the number of people, and s represents the number of slices for each person, we see that $s = \dfrac{24}{p}$.

A quantity Q is inversely proportional, or varies inversely, to a quantity t if $Q = \dfrac{k}{t}$, where k is the constant of proportionality.

Now let's examine the function $y = \dfrac{12}{x}$. By converting this to the form $xy = 12$, we can see that the product of these two variables must equal 12. If x is 3, y must be 4; if x doubles to 6, y is halved to 2. (We see that the operations performed on the variables are inverse operations.)

To draw the graph of this function we can create a table of values, as shown below.

x	−12	−6	−4	−3	−2	−1	1	2	3	4	6	12
y	−1	−2	−3	−4	−6	−12	12	6	4	3	2	1

We can plot the points and connect them with a smooth curve to form the graph shown below.

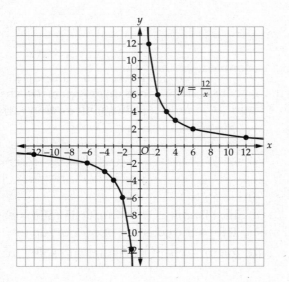

The graph of an inverse variation is a **rectangular hyperbola**. This function has two branches, appearing in the first and third quadrants when k is positive and in the second and fourth quadrants when k is negative. The graph can never cross either axis because there is no x-value that produces a y-value of 0 and no y-value that corresponds to an x-value of 0.

Notice that the graph gets closer and closer to the x- and y-axes, but it can never reach them since a product of zero is unattainable. When the graph of a function gets closer and closer to a value but never reaches it, it is said to be **asymptotic** to that value. Rectangular hyperbolas are asymptotic to both the x- and y-axes.

Looking at the graph, we see that the domain and range are both the set of nonzero real numbers. We also see that no horizontal line intersects the graph at more than one point. Thus, the function is one-to-one. Also, if we interchange the x and y, the function remains the same. This function is its own inverse.

MODEL PROBLEMS

1 If y varies inversely as x, and $y = 24$ when $x = 6$, what is the value of y when x is 12?

(1) 144   (3) 16
(2) 48   (4) 12

SOLUTION

Since y varies inversely as x, we know that $y = \dfrac{k}{x}$ or $xy = k$.

You can solve for k and then create a second equation equal to k.

$xy = k$

$6 \bullet 24 = 144$

Once you have found k, solve for y.

$12 \bullet y = 144$

$y = 12$

As an alternative, you can set the two pairs of elements that vary inversely equal to each other and solve: $6 \bullet 24 = 12 \bullet y$. In either case, $y = 12$.

Answer: (4)

Remember: In an inverse variation, when x is doubled, y is halved.

2 The rate at which Ishmir travels from home to his college varies inversely as the time it takes to make the trip. If Ishmir can make the trip in 4 hours at 45 miles per hour, how many miles per hour must he travel to make the trip in 3 hours?

(1) 65   (3) 55
(2) 60   (4) 50

SOLUTION

Use the formula: rate $\bullet$ time = distance, $rt = d$. Since Ishmir is traveling at 45 miles per hour for 4 hours, he must travel a distance of $45 \bullet 4 = 180$ miles. This is the constant of proportionality.

We use $d = 180$ as the constant, substitute 3 for the time spent traveling, and solve for the rate.

$rt = d$

$r(3) = 180$

$3r = 180$

$r = 60$

Thus, Ishmir must travel at 60 miles per hour to cover the 180 miles in 3 hours.

Answer: (2)

3 The amount of the tip each waiter receives after a wedding is inversely proportional to the number of waiters serving the event. If the total amount of tips at the Klaiwith-Sims wedding was \$1,200 and n represents the number of waiters and t represents the tip each waiter received, which represents the relationship between n and t?

(1) $n = \dfrac{t}{1{,}200}$ (3) $1{,}200 = \dfrac{t}{n}$

(2) $1{,}200 = \dfrac{n}{t}$ (4) $n = \dfrac{1{,}200}{t}$

SOLUTION

Since the amount of the tip each waiter receives is inversely proportional to the number of waiters, we have $t = \dfrac{1{,}200}{n}$.

Solving for n, we get $nt = 1{,}200$, and $n = \dfrac{1{,}200}{t}$.

Answer: (4)

4 If a varies inversely as b, what is the missing value in the table?

a	· 36	24	18
b	6	9	?

(1) 15   (3) 3
(2) 12   (4) 216

SOLUTION

We know that $a = \dfrac{k}{b}$ or $ab = k$. Thus, $36 \bullet 6 = 24 \bullet 9 = 216 = 18b$ and $b = 12$.

Answer: (2)

 **Practice**

Exercises 1–10: Write the numeral preceding the choice that best answers the question.

1 Kathleen has discovered that the elasticity of her hair tie varies inversely to the number of times she has used it. If her hair tie was only 25% stretchy the fourth time she used it, about how stretchy will it be when she uses it for a twelfth time

(1) 73 %   (3) 16%
(2) 50%   (4) 8%

2 TJ's Brick Works found that within reason, the number of workers on a job varies inversely to the time needed to finish a project. If 4 workers can complete a brick patio in 20 hours, how many workers are needed to finish the job in 5 hours?

(1) 20   (3) 12
(2) 16   (4) 8

3 If x varies inversely as y and x measures 14 when y is 6, find x when y is 4.

(1) 84   (3) 21
(2) 56   (4) $\dfrac{28}{3}$

4 The efficiency department of a mail and phone order company discovered the accuracy of phone orders varied inversely to the number of hours in the operator's shift. If employees who worked two-hour shifts were 98% accurate, how many hours were worked by those with 24.5% accuracy?

(1) 8   (3) 3
(2) 6   (4) 4

5 Given the area of a rectangle to be 360 square inches, the length of the rectangle varies inversely as the width. If the length of the rectangle is 20 inches, what is its width?

(1) 7,200   (3) 72
(2) 180   (4) 18

6 If m varies inversely as n and m is 48 when n is 12, what is m when n is 18?

(1) 36   (3) 30
(2) 32   (4) 24

7 If p varies inversely as q, find the missing value in the table below.

p	40	30	20
q	9	?	18

(1) 4.5   (3) 15
(2) 12   (4) 16

8 Because Kelly's coach believes every player should have an equal opportunity to play, her playing time is inversely proportional to the number of players who show up for a game. When the whole team of 16 players attends, each player has 18 minutes of playing time. How many players must be absent for Kelly to play 24 minutes?

(1) 12   (3) 6
(2) 8   (4) 4

9 When David drives to college, his travel time varies inversely as his speed. If he drives at 56 miles per hour, he arrives in 3 hours. How many minutes would he save if he traveled at 60 miles per hour?

(1) 80   (3) 28
(2) 40   (4) 12

10 If a varies inversely as b and $a = 15$ when $b = 8$, what is a when $b = 12$?

(1) 10   (3) 30
(2) 16   (4) 120

11 Sketch the graph of the function $y = -\dfrac{8}{x}$.

12 Sketch the graph of the function $xy = 16$.

Exercises 13 and 14: Determine the equation of each graph.

13

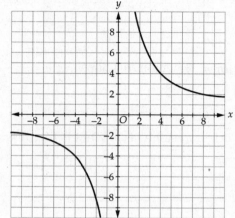

14

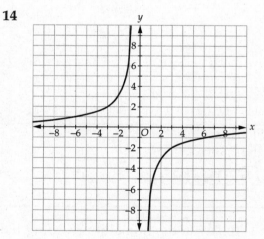

Your graphing calculator can be of great use in your study of functions.

Evaluating Functions

When you want to evaluate a function for a specific value, you have several possible approaches to verify (or obtain) your answer.

MODEL PROBLEM

If $g(x) = 2x^2 + 7x - 3$, evaluate $g(-5)$ and $g(7)$.

CALCULATOR SOLUTION

Method 1

Enter the function in Y_1 and then go to the home screen (2nd MODE)). Enter $Y_1(-5)$. To get Y_1, press VARS ▶ ENTER ENTER, enter -5 into the parentheses, and press ENTER. The calculator will produce the answer.

Then press 2nd ENTER, and the calculator will return the problem you just did. Edit that problem by replacing -5 with 7, press ENTER, and that answer appears as well.

```
Y₁(-5)
                        12
Y₁(7)
                       144
```

Method 2

Enter the function in Y_1, press 2nd TRACE, and then choose 1: value. The calculator will return to the graph of the function with an X = blinking in the lower left of the screen. Enter the value of x you want and press ENTER, and the corresponding y-value will appear on the screen.

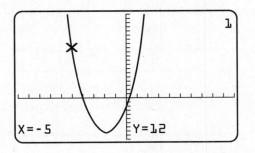

Method 3

Enter the function in Y_1 and graph. Press [TRACE] and then enter the x-value you are looking for, -5, and press [ENTER]. The calculator will TRACE that point and the corresponding y-value will appear on the screen. Repeat the procedure for $x = 7$.

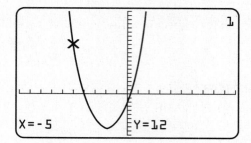

Method 4

Enter the function in Y_1 and press [2nd] [WINDOW] to set up your table. Set the Independent value to Ask, as shown in the screen below.

```
TABLE SETUP
 TblStart=0
 ΔTbl=1
Indpnt:    Auto    Ask
Depend:    Auto    Ask
```

When you go to the Table by pressing [2nd] [GRAPH] , you will see a blank table waiting for you to enter values for x.

```
  X    Y1

X=
```

Enter the two x-values we are using, -5 and 7. You will see the following results.

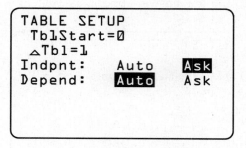

Domain and Range

When you are trying to find the domain and range of a function with undefined values, the calculator can help you determine the solution if you examine the graph for empty spots or the table for ERROR messages.

MODEL PROBLEM

Find the domain and range for the function $f(x) = \dfrac{4x - 1}{x}$.

CALCULATOR SOLUTION

Method 1

Enter the function in Y_1 and press **GRAPH**. Notice the graph does not cross the y-axis. Reset your window to view x from -2 to 2 and y from -20 to 20 with Yscl $= 2$ to enlarge the picture and verify this.

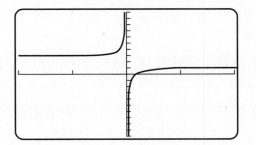

The domain would appear to be $\{x : x \neq 0\}$ while the range seems to be $\{y : y \neq 4\}$. Solving the problem algebraically, we'd set the denominator equal to zero, which means $x = 0$ would make the fraction undefined and, thus, is not an element in the domain.

Method 2

Enter the function in Y_1 and go to TABLE (**2nd** **GRAPH**).

X	Y₁
-2	4.5
-1	5
0	ERROR
1	3
2	3.5
3	3.6667
4	3.75
X = -2	

Notice the ERROR message at $x = 0$. This tells you that the function is undefined when $x = 0$. If you scroll up or down on the table of values, however, there are no other values for which that occurs, so you can speculate that the domain is $\{x : x \neq 0\}$ and then verify it algebraically.

Composition

The graphing calculator is also capable of performing composition of functions.

MODEL PROBLEM

If $f(x) = 3x + 4$ and $g(x) = x^2 - 2$, evaluate

  a $f(g(3))$
  b $g(f(3))$

CALCULATOR SOLUTION

Enter the $f(x)$ function in Y_1 and the $g(x)$ function in Y_2. Go to the home screen and enter

a $Y_1(Y_2(3))$. Press $\boxed{\text{ENTER}}$. The value of $f(g(3))$ is 25.

b   Now enter $Y_2(Y_1(3))$ and press $\boxed{\text{ENTER}}$. The value of $g(f(3))$ is 167.

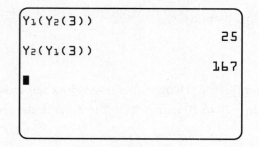

Practice

Try some of the problems within the chapter's exercises to test your understanding and get comfortable with these calculator approaches.

CHAPTER REVIEW

Exercises 1–10: Determine if each of the given relations is or is not a function and explain why. If the relation is a function, state its domain and range.

1   {(−2, 5), (3, 7), (8, 9), (13, 11)}

2   {(8, −3), (5, −3), (3, −3), (0, −3)}

3   {(Drew Carey, *Power of 10*)}, (Howie Mandel, *Deal or No Deal*), (Drew Carey, *The Price Is Right*), (Jeff Foxworthy, *Are You Smarter Than a 5th Grader?*)}

4   {(9, 4), (8, 5), (9, 7), (0, 4)}

5

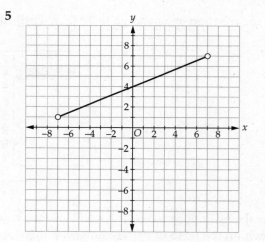

6

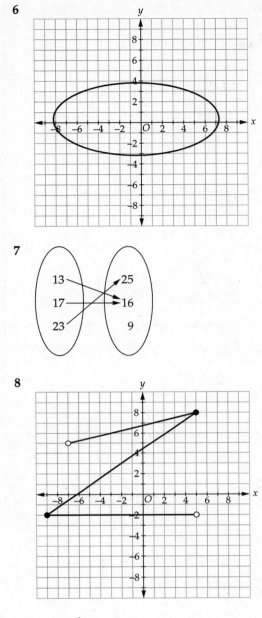

7

8

9 $y = -\dfrac{1}{2}(x + 4)^2 + 8$

10 $3x + 2y = -12$

Exercises 11–28: Select the numeral preceding the choice that best completes the statement or answers the question.

11 The function $g(t)$ is defined as $g(t) = 4 - 2t$ with the domain $-6 \le t \le 2$. What is the *least* element in the range?

(1) -8 (3) 0
(2) -2 (4) 16

12 Which value is *not* in the domain of $y = \sqrt{x^2 - 4}$?

(1) 1 (3) 3
(2) 2 (4) 4

13 If function A consists of {(3, 7), (5, 9), (7, 11), (9, 13)}, which point could be added to the set A while keeping it a function?

(1) $(9, -7)$ (3) $(5, 8)$
(2) $(8, 12)$ (4) $(3, 2)$

14 What is the domain of the relation shown below?

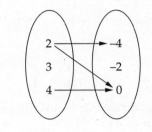

(1) {2, 4}   (3) {−4, −2, 0}
(2) {2, 3, 4}   (4) {2, 4, 44}

15 Which does *not* have a domain of all real numbers?

(1) $y = 3x - 8$ (3) $f(x) = 3x^2 - 4x - 1$
(2) $y = |6x - 7|$ (4) $g(x) = \dfrac{8 - 3x}{x + 5}$

16 If $g(x) = x^2 - 4x - 12$, evaluate $g(2)$.

(1) 6 (3) -8
(2) 2 (4) -16

17 If $f(n) = 2 + \sqrt{n}$ and $k(n) = 10 - 3n$, evaluate $(k \circ f)(9)$.

(1) -8 (3) 0
(2) -5 (4) not a real number

18 What is the inverse of $f(x) = 4x + 16$?

(1) $f^{-1}(x) = -\dfrac{x}{4} + 4$

(2) $f^{-1}(x) = \dfrac{1}{4}x + 4$

(3) $f^{-1}(x) = x - 4$

(4) $f^{-1}(x) = \dfrac{1}{4}x - 4$

19 Which set of ordered pairs does *not* represent a function?

   (1) $\{(3, -2), (-2, 3), (3, -1), (-2, 4)\}$
   (2) $\{(3, -2), (4, -3), (5, -4), (6, -5)\}$
   (3) $\{(3, -7), (4, -4), (7, -3), (9, -2)\}$
   (4) $\{(3, -2), (5, -2), (4, -2), (-1, -2)\}$

20 If $h(x) = \dfrac{6 - 3x}{2}$, evaluate $h^{-1}(-3)$.

   (1) 1   (3) 0
   (2) 2   (4) 4

21 For what value(s) of x is the function $f(x) = \dfrac{x^2 - 4}{2x + 6}$ undefined?

   (1) -3 (3) 3
   (2) $\{-2, -2\}$ (4) $\{-3, -2, 2\}$

22 Which type of transformation will produce the inverse of a function?

   (1) reflection in $y = x$
   (2) reflection in the origin
   (3) reflection in x-axis
   (4) reflection in y-axis

23 If $f(x) = 3x + 2$ and $g(x) = x^2 + 1$, find $f(g(x))$.

   (1) $9x^2 + 5$ (3) $3x^2 + 5$
   (2) $3x^2 + 3$ (4) $(3x + 2)^2 + 1$

24 The accompanying graph is a sketch of the function $y = f(x)$.

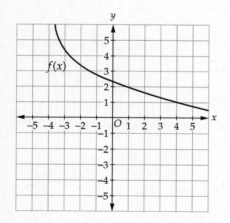

What is the value of $(f \circ f)(4)$?

   (1) 1   (3) 0
   (2) 2   (4) -2

25 If x varies inversely as y and y is multiplied by 3, x is

   (1) tripled   (3) unchanged
   (2) divided by 3   (4) divided by 9

Exercises 26–28: Consider the functions whose graphs are shown below.

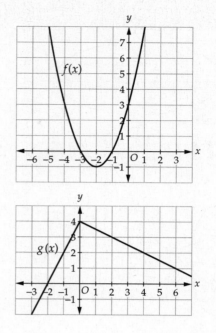

26 The composition $(g \circ f)(0)$ is

   (1) 1   (3) not visible on graph
   (2) 2.5   (4) 4

27 The composition $(f(g(-3)))$ is

   (1) -1 (3) 8
   (2) 0   (4) not visible on graph

28 Based on the graphs of functions $f(x)$ and $g(x)$, which composition is *not* true?

   (1) $g(f(-1)) = 4$ (3) $(g \circ f)(-4) = 4$
   (2) $f(g(6)) = 8$ (4) $(g \circ f)\left(\dfrac{1}{2}\right) = \dfrac{3}{2}$

Quadratic Functions and Complex Numbers

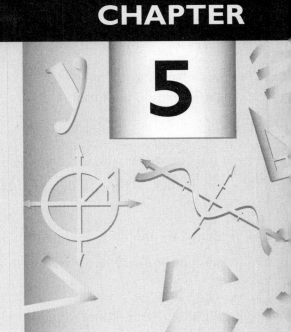

5.1 Alternate Methods of Solving Quadratics

Completing the Square

We have already discussed how to solve quadratic equations by factoring. Another method of solving quadratic equations is to make the quadratic a perfect square trinomial, thereby simplifying the analysis and solution. This is called **completing the square**. Completing the square will find both rational and irrational solutions exactly. A perfect square trinomial like $x^2 - 6x + 9$ is simplified quite easily into $(x - 3)(x - 3)$. If we can turn any given trinomial into a perfect square, the factoring becomes almost automatic.

MODEL PROBLEMS

1 Solve for x: $x^2 + 6x - 11 = 0$

SOLUTION

The expression $x^2 + 6x - 11$ is clearly not factorable, so we shall use the method of completing the square to turn it into a square expression. Step-by-step instructions for completing the square are below.

Step 1: Arrange the equation to be in the form $ax^2 + bx = c$. $\qquad x^2 + 6x = 11$

(If $a \neq 1$, divide each term of the equation by a to make $a = 1$.)

Step 2: Take $\dfrac{1}{2}b$ and square it.

$$\dfrac{1}{2}(6) = 3$$

$$3^2 = 9$$

163

Step 3: Add $\left(\dfrac{1}{2}b\right)^2$ to both sides of the equation. $\qquad\qquad x^2 + 6x + 9 = 20$

Step 4: Write as a perfect square in factored form. $\qquad\qquad (x + 3)^2 = 20$

Step 5: Take the square root of each side of the equation. $\qquad x + 3 = \pm\sqrt{20}$

Step 6: Solve for x. $\qquad\qquad\qquad\qquad\qquad\qquad\qquad\qquad x = -3 \pm \sqrt{20}$

Step 7: Simplify, if possible.

Answer: $x = -3 \pm 2\sqrt{5}$

Even if the roots are rational values, you can find them by completing the square.

2 Find all roots of the equation $x^2 - 2x - 24 = 0$.

SOLUTION

$x^2 - 2x - 24 = 0$

$\qquad x^2 - 2x = 24$ $\qquad\qquad\qquad\qquad$ Move the c term to the right side of equal sign.

$x^2 - 2x + 1 = 25$ $\qquad\qquad\qquad\qquad$ Find $\dfrac{1}{2}b$, square it, and add to both sides.

$\qquad (x - 1)^2 = 25$ $\qquad\qquad\qquad\qquad$ Take the square root of each side.

$\qquad\quad x - 1 = \pm 5$ $\qquad\qquad\qquad\qquad$ Solve for x.

$\qquad\qquad x = 1 \pm 5$

$\qquad\qquad x = 1 + 5 \qquad\quad x = 1 - 5$

$\qquad\qquad x = 6 \qquad\qquad\quad x = -4$

Answer: $x = 6, -4$

> **Note:** When the value on the right side of the equal sign is a perfect square after you've added $\left(\dfrac{1}{2}b\right)^2$, it means the equation could have been solved by factoring.

3 Find all roots of the function $3x^2 - 12x - 21 = 0$.

SOLUTION

First, divide out the common factor of 3.

$\dfrac{3x^2 - 12x - 21}{3} = \dfrac{0}{3}$

$\quad x^2 - 4x - 7 = 0$

$\qquad x^2 - 4x = 7$

$x^2 - 4x + 4 = 11$

$\qquad (x - 2)^2 = 11$

$\qquad\quad x - 2 = \pm\sqrt{11}$

$\qquad\qquad x = 2 \pm \sqrt{11}$

Answer: $x = 2 \pm \sqrt{11}$

Remember: The coefficient of x^2 must be 1 if you wish to use the process of completing the square.

 **Practice**

Solve the following quadratic equations by completing the square.

1 $x^2 + 6x - 8 = 0$

2 $x^2 + 9 = 8x$

3 $x^2 - 12x + 12 = 0$

4 $\dfrac{23}{x} = x - 10$

5 $2x^2 - 12x = 6$

6 $3x^2 = 6x + 15$

7 $2x^2 - 8x = -4$

8 $-x^2 + 6x + 7 = 0$

9 $-3x^2 + 6x - 2 = 3x - 8$

10 $x^2 + 12x + 5 = 0$

The Quadratic Formula

Quadratic equations can always be solved by using the quadratic formula. The quadratic formula can find every solution to a quadratic equation; it does not matter whether the roots are rational or irrational. The quadratic formula is derived from the general equation of a quadratic by completing the square, as shown below.

$$ax^2 + bx + c = 0$$

$$ax^2 + bx = -c$$

$$x^2 + \frac{b}{a}x = -\frac{c}{a}$$

$$x^2 + \frac{b}{a}x + \left(\frac{b}{2a}\right)^2 = \left(\frac{b}{2a}\right)^2 - \frac{c}{a}$$

$$x^2 + \frac{b}{a}x + \frac{b^2}{4a^2} = \frac{b^2}{4a^2} - \frac{c}{a}$$

$$x^2 + \frac{b}{a}x + \frac{b^2}{4a^2} = \frac{b^2 - 4ac}{4a^2}$$

$$\left(x + \frac{b}{2a}\right)^2 = \frac{b^2 - 4ac}{4a^2}$$

$$x + \frac{b}{2a} = \pm\sqrt{\frac{b^2 - 4ac}{4a^2}}$$

$$x + \frac{b}{2a} = \pm\frac{\sqrt{b^2 - 4ac}}{2a}$$

$$x = \frac{-b \pm \sqrt{b^2 - 4ac}}{2a}$$

To solve an equation using the quadratic formula, simply substitute the appropriate values for a, b, and c, and simplify the radical expression as much as possible, or round the answer as instructed.

1 Use the quadratic formula to find all roots of the equation $2x^2 - 3x - 2 = 0$.

SOLUTION

First identify the a, b, and c values.

$a = 2 \quad b = -3 \quad c = -2 \qquad x = \dfrac{-b \pm \sqrt{b^2 - 4ac}}{2a}$

$x = \dfrac{-(-3) \pm \sqrt{(-3)^2 - 4(2)(-2)}}{2(2)}$

$x = \dfrac{3 \pm \sqrt{9 - (8)(-2)}}{4}$

$x = \dfrac{3 \pm \sqrt{25}}{4}$

$x = \dfrac{3 \pm 5}{4}$

$x_1 = \dfrac{3 + 5}{4} \qquad\qquad x_2 = \dfrac{3 - 5}{4}$

$x_1 = 2 \qquad\qquad\qquad x_2 = -\dfrac{1}{2}$

The solutions to this equation are $\left\{ -\dfrac{1}{2}, 2 \right\}$.

This equation could also have been solved by factoring, as shown below.

$2x^2 - 3x - 2 = 0$

$(2x + 1)(x - 2) = 0$

$\qquad\quad 2x + 1 = 0 \qquad\quad x - 2 = 0$

$\qquad\qquad\quad 2x = -1 \qquad\quad\;\; x = 2$

$\qquad\qquad\qquad x = -\dfrac{1}{2}$

Check: $\quad 2x^2 - 3x - 2 = 0$

$\qquad x_1 = 2 \qquad\qquad\qquad\qquad x_2 = -\dfrac{1}{2}$

$2(4) - 3(2) - 2 \stackrel{?}{=} 0 \qquad 2\left(-\dfrac{1}{2}\right)^2 - 3\left(-\dfrac{1}{2}\right) - 2 \stackrel{?}{=} 0$

$\quad\; 8 - 6 - 2 \stackrel{?}{=} 0$

$\qquad\qquad 0 = 0 ✔ \qquad\qquad\qquad \dfrac{1}{2} + \dfrac{3}{2} - 2 \stackrel{?}{=} 0$

$\qquad\qquad\qquad\qquad\qquad\qquad\qquad\qquad 2 - 2 \stackrel{?}{=} 0$

$\qquad\qquad\qquad\qquad\qquad\qquad\qquad\qquad\quad 0 = 0 ✔$

Answer: $\left\{ -\dfrac{1}{2}, 2 \right\}$

2 Find the roots of $2x - 6 = \dfrac{3}{x}$.

SOLUTION

$$2x - 6 = \dfrac{3}{x} \qquad \text{Multiply by } x \text{ to put the equation in standard form.}$$

$$2x^2 - 6x = 3$$

$$2x^2 - 6x - 3 = 0$$

$$a = 2 \quad b = -6 \quad c = -3 \qquad x = \dfrac{-b \pm \sqrt{b^2 - 4ac}}{2a}$$

$$x = \dfrac{-(-6) \pm \sqrt{(-6)^2 - 4(2)(-3)}}{2(2)}$$

$$x = \dfrac{6 \pm \sqrt{36 + 24}}{4}$$

$$x = \dfrac{6 \pm \sqrt{60}}{4}$$

$$x = \dfrac{6 \pm 2\sqrt{15}}{4}$$

Answer: $x = \dfrac{3 \pm \sqrt{15}}{2}$

Radical Equations

You may also encounter radical equations that can be written as quadratics. The most important rule to remember in solving radical equations is to isolate the radical before you square both sides of the equation.

MODEL PROBLEM

3 Solve for x: $\sqrt{3x + 1} - 1 = x - 4$

SOLUTION

$\sqrt{3x + 1} - 1 = x - 4$	Isolate the radical.
$\sqrt{3x + 1} = x - 3$	
$3x + 1 = x^2 - 6x + 9$	Square both sides of the equation.
$0 = x^2 - 9x + 8$	Set the equation equal to zero.
$0 = (x - 8)(x - 1)$	Factor.
$0 = x - 8 \qquad\qquad 0 = x - 1$	Set each factor equal to zero and solve for x.
$8 = x \qquad\qquad\quad 1 = x$	

When you check the answers, however, the solution $x = 1$ does not check. The only solution to this equation is $x = 8$.

Answer: $x = 8$

Exercises 1–9: Solve each equation using the quadratic formula. If roots are irrational, leave the answer in simplest radical form.

1 $x^2 + 1 = 4x$

2 $x - 2 = \dfrac{5}{4x}$

3 $x^2 + 10 = 8x$

4 $\dfrac{1}{2}x^2 - 3x + 2 = 0$

5 $x - 1 = \dfrac{7}{4x}$

6 $5x^2 - 3x - 2 = 0$

7 $x^2 + 2x = 2$

8 $x - 1 = \dfrac{31}{2x}$

9 $3x(3x + 4) = 14$

Exercises 10–15: Solve each equation by whichever method you choose.

10 $6 + 2\sqrt{x - 3} = x$

11 $x - 2 = \dfrac{17}{x}$

12 $2(x + 4) = 3x^2$

13 $\sqrt{10 - 2x} - 7 = x$

14 $3x^2 + 5x + 2 = 0$

15 $2x - 1 = -\dfrac{5x^2}{2}$

5.2 The Complex Number System

Imaginary Numbers

An equation such as $x = \sqrt{-9}$ has no solution in the real number system. However, a solution does exist in the system of **imaginary numbers**. By definition, $\sqrt{-1}$ is defined as i, the imaginary unit. Since $\sqrt{-9} = \sqrt{9}\sqrt{-1}$, and $\sqrt{-1} = i$, we can simplify $\sqrt{-9}$ as $3i$. Similarly, $\sqrt{-5} = \sqrt{5}\sqrt{-1} = \sqrt{5}i = i\sqrt{5}$. We generally write $i\sqrt{5}$ rather than $\sqrt{5}i$ to make it clear that i is not under the radical sign.

MODEL PROBLEM

1 Simplify each number and express in terms of i.

   a $\sqrt{-100}$
   b $\sqrt{-18}$
   c $5\sqrt{-12}$

SOLUTION

   a $\sqrt{-100} = \sqrt{100}\sqrt{-1} = 10i$
   b $\sqrt{-18} = \sqrt{-9}\sqrt{2} = 3i\sqrt{2}$
   c $5\sqrt{-12} = 5\sqrt{-4}\sqrt{3} = 5(2i)\sqrt{3} = 10i\sqrt{3}$

Since $\sqrt{-1} = i$, by squaring both sides of the equation, we get $i^2 = -1$. Continuing with this process we get: $i^3 = (i^2)(i) = -1i = -i$ and $i^4 = (i^2)(i^2) = (-1)(-1) = 1$, $i^5 = (i^4)(i) = i$, $i^6 = (i^4)(i^2) = (1)(-1) = -1$, etc. By definition, $i^0 = 1$.

Putting this all together, we get:

$i^0 = 1$	$i^4 = 1$	$i^8 = 1$	$i^{12} = 1$
$i^1 = i$	$i^5 = i$	$i^9 = i$	$i^{13} = i$
$i^2 = -1$	$i^6 = -1$	$i^{10} = -1$	$i^{14} = -1$
$i^3 = -i$	$i^7 = -i$	$i^{11} = -i$	$i^{15} = -i$

Look at the pattern of the powers of i. They all simplify to either 1, i, -1, or $-i$. Any power of i that is a multiple of 4 (such as i^4, i^8, and i^{12}) will simplify to equal 1. To simplify other powers of i, divide the exponent by 4 and find the remainder. Use the remainder as the power of i to simplify. By learning that $i^1 = i$, $i^2 = -1$, and $i^3 = -i$, you can then determine the value of any power of i.

MODEL PROBLEM

2 Write i^{43} as a power of i in simplest terms.

SOLUTION

When 43 is divided by 4, the remainder is 3, so $i^{43} = (1)(i^3) = -i$.

Answer: $i^{43} = i^3 = -i$

Helpful Hint:
A tool to help you remember the basic powers of i is the phrase "I won, I won, plus, minus, minus, plus." You can use this to create an "i chart":

The i Chart

Power of i	Value	
i^1	i	← I (+)
i^2	-1	← won (−)
i^3	$-i$	← I (−)
i^4	1	← won (+)

MODEL PROBLEM

3 Write i^{22} as a power of i in simplest terms.

SOLUTION

When 22 is divided by 4, the remainder is 2, so $i^{22} = (i^{20})(i^2) = (1)(i^2)$.

We know that $i^2 = -1$.

Thus, $i^{22} = (1)(i^2) = (1)(-1) = -1$.

Answer: $i^{22} = -1$

Once you know the powers of i, you will be able to perform various operations on imaginary numbers.

MODEL PROBLEMS

4 What is the sum of $7i^7$ and $15i^{15}$?

SOLUTION

$7i^7 + 15i^{15} = 7i^4i^3 + 15i^{12}i^3 = 7(1)(-i) + 15(1)(-i) = -7i - 15i = -22i$

Answer: $-22i$

5 What is the product of $4i^{20}$ and $6i^{13}$?

SOLUTION

$4i^{20} \cdot 6i^{13} = (4)(i^0) \cdot 6(i^{12}i^1) = 4(1) \cdot 6(i) = 24i$

Note: You can simplify and then multiply, or multiply and then simplify.

$4i^{20} \cdot 6i^{13} = 24i^{33} = 24i^{32}i^1 = 24(1)i = 24i$

Answer: $24i$

Exercises 1–12: Express each number in terms of i.

1 $\sqrt{-49}$

2 $8\sqrt{-121}$

3 $\dfrac{1}{2}\sqrt{-64}$

4 $-\dfrac{7}{10}\sqrt{-100}$

5 $4\sqrt{-5}$

6 $-4\sqrt{-20}$

7 $6\sqrt{-44}$

8 $\dfrac{4}{5}\sqrt{-200}$

9 $\sqrt{\dfrac{-1}{4}}$

10 $\dfrac{2}{3}\sqrt{-27}$

11 $6\sqrt{\dfrac{-25}{36}}$

12 $8\sqrt{\dfrac{-3}{8}}$

Exercises 13–20: Write the given power of i in simplest terms.

13 i^7

14 i^{33}

15 i^{49}

16 i^{103}

17 i^{24}

18 i^{66}

19 i^{201}

20 i^{18}

Exercises 21–24: Simplify each of the following.

21 $4i^6 \cdot 3i^{11}$

22 $16i^5 + 13i^{23}$

23 $32i^{32} - 40i^{10}$

24 $\dfrac{-20i^{23}}{10i^{16}}$

Exercises 25–30: Select the numeral preceding the choice that best completes the statement or answers the question.

25 The sum of $6i^6$ and $13i^{34}$ is

   (1) $-19i$ (3) -19
   (2) $19i$ (4) 19

26 Find the product of $10i^{18}$ and $7i^{33}$.

   (1) $-70i$ (3) -70
   (2) $70i$ (4) 70

27 Simplify: $(10i^{13})^2$

   (1) $-100i$ (3) -100
   (2) $100i$ (4) 100

28 Which of the following is *not* equal to the other three?

   (1) i^{19} (3) i^{27}
   (2) i^9 (4) i^{35}

29 When $6i^{18}$ is multiplied by $8i^6$, the result is

   (1) $-48i$ (3) -48
   (2) $48i$ (4) 48

30 The expression $\dfrac{3}{4}\sqrt{-48}$ is equivalent to

   (1) $-3\sqrt{3}$ (3) $-3i\sqrt{3}$
   (2) $3i\sqrt{3}$ (4) $-\dfrac{3}{2}i\sqrt{3}$

Complex Numbers

A **complex number** is any number that can be expressed in the form $a + bi$, where a and b are real numbers and $i = \sqrt{-1}$. The number a is the real part and b is the imaginary part of the complex number. Examples of complex numbers are $3 + 2i$, $4 - 6i$, $-5 - 2i$, $9 + 0i$, and $0 + 7i$. When $b = 0$, the complex number is a real number. Thus, the set of real numbers is a subset of the set of complex numbers. When $a = 0$, the complex number becomes a pure imaginary number. Thus, the set of imaginary numbers is also a subset of the set of complex numbers.

Now that we know about complex numbers, we can illustrate our number system by the chart below:

Complex Numbers

Real Numbers   Imaginary Numbers

Rational Numbers   Irrational Numbers

Integers

Whole Numbers

Counting Numbers

Complex numbers are used in the study of electricity, specifically, electricity involving alternating currents.

Two complex numbers are equal if and only if their real parts are equal and their imaginary parts are also equal.

MODEL PROBLEM

If $(c + d) + ci = 5 + 3i$, find d.

SOLUTION

Since the two numbers are equal, we know that the real parts of both numbers are equal, that is, $c + d = 5$.

The imaginary parts of the numbers must also be equal, so $ci = 3i$. Thus, $c = 3$.

Substituting the value of 3 for c into our first equation, we determine that $d = 2$.

Answer: $d = 2$

Just as every real number can be represented on a number line, every complex number can be represented on the complex plane. (The complex plane is sometimes called the Argand plane after the Swiss mathematician Jean Robert Argand.)

In the complex plane, the horizontal axis is the real axis (the x-axis) and the vertical axis is the imaginary axis (the yi-axis). To plot the point $2 + 3i$, we go 2 units across and 3 units up. The number $5 + 0i$ would be plotted by proceeding 5 units on the real axis. This will graphically illustrate that the number $5 + 0i$ is a real number, since its graph lies on the real axis. The number $0 + 4i$ is plotted by proceeding 4 units on the imaginary axis. This graphically illustrates that the number $0 + 4i$ is a pure imaginary number since its graph lies on the imaginary axis. A complex number such as $-3 + 2i$ is represented by a number on the complex plane that is neither on the real axis nor the imaginary axis.

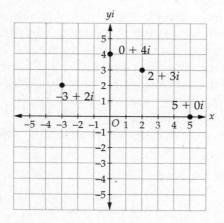

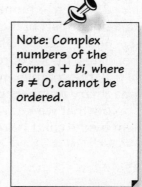

Note: Complex numbers of the form $a + bi$, where $a \neq 0$, cannot be ordered.

Besides being represented by a point in the complex number plane, a complex number can be represented by a *vector* in the complex number plane. A **vector** shows magnitude (length) and direction with an arrow.

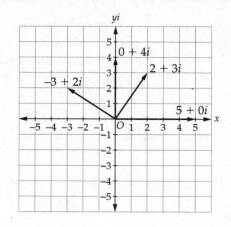

 **Practice**

Exercises 1–7: Find the real numbers *a* and *b* that will make the equation true.

1 $a + bi = 2 + 5i$

2 $a + bi = 7i$

3 $a + bi = 12$

4 $(a - 2b) + bi = -3 + 7i$

5 $a + (a - b)i = 6 + 4i$

6 $2a + 3bi = 10 - 6i$

7 $a + bi = 2 + 5i - 4 + 7i$

Exercises 8–12: Write in standard $a + bi$ form.

8 $6 + \sqrt{-25}$

9 $3 + \sqrt{-49} - 5$

10 $7 - \sqrt{-27}$

11 $5 + 3\sqrt{-8}$

12 $4i + 6i^2$

Exercises 13–18: State whether the statement is *true* or *false*, and explain your answer.

13 All real numbers are complex numbers.

14 All complex numbers are real numbers.

15 All integers are complex numbers.

16 A real number cannot be an imaginary number.

17 An imaginary number cannot be a complex number.

18 A complex number cannot be imaginary.

19 What complex number does each point in the accompanying diagram represent?

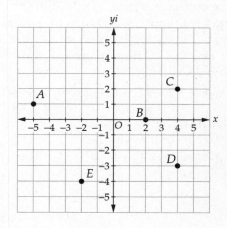

20 What complex number does each vector in the accompanying diagram represent?

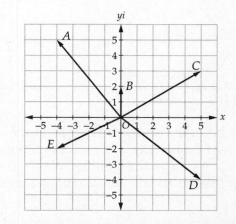

5.3 Operations with Complex Numbers

Addition and Subtraction of Complex Numbers

Adding and subtracting complex numbers is very similar to adding and subtracting binomials—we simply combine like terms. For example, to add $3 + 5i$ to $4 + 7i$ we add the 3 and the 4 and the $5i$ and the $7i$ to get $7 + 12i$. To subtract $3 + 5i$ from $4 + 7i$ we can write this as $(4 + 7i) - (3 + 5i) = 4 + 7i - 3 - 5i = (4 - 3) + (7i - 5i) = 1 + 2i$.

MODEL PROBLEM

1 Perform the indicated operation and express the answer in simplest $a + bi$ form.

  a $(2 + 4i) + (-5 - 6i)$
  b $(-3 - 8i) - (-2 + 4i)$
  c $\left(4 + \sqrt{-9}\right) - \left(\sqrt{-25}\right)$
  d $\left(5 - 2\sqrt{-12}\right) + \left(4 + \sqrt{-27}\right)$
  e $\left(2 - \sqrt{-8}\right) - \left(-4 - 3\sqrt{-32}\right)$

SOLUTION

  a $(2 + 4i) + (-5 - 6i) = (2 - 5) + (4i - 6i)$
  $$= -3 - 2i$$

  b $(-3 - 8i) - (-2 + 4i) = -3 - 8i + 2 - 4i$
  $$= (-3 + 2) + (-8i - 4i)$$
  $$= -1 - 12i$$

  c $\left(4 + \sqrt{-9}\right) - \left(\sqrt{-25}\right) = (4 + 3i) - (5i)$
  $$= 4 + 3i - 5i$$
  $$= 4 - 2i$$

  d $\left(5 - 2\sqrt{-12}\right) + \left(4 + \sqrt{-27}\right) = \left(5 - 2\sqrt{-4}\sqrt{3}\right) + \left(4 + \sqrt{-9}\sqrt{3}\right)$
  $$= \left(5 - 2(2i)\sqrt{3}\right) + \left(4 + 3i\sqrt{3}\right)$$
  $$= \left(5 - 4i\sqrt{3}\right) + \left(4 + 3i\sqrt{3}\right)$$
  $$= (5 + 4) + \left(-4i\sqrt{3} + 3i\sqrt{3}\right)$$
  $$= 9 - i\sqrt{3}$$

  e $\left(2 - \sqrt{-8}\right) - \left(-4 - 3\sqrt{-32}\right) = \left(2 - \sqrt{-4}\sqrt{2}\right) - \left(-4 - 3\sqrt{-16}\sqrt{2}\right)$
  $$= \left(2 - 2i\sqrt{2}\right) - \left(-4 - 3(4i)\sqrt{2}\right)$$
  $$= \left(2 - 2i\sqrt{2}\right) - \left(-4 - 12i\sqrt{2}\right)$$
  $$= 2 - 2i\sqrt{2} + 4 + 12i\sqrt{2}$$
  $$= 6 + 10i\sqrt{2}$$

We can use vector addition to graphically illustrate how to add and subtract complex numbers. To add two complex numbers, we represent each complex number by a vector in the complex plane. The sum of the two vectors is the resultant vector (that is, the diagonal of the parallelogram determined by the two vectors).

2 Let $Z_1 = 1 + 5i$ and $Z_2 = 6 + 2i$.

   a Graph the sum of Z_1 and Z_2.

   b Express the sum of Z_1 and Z_2 as a complex number.

SOLUTION

   a Graph Z_1 and Z_2. Then draw the parallelogram determined by the two vectors. The sum of the two vectors is the resultant vector (that is, the diagonal of the parallelogram).

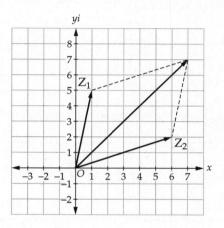

   b From the graph, we can see that the resultant vector represents the number $7 + 7i$.

Since subtraction is simply the addition of an additive inverse, we can also subtract complex numbers using vector addition. To subtract one complex number from another, rewrite the difference as the sum of the first complex number and the additive inverse of the second. Then proceed in the same manner as illustrated above.

3 Let $Z_3 = 3 - 4i$ and $Z_4 = -3 + i$.

   a Graph the difference $Z_3 - Z_4$.

   b Express the difference $Z_3 - Z_4$ as a complex number.

SOLUTION

   a $Z_3 - Z_4 = (3 - 4i) - (-3 + i)$

To subtract the two complex numbers, we rewrite the difference and add the additive inverse of the second number.

$(3 - 4i) - (-3 + i) = (3 - 4i) + (3 - i)$

Graph $(3 - 4i)$ and $(3 - i)$ and draw the parallelogram determined by the two vectors. The sum of the two vectors is the resultant vector (that is, the diagonal of the parallelogram).

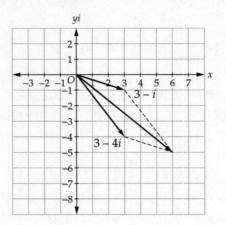

b From the graph, we can see that the resultant vector represents the number $6 - 5i$.

Practice

Exercises 1–10: Simplify.

1 $(-6 + 5i) + (6 - i)$

2 $(6 - 2i) + (-4 + 5i)$

3 $(3 - 5i) - (2 - 4i)$

4 $(-1 + 8i) - (-5 - 2i)$

5 $\left(6 + \sqrt{-49}\right) + \left(3 + \sqrt{-64}\right)$

6 $\left(-11 + \sqrt{-25}\right) - \left(-4 + 5\sqrt{-81}\right)$

7 $\left(2 + \sqrt{-18}\right) + \left(5 + \sqrt{-200}\right)$

8 $\left(-1 + 2\sqrt{-12}\right) - \left(8 + 5\sqrt{-48}\right)$

9 $\left(11 + 6\sqrt{-45}\right) - \left(-3 - 2\sqrt{-20}\right)$

10 $\left(-5 + \dfrac{2}{3}\sqrt{-27}\right) + \left(-2 + \dfrac{3}{2}\sqrt{-12}\right)$

Exercises 11–14: Find values for a and b that will make each statement true.

11 $(a + bi) + (4 + 6i) = 9 + 11i$

12 $(3 - 4i) + (a + bi) = 7 - 6i$

13 $(a + bi) - (2 + 5i) = 8 - 3i$

14 $(10 + 3i) - (a + bi) = 7 - 6i$

Exercises 15–20: Choose the numeral preceding the choice that best completes the statement or answers the question.

15 Express the sum of $(-5 - 6i)$ and $(10 - 4i)$ in simplest $a + bi$ form.

(1) $-5 - 10i$ (3) $5 - 2i$
(2) $15 - 2i$ (4) $5 - 10i$

16 In which quadrant does the sum of $(4 + 7i)$ and $(-3 - 5i)$ lie?

(1) I   (3) III
(2) II   (4) IV

17 If $(a + bi) - (2 + 4i) = 6 + 8i$, find the sum of a and b.

(1) 20   (3) 8
(2) 14   (4) 6

18 In which quadrant does the difference $(-5 + 11i) - (-2 + 7i)$ lie?

(1) I   (3) III
(2) II   (4) IV

19 Expressed in simplest form, $2\sqrt{-50} - 3\sqrt{-8}$ is equivalent to

(1) $4i\sqrt{2}$ (3) $-\sqrt{-42}$
(2) $16i\sqrt{2}$ (4) $3i\sqrt{2}$

20 Simplify $\left(5 - 3\sqrt{-20}\right) + \left(3 - 2\sqrt{-45}\right)$.

(1) $7 + 2i\sqrt{5}$ (3) $2 + i\sqrt{5}$
(2) $8 + 12i\sqrt{5}$ (4) $8 - 12i\sqrt{5}$

Exercises 21 and 22:
a Graph Z_1 and Z_2.
b Graph the sum of Z_1 and Z_2 and express the sum as a complex number.

21 $Z_1 = -2 + i,\ Z_2 = 1 + 4i$

22 $Z_1 = 3 - 2i,\ Z_2 = 2 + 3i$

Exercises 23 and 24:
a Graph Z_1 and Z_2.
b Graph the difference of Z_1 and Z_2 and express the difference as a complex number.

23 $Z_1 = 4 - i,\ Z_2 = -2 + 5i$

24 $Z_1 = 2 + 2i,\ Z_2 = -2 + 4i$

Multiplication and Division of Complex Numbers

Multiplying complex numbers is very similar to multiplying binomials: we multiply the binomials, simplify, and combine like terms. For example, to multiply $(2 + 3i)$ by $(4 + 5i)$, multiplying the binomials gives us $8 + 10i + 12i + 15i^2$. Since $i^2 = -1$, we can rewrite this as $8 + 10i + 12i + 15(-1) = 8 + 10i + 12i - 15 = -7 + 22i$.

To multiply $(3 - 6i)$ by $2i$, we distribute the $2i$, that is: $2i(3 - 6i) = 6i - 12i^2$. Since $i^2 = -1$, we can simplify this as $6i - 12(-1) = 6i + 12$. We can rewrite this as $12 + 6i$.

To multiply binomials containing radicals, be sure to simplify before multiplying.

MODEL PROBLEMS

1 Multiply $\left(6 + \sqrt{-100}\right)$ by $\left(3 + \sqrt{-4}\right)$.

SOLUTION

$$
\begin{aligned}
\left(6 + \sqrt{-100}\right)\left(3 + \sqrt{-4}\right) &= (6 + 10i)(3 + 2i) \\
&= 18 + 12i + 30i + 20i^2 \\
&= 18 + 42i + 20(-1) \\
&= 18 + 42i - 20 \\
&= -2 + 42i
\end{aligned}
$$

Answer: $-2 + 42i$

2 Find the product of $\left(2 + 3\sqrt{-8}\right)$ and $\left(-1 + \sqrt{-18}\right)$.

SOLUTION

$$
\begin{aligned}
\left(2 + 3\sqrt{-8}\right)\left(-1 + \sqrt{-18}\right) &= \left(2 + 3\sqrt{-4}\sqrt{2}\right)\left(-1 + \sqrt{-9}\sqrt{2}\right) \\
&= \left(2 + 3(2i)\sqrt{2}\right)\left(-1 + 3i\sqrt{2}\right) \\
&= \left(2 + 6i\sqrt{2}\right)\left(-1 + 3i\sqrt{2}\right) \\
&= -2 + 6i\sqrt{2} - 6i\sqrt{2} + 18i^2(2) \\
&= -2 + 36i^2 \\
&= -2 - 36 \\
&= -38
\end{aligned}
$$

Answer: -38

3 Multiply $6 - 4i$ by its conjugate.

SOLUTION

The conjugate of $6 - 4i$ is $6 + 4i$. Thus, we must find the product $(6 - 4i)(6 + 4i)$.

$$(6 - 4i)(6 + 4i) = 36 + 24i - 24i - 16i^2$$
$$= 36 - 16(-1)$$
$$= 36 + 16$$
$$= 52$$

Answer: 52

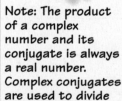

Note: The conjugate of the complex number $a + bi$ is the number $a - bi$. For example, the conjugate of $4 + 9i$ is the number $4 - 9i$.

4 Perform the indicated division and express your answer in simplest $a + bi$ form:

$$\frac{1 + 2i}{2 + 3i}$$

SOLUTION

This is very similar to rationalizing the denominator of a fraction. Multiply numerator and denominator by the conjugate of the denominator. The conjugate of $2 + 3i$ is $2 - 3i$.

$$\frac{1 + 2i}{2 + 3i} = \left(\frac{1 + 2i}{2 + 3i}\right)\left(\frac{2 - 3i}{2 - 3i}\right)$$
$$= \frac{2 - 3i + 4i - 6i^2}{4 - 6i + 6i - 9i^2}$$
$$= \frac{2 + i - 6(-1)}{4 - 9(-1)}$$
$$= \frac{2 + i + 6}{4 + 9}$$
$$= \frac{8 + i}{13}$$
$$= \frac{8}{13} + \frac{1}{13}i$$

Notice that we break the fraction $\dfrac{8 + i}{13}$ into $\dfrac{8}{13} + \dfrac{1}{13}i$ to satisfy the requirement of expressing the answer in "simplest $a + bi$ form."

Answer: $\dfrac{8}{13} + \dfrac{1}{13}i$

Note: The product of a complex number and its conjugate is always a real number. Complex conjugates are used to divide complex numbers.

5 Perform the indicated division and express your answer in simplest $a + bi$ form:

$$\frac{2 + \sqrt{-3}}{3 + \sqrt{-3}}$$

Note: When dividing radicals containing negative numbers, "take out the i's" before you begin.

SOLUTION

Be sure to simplify before you begin.

$$\frac{2 + \sqrt{-3}}{3 + \sqrt{-3}} = \frac{2 + \sqrt{-1}\sqrt{3}}{3 + \sqrt{-1}\sqrt{3}}$$

$$= \frac{2 + i\sqrt{3}}{3 + i\sqrt{3}}$$

$$= \frac{2 + i\sqrt{3}}{3 + i\sqrt{3}} \cdot \frac{3 - i\sqrt{3}}{3 - i\sqrt{3}}$$ $\qquad$ (**Note:** $3 - i\sqrt{3}$ is the conjugate of $3 + i\sqrt{3}$.)

$$= \frac{6 - 2i\sqrt{3} + 3i\sqrt{3} - 3i^2}{9 - 3i^2}$$

$$= \frac{6 + i\sqrt{3} - 3(-1)}{9 - 3(-1)}$$

$$= \frac{6 + i\sqrt{3} + 3}{12}$$

$$= \frac{9 + i\sqrt{3}}{12}$$

$$= \frac{9}{12} + \frac{\sqrt{3}}{12}i$$

$$= \frac{3}{4} + \frac{\sqrt{3}}{12}i$$

Answer: $\dfrac{3}{4} + \dfrac{\sqrt{3}}{12}i$

✏️ **Practice**

Exercises 1–15: Perform the indicated operations and express your answer in simplest $a + bi$ form.

1 $(2 - 5i)(6 + 7i)$

2 $\dfrac{2 - i}{3 + i}$

3 $3i(2i^2 + 4i - 6)$

4 $\dfrac{4 - 6i}{5i}$

5 $(3 + 4i)(-1 - 9i)$

6 $(7 + 3i)^2$

7 $\left(2 - \sqrt{-9}\right)\left(3 + \sqrt{-16}\right)$

8 $\dfrac{1}{2 - 5i}$

9 $4i^2(6 + 8i + 5i^2 - 3i^4)$

10 $\dfrac{1 + \sqrt{-4}}{2 + \sqrt{-9}}$

11 $(3 - i)(1 + 2i) + (1 - i)(2 + i)$

12 $\dfrac{5 + i}{3 - 4i}$

13 $\left(3 - \sqrt{-8}\right)\left(1 - \sqrt{-18}\right)$

14 $\dfrac{3 - 2i}{2i}$

15 $\left(4 - \sqrt{-27}\right)\left(3 + \sqrt{-12}\right)$

16 Find the product of $6 + 8i$ and its conjugate.

17 What is the multiplicative inverse of $5 + 3i$?

Exercises 18–24: Select the numeral preceding the choice that best completes the statement or answers the question.

18 The expression $\dfrac{1}{7 - 4i}$ is equivalent to

(1) $\dfrac{7}{65} - \dfrac{4i}{65}$ (3) $\dfrac{7}{65} + \dfrac{4i}{65}$

(2) $\dfrac{7}{33} - \dfrac{4i}{33}$ (4) $\dfrac{7}{33} + \dfrac{4i}{33}$

19 What is the product of $6 - 7i$ and its conjugate?

(1) -13 (3) 13

(2) 0 (4) 85

20 The expression $(2 + i)^2$ is equivalent to

(1) $3 + 4i$ (3) 3

(2) $3 - 4i$ (4) 5

21 Express $\dfrac{3}{2 + 2i}$ in simplest $a + bi$ form.

(1) $\dfrac{3}{2} + \dfrac{3}{2}i$ (3) $\dfrac{3}{4} + \dfrac{3}{4}i$

(2) $\dfrac{3}{2} - \dfrac{3}{2}i$ (4) $\dfrac{3}{4} - \dfrac{3}{4}i$

22 What is the reciprocal of $3 - \sqrt{-5}$?

(1) $\dfrac{3}{14} + \dfrac{i\sqrt{5}}{14}$ (3) $\dfrac{3}{4} + \dfrac{i\sqrt{5}}{4}$

(2) $\dfrac{3}{14} - \dfrac{i\sqrt{5}}{14}$ (4) $\dfrac{3}{4} - \dfrac{i\sqrt{5}}{4}$

23 What is the product of $5 + \sqrt{-36}$ and $1 - \sqrt{-49}$, expressed in simplest $a + bi$ form?

(1) $47 + 41i$ (3) $-37 + 41i$

(2) $47 - 29i$ (4) $5 - 71i$

24 The expression $(1 + i)^2$ in simplest form is

(1) 1 (3) $-i$

(2) 2 (4) $2i$

5.4 Nature of the Roots and the Discriminant

The graph of a quadratic equation, $y = ax^2 + bx + c$, where a, b, and c are real numbers and $a \neq 0$, is a parabola. A parabola may have several different appearances. When a is negative, the parabola opens downward from a maximum point and when a is positive, the parabola opens upward from a minimum point.

The graph of a parabola may not intersect the x-axis but remains totally above or below it depending on the positive or negative value of a. In this case, the roots of the equation $ax^2 + bx + c = 0$ are *not* real numbers.

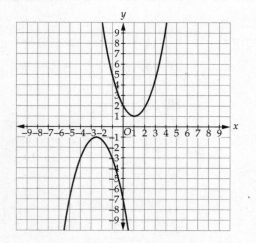

The graph of a parabola may intersect the x-axis in two distinct points, as shown in the two examples below. Thus, the roots of each equation are real and either rational or irrational.

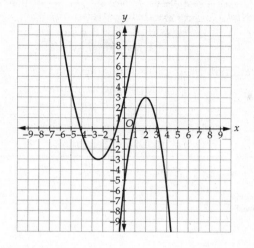

While the roots might appear to be 0.8 and 3.2 for the downward parabola, they could just as easily be $\sqrt{0.75}$ or $\sqrt{11}$. It is difficult to determine exact roots from a graph.

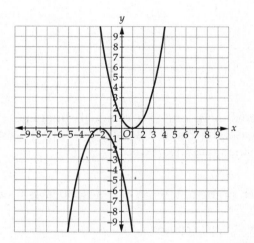

A parabola that is tangent to the x-axis, intersects it in just one point. Two examples of tangent parabolas are shown above. In each case, the roots of the equation will be real, rational, and equal.

By the quadratic formula, the two roots of $ax^2 + bx + c = 0$ are

$$x_1 = \frac{-b + \sqrt{b^2 - 4ac}}{2a} \qquad x_2 = \frac{-b - \sqrt{b^2 - 4ac}}{2a}$$

The **discriminant** is an expression that determines the nature of the roots of a quadratic equation and, by extension, the preferable method of solving a particular quadratic equation. The formula for the discriminant is $b^2 - 4ac$, the radicand of the quadratic formula. If you know the nature of the roots from examining the discriminant, you can choose the most efficient method of solving the quadratic to find those roots. This information is summarized in the table on page 182.

If the discriminant is	The roots will be	Method of solution is
a negative number	imaginary	completing the square or quadratic formula
zero	real, equal, rational	factoring, graphing, completing the square, or quadratic formula
a positive perfect square	real, unequal, rational	factoring, graphing, completing the square, or quadratic formula
a positive nonperfect square	real, unequal, irrational	completing the square or quadratic formula

MODEL PROBLEMS

1 Describe the roots of the equation $2x^2 - 3x + 4 = 0$.

SOLUTION

Rather than solving the equation, find the discriminant and interpret it.

$a = 2 \quad b = -3 \quad c = 4$

$$\text{discriminant} = b^2 - 4ac$$
$$= (-3)^2 - 4(2)(4)$$
$$= 9 - 32$$

-23 is the discriminant.

Answer: Since -23 is a negative number, there are two unequal, imaginary roots, meaning the parabola does not cross the x-axis; in this case, the graph lies entirely above the x-axis. The roots could best be found by completing the square or the quadratic formula.

2 Given the quadratic $3x^2 - 2x = 4$, which of the following best describes its roots?

    (1) two unequal, imaginary roots
    (2) two real, unequal, irrational roots
    (3) two real, equal, rational roots
    (4) two real, unequal, rational roots

SOLUTION

Rewrite the equation as $3x^2 - 2x - 4 = 0$. Find the discriminant and interpret it.

$a = 3 \quad b = -2 \quad c = -4$

$$\text{discriminant} = b^2 - 4ac$$
$$= (-2)^2 - 4(3)(-4)$$
$$= 4 - (-48)$$

52 is the discriminant. The roots are real, unequal, and irrational.

Answer: (2)

3 If the parabola $y = ax^2 + bx + c$, $a \neq 0$, has two equal roots, what can be said about its graph?

    (1) The graph lies totally below the x-axis.
    (2) The graph is tangent to the x-axis.
    (3) The graph intersects the x-axis at two points.
    (4) The graph lies totally above the x-axis.

SOLUTION

Since the equation has two equal roots, the discriminant must be zero. Therefore, the graph is tangent to the x-axis.

Answer: (2)

4 Find the smallest possible integer value of c such that $6x^2 - 4x + c = 0$ will have imaginary roots.

SOLUTION

For an equation to have imaginary roots, its discriminant must be negative. Set the discriminant, $b^2 - 4ac$, to be less than zero, substitute the values of a and b, and solve for c.

$a = 6 \quad b = -4$

$$b^2 - 4ac < 0$$
$$(-4)^2 - 4(6)c < 0$$
$$16 - 24c < 0$$
$$-24c < -16$$
$$c > \frac{-16}{-24}$$
$$c > \frac{2}{3}$$

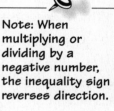

Note: When multiplying or dividing by a negative number, the inequality sign reverses direction.

To find the smallest possible *integer* value of c, as requested in the problem, we look for the smallest integer greater than $\frac{2}{3}$. That is 1.

Answer: $c = 1$

Practice

Exercises 1–6: Find the discriminant for each equation and explain its significance.

1. $3x^2 + 7 = -2x$

2. $10 - 3x = x^2$

3. $\dfrac{2x + 1}{x} = \dfrac{3x - 4}{2}$

4. $4x - 1 = \dfrac{-9}{x}$

5. $\dfrac{1}{3}x^2 - x = 6$

6. $4x = \dfrac{12x - 9}{x}$

Exercises 7–19: Select the numeral preceding the choice that best completes the sentence or answers the question.

7 Which equation has a discriminant of 64?

(1) $x^2 - 4x + 12 = 0$
(2) $3x^2 - 2x - 5 = 0$
(3) $2x^2 - x + 7 = 0$
(4) $6 - 4x = 3x^2$

8 Which methods would produce *exact* solutions to $x^2 + 25 = 6x$?

I. graphing
II. completing the square
III. quadratic formula
IV. factoring

(1) I and III
(2) II and III
(3) II and IV
(4) III and IV

9 For what integer value of a would $ax^2 - 6x + 8 = 0$ produce imaginary roots?

(1) 1   (3) 0
(2) 2   (4) −1

10 Which describes the graph of $4x^2 - 3x - 1 = 0$?

(1) The parabola is tangent to the x-axis.
(2) The parabola lies entirely above the x-axis.
(3) The parabola lies entirely below the x-axis.
(4) The parabola intersects the x-axis at two distinct points.

11 Which equation has real, rational, equal roots?

(1) $9x^2 + 6x + 1 = 0$
(2) $2x^2 + 7x - 10 = 0$
(3) $4x^2 - 9 = 0$
(4) $5x^2 - 25 = 0$

12 If the discriminant of an equation equals 17, what can be said of the roots?

(1) two real, unequal, irrational roots
(2) two real, equal, rational roots
(3) two imaginary, unequal roots
(4) two real, unequal, rational roots

13 Which might be the discriminant of a parabola that does *not* intersect the x-axis?

(1) 143   (3) 0
(2) 36   (4) −11

14 For what value of b will the roots of $2x^2 - bx + 9 = 0$ produce two real, unequal, irrational roots?

(1) −1   (3) 5
(2) 0   (4) 10

15 Find the largest integral value of k for which the roots of $2x^2 + 7x + k = 0$ are real.

(1) 7   (3) 0
(2) 6   (4) −2

16 Which equation has roots that are irrational?

(1) $x^2 - 4 = 0$
(2) $x^2 - 5x + 2 = 0$
(3) $x^2 + 4x - 5 = 0$
(4) $x^2 + 7x + 12 = 0$

17 The roots of $ax^2 + 6x + 9 = 0$ are imaginary if

(1) $-1 < a < 1$ (3) $a < 1$ only
(2) $a > 1$ only   (4) $a < -1$

18 The roots of $2x^2 + 8x + n = 0$ are real and unequal if n equals

(1) 12   (3) 8
(2) 10   (4) 6

19 Which equation has imaginary roots?
(1) $x(5 + x) = 8$ (3) $x(x + 6) = -10$
(2) $x(5 - x) = -3$ (4) $(2x - 1)(x - 3) = 7$

Exercises 20–25: Use any method you choose to solve for x.

20 $2x^2 - 7x + 3 = 0$

21 $x - 8 = \dfrac{20}{x}$

22 $\sqrt{2x - 1} - x = -2$

23 $4x(x - 3) = -1$

24 $x^2 = 2(7x - 12)$

25 $x - 3 = \dfrac{5}{2x}$

5.5 Complex Roots of Quadratic Equations

When we first solved quadratic equations by completing the square, or by using the quadratic formula, none of the equations had imaginary or complex roots. Now we will see that examples of this kind may be handled easily.

MODEL PROBLEMS

1 Find all roots of the equation $x^2 + 4x + 13 = 0$.

SOLUTION

Check the value of the discriminant for this equation, $b^2 - 4ac = -36$. This means the roots are imaginary. Therefore, we cannot use factoring or graphing to solve, but must use completing the square or the quadratic formula. Below both methods of solution are demonstrated.

METHOD 1 (COMPLETING THE SQUARE)

$x^2 + 4x + 13 = 0$

$x^2 + 4x = -13$

$x^2 + 4x + 4 = -9$

$(x + 2)^2 = -9$

$x + 2 = \pm 3i$

$x = -2 \pm 3i$

METHOD 2 (USING THE QUADRATIC FORMULA)

$x^2 + 4x + 13 = 0$ $\qquad\qquad a = 1 \quad b = 4 \quad c = 13$

$$x = \frac{-4 \pm \sqrt{4^2 - 4(1)(13)}}{2(1)}$$

$$x = \frac{-4 \pm \sqrt{16 - 52}}{2}$$

$$x = \frac{-4 \pm \sqrt{-36}}{2}$$

$$x = \frac{-4 \pm 6i}{2}$$

$$x = -2 \pm 3i$$

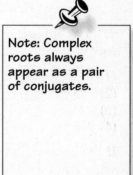

Note: Complex roots always appear as a pair of conjugates.

Notice that both methods produce the same roots.

Answer: $\{-2 - 3i, -2 + 3i\}$

2 Find the roots of $x - 6 = -\dfrac{11}{x}$.

SOLUTION

First multiply each side of the equation by x and get the equation in standard quadratic form.

$$x - 6 = -\dfrac{11}{x}$$
$$x^2 - 6x = -11$$
$$x^2 - 6x + 11 = 0$$

Again, if you check the discriminant, $b^2 - 4ac = -8$, so we must solve by completing the square or using the quadratic formula. In this example, we'll complete the square since the value of a is 1.

$$x^2 - 6x = -11$$
$$x^2 - 6x + 9 = -11 + 9$$
$$x^2 - 6x + 9 = -2$$
$$(x - 3)^2 = -2$$
$$x - 3 = \pm\sqrt{-2}$$

Answer: $x = 3 \pm i\sqrt{2}$

3 Solve: $4x^2 - 12x + 25 = 0$

SOLUTION

Once again, the discriminant is a negative number, -256, so we know that we cannot factor or graph to find the roots. Since $a \neq 1$, we'll use the quadratic formula this time.

$$4x^2 - 12x + 25 = 0 \qquad\qquad a = 4 \quad b = -12 \quad c = 25$$

$$x = \dfrac{-(-12) \pm \sqrt{(-12)^2 - 4(4)(25)}}{2(4)}$$

$$x = \dfrac{12 \pm \sqrt{144 - 400}}{8}$$

$$x = \dfrac{12 \pm \sqrt{-256}}{8}$$

$$x = \dfrac{12 \pm 16i}{8}$$

$$x = \dfrac{3}{2} \pm 2i$$

Answer: The roots of this function are $\left\{\dfrac{3}{2} + 2i, \dfrac{3}{2} - 2i\right\}$.

 **Practice**

Solve each of the following equations using the quadratic formula or completing the square. Express your answers in simplest $a + bi$ form.

1 $x^2 + 7 = 4x$

2 $x - 6 = \dfrac{-13}{x}$

3 $2x - 1 = -\dfrac{5}{2x}$

4 $x^2 + 5 = 4x$

5 $2x^2 - 6x + 5 = 0$

6 $\dfrac{9x^2}{2} = 3x - 1$

7 $2x^2 - 4x + 3 = 0$

8 $x^2 - x = \dfrac{-13}{2}$

9 $x^2 - 2x = -2$

10 $3x(x - 4) = -40$

11 $x^2 = 5x - 9$

12 $x^2 - 2x + 17 = 0$

13 $x - 2 = \dfrac{-5}{4x}$

14 $3x^2 + 7 = 8x$

15 $4x^2 + 37 = 4x$

16 $x^2 - x = -\dfrac{1}{2}$

17 $x^2 - 2(x - 2) = 0$

18 $\dfrac{x - 4}{10} = \dfrac{x - 5}{x}$

19 $4x(x - 3) + 25 = 0$

20 $x - 1 = -\dfrac{17}{4x}$

5.6 Sum and Product of the Roots

If we know the roots of an equation, we can work backward to find the equation. If the roots of the equation are 3 and -2, we know the factors of the equation are $(x - 3)$ and $(x + 2)$. The product $(x - 3)(x + 2)$ is $x^2 - x - 6$, so the original equation is $x^2 - x - 6 = 0$. Sometimes, however, the roots are not rational and the factors are more complicated to find, such as when the roots given are $3 + 2\sqrt{5}$ and $3 - 2\sqrt{5}$.

A better method with irrational or complex roots is to use formulas for the sum and product of the roots derived from the quadratic formula. We know that the roots of any quadratic equation are

$$x = \frac{-b}{2a} + \frac{\sqrt{b^2 - 4ac}}{2a} \quad \text{and} \quad x = \frac{-b}{2a} - \frac{\sqrt{b^2 - 4ac}}{2a}$$

Adding these roots together we get $\dfrac{-2b}{2a}$ or $\dfrac{-b}{a}$. Therefore, in any quadratic equation, the sum of the roots is $\dfrac{-2b}{2a}$ or $\dfrac{-b}{a}$.

Multiplying the two roots together, we get

$$\frac{b^2}{4a^2} - \frac{b\sqrt{b^2 - 4ac}}{4a^2} + \frac{b\sqrt{b^2 - 4ac}}{4a^2} - \frac{b^2 - 4ac}{4a^2}$$

$$= \frac{b^2}{4a^2} - \frac{b^2 - 4ac}{4a^2}$$

$$= \frac{b^2 - b^2 + 4ac}{4a^2}$$

$$= \frac{4ac}{4a^2}$$

$$= \frac{c}{a}$$

Therefore, the product of the roots of any quadratic equation is $\frac{c}{a}$. To find a quadratic equation when given the roots, use the sum of the roots and the product of the roots to determine the values of a, b, and c and then insert them into the general form of the quadratic equation, $ax^2 + bx + c = 0$.

MODEL PROBLEMS

1 Find the quadratic equation whose roots are $3 + \sqrt{2}$ and $3 - \sqrt{2}$.

SOLUTION

Sum of the roots: $3 + \sqrt{2} + 3 - \sqrt{2} = 6 = \frac{6}{1}$

$$\frac{-b}{a} = \frac{6}{1}$$

Product of the roots: $\left(3 + \sqrt{2}\right)\left(3 - \sqrt{2}\right) = 9 + 3\sqrt{2} - 3\sqrt{2} - 2 = 7 = \frac{7}{1}$

$$\frac{c}{a} = \frac{7}{1}$$

So $a = 1$, $b = -6$, $c = 7$, and the equation is $x^2 - 6x + 7 = 0$.

Answer: $x^2 - 6x + 7 = 0$

2 Find the quadratic equation whose roots are $5 + 2i$ and $5 - 2i$.

SOLUTION

Sum of the roots: $5 + 2i + 5 - 2i = \frac{-b}{a} = 10 = \frac{10}{1}$

Product of the roots: $(5 + 2i)(5 - 2i) = 25 - 4i^2 = 25 + 4 = 29 = \frac{29}{1} = \frac{c}{a}$

So $a = 1$, $b = -10$, $c = 29$. The equation is $x^2 - 10x + 29 = 0$.

Answer: $x^2 - 10x + 29 = 0$

3 If one root of a quadratic equation is $2 - i\sqrt{3}$, find the other root and write the quadratic equation that would produce these roots.

SOLUTION

Since complex roots always appear as a pair of conjugates, the second root must be $2 + i\sqrt{3}$.

Sum of the roots $= 4 = \dfrac{4}{1} = \dfrac{-b}{a}$

Product of roots $= 4 - 3i^2 = 4 - 3(-1) = 4 + 3 = 7 = \dfrac{7}{1} = \dfrac{c}{a}$

Therefore, $a = 1$, $b = -4$, and $c = 7$. The equation is $x^2 - 4x + 7 = 0$.

Answer: $x^2 - 4x + 7 = 0$

 **Practice**

1 Find the sum and product of the roots of the equation $2x^2 - 6x + 10 = 0$.

2 If the sum of two roots is 12 and one root is 5, find the other root and the pertinent quadratic equation.

3 Find the sum and product of the roots of the equation $4x^2 - 12 = 3x$.

4 If one root of a quadratic equation is $6 + 2i$, find the other root and the equation.

5 If $x^2 - 12x + k = 28$ and one root is 2, find the other root and the value of k.

6 If $r_1 = 2 - \sqrt{5}$, find the other root and the quadratic equation from which these roots are derived.

7 If one root of the equation $2x^2 + kx - 5 = 0$ is $\dfrac{1}{2}$, find the other root and k.

8 Write the equation of the quadratic whose roots are $-\dfrac{1}{3}$ and 4.

9 Write the equation of the quadratic whose roots are $3 - 4i$ and $3 + 4i$.

10 Write the quadratic equation whose roots are $\left\{ \dfrac{2}{9} + \dfrac{i}{9}, \dfrac{2}{9} - \dfrac{i}{9} \right\}$.

Exercises 11–15: Choose the numeral preceeding the choice that best answers the question or completes the statement.

11 If the sum of the roots of $2x^2 + 2 = 8x$ is added to the product of the roots, the result is

(1) -5 (3) 3
(2) -3 (4) 5

12 For which equation does the sum of the roots equal the product of the roots?

(1) $3x^2 - 3x + 1 = 0$
(2) $x^2 - 13 = 13x$
(3) $x^2 + 13 = 13x$
(4) $2x^2 + 2x + 2 = 0$

13 One root of a quadratic equation is $7 - i$. Determine the equation that has this root as its solution.

(1) $x^2 + 14x + 50 = 0$
(2) $x^2 - 14x + 50 = 0$
(3) $x^2 + 14x - 50 = 0$
(4) $x^2 - 14x - 50 = 0$

14 If the product of the roots of $4x^2 - 20 = 8x$ is subtracted from the sum of the roots, the result is

(1) -7 (3) 7
(2) -4 (4) 9

15 Identify the sum and product of the roots in the equation $\dfrac{2x - 1}{2x} = \dfrac{3x + 4}{x - 3}$.

(1) sum: $-\dfrac{15}{4}$, product: $-\dfrac{3}{4}$

(2) sum: $\dfrac{15}{4}$, product: $\dfrac{3}{4}$

(3) sum: $-\dfrac{15}{4}$, product: $\dfrac{3}{4}$

(4) sum: $\dfrac{15}{4}$, product: -5

5.7 Solving Higher Degree Polynomial Equations

Algebraic Solutions

We have solved quadratic equations algebraically by factoring. We can also solve higher degree equations using factoring. Until now the primary methods of factoring that you've used have been the greatest common factor, the difference of two squares, and trinomial factoring. However, in equations of degree three or higher, we need some additional tools. Among these are factoring by grouping as well as factoring the sum and difference of cubes.

Factoring by grouping is sometimes referred to as *double greatest common factor* because it often contains four terms that can be factored in pairs.

Consider the expression $2x^3 + 7x^2 + 8x + 28$.

- Examine this as two sets of binomials: $2x^3 + 7x^2 \quad + 8x + 28$
  When viewed independently, each binomial contains a different greatest common factor.
- Rewrite the expression in factored form: $x^2(2x + 7) + 4(2x + 7)$.
  Notice that the two binomials now contain a common factor $(2x + 7)$ in the parentheses.
- The factor $(2x + 7)$ becomes the new GCF and the "leftovers" go in the other parentheses.
- Your answer is $(2x + 7)(x^2 + 4)$.

Practice

Factor each expression by grouping.

1 $3x^3 + 5x^2 - 12x - 20$

2 $6a^3 + 4a^2 - 9a - 6$

3 $8x^3 + 6x^2 + 4x + 3$

4 $3y^3 + 4y^2 + 6y + 8$

5 $2x^3 + 7x^2 - 8x - 28$

6 $d^3 - 2d^2 - 9d + 18$

7 $3x^3 + x^2 - 3x - 1$

8 $3c^3 - 2c^2 - 12c + 8$

9 $2x^3 - 3x^2 - 18x + 27$

Two additional types of factoring that are commonly used for polynomials are **factoring the sum of two cubes** and **factoring the difference of two cubes**. To recognize this type of factoring, you first must know the most common cubic numbers:

$$1^3 = 1 \qquad 3^3 = 27 \qquad 5^3 = 125 \qquad 7^3 = 343$$
$$2^3 = 8 \qquad 4^3 = 64 \qquad 6^3 = 216 \qquad 10^3 = 1{,}000$$

To factor the sum of two cubes, consider the problem $x^3 + 8$.

Many students will incorrectly believe that this is equivalent to $(x + 2)^3$. Note that the original problem contains no x^2 or x term, which means that those terms must have been canceled because of a negative term somewhere in the multiplication process. To find the factors of the original expression, start with the binomial that is the cube root of each term in the cubic binomial, $x + 2$, and then divide to find the other factor, being careful to hold places for the x^2 and x terms with zeros.

$$
\begin{array}{r}
x^2 - 2x + 4 \\
x + 2 \overline{)\, x^3 + 0x^2 + 0x + 8} \\
\underline{x^3 + 2x^2} \\
-2x^2 + 0x \\
\underline{-2x^2 - 4x} \\
4x + 8 \\
\underline{4x + 8} \\
0
\end{array}
$$

The quotient of the polynomial division is $x^2 - 2x + 4$, a trinomial that cannot be factored. To check your answer, multiply $(x + 2)(x^2 - 2x + 4)$.

$$
\begin{aligned}
(x + 2)(x^2 - 2x + 4) &= x^3 - 2x^2 + 4x + 2x^2 - 4x + 8 \\
&= x^3 + 8
\end{aligned}
$$

To factor the sum of two cubes, one factor is a binomial whose terms are the cube roots of the terms in the original binomial, and the other factor is a trinomial whose first term is the square of the first term of the binomial, whose second term is the negative product of the two terms of the binomial, and whose third term is the second term of the binomial squared. That is,

$$x^3 + a^3 = (x + a)(x^2 - ax + a^2)$$

MODEL PROBLEM

1   Factor $8c^3 + 27$.

SOLUTION

The binomial is composed of the cube roots of each term, $(2c + 3)$.

The trinomial is the first term of the binomial squared, $(2c)^2$ or $4c^2$, the product of the two terms of the binomial negated, $-3(2c) = -6c$, and the second term of the binomial squared, 3^2 or 9.

Answer: $8c^3 + 27 = (2c + 3)(4c^2 - 6c + 9)$

Notice that once again the trinomial cannot be factored any further.

Factoring the difference of cubes is the same process, except that the sign of the binomial will be negative and both signs in the trinomial will be positive.

$$x^3 - a^3 = (x - a)(x^2 + ax + a^2)$$

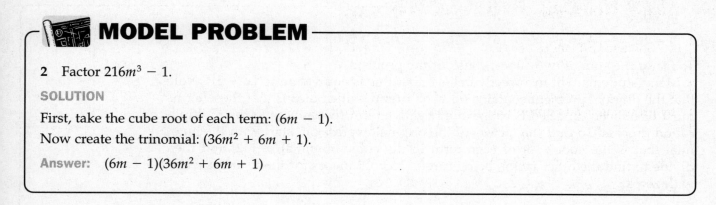

MODEL PROBLEM

2 Factor $216m^3 - 1$.

SOLUTION

First, take the cube root of each term: $(6m - 1)$.

Now create the trinomial: $(36m^2 + 6m + 1)$.

Answer: $(6m - 1)(36m^2 + 6m + 1)$

Practice

Exercises 1–8: Factor completely using the sum and difference of cubes.

1 $a^3 + 64b^3$

2 $\dfrac{1}{8} - 125a^3$

3 $27x^6 + 64$

4 $\dfrac{x^3}{1,000} - 343$

5 $1 - y^{12}$

6 $\dfrac{27}{8}b^3 - 125$

7 $c^3d^3 + 125$

8 $216 + \dfrac{x^9}{64}$

Exercises 9–15: Factor using whichever method is applicable.

9 $6x^3 - 8x^2 + 15x - 20$

10 $3x^3 + 2x^2 - 27x - 18$

11 $16a^6 - 2b^3$

12 $3x^3 + x^2 - 15x - 5$

13 $p^3 - 125q^3$

14 $4x^3 + 12x^2 - 16x$

15 $64z^6 + 27$

Knowing these additional methods of factoring, we can now solve higher degree equations by factoring.

MODEL PROBLEMS

1 Solve for all values of x: $2x^3 - 3x^2 - 8x + 12 = 0$

SOLUTION

Examining the equation, we see that it contains two binomials with common factors. Hence, factoring by grouping is an appropriate method to solve this equation.

$2x^3 - 3x^2 - 8x + 12 = 0$

$2x^3 - 3x^2 \qquad - 8x + 12 = 0$

$x^2(2x - 3) - 4(2x - 3) = 0$

$(2x - 3)(x^2 - 4) = 0$

$2x - 3 = 0 \qquad\qquad x^2 - 4 = 0$

$\qquad x = \dfrac{3}{2} \qquad (x - 2)(x + 2) = 0$

$\qquad\qquad\qquad\qquad x = 2, -2$

The solution set for this problem is $\left\{-2, \dfrac{3}{2}, 2\right\}$. Naturally, you should check each individual solution in the original equation to verify these answers.

Answer: $\left\{-2, \dfrac{3}{2}, 2\right\}$

2 Solve for all values of x, expressing complex roots in $a + bi$ form: $3x^4 - 81x = 0$

SOLUTION

First, factor out the GCF: $3x(x^3 - 27) = 0$

Now use difference of cubes: $3x(x - 3)(x^2 + 3x + 9) = 0$

$3x = 0 \qquad x - 3 = 0 \qquad x = \dfrac{-3 \pm \sqrt{3^2 - 4(1)(9)}}{2(1)}$

$\quad x = 0 \qquad\quad x = 3 \qquad\quad x = \dfrac{-3 \pm \sqrt{-27}}{2}$

$\qquad\qquad\qquad\qquad\qquad\qquad x = -\dfrac{3}{2} \pm \dfrac{3i\sqrt{3}}{2}$

Since the trinomial factor of the difference of squares is not factorable, we must use the quadratic formula to solve that piece of the factored problem. Notice that we have four solutions, two real roots and two imaginary roots for this fourth-degree equation.

Answer: $\left\{-\dfrac{3}{2} \pm \dfrac{3i\sqrt{3}}{2}, 0, 3\right\}$

Use your factoring skills to find all solutions for x. Express complex roots in simplest $a + bi$ form.

1 $8x^3 - 20x^2 + 8x = 0$

2 $4x^4 - 52x^2 + 144 = 0$

3 $3x^3 + x^2 = 10x$

4 $4x^3 + 3x^2 = 4x + 3$

5 $3x^3 - 27x^2 - 3x + 27 = 0$

6 $2x^5 - 162x = 0$

7 $6x^4 - 21x^3 + 18x^2 = 0$

8 $4x^2 - 5 = -\dfrac{1}{x^2}$

9 $\dfrac{3}{4}x^4 = x^3 + x^2$

10 $5x^4 = 5x$

11 $x^5 + 16x = 17x^3$

12 $27x^3 + 45x^2 = 3x + 5$

Graphic Solutions

To solve polynomial equations, you should first determine the number of possible solutions. As we saw when solving equations algebraically, the degree of the equation indicates the greatest possible number of solutions. The only problem is that some of those solutions may be complex numbers. Consider the graphs of the two functions shown below.

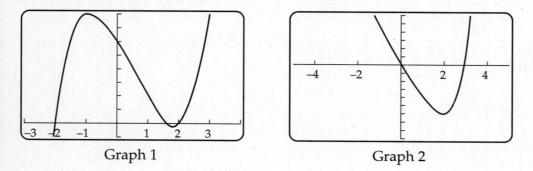

Graph 1   Graph 2

It appears that Graph 1 represents a third-degree equation, since it crosses the x-axis three times, indicating three real solutions. Graph 2 crosses the axis twice, so it appears there are only two solutions. These are actually the graphs of Model Problems 1 and 2 from page 193, which have three solutions and four solutions respectively.

Graph 1 represents the function $y = 2x^3 - 3x^2 - 8x + 12$. This equation has three real solutions: $-2, \dfrac{3}{2}, 2$.

Graph 2 represents the function $y = 3x^4 - 81x$, which has four roots, two real and two imaginary: $0, 3, -\dfrac{3}{2} \pm \dfrac{3i\sqrt{3}}{2}$.

We cannot use the calculator to find complex roots. However, we are able to identify real roots using the calculator's [2nd] [TRACE] function, which takes us to the Calculate menu.

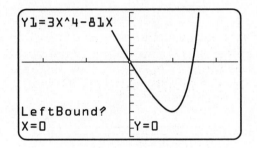

To locate the roots of any equation graphically, that is, to find the zeros of the function, choose 2 from this menu. The next screen you see will look like this when you have entered $3x^4 - 81x$ in Y_1:

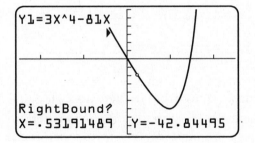

You must identify the left bound of the zero, so move your cursor to the left of the first zero and press [ENTER].

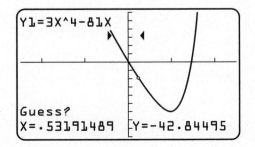

Now move your cursor to the right of the zero you wish to identify. Then press [ENTER].

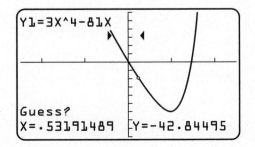

To guess, press (ENTER) again and you will see the solution on the calculator as below.

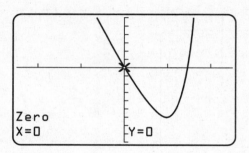

The leftmost zero on the graph is 0. To find the other visible zeros, repeat the steps above.

MODEL PROBLEM

Solve for all values of x: $3x^4 - 10x^3 + 8x^2 = 0$

SOLUTION

Looking at the equation to be solved, we see that it is a fourth-degree equation, so we know we will find, at most, four zeros. Consider the graph of this function show below:

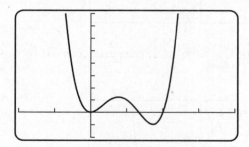

It appears that this graph has only three zeros, yet it is a fourth-degree equation. The reason for this is that when the function touches the x-axis but does not cross it, there are two equal roots at that point.

Now use the calculator to find the four zeros as described on pages 195 and 196.

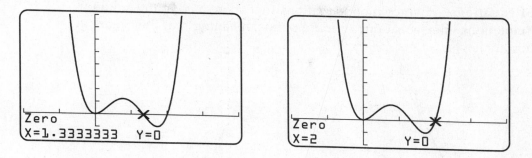

Notice that if you try to use the [2nd] [TRACE] function to identify the leftmost point, the calculator gives an error message that says "No Sign Change." Because the graph of the equation does not cross the x-axis, this approach will not provide that answer. Checking the table may give you the information you need if you are able to manipulate the Δ value on the table, or you can solve for this root algebraically.

Answer: The zeros are $\left\{0, 0, \dfrac{4}{3}, 2\right\}$, commonly written $\left\{0, \dfrac{4}{3}, 2\right\}$.

X	Y₁	
0	0	
1	1	
2	0	
3	45	
4	256	
5	825	
6	2016	
X=0		

Practice

Solve each equation for all real zeros, using the graphing calculator.

1 $2x^4 + 3x^3 - 28x^2 - 12x + 80 = 0$

2 $x^4 + x^3 - 3x^2 - x + 2 = 0$

3 $8x^4 - 12x^3 - 22x^2 + 3x + 5 = 0$

4 $3x^5 + 2x^4 - 35x^3 - 18x^2 + 72x = 0$

5 $3x^4 - 5x^3 - 5x^2 + 5x + 2 = 0$

6 $8x^4 + 18x^3 - 3x^2 - 17x - 6 = 0$

7 $8x^3 - 12x^2 - 72x + 108 = 0$

8 $15x^3 - 2x^2 - 48x + 32 = 0$

9 $3x^4 + 7x^3 - 18x^2 - 28x + 24 = 0$

10 $x^4 + 6x^3 - 7x^2 - 96x - 144 = 0$

5.8 Systems of Equations

A **system of equations** is two or more equations that share a common solution. That is, the equations intersect at one or more points, meaning that they share at least one coordinate pair.

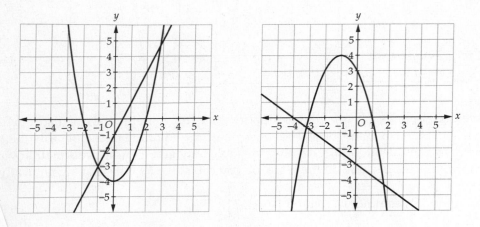

his section we will deal only with linear and quadratic systems. The com-
olution to any system may be found using either algebraic or graphic
and we will explore both methods.

ic Solutions to Systems

ystem of equations algebraically, we will restructure the system so
ation contains only one variable rather than two. One way to do this
of the equations in terms of one variable and substitute that defin-
riable into the other equation. That way, the second equation con-
ariable and can be solved by factoring, completing the square, or
a.

EL PROBLEM

ystem of equations: $y = x^2 - 2x - 8$, $y + 8 = x$

already solved for x, but it would be simpler to replace y in the quadratic equa-
e binomial $(y + 8)$. If $y + 8 = x$, then $y = x - 8$.

$x^2 - 2x - 8$, then

$= 0$

$= 3$

and Complex Numbers

To find the y-values of the intersection points, substitute the x-values in either equation.

$$y + 8 = x$$

$x = 0$	$x = 3$
$y + 8 = 0$	$y + 8 = 3$
$y = -8$	$y = -5$

The coordinate points at which the quadratic and linear equations intersect are therefore $(0, -8)$ and $(3, -5)$. To verify these solutions, it is necessary to check both pairs of points in both equations.

$$y = x^2 - 2x - 8$$

Check: $(0, -8)$ Check: $(3, -5)$

$-8 \stackrel{?}{=} 0^2 - 2(0) - 8$ $-5 \stackrel{?}{=} (3)^2 - 2(3) - 8$

$-8 = -8$ ✔ $-5 \stackrel{?}{=} 9 - 6 - 8$

                     $-5 = -5$ ✔

Checks:

$$y + 8 = x$$

$-8 + 8 \stackrel{?}{=} 0$ $-5 + 8 \stackrel{?}{=} 3$

     $0 = 0$ ✔ $3 = 3$ ✔

Answer: $(0, -8)$ and $(3, -5)$

Practice

Solve each system algebraically.

1. $y + 13 = x$
   $y + 3 = x^2 - 6x$

2. $2x^2 - y = 10$
   $y = -2x^2 - 3x + 12$

3. $y - x = 2$
   $y = x^2 - 2x + 4$

4. $y = 2 - x$
   $y + 1 = x^2 + x - 5$

5. $x^2 = y + 10 - 3x$
   $y + 4 = 2x$

6. $y = 2x^2 - 7x + 3$
   $x - 3 = y$

7. $y = x^2 - 5x + 6$
   $y + 1 = 3x$

8. $y + 2x^2 = 4x + 7$
   $y + 4x = x^2 + 4$

9. $y = x^2 + 1$
   $2x + 3 + y = 3x^2$

Graphic Solutions to Systems

To solve systems graphically, you can graph the equations by hand using graph paper or use a graphing calculator. With either method, the common solution must be checked in both equations.

To solve using a graphing calculator, follow these steps:

- Press (Y=).
- Enter the first equation in Y_1 and the second equation in Y_2. (Note: The equations must be solved for y in order to graph them on the calculator.)
- Press (WINDOW) and set reasonable boundaries for x and y. You will be asked to enter Xmin and Xmax as well as Ymin and Ymax. (An alternate approach is to start with the standard viewing window. Press (ZOOM) (6) to produce a window that is 10 units in each direction.)
- Once the equations are shown on the screen, if the window is not appropriate, go back to the window settings and adjust the x- and y- values so you can see the full graph of both equations. Remember, you are looking for their intersection.
- To locate the intersection of the graphs, press (2nd) (TRACE), which brings you to the CALCULATE screen
- Choose 5: intersect. You will be asked to verify the curves being explored. Press (ENTER) after each question: First curve? (ENTER). Second curve? (ENTER). Guess? (ENTER). The calculator will then locate one of the solutions. To find the other solution, go back to the CALCULATE screen and press (5) again. This time, move the cursor closer to the other intersection point shown when you are asked about the curves. Use these steps to follow the model problem below.

MODEL PROBLEM

Solve the following system of equations: $y = x^2 + x - 6, y = x - 5$

SOLUTION

Step 1: Enter the equations in Y_1 and Y_2.

```
Plot1  Plot2  Plot3
\Y1=X²+X-6
\Y2=X-5
\Y3=█
\Y4=
\Y5=
\Y6=
\Y7=
```

Step 2: Select (ZOOM) (6) for a standard window.

```
ZOOM MEMORY
1:ZBox
2:Zoom In
3:Zoom Out
4:ZDecimal
5:ZSquare
6:ZStandard
7↓ZTrig
```

Step 3: Check the graphs to be sure they are visible in the standard window.

Step 4: 2nd TRACE brings you to the CALCULATE screen.

```
CALCULATE
1:value
2:zero
3:minimum
4:maximum
5:intersect
6:dy/dx
7:∫f(x)dx
```

Step 5: Select 5: intersect; ENTER ENTER ENTER to have the calculator display the first solution.

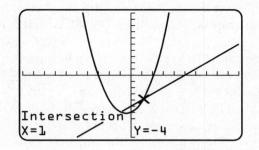

Step 6: Repeat Steps 4 and 5 to find the second solution.

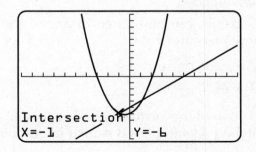

As you've discovered, the solutions to this system are the points whose coordinates are $(1, -4)$ and $(-1, -6)$. Again, this should be checked in each of the equations.

Answer: $(1, -4)$ and $(-1, -6)$

Exercises 1–6: Solve each system by graphing.

1 $x + 2 = y$
$y = -x^2 - 3x + 7$

2 $y = 3x^2 - 2x + 4$
$x + y = 6$

3 $y = 2x^2 - 5x + 1$
$y = 1 - x$

4 $y = x^2 - 4x$
$y = \dfrac{1}{2}x - 2$

5 $y + 3 = x^2 - x$
$y = 2x - 3$

6 $x^2 - y = 3x - 2$
$x + y = 5$

Exercises 7–12: Solve each system by whichever method you prefer.

7 $y = x^2 - 2x + 5$
$y - 2 = 2x$

8 $y = x^2 + x - 6$
$y = x^2 + 4x + 3$

9 $y = 2x^2 - 3x - 2$
$x^2 + y = 4$

10 $y = \dfrac{1}{2}x^2 - 6x - 9$
$y = 1 - 2x$

11 $y = 2x^2 - 5x - 3$
$y = 3x - 3$

12 $y = 3x^2 + 7x - 2$
$y = 2x - 4$

5.9 Quadratic Inequalities

Quadratic Inequalities in Two Variables

A quadratic inequality in two variables can be written in one of the following forms, where a, b, and c are real numbers and $a \neq 0$:

$y < ax^2 + bx + c$ $\qquad$ $y \leq ax^2 + bx + c$

$y > ax^2 + bx + c$ $\qquad$ $y \geq ax^2 + bx + c$

Its graph consists of all solutions (x, y) of the inequality.

Graphing a quadratic inequality in two variables is similar to graphing a linear inequality in two variables.

Let's review how to graph the inequality $y < 2x + 3$. First, we graph $y = 2x + 3$, which is the boundary line for the inequality. Since the inequality sign does *not* include the line $y = 2x + 3$, we use a dashed line. (If the inequality was $y \leq 2x + 3$, we would draw a solid line, since the boundary line is included in the solution.)

We select two test points, one on either side of the boundary line, and shade the region that includes the test point that is a solution of the inequality. The shaded region in the graph below contains all of the solutions (x, y) of the inequality.

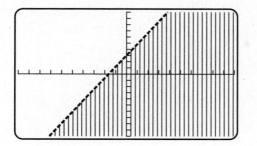

We will follow a similar procedure to graph the quadratic inequality $y < x^2 - x - 6$. First we graph $y = x^2 - x - 6$, which defines the boundary for the inequality. We make the parabola dashed since the boundary is not included in the solution.

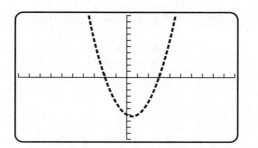

We select two test points, one inside the parabola and one outside the parabola, and shade the region that includes the test point that is a solution of the inequality.

For a point inside the parabola, let's choose $(0, 0)$ and test it by substituting the x- and y-values into the inequality.

$y < x^2 - x - 6$

$0 < 0^2 - 0 - 6$

$0 < -6$ False

For a point outside the parabola, let's choose $(5, 1)$ and test it.

$y < x^2 - x - 6$

$1 < 5^2 - 5 - 6$

$1 < 14$ True

Since (0, 0) is not a solution of the inequality, and (5, 1) is, we shade the region outside the parabola.

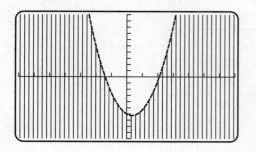

MODEL PROBLEM

Graph the inequality $y \geq 2x^2 - x - 6$.

SOLUTION

First graph the parabola $y = 2x^2 - x - 6$. This is shown as a solid parabola since the boundary is included in the solution.

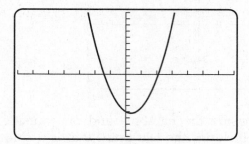

Now, test two different points, one point inside the parabola, and the other point outside the parabola. Choose the point (0, 4). We see that $4 \geq 2(0) - 0 - 6$ or $4 \geq -6$, which is true. We will shade inside the parabola.

To verify this, we can test another point outside the parabola. If we choose the point (5, 2), we can see that $2 \not\geq 2(5^2) - 5 - 6$ or $2 \not\geq 39$.

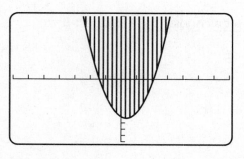

Revisiting Quadratic Inequalities in One Variable

In Section 1.8, we learned how to solve quadratic inequalities in one variable by factoring, and we graphed the solutions on number lines. For example, to solve the inequality $x^2 - 3x \leq x + 12$ algebraically, we rewrite the inequality so that all terms are on one side of the inequality symbol. We find the zeros of the equation $x^2 - 4x - 12 = 0$ and plot these points on a number line.

$$x^2 - 3x \leq x + 12$$

$$x^2 - 4x - 12 \leq 0$$

$$x^2 - 4x - 12 = 0$$

$$(x + 2)(x - 6) = 0$$

$$x = -2 \quad \text{or} \quad x = 6$$

Once we know these two values, we test three points, one to the left of -2, one between -2 and 6, and one to the right of 6. The solution falls in the areas in which our test points make the original inequality true.

Test value: $x = -3$

$$x^2 - 3x \leq x + 12$$

$$(-3)^2 - 3(-3) \overset{?}{\leq} -3 + 12$$

$$9 + 9 \overset{?}{\leq} 9$$

$$18 \leq 9 \text{ False}$$

Test value: $x = 0$

$$x^2 - 3x \leq x + 12$$

$$(0)^2 - 3(0) \overset{?}{\leq} 0 + 12$$

$$0 - 0 \overset{?}{\leq} 12$$

$$0 \leq 12 \text{ True}$$

Test value: $x = 8$

$$x^2 - 3x \leq x + 12$$

$$(8)^2 - 3(8) \overset{?}{\leq} 8 + 12$$

$$64 - 24 \overset{?}{\leq} 8 + 12$$

$$40 \leq 20 \text{ False}$$

Only the test value of x between -2 and 6 makes the inequality true, so the solution to this inequality is the shaded region on the number line below.

We can also use a calculator to illustrate the solution.

First, enter the left side of the inequality into Y_1 and the right side into Y_2 as shown below.

```
Plot1  Plot2  Plot3
\Y1=X2-3X
\Y2=X+12
\Y3=
\Y4=
\Y5=
\Y6=
\Y7=
```

Find the *x*-values for which $Y_1 \le Y_2$, by using the calculator to find the intersection points.

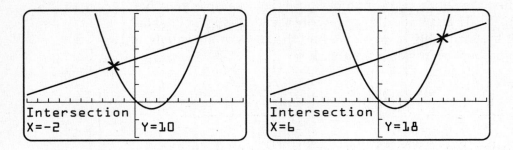

The parabola is below the line when *x* is between -2 and 6.

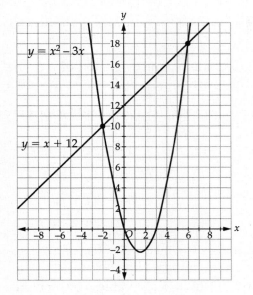

We can see from the graph above that when $-2 \le x \le 6$, $x^2 - 3x \le x + 12$ is true. This is consistent with the solution shown on the number line.

Alternatively, we could have rewritten the inequality as $x^2 - 4x - 12 \le 0$, entered the expression $x^2 - 4x - 12$ into Y_1, and graphed the parabola as shown below.

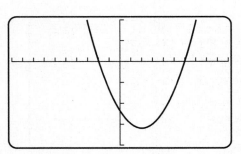

We find the two values of x for which $x^2 - 4x - 12 = 0$.

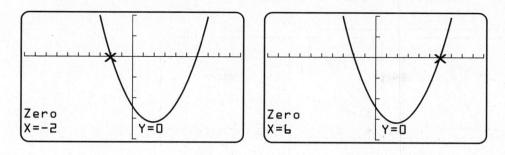

Since the parabola lies below the x-axis when x is between -2 and 6, the solution to the inequality $x^2 - 4x - 12 \leq 0$ is $-2 \leq x \leq 6$.

MODEL PROBLEM

Solve the inequality $7x > 2x^2 + 3$.

SOLUTION

To solve algebraically, regroup terms on one side of the inequality and factor as you would an equation to find the boundary values.

$7x > 2x^2 + 3$

$0 > 2x^2 - 7x + 3$

$0 = (2x - 1)(x - 3)$

$x = \dfrac{1}{2} \qquad x = 3$

The boundaries to the solution set are $\dfrac{1}{2}$ and 3. Now we test values between these boundaries as well as outside.

Test value: $x = 0$

$7x > 2x^2 + 3$

$7(0) \overset{?}{>} 2(0)^2 + 3$

$0 \overset{?}{>} 0 + 3$

$0 > 3$ False

Test value: $x = 1$

$7x > 2x^2 + 3$

$7(1) \overset{?}{>} 2(1)^2 + 3$

$7 \overset{?}{>} 2 + 3$

$7 > 5$ True

Test value: $x = 4$

$7x > 2x^2 + 3$

$7(4) \overset{?}{>} 2(4)^2 + 3$

$28 \overset{?}{>} 32 + 3$

$28 > 35$ False

Answer: Therefore, the solution is $\dfrac{1}{2} < x < 3$.

To solve the inequality from the model problem on page 207 graphically, enter the left side of the inequality in Y_1 and the right side in Y_2 and graph.

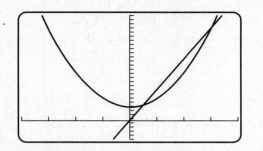

(Window: Xmin = –4, Xmax = 4; Ymin = –4, Ymax = 24)

Use the calculator to find the intersection points.

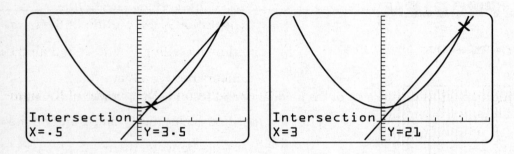

We can see that the line is above the parabola when x is between $\dfrac{1}{2}$ and 3. This is consistent with the solution shown on the number line in the answer.

Practice

Exercises 1–10: Graph each inequality.

1 $y > 3x^2 - 2x - 1$

2 $y \le 4x^2 + x - 5$

3 $y < 2x^2 + 5x + 2$

4 $y \ge 2x^2 - x - 15$

5 $y < -x^2 + 3x - 2$

6 $y \le x^2 - 6x - 16$

7 $y > x^2 - 4$

8 $y \le x^2 - 3x$

9 $y < -2x^2 + x + 3$

10 $y \le 5 - 3x - 2x^2$

Exercises 11–15: Select the numeral preceding the choice that best answers the question.

11 Which ordered pair is a solution to the inequality $y \ge x^2 - 3x - 5$?

(1) $(-10, -1)$
(2) $(-10, 1)$
(3) $(4, -5)$
(4) $(4, 5)$

12 Which inequality corresponds to the solution set shown below?

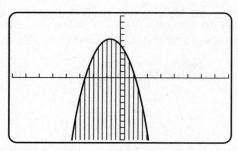

(Window: Xmin = –8, Xmax = 8; Ymin = –10, Ymax = 10)

(1) $y \geq -2x^2 + 5x + 2$
(2) $y \geq -2x^2 - 5x + 2$
(3) $y \leq -2x^2 + 5x + 2$
(4) $y \leq -2x^2 - 5x + 2$

13 Which graph shows the solution to the inequality $-3x^2 - 2x + 8 > 0$?

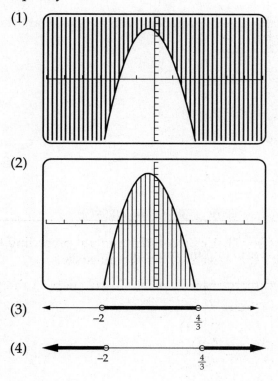

(1)

(2)

(3)

(4)

14 Which point is *not* in the solution set of $y < 3x^2 + 4x - 4$?

(1) $(0, 0)$
(2) $(-2, 0)$
(3) $(0, -2)$
(4) $\left(\dfrac{3}{4}, \dfrac{11}{16} \right)$

15 Given the inequality $y \geq 3x^2 - 5x + 2$, which statement is true?

(1) The solution includes all values of (x, y) that lie within the parabola, including those values on the parabola.
(2) The solution includes all values of (x, y) that lie outside the parabola, including those values on the parabola.
(3) The solution is the portion of the number line including $\dfrac{1}{3}$ and 2, and all the numbers between them.
(4) The solution is the portion of the number line excluding $\dfrac{1}{3}$ and 2 and all the numbers between them.

Exercises 16–20: Use a graph to solve each of the following inequalities.

16 $x^2 + 5x \leq 6$

17 $2x^2 + 7x \geq 4$

18 $x^2 - 4x > x + 14$

19 $3x^2 - 11x < 4$

20 $-x^2 + 12 > 5x - 12$

Exercises 21–23: Make a number line to illustrate the solution set to each of the inequalities in questions 16–18. Check your solution by solving the inequalities algebraically.

FYI

Many of the calculations we have done in this chapter can be performed using a graphing calculator. This section will illustrate how to utilize the calculator to perform some of these computations. First press (MODE) and then select $a + bi$, as shown below.

Note: Although some calculations do not require complex mode, this setting is needed for other calculations.

```
Normal Sci Eng
Float 0123456789
Radian Degree
Func Par Pol Seq
Connected Dot
Sequential Simul
Real a+bi re^θi
Full Horiz G-T
```

To add, subtract, multiply, or divide two complex numbers, simply enter the numbers with the operation symbol. The symbol for "i" is located on the bottom row of the calculator above the decimal point. To use it, you must press (2nd) (.).

The following screen illustrates how to enter into your calculator several operations with complex numbers.

```
(2-6i)+(-5-9i)
                    -3-15i
(1+7i)(2-4i)
                    30+10i
(3+i)/(2-i)
                       1+i
```

For some added features, go to the MATH CPX menu by pressing (MATH) (►) (►) (ENTER).

Option 1: conj (returns the complex conjugate of a complex number)

The example below illustrates how to use the graphing calculator to find the conjugate of $3 + 5i$.

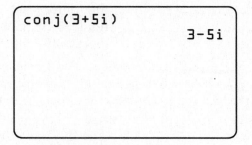

Thus, we can utilize the calculator to multiply a complex number by its conjugate. Enter the information as shown in the screen below.

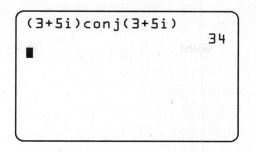

Option 2: real (returns the real part of a complex number)

Option 3: imag (returns the imaginary part of a complex number)

These are illustrated in the screen below.

```
real(5+6i)
                        5
imag(5+6i)
                        6
```

Limitations: The graphing calculator can help with many of your complex calculations. However, notice the two examples given below.

```
(2+√(-9))+(5+√(-4))
                     7+5i
(2+√(-5))+(5+√(-20))
            7+6.708203932i
```

The first example: $\left(2 + \sqrt{-9}\right) + \left(5 + \sqrt{-4}\right)$ is easily computed as $7 + 5i$ by the calculator. However, the second answer, to $\left(2 + \sqrt{-5}\right) + \left(5 + \sqrt{-20}\right)$, is given as a decimal equivalent to the exact answer of $7 + 3i\sqrt{5}$. Please be aware that, if you are asked for an *exact answer*, a decimal equivalent will be marked wrong.

Our advice to you: Master the skills in this, and every, chapter. Your calculator is a valuable tool. Learn how to use the calculator, but more important, learn *when* to use it and when not to use it.

Go back over the problems from the Practice sections of this chapter. See how the calculator can assist you in answering some of the questions, and when the calculator should not be used.

Exercises 1–22: Select the numeral preceding the choice that best completes the statement or answers the question.

1 The roots of the quadratic equation $3x^2 - x - 3 = x^2 - 5x - 7$ are

(1) real, rational, and equal
(2) real, rational, and unequal
(3) real, irrational, and unequal
(4) imaginary

2 What is the product of the roots of the equation $x^2 - 6x - 2 = 0$?

(1) 6   (3) −2
(2) 2   (4) −6

3 The expression $2i^6 - 3i^2$ equals

(1) 1   (3) $-1i^4$
(2) −1   (4) $-6i^{12}$

4 Which represents the product of $3 - 4i$ and its conjugate?

(1) −7   (3) $\dfrac{25}{3 + 4i}$
(2) $\dfrac{3 + 4i}{25}$ (4) 25

5 The value of $\sqrt{-9} \cdot \sqrt{-16}$ is

(1) −12   (3) $12i$
(2) 12   (4) ± 12

6 In which quadrant would you find the sum of $\left(2 - \sqrt{-4}\right) + \left(-5 + \sqrt{-36}\right)$?

(1) I   (3) III
(2) II   (4) IV

7 The expression $i^3 + i(2 - i)$ is equivalent to

(1) $-1 + 3i$ (3) $1 + i$
(2) $1 - i$ (4) $1 + 3i$

8 Which is a factor of $x^3 - 125$?

(1) $x + 5$ (3) $x + 25$
(2) $x - 5$ (4) $x - 25$

9 If a quadratic equation with real coefficients has a discriminant whose value is 25, then the two roots must be

(1) real, rational, and equal
(2) real, irrational, and unequal
(3) real, rational, and unequal
(4) imaginary

10 Which might be the value of the discriminant of a quadratic equation whose graph lies entirely above the x-axis?

(1) −10   (3) 6
(2) 0   (4) 9

11 For which value of k will the roots of $3x^2 + kx + 2 = 1$ be real?

(1) 1   (3) 3
(2) 2   (4) 4

12 What is the solution set of the equation $x^2 + 25 = 0$?

(1) { }   (3) $\{5i\}$
(2) $\{-5i\}$ (4) $\{-5i, 5i\}$

13 The expression $\dfrac{3}{2 + 3i}$ is equivalent to which of the following?

(1) $\dfrac{6 - 9i}{13}$ (3) $-\dfrac{6 - 9i}{5}$
(2) $\dfrac{-6 + 9i}{13}$ (4) $\dfrac{2 - 3i}{3}$

14 Which represents a real number?

(1) $-5 + 3i$ (3) $2 - \sqrt{5}$
(2) $5i\sqrt{2}$ (4) $0 - 7i$

15 The reciprocal of $12 - 3i$ is

(1) $12 + 3i$ (3) $\dfrac{12 + 3i}{153}$
(2) $-9i$ (4) $\dfrac{12 + 3i}{135}$

16 How many solutions does the following system of equations have?

$y = x^2 - x - 2$
$y = -x^2 + 3x - 5$

(1) 1   (3) 3
(2) 2   (4) 0

17 The expression $\dfrac{\sqrt{-50}}{\sqrt{-2}}$ is equivalent to

(1) 5   (3) −5
(2) $5i$ (4) $-5i$

18 When simplified, $(1 + 2i)^2 - 4i$ equals

(1) $1 + 4i$ (3) 5
(2) $1 - 4i^2$ (4) −3

19 Which is *not* a factor of the expression $x^3 + 3x^2 - 4x - 12$?

(1) $x + 4$ (3) $x + 2$
(2) $x + 3$ (4) $x - 2$

20 The product of $12i^7 \cdot 3i^3$ is
(1) -36 (3) 36
(2) $36i$ (4) $-36i$

21 When simplified, $4\sqrt{-18} + \dfrac{3}{2}\sqrt{-32}$ becomes

(1) $18i\sqrt{2}$ (3) $6i\sqrt{50}$
(2) $36i$ (4) $36i\sqrt{2}$

22 In which quadrant would you find the difference $\left(4 - 2\sqrt{-9}\right) - \left(5 + 3\sqrt{-4}\right)$?

(1) I   (3) III
(2) II   (4) IV

23 Solve by completing the square.

a $x^2 - 6x + 5 = 0$
b $x^2 - 2x + 3 = 2x + 6$
c $x^2 + 3x = x + 7$

24 Solve by using the quadratic formula.

a $x^2 - 10x + 5 = 0$
b $x^2 + 2x - 4 = 3x - 8$
c $2x^2 = 3x - 2$

25 Solve by using any method you prefer.

a $x^2 - 3x + 2 = 0$
b $x^2 + x + 5 = 0$
c $x^2 + 4x + 1 = 0$
d $x^2 - 4x = 2$
e $2x^2 - x = x^2 + 2x + 40$
f $2x^2 + 5x = x - 4$
g $3x^2 - 2x + 1 = 4$
h $x^3 - 7x^2 = -12x$
i $x^3 + 4x^2 = 4x + 16$

26 Olivia is standing on the 102nd floor of the Empire State Building, thinking about mathematics. She realizes that, if she were able to throw a ball from her present position, the height of the ball in feet, h, at time t seconds could be modeled by the equation $h = -16t^2 + 64t + 1{,}224$.

a How high above the ground, in feet, is the 102nd floor?
b What is the greatest height the ball would reach?
c How long would it take to reach that height?
d How long would it take the ball to hit the ground?

27 Express in simplest $a + bi$ form: $(4 - i)^2 + 5i^2 - 4i(3 + 2i^3)$

28 Solve each system of equations for x and y, and check.

a $y = x^2 + 2x + 7$
  $y = x + 13$
b $y^2 - x^2 = 11$
  $y = x + 1$
c $y = 2x^2 + 6x + 3$
  $y = x^2 - x - 7$

29 The Verrazano-Narrows Bridge, which connects Brooklyn to Staten Island, is the eighth longest suspension bridge in the world. The length of the main span is 4,260 feet. The roadway is suspended by cables that are supported by two towers that are 700 feet tall. The clearance at the center is 228 feet.

a The parabola graphed below represents the height of the cables above the water. The y-axis represents the center of the bridge. What are the coordinates of point P? What do these coordinates represent?

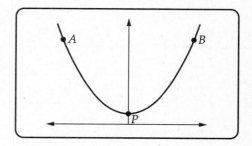

b Points A and B represent the height of each of the two towers. What are the coordinates of points A and B?
c The height of the cables above water can be represented by the equation $y = 0.000104x^2 + 228$, where x is the distance from the center of the bridge. What do the coordinates $(100, 229.04)$ represent?
d Find y when $x = 1{,}000$. Explain what x and y represent.
e Find y when $x = -1{,}000$. Explain what x and y represent.
f Find x when $y = 500$. Explain what x and y represent.

30 Simplify $\dfrac{3 - 2i}{-1 + 2i}$.

31 Express the roots of the equation $x^2 + 5x = 3x - 3$ in simplest $a + bi$ form.

32 Given $y = x^2 - 6x - 3$. Complete the square to determine the vertex of the parabola.

33 Write an equation whose roots are -8 and 6.

34 Solve, to the nearest tenth.

    a $x^3 + 2x^2 - 5x = 2$
    b $x^4 + 3x^3 = 5x + 6$

35 Write an equation that has a root of $2 - 5i$.

36 Find the solution, to the nearest tenth, of $x - 4 = \sqrt{x + 4}$.

37 What is the sum of the roots of the equation $3x^2 - 4x = x^2 - 8x + 5$?

38 If $z_1 = 5 - 2i$ and $z_2 = -3 - 5i$

    a Graphically show the vectors z_1 and z_2.
    b Graphically show the sum of z_1 and z_2.

39 Solve $4x^2 + 3x - 10 \le 0$ for x and graph the solution set on a number line.

40 Solve $y < -2x^2 + 3x + 14$ for x and graph the solution set.

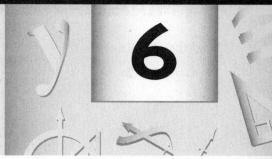

CHAPTER 6

Sequences and Series

6.1 Sequences

Look at the following figure and see if you can recognize the pattern.

Stage 1   Stage 2   Stage 3   Stage 4   Stage 5

☆   ☆☆☆   ☆☆☆   ☆☆☆☆   ☆☆☆☆☆
                  ☆☆   ☆☆☆   ☆☆☆☆

Let a_n be the number of stars in the nth stage. Thus, $a_1 = 1$, $a_2 = 3$, $a_3 = 5$, $a_4 = 7$, and $a_5 = 9$. Each stage has 2 more stars than the previous stage.

Therefore, the number of stars in stage n would be 2 more than the number of stars in stage $(n - 1)$, or $a_n = a_{n-1} + 2$. This is a **recursive** definition of the number of stars in each stage, because it is dependent on the number of stars in the previous stage.

A recursive definition is obtained by looking at the pattern formed. Each term is defined as a function of preceding terms. It is an example of an **iterative procedure**. When a recursive definition is supplied, the value of at least one term in the sequence must be supplied as well.

We could also give an **explicit** definition of the number of stars in each stage by noticing that $a_n = 2n - 1$ where n is the number of the term in the sequence. An explicit definition gives the formula based on the general term a_n. It enables us to directly compute any term.

The number of stars in each stage, 1, 3, 5, 7, 9, forms a sequence. A **sequence** is an ordered set of mathematical objects. It is a function whose domain is a set of consecutive integers. However, we usually represent a sequence by subscript notation rather than by function notation. The subscripts make up the domain of the sequence, and they serve to identify the location of a term within the sequence. In the example above, the domain is {1, 2, 3, 4, 5}. We see that a_3 is the third term of the sequence, and $a_3 = 5$ indicates the number of stars in the third stage.

Each number in the sequence is said to be a **term** of the sequence. The terms of the sequence form the range of the function. In the example above, the range is {1, 3, 5, 7, 9}. This is illustrated in the table below.

Stage Number	n	1	2	3	4	5	Domain
Number of Stars	a_n	1	3	5	7	9	Range

A **finite sequence** has a limited number of terms. An **infinite sequence** continues on forever.

MODEL PROBLEMS

1 List the first three terms of each sequence.

   a $a_n = n^2 + 2$
   b $a_n = (n + 1)(n + 2)$
   c $a_n = 2a_{n-1} + 3, \quad a_1 = 5$
   d $a_n = (a_{n-1})^2, \quad a_1 = 3$

SOLUTION

   a $a_n = n^2 + 2$

To find the first three terms, we substitute 1, 2, and 3 into the formula.

$a_1 = 1^2 + 2 = 1 + 2 = 3$

$a_2 = 2^2 + 2 = 4 + 2 = 6$

$a_3 = 3^2 + 2 = 9 + 2 = 11$

The first three terms are 3, 6, 11.

   b $a_n = (n + 1)(n + 2)$

To find the first three terms, we substitute 1, 2, and 3 into the formula.

$a_1 = (1 + 1)(1 + 2) = (2)(3) = 6$

$a_2 = (2 + 1)(2 + 2) = (3)(4) = 12$

$a_3 = (3 + 1)(3 + 2) = (4)(5) = 20$

The first three terms are 6, 12, 20.

   c $a_n = 2a_{n-1} + 3, \quad a_1 = 5$

We are given that the first term, a_1, is 5.

To find the second term, we multiply a_1 by 2 and then add 3.

$a_2 = 2a_1 + 3 = 2(5) + 3 = 10 + 3 = 13$

We continue in this manner to find additional terms.

$a_3 = 2a_2 + 3 = 2(13) + 3 = 26 + 3 = 29$

The first three terms are 5, 13, 29.

   d $a_n = (a_{n-1})^2, \quad a_1 = 3$

We are given that the first term, a_1, is 3.

To find the second term, we square a_1.

$a_2 = (a_1)^2 = 3^2 = 9$

We continue in this manner to find additional terms.

$a_3 = (a_2)^2 = 9^2 = 81$

The first three terms are 3, 9, 81.

Answers: **a** 3, 6, 11   **b** 6, 12, 20   **c** 5, 13, 29   **d** 3, 9, 81

2 Write both a recursive and an explicit definition for each of the following sequences.

    a 4, 8, 12, 16, 20
    b 5, 8, 11, 14, 17

SOLUTION

    a 4, 8, 12, 16, 20

To find a recursive definition, we must determine how each term is formed based on the preceding term. We begin with the first term, $a_1 = 4$. We see that each term is 4 more than the preceding term.

The recursive definition is $a_1 = 4$, $a_n = a_{n-1} + 4$.

To find an explicit definition, we see that $4 = 4 \bullet 1$, $8 = 4 \bullet 2$, $12 = 4 \bullet 3$, $16 = 4 \bullet 4$, and $20 = 4 \bullet 5$.

$a_n = 4n$

    b 5, 8, 11, 14, 17

As above, to find a recursive definition, we must determine how each term is formed based on the preceding term. We begin with $a_1 = 5$. We see that each term is 3 more than the preceding term.

$a_n = a_{n-1} + 3$

The recursive definition is $a_1 = 5$, $a_n = a_{n-1} + 3$.

To find an explicit definition, we see that $5 = 3 \bullet 1 + 2$, $8 = 3 \bullet 2 + 2$, $11 = 3 \bullet 3 + 2$, $14 = 3 \bullet 4 + 2$, and $17 = 3 \bullet 5 + 2$.

$a_n = 3n + 2$

Answers: **a** recursive: $a_1 = 4$, $a_n = a_{n-1} + 4$ explicit: $a_n = 4n$
                b recursive: $a_1 = 5$, $a_n = a_{n-1} + 3$ explicit: $a_n = 3n + 2$

✏️ Practice

Exercises 1–5: Describe in words each pattern formed. Find the next three terms.

1 5, 10, 15, 20, 25, 30

2 7, 12, 17, 22, 27, 32

3 11, 22, 44, 88, 176

4 1, 8, 27, 64, 125

5 2, 9, 28, 65, 126

Exercises 6–10: List the first three terms of each sequence.

6 $a_n = 4n - 1$

7 $a_n = 3(n + 1)$

8 $a_n = (n + 6)(n - 2)$

9 $a_n = 3a_{n-1} - 1, a_1 = 2$

10 $a_n = 2a_{n-1} - n, a_1 = 6$

Exercises 11–15: Write a possible recursive definition for the nth term of each sequence.

11 4, 6, 8, 10, 12, 14

12 5, 7, 9, 11, 13, 15

13 5, 10, 20, 40, 80

14 2, 5, 11, 23, 47, 95

15 1, 2, 5, 14, 41, 122

Exercises 16–20: Write a possible explicit definition for the nth term of each sequence.

16 2, 4, 6, 8, 10

17 1, 3, 5, 7, 9

18 1, 4, 9, 16, 25

19 0, 3, 8, 15, 24

20 2, 6, 12, 20, 30

21 Leonardo of Pisa, better known as Fibonacci, studied a sequence of numbers with a unique type of rule for determining the next number in the sequence. He began the sequence with 1, 1, 2, 3, 5, 8, and then calculated each successive number from the sum of the previous two. His *Liber Abaci*, published in 1202, introduced this sequence to Western European mathematics.

The original problem Fibonacci investigated was how fast rabbits could breed in ideal circumstances. Suppose we begin with a newly born pair of rabbits, one male and one female. Assume that the rabbits are able to mate at the age of one month, so at the end of its second month a female can produce another pair of rabbits. Suppose that our rabbits never die and that each female always produces one new pair (one male, one female) every month from the second month on.

a How many pairs will there be in one year?

b Write a recursive formula to be used in calculating this sequence.

22 A supermarket employee is stocking cans in the shape of a pyramid with a square base, as shown in the diagram below.

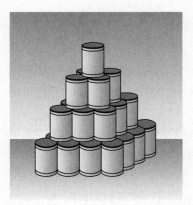

There is 1 can in the top layer, 4 cans in the second layer, 9 cans in the third layer, 16 cans in the fourth layer, 25 cans in the fifth layer, etc.

a If the pyramid were extended to the tenth layer, how many cans would be in that layer?

b Write a formula to model the number of cans in the nth layer.

6.2 Arithmetic Sequences

We will now look at a special type of sequence, called an **arithmetic sequence**. In an arithmetic sequence, the difference between consecutive terms is constant. A recursive definition of an arithmetic sequence will show that each term in the sequence is obtained by adding a constant value to the previous term. This constant value is known as d, the **common difference**. Let us look at an example.

In the Marquis Theater in New York City, there are 12 seats in the center orchestra seating of row A, 13 seats in the center orchestra seating of row B, 14 seats in row C, and so on. This pattern continues until row O. There is no row I in this theater. Jennifer and Evan plan to visit New York City and would like to take all of their relatives to the Marquis Theater to see a Broadway show. If there are 20 people who would like to sit together in center orchestra seating, what is the first row that would accommodate them?

To solve this problem, we can certainly count: 12 seats in row A, 13 in row B, 14 in row C, . . . 20 in row J. (Remember, there is no row I.)

We could use a recursive formula to determine which row would contain 20 seats:

$$a_1 = 12$$
$$a_2 = 13$$
$$a_3 = 14$$
$$\cdot$$
$$\cdot$$
$$\cdot$$
$$a_n = a_{n-1} + 1$$

By following through with this formula, we would see that $a_9 = 20$. Since there is no row I, we could then determine that row J contains 20 seats.

However, there is an easier way to calculate a_n.

When we list the successive terms in the arithmetic sequence, we see a pattern. This is an arithmetic sequence with a common difference of 1.

$$12, 12 + 1, 12 + 2(1), 12 + 3(1), 12 + 4(1) \ldots$$

$a_1, a_1 + d, a_1 + 2d, a_1 + 3d, a_1 + 4d, \ldots, a_1 + (n-1)d$. Thus, the formula for the nth term of an arithmetic sequence is

$$a_n = a_1 + (n-1)d.$$

To solve the problem above, we know that $a_n = 20$, $a_1 = 12$, and $d = 1$. We can substitute the information into the formula and solve for n.

$$a_n = a_1 + (n-1)d$$
$$20 = 12 + (n-1)(1)$$
$$8 = n - 1$$
$$n = 9$$

We see that there are 20 seats in the ninth row, which is row J.

MODEL PROBLEMS

1 Determine whether each sequence is arithmetic, and if so, find the common difference.

   a 5, 11, 17, 23, 29, . . .
   b 4, 8, 16, 32, 64, . . .
   c 20, 16, 12, 8, 4, . . .
   d 1, 4, 9, 16, 25, 36, . . .

SOLUTION

   a 5, 11, 17, 23, 29, . . .

By looking at any two consecutive terms, we see that the difference is always 6. Yes, this is an arithmetic sequence. The common difference is 6.

   b 4, 8, 16, 32, 64, . . .

The difference between the first and second terms is 4, but the difference between the second and third terms is 8. The difference is not constant. This is not an arithmetic sequence.

   c 20, 16, 12, 8, 4, . . .

The difference between any two consecutive terms is -4. Yes, this is an arithmetic sequence. The common difference is -4.

d 1, 4, 9, 16, 25, 36, . . .

The difference between the first and second terms is 3. The difference between the second and third terms is 5. The difference is not constant. This is not an arithmetic sequence.

2   Given the arithmetic sequence 6, 10, 14, 18, 22 . . . , find the 20th term.

SOLUTION

We will use the formula $a_n = a_1 + (n - 1)d$ to find a_{20}.

We see that $a_1 = 6, n = 20, d = 4$.

$a_n = a_1 + (n - 1)d$

$a_{20} = 6 + (19)(4)$

$a_{20} = 6 + 76$

$a_{20} = 82$

Answer: $a_{20} = 82$

3   Write a rule for the *n*th term of an arithmetic sequence that has two given terms of $a_4 = 36$ and $a_9 = 61$.

SOLUTION

Use the general formula for arithmetic sequences:

$a_n = a_1 + (n - 1)d$

Thus, $a_4 = a_1 + (4 - 1)d = a_1 + 3d$ and $a_9 = a_1 + (9 - 1)d = a_1 + 8d$.

Using the two equations above, solve for *d*:

$a_4 = a_1 + 3d$

Since $a_4 = 36$,

$36 = a_1 + 3d$

Since $a_9 = 61$,

$a_9 = a_1 + 8d$

$61 = a_1 + 8d$

Write the two equations as a system and subtract.

$61 = a_1 + 8d$

$\underline{-36 = a_1 + 3d}$

$25 = 5d$

$5 = d$

Since $a_1 = 36 - 3d$ and $d = 5, a_1 = 36 - 15 = 21$.

Substitute $a_1 = 21$ and $d = 5$ into the formula:

$a_n = a_1 + (n - 1)d$

$a_n = 21 + 5(n - 1)$

Answer: $a_n = 16 + 5n$

The terms between any two nonconsecutive terms of an arithmetic sequence are called **arithmetic means**. In the sequence 10, 20, 30, 40, 50, 60, 70, 80, the numbers 40 and 50 are the arithmetic means between 30 and 60.

MODEL PROBLEM

4 Form a sequence that has three arithmetic means between 7 and 27.

SOLUTION

If there are three arithmetic means between 7 and 27, there will be five terms in our sequence. Thus, $a_1 = 7$ and $a_5 = 27$. (Alternatively, the sequence could begin with 27 and end with 7. This will not affect the means.)

$a_n = a_1 + (n - 1)d$

$a_5 = a_1 + 4d$

$27 = 7 + 4d$

$20 = 4d$

$d = 5$

Our sequence begins with 7 and ends with 27, with a common difference of 5.

Answer: 7, 12, 17, 22, 27

 **Practice**

Exercises 1–10: Determine if each sequence is arithmetic. If it is arithmetic, give the common difference and the next two terms.

1 6, 12, 18, 24, . . .

2 1, 3, 9, 27, . . .

3 7, 3, −1, −5, . . .

4 $n, 5n, 9n, 13n, . . .$

5 $4, 2, 1, \dfrac{1}{2}, . . .$

6 −8, 8, 24, 40, . . .

7 $-b, 0, b, 2b, . . .$

8 −12, −18, −24, −30, . . .

9 31, 27, 23, 19, . . .

10 $2c, 4c, 8c, 16c, . . .$

11 Write the first four terms of an arithmetic sequence that has a first term of 12 and a common difference of −3.

12 Find d if $a_2 = 6$ and $a_6 = 30$.

13 Find the 20th term of the sequence −12, −7, −2, 3, ...

14 Form a sequence that has two arithmetic means between 18 and 30, and obtain a formula for a_n.

15 Find the first term of an arithmetic sequence for which $d = 3$ and $a_5 = 25$.

16 Write a rule for the nth term of an arithmetic sequence if $d = -4$ and $a_{10} = 66$.

17 When Johnny was a year old, his grandparents gave him $50. For each birthday, they increased their previous gift amount by $50: they gave him $100 for his second birthday, $150 for his third birthday, etc. If this pattern continued, how much would they give Johnny for his eighteenth birthday?

18 Sol is trying to get into shape for his Caribbean cruise. He will begin his exercise routine by doing 3 crunches today. He will do 2 additional crunches each day until he leaves for his cruise in 30 days. How many crunches will he do on the 30th day?

19 The bottom step of a brick staircase is made of 50 bricks. The second step has 47 bricks, the third step has 44 bricks, etc. This pattern continues up to the 15th step. How many bricks does the 15th step contain?

20 If the first term of an arithmetic sequence is doubled, but the common difference remains the same, would the nth term be doubled? Explain.

6.3 Sigma Notation

Sometimes we want to find the sum of the terms a sequence. For example, in Section 6.2 we examined the seating available in a theater. As you may recall, there are 12 seats in row A, 13 seats in row B, 14 seats in row C, etc. This pattern continues until row O. There is no row I in this theater. To find the total number of seats available in the center orchestra section of rows A through O, we have to add the number of seats in each row, $12 + 13 + 14 + 15 + \cdots + 24 + 25$. A sum of all the terms in a sequence, like this one, is called a **series**.

The Greek capital letter sigma, written $\sum$, is used to indicate **summation**. The

sigma notation $\sum\limits_{n=1}^{14} (12 + 1(n - 1)) = \sum\limits_{n=1}^{14} (12 + n - 1) = \sum\limits_{n=1}^{14} (11 + n)$ means find the sum of all the $(11 + n)$ terms for every consecutive integer n, from $n = 1$ through $n = 14$. The n in this notation represents the **index**. The lower limit or starting value of the index appears below the sigma, and the upper limit or ending value of the index is found above the sigma. We can calculate

$$\sum\limits_{n=1}^{14} (11 + n) = (11 + 1) + (11 + 2) + (11 + 3) + (11 + 4) + \cdots (11 + 14)$$

$$= 12 + 13 + 14 + 15 + \cdots + 25$$

$$= 259$$

There are 259 seats in rows A through O of this section of the theater.

> Note: When using sigma notation, i does not indicate the imaginary unit equivalent to $\sqrt{-1}$. Any letter can be used to represent the index, but mathematical convention usually assigns the letters i, j, k, or n.

MODEL PROBLEMS

1 Evaluate $\sum\limits_{i=4}^{7} (3i - 2)$.

SOLUTION

$$\sum\limits_{i=4}^{7} (3i - 2) = (3(4) - 2) + (3(5) - 2) + (3(6) - 2) + (3(7) - 2) = 10 + 13 + 16 + 19 = 58$$

Answer: 58

2 Evaluate $\sum\limits_{k=1}^{5} k^3$.

SOLUTION

$$\sum_{k=1}^{5} k^3 = 1^3 + 2^3 + 3^3 + 4^3 + 5^3 = 1 + 8 + 27 + 64 + 125 = 225$$

Answer: 225

3 Evaluate $2 \sum\limits_{j=1}^{3} (j^{j-1})$

SOLUTION

In the expression $2 \sum\limits_{j=1}^{3} (j^{j-1})$, the 2 is the coefficient of the sigma term, indicating that the sum is to be multiplied by 2.

$$2 \sum_{j=1}^{3} (j^{j-1}) = 2(1^{1-1} + 2^{2-1} + 3^{3-1})$$
$$= 2(1^0 + 2^1 + 3^2)$$
$$= 2(1 + 2 + 9)$$
$$= 24$$

Note that $\sum\limits_{j=1}^{3} 2(j^{j-1}) = 2(1^0) + 2(2^1) + 2(3^2) = 24$.

Therefore, $2 \sum\limits_{j=1}^{3} (j^{j-1}) = \sum\limits_{j=1}^{3} 2(j^{j-1})$.

Answer: 24

4 If $x_1 = 19$, $x_2 = 20$, $x_3 = 26$, $x_4 = 30$, and $\dfrac{1}{5} \sum\limits_{i=1}^{5} x_i = 24$, what is the value of x_5?

   (1) 20   (2) 24   (3) 25   (4) 26

SOLUTION

The data in this problem are defined with subscripted terms, $x_1 = 19$, $x_2 = 20$, $x_3 = 26$, and $x_4 = 30$. We are looking for the fifth term, x_5. The expression $\dfrac{1}{5} \sum\limits_{i=1}^{5} x_i$ indicates that the average of the five terms equals 24. Hence, we want to find the sum of the four terms that we do know and solve for the fifth term.

$$\frac{1}{5} \sum_{i=1}^{5} x_i = \frac{1}{5}(x_1 + x_2 + x_3 + x_4 + x_5)$$
$$= \frac{1}{5}(19 + 20 + 26 + 30 + x_5)$$
$$= \frac{1}{5}(95 + x_5)$$

Based on the question, we know this equals 24.

Substitute 24 for $\frac{1}{5} \sum_{i=1}^{5} x_i$ into the left side of the equation and solve:

$$24 = \frac{1}{5}(95 + x_5)$$

$$120 = 95 + x_5$$

$$25 = x_5$$

Answer: 25

5 Using sigma notation, write an expression that indicates the sum $\frac{4}{3} + \frac{9}{4} + \frac{16}{5} + \frac{25}{6} + \frac{36}{7}$.

SOLUTION

To solve this problem, look for patterns. Examine the numerators and denominators of these fractions separately.

$$\frac{4}{3} \qquad \frac{9}{4} \qquad \frac{16}{5} \qquad \frac{25}{6} \qquad \frac{36}{7}$$

The numerators are all perfect squares and the denominators are consecutive integers. One approach is to set the index to begin at 3 and include all integer values through 7. Looking at the numerators again, we can observe that the numerators are the squares of 1 less than each denominator. Therefore, one way of writing this summation is: $\sum_{j=3}^{7} \frac{(j-1)^2}{j}$.

This sigma notation, however, is not unique. An alternate, equally correct solution would be to start with $k = 2$ and restate the summation as $\sum_{k=2}^{6} \frac{k^2}{(k+1)}$. To check that these are equivalent summations, you may want to write them out for yourself. There is often more than one way to express a series in sigma notation.

 **Practice**

Exercises 1–12: Find the value of each expression indicated in sigma notation.

1 $\sum_{i=0}^{4} (i + 2)$

2 $\sum_{j=4}^{8} (3j - 5)$

3 $\frac{1}{2} \sum_{k=1}^{4} (13 - 3k)$

4 $3 \sum_{n=2}^{5} n$

5 $\sum_{k=7}^{10} (k - 6)^2$

6 $\sum_{k=1}^{4} \left(\frac{2k + 3}{k} \right)$

7 $\sum_{n=0}^{4} 3^n$

8 $\sum_{i=1}^{5} (2i^2)$

9 $2 \sum_{k=3}^{5} (k^2 + k)$

10 $\displaystyle\sum_{j=1}^{4} 4\left(\frac{1}{2}\right)^j$

11 $\displaystyle\frac{1}{3}\sum_{i=0}^{3} i^3$

12 $\displaystyle\sum_{n=1}^{3} (3 - n)^2$

Exercises 13–16: Use the summation symbol to write each sum in sigma notation.

13 $5 + 9 + 13 + 17 + 21 + 25$

14 $35 + 48 + 63 + 80 + 99$

15 $1 + \dfrac{1}{2} + 0 + \left(-\dfrac{1}{2}\right) + (-1)$

16 $\left(\dfrac{-2}{5}\right) + \left(\dfrac{-3}{7}\right) + \left(\dfrac{-4}{9}\right) + \left(\dfrac{-5}{11}\right)$

Exercises 17–23: Select the numeral preceding the choice that best answers the question.

17 Which is equivalent to $3\displaystyle\sum_{j=2}^{5} (j - 4)$?

(1) $\displaystyle\sum_{j=2}^{5} (3j - 4)$　　(3) $\displaystyle\sum_{j=2}^{5} (3j - 12)$

(2) $\displaystyle\sum_{j=2}^{5} \left(\dfrac{j - 4}{3}\right)$　　(4) $3\displaystyle\sum_{j=-2}^{-5} (4 - j)$

18 If $x_1 = 9$, $x_2 = 12$, $x_3 = 17$, $x_4 = 23$, and $\displaystyle\sum_{i=1}^{5} x_i = 81$, what is the value of x_5?

(1) 30　　　　(3) 19
(2) 20　　　　(4) 5

19 If $x_1 = 91$, $x_2 = 72$, $x_3 = 86$, and $\displaystyle\sum_{j=1}^{4} \dfrac{x_j}{4} = 85$, what is the value of x_4?

(1) 100　　　(3) 91
(2) 94　　　　(4) 85

20 Which represents the sum of $6 + 15 + 26 + 39$?

(1) $\displaystyle\sum_{n=4}^{7} (2n - 2)$　　(3) $\displaystyle\sum_{n=2}^{5} (n^2 + n)$

(2) $\displaystyle\sum_{n=4}^{7} (n^2 - 10)$　(4) $\displaystyle\sum_{n=2}^{5} \left(\dfrac{3n^2}{2}\right)$

21 Zach graduated from college after borrowing money to pay his tuition for 4 years. If he borrowed $20,000 for the first year and an additional $5,000 each year thereafter, which represents the total college loans he must repay?

(1) $\displaystyle\sum_{k=1}^{4} (20{,}000 + 5{,}000k)$

(2) $\displaystyle\sum_{k=1}^{4} (25{,}000k)$

(3) $\displaystyle\sum_{k=0}^{4} (5{,}000k + 25{,}000)$

(4) $\displaystyle\sum_{k=1}^{4} (20{,}000 + 5{,}000(k - 1))$

22 Fiona is training to run the marathon in New York City next year. Each week she increases the distance she runs by 0.5 mile. If she initially started running a 4-mile route, which expression represents the total number of miles she will run in 52 weeks of training?

(1) $\displaystyle\sum_{i=0}^{51} (4 + 0.5i)$　　(3) $\displaystyle\sum_{i=0}^{51} (4.5i)$

(2) $\displaystyle\sum_{i=0}^{51} (0.5 + 4i)$　　(4) $\displaystyle\sum_{i=0}^{51} (4 - 0.5i)$

23 As the number of days before the holidays decreases, the number of shoppers at the mall increases. If the sum $\displaystyle\sum_{n=1}^{25} 300(85 + n)$ represents the total number of shoppers at the Snowy North Pole Mall from December 1 to December 25, how many additional shoppers appear each successive day?

(1) 60　　　　(3) 300
(2) 85　　　　(4) 25,500

6.4 Arithmetic Series

Carl Friedrich Gauss (1777–1855) was a German mathematician and scientist. A popular legend about the young Gauss is that when his teacher tried to occupy his elementary school class by having them add up the integers from 1 to 100, Gauss was able to produce the correct answer within seconds. Instead of attempting to add the integers in order, he realized that adding terms from opposite ends of the list produced identical intermediate sums: $1 + 100 = 101, 2 + 99 = 101, 3 + 98 = 101$, and so on, for a total of 50 sums of $101 = 5,050$.

As you know, the sequence $1, 2, 3, 4, 5, \ldots, 99, 100$ is an arithmetic sequence. The sum of an arithmetic sequence is called an **arithmetic series**. Thus, $1 + 2 + 3 + 4 + 5 + \cdots + 99 + 100$ is an arithmetic series. Gauss found the sum of the arithmetic series $1 + 2 + 3 + 4 + 5 + \cdots + 99 + 100$ by realizing that there were $\dfrac{100}{2} = 50$ pairs of terms whose sum is 101.

Let's look at a general form of an arithmetic series of n terms. We will call this sum, S_n. We see that $S_n = a_1 + a_2 + a_3 + \cdots + a_{n-2} + a_{n-1} + a_n$. To find a formula for S_n, we'll rewrite the series in two ways, add the terms, and then simplify. The second equation for S_n is obtained by reversing the order of the terms in the first equation.

$$
\begin{array}{l}
S_n = \quad a_1 \; + (a_1 + d) \; + (a_1 + 2d) + (a_1 - 3d) + \cdots + (a_n - 3d) + (a_n - 2d) + (a_n - d) + \quad a_n \\
+S_n = \quad a_n \; + (a_n - d) \; + (a_n - 2d) + (a_n - 3d) + \cdots + (a_1 + 3d) + (a_1 + 2d) + (a_1 + d) + \quad a_1 \\
\hline
2S_n = (a_1 + a_n) + (a_1 + a_n) + (a_1 + a_n) + (a_1 + a_n) + \cdots + (a_1 + a_n) + (a_1 + a_n) + (a_1 + a_n) + (a_1 + a_n)
\end{array}
$$

Since there are n terms in the series,

$$2S_n = n(a_1 + a_n)$$

Dividing by 2, we get the formula for the sum of the first n terms of an arithmetic series:

$$S_n = \frac{n}{2}(a_1 + a_n)$$

As you can see, this is exactly what the legend says Gauss did in elementary school. To find the sum of the first 100 integers, we can use the formula above:

$$S_n = \frac{n}{2}(a_1 + a_n)$$

$$S_{100} = \frac{100}{2}(1 + 100) = 50(101) = 5,050$$

Let's now revisit the example from Section 6.3. To find the number of seats in the first fourteen rows of the center orchestra section of the Marquis Theater, we determined that $\sum\limits_{n=1}^{14}(11 + n) = 259$. Since this is the sum of an arithmetic series, we can also obtain the answer by utilizing our formula, using the values $n = 14$, $a_1 = 12$, $a_{14} = 25$.

$$S_n = \frac{n}{2}(a_1 + a_n)$$

$$S_{14} = \frac{14}{2}(12 + 25) = 259$$

MODEL PROBLEMS

1 Find the sum of the series $26 + 31 + 36 + 41 + 46 + 51 + 56 + 61 + 66 + 71 + 76$.

SOLUTION

$a_1 = 26, n = 11, a_{11} = 76$

$S_n = \dfrac{n}{2}(a_1 + a_n)$

$S_{11} = \dfrac{11}{2}(26 + 76) = 561$

Answer: 561

2 Find the sum of the first ten terms of the series $5 - 2 - 9 - 16 - \cdots$.

SOLUTION

$a_1 = 5, n = 10, a_{10} = ?$

To find a_{10}, we utilize the formula $a_n = a_1 + (n - 1)d$ and substitute the values for n, a_1, and $d = -7$.

$a_n = a_1 + (n - 1)d$

$a_{10} = 5 + (10 - 1)(-7)$

$\quad\ = 5 - 63$

$\quad\ = -58$

We can now utilize our formula for the sum of an arithmetic series.

$S_n = \dfrac{n}{2}(a_1 + a_n)$

$S_{10} = \dfrac{10}{2}(5 - 58) = -265$

Answer: -265

3 Find the sum of the series indicated by $\displaystyle\sum_{n=2}^{10}(10n - 4)$.

SOLUTION

This is the arithmetic series $16 + 26 + 36 + \cdots + 86 + 96$. There are nine terms in this series.

$a_1 = 16, n = 9, a_9 = 96$

$S_n = \dfrac{n}{2}(a_1 + a_n)$

$S_9 = \dfrac{9}{2}(16 + 96) = 504$

Answer: 504

Exercises 1–5: Write the sum in sigma notation and find the sum of each series.

1 $7 + 15 + 23 + 31 + 39 + 47 + 55 + 63$

2 $1.5 + 3 + 4.5 + 6 + 7.5 + 9 + 10.5$

3 $150 + 140 + 130 + 120 + 110 + 100$

4 $k + 3k + 5k + 7k + 9k + 11k + 13k + 15k + 17k + 19k$

5 $-\dfrac{1}{2} - 1 - \dfrac{3}{2} - 2 - \dfrac{5}{2} - 3 - \dfrac{7}{2} - 4 - \dfrac{9}{2}$

Exercises 6–12: Write the first three terms of the series and find the indicated sum.

6 $\displaystyle\sum_{i=1}^{12} (4 + i)$

7 $\displaystyle\sum_{j=1}^{15} (4j - 3)$

8 $\displaystyle\sum_{n=7}^{12} (4n)$

9 $\displaystyle\sum_{k=5}^{20} (6k + 2)$

10 $\displaystyle\sum_{k=3}^{14} \left(\dfrac{k}{2}\right)$

11 $\displaystyle\sum_{i=0}^{11} (7i + 3)$

12 $\displaystyle\sum_{n=1}^{100} (3n)$

13 Find the sum of the first 50 positive odd integers. Find the sum of the first 50 positive even integers. Add the two sums together. What do you get? Does this number look familiar?

14 Find the sum of the first 15 terms of the series $6 + 9 + 12 + 15 + \cdots$.

15 A supermarket clerk is stacking 60 cans in a trapezoidal formation. He has to make 6 rows with 5 cans on the top row. How many cans should he put on the bottom row? List the number of cans in each row.

16 Mario is saving up to go to the prom. If he saves $50 in June and increases the amount he saves by $5 per month, how much money will he have the following May? (Since the prom is in May, he will stop saving money after April.)

17 Will and Sunhil are driving back to college after spring break. They plan to drive 120 miles on the first day. They would like to add the same amount to their driving distance each day and would like to complete the 1,200-mile trip in 5 days. How many miles should they drive on each day?

18 Find the sum of the first one thousand positive integers.

19 A football stadium has 20 seats in the first row of a section in the corner of the end zone. Each successive row has 3 more seats than the row before it. If there are 15 rows in the section, how many seats are there?

20 A school district has to buy calculators for all of its students. They have enough money to buy only 300 calculators this year. They are hoping to increase their budget each year to have enough money to buy 80 more calculators than the preceding year. However, they estimate that they will have to replace 30 calculators each year. The net result is that they would have an additional 50 calculators per year. If this pattern continues, will they have enough calculators for all of their 1,600 students in three more years? (Assume that the enrollment remains the same during this period.)

6.5 Geometric Sequences

Take a piece of paper, fold it in half, then fold it in half again, and again. How many times do you think that you can continue to fold the paper in half?

To answer this question, we will assume that the average sheet of paper is approximately 0.0038 inch thick. Beginning with a thickness of 0.0038 inch, the folded paper would measure $2(0.0038) = 0.0076$ inch after the first fold. After the second fold the thickness would double again and be $2(0.0076) = 0.0152$ inch, etc. The table below illustrates the thickness of the paper after each fold.

Fold	1	2	3	4	5
Thickness (in inches)	0.0076	$2(0.0076)$ $= 2^1(0.0076)$ $= 0.0152$	$2(0.0152)$ $= 2^2(0.0076)$ $= 0.0304$	$2(0.0304)$ $= 2^3(0.0076)$ $= 0.0608$	$2(0.0608)$ $= 2^4(0.0076)$ $= 0.1216$

By continuing with this pattern, we can see that after the 20th fold, the thickness of the folded paper would be $2^{19}(0.0076) = 3,984.6$ inches thick. This is a little more than 330 feet, or approximately the height of a 33-story building!

It had previously been believed that, regardless of the thickness of the paper, a piece of paper could be folded in half only eight times. However, in January 2002, Britney Gallivan, a high school student in California, set a new world record by folding a single sheet of paper in half twelve times. She also derived a formula to determine the thickness of a piece of paper needed to complete this task.

Our paper-folding experiment is an example of a **geometric sequence**. A geometric sequence is a sequence that, for all n, there is a constant ratio, r, such that

$$\frac{a_n}{a_{n-1}} = r$$

The value r is called the **common ratio** of the geometric sequence.

In the example above, we used a recursive definition to find each term of the sequence. We saw that each fold produced a thickness twice as much as the thickness produced by the previous fold. Thus, $a_n = a_{n-1}(2)$. In general, $a_n = a_{n-1}r$.

Therefore, a geometric sequence can be written as a_1, $a_2 = a_1 r$, $a_3 = a_2 r$, $a_4 = a_3 r$, ... We can rewrite this in terms of a_1 as

$$a_1, \quad a_2 = a_1 r, \quad a_3 = a_2 r = (a_1 r) \bullet r = a_1 r^2, \quad a_4 = a_3 r = (a_1 r^2) \bullet r = a_1 r^3, \ldots$$

We see that each term after the first is the product of a_1 times r raised to a power that is 1 less than n, the number of the term. Therefore, the nth term of a geometric sequence is

$$a_n = a_1 r^{n-1}$$

MODEL PROBLEMS

1 Determine which sequences are geometric, and for those, identify the common ratio.

   a 5, 10, 15, 20, 25, . . .
   b 10, 30, 90, 270, 810, . . .
   c 64, 32, 16, 8, 4, . . .
   d 1, 4, 9, 16, 25, . . .

SOLUTION

a 5, 10, 15, 20, 25, . . .

By looking at any two consecutive terms, we see that the ratio does not remain constant.

$$\frac{a_2}{a_1} = \frac{10}{5} = 2 \qquad \frac{a_3}{a_2} = \frac{15}{10} = \frac{3}{2} \qquad \frac{a_4}{a_3} = \frac{20}{15} = \frac{4}{3} \qquad \frac{a_5}{a_4} = \frac{25}{20} = \frac{5}{4}$$

This is not a geometric sequence. (Since there is a common difference of 5 between consecutive terms, this is an arithmetic sequence.)

b 10, 30, 90, 270, 810, . . .

This is a geometric sequence since the ratio between any two consecutive terms is always 3:

$$\frac{a_2}{a_1} = \frac{30}{10} = 3 \qquad \frac{a_3}{a_2} = \frac{90}{30} = 3 \qquad \frac{a_4}{a_3} = \frac{270}{90} = 3 \qquad \frac{a_5}{a_4} = \frac{810}{270} = 3$$

c 64, 32, 16, 8, 4, . . .

This is a geometric sequence since the ratio between any two consecutive terms is always $\frac{1}{2}$:

$$\frac{a_2}{a_1} = \frac{32}{64} = \frac{1}{2} \qquad \frac{a_3}{a_2} = \frac{16}{32} = \frac{1}{2} \qquad \frac{a_4}{a_3} = \frac{8}{16} = \frac{1}{2} \qquad \frac{a_5}{a_4} = \frac{4}{8} = \frac{1}{2}$$

d 1, 4, 9, 16, 25, . . .

By looking at any two consecutive terms, we see that the ratio does not remain constant. This is not a geometric sequence.

Answers: **a** No **b** Yes; $r = 3$ **c** Yes; $r = \frac{1}{2}$ **d** No

2 Given the geometric sequence 1, 5, 25, 125, . . . , find the 8th term.

SOLUTION

We will use the formula $a_n = a_1 r^{n-1}$ to find a_8.

We see that $a_1 = 1$ and $r = 5$.

$$a_n = a_1 r^{n-1}$$

$$a_8 = 1(5)^7$$

$$a_8 = 78{,}125$$

Answer: $a_8 = 78{,}125$

3 Write a rule for the nth term of geometric sequence that has two given terms of $a_4 = 4$ and $a_7 = 32$.

SOLUTION

$$a_n = a_1 r^{n-1}$$

$$a_7 = 32 = a_1 r^6$$

$$a_4 = 4 = a_1 r^3$$

If we divide the first equation by the second, we can eliminate a_1.

$$\frac{32}{4} = \frac{a_1 r^6}{a_1 r^3}$$

$$8 = r^3$$

$$r = \sqrt[3]{8} = 2$$

Substitute 2 for r in either of the equations and solve for a_1.

$$4 = a_1 r^3$$

$$4 = a_1 (2)^3$$

$$4 = 8a_1$$

$$a_1 = \frac{1}{2}$$

By substituting the values for a_1 and r into the formula, we see that

$$a_n = a_1 r^{n-1} = \frac{1}{2}(2)^{n-1} = \frac{2^{n-1}}{2} = 2^{n-2}$$

Answer: $a_n = 2^{n-2}$

The terms between any two nonconsecutive terms of a geometric sequence are called **geometric means**. In the sequence, 3, 6, 12, 24, the numbers 6 and 12 are the geometric means between 3 and 24.

MODEL PROBLEM

4 Form a sequence that has three geometric means between 4 and 324.

SOLUTION

If there are three geometric means between 4 and 324, there will be five terms in our sequence. So, $a_1 = 4$ and $a_5 = 324$.

$$a_n = a_1 r^{n-1}$$

$$a_5 = a_1 r^4$$

$$324 = 4r^4$$

$$81 = r^4$$

$$r = \pm 3$$

Our sequence begins with 4 and ends with 324, with a common ratio of 3. Our sequence could be 4, 12, 36, 108, 324, or 4, −12, 36, −108, 324.

Exercises 1–10: Determine if each sequence is geometric. If it is geometric, give the common ratio and the next two terms.

1 6, 12, 18, 24, . . .

2 1, 3, 9, 27, . . .

3 99, 33, 11, . . .

4 $1, n, n^2, n^3, \ldots$

5 $4, -2, 1, -\dfrac{1}{2}, \ldots$

6 $\dfrac{1}{3}, \dfrac{2}{3}, \dfrac{4}{3}, \dfrac{8}{3}, \ldots$

7 $1, g, 2g, 4g, \ldots$

8 $-2, -0.8, -0.32, -0.128, \ldots$

9 $\dfrac{3}{4}, \dfrac{9}{16}, \dfrac{27}{64}, \dfrac{81}{256}, \ldots$

10 $\sqrt{2}, 2, \sqrt{8}, 4, \ldots$

11 Write the first three terms of a geometric sequence that has a first term of 12 and a common ratio of -3.

12 Find r if $a_2 = 6$ and $a_5 = 0.048$.

13 Find the 10th term of the sequence $1, \dfrac{1}{2}, \dfrac{1}{4}, \ldots$.

14 Form a sequence that has two geometric means between 13 and 4,459.

15 Find the first term of a geometric sequence for which $r = 3$ and $a_5 = 972$.

16 Write a rule for the nth term of a geometric sequence with $r = -4$ and $a_7 = 40,960$.

17 Danny decided to donate money to a food bank each year. The first year, he donated $10. In each year after that, he doubled his previous donation, that is, he donated $20 the second year, $40 the third year, and so on. If this pattern continued, how much did Danny donate in the eighteenth year?

18 If the first term of a geometric sequence is doubled, but the common ratio remains the same, would the nth term be doubled? Explain.

19 The cost of a 2008 luxury car was $56,890. If the value of the car depreciated by 10% each year, that is, the value of the car each year was 0.9 times the value the previous year, find the value of the car, to the nearest cent, at the end of each of its first five years.

20 A "superball" bounces to three-fourths of its initial height. If the ball is dropped from a height of 12 feet, how high does it go on the first bounce? The fifth bounce? Round all answers to the nearest tenth.

6.6 Geometric Series

There is an old English children's rhyme titled "As I was Going to St. Ives." The words are:

> *As I was going to St. Ives*
> *I met a man with seven wives,*
> *Every wife had seven sacks,*
> *Every sack had seven cats,*
> *Every cat had seven kits,*
> *Kits, cats, sacks, wives:*
> *How many were going to St. Ives?*

There are numerous interpretations of the answer to this rhyme, but we will assume that the man and his traveling companions were all going to St. Ives, and that the number going to St. Ives would include the man, his 7 wives,

7 sacks (7 wives), 7 cats (7 sacks (7 wives)), and 7 kits (7 cats (7 sacks (7 wives))). Using our mathematical knowledge, this is $1 + 7 + 7 \cdot 7 + 7 \cdot 7 \cdot 7 + 7 \cdot 7 \cdot 7 \cdot 7 = 7^0 + 7^1 + 7^2 + 7^3 + 7^4 = 2{,}801$. (Including the narrator, there would be a total of 2,802.)

This is an example of a **geometric series**. A geometric series is the sum of the terms of a geometric sequence. We will examine the general form of a geometric series of n terms whose sum is S_n with an nth term of $a_1 r^{n-1}$. We see that $S_n = a_1 + a_1 r + a_1 r^2 + \cdots + a_1 r^{n-2} + a_1 r^{n-1}$. To find a formula for S_n, we'll rewrite the series in two ways, subtract the terms, and then simplify. The second equation is obtained by multiplying the entire series by the common ratio, r.

$$
\begin{aligned}
S_n &= a_1 + a_1 r + a_1 r^2 + \cdots + a_1 r^{n-2} + a_1 r^{n-1} \\
-\ rS_n &= \qquad\ a_1 r + a_1 r^2 + \cdots + a_1 r^{n-2} + a_1 r^{n-1} + a_1 r^n \\
\hline
S_n - rS_n &= a_1 \qquad\qquad\qquad\qquad\qquad\qquad\quad\ -\ a_1 r^n
\end{aligned}
$$

We factor out the common factor of S_n and then divide to solve for S_n.

$$S_n(1 - r) = a_1 - a_1 r^n$$

$$S_n = \frac{a_1 - a_1 r^n}{1 - r}, (r \neq 1)$$

Looking at the example above, and making the appropriate substitutions, we can obtain a possible answer to the rhyme.

$$S_n = \frac{a_1 - a_1 r^n}{1 - r}$$

$$S_5 = \frac{1 - 1(7^5)}{1 - 7} = \frac{1 - 16{,}807}{-6} = \frac{-16{,}806}{-6} = 2{,}801$$

Counting the narrator, man, kits, cats, sacks, and wives, the total is 2,802.

MODEL PROBLEMS

1 Find the sum of the series $16 + 8 + 4 + 2 + 1 + \dfrac{1}{2} + \dfrac{1}{4} + \dfrac{1}{8} + \dfrac{1}{16}$.

SOLUTION

$$a_1 = 16, n = 9, r = \frac{1}{2}$$

$$S_n = \frac{a_1 - a_1 r^n}{1 - r}$$

$$S_9 = \frac{16 - 16\left(\dfrac{1}{2}\right)^9}{1 - \dfrac{1}{2}} = \frac{16 - \dfrac{1}{32}}{\dfrac{1}{2}} = \frac{511}{16} = 31.9375$$

Answer: 31.9375 or $31\dfrac{15}{16}$

2 Find the sum of the first ten terms of the series $5 + 15 + 45 + 135 + \cdots$.

SOLUTION

$a_1 = 5, n = 10, r = 3$

$$S_n = \frac{a_1 - a_1 r^n}{1 - r}$$

$$S_{10} = \frac{5 - 5(3)^{10}}{1 - 3} = \frac{5 - 295,245}{-2} = \frac{-295,240}{-2} = 147,620$$

Answer: 147,620

3 Find the sum of the series indicated by $\sum_{n=3}^{9} 2(5)^n$.

SOLUTION

$a_1 = 2(5)^3 = 250, n = 7, r = 5$

$$S_n = \frac{a_1 - a_1 r^n}{1 - r}$$

$$S_7 = \frac{250 - 250(5)^7}{1 - 5} = \frac{250 - 19,531,250}{-4} = \frac{-19,531,000}{-4} = 4,882,750$$

Answer: $\sum_{n=3}^{9} 2(5)^n = 4,882,750$

4 Find the sum of the first six terms of the geometric series whose first term is 3 and whose sixth term is 3,072.

SOLUTION

$a_1 = 3, n = 6, r = ?$

To find r, we utilize the formula $a_n = a_1 r^{n-1}$ and substitute the values for a_1 and n.

$$a_n = a_1 r^{n-1}$$
$$a_6 = 3r^{6-1}$$
$$3,072 = 3r^5$$
$$1,024 = r^5$$
$$r = \sqrt[5]{1,024}$$
$$r = 4$$

We can now utilize our formula for the sum of a geometric series.

$$S_n = \frac{a_1 - a_1 r^n}{1 - r}$$

$$S_6 = \frac{3 - 3(4)^6}{1 - 4} = \frac{3 - 12,288}{-3} = \frac{-12,285}{-3} = 4,095$$

Answer: 4,095

 **Practice**

Exercises 1–5: Find the sum of each series.

1 $2 + 4 + 8 + 16 + 32 + 64 + 128 + 256$

2 $6 - 12 + 24 - 48 + 96 - 192 + 384 - 768$

3 $\dfrac{1}{81} + \dfrac{1}{27} + \dfrac{1}{9} + \dfrac{1}{3} + 1 + 3$

4 $-5 - 20 - 80 - 320 - 1{,}280 - 5{,}120$

5 $64 + 16 + 4 + 1 + \dfrac{1}{4} + \dfrac{1}{16} + \dfrac{1}{64}$

Exercises 6–12: Write the first three terms of the series and find the indicated sum.

6 $\displaystyle\sum_{i=1}^{10} (5)^i$

7 $\displaystyle\sum_{j=1}^{12} 7(3)^j$

8 $\displaystyle\sum_{n=6}^{10} (-4)^n$

9 $20\displaystyle\sum_{k=2}^{6} \left(\dfrac{3}{4}\right)^k$

10 $\displaystyle\sum_{k=3}^{10} \left(-\dfrac{5}{2}\right)^{k-2}$

11 $\displaystyle\sum_{i=0}^{6} 9\left(\dfrac{1}{3}\right)^i$

12 $\displaystyle\sum_{n=1}^{5} 5(6)^{n-1}$

13 Use sigma notation to write a rule for the sum of the first eight terms of the geometric series $7 + 21 + 63 + 189 + \cdots$ and find its sum.

14 Find the sum of the first nine terms of the series $54 + 18 + 6 + 2 + \cdots$.

15 A basketball league has a single-elimination tournament that begins with 32 teams playing in 16 games. After the first game, only 16 teams remain in the tournament to play 8 games. This continues until there is a winner. How many total games were played in the tournament?

16 Find the sum of $\dfrac{3}{10} + \dfrac{3}{100} + \dfrac{3}{1{,}000} + \cdots + \dfrac{3}{1{,}000{,}000}$.

17 A pendulum swings through an arc of 20 inches. The length of the arc on each successive swing is 95 percent of the previous swing. After ten additional swings, what is the total distance through which the pendulum has swung?

18 When school is closed for a snow day, the PTSA activates a phone chain. The president of the PTSA calls two people, each of whom calls two people, each of whom calls two people, etc. If there are approximately 1,000 families that have to be called, how many rounds of phone calls will have to be made?

19 In the first week, a movie earned a total of $6,140,000. The studio expects the earnings for each of the next six weeks to be approximately 5 percent less than the previous week. What does the studio expect the movie to earn for the seven weeks?

20 When Caroline was born, her grandparents deposited $200 in a bank account that paid 3% interest per year, compounded annually. They deposited another $200 for each of her first three birthdays. At that point, Caroline had received $200 for her third birthday gift, one year of interest on her second birthday gift, two years of interest on her first birthday gift, and three years of interest on the $200 she received when she was born. This means that she had $200 + $200(1.03) + $200(1.03)^2 + $200(1.03)^3 = $836.73 in her bank account. If her grandparents continued to make the same deposit and receive the same interest, how much would Caroline have in her account after her grandparents made the deposit for her 18th birthday?

6.7 Infinite Series

If we took a 1-inch-by-1-inch square and divided it in half, then divided half of the half in half, and then half of one of those halves in half, etc., what would the area of the square be?

The length of each side of the square below is 1 unit. Thus, the area of the square is 1 square unit. When we divide the square in half, the area of the left portion is one-half square unit. When we divide the right portion in half, the area of the upper portion is one-fourth square unit, etc.

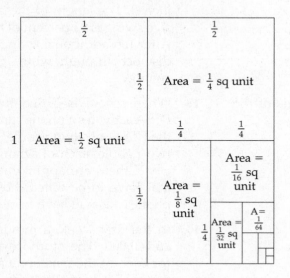

The sum of the areas of the resulting figures is $\dfrac{1}{2} + \dfrac{1}{4} + \dfrac{1}{8} + \dfrac{1}{16} + \dfrac{1}{32} + \dfrac{1}{64} + \cdots$. Since we know that the area of the square is 1, then $\dfrac{1}{2} + \dfrac{1}{4} + \dfrac{1}{8} + \dfrac{1}{16} + \dfrac{1}{32} + \dfrac{1}{64} + \cdots$ must equal 1. How can this be?

The series $\dfrac{1}{2} + \dfrac{1}{4} + \dfrac{1}{8} + \dfrac{1}{16} + \dfrac{1}{32} + \dfrac{1}{64} + \cdots$ is an example of an infinite geometric series. We can find the sum of a finite geometric series, but what do we do about an infinite one?

The sum of the first n terms of a finite geometric series is $S_n = \dfrac{a_1 - a_1 r^n}{1 - r}, (r \neq 1)$.

In the series above, $a_1 = \dfrac{1}{2}$ and $r = \dfrac{1}{2}$. Substituting this information in the formula, we get $S_n = \dfrac{\dfrac{1}{2} - \dfrac{1}{2}\left(\dfrac{1}{2}\right)^n}{1 - \dfrac{1}{2}}$. As the number of terms increases, and n becomes a very large number, $\left(\dfrac{1}{2}\right)^n$ becomes a very small number. Look at the calculator screen below to see what happens as we input larger and larger values for n into the expression $\left(\dfrac{1}{2}\right)^n$.

```
(1/2)^20
   9.536743164E-7
(1/2)^40
   9.094947020E-13
(1/2)^80
   8.271806130E-25
```

As you can see, $\left(\dfrac{1}{2}\right)^{80}$ is a decimal that begins with 24 zeros. Thus, as n contin-

ues to increase, $\left(\dfrac{1}{2}\right)^n$ gets closer and closer to zero, and $S_n \approx \dfrac{\dfrac{1}{2} - \dfrac{1}{2}\,(0)}{1 - \dfrac{1}{2}} =$

$\dfrac{\dfrac{1}{2}}{\dfrac{1}{2}} = 1$. A similar result will hold whenever $-1 < r < 1$. If $r \geq 1$ or $r \leq -1$, r^n will not get smaller as n gets larger, so our formula will not hold true. Geometric series in which $-1 < r < 1$ are called **convergent**, because the sum of the infinite number of their terms approaches a real, finite value.

The formula for the sum, S, of an infinite geometric series whose first term is a_1 and whose ratio is r is

$$S = \frac{a_1}{1 - r}, \quad -1 < r < 1$$

Note: A finite sum of an infinite series can be found only when $-1 < r < 1$.

MODEL PROBLEMS

1 Find the sum of each infinite geometric series, if it exists.

a $6 + 2 + \dfrac{2}{3} + \dfrac{2}{9} + \cdots$

b $\dfrac{2}{5} + \dfrac{4}{5} + \dfrac{8}{5} + \cdots$

c $\displaystyle\sum_{i=3}^{\infty} \left(\dfrac{4}{7}\right)^i$

d $\displaystyle\sum_{k=1}^{\infty} \left(\dfrac{8}{5}\right)^k$

SOLUTION

a $6 + 2 + \dfrac{2}{3} + \dfrac{2}{9} + \cdots$

$a_1 = 6$ and $r = \dfrac{1}{3}$

$S = \dfrac{a_1}{1 - r}$

$S = \dfrac{6}{1 - \dfrac{1}{3}} = \dfrac{6}{\dfrac{2}{3}} = 9$

Answer: $S = 9$

b $\dfrac{2}{5} + \dfrac{4}{5} + \dfrac{8}{5} + \cdots$

$a_1 = \dfrac{2}{5}$ and $r = 2$

Answer: Since $r > 1$, this series is not convergent and does not have a sum.

c $\displaystyle\sum_{i=3}^{\infty} \left(\dfrac{4}{7}\right)^i$

$a_1 = \dfrac{64}{343}$ and $r = \dfrac{4}{7}$

$S = \dfrac{a_1}{1 - r}$

$S = \dfrac{\dfrac{64}{343}}{1 - \dfrac{4}{7}} = \dfrac{\dfrac{64}{343}}{\dfrac{3}{7}} = \dfrac{64}{147}$

Answer: $S = \dfrac{64}{147}$

d $\displaystyle\sum_{k=1}^{\infty} \left(\dfrac{8}{5}\right)^k$

$a_1 = \dfrac{8}{5}$ and $r = \dfrac{8}{5}$

Answer: Since $r > 1$, this series is not convergent and does not have a sum.

2 Write each repeating decimal as a fraction.

   a 0.55555 . . .
   b 0.24242424 . . .

SOLUTION

Each repeating decimal forms an infinite geometric series.

a $0.55555\ldots = \dfrac{5}{10} + \dfrac{5}{100} + \dfrac{5}{1,000} + \dfrac{5}{10,000} + \dfrac{5}{100,000} + \cdots$

$a_1 = \dfrac{5}{10}$ and $r = \dfrac{1}{10}$

$S = \dfrac{a_1}{1 - r}$

$S = \dfrac{\dfrac{5}{10}}{1 - \dfrac{1}{10}} = \dfrac{\dfrac{5}{10}}{\dfrac{9}{10}} = \dfrac{5}{9}$

Answer: $S = \dfrac{5}{9}$

b $0.24242424\ldots = \dfrac{24}{100} + \dfrac{24}{10,000} + \dfrac{24}{1,000,000} + \dfrac{24}{100,000,000} + \cdots$

$a_1 = \dfrac{24}{100}$ and $r = \dfrac{1}{100}$

$S = \dfrac{a_1}{1 - r}$

$S = \dfrac{\dfrac{24}{100}}{1 - \dfrac{1}{100}} = \dfrac{\dfrac{24}{100}}{\dfrac{99}{100}} = \dfrac{24}{99} = \dfrac{8}{33}$

Answer: $S = \dfrac{8}{33}$

Exercises 1–10: Find the sum of each infinite geometric series, if it is convergent.

1 $80 + 20 + 5 + \cdots$

2 $2 + 3 + \dfrac{9}{2} + \cdots$

3 $1 + 5 + 25 + \cdots$

4 $0.6 + 0.06 + 0.006 + \cdots$

5 $8 + 1.6 + 0.32 + \cdots$

6 $\displaystyle\sum_{i=2}^{\infty} 2\left(\dfrac{5}{6}\right)^{i}$

7 $\displaystyle\sum_{k=4}^{\infty} \left(\sqrt{2}\right)^{k}$

8 $5 \displaystyle\sum_{n=1}^{\infty} \left(\dfrac{3}{2}\right)^{n}$

9 $\displaystyle\sum_{j=1}^{\infty} (0.32)^{j}$

10 $\displaystyle\sum_{i=2}^{\infty} (0.15)^{i}$

Exercises 11–20: Write each repeating decimal as a fraction.

11 $0.66666\ldots$

12 $0.7777\ldots$

13 $0.31313131\ldots$

14 $0.5252525\ldots$

15 $0.123123123\ldots$

16 $0.634634634\ldots$

17 $5.6666666\ldots$

18 $1.54545454\ldots$

19 $0.2444444444\ldots$

20 $0.52121212121\ldots$

21 A pendulum swings through an arc of 26 inches. The length of the arc on each successive swing is 92 percent of the previous swing. By the time the pendulum stops, what is the total distance that it will have swung?

 **FYI**

The graphing calculator utilizes the sequence mode to find the terms of a sequence, graph the sequence, and find the sum of the terms of the sequence.

First, Press (**MODE**) and put your calculator in sequence mode and dot mode, as shown below.

```
NORMAL   SCI  ENG
FLOAT   0123456789
RADIAN   DEGREE
FUNC  PAR  POL  SEQ
CONNECTED  DOT
SEQUENTIAL  SIMUL
REAL  a+bi  re^θi
FULL  HORIZ  G-T
```

We'll use a sequence that we discussed in several sections of this chapter: 12, 13, 14, 15, . . . , 24, 25. We must write a formula for the sequence function, $u(n)$, with the independent variable, n. When $n = 1$, $u(n) = 11 + n$. Press (**Y=**) and enter the information as shown on the following page.

Since we are in sequence mode, to enter n, press $\boxed{\text{X,T,θ,n}}$. The letter produced by this button is determined by the mode settings. Function mode has an independent variable of x, while sequence mode has an independent variable of n.

It is not necessary to enter anything into $u(n\text{Min})$ unless we are working with a recursive sequence.

```
Plot1  Plot2  Plot3
 nMin=1
\u(n)■11+n
 u(nMin)■
\v(n)=
 v(nMin)=
\w(n)=
 w(nMin)=
```

To see the values in the sequence, press $\boxed{\text{2nd}}$ $\boxed{\text{WINDOW}}$ and set the table to begin with $n = 1$ and increase by increments of 1, as shown in the screen shot below.

```
TABLE SETUP
 TblStart=1
 △Tbl=1
Indpnt: Auto   Ask
Depend: Auto   Ask
```

Press $\boxed{\text{2nd}}$ $\boxed{\text{GRAPH}}$ to view the table shown below.

n	$u(n)$	
1	12	
2	13	
3	14	
4	15	
5	16	
6	17	
7	18	
$n=5$		

We can also look at the data on a graph. Set your viewing window with $1 \le n \le 14$, $0 \le x \le 16$, $0 \le y \le 30$. (Plot Start is the first term number to be plotted and Plot Step is the incremental n value.) The figures below show all of the window settings.

```
WINDOW
 nMin=1
 nMax=14
 PlotStart=1
 PlotStep=1
 Xmin=0
 Xmax=16
↓Xscl=■
```

```
WINDOW
↑PlotStep=1
 Xmin=0
 Xmax=16
 Xscl=1
 Ymin=0
 Ymax=30
 Yscl=5
```

Press **GRAPH** to obtain the graph below.

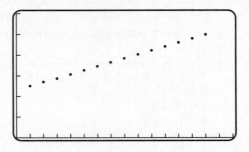

Press **TRACE** to see the values of the sequence.

We can also use the calculator to find the sum of the terms of a sequence. Press **2nd** **MODE** to exit from the graphing window and then **2nd** **STAT** to display the LIST menu shown below.

```
 NAMES  OPS  MATH
 1:L1
 2:L2
 3:L3
 4:L4
 5:L5
 6:L6
 7↓L10
```

Right arrow over to MATH. The following menu appears.

```
 NAMES  OPS  MATH
 1:min(
 2:max(
 3:mean(
 4:median(
 5:sum(
 6:prod(
 7↓stdDev(
```

Choose option 5, as shown above. Press **ENTER** and the summation notation, sum(, will appear on your home screen. Now go back to **2nd** **STAT** and choose OPS, as shown below.

```
 NAMES  OPS  MATH
 1:SortA(
 2:SortD(
 3:dim(
 4:Fill(
 5:seq(
 6:cumSum(
 7↓ΔList(
```

Choose option 5: seq(. Press (ENTER). The seq(command will now appear on your home screen adjacent to the sum(command.

```
sum(seq(█
```

Now enter the sequence to be summed, followed by the variable used, the starting value, the ending value, and the desired increment. Using the series $12 + 13 + 14 + \cdots + 24 + 25$ or $\sum_{n=1}^{14} (11 + n)$, the command would look like this.

```
sum(seq((11+n),n
,1,14,1)
                259
█
```

In the above command, notice that the first entry is the expression for the sequence enclosed in parentheses; the second is the variable, then the lower limit, followed by the upper limit, and finally the increment.

If the increment is 1, there is no need to include it.

 **Practice**

Go back to some of the problems in the chapter and perform the calculations by using the calculator functionality as described in this section.

Exercises 1–10: Determine if the following sequences are arithmetic, geometric, or neither. If a sequence is arithmetic, find the common difference and the next three terms. If a sequence is geometric, find the common ratio and the next three terms.

1 $-3, 4, 11, 18$

2 $144, -72, 36, -18$

3 $243, 162, 108, 72$

4 $9, 16, 25, 36$

5 $74, 65, 56, 47$

6 $\dfrac{16}{9}, \dfrac{8}{9}, \dfrac{4}{9}, \dfrac{2}{9}$

7 $13, 24, 35, 46$

8 $\dfrac{32}{7}, -\dfrac{48}{7}, \dfrac{72}{7}, -\dfrac{108}{7}$

9 $\sqrt{3}, \sqrt{6}, 2\sqrt{3}, 2\sqrt{6}$

10 $500, 400, 325, 275$

Exercises 11–24: Select the numeral preceding the choice that best answers the question.

11 Given the sequence $17, 23, 29, 35, \ldots$, which rule can be used to find the nth term of the sequence?

   (1) $a_n = 23 - 6n$
   (2) $a_n = 35 - 6n$
   (3) $a_n = 6 + 17n$
   (4) $a_n = 11 + 6n$

12 If $a_3 = 17$ and $a_8 = 37$ are terms in an arithmetic sequence, find a_1 and d.

   (1) $a_1 = 7 \quad d = 5$
   (2) $a_1 = 9 \quad d = 4$
   (3) $a_1 = 17 \quad d = 4$
   (4) $a_1 = 11 \quad d = 3$

13 Given that $a_3 = 408$ and $a_6 = 564$ in an arithmetic sequence, find a_7.

   (1) 610
   (2) 612
   (3) 616
   (4) 618

14 Which rule represents an arithmetic sequence with two arithmetic means between 25 and 43?

   (1) $a_n = 17 + 8(n - 1)$
   (2) $a_n = 25 + 6(n - 1)$
   (3) $a_n = 28 - 3(n - 1)$
   (4) $a_n = 43 - 6(n - 1)$

15 The sum of the arithmetic sequence $19 + 27 + 35 + 43 + 51$ can be represented as which of the following?

   (1) $\displaystyle\sum_{n=1}^{5} (11 + 8n)$

   (2) $\displaystyle\sum_{n=19}^{51} \left(19 + \dfrac{n - 1}{2}\right)$

   (3) $\displaystyle\sum_{n=5}^{1} (51 - 8n)$

   (4) $\displaystyle\sum_{n=5}^{1} (19 - 8n)$

16 If $x_1 = 18$, $x_3 = 42$, $x_4 = 54$, and $\dfrac{2}{3}\displaystyle\sum_{j=1}^{4} x_j = 96$, what is the value of x_2?

   (1) 24   (3) 96
   (2) 30   (4) 144

17 In a geometric sequence, if $a_2 = 162$ and $a_5 = -6$, what is the value of r?

   (1) $-\dfrac{1}{2}$ (3) $\dfrac{1}{3}$

   (2) $-\dfrac{1}{3}$ (4) $\dfrac{1}{2}$

18 In a geometric sequence, if $r = \sqrt{3}$ and $a_4 = 27$, what is the value of a_1?

   (1) $-3\sqrt{3}$ (3) 3
   (2) $-\sqrt{3}$ (4) $3\sqrt{3}$

19 What is the sixth term of a geometric sequence defined as $a_n = 5(0.4)^{n-1}$?

   (1) 32   (3) 0.0512
   (2) 0.1024   (4) 0.02048

20 Given that $a_3 = -256$ and $a_6 = 32$ in a geometric sequence, find r.

   (1) -2 (3) $\dfrac{1}{4}$

   (2) $-\dfrac{1}{2}$ (4) $\dfrac{1}{2}$

21 For which infinite series can we *not* calculate a sum?

(1) $343 + 98 + 28 + 8 + \cdots$

(2) $2{,}187 + 729 + 243 + 81 + \cdots$

(3) $4 + 5 + \dfrac{25}{4} + \dfrac{125}{16} + \cdots$

(4) $64 + 16 + 4 + 1 + \cdots$

22 What is the sum of the infinite geometric series $\displaystyle\sum_{k=4}^{\infty} \left(\dfrac{7}{8}\right)^k$?

(1) $\dfrac{1}{3{,}584}$

(3) 7

(2) $\dfrac{2{,}401}{512}$

(4) 128

23 Which fraction is equivalent to $0.378378378\ldots$?

(1) $\dfrac{378}{1{,}000}$

(3) $\dfrac{189}{500}$

(2) $\dfrac{622}{999}$

(4) $\dfrac{14}{37}$

24 Which sequence is expressed by the rule $a_n = \dfrac{3n}{n+1}$?

(1) $\dfrac{3}{2}, \dfrac{9}{4}, \dfrac{27}{8}, \dfrac{81}{16}, \ldots$

(2) $\dfrac{3}{2}, 2, \dfrac{9}{4}, \dfrac{12}{5}, \ldots$

(3) $2, \dfrac{8}{3}, 3, \dfrac{16}{5}, \ldots$

(4) $1, \dfrac{3}{2}, \dfrac{9}{5}, 2, \ldots$

25 Savannah has $150 in her bank account and gets $10 a week for allowance. She puts all of her allowance in her bank account.

a Write an arithmetic series to indicate the amount of money she will have after one year (52 weeks) and evaluate it.

b If Savannah wants to go on a $375 horseback riding weekend after 40 weeks of saving, will she have enough in her bank account to cover the cost? Explain.

26 In an Online game, 10 grains of rice are donated to the needy for each vocabulary word a player defines correctly. Abram plays the game each day of the month of December. On December 1, Abram defines correctly one word. Each day that follows, Abram defines correctly one word more than the previous day. How many grains of rice will he have donated in total on December 31?

27 The Chamber of Commerce does a holiday display of poinsettias. If the poinsettias form the shape of a tree with one pot of flowers in the top row, 4 pots in the second row, 7 pots of flowers in the third row and so on, find the total number of poinsettia plants needed to build a poinsettia tree of 8 rows.

28 The clinic in Henderson reported that on the first day of the flu outbreak, 11 people sought treatment. On each consecutive day, the number of new patients increased by 6.

a Write the arithmetic sequence for the number of new patients admitted to the hospital during the 10-day flu outbreak.

b Over the 10 days, how many citizens of Henderson were treated?

c If the population of Henderson is 1,900, what percent of the citizens came in for treatment for the flu?

29 The trapeze at the McDougal Circus swings a distance of 48 feet on its first release. The distance the trapeze travels decreases by 40 percent on each swing.

a Write a rule to find a_n in this geometric sequence.

b How far from the point of release does the trapeze travel on the third swing?

c If the trapeze artist Helena grabs the trapeze after its seventh swing, how many feet, to the *nearest hundredth of a foot*, had the trapeze traveled in total over the seven swings?

30 Mallory e-mailed a funny cartoon to Ann. She told Ann to send it to five friends with instructions for each of them to send it to five other friends. After four cycles of e-mailing, how many cartoons will have been sent?

CHAPTER 7

Exponential Functions

7.1 Review of Exponents

Laws of Exponents

In a term such as x^4, x is the base and 4 is the exponent that tells us how many times the base is used as a factor. An exponent is a shortcut way of writing multiplication. For example, instead of writing $xxxx$, we can write x^4. Therefore, if we multiply $x^4 \times x^3$, it is the same as multiplying $xxxx \times xxx = xxxxxxx = x^7$. Remember the rule for multiplication: keep the base the same, and add the exponents.

When we divide $x^4 \div x^3$, we can rewrite this as $\dfrac{xxxx}{xxx}$ and "cancel" the common

factors: $\dfrac{xxxx}{xxx} = \dfrac{\cancel{x}\cancel{x}\cancel{x}x}{\cancel{x}\cancel{x}\cancel{x}} = x^{4-3} = x$. Remember the rule for division: keep the base the same and subtract the exponents.

To raise x^3 to the second power, we have $(x^3)^2$. We can rewrite this and follow our rules for multiplication: $(x^3)^2 = (x^3)(x^3) = x^6$. However, it is easier to remember that we keep the bases the same and multiply the exponents.

Make sure that you know these rules:

$x^a \bullet x^b = x^{a+b}$ Multiplication Rule

$x^a \div x^b = x^{a-b}$ Division Rule

$(x^a)^b = x^{ab}$ Power Rule

These rules can be used to verify two other rules:

$(xy)^a = x^a y^a$ Power of a Product Rule

$\left(\dfrac{x}{y}\right)^a = \dfrac{x^a}{y^a}$ Power of a Quotient Rule

We can apply our division rule to the following problem: $x^a \div x^a = x^{a-a} = x^0$. We know that if we divide any nonzero number by itself, we always get 1. Therefore, $x^a \div x^a = 1$. Since $x^a \div x^a = x^0$ and $x^a \div x^a = 1$, we can conclude that $x^0 = 1$.

Negative Exponents

We know that $x^4 \div x^3 = x$. What happens if we have $x^3 \div x^4$?

$$x^3 \div x^4 = x^{3-4} = x^{-1}$$

We also know that $x^3 \div x^4 = \dfrac{\cancel{x}\cancel{x}\cancel{x}}{\cancel{x}\cancel{x}\cancel{x}x} = \dfrac{1}{x}$.

Therefore, we can conclude that $x^{-1} = \dfrac{1}{x}$.

Similarly, $x^{-2} = \dfrac{1}{x^2}$ and $\dfrac{1}{x^{-1}} = \dfrac{1}{\frac{1}{x}} = \dfrac{1}{1} \cdot \dfrac{x}{1} = x.$

A negative exponent tells us to "flip": $x^{-1} = \dfrac{1}{x}$ and $\dfrac{1}{x^{-1}} = x$, $(x \neq 0)$. The rules for operations with positive exponents can also be applied to negative exponents.

MODEL PROBLEM

1 Simplify each expression.

a $3a^2b^3c^4 \cdot 5ab^2c^6$

b $\dfrac{35x^4y^5z^{10}}{7xy^7z^{10}}$

c $\left(\dfrac{1}{2}\right)^{-2} \cdot 3^0 \cdot 4^{-3}$

d $-2^{-4} \cdot (-2)^{-4}$

SOLUTION

a $3a^2b^3c^4 \cdot 5ab^2c^6$

We multiply the 3 by 5, leave the bases the same for a, b, and c, and add the exponents of like variables.

$3a^2b^3c^4 \cdot 5ab^2c^6 = 3 \cdot 5a^{2+1}b^{3+2}c^{4+6} = 15a^3b^5c^{10}$

Answer: $15a^3b^5c^{10}$

b $\dfrac{35x^4y^5z^{10}}{7xy^7z^{10}}$

We divide the 35 by 7, leave the bases the same for x, y, and z, and subtract the exponents.

$\dfrac{35x^4y^5z^{10}}{7xy^7z^{10}} = 5x^{4-1}y^{5-7}z^{10-10} = 5x^3y^{-2}$

Answer: $5x^3y^{-2}$ or $\dfrac{5x^3}{y^2}$

Note: If a problem asks for answers with only positive exponents, then a result such as $5x^3y^{-2}$ should be expressed as $\dfrac{5x^3}{y^2}$.

c $\left(\dfrac{1}{2}\right)^{-2} \cdot 3^0 \cdot 4^{-3}$

We can rewrite the expression as follows:

$$\left(\dfrac{1}{2}\right)^{-2} \cdot 3^0 \cdot 4^{-3} = \left(\dfrac{2}{1}\right)^2 \cdot 1 \cdot \dfrac{1}{4^3}$$

$$= \dfrac{\cancel{4}}{1} \cdot \dfrac{1}{\underset{16}{\cancel{64}}}$$

$$= \dfrac{1}{16}$$

Answer: $\dfrac{1}{16}$

d $-2^{-4} \cdot (-2)^{-4}$

Notice the difference between the two expressions in the product, and remember the order of operations. When we see -2^{-4}, we follow the order of operations, which tells us to raise the 2 to the -4 power, and then negate the answer. It may help you to think of -2^{-4} as

$$-1(2^{-4}) = -1\left(\dfrac{1}{2^4}\right) = -1\left(\dfrac{1}{16}\right) = -\dfrac{1}{16}.$$

The expression $(-2)^{-4}$ tells us to take the number -2 and raise it to the -4 power.

$$-2^{-4} \cdot (-2)^{-4} = -\dfrac{1}{2^4} \cdot \dfrac{1}{(-2)^4}$$

$$= -\dfrac{1}{16} \cdot \dfrac{1}{16}$$

$$= -\dfrac{1}{256}$$

Answer: $-\dfrac{1}{256}$

Fractional Exponents

How can we rewrite $\sqrt{x}$ as x to some power?

We know that $\sqrt{x} \cdot \sqrt{x} = x$.

Let the square root function equal some power, p.

Then $x^p \cdot x^p = x^1$.

$$x^p \bullet x^p = x^1$$

$$x^{p+p} = x^1 \qquad \text{When we multiply, we add the exponents:}$$

$$x^{2p} = x^1$$

$$2p = 1 \qquad \text{Since the bases are the same, equate the exponents.}$$

$$p = \frac{1}{2} \qquad \text{Solve.}$$

Therefore, $\sqrt{x} = x^{\frac{1}{2}}$.

$$x^{\frac{1}{2}} = \sqrt{x}$$

$$x^{\frac{1}{3}} = \sqrt[3]{x}$$

$$x^{\frac{1}{4}} = \sqrt[4]{x}, \text{ etc.}$$

> Note: Fractional powers are roots.

MODEL PROBLEM

2 Simplify.

   a $16^{\frac{3}{4}}$

   b $16^{-\frac{3}{4}}$

   c $-8^{\frac{2}{3}}$

   d $(-8)^{\frac{2}{3}}$

   e $(-8)^{-\frac{2}{3}}$

SOLUTION

   a $16^{\frac{3}{4}}$

We find the 4th root of 16 and then raise it to the 3rd power. (Alternatively, we could raise 16 to the 3rd power and then find the 4th root of that number, but it is usually easier to find the root first.)

$$16^{\frac{3}{4}} = \left(\sqrt[4]{16}\right)^3 = 2^3 = 8$$

Answer: 8

   b $16^{-\frac{3}{4}}$

This is the same question as above except the exponent is negative. We need to find the reciprocal of our answer to part **a**.

Thus $16^{-\frac{3}{4}} = \dfrac{1}{8}$

Answer: $\dfrac{1}{8}$

   c $-8^{\frac{2}{3}}$

We must find the cube root of 8, raise that to the 2nd power, and then negate our answer.

$$-8^{\frac{2}{3}} = -\left(\sqrt[3]{8}\right)^2$$

$$= -2^2 = -4$$

Answer: -4

d $(-8)^{\frac{2}{3}}$

This time we are finding the cube root of -8 and raising that to the 2nd power.

$$(-8)^{\frac{2}{3}} = \left(\sqrt[3]{-8}\right)^2$$
$$= (-2)^2 = 4$$

Answer: 4

e $(-8)^{-\frac{2}{3}}$

This is the same question as in part **d** except the exponent is negative. We need to find the reciprocal of our previous answer.

$$(-8)^{-\frac{2}{3}} = \frac{1}{4}$$

Answer: $\dfrac{1}{4}$

 # Practice

Exercises 1–15: Simplify each expression without using a calculator.

1 $5x^0$

2 $(5x)^0$

3 $\left(3a^2b^4c\right)\left(2.5a^{-4}bc\right)$

4 $3^{-2} \bullet -2^3$

5 $32^{\frac{3}{5}}$

6 $\dfrac{16r^3s^{10}t^{-2}}{24r^3s^{-3}t^2}$

7 $-3y^0$

8 $(-3y)^0$

9 $(-2)^{-2}$

10 -2^{-2}

11 $\left(5c^{-3}d^{-6}e^2\right)\left(2c^{-4}d^{-2}e^{-2}\right)$

12 $-81^{-\frac{3}{4}}$

13 $(-81)^{-\frac{3}{4}}$

14 $\dfrac{2.25s^{-4}r^5}{0.5s^{-4}r^{-2}}$

15 $\left(-0.35x^4y^{-4}z^8\right)\left(0.2xy^4z^{-6}\right)$

16 If $f(x) = 18x^{-3}$, find $f(3)$.

17 Evaluate $g(4)$ if $g(x) = 12x^0$.

18 If $h(x) = 16x^{-\frac{2}{5}}$, find $h(32)$.

19 If $j(x) = -x^{-2}$, find $j(-3)$.

20 Evaluate $r(27)$ if $r(x) = \dfrac{2}{3}x^{-\frac{2}{3}}$.

Exercises 21–25: Rewrite as a radical expression.

21 $4x^{\frac{3}{2}}$

22 $(3xy)^{\frac{4}{5}}$

23 $-64^{\frac{2}{3}}$

24 $9^{-\frac{3}{2}}$

25 $(-8)^{-\frac{4}{3}}$

Exercises 26–30: Rewrite with fractional exponents.

26 $\sqrt[6]{x^5}$

27 $\dfrac{2}{3\sqrt[5]{ab^2}}$

28 $\left(\sqrt[3]{125}\right)^2$

29 $\left(\sqrt{de}\right)^3$

30 $-\left(\dfrac{1}{\sqrt[3]{cd}}\right)^2$

Exercises 31–40: Select the numeral preceding the choice that best completes the sentence or answers the question.

31 If $f(x) = 4^x$, then $f(-2)$ equals

(1) -16
(2) -8
(3) $\dfrac{1}{16}$
(4) $\dfrac{1}{8}$

32 For what value of x is the expression $(x + 1)^{-2}$ undefined?

(1) 1
(2) 0
(3) -1
(4) It's never undefined.

33 If $f(x) = x^{\frac{2}{3}}$ and $g(x) = x^{\frac{1}{2}}$, what is $(f \circ g)(64)$?

(1) 8
(2) 2
(3) -2
(4) 4

34 If $h(x) = x^0 + x^{\frac{2}{3}} + x^{-\frac{2}{3}}$, evaluate $h(27)$.

(1) 1
(2) 9
(3) $9\dfrac{8}{9}$
(4) $10\dfrac{1}{9}$

35 What is the product of 4^2 and 4^4?

(1) 4^6
(2) 4^8
(3) 16^6
(4) 16^8

36 If $f(x) = (10x)^0 + x^{-2} + x^{\frac{1}{2}}$, evaluate $f(9)$.

(1) -5
(2) -3.5
(3) $3\dfrac{1}{81}$
(4) $4\dfrac{1}{81}$

37 The expression $\dfrac{2^{\frac{1}{2}}}{2^{-\frac{1}{2}}}$ is equivalent to

(1) 1
(2) 2
(3) -1
(4) -2

38 Evaluate $(x + 3)^0 + (x + 4)^{-\frac{1}{2}}$ when $x = 5$.

(1) -5
(2) -2
(3) $\dfrac{1}{3}$
(4) $\dfrac{4}{3}$

39 If $f(x) = x^{\frac{1}{3}}$ and $g(x) = 5x^2$, find $(f \circ g)(5)$.

(1) $5^{\frac{2}{3}}$
(2) 5
(3) $5^{\frac{5}{3}}$
(4) $5^{\frac{10}{3}}$

40 Which is equivalent to $3^x + 3^x + 3^x$?

(1) 3^{x+1}
(2) 3^{3x}
(3) 9^x
(4) 9^{3x}

7.2 Exponential Functions and Their Graphs

If you won a contest and were given the choice of the following prizes, which one would you choose?

Option 1: $1,000 if you collected the money on day 1, $2,000 if you waited until day 2 to collect your money, $3,000 if you waited until day 3 to collect your money, $4,000 if you waited until day 4 to collect your money, and so on. You could collect your money at any time, or wait until the end of 20 days and collect the money at that time.

Option 2: $1 if you collected the money on day 1, $2 if you waited until day 2 to collect your money, $4 if you waited until day 3 to collect your money, $8 if you waited until day 4 to collect your money, and so on. You could collect your money at any time, or wait until the end of 20 days and collect the money at that time.

At first glance, it appears that the first choice is a much better offer. If you collected your money on day 5, you would receive $5,000 from the first option, while receiving only $16 from the second one. However, how much would you collect from each offer if you waited 20 days?

Option 1 pays $1,000 times the number of days you wait to collect the money. For example, the money paid on the 3rd day is $1,000(3) = $3,000. So if you left your money for 20 days, it would pay $1,000(20) = $20,000.

The numbers in Option 2 are all powers of 2. For example, if you collected your money on day 1, you would receive 2^0 = $1. The money paid on day 2 is 2^1, the money paid on day 3 is 2^2, and the money paid on day 4 is 2^3. So the money paid on day 20 would be 2^{19}. Enter this number in your calculator. Are you surprised by the result?

If you chose the second option, and waited 20 days to collect your money, you would receive 2^{19} = $524,288. This is certainly quite amazing!

Let's look at the equations for the two options.

Option 1: $1,000(number of days)
If we let x represent the number of days, the equation for this option would be

$y = 1,000x$.

Option 2: $2^{\text{number of days} - 1}$
If we let x represent the number of days, the equation for this option would be

$y = 2^{x-1}$.

We can make a table of values for each of the options.

x	1	2	3	4	5	6	7	8	9	10
1,000x	1,000	2,000	3,000	4,000	5,000	6,000	7,000	8,000	9,000	10,000
2^{x-1}	1	2	4	8	16	32	64	128	256	512

Notice that, although Option 1 still pays more money, Option 2 seems to be "catching up." We can continue our table to see if Option 2 will ever pay more money than Option 1.

x	11	12	13	14	15	16	17	18	19	20
1,000x	11,000	12,000	13,000	14,000	15,000	16,000	17,000	18,000	19,000	20,000
2^{x-1}	1,024	2,048	4,096	8,192	16,384	32,768	65,536	131,072	262,144	524,288

We can also solve the problem by graphing the two equations on the calculator.

Enter the functions as follows, being sure to put the $x - 1$ into parentheses.

```
Plot1  Plot2  Plot3
\Y1■1000X
\Y2■2^(x-1)
\Y3=
\Y4=
\Y5=
\Y6=
\Y7=
```

Be aware that our equations are valid only for integer values of x from 1 to 20. We could enter the values as *discrete data*, that is, just the 20 points. However, it is easier for us to enter the two equations and just focus on the values we need.

Let's look at the first 16 days. Set Xmin to 0, Xmax to 16, and press ‭ZOOM‬ ‭0‬. This will adjust the y-values to correspond with values of x from 0 to 16. You should obtain the following graph.

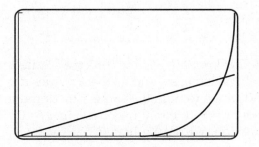

You should recognize the first equation as a linear function. The dollar amount increases at a constant rate of $1,000 per day. The slope of this function is the same between each pair of points. The second equation is an **exponential function**. Although each day's prize money doubles the previous day's money, the dollar amount of the increase is constantly increasing. The linear function will never "catch up" to the exponential function.

Let us now focus on the concept of exponential functions in general. An exponential function has the form $y = b^x$ where $b > 0$, $b \neq 1$, and x is a variable. The functions $y = 2^x$, $y = 2^{x-1}$, $y = 3^x$, $y = 3^{x+1}$ are examples of exponential functions. If $b > 1$, then as the x-values increase, the y-values also increase. What happens as the x-values decrease? Look at the function $y = 3^x$ and its table of values.

x	-3	-2	-1	0	1	2	3
3^x	$\dfrac{1}{27}$	$\dfrac{1}{9}$	$\dfrac{1}{3}$	1	3	9	27

Since 3 raised to any power is always a positive number, as the x-values decrease (go in the negative direction), the y-values get smaller and smaller but remain positive, never actually reaching 0. Since $y = 3^x$ is defined for all real values of x, our domain is the set of real numbers; our range is the set of positive real numbers: $\{y : y > 0\}$.

Let's look at the graph of $y = 3^x$ in the window set to $-3 \leq x \leq 3$ and $0 \leq y \leq 30$.

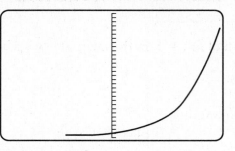

The curve is very similar to the graph of $y = 2^{x-1}$.

Next, consider the function $y = \left(\dfrac{1}{2}\right)^x$. In this case, the value of the base is positive but less than 1. A table of values will help us to determine what we expect to see in the graph.

x	-3	-2	-1	0	1	2	3
$\left(\dfrac{1}{2}\right)^x$	8	4	2	1	$\dfrac{1}{2}$	$\dfrac{1}{4}$	$\dfrac{1}{8}$

The pattern is the opposite of the two previous exponential functions we studied. In this case, as the x-values increase the y-values decrease, and as the x-values decrease the y-values increase. The domain and range remain the same. The domain is the set of real numbers; the range is the set of positive real numbers: $\{y : y > 0\}$.

Examine the graph of this exponential function. We set Ymin = 5.

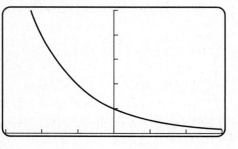

The graph of $y = \left(\dfrac{1}{2}\right)^x$ is the reflection in the y-axis of $y = 2^x$. The line $y = 0$ (the x-axis) is a horizontal asymptote for both functions. Each graph intersects the y-axis at the point $(0, 1)$. Recall that when we reflect in the y-axis, we negate the x-values. Therefore, for each point (x, y) on the graph of $y = 2^x$, there is a corresponding point $(-x, y)$ on the graph of $y = 2^{-x} = \dfrac{1}{2^x} = \left(\dfrac{1}{2}\right)^x$. We can say that the graph is *asymptotic* to the x-axis, or that the x-axis (whose equation is $y = 0$) is an *asymptote*.

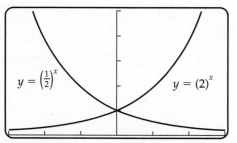

1 **a** On a coordinate plane, sketch the graph of $f(x) = 2^x$ in the interval $-3 \leq x \leq 3$.
   b Evaluate $f(2)$.
   c Evaluate $f(2.5)$, to the nearest thousandth.
   d Solve for x: $f(x) = 2$.
   e Solve for x: $f(x) = 2.5$, to the nearest thousandth.

SOLUTION

a

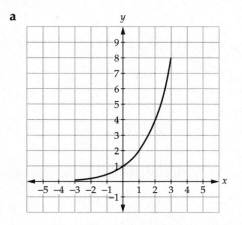

b We can substitute 2 for the value of x in the function $f(x) = 2^x$ and obtain $f(2) = 2^2 = 4$.
c We can substitute 2.5 for the value of x in the function $f(x) = 2^x$ and obtain $f(2.5) = 2^{2.5}$. This is the same as $2^{\frac{5}{2}} = \left(\sqrt{2}\right)^5$ or $\sqrt{32}$. We need the calculator to evaluate this: $f(2.5) \approx 5.657$.

Note: We could also utilize the tracing feature of the calculator. Press (**TRACE**) and enter 2.5 as the value of x.

d The equation $f(x) = 2$ requires a value of x such that $2^x = 2$. We know that $2^1 = 2$. Therefore, $x = 1$.
e The equation $f(x) = 2.5$ requires a value of x such that $2^x = 2.5$. We know that $2^1 = 2$ and $2^2 = 4$. Therefore, our answer is between 1 and 2. We must use a calculator to solve this equation.

Since we are being asked to find an x-value that would produce a y-value of 2.5, graph $y = 2^x$ in Y_1 and $y = 2.5$ in Y_2. Find the intersection of the two graphs. After both equations are graphed, press (**2nd**) (**TRACE**) (**5**) (intersect). We see that $x \approx 1.322$.

We can generalize what we have noticed through our exploration of exponential functions.

- The equation $y = b^x$, where $b > 0$ and $b \neq 1$, is an exponential function.
- Domain: $\{x : x \in \mathbb{R}\}$
- Range: $\{y : y > 0\}$
- If $b > 1$, as the x-values increase, the y-values increase.
- If $0 < b < 1$, as the x-values increase, the y-values decrease.

The function $y = b^x$ is a one-to-one function that is asymptotic to the x-axis and has a y-intercept of 1.

2 Graph $y = 2^x$, $y = 3^x$, and $y = 4^x$ on the same set of axes. Describe their similarities and differences.

SOLUTION

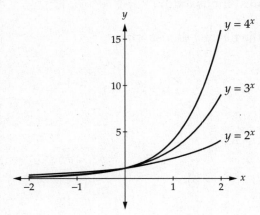

Notice that the graphs are quite similar and that the domain and range for each function are the same.

Domain: $\{x : x \in \mathbb{R}\}$

Range: $\{y : y > 0\}$

For each graph, as the x-values increase, the y-values increase also.

The y-intercept for each function is the same point, $(0, 1)$.

When $x > 0$, the function $y = 4^x$ increases more quickly than the other two. When $x < 0$, the function $y = 4^x$ decreases more quickly.

 Practice

Exercises 1–10: Write the numeral preceding the choice that best completes the statement or answers the question.

1 The graph of the equation $y = b^x$, where $b > 0$, lies in quadrants

(1) I and II
(2) II and III
(3) III and IV
(4) I and IV

2 If the graphs of $y = x$ and $y = 2^x$ are drawn on the same set of axes, they will intersect when x is equal to

(1) 1
(2) 2
(3) 0
(4) They will never intersect.

3 If the graphs of $y = 2x$ and $y = 2^x$ are drawn on the same set of axes, they will intersect when x is equal to

(1) 1
(2) 2
(3) 1 and 2
(4) They will never intersect.

4 Which is an exponential function?

I $y = x^2$ II $y = 0.6^x$

(1) I only
(2) II only
(3) I and II
(4) neither of these

5 Which is *not* a function?

(1) $y = \left(\dfrac{1}{3}\right)^x$

(2) $xy = 16$

(3) $y = (x - 3)^2$

(4) $x^2 + y^2 = 5$

6 Which is *not* in the domain of $y = 2^x$?

(1) -2

(2) 0

(3) 3

(4) They are all in the domain.

7 Which is *not* in the range of $y = 2^x$?

(1) 1

(2) -2

(3) 3

(4) They are all in the range.

8 If $f(x) = 5^x$, find $f(-2)$.

(1) -25

(2) -10

(3) $\dfrac{1}{25}$

(4) $\dfrac{1}{10}$

9 If $f(x) = 4^x$, what x-value would satisfy the equation $f(x) = 64$?

(1) 16

(2) 8

(3) 3

(4) 4

10 The graph of $y = \left(\dfrac{1}{b}\right)^x$ for $b > 0$ is a reflection of the graph of $y = b^x$ in the

(1) x-axis

(2) y-axis

(3) line $y = x$

(4) line $y = -x$

11 **a** Complete the table for the values of y for the equation $y = 4^x$.

x	-2	-1	0	1	2
y					

b Use the completed table to graph the equation $y = 4^x$ on a coordinate plane for the interval $-2 \le x \le 2$. Label the graph A.

c Reflect the graph in the y-axis. Label the graph B.

d Write an equation for the function whose graph is B.

12 **a** On a coordinate plane, sketch the graph of $f(x) = 3^x$ in the interval $-3 \le x \le 2$.

b Use your calculator to find $f(-1.6)$.

c Use your calculator to graph the function and find the value of x that would satisfy the equation $f(x) = 1.6$.

13 **a** On a coordinate plane, sketch the graph of $y = \left(\dfrac{1}{4}\right)^x$ in the interval $-2 \le x \le 2$.

b On the same set of axes, sketch the graph of $y = x + 5$.

c Use your calculator to find the value of x that would satisfy the equation $\left(\dfrac{1}{4}\right)^x = x + 5$.

14 **a** Graph and label the function $y = 2^x$ in the interval $-3 \le x \le 3$. Label the graph A.

b On the same set of axes, sketch the reflection of $y = 2^x$ in the x-axis and label the image B.

c Write an equation for the function whose graph is B.

15 **a** Graph and label the function $y = \left(\dfrac{1}{2}\right)^x$ in the interval $-3 \le x \le 3$.

b On the same set of axes, sketch the translation of $y = \left(\dfrac{1}{2}\right)^x$ under $T_{(0, -3)}$.

c What are the x- and y-intercepts of the graphs drawn in part **a**?

d What are the x- and y-intercepts of the graphs drawn in part **b**?

16 One of the graphs shown below is the graph of $y = \left(\dfrac{2}{3}\right)^x$, the other is the graph of $y = \left(\dfrac{3}{2}\right)^x$. Identify each of the graphs and explain your reasoning.

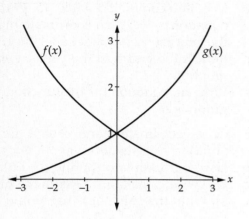

17 Graph $y = \left(\dfrac{1}{2}\right)^x$, $y = \left(\dfrac{1}{3}\right)^x$, and $y = \left(\dfrac{1}{4}\right)^x$. Discuss the similarities and differences of the three graphs.

18 **a** Graph $y = 3^x$.
   b On the same set of axes, sketch the transformation of the graph drawn in part **a** under $r_{x\text{-}axis}$ and label it B.
   c Write an equation for the graph drawn in part **b**.

19 **a** Graph $y = \left(\dfrac{3}{4}\right)^x$.
   b On the same set of axes, sketch the transformation of the graph drawn in part **a** under $r_{y\text{-}axis}$ and label it B.
   c Write an equation for the graph drawn in part **b**.

20 **a** Graph $y = 2^x$.
   b On the same set of axes, sketch the transformation of the graph drawn in part **a** under $T_{0,3}$ and label it B.
   c Write an equation for the graph drawn in part **b**.

21 Match the graphs drawn below with one of the following equations:
$$y = 2^x, y = 2^{-x}, y = 3^x, y = 3^{-x}, y = -3^x$$

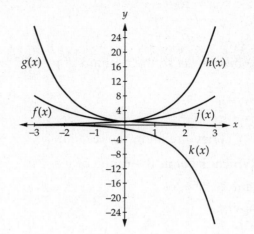

Explain how you could match the graphs with the equations without using your calculator.

22 Given the functions $f(x) = 2^x$ and $g(x) = 4^x$, answer the following questions without using your calculator.

   a For what value(s) of x are the two functions equal?
   b Which function has greater values when $x > 0$? Explain.
   c Which function has greater values when $x < 0$? Explain.

23 Given the functions $h(x) = 2^x$ and $j(x) = \left(\dfrac{1}{2}\right)^x$, answer the following questions without using your calculator.

   a For what value(s) of x are the two functions equal?
   b Which function has greater values when $x > 0$? Explain.
   c Which function has greater values when $x < 0$? Explain.
   d Rewrite $j(x)$ using a negative exponent.
   e What transformation would map $h(x)$ onto $j(x)$?

7.3 Solving Equations Involving Exponents

Let's recall the process used in solving equations containing radicals.

🗂 MODEL PROBLEM

1 Solve for x: $\sqrt{2x - 4} + 3 = 5$

SOLUTION

$$\sqrt{2x - 4} + 3 = 5$$

Isolate the radical: $\quad\quad\sqrt{2x - 4} = 2$

Square both sides: $\quad\left(\sqrt{2x - 4}\right)^2 = 2^2$

Simplify: $\quad\quad\quad\quad\quad 2x - 4 = 4$

$$2x = 8$$

$$x = 4$$

Check for extraneous roots.

$$\sqrt{2x - 4} + 3 = 5$$

$$\sqrt{2(4) - 4} + 3 \stackrel{?}{=} 5$$

$$\sqrt{4} + 3 \stackrel{?}{=} 5$$

$$5 = 5 \checkmark$$

Answer: $x = 4$

We know that radicals can be written as fractional exponents. So we can rewrite $\sqrt{2x - 4}$ as $(2x - 4)^{\frac{1}{2}}$ and the equation above as $(2x - 4)^{\frac{1}{2}} + 3 = 5$.

To solve this equation, we first isolate the expression with the exponent. Then, we raise both sides of the equation to the second power and continue as we did in the model problem above. If the exponent had been $\frac{1}{3}$ instead of $\frac{1}{2}$, we would have raised both sides of the equation to the third power.

What do we do if we have an exponent of $\frac{3}{4}$? Look at the following example.

🗂 MODEL PROBLEM

2 Solve for x: $x^{\frac{3}{4}} = 8$

SOLUTION

We want to eliminate the exponent to leave us with $x^1 = x$.

Recall that when raising a power to a power, we multiply the exponents.

What number when multiplied by $\frac{3}{4}$ will give us 1? The answer is $\frac{4}{3}$, which is the reciprocal of $\frac{3}{4}$.

Now solve the equation.

Note:
$$\left(x^{\frac{3}{4}}\right)^{\frac{4}{3}} = x^{\frac{3}{4} \cdot \frac{4}{3}}$$
$$= x^1 = x$$

Raise both sides to the $\frac{4}{3}$ power: $(x^{\frac{3}{4}})^{\frac{4}{3}} = 8^{\frac{4}{3}}$

Simplify: $x = 16$

Check the solution in the original equation.

$x^{\frac{3}{4}} = 8$

$16^{\frac{3}{4}} \stackrel{?}{=} 8$

$8 = 8 \checkmark$

Answer: $x = 16$

To solve equations with fractional or negative exponents:

1. Isolate the expression containing the exponent.
2. Raise both sides to the reciprocal of the power.
3. Solve the resulting equation.
4. Check your answer in the original equation.

MODEL PROBLEM

3 Solve for y.

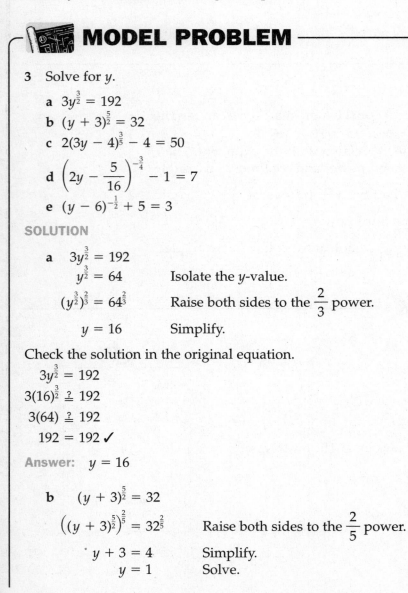

a $3y^{\frac{3}{2}} = 192$

b $(y + 3)^{\frac{5}{2}} = 32$

c $2(3y - 4)^{\frac{3}{5}} - 4 = 50$

d $\left(2y - \dfrac{5}{16}\right)^{-\frac{3}{4}} - 1 = 7$

e $(y - 6)^{-\frac{1}{2}} + 5 = 3$

SOLUTION

a $3y^{\frac{3}{2}} = 192$

$\quad\quad y^{\frac{3}{2}} = 64$ Isolate the y-value.

$\quad (y^{\frac{3}{2}})^{\frac{2}{3}} = 64^{\frac{2}{3}}$ Raise both sides to the $\frac{2}{3}$ power.

$\quad\quad\quad y = 16$ Simplify.

Check the solution in the original equation.

$3y^{\frac{3}{2}} = 192$

$3(16)^{\frac{3}{2}} \stackrel{?}{=} 192$

$3(64) \stackrel{?}{=} 192$

$192 = 192 \checkmark$

Answer: $y = 16$

b $(y + 3)^{\frac{5}{2}} = 32$

$\quad \left((y + 3)^{\frac{5}{2}}\right)^{\frac{2}{5}} = 32^{\frac{2}{5}}$ Raise both sides to the $\frac{2}{5}$ power.

$\quad\quad\quad y + 3 = 4$ Simplify.

$\quad\quad\quad\quad y = 1$ Solve.

Check the solution in the original equation.

$(y + 3)^{\frac{5}{2}} = 32$

$(1 + 3)^{\frac{5}{2}} \stackrel{?}{=} 32$

$4^{\frac{5}{2}} \stackrel{?}{=} 32$

$32 = 32 ✓$

Answer: $y = 1$

    c $2(3y - 4)^{\frac{3}{5}} - 4 = 50$

$2(3y - 4)^{\frac{3}{5}} = 54$ Isolate the expression containing the exponent.

$(3y - 4)^{\frac{3}{5}} = 27$

$\left((3y - 4)^{\frac{3}{5}}\right)^{\frac{5}{3}} = 27^{\frac{5}{3}}$ Raise both sides to the $\dfrac{5}{3}$ power.

$3y - 4 = 243$ Simplify.

$3y = 247$ Solve.

$y = \dfrac{247}{3}$

Check the solution in the original equation.

$2(3y - 4)^{\frac{3}{5}} - 4 = 50$

$2\left(3\left(\dfrac{247}{3}\right) - 4\right)^{\frac{3}{5}} - 4 \stackrel{?}{=} 50$

$2(247 - 4)^{\frac{3}{5}} - 4 \stackrel{?}{=} 50$

$2(243)^{\frac{3}{5}} - 4 \stackrel{?}{=} 50$

$2(27) - 4 \stackrel{?}{=} 50$

$50 = 50 ✓$

Answer: $y = \dfrac{247}{3}$

    d $\left(2y - \dfrac{5}{16}\right)^{-\frac{3}{4}} - 1 = 7$

$\left(2y - \dfrac{5}{16}\right)^{-\frac{3}{4}} = 8$ Isolate the expression containing the exponent.

$\left(\left(2y - \dfrac{5}{16}\right)^{-\frac{3}{4}}\right)^{-\frac{4}{3}} = 8^{-\frac{4}{3}}$ Raise both sides to the $-\dfrac{4}{3}$ power.

$2y - \dfrac{5}{16} = \dfrac{1}{16}$ Simplify.

$2y = \dfrac{6}{16}$ Solve.

$y = \dfrac{3}{16}$

Check the solution in the original equation.

$$\left(2y - \frac{5}{16}\right)^{-\frac{3}{4}} - 1 = 7$$

$$\left(2\left(\frac{3}{16}\right) - \frac{5}{16}\right)^{-\frac{3}{4}} - 1 \stackrel{?}{=} 7$$

$$\left(\frac{6}{16} - \frac{5}{16}\right)^{-\frac{3}{4}} - 1 \stackrel{?}{=} 7$$

$$\left(\frac{1}{16}\right)^{-\frac{3}{4}} - 1 \stackrel{?}{=} 7$$

$$8 - 1 \stackrel{?}{=} 7$$

$$7 = 7 \checkmark$$

Answer: $y = \dfrac{3}{16}$

e $(y - 6)^{-\frac{1}{2}} + 5 = 3$

$\qquad (y - 6)^{-\frac{1}{2}} = -2$ Isolate the y-value.

$\qquad \left((y - 6)^{-\frac{1}{2}}\right)^{-2} = (-2)^{-2}$ Raise both sides to the -2 power.

$\qquad\qquad y - 6 = \dfrac{1}{4}$ Simplify.

$\qquad\qquad y = 6\dfrac{1}{4}$ Solve.

Check the solution in the original equation.

$$(y - 6)^{-\frac{1}{2}} + 5 = 3$$

$$\left(6\frac{1}{4} - 6\right)^{-\frac{1}{2}} + 5 \stackrel{?}{=} 3$$

$$\left(\frac{1}{4}\right)^{-\frac{1}{2}} + 5 \stackrel{?}{=} 3$$

$$2 + 5 \stackrel{?}{=} 3$$

$$7 \neq 3$$

Our solution does not check in the original equation. We could have determined this as we were solving the equation when we obtained $(y - 6)^{-\frac{1}{2}} = -2$, because no real number has a negative square root. Since our equation does not have a solution, we indicate the solution set with the symbol for the empty set, $\varnothing$.

Answer: $\varnothing$ or $\{\ \ \}$

Practice

Exercises 1–16: Solve and check. All variables represent positive numbers.

1 $x^{\frac{5}{3}} = 25$

2 $y^{\frac{3}{4}} = 125$

3 $z^{-\frac{5}{3}} = 243$

4 $2a^{-\frac{1}{4}} = 12$

5 $a^{\frac{3}{5}} - 2 = 25$

6 $2b^{-\frac{1}{3}} + 5 = 15$

7 $3r^{-\frac{3}{4}} = 81$

8 $-4s^{-\frac{3}{5}} - 1 = 31$

9 $(g - 1)^{\frac{1}{2}} = 5$

10 $(w + 1)^{-\frac{1}{3}} = 2$

11 $(r - 4)^{-\frac{1}{2}} - 1 = 5$

12 $2(v - 1)^{\frac{3}{4}} = 16$

13 $(3x - 1)^{\frac{3}{5}} = 125$

14 $(5z - 2)^{\frac{5}{3}} - 1 = 31$

15 $3(2m + 3)^{\frac{3}{2}} + 2 = 26$

16 $2(3y + 2)^{-\frac{5}{2}} = \dfrac{1}{16}$

Exercises 17–20: Select the numeral preceding the choice that best completes the statement or answers the question.

17 Which of the following equations does *not* have a solution in the set of real numbers?

(1) $y^{\frac{2}{3}} = -4$
(2) $y^{\frac{1}{3}} = -8$
(3) $y^{-\frac{2}{3}} = 4$
(4) $y^{-\frac{1}{2}} = 5$

18 A root of $(z - 2)^{-\frac{3}{4}} = 8$ is

(1) -2
(2) $-\dfrac{31}{16}$
(3) $\dfrac{31}{16}$
(4) $\dfrac{33}{16}$

19 To solve the equation $\sqrt{(x + 1)^3} = 4$, we can rewrite the equation as

(1) $\dfrac{2}{3}(x + 1) = 4$
(2) $\dfrac{3}{2}(x + 1) = 4$
(3) $(x + 1)^{\frac{2}{3}} = 4$
(4) $(x + 1)^{\frac{3}{2}} = 4$

20 The solution of the equation $y^{\frac{5}{3}} = 8$ is

(1) rational
(2) irrational
(3) imaginary
(4) nonexistent

7.4 Solving Exponential Equations

Just as an exponential function is a function in which the variable is in the exponent, an **exponential equation** is an equation in which the variable appears in an exponent.

Let's look at an example:

Solve for x: $3^x = 9$

We know that $9 = 3^2$, so we know that x must be equal to 2.

What if we had to solve the equation $3^{x-1} = 9$? We know that $9 = 3^2$, so $3^{x-1} = 3^2$, $x - 1 = 2$, and $x = 3$.

What if we had $3^{2x-3} = 9$? Again, since $9 = 3^2$, we know that $3^{2x-3} = 3^2$, so $2x - 3 = 2$, and $x = \dfrac{5}{2}$.

Think about how we are solving these equations. We are rewriting both sides of the equations with the same base, setting the exponents equal to each other, and solving the resulting equation.

Remember: If $b^x = b^y$, $b \neq 0, 1$, then $x = y$.

1 Solve for y: $2^{3y-6} = 8$

SOLUTION

$2^{3y-6} = 8$

$2^{3y-6} = 2^3$ Rewrite 8 as a power of 2 since $8 = 2^3$.

$3y - 6 = 3$ The bases are the same, so we can now equate the exponents.

   $3y = 9$ Solve the equation.

    $y = 3$

Check:

$2^{3y-6} = 8$

$2^{3(3)-6} \stackrel{?}{=} 8$

  $2^3 \stackrel{?}{=} 8$

  $8 = 8$ ✓

Answer: $y = 3$

Sometimes we have to rewrite both sides of the equation, as shown in the examples below.

2 Solve.

   a $9^x = 27$

   b $4^{x+1} = 8^x$

   c $\left(\dfrac{1}{9}\right)^x = 27^{1-x}$

SOLUTION

   a $9^x = 27$

      $(3^2)^x = 3^3$ Rewrite both sides of the equation as powers of 3.

        $3^{2x} = 3^3$ Simplify the left side by multiplying the exponents.

        $2x = 3$ Since the bases are the same, equate the exponents.

         $x = \dfrac{3}{2}$ Solve the resulting equation.

Check:

$9^x = 27$

$9^{\frac{3}{2}} \stackrel{?}{=} 27$

$27 = 27$ ✓

Answer: $x = \dfrac{3}{2}$

   b $4^{x+1} = 8^x$

      $(2^2)^{x+1} = 2^{3x}$ Rewrite both sides of the equation as powers of 2.

    $2(x + 1) = 3x$ Since the bases are the same, equate the exponents.

      $2x + 2 = 3x$ Solve the resulting equation.

           $x = 2$

Check:

$4^{x+1} = 8^x$

$4^{2+1} \overset{?}{=} 8^2$

$4^3 \overset{?}{=} 8^2$

$64 = 64 \checkmark$

Answer: $x = 2$

c $\left(\dfrac{1}{9}\right)^x = 27^{1-x}$

$(3^{-2})^x = (3^3)^{1-x}$ Rewrite both sides of the equation as powers of 3.

$-2x = 3(1 - x)$ Since the bases are the same, equate the exponents.

$-2x = 3 - 3x$ Solve the resulting equation.

$x = 3$

Check:

$\left(\dfrac{1}{9}\right)^x = 27^{1-x}$

$\left(\dfrac{1}{9}\right)^3 \overset{?}{=} 27^{1-3}$

$\left(\dfrac{1}{9}\right)^3 \overset{?}{=} 27^{-2}$

$\dfrac{1}{729} = \dfrac{1}{729} \checkmark$

Answer: $x = 3$

In solving exponential equations, it is not always possible to rewrite both sides of the equation in terms of the same base. The method for solving such equations algebraically will be discussed in Chapter 8. At this point, you can use your graphing calculator as illustrated in the model problems that follow.

MODEL PROBLEMS

3 Solve $2^{-2x} = 3^{x+1}$ for x. Round to the nearest hundredth.

SOLUTION

We cannot change both sides of the equation to the same base. We can, however, use a graphing calculator to solve the equation.

First, enter both sides of the equation into the $\boxed{\text{Y=}}$ editor of the calculator. Be sure to put the $-2x$ and the $x + 1$ into parentheses.

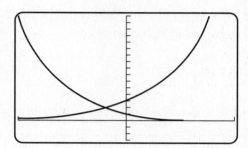

When the two equations are graphed in the window set to $-2 \le x \le 2$ and $-3 \le y \le 16$, we obtain the graph shown below.

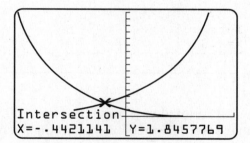

We can see that the two graphs intersect. Enter (2nd) (TRACE), 5: intersect, and obtain the point of intersection.

Answer: $x \approx -0.44$

Of course, we could also use the calculator to solve exponential equations that can be expressed as integral powers of the same base.

2   Solve for x: $2^{-2x} = 4^{x+1}$

SOLUTION

Since 4 is a power of 2, we could solve this problem algebraically by rewriting the right side of the equation as a power of 2 and then proceeding as explained above.

$2^{-2x} = 4^{x+1}$

$2^{-2x} = (2^2)^{x+1}$ Rewrite the right side of the equation as a power of 2.

$-2x = 2x + 2$ Since the bases are the same, equate the exponents.

$-4x = 2$ Solve.

$x = -\dfrac{1}{2}$

Check:
$$2^{-2x} = 4^{x+1}$$
$$2^{-2\left(-\frac{1}{2}\right)} \stackrel{?}{=} 4^{-\frac{1}{2}+1}$$
$$2^1 \stackrel{?}{=} 4^{\frac{1}{2}}$$
$$2 = 2 \checkmark$$

This equation can also be solved graphically.

First enter the two sides of the equation into the $\boxed{\text{Y=}}$ editor of the calculator, as shown.

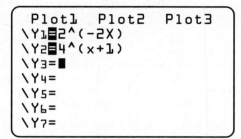

Graph both equations and use your calculator to find the point of intersection.

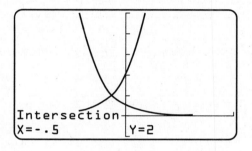

The point of intersection occurs at $x = -0.5$.

Answer: $x = -\dfrac{1}{2}$

![Pencil icon] **Practice**

Exercises 1–15: Solve and check.

1 $5^x = 125$

2 $6^{z-2} = 216$

3 $2^{r+1} = 4^r$

4 $3^{2x} = 27^{x+1}$

5 $5^{x+1} = \dfrac{1}{125}$

6 $\dfrac{1}{36} = 6^{2x}$

7 $4^s = 8^{s-2}$

8 $25^{x-1} = 125^x$

9 $\dfrac{1}{8} = 16^x$

10 $9^{x-1} = 27^{x+1}$

11 $216 = 36^n$

12 $100^p = 1{,}000^{p+1}$

13 $16^{x-2} = 64^{x-3}$

14 $2^{x^2-x} = 4$

15 $\left(\dfrac{1}{49}\right)^{x+1} = 343^x$

Exercises 16–20: Select the numeral preceding the choice that best completes the statement or answers the question.

16 Solve for y: $4^y = 8^{y-1}$

(1) 1   (3) 3
(2) 2   (4) 4

17 The solution set of $3^{x^2-x} = 9^x$ is

(1) $\{0\}$ (3) $\{3\}$
(2) $\{0, 2\}$ (4) $\{0, 3\}$

18 Solve for z: $16^{z-2} = \left(\dfrac{1}{8}\right)^z$

(1) -2
(2) -1
(3) $\dfrac{7}{8}$
(4) $\dfrac{8}{7}$

19 Solve for x: $\left(\dfrac{9}{16}\right)^x = \dfrac{27}{64}$

(1) $\dfrac{2}{3}$
(2) $\dfrac{3}{2}$
(3) 3
(4) 4

20 Solve for y: $125^{-2x} = 25^{x+1}$

(1) $-\dfrac{1}{4}$
(2) $\dfrac{1}{4}$
(3) $\dfrac{5}{2}$
(4) 4

Exercises 21–30: Solve each equation using your graphing calculator. If possible, solve algebraically as well as graphically. Round to the *nearest hundredth*.

21 $9^{r+1} = 27$

22 $4^{w-1} = 5$

23 $36^p = 216^{p-1}$

24 $12^x = 24^{x-2}$

25 $0.25^v = 16$

26 $0.35^w = 12$

27 $25^{x+1} = 5^x$

28 $6^{2r} = 4^{r+3}$

29 $2^{x-2} = 6^x$

30 $3^m = 6^{m-2}$

7.5 Applications of Exponential Equations

Many real-world situations can be modeled as exponential functions. One of the most familiar examples of exponential growth is compound interest.

If you invested $1 in the bank at 4% annual interest and you earned *simple interest* on your money, you would receive 4% of $1 = $0.04 each year. If you left your money in the bank for ten years you would have gained $0.04 each year for the ten years, giving you a total of $0.40 interest. The amount you would have in the bank would be $1.40.

However, if you earned interest that was *compounded* each year, you would earn interest not only on the original $1 but also on the interest you gained each year.

In the first year, you earn 4% interest on $1. This is a 4% increase on your $1 investment, so you would receive 104% of your $1 = 1(1.04) = $1.04.

In the second year, you receive a 4% increase on the previous year's money. So you would have

$$1(1.04) \times (1.04) = 1.04^2 = 1.0816 = \$1.08.$$
<small>from year 1</small>

This would continue in the third year, where you would have

$$1(1.04)(1.04) \times (1.04) = 1.04^3 = 1.124864 = \$1.12.$$
<small>from the first two years</small>

In ten years, you would have $1.04^{10} = \$1.48$. You would receive $0.48 interest over the ten-year period if the interest were compounded annually. Of course, if you had more than $1 in the bank, this would make a significant difference in the amount of interest you received.

In general, exponential functions are in the form $f(x) = ab^x$, where $a \neq 0$, $b > 0$, and $b \neq 1$. Since $f(0) = ab^0 = a(1) = a$, a is called the **initial value** and b is called the **growth factor**. If $b > 1$, the model is increasing, or growing; if $0 < b < 1$, the model is decreasing, or decaying.

In our interest example, if you had $100 in the bank gaining 4% annual interest, compounded annually, the equation $f(x) = 100(1.04)^x$ would model the amount of money you would have in the bank after x years. To find the amount of money you would have after ten years, substitute 10 for x. Thus, $f(10) = 100(1.04)^{10} = 148.02$. You would have $148.02 in ten years.

> **Note:** Given an exponential function in the form $y = ab^x$, the y-intercept is $(0, a)$.

MODEL PROBLEMS

1 In the 2007–2008 academic year, the average cost for one year at a four-year private college was $23,712, which was an increase of 6.3% from the previous year. If this trend were to continue, the function $C(x) = 23{,}712(1.063)^x$ could be used to model the cost, $C(x)$, of a college education x years from 2007.

   a Find $C(4)$.

   b If this trend continues, how much would parents expect to pay for their new baby's first year of college? (Assume the child would enter college in 18 years.)

   c If this trend continues, when will one year of a private college cost an average of $50,000?

SOLUTION

   a To find $C(4)$, substitute 4 for x in the formula $C(x) = 23{,}712(1.063)^x$.
   Thus, $C(4) = 23{,}712(1.063)^4 = 30{,}276.19$.
   This means that the average cost would be $30,276.19 in the 2011–2012 school year.

   b To find the average cost of a year of college 18 years from now, substitute 18 for x in the formula $C(x) = 23{,}712(1.063)^x$ to get $C(18) = 23{,}712(1.063)^{18} = 71{,}214.26$. It would cost the parents $71,214.26 for their child's first year of college.
   Alternatively, you could obtain an answer by graphing the function and evaluating the function for $x = 18$, as shown below.

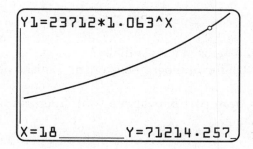

c To find when the average cost will be $50,000, set $C(x) = 50,000$ and solve for x.

We will have to use a graphing calculator to solve this equation.

Graph $y = 23{,}712(1.063)^x$ and also graph $y = 50{,}000$.

Use the calculator to determine when the two graphs intersect, as shown below.

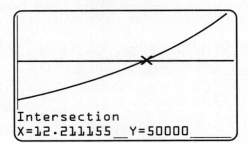

```
Intersection
X=12.211155  Y=50000
```

According to our graph, one year of a private college will cost an average of $50,000 in approximately 12 years from the 2007–2008 academic year. That will be the 2019–2020 school year.

We can gain quite a bit of information from reading graphs, including determining a possible equation for our function.

2 Tanisha is a talented artist who has begun her own business designing and printing custom greeting cards. The number of customers has grown steadily, as illustrated in the graph below.

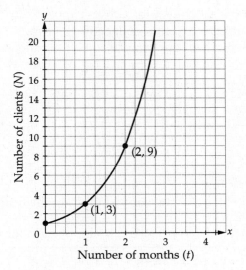

a How many customers did Tanisha have initially?

b Write an equation for $N(t)$, the number of customers Tanisha has t months after she began her business.

c Based on your formula from part **b**, evaluate $N(3)$. Interpret what this means in terms of the number of clients Tanisha has.

SOLUTION

a By looking at the graph, at time 0, we see that Tanisha has 1 client.

b We now have 3 points on the graph: (0, 1), (1, 3), and (2, 9). We can see that the graph is an exponential function. The y-coordinate is always a power of 3: $1 = 3^0$, $3 = 3^1$, and $9 = 3^2$. So our equation is $N(t) = 3^t$.

We can also determine the formula algebraically.

First, the formula for an exponential function is $N(t) = ab^t$, where a is the initial value.

Since our initial value is 1, we know that our formula is $N(t) = 1 \cdot b^t = b^t$.

Now we can substitute values for t and $N(t)$, giving us $3 = b^1$.
Thus, $b = 3$ and our equation is $N(t) = 3^t$.

c Substitute 3 for the t in the above formula: $N(3) = 3^3 = 27$. Tanisha has 27 customers 3 months after she began her business.

Let's go back and reexamine our interest example from the start of this section. We concluded that if you had \$100 in the bank gaining 4% annual interest, compounded annually, the equation $f(x) = 100(1.04)^x$ would model the amount of money you would have in the bank after x years.

What if the interest was compounded quarterly, instead of annually? You would receive 1% interest every quarter, and interest would be compounded four times a year, for x years.

The formula would be $g(x) = 100(1.01)^{4x}$. To see what difference this would make, let's find how much money you would receive after 10 years using this new formula.

$$g(10) = 100(1.01)^{4 \cdot 10} = 100(1.01)^{40} = 148.89$$

You would have \$148.89, which is \$0.87 more than the \$148.02 when the interest was compounded annually.

What if the interest was compounded monthly? We would divide the 4% interest by 12 and change the exponent to $12x$, since interest is compounded 12 times per year, for x years.

$$h(x) = 100\left(1 + \frac{0.04}{12}\right)^{12x}, \text{ and } h(10) = 100\left(1 + \frac{0.04}{12}\right)^{12 \cdot 10} = 100\left(1 + \frac{0.04}{12}\right)^{120}$$
$$= 149.08$$

In general, for an interest rate r per year, compounded n times per year for t years, the rate per period is $\frac{r}{n}$ and the number of periods in t years is nt.

The formula for the value of the total amount, A, when P dollars are invested at an interest rate r per year, compounded n times per year for t years is $A = P\left(1 + \frac{r}{n}\right)^{nt}$.

Let's see what happens when we continue to increase the number of times the investment is compounded. We have $A = P\left(1 + \frac{r}{n}\right)^{nt}$.

To make our algebra simpler, let $\frac{r}{n} = \frac{1}{k}$. Therefore, $n = rk$.

$$A = P\left(1 + \frac{r}{n}\right)^{nt} = P\left(1 + \frac{1}{k}\right)^{rkt} = P\left(\left(1 + \frac{1}{k}\right)^k\right)^{rt}$$

Since $n = rk$, and r is a fixed number, as n increases, k increases. The table below shows what happens to the expression $\left(1 + \frac{1}{k}\right)^k$ as k continues to increase.

k	10	100	1,000	10,000	100,000	1,000,000	10,000,000
$\left(1 + \dfrac{1}{k}\right)^k$	2.59374	2.70481	2.71692	2.71815	2.71827	2.71828	2.71828

As k becomes infinitely large, the expression $\left(1 + \dfrac{1}{k}\right)^k$ becomes approximately equal to 2.71828. The expression is approaching the value of the irrational number e, named after the mathematician Leonhard Euler.

When we substitute this into our formula and simplify, we get $P\left(\left(1 + \dfrac{1}{k}\right)^k\right)^{rt} = Pe^{rt}$.

The formula for continuously compounded interest is $A = Pe^{rt}$, where A is the total amount, when P dollars are invested at an interest rate r per year, for t years.

MODEL PROBLEM

3 Susie has invested $2,000 at a rate of 3.5% per year, compounded continuously.

    a How much will she have after 10 years?
    b How long will it take until she has $3,000 in her account?

SOLUTION

    a Using the formula $A = Pe^{rt}$, we substitute 2,000 for P, and 0.035 for r.

$A = 2,000e^{0.035t}$

To determine how much money Susie has after 10 years, replace the t with 10.

$A = 2,000e^{0.035t}$

$ = 2,000e^{0.035 \cdot 10}$

$ = 2,838.14$

Answer: Susie will have $2,838.14 after 10 years.

    b To see when Susie will have $3,000 in her account, we must solve the equation $3,000 = 2,000e^{0.035t}$. Let's graph the two functions $y_1 = 2,000e^{0.035x}$ and $y_2 = 3,000$ and see where the functions intersect. (Set Xmin = 0, Xmax = 20, Ymin = 1,000, Ymax = 3,500, and Yscl = 500.)

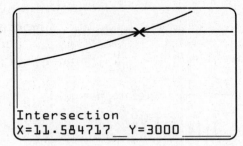

```
Intersection
X=11.584717   Y=3000
```

As we can see from the graph above, $2,000e^{0.035x} = 3,000$ when $x = 11.5847$.

Answer: Susie will have $3,000 in her account approximately $11\dfrac{1}{2}$ years after her initial investment.

Note: Exponential functions with base e have the same properties as other exponential functions. Since $2 < e < 3$, the graph of $f(x) = e^x$ is similar to the graphs of $g(x) = 2^x$ and $h(x) = 3^x$.

Exercises 1–8: Select the numeral preceding the choice that best answers the question.

1 A population increases from 15,000 at an annual rate of 2% per year. Which function would model this?

(1) $P(t) = 15{,}000(0.02)^t$
(2) $P(t) = 15{,}000(0.2)^t$
(3) $P(t) = 15{,}000(1.02)^t$
(4) $P(t) = 15{,}000(1.2)^t$

2 A population decreases from 15,000 at an annual rate of 2% per year. Which function would model this?

(1) $P(t) = 15{,}000(-0.2)^t$
(2) $P(t) = 15{,}000(-0.02)^t$
(3) $P(t) = 15{,}000(0.8)^t$
(4) $P(t) = 15{,}000(0.98)^t$

3 A population increases from 15,000 at a continuous rate of 2% per year. Which function would model this?

(1) $P(t) = 15{,}000e^{0.02t}$
(2) $P(t) = 15{,}000e^{0.2t}$
(3) $P(t) = 15{,}000e^{1.02t}$
(4) $P(t) = 15{,}000e^{1.2t}$

4 A population decreases from 15,000 at a continuous rate of 2% per year. Which function would model this?

(1) $P(t) = 15{,}000e^{-0.2t}$
(2) $P(t) = 15{,}000e^{-0.02t}$
(3) $P(t) = 15{,}000e^{0.8t}$
(4) $P(t) = 15{,}000e^{0.98t}$

5 José took a piece of paper and cut it in half. He put the two pieces together and cut them in half again. He put the four pieces of paper together and cut them in half again. If he continued to do this over and over again, the number of pieces obtained after each cut could be represented by the graph shown below.

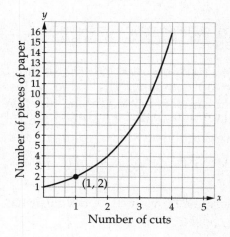

Which equation could be used to represent the graph?

(1) $y = 2x$
(2) $y = 2x + 1$
(3) $y = 2^x$
(4) $y = 2^x + 1$

6 The population of Lonely, NY, can be modeled by the equation $P(t) = 2{,}300(0.85)^t$, where $t = 0$ represents the year 2008. In what year will the population of Lonely be approximately half the size it was in the year 2008?

(1) 2010
(2) 2012
(3) 2014
(4) 2016

7 The table below represents the number of people who are living in Fun Town, NY.

Time (in years since 2000)	0	1	2	3	4
Population (in thousands)	1	3	9	27	81

Which equation can be used to represent the number of people living in Fun Town, NY?

(1) $P(t) = 3t$
(2) $P(t) = 3t^2$
(3) $P(t) = 3^t$
(4) $P(t) = 3(3)^t$

8 Sumil has invested $1,000 in an Internet start-up company. The value of his investment can be modeled by the function $V(t) = 1,000(0.70)^t$, where t is the time, in years, since Sumil made his investment. If the trend continues, how much will Sumil's investment be worth after 5 years?

(1) $3,500
(2) $700
(3) $437.28
(4) $168.07

9 Suppose you receive an inheritance of $5,000 and invest it at 5% interest, compounded annually. The equation $A(x) = 5,000(1.05)^x$ can be used to model this investment, where x is the number of years your money is invested and $A(x)$ represents the amount of money you have.

a How much will you have in 5 years?
b How long will it take for your money to double?

10 Suppose you receive an inheritance of $5,000 and invest it at 5% interest, compounded continuously. The equation $C(x) = 5,000e^{0.05x}$ can be used to model this investment, where x is the number of years your money is invested and $C(x)$ represents the amount of money you have.

a How much will you have in 5 years?
b How long will it take for your money to double?

11 Marissa invests $20,000 at an annual rate of 4.25%, compounded continuously.

a How much money will she have after 6 years?
b To the *nearest year*, how many years will it take for Marissa to double her investment?

12 MacArthur High School is holding a mathematics contest. Each week, students are given mathematics problems to solve. At the end of the week, only the top half of participants is invited to continue with the contest. If 200 students initially participate in the contest, the equation $N(t) = 200(0.5)^t$ can be used to determine the number of students, $N(t)$, participating in the contest after t weeks. This will continue until there is only one student left, who will be declared the winner.

a When will there be only 25% of the original 200 students remaining?
b How many participants will be left after 3 weeks?

13 Given the function $P(t) = 20(1.15)^t$, where $P(t)$ is the population, in thousands, of people in a town, t years after 1990.

a What was the initial population of the town?
b At what rate is the population growing?

14 A used car was purchased in January 2008 for $18,400. If the car loses 12% of its value each year, what will be the value of the car in January 2012?

15 Given the function $F(x) = 20(0.90)^x$, where $F(x)$ is the number of fish in Jason's fish tank and x is the number of days since Jason set up the tank.

a How many fish did Jason have to start?
b What is happening to Jason's fish? Explain.

16 In his second State of the Union address, given on December 1, 1862, Abraham Lincoln wrote that there was an "average decennial increase of 34.60 per cent in population through the seventy years from our first to our last census yet taken. It is seen that the ratio of increase at none of these seven periods is either 2 per cent below or 2 per cent above the predicted average, thus showing how inflexible, and consequently how reliable, the law of increase in our case is." Based on this information, President Lincoln made predictions about the population of the United States for every decade from 1870 to 1930. If the population of the United States in 1860 was estimated to be 31,443,790, and using Lincoln's prediction of a 34.6 percent increase every decade,

a Write an equation for the exponential function that would model the population of the United States x decades after 1860.

b Use your equation from part **a** to predict the population of the United States in 1930, to the *nearest thousand*.

c Use your equation from part **a** to predict when the population of the United States would reach 400,000,000.

d According to the U.S. Census Bureau, the population in the United States in November 2007 was 303,452,900. How does this information fit in with your answers to parts **b** and **c** above?

17 Carbon-14 is used to estimate the age of organic compounds. The formula $f(x) = 100e^{-0.00012101x}$ can be used to estimate the amount of carbon-14 present in a quantity that originally contained 100 micrograms of carbon-14 x years ago.

a How much carbon-14 would you expect to be present if the compound is 1,000 years old?

b To the *nearest year*, how old is the sample if there are 75 micrograms of carbon-14 present?

c According to this formula, to the *nearest year*, how long does it take for a sample of carbon-14 to lose half of its mass?

18 Match each situation to the graph that models it best, without using a calculator. Explain how you arrived at your conclusion.

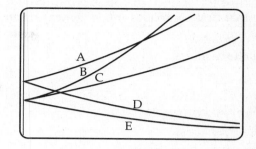

i Melissa deposited $200 in the bank. She received 4% interest, compounded annually.

ii Tom deposited $300 in the bank. He received 4% interest, compounded annually.

iii Sara deposited $200 in the bank. She received 7% interest, compounded continuously.

iv Jeff invested $300 in the stock market. Unfortunately, he lost approximately 5% of his investment each year.

v Jennifer invested $200 in the stock market. Unfortunately, she lost approximately 5% of her investment each year.

19 Give an example of an exponential function that would occur in the real world. How do you know your function is exponential?

20 Sketch the graphs of $y = 2^x$, $y = 3^x$, and $y = e^x$. Explain the similarities and differences of the three graphs.

21 Good news! Your parents have decided to give you an allowance to help with your school expenses. You have two options. Option 1: $1 per day. Option 2: one penny on day 1, two pennies on day two, three pennies on day three, and so forth. For the first option, use the equation $y = x$ to model the amount earned each day and use the equation $y = 0.01(2)^x$ to model the amount earned each day for the second option.

a For how many days will the first option be a better choice?

b When will the two options be worth the same amount? What happens after that?

Exercises 1–24: Select the numeral preceding the choice that best completes the statement or answers the question.

1 Evaluate $6^0 - 9^{\frac{1}{2}}$.

  (1) -3.5
  (2) -2
  (3) 1.5
  (4) 4.5

2 Simplify $(4x^3y^2)(-3x^4y^{-2})$.

  (1) $-12x^7y$
  (2) $-12x^7$
  (3) $-12x^{12}$
  (4) $-12x^{12}y^4$

3 If $m = 4$, evaluate $3(m^3)^{\frac{2}{3}}$.

  (1) $\dfrac{3}{2}$
  (2) 16
  (3) 24
  (4) 48

4 Expressed without negative exponents, the expression $\dfrac{(2a^2b^4)^2}{2a^3b^{-5}}$ equals

  (1) $1ab^3$
  (2) $\dfrac{2b^3}{a}$
  (3) $2ab^{13}$
  (4) $\dfrac{2b^{13}}{a}$

5 The growth of bacteria in a petri dish is modeled by the function $g(t) = 2^{\frac{t}{3}}$. For what value of t is $g(t) = 32$?

  (1) 1
  (2) 9
  (3) 15
  (4) 48

6 Simplify $\dfrac{4^x}{4^2}$.

  (1) 4^{x-2}
  (2) 16^{x-2}
  (3) $x - 2$
  (4) $\dfrac{x}{2}$

7 If $k = 64$, evaluate $\dfrac{1}{2}k^{\frac{2}{3}} + 5(k^{\frac{1}{2}})^{\frac{2}{3}}$.

  (1) 96
  (2) 84
  (3) 28
  (4) 9

8 When $x = 8$, the value of $\left((x^{-2})(27x^0)\right)^{\frac{1}{3}}$ is equivalent to

  (1) $\dfrac{1}{8}$
  (2) $\dfrac{3}{4}$
  (3) 12
  (4) 4

9 To solve the equation $\left(\sqrt[3]{x^2 + 3x}\right)^4 = 16$, we can rewrite the equation as

  (1) $(x^2 + 3x)^{-\frac{4}{3}} = 16$
  (2) $(x^2 + 3x)^{\frac{3}{4}} = 16$
  (3) $(x^2 + 3x)^{\frac{4}{3}} = 16$
  (4) $(x^2 + 3x)^{\frac{2}{3}} = 4$

10 Solve for y: $(y + 3)^{\frac{3}{2}} - 8 = 19$

  (1) 27
  (2) 12
  (3) 9
  (4) 6

11 Solve for x: $3x^{\frac{3}{2}} - 6 = 75$

  (1) $\left(\sqrt[2]{23}\right)^3$
  (2) $\left(\sqrt[3]{23}\right)^2$
  (3) 9
  (4) 27

12 Solve for x: $8^x = 2^{x+6}$

  (1) $\dfrac{1}{2}$
  (2) 2
  (3) 3
  (4) 4

13 Solve for x: $3^{x^2 - 3} = 3^{2x}$

  (1) $\{-1\}$
  (2) $\{-3, 1\}$
  (3) $\{3\}$
  (4) $\{3, -1\}$

14 If x is a positive integer, $(9x)^{\frac{1}{2}}$ is equivalent to

(1) $3x$
(2) $3\sqrt{x}$
(3) $\sqrt{3x}$
(4) $4.5\sqrt{x}$

15 If $2^a = b$, then 2^{a+3} equals

(1) $b + 3$
(2) b^3
(3) $6b$
(4) $8b$

16 Solve for x: $4^{x^2 + 4x} = 4^{-3}$

(1) -1
(2) -3
(3) $\{-3, -1\}$
(4) $\{\ \}$

17 Find the value of $(x + 2)^0 + (x - 1)^{-2}$ when $x = 3$.

(1) -3
(2) -1
(3) $\dfrac{3}{4}$
(4) $\dfrac{5}{4}$

18 Which could *not* be described as an exponential function?

(1) the medication remaining in the body t hours after it is administered
(2) the number of bacteria in a culture that increases 8.3% every hour
(3) the amount of a person's salary if she gets a $1,500 raise every year
(4) the amount of money in a bank account compounded continuously

19 The amount of money, A, accrued at the end of n years when a certain amount, P, is invested at a compound rate is $A = P\left(1 + \dfrac{r}{n}\right)^{nt}$. If a person invests $390 at 6% interest compounded quarterly, find the approximate amount obtained at the end of 15 years.

(1) $923
(2) $952
(3) $1,950
(4) $12,694

20 Solve for a: $16^{a-2} = \left(\dfrac{1}{8}\right)^a$

(1) 1
(2) -2
(3) $\dfrac{7}{8}$
(4) $\dfrac{8}{7}$

21 In 2006, five students wanted to start a Key Club in their school. Each year, the number of members of the club has increased by 8%. Which equation could be used to express the number of members of the Key Club since 2006?

(1) $N(t) = 5(1.08)^t$
(2) $N(t) = 5(1.8)^t$
(3) $N(t) = 5(0.8)^t$
(4) $N(t) = 8(1.05)^t$

22 The increase in population of a bacteria culture can be represented by the exponential formula $h(t) = 14(e^{0.0889t})$, where h = the number of bacteria in thousands and t is time in hours. Approximately how many thousand bacteria will be present in the culture after twelve hours?

(1) 14
(2) 41
(3) 53
(4) 63

23 Every year, the cost of the bowling league dinner increases by 5%. If the initial cost of the dinner is represented by c, which equation shows this relationship?

(1) $y = c(1.5)^x$
(2) $y = c(1.05)^x$
(3) $y = 0.05^x$
(4) $y = c(.95)^x$.

24 Minerva did a study of baby-sitting rates in her neighborhood over the last three years and discovered that the function $b(t) = 7.50(1.2)^t$ represents the average price charged per hour, where t is the number of years since 2006. What was the average price charged per hour in Minerva's neighborhood in 2006?

(1) $9.00
(2) $7.50
(3) $6.30
(4) $1.20

25 Mai Lyn is a talented artist who has begun her own business designing and printing unique business cards. She initially had 10 customers and the number of customers increased by 7.9% per week.

a Write the equation that models this situation.
b Determine the number of customers she had at the end of her *first year*.
c If her financial adviser told her to incorporate the business when her client list reached 1,000 customers, in what week will Mai Lyn file the incorporation papers?

26 Since January 2007, the population of the city of Halycon has grown according to the mathematical model $y = 720{,}500(1.022)^x$, where x is the number of years since January 2007.

   a Explain what the numbers 720,500 and 1.022 represent in this model.

   b If this trend continues, use this model to predict the year in which the population of Halcyon will reach 1,000,000.

27 As cars get older, they are worth less than when they were new. This is called *depreciation*. Suppose you bought a new 2009 Expedition for \$39,389 that depreciates approximately 18% per year.

   a Write the equation that models this situation.

   b Determine the value, to the *nearest dollar*, of the car after 1 year.

   c When will the car first be worth less than \$5,000?

28 P dollars is deposited in an account paying an annual interest rate, r, compounded n times per year. After t years, the amount of money in the account, in dollars, is given by the equation $A = P\left(1 + \dfrac{r}{n}\right)^{nt}$.

   a Rachel deposited \$3,500 at 3.8% annual interest, compounded monthly. How much money, to the *nearest cent*, will she have after 4 years?

   b If the account is untouched, in how many years, to the *nearest tenth of a year*, will she have \$5,000 in the account?

29 Jordan invests \$7,500 at an annual rate of 4.25% compounded continuously, according to the formula $A = Pe^{rt}$, where A is the amount, P is the principal, r is the rate of interest, and t is the time in years.

   a Determine, to the *nearest dollar*, the amount of money he will have in 10 years.

   b Determine how many years, to the *nearest tenth of a year*, it will take for the initial investment to triple.

30 The population of Elfdom in the North Pole suburbs can be represented by the exponential function $P(t) = 47{,}827(e^{-0.1779t})$, where t is time in years when $t = 0$ is 2008.

   a Explain the meaning of 47,827 and $e^{-0.1779t}$ in this function.

   b Since the young elves are leaving Elfdom for the big cities, in how many years, to the *nearest tenth of a year*, will there first be fewer than 15,000 elves in Elfdom?

31 Americans have been steadily increasing their usage of bottled water. In fact, between 1987 and 1996, our use of bottle water doubled. The yearly usage of water, in billions of gallons sold, can be represented by the function $y = 1.55(1.08006)^t$, where t represents the number of years since 1987.

   a How many billions of gallons of water were sold in 1987?

   b What is the yearly rate of growth in sales of bottled water?

   c If this trend continued, how many gallons were sold in 2008?

   d If Americans continue to prefer bottled water at a similar rate, in what year will sales top 100 billion gallons of bottled water?

Logarithmic Functions

8.1 Inverse of an Exponential Function

A **logarithmic function** can be defined as the inverse of an exponential function. Specifically, the word **logarithm** means exponent.

Given the exponential function $y = 4^x$, to find its inverse, we interchange the domain and range:

$$y = 4^x$$

$$x = 4^y$$

Graphically, the function $y = 4^x$, as shown below, lies in Quadrants I and II while its inverse $x = 4^y$ appears in Quadrants I and IV.

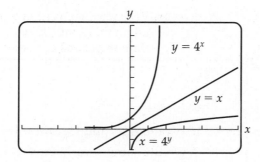

Note: To find an inverse graphically, simply reflect the function in the line $y = x$.

The values of the domain and range are interchanged in any inverse, as demonstrated by this table of values for these two functions.

$y = 4^x$		$x = 4^y$	
x	y	x	y
$-\dfrac{3}{2}$	$\dfrac{1}{8}$	$\dfrac{1}{8}$	$-\dfrac{3}{2}$
-1	$\dfrac{1}{4}$	$\dfrac{1}{4}$	-1
$-\dfrac{1}{2}$	$\dfrac{1}{2}$	$\dfrac{1}{2}$	$-\dfrac{1}{2}$
0	1	1	0
$\dfrac{1}{2}$	2	2	$\dfrac{1}{2}$
1	4	4	1
$\dfrac{3}{2}$	8	8	$\dfrac{3}{2}$

Usually we prefer to write equations that define functions in terms of x.

The expression $x = 4^y$ can be translated as:

y is the exponent to base 4 that produces the result x.

Since a logarithm is an exponent, this can be rewritten as:

y is the logarithm to base 4 of x.

In mathematical notation we write: $y = \log_4 x$. Thus, $y = \log_4 x$ is the inverse of the function $y = 4^x$.

We can summarize this rule as follows:

For $b > 0$ and $b \neq 1$, $x = b^y \leftrightarrow y = \log_b x$.

MODEL PROBLEMS

1 For the function $y = 2^x$:

   a Find the inverse of the function and express it in exponential and logarithmic form.

   b Sketch the graph of $y = 2^x$ such that $-3 \leq x \leq 3$. On the same axes, sketch its inverse.

SOLUTION

   a Both $x = 2^y$ and $y = \log_2 x$ represent the inverse of $y = 2^x$.

   b

When we make a table of values, notice that once again the values of the domain and range are interchanged, indicating that the functions are inverses.

$y = 2^x$		$y = \log_2 x$	
x	y	x	y
-3	$\dfrac{1}{8}$	$\dfrac{1}{8}$	-3
-2	$\dfrac{1}{4}$	$\dfrac{1}{4}$	-2
-1	$\dfrac{1}{2}$	$\dfrac{1}{2}$	-1
0	1	1	0
1	2	2	1
2	4	4	2
3	8	8	3

An excellent way of checking a logarithmic graph is to examine its inverse, the exponential function, verifying that the values of the x- and y-coordinates are properly interchanged.

Remember: Since an exponential function has a range of $y > 0$, its inverse, a logarithmic function, will have a domain of $x > 0$. The x-axis (the line $y = 0$) is a horizontal asymptote for the graph of the exponential function $y = b^x$, while the y-axis (the line $x = 0$) is a vertical asymptote for the graph of the logarithmic function $y = \log_b x$.

2   Determine the equation of the function shown in the graph below.

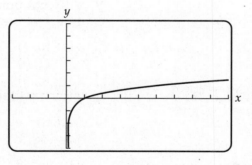

(1) $y = \log_2 x$
(2) $y = 3^x$
(3) $y = \log_4 x$
(4) $y = \log_6 x$

SOLUTION

Since the graph contains the point $(1, 0)$ and is in Quadrants I and IV, it must be a logarithmic function. The standard form of a logarithmic equation, $y = \log_b x$, is equivalent to $x = b^y$, so if $y = 1$, the x-value will be the base of the logarithm. Therefore, to determine the logarithmic equation, look for the value of x when $y = 1$. The graph represents the function $y = \log_4 x$.

Answer: (3)

Exercises 1–10: Select the numeral preceding the choice that best completes the sentence or answers the question.

1 Which equation represents the inverse of $y = 3^x$?

(1) $y = x^3$
(2) $3^x = y$
(3) $x = \log_3 y$
(4) $y = \log_3 x$

2 The graph of the function $y = \log_5 x$ appears in which quadrants?

(1) I and II
(2) I and IV
(3) II and III
(4) III and IV

3 The point $(1, 0)$ is always a point on the graph of which type of function?

(1) $f(x) = ax^2 + bx + c$
(2) $f(x) = b^x$
(3) $f(x) = \log_b x$
(4) $f(x) = mx + b$

4 Which number is *not* in the domain of the function $f(x) = \log_5 x$?

(1) 1
(2) 2
(3) 3
(4) 0

5 The inverse of the function $y = \log_2 x$ is

(1) $y^2 = x$
(2) $y = 2^x$
(3) $x = 2^y$
(4) $y = \log_x 2$

6 If $y = 2^x$ and $y = \left(\dfrac{1}{2}\right)^x$ are graphed on the same set of axes, which transformation would map one of them onto the other?

(1) reflection in the y-axis
(2) rotation of $180°$
(3) reflection in the origin
(4) reflection in the line $y = x$

7 If $y = \log_{10} x$ and $1 < y < 2$, then which is a true statement?

(1) $x < 0$
(2) $x = 0$
(3) $0 < x < 10$
(4) $10 < x < 100$

8 Which equation represents the graph shown below?

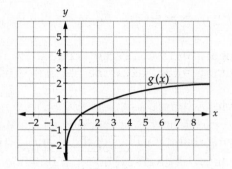

(1) $g(x) = 2^x$
(2) $g(x) = 3^x$
(3) $g(x) = \log_2 x$
(4) $g(x) = \log_3 x$

9 At what point will the graph of $f(x) = \log_5 x$ intersect the y-axis?

(1) $(0, 1)$
(2) $(1, 0)$
(3) $(0, 5)$
(4) It will not intersect the y-axis.

10 Which equation is *not* equivalent to $y = \log_2 x$?

(1) $y = 2^x$
(2) $x = 2^y$
(3) $x = \left(\dfrac{1}{2}\right)^{-y}$
(4) All are equivalent.

Exercises 11–16: Write the inverse of each function.

11 $y = 6^x$

12 $f(x) = \log_4 x$

13 $y = 3^x$

14 $f(x) = \log_{10} x$

15 $y = \log_2 x$

16 $f(x) = 10^x$

17 **a** Sketch the graph of the function $f(x) = 3^x$ in the interval $-2 \leq x \leq 2$.

b On the same set of axes, sketch the inverse of the function in part **a** and label it $g(x)$.

c What is the equation of $g(x)$?

18 **a** Sketch the graph of $y = \log_5 x$ in the interval $-2 \leq y \leq 2$.

b Find the intersection of $y = \log_5 x$ and the line $x = 1$.

8.2 Logarithmic Form of an Exponential Equation

Both logarithmic and exponential functions give information about a power. The statement $y = \log_2 16$ can be translated into the exponential form $2^y = 16$ (where $y = 4$).

Any logarithmic equation can be rewritten in exponential form.

Logarithmic Form	Exponential Form
$2 = \log_5 25$	$5^2 = 25$
$3 = \log_4 64$	$4^3 = 64$
$\dfrac{1}{2} = \log_9 3$	$9^{\frac{1}{2}} = 3$
$-1 = \log_{10} \dfrac{1}{10}$	$10^{-1} = \dfrac{1}{10}$

The general rule for logarithms and exponents says

$$\log_b c = a \quad \leftrightarrow \quad b^a = c \text{ (where } b > 0 \text{ and } b \neq 1)$$

MODEL PROBLEMS

1 Rewrite $y = \log_4 16$ in exponential form.

SOLUTION

The equation $y = \log_4 16$ means "4 to the y power is equal to 16." Therefore, the exponential equation is $4^y = 16$.

Answer: $y = 2$

Remember: The number to the right and below the word *log* will be the base of the exponential equation.

2 Rewrite $81 = 3^4$ as a logarithmic statement.

SOLUTION

Since 4 is the exponent in the expression $81 = 3^4$, the logarithmic equation would be $4 = \log_3 81$.

Answer: $4 = \log_3 81$

3 Solve for x: $2 = \log_{12} x$

SOLUTION

To solve, first rewrite the equation in exponential form: $12^2 = x$. Then evaluate by performing the indicated operation. Since $12^2 = 144$, $x = 144$.

Answer: $x = 144$

4 Solve for x: $x = \log_4 8$

SOLUTION

To solve, first rewrite the equation in exponential form: $4^x = 8$. In this case, we must solve for the exponent x, so we must rewrite the equation to make the bases equal. As you learned in the last chapter, when the bases are equal, the exponents will also be equal.

$$4^x = 8$$
$$(2^2)^x = 2^3$$
$$2^{2x} = 2^3$$
$$2x = 3$$

Answer: $x = \dfrac{3}{2}$

5 Solve for x: $\dfrac{1}{2} = \log_x 16$

SOLUTION

First, we rewrite the equation as an exponential equation: $x^{\frac{1}{2}} = 16$. To solve for x, we raise each side of the equation to the reciprocal of the power.

$$x^{\frac{1}{2}} = 16$$
$$\left(x^{\frac{1}{2}}\right)^2 = 16^2$$

Answer: $x = 256$

6 If $f(x) = \log_8 x$, evaluate $f(4)$.

SOLUTION

First we replace x with 4: $f(4) = \log_8 4$ or $y = \log_8 4$.

Rewrite as an exponential equation and solve: $\qquad 8^y = 4$

Again, we need to make the bases the same: $\qquad 2^{3y} = 2^2$

$$3y = 2$$

Answer: $y = \dfrac{2}{3}$

Note that $8^{\frac{2}{3}} = \left(8^{\frac{1}{3}}\right)^2 = \left(\sqrt[3]{8}\right)^2 = 2^2 = 4$.

 **Practice**

Exercises 1–8: Write the exponential equation in logarithmic form.

1 $3^5 = 243$

2 $16^{\frac{1}{2}} = 4$

3 $36 = 6^2$

4 $\dfrac{1}{4} = 2^{-2}$

5 $\left(\dfrac{5}{6}\right)^2 = \dfrac{25}{36}$

6 $10^{-2} = 0.01$

7 $7 = 49^{\frac{1}{2}}$

8 $b^a = c$

Exercises 9–14: Write the logarithmic equation in exponential form.

9 $6 = \log_2 64$

10 $3 = \log_5 125$

11 $-3 = \log_{10} 0.001$

12 $\dfrac{1}{2} = \log_4 2$

13 $2 = \log_{11} 121$

14 $-2 = \log_2 \dfrac{1}{4}$

Exercises 15–32: Solve for x.

15 $x = \log_3 81$

16 $x = \log_4 \dfrac{1}{2}$

17 $x = \log_9 27$

18 $x = \log_{10} 10,000$

19 $x = \log_5 \dfrac{1}{25}$

20 $x = \log_2 8$

21 $\log_4 x = 3$

22 $\log_9 x = -2$

23 $\log_{25} x = \dfrac{1}{2}$

24 $\log_{10} x = -3$

25 $\log_{\sqrt{3}} x = 6$

26 $\log_7 x = -1$

27 $\log_x 32 = 5$

28 $\log_x 27 = \dfrac{3}{2}$

29 $\log_x 100 = 2$

30 $\log_x \dfrac{1}{2} = -1$

31 $\log_x 216 = 3$

32 $\log_x \sqrt{2} = \dfrac{1}{2}$

Exercises 33–40: Select the numeral preceding the choice that best completes the sentence or answers the question.

33 If $f(x) = \log_{10} x$, the value of $f(10,000)$ is

(1) 1,000
(2) 100
(3) 10
(4) 4

34 The value of x in the equation $\log_8 x = -\dfrac{2}{3}$ is

(1) 64
(2) 16
(3) $\dfrac{1}{4}$
(4) 4

35 The value of x in the equation $x = \log_{10} 0.0001$ is

(1) 1
(2) -2
(3) -3
(4) -4

36 If $\log_{(x+1)} 64 = 2$, find the value of x.

(1) 8
(2) 2
(3) 3
(4) 7

37 If $x = \log_2 6$, then 4^x equals

(1) 1
(2) 16
(3) 36
(4) 256

38 If $\log_a \dfrac{2}{b} = -1$, then a equals

(1) $-b$

(2) $\dfrac{2}{b}$

(3) $\dfrac{b}{2}$

(4) $\dfrac{-2}{b}$

39 If $\log_b n = y$, then n equals

(1) yb

(2) $\dfrac{y}{b}$

(3) y^b

(4) b^y

40 If $\log_{25} x = \dfrac{-3}{2}$, the value of x is

(1) -125

(2) $-\dfrac{1}{125}$

(3) $\dfrac{1}{125}$

(4) 125

8.3 Logarithmic Relationships

Since logarithms are exponents, all of the rules of exponents apply to logarithms for all positive numbers m, n, and b, where $b \neq 1$.

	Exponential Rule	**Logarithmic Rule**	**Example of Logarithmic Rule**
Product	$(x^m)(x^n) = x^{m+n}$	$\log_b mn = \log_b m + \log_b n$	$\log_b (5 \bullet 7) = \log_b 5 + \log_b 7$
Quotient	$\dfrac{x^m}{x^n} = x^{m-n}$	$\log_b \dfrac{m}{n} = \log_b m - \log_b n$	$\log_b \dfrac{145}{12} = \log_b 145 - \log_b 12$
Power	$(x^m)^n = x^{mn}$	$\log_b m^n = n\log_b m$	$\log_b 10^2 = 2\log_b 10$

In words, the product rule of logarithms says that if two numbers are being multiplied, we add their logarithms together. For example,

$\log_b (793 \bullet 915) = \log_b 793 + \log_b 915$

$\log_2 (16 \bullet 64) = \log_2 16 + \log_2 64 = 4 + 6 = 10$

We could also have performed the second calculation using the power rule:

$\log_2 (16 \bullet 64) = \log_2 (2^4 \bullet 2^6) = \log_2 (2^{4+6}) = \log_2 (2^{10}) = 10\log_2 2 = 10$

In today's technological world, it does not seem to make much difference whether we multiply and then take the logarithm of the result or find the two logarithms and then add, but logarithms were first used in the seventeenth century before mechanical machines existed to facilitate mathematics operations. As recently as the latter half of the twentieth century, logarithms were invaluable to engineers in forming the basis of operations for the slide rule.

The quotient rule of logarithms says that if two numbers are being divided, we subtract the logarithm of the denominator from the logarithm of the numerator.

For example, $\log_b \dfrac{57}{8} = \log_b 57 - \log_b 8$.

The power rule of logarithms says that if a number is being raised to a power, its logarithm is the product of the power and the logarithm of the number.

For example, $\log_b 1{,}324^{\frac{1}{2}} = \dfrac{1}{2} \log_b 1{,}324$.

Two other basic relationships are important:

$\log_b 1 = 0$

$\log_b b = 1 \qquad b > 0, b \neq 1$

MODEL PROBLEMS

1 If $\log_b 3 = g$ and $\log_b 2 = h$, express each of the following in terms of g and h:

a $\log_b 6$

b $\log_b 12$

c $\log_b \dfrac{3}{2}$

d $\log_b 36$

SOLUTION

We need to rewrite each expression in terms of $\log_b 3$ and $\log_b 2$ and then substitute the values we know.

a $\log_b 6 = \log_b (2 \bullet 3)$

$\qquad = \log_b 2 + \log_b 3$

$\qquad = h + g$

b $\log_b 12 = \log_b (2 \bullet 2 \bullet 3)$

$\qquad = \log_b 2 + \log_b 2 + \log_b 3$

$\qquad = h + h + g$

$\qquad = 2h + g$

c $\log_b \dfrac{3}{2} = \log_b 3 - \log_b 2$

$\qquad = g - h$

d $\log_b 36 = \log_b (4 \bullet 9)$ $\qquad$ or $\qquad$ $\log_b 36 = \log_b 6^2$

$\qquad = \log_b (2^2 \bullet 3^2)$ $\qquad\qquad\qquad\qquad = 2\log_b 6$

$\qquad = \log_b 2^2 + \log_b 3^2$ $\qquad\qquad$ Using results from part **a**,

$\qquad = 2\log_b 2 + 2\log_b 3$ $\qquad\qquad\qquad\quad = 2(h + g)$

$\qquad = 2h + 2g$ $\qquad\qquad\qquad\qquad\qquad\quad = 2h + 2g$

2 If $\log_b 5 = 1.367$, which of the following represents $\log_b 25$?

    (1) 26.367

    (2) 2.734

    (3) 1.868689

    (4) 0.6835

SOLUTION

Again, we simplify the logarithmic expression given and then substitute.

$$\begin{aligned} \log_b 25 &= \log_b 5^2 \\ &= 2\log_b 5 \\ &= 2(1.367) = 2.734 \end{aligned}$$

Answer: (2)

3 If $\log_b x = \log_b p + \log_b t - \dfrac{1}{2}\log_b q$, which expression represents x?

    (1) $pt\sqrt{q}$

    (2) $p + t - q^2$

    (3) $\dfrac{pt}{\sqrt{q}}$

    (4) $\dfrac{p}{tq}$

SOLUTION

We have to "undo" the logarithmic rules in this expression. In this case, we know the logarithm and are finding the number that has that logarithm. This number is called the **antilogarithm** or antilog.

$$\log_b x = \log_b p + \log_b t - \frac{1}{2}\log_b q$$

$\log_b x = \log_b pt - \dfrac{1}{2}\log_b q$ Addition of logarithms indicates multiplication of terms.

$\log_b x = \log_b pt - \log_b q^{\frac{1}{2}}$ Multiplication of a logarithm by a number indicates raising to a power.

$\log_b x = \log_b \dfrac{pt}{q^{\frac{1}{2}}}$ Subtraction of logarithms indicates division of terms.

$\log_b x = \log_b \dfrac{pt}{\sqrt{q}}$ An exponent of $\dfrac{1}{2}$ indicates square root.

$x = \dfrac{pt}{\sqrt{q}}$ Take the antilog of each side.

Answer: (3)

4 If $x = \dfrac{m^2 n}{p\sqrt{s}}$, which expression represents $\log_b x$?

(1) $2\log_b m + \log_b n - \dfrac{1}{2}\, p\, \log_b s$

(2) $2\log_b m + \log_b n - \log_b p + \dfrac{1}{2}\log_b s$

(3) $2\log_b mn - \left(\log_b p + \dfrac{1}{2}\log_b s\right)$

(4) $2\log_b m + \log_b n - \left(\log_b p + \dfrac{1}{2}\log_b s\right)$

SOLUTION

Here we need to take the log of each side of the equation and apply the appropriate logarithmic rules to the right-hand side.

$\log_b x = \log_b \dfrac{m^2 n}{p\sqrt{s}}$

$\log_b x = \log_b m^2 n - \log_b p\sqrt{s}$ Division of terms uses subtraction of logs.

$\log_b x = \log_b m^2 + \log_b n - \left(\log_b p + \log_b \sqrt{s}\right)$ Multiplication of terms uses addition of logs.

$\log_b x = 2\log_b m + \log_b n - \left(\log_b p + \dfrac{1}{2}\log_b s\right)$ Powers become products of logs.

Answer: (4)

5 If $\log_4 (4x) + \log_4 x = \log_4 64$, find the value of x.

SOLUTION

$\log_4 (4x) + \log_4 x = \log_4 64$

    $\log_4 (4x \bullet x) = \log_4 64$ Simplify the left-hand side of the equation.

      $\log_4 (4x^2) = \log_4 64$

         $(4x^2) = 64$

           $x^2 = 16$ Since the domain of logarithms is $x > 0$, there is one solution.

Answer: $x = 4$

6 Evaluate $\log_2 32 - \log_2 1$.

SOLUTION

The expression $\log_2 32 - \log_2 1$ can be rewritten as $\log_2 \dfrac{32}{1} = \log_2 32 = 5$. Since $\log_2 1 = 0$, we could have rewritten this expression as $\log_2 32 - \log_2 1 = \log_2 32 - 0 = \log_2 32 = 5$.

Answer: 5

7 Solve for x: $\log_2 x + \log_2 (x - 4) = 5$

SOLUTION

$\log_2 x + \log_2 (x - 4) = 5$

$\qquad \log_2 x(x - 4) = 5$ Undo the logarithmic operations.

$\qquad\qquad x(x - 4) = 2^5$ Rewrite as an exponential equation.

$\qquad\quad x^2 - 4x - 32 = 0$ Solve the resulting quadratic equation.

$\qquad (x - 8)\,(x + 4) = 0$

$x = 8 \qquad x \neq -4$ Remember, you cannot take the logarithm of a negative number.

Answer: $x = 8$

Note that $\log_2 8 = 3$ and $\log_2 (8 - 4) = \log_2 4 = 2$ and $3 + 2 = 5$.

 **Practice**

Exercises 1–16: Select the numeral preceding the choice that best completes the sentence or answers the question.

1 If $\log_b 5 = m$ and $\log_b 2 = n$, then $\log_b 20$ can be represented as

(1) $m + n^2$
(2) $m + 2n$
(3) $2mn$
(4) $2m + n$

2 If $x = \dfrac{a\sqrt{b}}{c}$, then $\log_{10} x$ equals

(1) $\dfrac{\log_{10} a \bullet \log_{10} \sqrt{b}}{\log_{10} c}$

(2) $\log_{10} a + \dfrac{1}{2}\log_{10} b + \log_{10} c$

(3) $\dfrac{\log_{10} a + \dfrac{1}{2}\log_{10} b}{\log_{10} c}$

(4) $\log_{10} a + \dfrac{1}{2}\log_{10} b - \log_{10} c$

Exercises 3–5: Use the following:

$\log_a 7 = 4.61 \quad \log_a 2 = 1.73 \quad \log_a 3 = 2.14$

3 Which represents $\log_a 12$?

(1) 3.87
(2) 5.6
(3) 6.404806
(4) 14.9769

4 Which represents $\log_a 42$?

(1) 3.87
(2) 8.48
(3) 17.03
(4) 27.66

5 Which is equal to $\log_a \sqrt{6}$?

(1) 1.935
(2) 1.967
(3) 2.4495
(4) 3.87

6 Evaluate $\log_4 1 - 3\log_4 2 + \dfrac{1}{2}\log_4 16$.

(1) $-\dfrac{3}{2}$ (3) $\dfrac{1}{2}$

(2) $-\dfrac{1}{2}$ (4) $\dfrac{3}{2}$

7 If $2\log_{10} x = \log_{10} 2x$, then x equals

(1) 1
(2) 2
(3) 3
(4) 4

8 If $x = \dfrac{8^2 \sqrt[3]{5}}{21}$, which represents $\log_c x$?

(1) $2\log_c 8 + \dfrac{1}{3}\log_c 5 - 2\log_c 21$

(2) $\dfrac{\log_c 8^2 \cdot \dfrac{1}{3}\log_c \sqrt{5}}{\log_c 21}$

(3) $2\log_c 8 - 2\log_c 5 - \log_c 21$

(4) $2\log_c 8 + \dfrac{1}{3}\log_c 5 - \log_c 21$

9 If $\log_c x = 2\log_c a - \left(3\log_c b + \dfrac{1}{2}\log_c d\right)$, which is equivalent to x?

(1) $a^2 b^3 c^{\frac{1}{2}}$

(2) $\dfrac{a^2}{\sqrt{b^3 d}}$

(3) $\dfrac{a^2}{b^3 \sqrt{d}}$

(4) $\dfrac{a^2 b^3}{\sqrt{d}}$

10 The value of $\log_2 16 - \log_2 4$ is

(1) 1
(2) 2
(3) 3
(4) 4

11 If $\log_c 3 = p$ and $\log_c 6 = q$, express $\log_c \sqrt{\dfrac{1}{2}}$ in terms of p and q.

(1) $p - q$

(2) $\dfrac{1}{2}pq$

(3) $\dfrac{1}{2}p - q$

(4) $\dfrac{1}{2}(p - q)$

12 To simplify the expression $\log_z 45^2 \cdot \sqrt{873}$, which logarithm rules would you use?

(1) quotient and power rules
(2) product and power rules
(3) quotient and power rules
(4) product, quotient, and power rules

13 Solve for x: $\log_6 x = \log_6 36 - \log_6 \left(\dfrac{1}{6}\right)$

(1) 216
(2) 36
(3) 3
(4) 0

14 Solve for x: $\log_5 (125x) = \log_5 (25x) + \log_5 x$

(1) 625
(2) 125
(3) 25
(4) 5

15 Solve for x: $2\log_4 x - \log_4 (x + 3) = 1$

(1) $\{-2, 6\}$
(2) $\{-2\}$
(3) $\{6\}$
(4) $\{\ \}$

16 Solve for a: $2\log_3 a - \log_3 (a + 4) = 2$

(1) $\{-3\}$
(2) $\{-3, +12\}$
(3) $\{3, -12\}$
(4) $\{12\}$

Exercises 17 and 18: Express x in terms of p, q, and r.

17 $\log_z x = 3\log_z p + \dfrac{1}{2}\log_z r - \log_z q$

18 $\log_z x = \dfrac{1}{3}(\log_z q + \log_z r) - 2\log_z p$

Exercises 19 and 20: Rewrite as an equivalent logarithmic expression.

19 $x = p^2 q^3 r$

20 $x = \dfrac{\sqrt{pr}}{q^3}$

8.4 Common and Natural Logarithms

Since there are many different exponents and bases available in the set of real numbers, there are also many different logarithms. One of the most often used is the **common logarithm**, in which the base is 10. In fact, the absence of a base in a logarithmic expression or equation signals that the logarithm is in base 10. If x is a positive number, log x is the exponent of 10 that gives a value of x. That is, if $y = \log x$, then $10^y = x$. For example, log 10 = 1 because $10^1 = 10$. In the same manner, log 100 = 2 and log 1,000 = 3.

If we want to find log 532, we know the answer is somewhere between 2 and 3, since $10^2 = 100$ and $10^3 = 1,000$. To find log 532, however, we need a calculator. On a calculator, simply press (LOG) (5) (3) (2) (ENTER) and you will see that log 532 ≈ 2.725911632.

To check, we must store the value of log 532 as x in the calculator by pressing (STO▶) (X,T,θ,n) (ENTER). Then raise 10^x to get 532. (Since the calculator only has space to show the approximation 2.2725911632, raising $10^{2.2725911632}$ will *not* give you 532.)

In the equation x (≈2.725911632) is the logarithm of 532 and 532 is the antilogarithm of x. The logarithm is the exponent and the antilogarithm is the power. The equation log $x = 4$ has the same meaning as $\log_{10} x = 4$ or $10^4 = x$. Thus, $x = 10,000$.

To solve the equation log $x = 1.2$, we have to use the calculator to find the antilogarithm of 1.2. Press (2nd) (LOG) (1) (.) (2) (ENTER) to get the answer of ≈15.84893192. Notice that when you press (2nd) (LOG), the calculator displays the following:

> Remember: If log x = y, then x = antilog y.

```
10^(
```

The reason is that the equation log $x = 1.2$ means $\log_{10} x = 1.2$. So we are trying to find the value of x such that $10^{1.2} = x$. (In this case, $x \approx 15.84893192$.)

MODEL PROBLEMS

1 Rewrite log 100,000 = 5 using an exponent instead of a logarithm.

SOLUTION

log 100,000 = 5 means that $10^5 = 100,000$.

2 Rewrite $10^{-2} = 0.01$ using a logarithm instead of an exponent.

SOLUTION

$10^{-2} = 0.01$ means that log 0.01 = −2.

3 Without a calculator, evaluate each of the following:

   a $\log 1$

   b $\log 0.1$

SOLUTION

   a $\log 1 = 0$ since $10^0 = 1$.

   b $\log 0.1 = -1$ since $10^{-1} = 0.1$.

4 Evaluate $\log 34.6$ to the nearest thousandth.

SOLUTION

This is a simple calculator question. Press $\boxed{\text{LOG}}$ $\boxed{3}$ $\boxed{4}$ $\boxed{.}$ $\boxed{6}$ $\boxed{\text{ENTER}}$ to get 1.539076099. Rounded, $\log 34.6 = 1.539$

5 If $\log x = -0.3124$, find x to the nearest thousandth.

SOLUTION

Use the calculator to find the antilogarithm of -0.3124. Press $\boxed{\text{2nd}}$ $\boxed{\text{LOG}}$ $\boxed{(-)}$ $\boxed{.}$ $\boxed{3}$ $\boxed{1}$ $\boxed{2}$ $\boxed{4}$ $\boxed{\text{ENTER}}$ to get 0.4870796665, which rounds to 0.487.

Another base that is often used for logarithms is base e where e is an irrational constant that is approximately equal to 2.718281828. In fact, "log base e" is used so frequently that it has its own notation, **ln** x, read as "the **natural log** of x." If x is a positive number, $\ln x$ is the exponent of e that gives a value of x. That is, if $y = \ln x$, then $e^y = x$. For example, $\ln e = 1$ because $e^1 = e$. In the same manner, $\ln e^2 = 2$ and $\ln e^3 = 3$. Also, $e^{\ln x} = x$, $x > 0$. Using this property, we can state, for example, that $e^{\ln(x+2)} = x + 2$ and $e^{\ln ab} = ab$.

MODEL PROBLEMS

6 Rewrite $\ln \dfrac{1}{e} = -1$ using an exponent instead of a logarithm.

SOLUTION

$\ln \dfrac{1}{e} = -1$ means that $e^{-1} = \dfrac{1}{e}$.

7 Rewrite $e^0 = 1$ using a logarithm instead of an exponent.

SOLUTION

$e^0 = 1$ means that $\ln 1 = 0$.

8 Without a calculator, evaluate each of the following:

   a $\ln e^0$

   b $\ln \sqrt{e}$

SOLUTION

   a $\ln e^0 = 0$ since $\ln e^0 = \ln 1 = 0$.

   b $\ln \sqrt{e} = \dfrac{1}{2}$ since $\ln \sqrt{e} = \ln e^{\frac{1}{2}} = \dfrac{1}{2} \ln e = \dfrac{1}{2}(1) = \dfrac{1}{2}$.

9 Evaluate ln 4.6 to the nearest ten-thousandth.

SOLUTION

Use a calculator. Press ⌈LN⌉ ⌈4⌉ ⌈.⌉ ⌈6⌉ ⌈ENTER⌉ to get 1.526056303.
ln 4.6 ≈ 1.5261

10 If ln $x = -0.128$, find x to the nearest hundredth.

SOLUTION

Use the calculator to find the antilogarithm of -0.128. Press ⌈2nd⌉ ⌈LN⌉ ⌈(−)⌉ ⌈.⌉ ⌈1⌉ ⌈2⌉ ⌈8⌉ ⌈ENTER⌉ to get an approximation of 0.8798533791, which rounds to 0.88.

 Practice

Exercises 1–10: Select the numeral preceding the choice that best completes the sentence or answers the question.

1 If log $N = 3.5777$, find N to the *nearest ten-thousandth*.

(1) 3,781.8126
(2) 3,898.8126
(3) 5,724.0049
(4) 6,781.9292

2 If ln $x = 2.156$, find x to the *nearest ten-thousandth*.

(1) 0.3336
(2) 0.7683
(3) 8.6365
(4) 143.2189

3 If log $3.87 = a$, then log 3,870 equals

(1) $3a$
(2) $3 + a$
(3) $1,000a$
(4) $1,000 + a$

4 If $f(x) = \log x$, then $f(100,000)$ is equal to

(1) 7
(2) 6
(3) 5
(4) 4

5 If $g(x) = \ln x$, then $g(856)$ is equal to

(1) 2.14710019
(2) 2.932473765
(3) 6.752270376
(4) 5,218.681172

6 If log $8 = w$, then log 640 equals

(1) $4w + 1$
(2) $10w^2$
(3) $w + 80$
(4) $2w + 1$

7 If ln $5 = b$, then ln $5e$ equals

(1) eb
(2) $e + b$
(3) $b + 1$
(4) $b - 1$

8 Log $\sqrt{\dfrac{100}{n}}$ equals

(1) $1 - \dfrac{\log n}{2}$

(2) $10 - \dfrac{\log n}{2}$

(3) $2 - \log n$

(4) $\dfrac{2}{\log n}$

9 ln $\sqrt{\dfrac{e^2}{n}}$ equals

(1) $1 - \dfrac{\ln n}{2}$

(2) $e - \dfrac{\ln n}{2}$

(3) $2 - \ln n$

(4) $\dfrac{e^2}{\ln n}$

10 If $\log N = 0.730812$, what is the value of N to the *nearest ten-thousandth*?

    (1)   0.7308
    (2)   5.3804
    (3)   538.0368
    (4)   53.8037

11 Write using exponents instead of logarithms.

    a $\log 3.29 = 0.5171959$
    b $\ln 7.65 = 2.0347056$
    c $\log a = b$
    d $\ln c = d$

12 Write using logarithms instead of exponents.

    a $10^{4.12} = 13{,}182.56739$
    b $e^{6.81} = 906.8708069$
    c $10^x = y$
    d $e^x = z$

13 Indicate if the statement is *true* or *false*. Justify your answer.

    a $\ln AB = \ln A + \ln B$
    b $\log (A + B) = \log A + \log B$
    c $\log 10^2 = 2$
    d $\ln \sqrt[3]{e} = 3$
    e $\log 1 = \ln 1$

14 Evaluate without using a calculator:

    a $\log 1{,}000{,}000$
    b $\log 0.0001$
    c $\ln e^5$
    d $\ln \dfrac{1}{e^3}$

8.5 Exponential Equations

In Chapter 7, you learned how to solve exponential equations by rewriting the expressions so they shared the same base. For example, in the equation $9^x = 27$, we can write both sides of the equation as powers of 3: $3^{2x} = 3^3$. Since the bases are the same, we are then able to set the exponents equal to one another: $2x = 3$ and $x = \dfrac{3}{2}$. So $9^{\frac{3}{2}} = 27$.

However, in some equations, like $7^x = 83$, the bases cannot be made equal. Neither 7 nor 83 can be written as powers of the same base. In such cases, we can solve by graphing as we did in the last chapter—or we can use logarithms to solve for x.

MODEL PROBLEMS

1   Solve $7^x = 83$ for x to the nearest ten-thousandth.

SOLUTION

$$7^x = 83$$

$\log 7^x = \log 83$ Take the logarithm of each side of the equation.

$x \log 7 = \log 83$ Apply the power rule of logs.

$x = \dfrac{\log 83}{\log 7}$ Isolate the x by dividing by $\log 7$.

$x \approx 2.270834864$ Use a calculator to solve for x.

Answer: To the nearest ten-thousandth, $x = 2.2708$.

Note: To evaluate $\dfrac{\log 83}{\log 7}$ correctly on a calculator, you must include the right parenthesis for the logs in the quotient: ⬚LOG⬚

83 ⬚) ⬚÷⬚

⬚LOG⬚ 7 ⬚)⬚

⬚ENTER⬚

2 Solve using logarithms: $9^x = 27$

SOLUTION

This equation was solved on the previous page by writing each side with a base of 3. It can also be solved using logarithms.

$$9^x = 27$$

$\log 9^x = \log 27$ Take the log of each side.

$x \log 9 = \log 27$ Apply the power rule of logs.

$$x = \frac{\log 27}{\log 9}$$ Use a calculator to evaluate the right side.

Answer: $x = 1.5 = \dfrac{3}{2}$

3 Jack and Jill were sightseeing in the desert when their camper ran out of gas along a level stretch of interstate highway. The speed of their camper decreased exponentially over time. The camper's speed function is represented by $P(t)$ where the speed P is measured in miles per minute, and t is expressed in minutes: $P(t) = 1.2(0.58697)^t$.

To the nearest minute, how long did it take until their speed was 0.01 mile per minute?

SOLUTION

To solve this problem, we set the camper's speed function, $P(t)$, equal to the desired speed, 0.01 mile per minute, and solve the equation.

$$P(t) = 1.2(0.58697)^t$$

$0.01 = 1.2(0.58697)^t$ Set the desired speed equal to $P(t)$.

$\dfrac{0.01}{1.2} = (0.58697)^t$ Isolate the base of the exponent.

$\log\left(\dfrac{0.01}{1.2}\right) = \log(0.58697)^t$ Take the logarithm of each side.

$\log\left(\dfrac{0.01}{1.2}\right) = t \log(0.58697)$ Use the power rule to simplify the equation.

$$t = \frac{\log\left(\dfrac{0.01}{1.2}\right)}{\log(0.58697)}$$ Isolate t.

$t \approx 8.985843415$ Use a calculator to find t.

Answer: Approximately 9 minutes

When our equation involves a base of e, we use the natural logarithm function to solve the equation.

MODEL PROBLEM

4   Solve $1 + 3e^{0.52x} = 37$ for x to the nearest ten-thousandth.

SOLUTION

$1 + 3e^{0.52x} = 37$

$3e^{0.52x} = 36$

$e^{0.52x} = 12$ Isolate the term containing the exponent.

$\ln(e^{0.52x}) = \ln 12$ Take the natural log of each side of the equation.

$0.52x(\ln e) = \ln 12$ Apply the power rule of logs.

$0.52x = \ln 12$ Since $\ln e = 1$, simplify the left side of the equation.

$x = \dfrac{\ln 12}{0.52}$ Divide by 0.52.

$x \approx 4.778666634$ Use a calculator to evaluate the right side.

Answer: $x = 4.7787$.

An exponential equation can be solved by taking the logarithm of each side of the equation and solving the resulting logarithmic equation for the variable. When the base in the equation is e, it is easier to use natural logs in solving the equation. However, if the base in the equation is not e, either common logarithms or natural logarithms can be used.

MODEL PROBLEM

5   Solve for x to the nearest tenth: $5.83^x = 892.56$

   a Using common logs

   b Using natural logs

SOLUTION

a $5.83^x = 892.56$

$\log 5.83^x = \log 892.56$ Take the log of each side.

$x \log 5.83 = \log 892.56$ Apply the power rule of logs.

$x = \dfrac{\log 892.56}{\log 5.83}$ Divide by $\log 5.83$.

$x \approx 3.853674546$ Use a calculator to evaluate the right side.

Answer: To the nearest tenth, $x = 3.9$.

b $5.83^x = 892.56$

$\ln 5.83^x = \ln 892.56$ Take the natural log of each side.

$x \ln 5.83 = \ln 892.56$ Apply the power rule of natural logs.

$x = \dfrac{\ln 892.56}{\ln 5.83}$ Divide by ln 5.83.

$x \approx 3.853674546$ Use a calculator to evaluate the right side.

Answer: Rounded to the nearest tenth, $x = 3.9$.

We can also solve any of these problems graphically. Let's look at Model Problem 5.

Solve for x to the nearest tenth: $5.83^x = 892.56$.

First, enter the left side of the equation in Y_1 and the right side in Y_2.

```
Plot1  Plot2  Plot3
\Y1■5.83^X
\Y2■892.56
\Y3=
\Y4=
\Y5=
\Y6=
\Y7=
```

To set the window, we look at the equation. We know that $5^3 = 125$ and $6^3 = 216$. We also know that $5^4 = 625$ and $6^4 = 1{,}296$. Since our base is between 5 and 6, our exponent, x, will be less than 5. Since we are looking for a solution of 892.56, we will set our y-values less than 1,000. We choose a window of $0 \le x \le 5$ and $0 \le y \le 1{,}000$, as shown below.

```
WINDOW
 Xmin=0
 Xmax=5
 Xscl=1
 Ymin=0
 Ymax=1000
 Yscl=100
 Xres=1
```

We graph the two equations and see that they intersect.

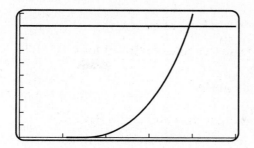

To find the intersection point, press **2nd** **TRACE** and choose 5: intersect.

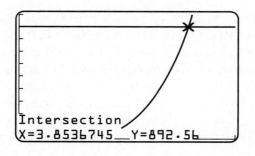

Since there are only two curves graphed, when we are asked for the first and second curves, we can just press **ENTER**. Since there is only one intersection point, when we are asked for a guess, we can again just press **ENTER**.

Notice that the solution is the same as the solution that we obtained by using logarithms.

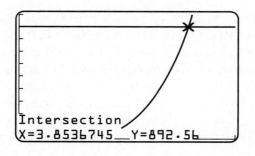

 **Practice**

Exercises 1–8: Solve each equation for x. Round to the *nearest hundredth*.

1 $5^x = 38$

2 $3^{2x} = 108$

3 $e^{0.52x} = 18$

4 $83^x = 29.1$

5 $12 + 4^x = 18$

6 $53 + 4e^{-0.21x} = 821$

7 $13.2^x = 4{,}719$

8 $1.45 + 6e^{0.32x} = 34.23$

9 Solve for x to the *nearest thousandth*: $2^x = \dfrac{3}{2}$

10 Solve for x to the *nearest ten-thousandth*: $6.3e^{-0.38x} = 873.92$

11 Solve for x to the *nearest ten-thousandth*: $10 + 4.5^x = 88$

12 Solve for x to the *nearest ten-thousandth*: $4.21 + 6.7e^{0.14x} = 783.23$

13 A misinformed criminal planted 37 ounces of radioactive krypton-85 in a safety-deposit box near *The Daily Planet* on January 1, 1989. (Superman is actually sensitive to *Kryptonite*.) The function showing the number of ounces of the remaining krypton-85 is $K(t) = 37(0.9376)^t$ where t represents the years since 1989. The criminal thinks any amount over 8 ounces will immobilize Superman.

  a Will there be more than 8 ounces of krypton-85 during the criminal's planned jewel robbery on New Year's Eve, 2010? Justify your answer.
  b What is the first year in which there will be fewer than 8 ounces of krypton-85 in the bank vault?
  c To the *nearest tenth of an ounce*, how much krypton-85 will remain on January 1, 2020?

14 Bacteria being grown for research programs at a university have a population modeled by the function $B(t) = 1.25(2)^t$ where $B(t)$ is in thousands of bacteria and t represents the time in hours. After how many hours will the bacteria population reach 1,000,000? (Round to the *nearest hundredth of an hour*.)

15 Use the formula $B(t) = 1.25e^{0.693147t}$ instead of the formula given in Exercise 14 to determine when the bacteria population would reach 1,000,000. Do the two formulas appear to be equivalent?

16 As cars get older, they are worth less than when they were new. This is called *depreciation*. Suppose you bought a new 2008 car for $32,640 that depreciates approximately 18% per year.

  a Write an equation that models this situation. Let V represent the value of the car.
  b To the nearest dollar, determine the value of the car after 1 year.
  c In what year will the car first be worth less than $5,000?

17 The number of Canada geese on a school's sports fields increases every year according to the function $G(t) = 24(1.2314)^t$, where t is years since 2008. The school board has suggested hiring dogs to chase the geese, but the dog squads will not work with geese populations less than 70. What is the first year the school will be able to hire the geese-chasing dogs?

18 The percentage of the United States population that is foreign born is growing at an exponential rate. The function is represented by the equation $P(t) = 4.7(1.027)^t$ where t is the number of years since 1970. If this trend continues, in what year is the number of people born outside the United States triple their population in 1970?

19 Many antiques *appreciate* or gain in value as they age. In 2004, an antique diamond necklace made in 1847 sold for $71,675.

  a Disregarding inflation and changes in currency, if the value of the necklace grew steadily at 5.4%, what was its initial selling price, to the nearest cent?
  b Based on the information given above, write an equation to model the value of the necklace t years after 1847.
  c Based on your equation from part **b**, in what year will the necklace be worth $100,000?

20 In 2007–2008, the average cost for one year at a four-year private college was $23,712, which was an increase of 6.3% from the previous year. If this trend continues, the cost of college for a newborn baby would be approximately $71,200 in eighteen years. Baby Jessica's grandparents have invested $10,000 for her college education. What interest rate, compounded continuously, would they need to receive to be able to finance her first year of college, in eighteen years? (Use the formula $A = Pe^{rt}$ to solve for r.) Do you think that this is a plausible interest rate? If not, determine what might be a reasonable rate and determine how much money Jessica's grandparents would have to invest to finance her first year of college.

21 The population of Ghostton, Nevada, is modeled by the function $G(t) = 1,824(0.896)^t$ where t is the number of years since 1980. In what year will the population be less than fifty people?

22 The Abrahams had an above-ground pool installed in their backyard and then went away for the weekend. On Saturday, the pool developed a leak and water has been leaking out of the pool at the rate of 3% per hour. The pool originally held 17,420 gallons.

  a Write an exponential equation that models the amount of water W left in the pool.

  b After how many hours, to the *nearest tenth of an hour,* will the pool be half full?

  c If the leak began at 8 A.M. on Saturday and the Abrahams are expected home Sunday at 9 P.M., how much water will be left in the pool, assuming the leak is at the very bottom of the pool?

23 A painting attributed to Dutch painter Jan Vermeer (1632–1675) contains 99.5% of its original carbon-14. The formula $f(x) = A_0 e^{-0.00012101x}$ can be used to estimate the amount of carbon-14 present where A_0 represents the original amount of carbon-14 that the paint contained x years ago.

  a Using the information above, write an equation that can be used to determine the age of the painting.

  b Solve the equation from part **a** to determine if the painting is a forgery or not.

24 Environmentalists in Ireland are concerned about the growth of the leprechaun population, represented by the function $L(t) = 1,208(1.265)^t$ where t is the number of years since 2008. Since leprechauns live at the base of rainbows, an increase in leprechauns without a corresponding increase in rainbows will be detrimental to the survival of the leprechauns. If there are enough rainbows for only 10,000 leprechauns, how many years, to the *nearest tenth,* do the environmentalists have to resolve this problem?

25 Deirdre and Alan graduated with master's degrees in business in May 2008 and accepted jobs at competing firms. Deirdre's salary is represented by the function $D(t) = 46,500(1.082)^t$ while Alan's salary is $A(t) = 51,000(1.065)^t$. Both are functions of time in years.

  a In how many years after being hired will Deirdre and Alan earn the same salary?

  b What will that salary be?

  c When will each of these employees first earn $100,000?

8.6 Logarithmic Equations

Sometimes an equation to be solved is written in logarithmic form. Our first step is to write the equation in exponential form to explore a means of solution.

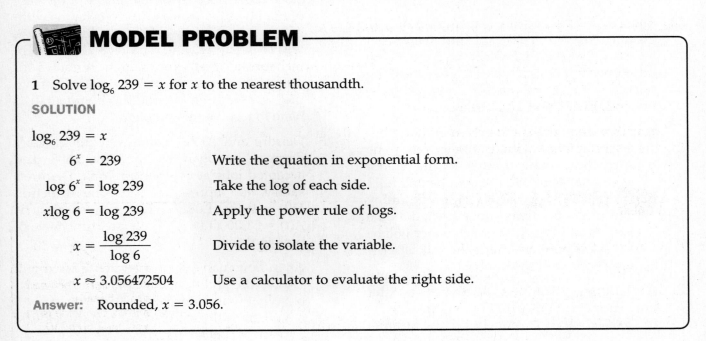

MODEL PROBLEM

1 Solve $\log_6 239 = x$ for x to the nearest thousandth.

SOLUTION

$\log_6 239 = x$

$6^x = 239$	Write the equation in exponential form.
$\log 6^x = \log 239$	Take the log of each side.
$x\log 6 = \log 239$	Apply the power rule of logs.
$x = \dfrac{\log 239}{\log 6}$	Divide to isolate the variable.
$x \approx 3.056472504$	Use a calculator to evaluate the right side.

Answer: Rounded, $x = 3.056$.

We can use the procedure outlined above to derive a formula that is helpful if we want to change from one base to another.

The equation $y = \log_a x$ can be written in exponential form:

$a^y = x$

Take the logarithm of both sides, but use base b: $\log_b a^y = \log_b x$.

Solve for y: $y\log_b a = \log_b x$

$$y = \frac{\log_b x}{\log_b a}$$

Since $y = \log_a x$, replace y with $\log_a x$: $\log_a x = \dfrac{\log_b x}{\log_b a}$.

This is called the **change of base formula**:

$$\log_a x = \frac{\log_b x}{\log_b a}$$

We can use this formula to solve Model Problem 1. We change $\log_6 239$ to common logarithms of base 10, and then use the calculator to evaluate.

$$\log_a x = \frac{\log_b x}{\log_b a}$$

$$\log_6 239 = \frac{\log_{10} 239}{\log_{10} 6} \qquad \text{Substitute 6 for } a \text{ and 239 for } x.$$

$$= \frac{\log 239}{\log 6} \qquad \begin{array}{l}\text{Since the logs are base 10, write them without} \\ \text{a base.}\end{array}$$

$$\approx 3.056472504 \qquad \text{Use a calculator to evaluate.}$$

Logarithmic equations are solved by "undoing" the log operations and replacing the given equation with its equivalent algebraic format.

MODEL PROBLEMS

2 Solve for all values of x: $\log (x - 1) + \log (2x - 3) = 1$

SOLUTION

> Remember: When no other base is shown, the base is assumed to be 10.

$$\log (x - 1) + \log (2x - 3) = 1$$

$$\log ((x - 1)(2x - 3)) = 1 \qquad \text{Apply the product rule of logs.}$$

$$(x - 1)(2x - 3) = 10^1 \qquad \text{Write as an exponential equation.}$$

$$2x^2 - 5x + 3 = 10 \qquad \text{Perform indicated operations.}$$

$$2x^2 - 5x - 7 = 0 \qquad \text{Set the equation equal to zero and solve.}$$

$$(2x - 7)(x + 1) = 0$$

$$2x - 7 = 0 \qquad x + 1 = 0$$

$$2x = 7 \qquad x \neq -1 \qquad \text{Reject the negative root.}$$

$$x = \frac{7}{2}$$

Because the domain of logarithmic functions is $x > 0$, the log of a negative number is not defined, so the only solution to this equation is $x = \frac{7}{2}$. The solution should be checked in the original equation.

Check:

$$\log (x - 1) + \log (2x - 3) = 1$$

$$\log \left(\frac{7}{2} - 1 \right) + \log \left(2 \cdot \frac{7}{2} - 3 \right) \overset{?}{=} 1$$

$$\log \left(\frac{5}{2} \right) + \log (4) \overset{?}{=} 1$$

$$\log \left(\frac{5}{2} \cdot 4 \right) \overset{?}{=} 1$$

$$\log 10 \overset{?}{=} 1$$

$$1 = 1 \checkmark$$

Answer: $x = \dfrac{7}{2}$

We solve equations involving natural logarithms in a similar manner.

3 Solve for x to the nearest hundredth: $3 + 2\ln x = 9$

SOLUTION

$$3 + 2\ln x = 9$$
$$2\ln x = 6$$
$$\ln x = 3 \qquad \text{Isolate } \ln x.$$
$$x = e^3 \approx 20.08553692 \qquad \text{Write as an exponential equation. Use a calculator to evaluate.}$$

Answer: $x = 20.09$

4 Solve for x: $\ln (x + 1) - \ln (x - 3) = \ln 5$

SOLUTION

$$\ln (x + 1) - \ln (x - 3) = \ln 5$$

$$\ln \frac{(x + 1)}{(x - 3)} = \ln 5 \qquad \text{Apply the quotient rule of logs.}$$

$$\frac{x + 1}{x - 3} = 5 \qquad \text{Take the antilog of both sides of the equation.}$$

$$x + 1 = 5x - 15 \qquad \text{Solve, using algebraic techniques.}$$

$$16 = 4x$$

Answer: $x = 4$

Note that logarithmic equations in base 10 or base e (natural logs) can also be solved graphically. Enter the left side of the equation as Y_1 and the right side of the equation as Y_2, then press [2nd] [TRACE] and choose 5: intersect to find the solution(s).

Practice

Exercises 1–8: Solve each equation for x. Round to the *nearest hundredth*.

1 $4\log x = 5$

2 $8\ln x = 16$

3 $x = \log_3 152$

4 $\log_2 x + \log_2 4 = 3$

5 $\ln 3x = 6$

6 $x = \log_7 513$

7 $2\log x - \log 3 = 5$

8 $\ln x + \ln 1 = 5$

Exercises 9–20: Solve each equation for all values of x. Check that your answers are valid.

9 $2\log_4 x - \log_4 (x + 3) = 1$

10 $\log x + \log (x + 1) = \log 12$

11 $\log_2 (4x + 10) - \log_2 (x + 1) = 3$

12 $\ln (x + 3) + \ln (x - 3) = \ln 16$

13 $\log_3 (2x - 1) + \log_3 (x + 7) = 3$

14 $\log_2 (x + 5) - \log_2 (x - 2) = 3$

15 $\ln x + \ln (2x - 1) = 0$

16 $\log (3x - 2) + \log (x - 1) = \log 2x$

17 $\log_4 (x^2 + 3x) - \log_4 (x + 5) = 1$

18 $\ln (x + 11) - \ln (x - 3) = \ln 3$

19 $\ln x + \ln (x + 1 - e) = 1$

20 $2 \log_3 x - \log_3 (x - 2) = 2$

CHAPTER REVIEW

Exercises 1–25: Write the numeral preceding the choice that best completes the statement or answers the question.

1 If $x = \dfrac{a\sqrt{b}}{cd}$, which expression is equivalent to $\log x$?

(1) $\log a + \dfrac{1}{2} \log b - \log c + \log d$

(2) $\dfrac{1}{2} \log a + \dfrac{1}{2} \log b - \log c + \log d$

(3) $\log a - \dfrac{1}{2} \log b - \log c + \log d$

(4) $\log a + \dfrac{1}{2} \log b - \log c - \log d$

2 The inverse of $y = 10^x$ is obtained by reflecting $y = 10^x$ in the line

(1) $y = x$
(2) $y = -x$
(3) $y = 0$
(4) $x = 0$

3 The graph of $y = \log_4 x$ lies entirely in quadrants

(1) I and II
(2) II and III
(3) III and IV
(4) IV and I

4 If $\log a = x$ and $\log b = y$, then $\log \sqrt{ab}$ is equal to

(1) $\dfrac{1}{2} xy$

(2) $\dfrac{1}{2} x + y$

(3) $\dfrac{1}{2} x + \dfrac{1}{2} y$

(4) $\dfrac{1}{2} x - \dfrac{1}{2} y$

5 If $\log_x 3 = \dfrac{1}{4}$, what is the value of x?

(1) 81
(2) 27

(3) $3\dfrac{1}{4}$

(4) $\sqrt[4]{3}$

6 The equation $y = a^x$ expressed in logarithmic form is

(1) $y = \log_a x$
(2) $x = \log_a y$
(3) $x = \log_y a$
(4) $a = \log_y x$

7 If $\log 6 = a$, then $\log 600 =$

(1) $100a$
(2) $a + 2$
(3) $a - 2$
(4) $2a$

8 If the graphs of $y = \log_4 x$ and $y = 3$ are drawn on the same set of axes, they will intersect when $x =$

(1) 64
(2) 12
(3) 3
(4) $3^{\frac{1}{4}}$

9 Which value is *not* in the range of the function $y = \log_5 x$?

(1) -2
(2) 0
(3) 3
(4) The range is $\{y : y \in \mathbb{R}\}$.

10 The inverse of $y = \log_4 x$ is

(1) $x = 4^y$
(2) $y = 4^x$
(3) $x = y^4$
(4) $y = x^4$

11 Which expression is *not* equivalent to $\log_b 36$?

(1) $6\log_b 2$
(2) $2\log_b 6$
(3) $\log_b 9 + \log_b 4$
(4) $\log_b 72 - \log_b 2$

12 Simplify the expression $e^x \bullet 2e^{3x-1}$.

(1) $2e^{3x^2-1}$
(2) $3e^{3x-1}$
(3) $2e^{3x+x}$
(4) $2e^{4x-1}$

13 In the equation $\log_x 5 + \log_x 20 = 2$, x is equivalent to

(1) $\sqrt{2}$
(2) 2
(3) 10
(4) 25

14 If $\log_x 3 = a$ and $\log_x 2 = b$, express $\log_x 18$ in terms of a and b.

(1) $a^2 b$
(2) $3ab$
(3) $2a + b$
(4) $a^2 + b$

15 If you know only the values of $\log_b 2$ and $\log_b 3$, which *cannot* be found?

(1) $\log_b 6$
(2) $\log_b 7$
(3) $\log_b 8$
(4) $\log_b 12$

16 For which value of x is the expression $\log_4 (x + 3)$ not defined?

(1) 0
(2) -2
(3) 3
(4) -4

17 If $\log 7 = a$, what is the value of $\log 490$ in terms of a?

(1) $a^2 + 2$
(2) $2a + 1$
(3) $2a + 10$
(4) $10a^2$

18 Solve for x: $\log_{64} x = -\dfrac{3}{2}$

(1) 16
(2) $\dfrac{1}{512}$
(3) -16
(4) -512

19 Solve for x: $\log_x 625 = -4$

(1) $\dfrac{1}{5}$
(2) $\dfrac{1}{2}$
(3) 5
(4) 25

20 Solve for x: $\log_{\frac{1}{3}} 81 = x$

(1) 27
(2) -1
(3) -3
(4) -4

21 For what value of k will the graph of $y = \log_7 x$ contain the point $(1, k)$?

(1) 1
(2) 0
(3) 7
(4) 49

22 If $y = \log_{10} x$ and $2 < y < 3$, then which is a true statement?

(1) $-1 < x < 0$
(2) $10 < x < 100$
(3) $100 < x < 1,000$
(4) $1,000 < x < 10,000$

23 Which is *not* a true statement?

(1) $\log_{10} 1 = 0$
(2) $\log_{10} 0 = 1$
(3) The range of $y = \log_{10} x$ is all real numbers.
(4) The domain of $y = \log_{10} x$ is $x > 0$.

24 If $\log_b 49 = 2.542$, which approximates the value of $\log_b 7$?

(1) 0.7969
(2) 1.271
(3) 1.3625
(4) 1.5937

25 If $\ln 17 = h$, which represents $\ln 17e$?

(1) $e + h$
(2) $h + 1$
(3) eh
(4) $h + 17$

26 Solve for x to the *nearest hundredth*: $5^x = 187$

27 Solve for x to the *nearest thousandth*: $11 + 5e^{0.24x} = 16.578$

28 Solve for x: $\log_x 16 = 4$

29 Evaluate $\log_a a$.

30 Write as a single logarithm: $\log 2 + 3\log x - \frac{1}{2} \log b$.

31 If $x = \log_2 6$, find the value of x to the *nearest thousandth*.

32 If $f(x) = \log_3 x$, what are the domain and range of $f(x)$?

33 Solve for x: $\log x + \log (x + 3) = 1$

34 If $\log_{x-2} 125 = 3$, find x.

35 Solve for x: $\log (x - 2) + \log (2x - 3) = 2\log x$

36 Evaluate $\log_b 1$.

37 Using logarithms, find x to the *nearest hundredth*: $x = \log_4 44.4$

38 In 2005, your great-aunt Marguerite retired after forty years of service to a Wall Street firm and received a retirement bonus of \$500,000. Because of the large sum, she was able to invest it at an annual rate of 7.25% compounded continuously. Use the formula $A = P_0 e^{rt}$ where P_0 is the initial investment, r = rate of investment, and t = time in years. In how many years, to the *nearest tenth of a year*, will your great-aunt's money have doubled?

39 Mouthwash manufacturers are constantly testing various chemicals on bacteria that thrive on human saliva. The death of the bacteria exposed to Antigen 223 can be represented by the function $P(t) = 2,000e^{-0.37t}$ where $P(t)$ represents the number of bacteria from a population of 2,000 surviving after t minutes.

a Determine the number of bacteria surviving 3 minutes after exposure to Antigen 223.

b Using logarithms, determine the number of minutes, to the *nearest tenth of a minute*, necessary to kill 90% of the bacteria.

40 Nurse Hatchet administers 150 milligrams of medication to Patient Curmudgeon at 8 A.M. The amount of medication a remaining in a patient's bloodstream t hours after it has been administered is given by the formula $a = 150e^{-0.4895t}$. If the next dose of medication is not given until less than 25 milligrams remain in the body, determine, to the *nearest tenth of an hour*, in how many hours Patient Curmudgeon will receive his next medication.

CHAPTER 9

Trigonometric Functions

9.1 Trigonometry of the Right Triangle

Trigonometry, a word taken from the Greek, means the measure of triangles. In this section, we will look specifically at the measurement of right triangles using trigonometry.

The side of the triangle opposite the right angle is known as the **hypotenuse**, which is always the longest side of a right triangle. The two perpendicular sides are called the **legs** of the triangle.

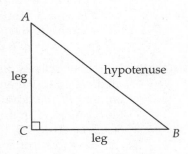

The three trigonometric ratios that we use to find the measure of sides or angles in a right triangle are:

$$\text{sine } \angle A = \frac{\text{length of the side opposite } \angle A}{\text{length of the hypotenuse}}$$

In the diagram above, this ratio would be: $\sin \angle A = \dfrac{BC}{AB}$.

$$\text{cosine } \angle A = \frac{\text{length of the side adjacent to } \angle A}{\text{length of hypotenuse}} \quad \text{or} \quad \cos \angle A = \frac{AC}{AB}$$

$$\text{tangent } \angle A = \frac{\text{length of the side opposite } \angle A}{\text{length of the side adjacent to } \angle A} \quad \text{or} \quad \tan \angle A = \frac{BC}{AC}$$

Remember: A side may be named by using its two endpoints (capital letters) or as a single letter, the lowercase letter of the angle opposite: $a = BC$, $b = AC$, and $c = AB$.

The acronym **SOHCAHTOA** is helpful for remembering the ratios. These are the first letters of the phrase **S**ine is **O**pposite leg over **H**ypotenuse, **C**osine is **A**djacent leg over **H**ypotenuse, and **T**angent is **O**pposite leg over **A**djacent leg.

If we know two sides of a right triangle, we can find its angles; if we know one side and one angle, we can find the remaining angles and sides by using these ratios.

Note: Remember to check the (MODE) screen of your calculator to be certain you are in degree mode before beginning these problems.

📖 MODEL PROBLEM

1 In triangle QPR, $\angle P$ is a right angle, $QR = 12$, and $m\angle Q = 30$. Find PR.

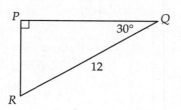

SOLUTION

Determine what information you have: $m\angle Q$ and QR, which is the length of the hypotenuse. Since you are looking for PR, the length of the leg opposite $\angle Q$, use the sine ratio.

$$\sin \angle Q = \frac{PR}{QR}$$

$$\sin 30° = \frac{PR}{12}$$

$$12 \sin 30° = PR$$

$$12(0.5) = PR$$

$$6 = PR$$

Answer: $PR = 6$

In some cases you are asked to find the measure of an angle, given two sides of the right triangle.

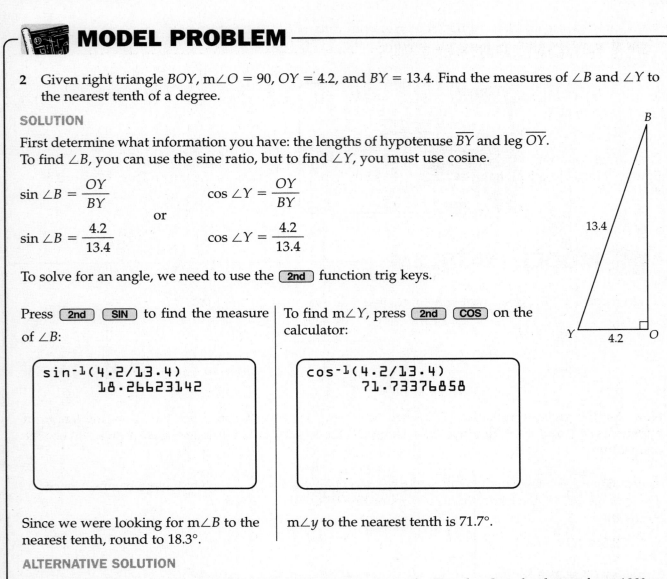

MODEL PROBLEM

2 Given right triangle BOY, m$\angle O = 90$, $OY = 4.2$, and $BY = 13.4$. Find the measures of $\angle B$ and $\angle Y$ to the nearest tenth of a degree.

SOLUTION

First determine what information you have: the lengths of hypotenuse $\overline{BY}$ and leg $\overline{OY}$.
To find $\angle B$, you can use the sine ratio, but to find $\angle Y$, you must use cosine.

$$\sin \angle B = \frac{OY}{BY} \qquad\qquad \cos \angle Y = \frac{OY}{BY}$$
$$\text{or}$$
$$\sin \angle B = \frac{4.2}{13.4} \qquad\qquad \cos \angle Y = \frac{4.2}{13.4}$$

To solve for an angle, we need to use the (2nd) function trig keys.

Press (2nd) (SIN) to find the measure of $\angle B$:

```
sin⁻¹(4.2/13.4)
        18.26623142
```

To find m$\angle Y$, press (2nd) (COS) on the calculator:

```
cos⁻¹(4.2/13.4)
        71.73376858
```

Since we were looking for m$\angle B$ to the nearest tenth, round to 18.3°.

m$\angle y$ to the nearest tenth is 71.7°.

ALTERNATIVE SOLUTION

Once the measure of $\angle B$ is found, simply add the measures of $\angle B$ and $\angle O$ and subtract from 180° to find m$\angle Y$:

$180° - (90° + 18.3°) = 71.7°$

Answer: m$\angle Y \approx 71.7$ and m$\angle B \approx 18.3$

Sometimes, rather than being given the diagram as well as the information for a problem, you are given a description of the situation and you must provide your own figure.

MODEL PROBLEMS

3 In triangle CTH, m$\angle T = 90$, m$\angle C = 48$, and $CH = 50$ cm. Find the length of $\overline{CT}$ to the nearest tenth of a centimeter.

SOLUTION

First, draw your diagram, being certain to place the information in the correct locations. As shown in the figures below, the orientation of the triangle is not significant as long as the information is accurate.

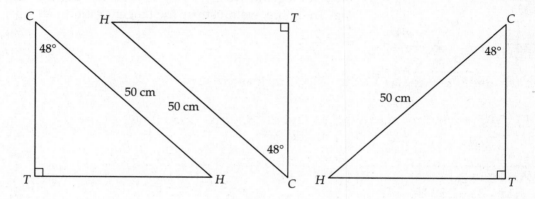

Now, use the given information to determine which trig ratio to use. Since we know the length of hypotenuse $\overline{CH}$ and m$\angle C$, and we are seeking CT, the length of the leg adjacent to $\angle C$, we will use the cosine ratio.

$$\cos 48° = \frac{CT}{50}$$

$$50 \cos 48° = CT$$

$$33.5 \approx CT$$

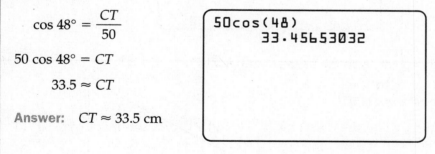

```
50cos(48)
        33.45653032
```

Answer: $CT \approx 33.5$ cm

4 Amelia Ann is standing on the beach looking up at a lighthouse whose base is 650 feet from where she is standing. If the angle of elevation from where Amelia Ann is standing to the top of the lighthouse measures 52°, to the nearest foot, how tall is the lighthouse?

SOLUTION

Recall that the angle of elevation is the angle formed by a horizontal line and the upward line of sight to an object (the line of sight is along the hypotenuse of the triangle).

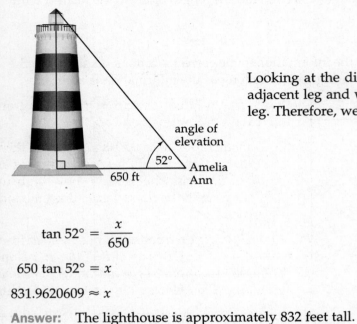

Looking at the diagram, we see that we know the length of the adjacent leg and we are trying to find the length of the opposite leg. Therefore, we must use the tangent ratio.

$$\tan 52° = \frac{x}{650}$$

$$650 \tan 52° = x$$

$$831.9620609 \approx x$$

Answer: The lighthouse is approximately 832 feet tall.

✏️ **Practice**

Exercises 1–12: Solve each triangle for x to the *nearest tenth of a degree* or to the *nearest tenth of a centimeter*.

1

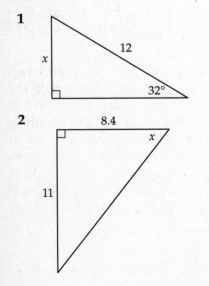

2

3

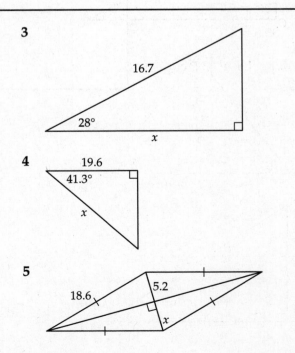

4

5

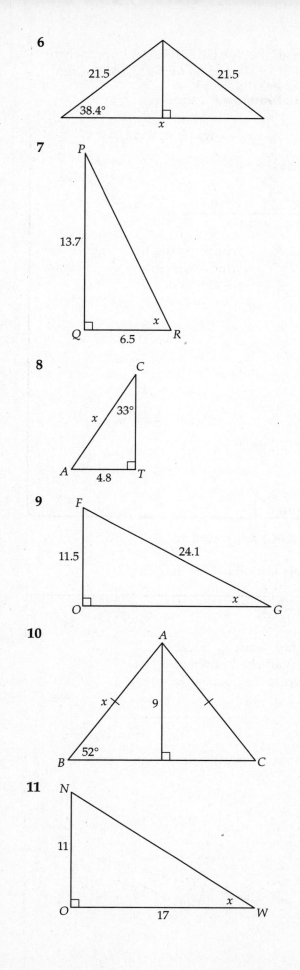

6

21.5   21.5

38.4°

x

7   P

13.7

x

Q   R
6.5

8   C

x   33°

A   T
4.8

9   F

11.5   24.1

x

O   G

10   A

x   9

52°

B   C

11   N

11

x

O   W
17

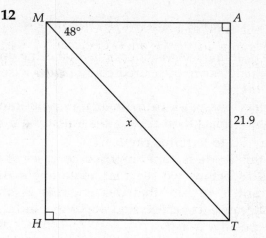

12   M   A

48°

x   21.9

H   T

Exercises 13–18: Draw the appropriate diagram for the situation described and solve.

13 A 96-inch ladder is leaning against the side of a building. If the foot of the ladder makes an angle of 53° with the ground, how high up the building, to the *nearest inch*, does the ladder reach?

14 Elena is lying on a beach blanket 60 feet from the base of a 150-foot cliff. Determine the angle of elevation, to the *nearest tenth of a degree*, at which Elena sights the top of the cliff.

15 The angle of elevation from a point 10 feet away from the base of a tree on level ground to the top of the tree is 36°. How tall is the tree to the *nearest tenth of a foot*?

16 A 10-foot utility pole is staked to the ground with a wire that makes an angle of 58° with the ground. To the *nearest tenth of a foot*, how long is the wire?

17 A 16-foot ladder, leaning against a restaurant, reaches the bottom of a sign that is 15 feet above the ground. To the *nearest degree*, find the angle the ladder makes with the ground.

18 Gaumar is playing ball in the stadium when he notices the shadow of the bleachers on the ground. Hoping to get extra credit in his math class, Gaumar measures the length of the shadow; it is 41 feet long. If Gaumar stands at the tip of the shadow farthest from the 17.5-foot bleachers, what is the angle of elevation from the point where Gaumar is standing to the top of the bleachers to the *nearest degree*?

9.2 Angles as Rotations

An **angle** is defined as a set of points that is the union of two rays having the same endpoint. Angles are measured counterclockwise from the **initial ray** toward the **terminal ray**.

From previous work in mathematics, you know that we can name this $\angle B$ or $\angle ABC$. It is measured from horizontal ray $\overrightarrow{BC}$ to terminal ray $\overrightarrow{BA}$.

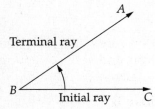

When this angle is superimposed on a set of coordinate axes as below, we see that acute angle ABC lies in Quadrant I. We say that this angle is in **standard position** because its vertex is on the origin and its initial ray is the positive x-axis.

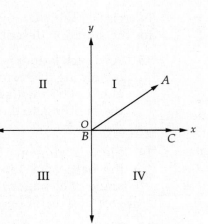

Since there are 360° in a full rotation, each quadrant contains 90°.

- **Acute** angles that measure *between* 0° and 90°, such as $\angle ABC$, are found in Quadrant I.
- **Obtuse** angles that measure *between* 90° and 180° have their terminal rays in Quadrant II.
- Quadrant III contains angles that measure *between* 180° and 270°.
- Quadrant IV contains angles that measure *between* 270° and 360°.

Notice that each of these definitions is for angles that fall *inside* a quadrant. The angles that measure exactly 0°, 90°, 180°, 270°, and 360° are known as **quadrantal angles** and are not "in" a quadrant, but rather separate the quadrants.

MODEL PROBLEM

1 Determine the quadrant in which each of the following angles lies.

    a 145°   **b** 303°   **c** 240°   **d** 412°   **e** 189°   **f** 270°

SOLUTION

Remember that angles are measured counterclockwise. We can place any size angle on the coordinate axes in standard position and see where its terminal ray falls. An angle is said to lie in the quadrant in which its terminal ray falls.

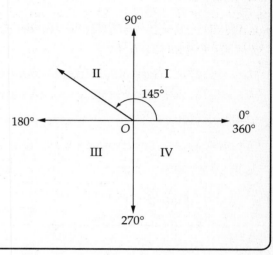

    a 145° is in Quadrant II.

    b 303° is in Quadrant IV.

    c 240° is in Quadrant III.

    d 412° has made one full revolution or rotation around the axes and is now in Quadrant I.

        412° − 360° = 52°

    e 189° is in Quadrant III.

    f 270° is not in a quadrant; it is a quadrantal angle.

When an angle has a negative measure, it has rotated clockwise rather than counterclockwise.

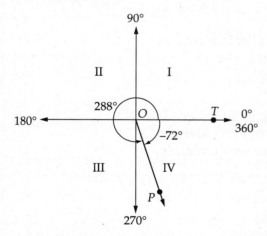

Angle *TOP* is in Quadrant IV. We can describe ∠*TOP* as an angle with a *clockwise* rotation of −72°. We can also describe ∠*TOP* as an angle with a *counterclockwise* rotation of 288°. Angles of −72° and 288° share the same initial and terminal rays, so they are called **coterminal angles**.

    Angles in the same position on the coordinate axes but with different measures are coterminal angles. Let *A* be the measure of an angle. Then its coterminal angles have the measure $A + 360n$, where *n* is the number of complete 360° rotations of the terminal ray. This means that ∠*TOP* is also coterminal with an angle measuring 288 + 360(2) = 1,008 degrees or an angle measuring 288 − 360(2) = −432 degrees.

MODEL PROBLEM

2 Which of the following angles is *not* coterminal to an angle that measures $-120°$?

    (1) $-480°$

    (2) $60°$

    (3) $240°$

    (4) $600°$

SOLUTION

Choice (1) $-480°$ has made an additional rotation of $360°$ clockwise from $-120°$.

$-480° = -120° + (-360°)$

Choice (2) $60°$ does not utilize the same terminal and initial rays as the original angle.

Choice (3) $240°$ is the counterclockwise angle on the same plane as $-120°$.

$240° = -120° + 360°$

Choice (4) $600°$ has completed two full revolutions from $-120°$.

$600° = -120° + (360°)2$

Answer: Choice (2)

Practice

Exercises 1–15: Determine in which quadrant an angle of the given measure lies.

1 $215°$

2 $-110°$

3 $318°$

4 $72°$

5 $95°$

6 $-45°$

7 $225°$

8 $150°$

9 $422°$

10 $-240°$

11 $680°$

12 $23°$

13 $812°$

14 $-300°$

15 $289°$

Exercises 16–18: Select the numeral preceding the choice that best completes the statement or answers the question.

16 Which angle is *not* coterminal to $112°$?

    (1) $-248°$

    (2) $68°$

    (3) $472°$

    (4) $832°$

17 An angle whose measure is $-214°$ is coterminal with all of the following *except*

    (1) $-574°$

    (2) $34°$

    (3) $146°$

    (4) $506°$

18 Which angle rotates clockwise?

    (1) $-104°$

    (2) $87°$

    (3) $128°$

    (4) $372°$

9.3 The Unit Circle

A **unit circle** is a circle whose center is at the origin and whose radius is 1 unit. Point P starts at the point $(1, 0)$. As P moves in a counterclockwise direction along the unit circle, the measure of the angle formed by the x-axis and the terminal side of $\overrightarrow{OP}$ starts at $0°$ and increases until it reaches $360°$. We use the Greek letter θ (theta) to represent the angles formed. (If P moved in a clockwise direction, the measure of the angle formed would start at $0°$ and *decrease* until it reached $-360°$ after one complete revolution.)

As P moves around the circle, not only does the angle θ change but the coordinates of point P also change. We will call the coordinates of point P (a, b). Since the distance from P to the origin remains at 1 unit, we can see that $\sqrt{a^2 + b^2} = 1$.

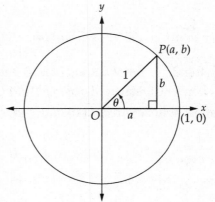

As we reviewed in Section 9.1:

$$\sin \theta = \frac{\text{opposite}}{\text{hypotenuse}} \qquad \cos \theta = \frac{\text{adjacent}}{\text{hypotenuse}}$$

In the unit circle, the length of the hypotenuse remains at a constant value of 1. Therefore,

$$\sin \theta = \frac{\text{opposite}}{\text{hypotenuse}} = \frac{b}{1} = b$$

$$\cos \theta = \frac{\text{adjacent}}{\text{hypotenuse}} = \frac{a}{1} = a$$

Note: In a unit circle, $\cos \theta$ is the x-coordinate and $\sin \theta$ is the y-coordinate of point P. You can write (x, y) in alphabetical order and $(\cos \theta, \sin \theta)$ in alphabetical order and match them up.

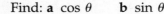 **MODEL PROBLEMS**

1   P is a point on a unit circle with coordinates $(0.6, 0.8)$ as shown below.

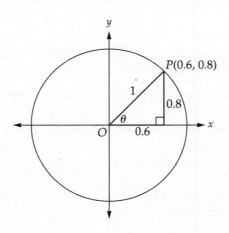

Find: **a** $\cos \theta$ **b** $\sin \theta$

SOLUTION

In a unit circle, the radius measures 1 unit.

a $\cos \theta = \dfrac{\text{adjacent}}{\text{hypotenuse}} = \dfrac{0.6}{1} = 0.6$ ($\cos \theta$ is the x-coordinate.)

b $\sin \theta = \dfrac{\text{opposite}}{\text{hypotenuse}} = \dfrac{0.8}{1} = 0.8$ ($\sin \theta$ is the y-coordinate.)

Since P is a point on the unit circle, when we see the coordinates of $(0.6, 0.8)$, we know that we have $(\cos \theta, \sin \theta)$.

Answers: **a** $\cos \theta = 0.6$ **b** $\sin \theta = 0.8$

> You **must** be working on a unit circle for the x- and y-coordinates to be $\cos \theta$ and $\sin \theta$.

2 In the accompanying diagram of a unit circle, $\overline{BD}$ is tangent to circle O at D, $\overline{AC}$ is perpendicular to the x-axis, and $\overline{OA}$ is a radius. Name a line segment whose directed distance is the value of:

a $\sin \theta$

b $\cos \theta$

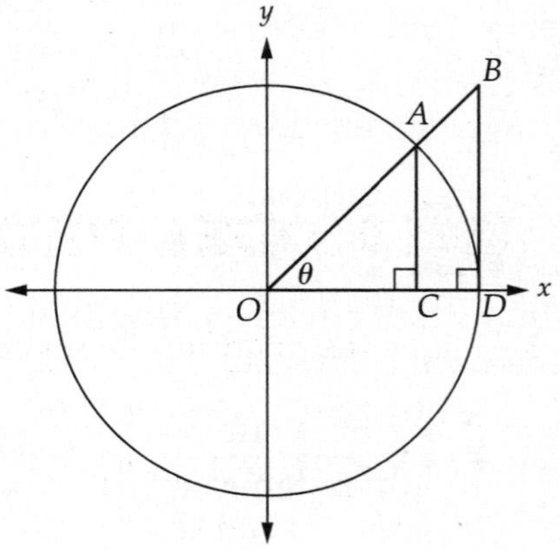

SOLUTION

a Since $\sin \theta = \dfrac{\text{opposite}}{\text{hypotenuse}}$, we need to find a triangle whose hypotenuse measures 1. In triangle OAC, $OA = 1$. Thus, $\sin \theta = \dfrac{AC}{OA} = \dfrac{AC}{1} = AC$.

Answer: $\overline{AC}$

b Since $\cos \theta = \dfrac{\text{adjacent}}{\text{hypotenuse}}$, we need to find a triangle whose hypotenuse measures 1. In triangle OAC, $OA = 1$. Thus, $\cos \theta = \dfrac{OC}{OA} = \dfrac{OC}{1} = OC$.

Answer: $\overline{OC}$

As point $P(a, b)$ moves around the unit circle, and θ increases from $0°$ to $360°$, a and b change signs, and thus the signs of $\sin \theta$ and $\cos \theta$ also change.

- In the first quadrant, since a and b are both positive numbers, $\sin \theta$ is positive and $\cos \theta$ is positive.
- In the second quadrant, since a is a negative number, and b is a positive number, $\sin \theta$ is positive and $\cos \theta$ is negative.
- In the third quadrant, since a and b are both negative numbers, $\sin \theta$ is negative and $\cos \theta$ is negative.
- In the fourth quadrant, since a is a positive number, and b is a negative number, $\sin \theta$ is negative and $\cos \theta$ is positive.

This information can be summed up in the following diagram:

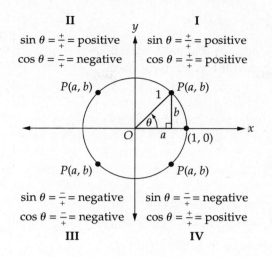

II
$\sin \theta = \frac{+}{+} = $ positive
$\cos \theta = \frac{-}{+} = $ negative

I
$\sin \theta = \frac{+}{+} = $ positive
$\cos \theta = \frac{+}{+} = $ positive

$P(a, b)$

$P(a, b)$

$(1, 0)$

$P(a, b)$

$P(a, b)$

$\sin \theta = \frac{-}{+} = $ negative
$\cos \theta = \frac{-}{+} = $ negative

$\sin \theta = \frac{-}{+} = $ negative
$\cos \theta = \frac{+}{+} = $ positive

III

IV

MODEL PROBLEM

3   Name the quadrant in which θ lies if:

a $\sin \theta > 0$ and $\cos \theta < 0$

b $\cos \theta > 0$ and $\sin \theta > 0$

c $\sin \theta < 0$ and $\cos \theta < 0$

SOLUTION

a $\sin \theta > 0$ and $\cos \theta < 0$

We are looking for a quadrant in which $\sin \theta$ is positive ($\sin \theta > 0$). This could occur in Quadrants I or II.

We also need $\cos \theta$ to be negative ($\cos \theta < 0$). This could occur in Quadrants II or III.

Both requirements are fulfilled in Quadrant II.

A diagram will make this much easier.

First, make a sketch of a Cartesian plane. Then, put a check mark in Quadrants I and II, the quadrants that have positive values for $\sin \theta$. Next, put a check mark in Quadrants II and III, the quadrants that have negative values for $\cos \theta$. Finally, look to see which quadrant fulfills both conditions (has two check marks).

Answer: Quadrant II

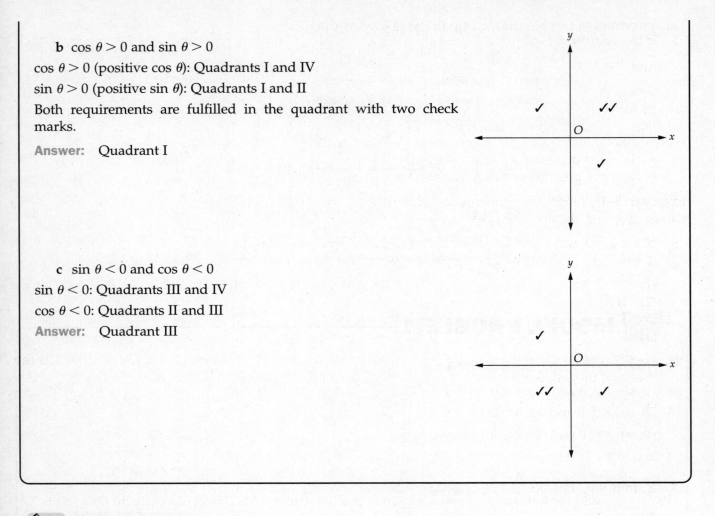

b $\cos \theta > 0$ and $\sin \theta > 0$

$\cos \theta > 0$ (positive $\cos \theta$): Quadrants I and IV

$\sin \theta > 0$ (positive $\sin \theta$): Quadrants I and II

Both requirements are fulfilled in the quadrant with two check marks.

Answer: Quadrant I

c $\sin \theta < 0$ and $\cos \theta < 0$

$\sin \theta < 0$: Quadrants III and IV

$\cos \theta < 0$: Quadrants II and III

Answer: Quadrant III

Practice

1 Copy and complete the following table by writing the sign of the function in each quadrant.

Quadrant	Sin θ	Cos θ
I		
II		
III		
IV		

Exercises 2 and 3: P is a point on the unit circle as shown in the figure below.

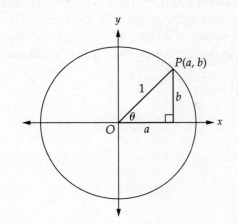

2   If the coordinates of point P are $(0.5, 0.5\sqrt{3})$, find

    a $\sin \theta$

    b $\cos \theta$

3 If the coordinates of point P are $\left(\dfrac{\sqrt{2}}{2}, \dfrac{\sqrt{2}}{2}\right)$, find

   a $\sin \theta$
   b $\cos \theta$

4 Given $m\angle A = 250$:

   a In what quadrant does $\angle A$ lie?
   b Is $\sin A$ positive or negative? Why?

Exercises 5–11: Select the numeral preceding the choice that best answers the question.

5 If $\sin \theta > 0$ and $\cos \theta < 0$, in what quadrant does θ lie?

   (1) I
   (2) II
   (3) III
   (4) IV

6 If $\cos \theta$ is positive, and $\sin \theta$ is negative, what could be the value of θ?

   (1) 70°
   (2) 100°
   (3) 195°
   (4) 303°

7 If $\sin B = \dfrac{3}{5}$ and $\cos B > 0$, in what quadrant does $\angle B$ lie?

   (1) I
   (2) II
   (3) III
   (4) IV

8 If $\cos A > 0$ and $(\cos A)(\sin A) < 0$, in what quadrant does $\angle A$ lie?

   (1) I
   (2) II
   (3) III
   (4) IV

9 If $\sin x = \dfrac{\sqrt{2}}{2}$ and $\cos x = -\dfrac{\sqrt{2}}{2}$, in what quadrant could angle x terminate?

   (1) I
   (2) II
   (3) III
   (4) IV

10 If $\sin \theta = -\dfrac{1}{2}$ and $\cos \theta = -\dfrac{\sqrt{3}}{2}$, which could be the measure of θ?

   (1) 30°
   (2) 150°
   (3) 210°
   (4) 330°

11 Which could be true?

   (1) $\sin 300° = \dfrac{\sqrt{3}}{2}$

   (2) $\sin 240° = \dfrac{\sqrt{3}}{2}$

   (3) $\sin 120° = \dfrac{\sqrt{3}}{2}$

   (4) $\sin 60° = -\dfrac{\sqrt{3}}{2}$

Exercises 12–15: $OA = 1$ and $m\angle AOB = \theta$ in the figure below.

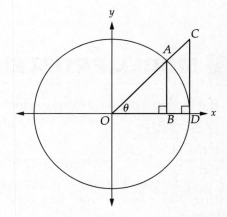

12 If the coordinates of point A are $\left(\dfrac{2}{3}, \dfrac{\sqrt{5}}{3}\right)$, find

   a $\sin \theta$
   b $\cos \theta$

13 Name a line segment whose directed distance is the value of

   a $\sin \theta$
   b $\cos \theta$

14 If the coordinates of point A are $\left(\dfrac{1}{2}, \dfrac{\sqrt{3}}{2}\right)$ and $\theta = 60°$, find $\cos 60°$.

15 If the coordinates of point A are $\left(\dfrac{\sqrt{2}}{2}, \dfrac{\sqrt{2}}{2}\right)$ and $\theta = 45°$, find $\sin 45°$.

9.4 The Tangent Function

In Section 9.3, we examined the unit circle with regard to the sine and cosine functions. Now, let us consider the tangent function on the unit circle.

Based on the work we did on right triangles in Section 9.1, we know that the tangent function is defined as: $\tan \theta = \dfrac{\text{opposite leg}}{\text{adjacent leg}}$. In this diagram, $\tan \theta = \dfrac{b}{a}$.

In the unit circle, however, we know that $\sin \theta = \dfrac{b}{1}$ and $\cos \theta = \dfrac{a}{1}$. Therefore, we can

define $\tan \theta$ as $\dfrac{b}{a} = \dfrac{\dfrac{b}{1}}{\dfrac{a}{1}} = \dfrac{\sin \theta}{\cos \theta}$.

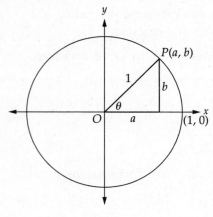

MODEL PROBLEM

1 In the diagram below, determine the value of

   a $\tan \angle LOM$

   b $\tan \angle LOA$

   c $\tan \angle LOT$

   d $\tan \angle LOH$

SOLUTION

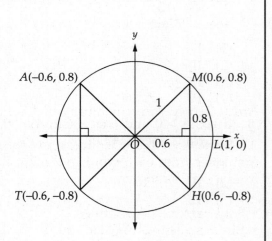

   a The y-value of point M, or the sine value, is 0.8 while the cosine or x-value is 0.6.

$$\tan \angle LOM = \frac{0.8}{0.6} = \frac{0.4}{0.3} = \frac{4}{3}$$

Since both the x- and the y-coordinates, or the sine and cosine values, are positive, the tangent is positive in Quadrant I.

   b Point A is in the second quadrant where the y-value of point A, or sine value, is 0.8 while the cosine or x-value is -0.6.

$$\tan \angle LOA = \frac{0.8}{-0.6} = -\frac{0.4}{0.3} = -\frac{4}{3}$$

Since the x-value or cosine is negative while the y-value or sine is positive, the tangent function is negative in Quadrant II.

c The y-value of point T, or sine, is -0.8 while the cosine or x-value is -0.6.

$$\tan \angle LOT = \frac{-0.8}{-0.6} = \frac{0.4}{0.3} = \frac{4}{3}$$

Since both the x- and the y-coordinates, or the sine and cosine values, are negative, the tangent is positive in Quadrant III.

d The y-value of point H, or sine, is -0.8 while the cosine or x-value is 0.6.

$$\tan \angle LOH = \frac{-0.8}{0.6} = \frac{-0.4}{0.3} = -\frac{4}{3}$$

Since the y-value or sine is negative while the x-value or cosine is positive, the tangent function is negative in Quadrant IV.

The diagram below illustrates the positive and negative values of all three functions in the four quadrants.

$$
\begin{array}{c|c}
\text{II} & \text{I} \\
\sin \theta = \frac{+}{+} = \text{positive} & \sin \theta = \frac{+}{+} = \text{positive} \\
\cos \theta = \frac{-}{+} = \text{negative} & \cos \theta = \frac{+}{+} = \text{positive} \\
\tan \theta = \frac{-}{+} = \text{negative} & \tan \theta = \frac{+}{+} = \text{positive} \\
\hline
\sin \theta = \frac{-}{+} = \text{negative} & \sin \theta = \frac{-}{+} = \text{negative} \\
\cos \theta = \frac{-}{+} = \text{negative} & \cos \theta = \frac{+}{+} = \text{positive} \\
\tan \theta = \frac{-}{-} = \text{positive} & \tan \theta = \frac{-}{+} = \text{negative} \\
\text{III} & \text{IV}
\end{array}
$$

Note: To help you remember which function is positive in each quadrant, remember that **All Students Take Calculus**, and write the first letter from each word in the quadrants from I to IV as shown.

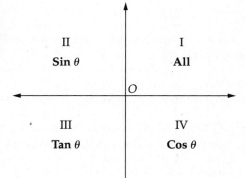

- **All** functions are positive in Quadrant I.
- **Sin** θ is positive in Quadrant II.
- **Tangent** θ is positive in Quadrant III.
- **Cos** θ is positive in Quadrant IV.

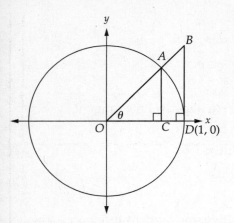

Look at the diagram of the unit circle. We see that $\tan \theta = \dfrac{AC}{OC}$. In geometry, you learned that a segment *tangent* to a circle touches the circle at exactly one point. By this definition, $\overline{BD}$ is tangent to the circle at $D(1, 0)$. Does $\tan \theta = BD$, too? Yes. In $\triangle BOD$, $\tan \theta = \dfrac{BD}{OD}$, but $OD = 1$, so $\tan \theta = \dfrac{BD}{1} = BD$.

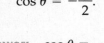 **MODEL PROBLEMS**

2 Determine the quadrant in which the terminal ray of θ lies if:

a $\tan \theta < 0$ and $\sin \theta > 0$.

b $\cos \theta < 0$ and $\tan \theta > 0$.

SOLUTION

a Tangent is negative in Quadrants II and IV; sine is positive in Quadrants I and II. Both conditions are true in Quadrant II.

Answer: Quadrant II

b Cosine is negative in Quadrants II and III; tangent is positive in Quadrants I and III. Both conditions are met in quadrant III.

Answer: Quadrant III

3 If point $P\left(-\dfrac{1}{2}, \dfrac{\sqrt{3}}{2}\right)$ lies on $\overline{OP}$ at the intersection with the unit circle as shown below, determine:

a $\cos \theta$

b $\sin \theta$

c $\tan \theta$

SOLUTION

a Since $\cos \theta$ corresponds to the *x*-value on the unit circle, $\cos \theta = -\dfrac{1}{2}$.

Answer: $\cos \theta = -\dfrac{1}{2}$

b Since $\sin \theta$ corresponds to the *y*-value on the unit circle, $\sin \theta = \dfrac{\sqrt{3}}{2}$.

Answer: $\sin \theta = \dfrac{\sqrt{3}}{2}$

c Since $\tan \theta$ corresponds to $\dfrac{\sin \theta}{\cos \theta}$, $\tan \theta = \dfrac{\dfrac{\sqrt{3}}{2}}{-\dfrac{1}{2}}$. When simplified, $\tan \theta = -\sqrt{3}$.

Answer: $\tan \theta = -\sqrt{3}$

Practice

1 Copy and complete the following table by writing the sign of the function in each quadrant.

Quadrant	$\sin \theta$	$\cos \theta$	$\tan \theta$
I			
II			
III			
IV			

Exercises 2–15: Select the numeral preceding the choice that best answers the question.

2 If $\tan x = -1$ and $\cos x = -\dfrac{\sqrt{2}}{2}$, in what quadrant could angle x terminate?

(1) I
(2) II
(3) III
(4) IV

3 If $\tan \theta$ is positive and $\cos \theta$ is negative, in what quadrant does θ terminate?

(1) I
(2) II
(3) III
(4) IV

4 If $\tan A > 0$ and $(\tan A)(\sin A) > 0$, in what quadrant does $\angle A$ lie?

(1) I
(2) II
(3) III
(4) IV

5 If $\tan \theta = \dfrac{2 - \sqrt{2}}{5}$, in what quadrant(s) can this angle terminate?

(1) I only
(2) I and II
(3) I and III
(4) II and IV

6 If $\sin \theta < 0$ and $\tan \theta < 0$, what might be the measure of θ?

(1) 81°
(2) 128°
(3) 207°
(4) 313°

7 If $\cos \theta = -\dfrac{1}{3}$ and $\tan \theta > 0$, which *must* be true?

(1) $\sin \theta < 0$
(2) $\sin \theta > 0$
(3) $\sin \theta = 0$
(4) $\sin \theta$ is undefined

8 If θ is an angle in standard position and its terminal side passes through the point $\left(\dfrac{\sqrt{3}}{2}, -\dfrac{1}{2} \right)$ on a unit circle, in what quadrant is θ?

(1) I
(2) II
(3) III
(4) IV

9 If the coordinates of point A are $(1, 0)$ and the coordinates of B are $\left(-\dfrac{\sqrt{2}}{2}, \dfrac{\sqrt{2}}{2}\right)$, what is the tangent of $\angle AOB$?

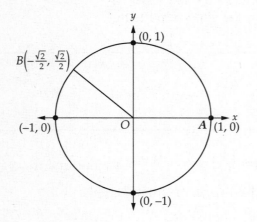

(1) 1

(2) -1

(3) $\dfrac{\sqrt{2}}{2}$

(4) $-\sqrt{2}$

10 Which *cannot* be true?

(1) $\sin 30° = \dfrac{1}{2}$

(2) $\tan 180° = 0$

(3) $\tan 240° = -\sqrt{3}$

(4) $\cos 300° = \dfrac{1}{2}$

11 If $\tan \theta > 0$, which of the following is *true*?

(1) Sin θ must be negative.

(2) Cos θ must be negative.

(3) θ must be in Quadrant I.

(4) Sin θ may be positive or negative.

12 If θ is an angle in standard position and $P\left(-\dfrac{5}{13}, \dfrac{12}{13}\right)$ is a point on the unit circle on the terminal side of θ, what is the value of $\tan \theta$?

(1) $-\dfrac{12}{5}$

(2) $-\dfrac{5}{13}$

(3) $-\dfrac{5}{12}$

(4) $\dfrac{12}{13}$

13 In the accompanying diagram, $\overline{PR}$ is tangent to circle O at R, $\overline{QS} \perp \overline{OR}$, and $\overline{PR} \perp \overline{OR}$.

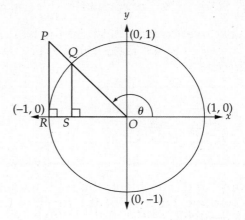

Which segment has the same measure as $\tan \theta$?

(1) $\overline{SO}$

(2) $\overline{RO}$

(3) $\overline{PR}$

(4) $\overline{QS}$

14 If $\tan \theta = 2.7$ and $\sin \theta < 0$, in which quadrant does θ lie?

(1) I

(2) II

(3) III

(4) IV

15 Which of the following is a *false* statement?

(1) Tan θ is undefined whenever cos θ equals zero.

(2) Tan θ equals zero whenever sin θ equals zero.

(3) Sin θ can equal cos θ in Quadrant I or Quadrant III of the unit circle.

(4) Sin θ can equal cos θ only in Quadrant I of the unit circle.

9.5 Special Angles and Reference Angles

Recall the relationships between the legs and hypotenuse of the 30°-60° right triangle and the 45°-45° right triangle. For your reference, they are shown in the figures below.

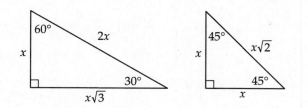

If we incorporate our knowledge of these special angles with our knowledge of the unit circle, we can extend our study of trigonometry to the other quadrants. In the accompanying diagram of a unit circle, $\overline{OA}$ is a radius, and $\overline{AC}$ is perpendicular to the x-axis. If $\theta = 30°$, we can determine that the coordinates of point A are $\left(\dfrac{\sqrt{3}}{2}, \dfrac{1}{2}\right)$

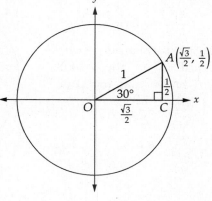

and that $\sin 30° = \dfrac{1}{2}$, $\cos 30° = \dfrac{\sqrt{3}}{2}$, and

$$\tan 30° = \dfrac{\dfrac{1}{2}}{\dfrac{\sqrt{3}}{2}} = \dfrac{1}{\cancel{2}} \cdot \dfrac{\cancel{2}}{\sqrt{3}} = \dfrac{1}{\sqrt{3}} = \dfrac{1}{\sqrt{3}} \cdot \dfrac{\sqrt{3}}{\sqrt{3}} = \dfrac{\sqrt{3}}{3}.$$

Now let us look at an angle in the second quadrant. Let $\theta = 150°$. If we draw a perpendicular segment from A to a point C on the x-axis, $m\angle AOC = 30$. We then know that the coordinates of point A are $\left(-\dfrac{\sqrt{3}}{2}, \dfrac{1}{2}\right)$.

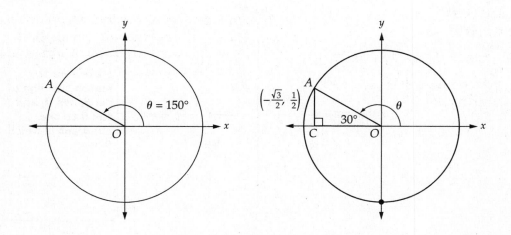

Since we are working in a unit circle, $\sin 150° = \dfrac{1}{2}$, $\cos 150° = -\dfrac{\sqrt{3}}{2}$, and $\tan 150° = -\dfrac{\sqrt{3}}{3}$.

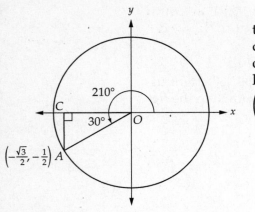

The procedure is the same for angles in the other two quadrants. Let $\theta = 210°$. If we draw a perpendicular from A to a point C on the x-axis, $m\angle AOC = 30$. We then know that the coordinates of point A are $\left(-\dfrac{\sqrt{3}}{2}, -\dfrac{1}{2}\right)$.

Thus, $\sin 210° = -\dfrac{1}{2}$, $\cos 210° = -\dfrac{\sqrt{3}}{2}$, and $\tan 210° = \dfrac{\sqrt{3}}{3}$.

Next, let $\theta = 330°$. If we draw a perpendicular from A to a point C on the x-axis, $m\angle AOC = 30$. We then know that the coordinates of point A are $\left(\dfrac{\sqrt{3}}{2}, -\dfrac{1}{2}\right)$.

Thus, $\sin 330° = -\dfrac{1}{2}$, $\cos 330° = \dfrac{\sqrt{3}}{2}$, and $\tan 330° = -\dfrac{\sqrt{3}}{3}$.

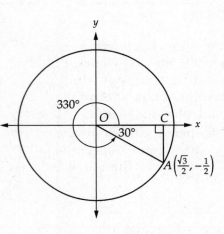

In each of these cases, we referred back to a 30° angle. The 30° angle is called the **reference angle** and is the basis for the other angles. When the terminal side of a 30° angle is reflected in the y-axis, it produces an angle in the second quadrant that measures 150° in standard position. When the terminal side is reflected through the origin, it forms an angle in the third quadrant that measures 210° in standard position. Similarly, a reflection in the x-axis produces an angle in the fourth quadrant that measures 330° in standard position.

For an angle whose degree measure is θ, if θ is in Quadrant

 II: reference angle is $180° - \theta$
III: reference angle is $\theta - 180°$
 IV: reference angle is $360° - \theta$

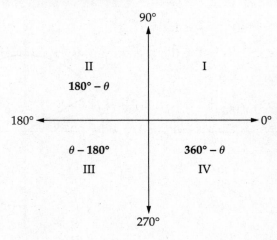

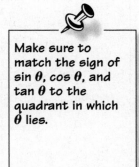

Make sure to match the sign of sin θ, cos θ, and tan θ to the quadrant in which θ lies.

Recall that angles that lie on the axes (0°, 90°, 180°, 270°, and 360°) are called quadrantal angles. By looking at their x- and y-coordinates on a unit circle, we can determine the sine and cosine of each of these angles.

For example, cos 90° = 0 and sin 90° = 1 since the coordinates for 90° are (0, 1). (Remember that the x-coordinate is the cosine of the angle and the y-coordinate is the sine of the angle.) To determine the tangent of a quadrantal angle, use the formula $\tan \theta = \dfrac{\sin \theta}{\cos \theta}$.

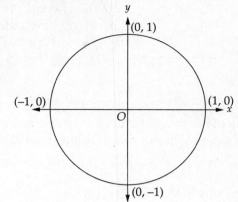

$$\tan 0° = \frac{0}{1} = 0 \qquad\qquad \tan 180° = \frac{0}{-1} = 0$$

$$\tan 90° = \frac{1}{0} = \textit{Undefined} \qquad \tan 270° = \frac{-1}{0} = \textit{Undefined}$$

Since division by zero is undefined, the values of tan 90° and tan 270° are *undefined*.

MODEL PROBLEMS

1 Express each of the following as a function of a positive acute angle.

   a sin 140°

   b cos 250°

   c tan 300°

SOLUTION

   a sin 140°: Since 140° is in the second quadrant, we know that sin 140° is positive.

sin 140° = sin (180° − 140°) = sin 40°

   b cos 250°: Since 250° is in the third quadrant, we know that cos 250° is negative.

cos 250° = −cos (250° − 180°) = −cos 70°

   c tan 300°: Since 300° is in the fourth quadrant, we know that tan 300° is negative.

tan 300° = −tan (360° − 300°) = −tan 60°

2 Find the exact value for each of the following.

    a $\sin 300°$

    b $\cos 135°$

    c $\tan 240°$

    d $\sin 270°$

    e $\cos 180°$

SOLUTION

Remember that a calculator *cannot* be used to obtain exact values of most trigonometric functions. A calculator will give only approximate values of these functions.

    a $\sin 300°$: Since $300°$ is in the fourth quadrant, we know that $\sin 300°$ is negative.

$$\sin 300° = -\sin (360° - 300°) = -\sin 60°$$

$$\sin 300° = -\sin 60° = -\frac{\sqrt{3}}{2}$$

> Refer to the 30°–60° right triangle on page 327.

    b $\cos 135°$: Since $135°$ is in the second quadrant, we know that $\cos 135°$ is negative.

$$\cos 135° = -\cos (180° - 135°) = -\cos 45° = -\frac{\sqrt{2}}{2}$$

    c $\tan 240°$: Since $240°$ is in the third quadrant, we know that $\tan 240°$ is positive.

$$\tan 240° = \tan (240° - 180°) = \tan 60° = \sqrt{3}$$

    d $\sin 270°$: Since the terminal ray of $270°$ lies on the y-axis, it is a quadrantal angle. The sine of the angle is its y-coordinate. Since the coordinates are $(0, -1)$, $\sin 270° = -1$.

    e $\cos 180°$: Since the terminal ray of $180°$ lies on the x-axis, it is also a quadrantal angle. The cosine of the angle is its x-coordinate. Since the coordinates are $(-1, 0)$, $\cos 180° = -1$.

How do we find $\tan (-240°)$? We use coterminal angles *and* reference angles. We know that moving $240°$ in a negative direction is the same as moving $120°$ in a positive direction, so the $-240°$ angle is coterminal with the $120°$ angle (see Section 9.2). Since $-240°$ is in the second quadrant, we know that $\tan (-240°)$ is negative.

$$\tan (-240°) = \tan 120° = -\tan (180° - 120°) = -\tan 60° = -\sqrt{3}$$

We can use similar reasoning to find $\cos 420°$. We know that a $420°$ angle is more than one complete rotation. Since $420° - 360° = 60°$, an angle of $420°$ is coterminal with an angle of $60°$. Since $420°$ is in the first quadrant, we know that $\cos 420°$ is positive.

$$\cos (420°) = \cos 60° = \frac{1}{2}$$

**Practice**

1 Copy and complete the table.

θ	0°	30°	45°	60°	90°	180°	270°	360°
$\sin \theta$								
$\cos \theta$								
$\tan \theta$								

2 Copy and complete the table as shown.

Angle	Quadrant	Reference Angle Formula	Reference Angle
210°	III	210° − 180°	30°
330°			
135°			
300°			
120°			
240°			
225°			

Exercises 3–7: Find the smallest positive angle that is coterminal with each angle.

3 −40°

4 390°

5 800°

6 −400°

7 −160°

Exercises 8–14: Find the exact value of each expression.

8 sin 120°

9 cos 300°

10 sin 315°

11 tan (−60°)

12 sin (−135°)

13 cos 90° + tan 225°

14 $(\tan 30°)^2 + (\cos 30°)^2$

15 If $g(x) = 2 \cos x$, find

   a $g(300°)$
   b $g(-45°)$
   c $g(0°)$

16 Express as a function of a positive acute angle.

   a sin 320°
   b tan (−50°)
   c cos 200°
   d tan 140°
   e sin 400°

Exercises 17–30: Write the numeral preceding the choice that best completes the statement or answers the question.

17 For what value of x is the expression $\dfrac{1}{1 - \sin x}$ undefined?

   (1) 1
   (2) 90°
   (3) 180°
   (4) 270°

18 If $f(x) = \sin 2x + \cos x$, then $f(180°) =$

   (1) 1
   (2) 2
   (3) −1
   (4) 0

19 Evaluate 2 sin 330° + cos (−60°).

   (1) $-1\dfrac{1}{2}$
   (2) $-\dfrac{1}{2}$
   (3) $\dfrac{1}{2}$
   (4) $1\dfrac{1}{2}$

20 If θ is an angle in standard position and its terminal side passes through the point $\left(-\dfrac{1}{2}, -\dfrac{\sqrt{3}}{2}\right)$ on the unit circle, then a possible value for θ is

(1) 60°
(2) 120°
(3) 240°
(4) 300°

21 The expression cos 290° is equivalent to

(1) cos 70°
(2) cos 20°
(3) −cos 20°
(4) −cos 70°

22 What single transformation moves a fourth-quadrant angle to its equivalent first-quadrant reference angle?

(1) reflection in the y-axis
(2) reflection in the origin
(3) reflection in the x-axis
(4) reflection in the line $y = x$

23 Which expression has the greatest value?

(1) sin 120°
(2) sin 150°
(3) tan 240°
(4) cos 315°

24 Which expression is *not* equal to sin 210°?

(1) −sin 30°
(2) sin (−30°)
(3) sin 30°
(4) −cos 60°

25 Evaluate:
$(\cos 315°)^2(\sin 30°) + (\tan 135°)(\cos 180°)$

(1) $-\dfrac{3}{4}$

(2) $\dfrac{1}{2}$

(3) $\dfrac{3}{4}$

(4) $\dfrac{5}{4}$

26 Find the exact value of $(\tan 120°)^2 - \cos 180°$.

(1) $\sqrt{3} + 1$
(2) 2
(3) 3
(4) 4

27 The value of tan 315° is the same as the value of

(1) cos 0°
(2) sin 90°
(3) tan 135°
(4) sin 180°

28 What is the reference angle for −132°?

(1) 42°
(2) 48°
(3) 138°
(4) 228°

29 If the coordinates of point A are $(1, 0)$ and the coordinates of B are $\left(-\dfrac{\sqrt{3}}{2}, \dfrac{1}{2}\right)$, what is the measure of $\angle AOB$?

(1) 120°
(2) 135°
(3) 150°
(4) 330°

30 The expression sin (360° − x) is equivalent to

(1) sin x
(2) −sin x
(3) cos x
(4) −cos x

31 The expression tan 180° has the same value as

(1) tan 90°
(2) cos 180°
(3) sin 270°
(4) sin 180°

32 Which is a *false* statement?

(1) Tan θ is undefined whenever cos θ equals zero.
(2) If sin $\theta = \dfrac{\sqrt{3}}{2}$, $|\cos \theta| = \dfrac{1}{2}$.
(3) If cos $\theta = 0$, then $|\sin \theta| = 1$.
(4) Sin $\theta = \cos \theta$ only in Quadrant I.

9.6 Reciprocal Trigonometric Functions

Each of the three basic trigonometric functions has a corresponding **reciprocal function**. The **secant** function (sec) is the reciprocal of the cosine function, the **cosecant** function (csc) is the reciprocal of the sine function, and the **cotangent** function (cot) is the reciprocal of the tangent function.

$\sec \theta = \dfrac{1}{\cos \theta}$, $\cos \theta \neq 0$ (sec θ is defined for all $\theta \neq 90° + 180°n$)

$\csc \theta = \dfrac{1}{\sin \theta}$, $\sin \theta \neq 0$ (csc θ is defined for all $\theta \neq 180°n$)

$\cot \theta = \dfrac{1}{\tan \theta}$, $\tan \theta \neq 0$ (cot θ is defined for all $\theta \neq 180°n$)

Note: $\cot \theta = 0$ if $\tan \theta$ is undefined.

An easy way to remember that the secant function is the reciprocal of the cosine function and the cosecant function is the reciprocal of the sine function is to notice that each function-reciprocal pair contains one c term and one s term. Thus, **sec** θ is the reciprocal of **cos** θ, and **csc** θ is the reciprocal of **sin** θ.

MODEL PROBLEMS

1 Name the quadrant in which $\angle A$ must lie if $\sec A > 0$ and $\csc A < 0$.

SOLUTION

If $\sec A > 0$, then $\cos A > 0$, and if $\csc A < 0$, then $\sin A < 0$.

Draw a set of axes and note that $\cos A > 0$ in Quadrants I and IV. Place check marks in Quadrants I and IV, as indicated in the figure. Sin $A < 0$ in Quadrants III and IV. Place check marks in Quadrants III and IV. Both conditions hold true in Quadrant IV.

Answer: Quadrant IV

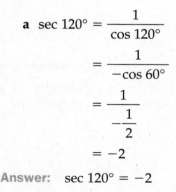

2 Find the exact value of   **a** sec 120°   **b** cot 210°

SOLUTION

a $\sec 120° = \dfrac{1}{\cos 120°}$

$= \dfrac{1}{-\cos 60°}$ (Cosine is negative in the second quadrant.)

$= \dfrac{1}{-\dfrac{1}{2}}$

$= -2$

Answer: $\sec 120° = -2$

b $\cot 210° = \dfrac{1}{\tan 210°}$

$\qquad\qquad = \dfrac{1}{\tan 30°}$ $\qquad$ (Tangent is positive in the third quadrant.)

$\qquad\qquad = \dfrac{1}{\dfrac{\sqrt{3}}{3}}$

$\qquad\qquad = \dfrac{3}{\sqrt{3}}$

$\qquad\qquad = \dfrac{3}{\sqrt{3}} \cdot \dfrac{\sqrt{3}}{\sqrt{3}}$

$\qquad\qquad = \dfrac{3\sqrt{3}}{3}$

$\qquad\qquad = \sqrt{3}$

Answer: $\cot 210° = \sqrt{3}$

We have not yet illustrated the use of calculators in our study of trigonometry. When you are asked to find an exact value for a trigonometric function, you may not give a decimal approximation of the answer. You should learn the functions of all of the special angles. However, for approximations you may use the calculator.

Remember to put your calculator in degree mode. (See page 309.)

There are no calculator keys for the reciprocal functions. Instead, you need to treat them as 1 *over* the basic function. For example, to find an approximate value for csc 120°, use these steps:

1. Make sure that your calculator is in degree mode.
2. Press 1 [÷] [SIN] 120 [ )] [ENTER].
3. The answer 1.154700530 is an approximation for $\dfrac{2\sqrt{3}}{3}$.

Note: The [2nd] [SIN] function, SIN^{-1}, is the inverse of the sine function, *not* its reciprocal.

 **Practice**

1 Copy and complete the table.

θ	0°	30°	45°	60°	90°	180°	270°	360°
$\sec \theta$								
$\csc \theta$								
$\cot \theta$								

2 In the interval $0 \le \theta \le 360°$, identify all values at which the function is undefined:

a $\sec \theta$
b $\csc \theta$
c $\cot \theta$

3 Determine the quadrant in which x lies if

    a $\sin x > 0$ and $\cot x < 0$
    b $\csc x < 0$ and $\cot x < 0$
    c $\sec x > 0$ and $\sin x < 0$
    d $\cot x < 0$ and $\sec x < 0$
    e $\cos x > 0$ and $\csc x > 0$

Exercises 4–10: Find the exact value of each expression.

4 $\sec 300°$

5 $\csc 225°$

6 $\cot 270°$

7 $\cot 420°$

8 $\csc (-210°)$

9 $(\sec 150°)(\cos 150°)$

10 $(\tan 300°)(\cot 300°)$

Exercises 11–15: Use a calculator and approximate each value to the *nearest thousandth*.

11 $\csc 238°$

12 $\sec 410°$

13 $\cot (-35°)$

14 $\cot 125°$

15 $\csc 325°$

Exercises 16–20: Select the numeral preceding the choice that best completes the statement or answers the question.

16 $(\sec \theta)(\cos \theta) =$

    (1) 1
    (2) 0
    (3) undefined
    (4) varies depending upon the value of θ

17 Which expression is equivalent to $\csc 45°$?

    (1) $\dfrac{1}{\sin 45°}$

    (2) $\dfrac{1}{\sec 45°}$

    (3) $\dfrac{1}{\tan 45°}$

    (4) $\sin (-45°)$

18 If $f(x) = 2 \sec x$, find $f(30°)$.

    (1) $\dfrac{2\sqrt{3}}{3}$

    (2) 2

    (3) $\sqrt{3}$

    (4) $\dfrac{4\sqrt{3}}{3}$

19 If $g(x) = \sin x + \csc x$, find $g(90°)$.

    (1) 1
    (2) 2
    (3) 0
    (4) −2

20 Which expression is equal in value to $\sec 180°$?

    (1) $\csc 180°$
    (2) $\tan 180°$
    (3) $\cot 135°$
    (4) $\cos 225°$

Select the numeral preceding the choice that best completes the statement or answers the question.

1 If $\csc \theta = 2$ and $\sec \theta < 0$, in which quadrant does θ terminate?

(1) I
(2) II
(3) III
(4) IV

2 A kite is flying 40 feet in the air. The kite string is 75 feet long and has been staked to the ground. To the *nearest degree*, what is the measure of the angle of elevation of the kite?

(1) 28°
(2) 32°
(3) 58°
(4) 75°

3 In which quadrant does a −285° angle lie?

(1) I
(2) II
(3) III
(4) IV

4 Express tan 150° as the function of a positive acute angle.

(1) tan 30°
(2) cot 60°
(3) −cot 30°
(4) −tan 30°

5 Evaluate: $(\sin 135°)^2(\sin 30°) + (\cos 225°)^2(\cos 120°)$

(1) −1
(2) $-\dfrac{1}{4}$
(3) 0
(4) $\dfrac{3}{4}$

6 Find the exact value of $(\cos 150°)(\tan 315°) - \sin 240°$.

(1) 0
(2) $\dfrac{\sqrt{3}}{4}$
(3) $\dfrac{\sqrt{3}}{2}$
(4) $\sqrt{3}$

7 Point P lies on the unit circle as shown in the diagram below. If the coordinates of point P are $\left(\dfrac{7}{25}, \dfrac{24}{25}\right)$, what is $\cos \theta$?

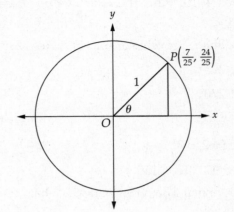

(1) $\dfrac{7}{25}$

(2) $\dfrac{7}{24}$

(3) $\dfrac{24}{25}$

(4) $\dfrac{24}{7}$

8 If $\sin \theta < 0$ and $\tan \theta < 0$, what might be the measure of θ?

(1) 45°
(2) 135°
(3) 330°
(4) 450°

9 As angle β increases from 90° to 180°, the value of $\sin \beta$

(1) decreases from 0 to −1
(2) decreases from 1 to 0
(3) increases from −1 to 0
(4) increases from 0 to 1

10 For which value of θ is the fraction $\dfrac{2}{1 - \tan \theta}$ undefined?

(1) 0°
(2) 135°
(3) 180°
(4) 225°

11 The coordinates of a point on the unit circle are $\left(\dfrac{\sqrt{2}}{2}, -\dfrac{\sqrt{2}}{2}\right)$. If the terminal side of angle θ in standard position passes through the given point, find m$\angle\theta$.

(1) 135
(2) 150
(3) 300
(4) 315

12 Find the exact value of $\sin 150° + (\cos 240°)^2$.

(1) 0
(2) $\dfrac{1}{4}$
(3) $\dfrac{1}{2}$
(4) $\dfrac{3}{4}$

13 The expression $1 - 2(\sin 45°)^2$ has the same value as

(1) $\sin 90°$
(2) $\cos 90°$
(3) $\cos 45°$
(4) $\sin 22.5°$

14 In the interval $0° \le \beta < 360°$, $\sin \beta = \cos \beta$ when β is

(1) 45° only
(2) 135° and 315°
(3) 225° only
(4) 45° and 225°

15 Express in radical form: $(\sin 90°)(\tan 30°) + (\tan 60°)(\cos 90°)$.

(1) $\sqrt{3}$
(2) $\dfrac{\sqrt{3}}{3}$
(3) $-\dfrac{\sqrt{3}}{3}$
(4) $-\sqrt{3}$

16 If $\tan \theta = \dfrac{-2 - \sqrt{3}}{5}$, in what quadrant(s) can this angle terminate?

(1) I or II
(2) I or III
(3) II or III
(4) II or IV

17 Which angle is *not* coterminal with an angle that measures 300°?

(1) −420°
(2) −300°
(3) −60°
(4) 660°

18 In standard position, an angle of 210° has the same terminal ray as an angle of

(1) −150°
(2) −30°
(3) 150°
(4) 240°

19 If $f(\theta) = 2 \sin \theta - \tan \dfrac{3\theta}{2}$, evaluate $f(30°)$.

(1) 1
(2) −1
(3) 3
(4) 0

20 For which value of θ is $\tan \theta$ undefined?

(1) 180°
(2) 450°
(3) 720°
(4) 960°

21 In right triangle DEF, the length of hypotenuse $\overline{DF}$ is 13 inches. If $DE = 5$ inches, to the *nearest degree*, what is m$\angle F$?

(1) 21
(2) 23
(3) 67
(4) 90

22 What is the reference angle for −512°?

(1) −208°
(2) −28°
(3) 28°
(4) 280°

23 If $f(x) = \cos 2\theta + \sin \theta$, then $f(180°)$ equals

(1) 1
(2) 2
(3) −2
(4) 0

24 If $\sin \theta = c$ and $c \ne 0$, then the value of the expression $(\sin \theta)(\csc \theta)$ is equivalent to

(1) 1
(2) c
(3) $\dfrac{1}{c^2}$
(4) c^2

25 P is the point at which the terminal side of an angle θ in standard position intersects the unit circle in the second quadrant. If the x-coordinate of point P is $-\dfrac{5}{13}$, what is the y-coordinate of P?

(1) $-\dfrac{12}{13}$

(2) $-\dfrac{5}{13}$

(3) $\dfrac{5}{13}$

(4) $\dfrac{12}{13}$

26 Which angle does *not* have the same reference angle as the other three?

(1) $120°$
(2) $150°$
(3) $240°$
(4) $300°$

27 Evaluate $2(\csc 210°)^2 + (\cot 225°)^2$.

(1) 1

(2) $\dfrac{3}{2}$

(3) 3
(4) 9

28 Which is *not* a quadrantal angle?

(1) $-540°$
(2) $-450°$
(3) $680°$
(4) $1{,}080°$

29 If $\sin \theta = -\dfrac{\sqrt{2}}{2}$, which of the following *must* be true?

(1) $\cos \theta = \dfrac{\sqrt{2}}{2}$

(2) $\tan \theta = -1$
(3) $\csc \theta = -\sqrt{2}$
(4) $\sec \theta = -\sqrt{2}$

30 For which values is the fraction $\dfrac{4\cos \theta}{\tan^2 \theta - 3}$ undefined?

(1) $30°$ and $180°$
(2) $120°$ and $240°$
(3) $210°$ and $330°$
(4) $150°$ and $300°$

31 If the terminal ray of angle θ, in standard position, passes through the point whose coordinates are $\left(-\dfrac{\sqrt{3}}{2}, -\dfrac{1}{2}\right)$, find $m\angle \theta$.

(1) $120°$
(2) $150°$
(3) $210°$
(4) $240°$

32 An angle whose measure is $-214°$ is coterminal with all of the following *except*

(1) $-574°$
(2) $34°$
(3) $146°$
(4) $506°$

33 Find the exact value of $(\csc 210°)(\cos 315°) + (\cos 135°)(\sec 300°)$.

(1) $-2\sqrt{2}$

(2) $-\dfrac{1}{2}$

(3) $\dfrac{1}{2}$

(4) $2\sqrt{2}$

CHAPTER 10

More Trigonometric Functions

10.1 Radian Measure

The two most common units used to measure angles are degrees and *radians*. The Babylonians were responsible for dividing the circle into 360°. The radian is more commonly used in advanced mathematics. A **radian** is the measure of a central angle that intercepts an arc equal in length to the radius of the circle. To help you understand the concept of radian measure, try the following.

Given the following circle:

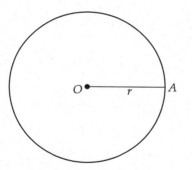

Step 1: Take a piece of string and place one end at point O, and cut it so the other end is at point A. Your string is now the length of the radius of the circle.

Step 2: Place one end of the string at A, and extend your string so that it lies along the circumference of the circle (the distance along the outside of the circle). Locate the point where the string ends, and label the point B. Connect B to O. Your angle should look like the figure below.

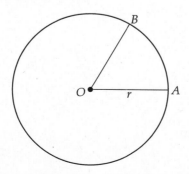

Angle BOA measures one radian.

Step 3: Now mark off the length of another radius along the circumference of your circle. Label the point C. $m\angle COA = 2$ radians, since its length is twice the radius of the circle.

We could continue on in the same manner marking off the length around the circumference of the circle. Therefore, the measure of the central angle θ, in radians, is the length of the intercepted arc, s, divided by the radius of the circle, r.

$$\theta = \frac{s}{r}$$

MODEL PROBLEMS

1 Given: θ is the measure of the central angle in radians, s is the length of the intercepted arc, and r is the radius of the circle.

   a If $s = 12$ and $r = 4$, find θ.
   b If $r = 5$ and $\theta = 10$, find s.
   c If $\theta = 3$ and $s = 15$, find r.

SOLUTION

   a Use the formula with $s = 12$ and $r = 4$:

$$\theta = \frac{s}{r}$$

$$\theta = \frac{12}{4}$$

$$\theta = 3$$

Answer: $\theta = 3$ radians

   b Use the formula with $r = 5$ and $\theta = 10$:

$$\theta = \frac{s}{r}$$

$$10 = \frac{s}{5}$$

$$s = 50$$

Answer: The length of s, the intercepted arc, is 50 units.

   c Use the formula with $\theta = 3$ and $s = 15$:

$$\theta = \frac{s}{r}$$

$$3 = \frac{15}{r}$$

$$3r = 15$$

$$r = 5$$

Answer: The radius r measures 5 units.

2 In a circle, a central angle of 2 radians intercepts an arc of 6 inches. Find the length of the radius of the circle.

SOLUTION

Use the formula: $\theta = \dfrac{s}{r}$

$$2 = \dfrac{6}{r}$$

$$2r = 6$$

$$r = 3$$

Answer: The length of the radius is 3 inches.

We know that the measure, in degrees, of the central angle formed by a complete rotation is 360°. To find the measure, in radians, of the central angle formed by a complete rotation we use the formula: $\theta = \dfrac{s}{r}$.

The circumference of a circle (the length of the arc that is formed by one complete rotation) is equal to 2π times the radius of the circle, or $C = 2\pi r$.

Substituting this for s in the formula, we get

$$\theta = \dfrac{2\pi r}{r} = 2\pi$$

Since a complete rotation is 360° and also 2π radians, 2π radians = 360°.
Dividing both sides of the equation by 2, we obtain π radians = 180°.
To find the measure of 1 radian, we divide both sides of the equation by π and obtain

$$1 \text{ radian} = \dfrac{180°}{\pi} \approx 57.3°$$

You can use 57° as a good approximation for 1 radian.
We can convert from degrees to radians and from radians to degrees.

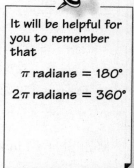

It will be helpful for you to remember that

π radians = 180°

2π radians = 360°

Converting Degrees to Radians

Since 180° = π radians, we can see that 90° = $\dfrac{\pi}{2}$ radians, 60° = $\dfrac{\pi}{3}$ radians, and so forth.

What about an angle that measures 40°? How can we convert 40° to radian measure? To convert 40° to radians we will multiply by 1 in the form $\dfrac{\pi \text{ radians}}{180°}$.

$$40° = 40° \cdot 1 = \dfrac{40 \text{ degrees}}{1} \cdot \dfrac{\pi \text{ radians}}{180 \text{ degrees}} = \dfrac{\overset{2}{\cancel{40}}}{\underset{9}{\cancel{180}}} \pi \text{ radians} = \dfrac{2}{9} \pi \text{ radians}$$

In general, when converting from degrees to radians, multiply by $\frac{\pi \text{ radians}}{180°}$.
The degrees in the numerator will "cancel" with the degrees in the denominator.

$$\frac{n \text{ degrees}}{1} \cdot \frac{\pi \text{ radians}}{180 \text{ degrees}} = \frac{n\pi}{180} \text{ radians}$$

Converting Radians to Degrees

To convert from radians to degrees, we also multiply the measure by 1, but we use
1 in the form $\frac{180°}{\pi \text{ radians}}$.
The radians in the numerator will "cancel" with the radians in the denominator.

$$\frac{\theta \text{ radians}}{1} \cdot \frac{180 \text{ degrees}}{\pi \text{ radians}} = \frac{180\theta}{\pi} \text{ degrees}$$

MODEL PROBLEMS

3 Express $\frac{5\pi}{3}$ radians in degrees.

SOLUTION

Multiply by 1 in the form $\frac{180°}{\pi \text{ radians}}$.

$$\frac{5\pi}{3} \cdot \frac{\overset{60}{\cancel{180°}}}{\cancel{\pi}} = 300°$$

Answer: 300°

4 Express 150° in radians.

SOLUTION

Multiply by 1 in the form $\frac{\pi \text{ radians}}{180°}$.

$$\frac{\overset{5}{\cancel{150°}}}{1} \cdot \frac{\pi}{\underset{6}{\cancel{180°}}} = \frac{5}{6}\pi$$

Answer: $\frac{5}{6}\pi$ or $\frac{5\pi}{6}$

 **Practice**

Exercises 1–10: Change each angle from degree measure to radian measure.

1 120°

2 270°

3 −50°

4 315°

5 −135°

6 80°

7 330°

8 −180°

9 −45°

10 240°

Exercises 11–20: Change each angle from radian measure to degree measure.

11 $\dfrac{3\pi}{2}$

12 $\dfrac{2\pi}{3}$

13 $\dfrac{5\pi}{4}$

14 $-\dfrac{\pi}{2}$

15 $\dfrac{5\pi}{6}$

16 $-\dfrac{7\pi}{4}$

17 $\dfrac{\pi}{5}$

18 $\dfrac{5\pi}{3}$

19 $-\dfrac{\pi}{6}$

20 π

21 Find the length of the radius of a circle in which a central angle of 4.5 radians intercepts an arc of 9 meters.

22 A pendulum makes an angle of 3 radians as its tip travels 18 feet. What is the length of the pendulum?

23 Place in order from smallest to largest: 1 radian, 1 revolution, 1 degree, 3 radians.

24 What is the measure of an angle formed by the hands of a clock at 2:30?

    a in degrees
    b in radians

25 If the minute hand of a clock measures 6 inches, how long is the arc traced by this hand from 1:00 to 1:30?

Exercises 26–30: Select the numeral preceding the choice that best completes the statement or answers the question.

26 An angle of $\dfrac{3\pi}{4}$ radians lies in quadrant

    (1) I
    (2) II
    (3) III
    (4) IV

27 Circle O has a radius of 10 inches. What is the length, in inches, of the arc subtended by a central angle measuring 2.5 radians?

    (1) 250
    (2) 40
    (3) 25
    (4) 4

28 In what quadrant does an angle whose measure is $\dfrac{5\pi}{4}$ lie?

    (1) I
    (2) II
    (3) III
    (4) IV

29 In standard position, an angle of $\dfrac{5\pi}{3}$ has the same terminal side as an angle of

(1) 60°
(2) 120°
(3) 240°
(4) 300°

30 A full revolution in the unit circle is how many radians?

(1) $\dfrac{\pi}{2}$
(2) 2
(3) π
(4) 2π

10.2 Trigonometric Functions with Radian Measure

Just as we explored various types of problems using degree measure, we will look at similar problems with radian measure.

For angles with degree measure, we used reference angles (corresponding positive acute angles) to find their trigonometric function values. We do the same for angles with radian measure.

Refer to the unit circle and table below to help you identify the reference angle for a given θ in each quadrant.

> Remember which functions are positive in each quadrant:
> I: All
> II: Sine
> III: Tangent
> IV: Cosine

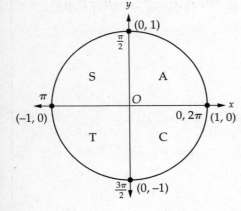

Angle Measure	Quadrant	Reference Angle
$0 < \theta < \dfrac{\pi}{2}$	I	θ
$\dfrac{\pi}{2} < \theta < \pi$	II	$\pi - \theta$
$\pi < \theta < \dfrac{3\pi}{2}$	III	$\theta - \pi$
$\dfrac{3\pi}{2} < \theta < 2\pi$	IV	$2\pi - \theta$

1   Express each as a function of a positive acute angle.

   a $\sin \dfrac{5\pi}{4}$ **b** $\tan \dfrac{7\pi}{6}$ **c** $\csc \dfrac{5\pi}{3}$

SOLUTION

The "positive acute angle" means the reference angle. To help you remember the formulas for the reference angles, consult the figure below.

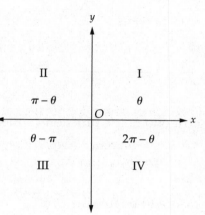

   a Since $\dfrac{5\pi}{4}$ can be written as $\dfrac{5}{4}\pi$, we see that this value is larger than π and smaller than $\dfrac{3\pi}{2}$, so the angle is in the third quadrant, where sine is negative. Thus, we apply the third quadrant formula to find the reference angle.

$$\sin \frac{5\pi}{4} = -\sin\left(\frac{5\pi}{4} - \pi\right)$$

$$= -\sin \frac{\pi}{4}$$

Answer: $-\sin \dfrac{\pi}{4}$

   b Since $\dfrac{7\pi}{6}$ is in the third quadrant $\left(\text{it is larger than } \pi \text{ and smaller than } \dfrac{3\pi}{2}\right)$, we know that the tangent is positive.

$$\tan \frac{7\pi}{6} = \tan\left(\frac{7\pi}{6} - \pi\right)$$

$$= \tan \frac{\pi}{6}$$

Answer: $\tan \dfrac{\pi}{6}$

> **Note:** The reference angle is formed by the terminal ray of θ and the horizontal axis.

c Since $\dfrac{5\pi}{3}$ is in the fourth quadrant $\left(\text{it is larger than } \dfrac{3\pi}{2} \text{ and less than } 2\pi\right)$, we know that cosecant will be negative since sine is negative in Quadrant IV. When we apply the formula for the reference angle, we see that

$$\csc \frac{5\pi}{3} = -\csc\left(2\pi - \frac{5\pi}{3}\right)$$

$$= -\csc \frac{\pi}{3} \quad \text{or} \quad -\frac{1}{\sin \dfrac{\pi}{3}}$$

Answer: $\quad -\csc \dfrac{\pi}{3}$

We have two methods for finding trigonometric function values of angles with radian measure:

Method 1

- Convert the angle from radian measure to degree measure.
- Evaluate the function for the angle in degrees.

Method 2

- Evaluate the function for the angle in radians.

You may evaluate trigonometric functions in radians by using reference angles or with your calculator. Be sure that your calculator is in radian mode.

```
Normal  Sci  Eng
Float   0123456789
Radian  Degree
Func  Par  Pol  Seq
Connected  Dot
Sequential  Simul
Real  a+bi  re^θi
Full  Horiz  G-T
```

2 Find the exact value for each of the following:

    a $\cos\dfrac{2\pi}{3}$ **b** $\tan\dfrac{11\pi}{6}$ **c** $\sin 2\pi$

SOLUTIONS

These problems can be solved by converting from radians to degrees or by evaluating in radian measure. We will vary the methods below.

    a Method 1: Convert to degrees.

$$\cos\dfrac{2\pi}{3} = \cos 120° \qquad\qquad \text{Since } 120° \text{ is in the second quadrant, cosine will be negative.}$$

$$= -\cos(180° - 120°)$$

$$= -\cos 60° \qquad\qquad \text{Now, we need to find this value.}$$

$$= -\dfrac{1}{2}$$

Answer: $-\dfrac{1}{2}$

    b Method 2: Evaluate in radians.

Since $\dfrac{11\pi}{6}$ is greater than $\dfrac{3\pi}{2}$ and less than 2π, the angle is in Quadrant IV. So tangent must be negative.

$$\tan\dfrac{11\pi}{6} = -\tan\left(2\pi - \dfrac{11\pi}{6}\right)$$

$$= -\tan\dfrac{\pi}{6}$$

$$= -\dfrac{\sqrt{3}}{3}$$

Answer: $-\dfrac{\sqrt{3}}{3}$

> **Note:** Since the exact value is required, the calculator cannot be used.

    c Since 2π or $360°$ is a quadrantal angle, we evaluate it directly rather than finding a reference angle.

$$\sin 2\pi = \sin 2(180°)$$

$$= \sin 360°$$

$$= 0$$

Answer: 0

Exercises 1– 8: Write each as a function of a positive acute angle.

1 $\sin \dfrac{5\pi}{3}$

2 $\cos \left(-\dfrac{3\pi}{4}\right)$

3 $\cot \dfrac{7\pi}{4}$

4 $\sec \dfrac{2\pi}{3}$

5 $\csc \dfrac{11\pi}{6}$

6 $\cos \dfrac{5\pi}{6}$

7 $\tan \left(-\dfrac{\pi}{4}\right)$

8 $\sin \dfrac{7\pi}{6}$

Exercises 9– 13: Evaluate each expression.

9 $\left(\sin \dfrac{3\pi}{4}\right)^2 + \left(\cos \dfrac{3\pi}{4}\right)^2$

10 $\sin \dfrac{7\pi}{6} + \cos \dfrac{2\pi}{3}$

11 $\left(\sec \dfrac{2\pi}{3}\right)\left(\sin \dfrac{2\pi}{3}\right)$

12 $\left(\csc \dfrac{3\pi}{4}\right)^2$

13 $\sin \left(\dfrac{3\pi}{2}\right) + \tan^2 \left(\dfrac{2\pi}{3}\right)$

Note: $(\tan \theta)^2$ can be written as $\tan^2 \theta$.

14 If $f(x) = \sin x$, find:

a $f\left(-\dfrac{\pi}{4}\right)$

b $f\left(\dfrac{5\pi}{3}\right)$

c $f(\pi)$

15 Evaluate $\tan \dfrac{7\pi}{4} - \sec \dfrac{5\pi}{3}$. Write your answer as an exact value.

Exercises 16–25: Select the numeral preceding the choice that best completes the statement or answers the question.

16 If $f(\theta) = 2 \cos \dfrac{1}{2}\theta - \tan \theta$, find the numerical value of $f\left(\dfrac{\pi}{3}\right)$.

(1) $\dfrac{\sqrt{3}}{2} - \dfrac{\sqrt{3}}{3}$

(2) $1 - \sqrt{3}$

(3) 0

(4) $\dfrac{1}{2} - \sqrt{3}$

17 Evaluate $\cos^2 \left(\dfrac{3\pi}{2}\right) + \tan^2 \left(\dfrac{5\pi}{3}\right)$ *exactly*.

(1) -1

(2) 0

(3) 3

(4) 4

18 If $g(x) = 2 \sin x - \cos (2x)$, find $g\left(\dfrac{\pi}{6}\right)$.

(1) $-1\dfrac{1}{2}$

(2) $-\dfrac{1}{2}$

(3) $\dfrac{1}{2}$

(4) $1\dfrac{1}{2}$

19 If $\sin x = \dfrac{\sqrt{2}}{2}$ and $\cos x = -\dfrac{\sqrt{2}}{2}$, then $x =$

(1) $\dfrac{\pi}{4}$

(2) $\dfrac{3\pi}{4}$

(3) $\dfrac{5\pi}{4}$

(4) $\dfrac{7\pi}{4}$

20 The expression $\cos \dfrac{7\pi}{4}$ has the same value as

(1) $\tan \dfrac{\pi}{4}$

(2) $\cos \dfrac{5\pi}{4}$

(3) $\sin \dfrac{3\pi}{4}$

(4) $\sec \dfrac{\pi}{4}$

21 Evaluate $\sin \dfrac{3\pi}{2} \cos \dfrac{\pi}{2} - \cos \pi \tan 2\pi$.

(1) 1
(2) 2
(3) 0
(4) −1

22 If $\csc \theta < 0$ and $\cos \theta > 0$, which might be the value of θ?

(1) $\dfrac{\pi}{6}$

(2) $\dfrac{2\pi}{3}$

(3) π

(4) $\dfrac{11\pi}{6}$

23 In a unit circle, the terminal ray of which angle contains the point $\left(-\dfrac{\sqrt{3}}{2}, \dfrac{1}{2}\right)$?

(1) $\dfrac{2\pi}{3}$

(2) $\dfrac{5\pi}{6}$

(3) $\dfrac{7\pi}{6}$

(4) $\dfrac{5\pi}{3}$

24 The value of $\sec^2\left(\dfrac{3\pi}{4}\right) - \tan^2\left(\dfrac{3\pi}{4}\right)$ is

(1) 1
(2) −1
(3) 3
(4) 0

25 The expression $\tan \pi$ has the same value as which of the following?

(1) $\tan \dfrac{\pi}{2}$

(2) $\cos \pi$

(3) $\sin \dfrac{3\pi}{2}$

(4) $\sin \pi$

10.3 Basic and Pythagorean Trigonometric Identities

Basic Identities

An **identity** is an equation that is true for *all* values of the variable for which the equation is defined. You are already familiar with some trigonometric identities, although we did not use the term at the time. The **reciprocal identities** and the **quotient identities** are shown below.

Reciprocal Identities

$$\sec \theta = \frac{1}{\cos \theta}$$

$$\csc \theta = \frac{1}{\sin \theta}$$

$$\cot \theta = \frac{1}{\tan \theta}$$

Quotient Identities

$$\tan \theta = \frac{\sin \theta}{\cos \theta}$$

$$\cot \theta = \frac{\cos \theta}{\sin \theta}$$

Pythagorean Identities

For any angle in standard position on the unit circle, the x-coordinate is the cosine of the angle and the y-coordinate is the sine of the angle. Looking at the figure below, we can see that $x^2 + y^2 = 1$.

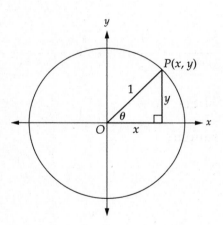

Substituting $\cos \theta$ for the x-coordinate and $\sin \theta$ for the y-coordinate, we obtain:

$$\cos^2 \theta + \sin^2 \theta = 1$$

Since this identity is based on the Pythagorean theorem, it is called a **Pythagorean identity**. We can rewrite this identity as $\sin^2 \theta + \cos^2 \theta = 1$. Using our algebra skills, we can solve this equation for $\cos^2 \theta$ or $\sin^2 \theta$.

$$\cos^2 \theta = 1 - \sin^2 \theta \qquad \sin^2 \theta = 1 - \cos^2 \theta$$

If we know the sine or cosine of an angle, even without knowing the angle measure, we can learn the other functions by using this Pythagorean identity.

MODEL PROBLEM

1   If θ is in Quadrant II and $\sin \theta = \dfrac{5}{13}$, find $\cos \theta$.

SOLUTION

Since we are looking for $\cos \theta$, we will use the $\cos^2 \theta = 1 - \sin^2 \theta$ version of the identity. Substitute $\dfrac{5}{13}$ into the equation in place of $\sin \theta$ and solve for $\cos \theta$. Since θ is in Quadrant II, remember that cosine must have a negative value.

$$\cos^2 \theta = 1 - \sin^2 \theta$$

$$\cos^2 \theta = 1 - \left(\frac{5}{13}\right)^2$$

$$\cos^2 \theta = 1 - \frac{25}{169}$$

$$\cos^2 \theta = \frac{144}{169}$$

$$\cos \theta = -\sqrt{\frac{144}{169}}$$

$$\cos \theta = -\frac{12}{13}$$

Answer: $-\dfrac{12}{13}$

We can derive two other Pythagorean identities from our original identity $\sin^2 \theta + \cos^2 \theta = 1$.

For the first, divide each term by $\cos^2 \theta$ and simplify.

$$\sin^2 \theta + \cos^2 \theta = 1$$

$$\frac{\sin^2 \theta}{\cos^2 \theta} + \frac{\cos^2 \theta}{\cos^2 \theta} = \frac{1}{\cos^2 \theta}$$

$$\tan^2 \theta + 1 = \sec^2 \theta$$

This is a second Pythagorean identity.

If we return to the original identity and divide each term by $\sin^2 \theta$ and simplify, we will produce a third identity.

$$\sin^2 \theta + \cos^2 \theta = 1$$

$$\frac{\sin^2 \theta}{\sin^2 \theta} + \frac{\cos^2 \theta}{\sin^2 \theta} = \frac{1}{\sin^2 \theta}$$

$$1 + \cot^2 \theta = \csc^2 \theta$$

We now have three Pythagorean identities whose use will be very important as we continue through trigonometry. It would be an excellent idea to memorize these.

$$\sin^2 \theta + \cos^2 \theta = 1$$

$$\tan^2 \theta + 1 = \sec^2 \theta$$

$$1 + \cot^2 \theta = \csc^2 \theta$$

We can use these identities to find the values of the other trigonometric functions when the value of one function is known.

MODEL PROBLEMS

2 If $\cos \theta = \dfrac{3}{5}$, and θ is an angle that terminates in Quadrant IV, find the values of the other five trigonometric functions.

SOLUTION

You could solve this problem using right triangle trigonometry or by using the identities. Both methods are illustrated below.

METHOD 1: Using Right Triangle Trigonometry

Sketch a right triangle with acute angle θ as shown, placing the 3 on the adjacent side and the 5 on the hypotenuse.

We can now use the Pythagorean theorem and find that the opposite side measures 4. Since sine is negative in Quadrant IV, its *directed distance* is -4. We can now use this information to find the remaining five trigonometric functions.

$$\sin \theta = \frac{\text{opposite}}{\text{hypotenuse}} = -\frac{4}{5} \qquad \tan \theta = \frac{\text{opposite}}{\text{adjacent}} = -\frac{4}{3}$$

Then, find all of the reciprocal functions.

$$\sec \theta = \frac{1}{\cos \theta} = \frac{5}{3} \qquad \csc \theta = \frac{1}{\sin \theta} = -\frac{5}{4}$$

$$\cot \theta = \frac{1}{\tan \theta} = -\frac{3}{4}$$

METHOD 2: Using Identities

Since $\sin^2 \theta + \cos^2 \theta = 1$, we can substitute into this equation as follows:

$$\sin^2 \theta + \left(\frac{3}{5}\right)^2 = 1$$

$$\sin^2 \theta = 1 - \frac{9}{25}$$

$$\sin^2 \theta = \frac{16}{25}$$

$$\sin \theta = \pm\frac{4}{5}$$

Since we are in Quadrant IV, where $\sin \theta$ is negative, we pick the negative value.

$$\sin \theta = -\frac{4}{5} \qquad \tan \theta = \frac{\sin \theta}{\cos \theta} = \frac{-\dfrac{4}{5}}{\dfrac{3}{5}} = -\frac{4}{3}$$

Now, find the reciprocal functions.

$$\sec \theta = \frac{1}{\cos \theta} = \frac{5}{3} \qquad \csc \theta = \frac{1}{\sin \theta} = -\frac{5}{4} \qquad \cot \theta = \frac{1}{\tan \theta} = -\frac{3}{4}$$

3 If $\sin \theta = -\dfrac{2}{3}$ and $\tan \theta > 0$, find $\cos \theta$.

SOLUTION

In this case, we will illustrate only the method using identities. Since $\sin^2 \theta + \cos^2 \theta = 1$, we can substitute into this equation.

$$\left(-\frac{2}{3}\right)^2 + \cos^2 \theta = 1$$

$$\cos^2 \theta = 1 - \frac{4}{9}$$

$$\cos^2 \theta = \frac{5}{9}$$

$$\cos \theta = \pm \frac{\sqrt{5}}{3}$$

Since $\sin \theta < 0$ and $\tan \theta > 0$, we are in Quadrant III, where $\cos \theta < 0$.

Answer: $-\dfrac{\sqrt{5}}{3}$

We can also use the identities to simplify more complicated trigonometric expressions.

MODEL PROBLEM

4 Write each expression in terms of a single function.

a $(\cos \theta)(\tan \theta)$

b $\sec^2 \theta - 1$

SOLUTION

a We know that $\tan \theta = \dfrac{\sin \theta}{\cos \theta}$, so we can substitute.

$$(\cos \theta)(\tan \theta) = \cos \theta \cdot \frac{\sin \theta}{\cos \theta} \qquad \text{"Cancel" } \cos \theta.$$

$$= \sin \theta$$

Our original expression, $(\cos \theta)(\tan \theta)$, is undefined when $\cos \theta = 0$, and our answer must show this.

Answer: $\sin \theta \ (\cos \theta \neq 0)$

b We know that $\tan^2 \theta + 1 = \sec^2 \theta$, so we can substitute.

$$\sec^2 \theta - 1 = (\tan^2 \theta + 1) - 1$$
$$= \tan^2 \theta$$

Answer: $\tan^2 \theta$

In Model Problem 4, we simplified expressions, but we can also use these basic trigonometric identities to prove other identities. This will be explored in Chapter 12.

 **Practice**

Exercises 1–10: Write each expression as a single function or a constant.

1 $1 - \cos^2 \theta$

2 $(\sin \theta)(\csc \theta)$

3 $(\tan \theta)(\cot \theta)$

4 $\sec^2 \theta - 1$

5 $\tan \theta \cdot \csc \theta$

6 $\dfrac{\csc x}{\sec x}$

7 $\cos \theta (\tan^2 \theta + 1)$

8 $\sin^2 \theta + \cot^2 \theta + \cos^2 \theta$

9 $1 - \dfrac{\tan^2 \alpha}{\sec^2 \alpha}$

10 $(\sin^2 \theta)(\cos \theta)(\tan \theta)(\csc \theta)$

11 If $\cos \theta = -\dfrac{5}{13}$ and θ lies in Quadrant II, find the values of the remaining five trigonometric functions.

12 If $\sin \theta = -\dfrac{7}{25}$ and $\cos \theta < 0$, find the values of the remaining five trigonometric functions.

13 If $\sec \theta = \dfrac{4}{3}$ and $\sin \theta > 0$, find the values of the remaining five trigonometric functions.

Exercises 14–20: Select the numeral preceding the choice that best completes the statement or answers the question.

14 The expression $\dfrac{\tan^2 \theta}{\sin^2 \theta}$ is equivalent to

(1) $\sin^2 \theta$
(2) $\cos^2 \theta$
(3) $\sec^2 \theta$
(4) $\csc^2 \theta$

15 If $\csc \theta = -\dfrac{5}{4}$ and θ is in the third quadrant, then $\cos \theta =$

(1) $-\dfrac{4}{5}$

(2) $-\dfrac{3}{5}$

(3) $\dfrac{3}{5}$

(4) $\dfrac{4}{5}$

16 $\sin^2 \theta + \cos^2 \theta + \tan^2 \theta =$

(1) $\sec^2 \theta$
(2) $\csc^2 \theta$
(3) $\cot^2 \theta$
(4) $\dfrac{1}{\cot^2 \theta}$

17 If $\sin \theta = 0.6$ and $\cos \theta < 0$, then $\tan \theta =$

(1) -1.333
(2) -0.75
(3) 0.75
(4) 1.333

18 If $\cos \theta = k$, then the value of $(\cos \theta)(\sin \theta)(\cot \theta) =$

(1) 1
(2) k
(3) k^2
(4) $\dfrac{1}{k}$

19 If $\sin \theta = \dfrac{3}{4}$ and θ is an acute angle, what is the value of $\tan \theta \cos \theta$?

(1) $\dfrac{3}{5}$
(2) $\dfrac{\sqrt{7}}{4}$
(3) $\dfrac{3}{4}$
(4) $\dfrac{3\sqrt{7}}{7}$

20 The expression $\sec^2 \theta + \csc^2 \theta$ is equivalent to

(1) 1
(2) $\sec \theta \csc \theta$
(3) $\dfrac{1}{\sin \theta \cos \theta}$
(4) $\dfrac{1}{\sin^2 \theta \cos^2 \theta}$

10.4 Range and Domain of Trigonometric Functions

When we use the unit circle in trigonometry, we can set a domain in which $0° \leq x \leq 360°$ or, in radians, $0 \leq x \leq 2\pi$. However, we can continue to move around the circle. Thus, the domain of both the sine and cosine functions is the set of all real numbers since we can move counterclockwise or clockwise without end.

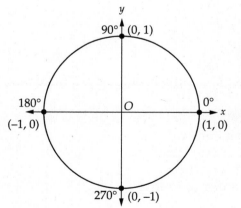

The range of sine and cosine function, however, is much more limited. Since the radius of the circle is 1, the range of the sine and cosine can only be $-1 \leq y \leq 1$.

Based on the unit circle, we can define the values of all six trigonometric functions for each of the quadrantal angles as shown in the table on the following page.

Degree Measure	0°	90°	180°	270°	360°
Radian Measure	0	$\dfrac{\pi}{2}$	π	$\dfrac{3\pi}{2}$	2π
sin θ	0	1	0	−1	0
cos θ	1	0	−1	0	1
tan θ	0	Undefined	0	Undefined	0
csc θ	Undefined	1	Undefined	−1	Undefined
sec θ	1	Undefined	−1	Undefined	1
cot θ	Undefined	0	Undefined	0	Undefined

Whenever a function has a value of zero, its reciprocal function value is *undefined*. This occurs because the reciprocal of zero is $\dfrac{1}{0}$, which cannot be measured.

 MODEL PROBLEM

Determine the values of tan 90° and cot 90°.

SOLUTION

$\tan 90° = \dfrac{\sin 90°}{\cos 90°}$

$= \dfrac{1}{0} \quad$ *undefined*

Therefore,

$\cot 90° = \dfrac{\cos 90°}{\sin 90°}$

$= \dfrac{0}{1}$

$= 0$

Answer: tan 90° is undefined, cot 90° = 0

When we consider the domain of the cosecant function, we must remember that cosecant will be undefined whenever the sine function equals zero. Hence, cosecant is undefined at 0°, 180°, 360°, and all subsequent multiples of 180°. The domain of cosecant is all real numbers except 180°n for all integral values of n. In radians, the domain of cosecant is all real numbers except πn.

Similarly, the domain of the secant function is all real numbers except 90° + 180°n or $\dfrac{\pi}{2} + \pi n$ for all integral values of n.

The following table summarizes the domains and ranges of the six functions.

Function	Domain	Range
$\sin \theta$	All real numbers	$-1 \le \sin \theta \le 1$
$\cos \theta$	All real numbers	$-1 \le \cos \theta \le 1$
$\tan \theta$	All real numbers *except* $90° + 180°n$ $\left(\dfrac{\pi}{2} + \pi n\right)$	All real numbers
$\csc \theta$	All real numbers *except* $180°n$ (πn)	$\csc \theta \le -1$ or $\csc \theta \ge 1$
$\sec \theta$	All real numbers *except* $90° + 180°n$ $\left(\dfrac{\pi}{2} + \pi n\right)$	$\sec \theta \le -1$ or $\sec \theta \ge 1$
$\cot \theta$	All real numbers *except* $180°n$ (πn)	All real numbers

 Practice

Exercises 1–4: Demonstrate why the following functions are *undefined* for the given angle measure.

1 $\sec \dfrac{3\pi}{2}$

2 $\csc 0°$

3 $\cot \pi$

4 $\sec 90°$

Exercises 5–18: Evaluate each function or explain why it is undefined.

5 $\tan 30°$

6 $\cos 180°$

7 $\sec \dfrac{4\pi}{3}$

8 $\csc \pi$

9 $\sin 240°$

10 $\cot 2\pi$

11 $\cos 150°$

12 $\tan \dfrac{11\pi}{6}$

13 $\csc 210°$

14 $\sec \dfrac{3\pi}{4}$

15 $\cot 330°$

16 $\tan \dfrac{5\pi}{4}$

17 $\sin 150°$

18 $\sec \dfrac{7\pi}{6}$

Exercises 19 and 20: Select the numeral preceding the choice that best answers the question.

19 For what value of θ is $\sec \theta$ *undefined*?

    (1) 0

    (2) $\dfrac{\pi}{2}$

    (3) π

    (4) $\dfrac{4\pi}{3}$

20 Which statement is *not* true?

    (1) The domain of the sine function is all real numbers.

    (2) The domain of the cosine function is all real numbers.

    (3) The domain of the tangent function is all real numbers.

    (4) The range of the tangent function is all real numbers.

10.5 Inverse Trigonometric Functions

From previous work with the trigonometric functions, we know that each function is positive in two quadrants of the unit circle and negative in two quadrants of the unit circle. Let's consider one revolution of the unit circle, 0° to 360°. If you were asked to find the angle that had a sine value of $\frac{1}{2}$, you would need to have two answers, 30° for the angle in the first quadrant and 150° for the angle in the second quadrant. Similarly, if you were asked for the angle that had a sine value of $-\frac{1}{2}$, there would have to be two answers, 210° for the third quadrant and 330° for the fourth. Recall that a one-to-one function can have only one element in the domain for each element in the range. Therefore, the sine function is not one-to-one. A function that is *not* one-to-one does not have an inverse function.

Mathematicians limited the domain of sine, cosine, and tangent so they could define functions that are the inverses of the trigonometric functions.

Note the limitations as shown in the table below.

Sine Function: $y = \sin x$	Inverse Sine Function: $y = \arcsin x$ or $y = \sin^{-1} x$
Restricted Domain: $-\frac{\pi}{2} \le x \le \frac{\pi}{2}$ or $-90° \le x \le 90°$	Domain: $-1 \le x \le 1$
Range: $-1 \le y \le 1$	Range: $-\frac{\pi}{2} \le y \le \frac{\pi}{2}$ or $-90° \le y \le 90°$

MODEL PROBLEMS

1 Find $\arcsin\left(\dfrac{\sqrt{3}}{2}\right)$.

SOLUTION

The range of the arcsine function is limited to $-\dfrac{\pi}{2} \le y \le \dfrac{\pi}{2}$, that is, to Quadrants I and IV. An angle whose sine is $\dfrac{\sqrt{3}}{2}$ is in the first quadrant. You should recall that $\sin\dfrac{\pi}{3} = \sin 60° = \dfrac{\sqrt{3}}{2}$, but if you do not, use your calculator.

Use the $\sin^{-1}$ (arcsine) function by pressing the following keys:

[2nd] [SIN] [(] [2nd] [x^2] [3] [)] [÷] [2] [)] [ENTER]

Note: You want your calculator in degree mode so you get 60 instead of a decimal approximation of $\dfrac{\pi}{3}$.

Answer: $\dfrac{\pi}{3}$ or 60°

2 Find $\arcsin\left(-\dfrac{\sqrt{2}}{2}\right)$.

Again, our range is limited, but since the sine function here is a negative number, our answer must be in the fourth quadrant. If $\sin^{-1}\theta = -\dfrac{\sqrt{2}}{2}$, $\theta = -\dfrac{\pi}{4}$ or $-45°$.

Answer: $-\dfrac{\pi}{4}$ or $-45°$

In a similar fashion, limiting the domain of the other trigonometric functions allows us to be certain the inverse trigonometric relations are functions.

Cosine Function: $y = \cos x$	Inverse Cosine Function: $y = \arccos x$
Restricted Domain: $0 \le x \le \pi$	Domain: $-1 \le y \le 1$
Range: $-1 \le y \le 1$	Range: $0 \le x \le \pi$

Tangent Function: $y = \tan x$	Inverse Tangent Function: $y = \arctan x$
Restricted Domain: $-\dfrac{\pi}{2} < x < \dfrac{\pi}{2}$	Domain: All real numbers
Range: All real numbers	Range: $-\dfrac{\pi}{2} < x < \dfrac{\pi}{2}$

MODEL PROBLEM

3 Evaluate $\arctan 1 + \arccos\left(-\dfrac{1}{2}\right)$.

SOLUTION

In this problem we are asked to find the sum of two angles, one whose tangent equals 1 and the other whose cosine equals $-\dfrac{1}{2}$. Since the tangent value is positive, with our limited range, we must be looking for a first-quadrant angle:

$\arctan 1 = 45° = \dfrac{\pi}{4}$

Because the cosine value is negative, with the limited range, we must be looking for a second-quadrant angle whose cosine is $-\dfrac{1}{2}$:

$\arccos\left(-\dfrac{1}{2}\right) = 120° = \dfrac{2\pi}{3}$

$45° + 120° = 165°$ or $\dfrac{\pi}{4} + \dfrac{2\pi}{3} = \dfrac{11\pi}{12}$

Answer: $165°$ or $\dfrac{11\pi}{12}$

We will explore this topic further when we look at graphing the trigonometric functions in Chapter 11.

Practice

Exercises 1–8: Find the value of θ. If θ is not an integer, round to the *nearest tenth of a degree*.

1 $\arctan(-1)$

2 $\arccos 0$

3 $\arcsin\left(-\dfrac{\sqrt{2}}{2}\right)$

4 $\arctan \dfrac{7}{8}$

5 $\arcsin\left(-\dfrac{\sqrt{3}}{2}\right)$

6 $\arccos \dfrac{3}{4}$

7 $\arcsin \dfrac{5}{13}$

8 $\arctan\left(-\sqrt{3}\right)$

Exercises 9–13: Find the value of θ in radian measure.

9 $\arcsin 0$

10 $\arctan\left(-\dfrac{\sqrt{3}}{3}\right)$

11 $\arccos\left(-\dfrac{\sqrt{3}}{2}\right)$

12 $\arcsin\left(-\dfrac{1}{2}\right)$

13 $\arctan\left(-\sqrt{3}\right)$

Exercises 14–20: Write the numeral preceding the choice that best completes the statement or answers the question.

14 If $\theta = \arctan(-1)$, what is the value of θ?

   (1) $\quad -\dfrac{1}{4}\pi$

   (2) $\quad \dfrac{1}{4}\pi$

   (3) $\quad \dfrac{3}{4}\pi$

   (4) $\quad \dfrac{7}{4}\pi$

15 If $\theta = \arccos \dfrac{1}{2}$, what is the measure of θ?

   (1)   30°
   (2)   60°
   (3)   300°
   (4)   330°

16 The value of $\arccos \dfrac{\sqrt{3}}{2} + \arcsin\left(-\dfrac{1}{2}\right)$ is

   (1)   0°
   (2)   30°
   (3)   60°
   (4)   90°

17 What is the value of y if $y = \arcsin\left(-\dfrac{\sqrt{3}}{2}\right)$?

   (1) $\quad -\dfrac{\pi}{6}$

   (2) $\quad -\dfrac{\pi}{3}$

   (3) $\quad \dfrac{\pi}{3}$

   (4) $\quad \dfrac{5}{3}\pi$

18 For which of the following does $\theta = \dfrac{2\pi}{3}$?

   (1) $\quad \arcsin\left(-\dfrac{\sqrt{3}}{2}\right) = \theta$

   (2) $\quad \arctan\left(-\sqrt{3}\right) = \theta$

   (3) $\quad \arccos\left(-\dfrac{1}{2}\right) = \theta$

   (4) $\quad \arccos\left(\dfrac{1}{2}\right) = \theta$

19 A value of y that is *not* in the range of $y =$ arccos x is

   (1) 0

   (2) $\dfrac{\pi}{2}$

   (3) $\dfrac{3\pi}{4}$

   (4) $\dfrac{5\pi}{3}$

20 Which has the same value as arctan (-1)?

   (1) $\arcsin\left(-\dfrac{\sqrt{2}}{2}\right)$

   (2) arctan 1

   (3) $\arccos\dfrac{1}{2}$

   (4) $\arcsin\left(-\dfrac{\sqrt{3}}{2}\right)$

10.6 Cofunctions

Recall that if two angles are complementary, their sum is 90°. We will now expand this concept into a discussion of *cofunctions*. The prefix *co-* gives us a hint about cofunctions. Sine and cosine are cofunctions, tangent and cotangent are cofunctions, and secant and cosecant are cofunctions. The function of an acute angle is equal to the **cofunction** of its complement. For example, since a 30° angle is complementary to a 60° angle, sin 30° = cos 60°, tan 30° = cot 60°, and sec 30° = csc 60°.

MODEL PROBLEMS

1 Write the expression as a function of an acute angle whose measure is less than 45° or $\dfrac{\pi}{4}$.

   a sin 70°   **b** tan 100°   **c** csc 410°   **d** $\cos\dfrac{3\pi}{8}$

SOLUTION

   a Since a 70° angle is complementary to a 20° angle, sin 70° = cos 20°.

Answer: sin 70° = cos 20°

   b 100° is in the second quadrant, where tangent is negative, and the reference angle is $(180° - 100°) = 80°$.

tan 100° = −tan 80°

Since an 80° angle is complementary to a 10° angle, −tan 80° = −cot 10°.

Answer: tan 100° = −cot 10°

c 410° is more than one complete revolution, so we subtract 360° from it:

$$\csc 410° = \csc (410° - 360°)$$
$$= \csc 50°$$

Since a 50° angle is complementary to a 40° angle, $\csc 50° = \sec 40°$.

Answer: $\csc 410° = \sec 40°$

d In radians, two angles are complementary if their sum is $\dfrac{\pi}{2}$.

$$\cos \frac{3\pi}{8} = \sin \left(\frac{\pi}{2} - \frac{3\pi}{8} \right)$$
$$= \sin \frac{\pi}{8}$$

Answer: $\cos \dfrac{3\pi}{8} = \sin \dfrac{\pi}{8}$

2 If x is the measure of a positive acute angle, solve for x.

   a $\sin (x + 15)° = \cos (2x)°$

   b $\sec (x + 15)° = \csc (2x - 6)°$

SOLUTION

   a Since sine and cosine are cofunctions, and the sine of one angle is equal to the cosine of another angle, then the two angles must be complementary.

$$x + 15 + 2x = 90$$
$$3x + 15 = 90$$
$$3x = 75$$
$$x = 25$$

Answer: $x = 25$

   b Since secant and cosecant are cofunctions, and the secant of an angle equals the cosecant of another angle, the two angles must be complementary.

$$x + 15 + 2x - 6 = 90$$
$$3x + 9 = 90$$
$$3x = 81$$
$$x = 27$$

Answer: $x = 27$

Note: Be careful not to confuse cofunctions and reciprocal functions. With reciprocal functions, we work with a single angle measure. With *co*functions, we work with complementary angles.

Exercises 1–10: Write the expression as a function of a positive acute angle whose measure is less than 45° or $\frac{\pi}{4}$.

1 sin 65°

2 cot $\frac{5\pi}{3}$

3 csc (−75°)

4 tan 110°

5 sec 47°

6 sin 254°

7 cot (−117°)

8 cos $\frac{13\pi}{30}$

9 tan (−71°)

10 csc 237°

Exercises 11–20: Solve each equation for θ.

11 cot $(3\theta - 6)° = $ tan $(\theta + 8)°$

12 sin $(3\theta)° = $ cos $(4\theta + 13)°$

13 tan $(\theta + 15)° = $ cot $(2\theta - 30)°$

14 sin $(23 + 4\theta)° = $ cos $(13 + 5\theta)°$

15 csc $(3\theta - 8)° = $ sec $(48 + 2\theta)°$

16 tan $(4\theta + 15)° = $ cot $(2\theta - 27)°$

17 cos $(2\theta + 18)° = $ sin $(57 + 3\theta)°$

18 sec $(4\theta - 5)° = $ csc $(2\theta - 13)°$

19 cot $(3\theta - 14)° = $ tan $(56 - \theta)°$

20 sin $(28 - 2\theta)° = $ cos $(3\theta + 50)°$

Exercises 21–26: Select the numeral preceding the expression that best completes the statement or answers the question.

21 If tan $x° = $ cot $(2x - 15)°$, then $x =$

   (1) 15
   (2) 25
   (3) 35
   (4) 45

22 Which expression is equivalent to sec $\frac{4\pi}{15}$?

   (1) csc $\frac{7\pi}{30}$

   (2) csc $\frac{4\pi}{15}$

   (3) cos $\frac{7\pi}{30}$

   (4) cos $\frac{4\pi}{15}$

23 If θ is the measure of an acute angle and tan $\theta = $ cot 2θ, then tan $\theta =$

   (1) $\frac{1}{2}$

   (2) $\frac{\sqrt{3}}{3}$

   (3) $\sqrt{3}$

   (4) 30

24 For what value of θ does cos $(3\theta + 25)° = $ sin $(37 - \theta)°$?

   (1) 28
   (2) 23
   (3) 14
   (4) 7

25 For what value of θ does $\frac{\sin \theta}{\cos 56°} = 1$?

   (1) 34°
   (2) 56°
   (3) 90°
   (4) 124°

26 Express sec 102° as the function of a positive acute angle less than 45°.

   (1) −sec 78°
   (2) −csc 12°
   (3) −sec 12°
   (4) csc 12°

CHAPTER REVIEW

Select the numeral preceding the choice that best completes the statement or answers the question.

1 Convert $120°$ to radian measure.

(1) $\dfrac{\pi}{6}$

(2) $\dfrac{2\pi}{3}$

(3) $\dfrac{5\pi}{6}$

(4) $\dfrac{3\pi}{2}$

2 If $f(\beta) = \cos 2\beta + 2\sin \beta$, the numerical value of $f\left(\dfrac{\pi}{6}\right)$ is

(1) 1

(2) 0

(3) $\dfrac{3}{2}$

(4) $\dfrac{\sqrt{3} + 1}{2}$

3 Find $\sin\left(\arccos \dfrac{1}{2}\right)$.

(1) 1

(2) $\dfrac{\sqrt{3}}{2}$

(3) $\dfrac{\sqrt{2}}{2}$

(4) $\dfrac{1}{2}$

4 What is the numerical value of $\left(\tan \dfrac{3\pi}{4}\right)\left(\csc \dfrac{7\pi}{6}\right)$?

(1) -1

(2) 2

(3) $\dfrac{\sqrt{3}}{2}$

(4) $\dfrac{2\sqrt{3}}{3}$

5 Simplify: $\sin^2 2\theta + \cos^2 2\theta$

(1) 1

(2) 2

(3) $\dfrac{1 + \sqrt{3}}{2}$

(4) 4

6 Which expression is *not* equal to $\sin \dfrac{5\pi}{3}$?

(1) $\csc \dfrac{5\pi}{3}$

(2) $\sin (-60)°$

(3) $-\sin 60°$

(4) $-\cos \dfrac{\pi}{6}$

7 If $\csc \theta < 0$ and $\cot \theta > 0$, what might be the measure of θ?

(1) $\dfrac{\pi}{15}$

(2) $\dfrac{8\pi}{9}$

(3) $\dfrac{7\pi}{6}$

(4) $\dfrac{23\pi}{12}$

8 Which is equivalent to $\tan x \cot x + \tan^2 x$?

(1) $\sin x \cos x$

(2) $\sin x \csc x + \sin^2 x$

(3) $\sec^2 x$

(4) $\csc^2 x$

9 For what value of θ is the fraction $\dfrac{\cos \theta}{1 - \tan \theta}$ undefined?

(1) $\dfrac{\pi}{6}$

(2) $\dfrac{\pi}{4}$

(3) $\dfrac{\pi}{3}$

(4) π

10 Which is *not* in the range of $y = \arcsin x$?

(1) $-\dfrac{\pi}{2}$

(2) $-\dfrac{\pi}{4}$

(3) $\dfrac{\pi}{3}$

(4) $\dfrac{5\pi}{6}$

11 Circle O has a radius of 9 inches. What is the length, in inches, of the arc subtended by a central angle measuring 1.5 radians?

(1) 0.1667
(2) 6
(3) 8.1667
(4) 13.5

12 The coordinates of a point on the unit circle are $\left(\frac{\sqrt{2}}{2}, -\frac{\sqrt{2}}{2}\right)$. If the terminal side of angle θ in standard position passes through the given point, find $m\angle\theta$.

(1) 135
(2) 150
(3) 300
(4) 315

13 Find the exact value of $\tan\pi + \cos^2\left(\frac{5}{3}\pi\right)$.

(1) 0
(2) $\frac{1}{4}$
(3) $\frac{1}{2}$
(4) $\frac{3}{4}$

14 If $\cos\theta = -\frac{5}{13}$ and $\sin\theta < 0$, find $\tan\theta$.

(1) $-\frac{12}{5}$
(2) $-\frac{5}{12}$
(3) $\frac{5}{12}$
(4) $\frac{12}{5}$

15 Solve for x: $\cos(4x - 10)° = \sin(5x + 10)°$

(1) 10
(2) 20
(3) 30
(4) 40

16 Which is equivalent to $\cot\alpha\,(\cot\alpha + \tan\alpha)$?

(1) 1
(2) $\cos^2\alpha$
(3) $\sec^2\alpha$
(4) $\csc^2\alpha$

17 Express in radical form:

$$\left(\sin\frac{\pi}{2}\right)\left(\tan\frac{\pi}{6}\right) - \left(\tan\frac{\pi}{4}\right)\left(\cos\frac{3\pi}{2}\right)$$

(1) $-\sqrt{3}$
(2) $-\frac{\sqrt{3}}{3}$
(3) $\frac{\sqrt{3}}{3}$
(4) $\sqrt{3}$

18 Which function does *not* include 4 in its range?

(1) $\sin\theta$
(2) $\csc\theta$
(3) $\cot\theta$
(4) $\tan\theta$

19 Which is *not* in the range of $y = \arccos x$?

(1) $-\frac{\pi}{6}$
(2) 0
(3) $\frac{\pi}{2}$
(4) $\frac{5\pi}{6}$

20 Express $240°$ in radian measure.

(1) $-\frac{4\pi}{3}$
(2) $\frac{2\pi}{3}$
(3) $\frac{7\pi}{6}$
(4) $\frac{4\pi}{3}$

21 If placed in standard position, an angle of $\frac{7\pi}{6}$ has the same terminal ray as an angle of

(1) $-150°$
(2) $-30°$
(3) $150°$
(4) $240°$

22 If $f(\theta) = 2\tan\theta - \sin\frac{3\theta}{2}$, evaluate $f(\pi)$.

(1) 1
(2) -1
(3) 3
(4) 0

23 In circle O, the length of radius $\overline{AB}$ is 8 centimeters. If central angle AOB measures 2.5 radians, what is the length of the intercepted arc AB?

(1) 1 centimeter
(2) 2.5 centimeters
(3) 3.2 centimeters
(4) 20 centimeters

24 If $\csc \alpha = 2$, which could be the measure of α?

(1) $\dfrac{\pi}{4}$

(2) $\dfrac{\pi}{3}$

(3) $\dfrac{5\pi}{6}$

(4) $\dfrac{3\pi}{2}$

25 If $\cot \theta = -\dfrac{3}{4}$ and $\cos \theta > 0$, find $\sin \theta$.

(1) $-\dfrac{4}{5}$

(2) $-\dfrac{3}{5}$

(3) $\dfrac{3}{5}$

(4) $\dfrac{4}{5}$

26 If $f(x) = \cos 2\theta + \sin \theta$, then $f\left(\dfrac{\pi}{2}\right)$ equals

(1) 1   (3) -2
(2) 2   (4) 0

27 Which pair of functions have the same domain and range?

(1) $\sin x$ and $\cos x$
(2) $\sin x$ and $\csc x$
(3) $\sec x$ and $\cos x$
(4) $\sec x$ and $\cot x$

28 If $\sin \theta = c$, then the value of the expression $\sin \theta \csc \theta$ is equivalent to

(1) 1
(2) c
(3) $\dfrac{1}{c^2}$
(4) c^2

29 Solve for θ: $\sec (5\theta + 14)° = \csc (2\theta - 1)°$

(1) -5 (3) 22
(2) 11   (4) 90

30 Evaluate: $2 \csc^2 \dfrac{5\pi}{6} + \tan^2 \dfrac{2\pi}{3}$

(1) 1

(2) $\dfrac{1}{2} + \sqrt{3}$

(3) $9\dfrac{1}{4}$

(4) 11

31 In circle O, the length of radius $\overline{OB}$ is 5 centimeters and the length of arc AB is 5 centimeters. The measure of angle AOB is

(1) 1 radian
(2) 60 degrees
(3) π radians
(4) more than 60 degrees

32 If the terminal side of angle θ in standard position on a unit circle passes through the point whose coordinates are $\left(-\dfrac{\sqrt{3}}{2}, \dfrac{1}{2}\right)$, find m$\angle \theta$.

(1) $\dfrac{5\pi}{6}$

(2) $\dfrac{7\pi}{6}$

(3) $\dfrac{5\pi}{3}$

(4) $-\dfrac{\pi}{6}$

33 One radian is equivalent to approximately how many degrees?

(1) 57°   (3) 189°
(2) 90°   (4) 360°

34 Which is *not* in the domain of the cotangent function?

(1) 0

(2) $\dfrac{2\pi}{3}$

(3) $\dfrac{7}{4}\pi$

(4) $\dfrac{3\pi}{2}$

35 What is arctan (-1)?

(1) $-\dfrac{\pi}{2}$

(2) $-\dfrac{\pi}{4}$

(3) $\dfrac{3\pi}{4}$

(4) $\dfrac{3\pi}{2}$

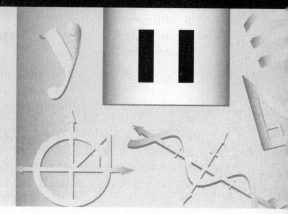

CHAPTER 11

Graphs of Trigonometric Functions

11.1 Graphs of the Sine and Cosine Functions

Just as other functions have graphs that illustrate them, so do trigonometric functions. When drawing trigonometric graphs by hand, we set the axes a bit differently than for other graphs. We use the horizontal axis for angle values in radians and the vertical axis for the values of the trigonometric functions.

What radian measures are familiar to us? From Chapter 10, we know the sine and cosine of special angles on the unit circle, such as $\frac{\pi}{6}, \frac{\pi}{3}, \frac{\pi}{2}, \frac{2\pi}{3}, \frac{5\pi}{6}$, and π, which are all *multiples of* $\frac{\pi}{6}$. Therefore, we divide our x-axis into intervals of $\frac{\pi}{6}$. $\left(\text{The negative } x\text{-axis is labeled } -\frac{\pi}{6}, -\frac{\pi}{3}, -\frac{\pi}{2}, -\frac{2\pi}{3}, -\frac{5\pi}{6}, -\pi, \ldots\right)$

We label the y-axis to clearly show the range of the trigonometric functions. For example, since $\sin x$ and $\cos x$ have values between -1 and 1, we focus in on this interval for these functions.

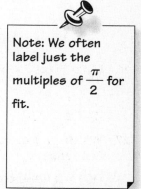

Note: We often label just the multiples of $\frac{\pi}{2}$ for fit.

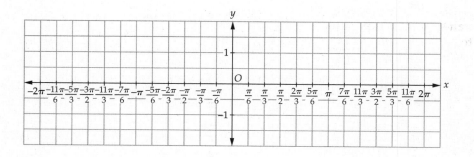

Graph of y = sin x

To graph the sine function, we explore the information the unit circle provides. Since we draw our trigonometric graphs using radians, angle measures on this unit circle are in radians.

Notice the values of sin x at the quadrantal angles.

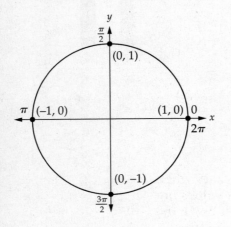

x	0	$\dfrac{\pi}{2}$	π	$\dfrac{3\pi}{2}$	2π
$\sin x$	0	1	0	-1	0

If we plot these points on a graph, we start to get an idea of the shape of $y = \sin x$.

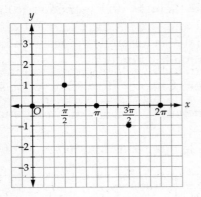

When we include other values of sin x that we know, we see the graph becoming more complete.

$$\sin \frac{\pi}{6} = \frac{1}{2} = 0.5 \qquad\qquad \sin \frac{\pi}{3} = \frac{\sqrt{3}}{2} \approx 0.87$$

$$\sin \frac{2\pi}{3} = \frac{\sqrt{3}}{2} \approx 0.87 \qquad\qquad \sin \frac{5\pi}{6} = \frac{1}{2} = 0.5$$

$$\sin \frac{7\pi}{6} = -\frac{1}{2} = -0.5 \qquad\qquad \sin \frac{4\pi}{3} = -\frac{\sqrt{3}}{2} \approx -0.87$$

$$\sin \frac{5\pi}{3} = -\frac{\sqrt{3}}{2} \approx -0.87 \qquad\qquad \sin \frac{11\pi}{6} = -\frac{1}{2} = -0.5$$

We have divided the horizontal axis into units of $\frac{\pi}{6}$, which makes the plotting of these points easy.

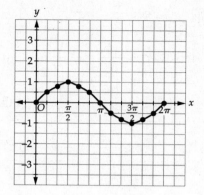

Now look at the sine curve. In the first and second quadrants, that is, when $0 < x < \pi$, the graph of $y = \sin x$ is above the x-axis, which means all values are positive. This matches what we know from the unit circle. When $\pi < x < 2\pi$, in the third and fourth quadrants, $y = \sin x$ is below the x-axis and therefore negative.

Note: The graph of $y = \sin x$ starts its cycle at zero, ends its cycle at zero, and is at zero halfway through the curve.

Graph of $y = \cos x$

To graph the cosine curve by hand, again we turn to the values shown on the unit circle, beginning with the quadrantal angles.

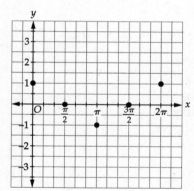

x	0	$\frac{\pi}{2}$	π	$\frac{3\pi}{2}$	2π
$\cos x$	1	0	-1	0	1

Once again, we can see more of the graph by including the cosine values of other known angles.

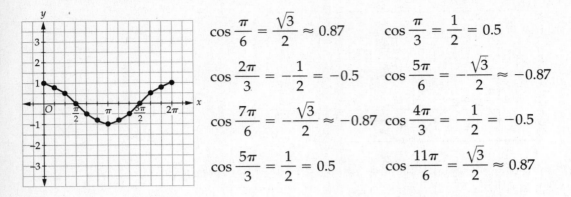

$$\cos \frac{\pi}{6} = \frac{\sqrt{3}}{2} \approx 0.87 \qquad \cos \frac{\pi}{3} = \frac{1}{2} = 0.5$$

$$\cos \frac{2\pi}{3} = -\frac{1}{2} = -0.5 \qquad \cos \frac{5\pi}{6} = -\frac{\sqrt{3}}{2} \approx -0.87$$

$$\cos \frac{7\pi}{6} = -\frac{\sqrt{3}}{2} \approx -0.87 \quad \cos \frac{4\pi}{3} = -\frac{1}{2} = -0.5$$

$$\cos \frac{5\pi}{3} = \frac{1}{2} = 0.5 \qquad \cos \frac{11\pi}{6} = \frac{\sqrt{3}}{2} \approx 0.87$$

Note: The graph of $y = \cos x$ starts its cycle at its maximum, ends its cycle at its maximum, and is at its minimum halfway through the curve. Halfway between each maximum and minimum, the cosine curve is at zero.

Now that you have seen the process of graphing trigonometric functions by hand, we can graph the same functions using the graphing calculator.

First, go to the (MODE) screen. Be certain that all options are highlighted on the left, particularly Radian.

```
Normal  Sci  Eng
Float   0123456789
Radian  Degree
Func  Par  Pol  Seq
Connected  Dot
Sequential  Simul
Real  a+bi  re^θi
Full  Horiz  G-T
```

To graph $y = \sin x$, go to the (Y=) screen and enter (SIN) (X,T,θ,n) ( )). Notice that the calculator gives you an open parenthesis for your variable when you press (SIN). Now go to the (WINDOW) screen. We want the calculator to give us a window to see our trigonometric graphs, so we set the parameters as shown

below. Notice that the calculator shows decimal equivalents for 2π and $\frac{\pi}{2}$.

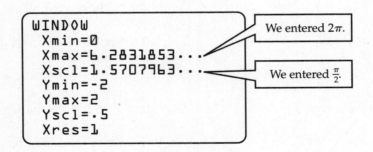

```
WINDOW
 Xmin=0
 Xmax=6.2831853...        We entered 2π.
 Xscl=1.5707963...        We entered π/2.
 Ymin=-2
 Ymax=2
 Yscl=.5
 Xres=1
```

Now press **GRAPH** and you should see a graph like this one (though it won't have the labels).

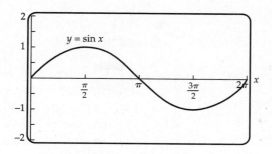

Once again, you can see how the graph of the sine function starts at zero, ends at zero, and passes through zero halfway through its cycle in the interval $[0, 2\pi]$.

To see the graph of $y = \cos x$, enter that equation as Y_1 in the **Y=** screen. Leave the window settings the same and press **GRAPH**.

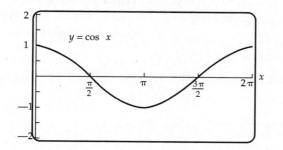

Here you can see the graph of the cosine function starts at its maximum, ends at its maximum, and is at its minimum halfway through its cycle in the interval $[0, 2\pi]$. Halfway between each of those maximum and minimum points, the curve is at zero.

1 Graph the function $y = \sin x$ in the closed interval $[-2\pi, 2\pi]$.

   a What is the maximum value of the function?

   b What is the minimum value of the function?

   c What are the zeros of the function?

2 Graph the function $y = \cos x$ in the closed interval $[-2\pi, 2\pi]$.

   a What is the maximum value of the function?

   b What is the minimum value of the function?

   c What are the zeros of the function?

3 Using a domain of $\{0 \le x \le 2\pi\}$, graph the functions $y = \sin x$ and $y = \cos x$ on the same set of axes.

   a For what values of x does $\sin x = \cos x$? What are these x-values in degree measure?

   b In what inverval(s) are both $y = \sin x$ and $y = \cos x$ negative?

   c In what interval(s) are both $y = \sin x$ and $y = \cos x$ positive?

   d In what interval(s) do the sine and cosine functions both increase?

   e In what interval(s) do the sine and cosine functions both decrease?

4 Using a domain of $\{-\pi \le x \le \pi\}$, graph the functions $y = \sin x$ and $y = \cos x$ on the same set of axes.

  a When does $\sin x - \cos x = 1$? (Hint: Look to see when the two graphs are one unit apart.)

  b Translate the graph of $y = \cos x$ a distance of $\dfrac{\pi}{2}$ units to the right. Describe what happens.

5 Graph the functions $y = \sin x$ and $y = \cos x$ on the same set of axes over the interval $-\dfrac{\pi}{2} \le x \le \dfrac{\pi}{2}$.

  a What fraction of a complete sine curve do you see in this interval?

  b What fraction of a complete cosine curve do you see?

  c For what value(s) of x does $\sin x - \cos x = -1$?

6 Graph the functions $y = \sin x$ and $y = \cos x$ on the same set of axes in the closed interval $[0, 4\pi]$.

  a How many complete sine curves do you see in this interval?

  b How many cosine curves do you see?

  c If you graphed the same functions in the interval $[0, 8\pi]$, how many complete sine and cosine curves would you see?

  d In what interval from part **c** would you see one complete sine and one complete cosine curve?

  e Name another interval, different from the one in part **d**, in which you can see one complete sine and cosine curve.

  f Compare your answers to parts **d** and **e** with the answers of some of your classmates. What is common about each of these intervals?

11.2 Amplitude, Period, and Phase Shift

In Section 11.1, we graphed the functions $y = \sin x$ and $y = \cos x$ in various intervals and discussed properties of the graphs. We will now explore what happens when we perform transformations on those basic sine and cosine functions.

Amplitude

Use your graphing calculator to graph the functions $f(x) = \sin x$, $g(x) = 2\sin x$, and $h(x) = \dfrac{1}{2}\sin x$ in the interval $0 \le x \le 2\pi$. In the graph below, $f(x) = \sin x$ is drawn in bold, while $g(x) = 2\sin x$ and $h(x) = \dfrac{1}{2}\sin x$ are both light. Observe that, in each case, the shape of the curve is the same. The sine curve starts at zero, ends at zero, and is at zero halfway through its cycle.

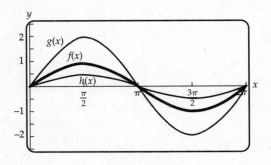

Note the y-values of these functions in the table below. Since zero times any value is still zero, the x-intercepts do not change. Other values are the original values of the $y = \sin x$ function multiplied by the coefficient of $\sin x$.

x	0	$\dfrac{\pi}{2}$	π	$\dfrac{3\pi}{2}$	2π
$f(x)$	0	1	0	-1	0
$g(x)$	0	2	0	-2	0
$h(x)$	0	$\dfrac{1}{2}$	0	$-\dfrac{1}{2}$	0

We see that all three equations are in the form $y = a\sin x$. By looking at both the graph and the table above, we can see the effect that the coefficient a has on the function. We call $|a|$ the **amplitude** of this function. In general, the amplitude is one-half the difference between the maximum and minimum values of the trigonometric function.

In each of the three functions shown above, the maximum value of the sine function equals the absolute value of a, the amplitude, while the minimum value of the function equals the negative of the absolute value of the amplitude. The amplitude of $f(x) = |1| = 1$, the amplitude of $g(x) = |2| = 2$, and the amplitude of $h(x) = \left|\dfrac{1}{2}\right| = \dfrac{1}{2}$.

In the graph below in the interval $[0, 2\pi]$, $f(x) = \sin x$ is drawn in bold, while $j(x) = -\sin x$ is light.

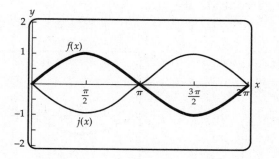

Observe that $j(x)$ is the function $f(x)$ reflected in the x-axis. Whenever a is negative, you are looking at a reflection of the original function in the x-axis. Since $|-1| = 1$, $j(x) = -\sin x$ has an amplitude of 1, the same as $f(x)$.

The cosine function curves follow similar patterns. If a is negative, the curve will be at its minimum point when x equals zero and be back at its minimum point when x equals 2π. In the graph below, $f(x) = \cos x$ is drawn in bold, while $g(x) = -\cos x$ and $h(x) = \dfrac{3}{2}\cos x$ are light.

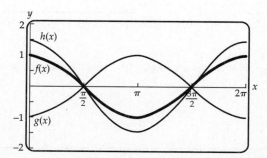

Once again, the x-intercepts remain unchanged for all of the cosine curves, and the basic cosine shape stays the same. The maximum and minimum values of the functions are $|a|$ and $-|a|$. The maximum value (and amplitude) of $f(x) = \cos x$ and $g(x) = -\cos x$ is 1, while the maximum and amplitude of $h(x) = \dfrac{3}{2}\cos x$ is $\dfrac{3}{2}$.

MODEL PROBLEMS

1 Given the function $f(x) = 3\sin x$, what is the maximum value of $f(x)$?

SOLUTION

In this function, the amplitude corresponds to the maximum value of $f(x)$. Since the amplitude is 3, the maximum value is 3.

2 Which function has a minimum value of -2?

(1) $y = \sin x$

(2) $y = 2\sin x$

(3) $y = -\sin x$

(4) $y = 4\sin x$

SOLUTION

If the minimum value in the range is to be -2, it means the function must have an "a value" of ± 2. The only function that meets that requirement is choice (2), $y = 2\sin x$.

3 Which graph shows a function with an amplitude of $\dfrac{1}{2}$?

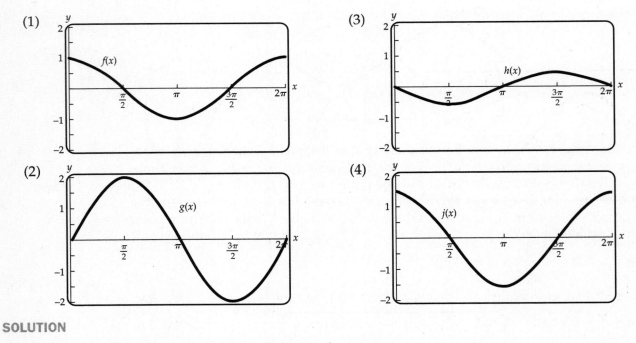

SOLUTION

An amplitude of $\dfrac{1}{2}$ means the range is $-\dfrac{1}{2} \le y \le \dfrac{1}{2}$. Looking at the graphs, we see the only function with that range is $h(x)$, choice (3).

Answer: Choice (3)

Period

The **period** of a trigonometric function is the length of the interval needed to see one complete cycle of the curve. In all of the examples thus far, the period of the graphs has been 2π. Let's examine two functions that have different periods. Use your graphing calculator to graph the functions $f(x) = \sin x$ and $g(x) = \sin 2x$ in the interval $0 \le x \le 2\pi$. Note that the amplitude, $|a|$, is 1.

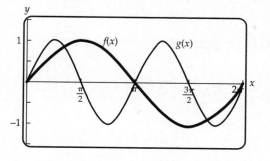

From the graph above, we see that the period of $f(x) = \sin x$ is 2π, while the period of $g(x) = \sin 2x$ is π, since one complete cycle of the curve is obtained in an interval of π.

Observe that in the interval $0 \le x \le 2\pi$, there is one complete cycle of the sine curve $f(x) = \sin x$ and two complete cycles of sine curve $g(x) = \sin 2x$. The **frequency** of a sine or cosine function is the number of complete cycles of the curve contained in the interval $0 \le x \le 2\pi$.

We say that the function $f(x) = \sin x$ has a frequency of 1, while the function $g(x) = \sin 2x$ has a frequency of 2.

Use your graphing calculator to graph the functions $f(x) = \sin x$ and $h(x) = \sin \frac{1}{2}x$ in the interval $0 \le x \le 2\pi$ and in the interval $0 \le x \le 4\pi$.

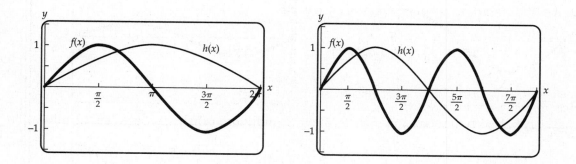

The period of $h(x) = \sin \frac{1}{2}x$ is 4π since an interval of 4π is needed to complete one curve.

Observe that in the interval $0 \le x \le 2\pi$, there is one complete cycle of the sine curve $f(x) = \sin x$ and *one-half* of a complete cycle of the sine curve $h(x) = \sin \frac{1}{2}x$. We say that the function $h(x) = \sin \frac{1}{2}x$ has a frequency of $\frac{1}{2}$.

In general:

- For the sine function $y = \sin bx$ or the cosine function $y = \cos bx$, $|b|$ is the frequency of the curve.
- The period of a sine or cosine function is calculated by dividing 2π by the frequency of the function. That is, for $y = \sin bx$ or $y = \cos bx$, period $= \dfrac{2\pi}{|b|}$.

MODEL PROBLEMS

4 Without using your graphing calculator, graph the function $y = 3\sin 2x$ over the interval $[0, 2\pi]$. On the same set of axes, graph the function $y = 2\cos x$. For what value(s) of x do both functions have a common zero?.

SOLUTION

First explore what you know about the two equations given.

Function	$y = 3\sin 2x$	$y = 2\cos x$
Amplitude	3	2
Min/Max	Min = -3, Max = 3	Min = -2, Max = 2
Frequency	2 (2 full cycles in 2π)	1 (1 full cycle in 2π)
Period	π	2π

Draw the basic trigonometric axes for the interval $[0, 2\pi]$ and put in the points you know for each curve.

$y = 3\sin 2x$

A sine curve has zeros at the start, middle, and end of each cycle:

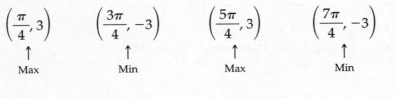

$$(0, 0) \qquad \left(\frac{\pi}{2}, 0\right) \qquad (\pi, 0) \qquad \left(\frac{3\pi}{2}, 0\right) \qquad (2\pi, 0)$$

| ↑ Start | ↑ Middle | ↑ End/Start | ↑ Middle | ↑ End |

The maximum is halfway between the start and middle, and the minimum is halfway between the middle and end:

$$\left(\frac{\pi}{4}, 3\right) \qquad \left(\frac{3\pi}{4}, -3\right) \qquad \left(\frac{5\pi}{4}, 3\right) \qquad \left(\frac{7\pi}{4}, -3\right)$$

| ↑ Max | ↑ Min | ↑ Max | ↑ Min |

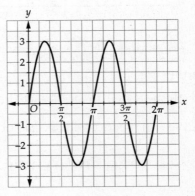

$y = 2\cos x$

A cosine curve starts and ends its cycle at its maximum. The minimum is halfway between the start and end:

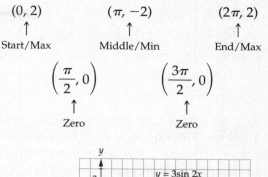

$(0, 2)$ $(\pi, -2)$ $(2\pi, 2)$
↑   ↑   ↑
Start/Max   Middle/Min   End/Max

The zeros are halfway between the maximum and minimum, and halfway between the minimum and maximum:

$\left(\dfrac{\pi}{2}, 0\right)$ $\left(\dfrac{3\pi}{2}, 0\right)$
↑   ↑
Zero   Zero

When we look at the graphs of the two functions, we see four points of intersection, two of which occur at $x = \dfrac{\pi}{2}$ and $x = \dfrac{3\pi}{2}$. These are the common zeros.

Answer: $x = \dfrac{\pi}{2}, \dfrac{3\pi}{2}$

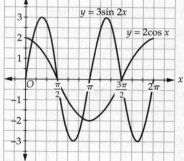

5   What is the period of the function $y = 3\sin 2x$?

SOLUTION

For a function $y = a\sin bx$, the period is $\dfrac{2\pi}{b}$. In this case, $|b| = 2$, so $\dfrac{2\pi}{|b|} = \dfrac{2\pi}{2} = \pi$.

Answer: π

6   Find the amplitude and period of the function $y = \dfrac{1}{2}\cos 4x$.

SOLUTION

Since amplitude $= |a|$ and period $= \dfrac{2\pi}{|b|}$, we look first at the values of a and b in this equation. Since $a = \dfrac{1}{2}$, the amplitude is $\left|\dfrac{1}{2}\right|$ or $\dfrac{1}{2}$. We see that $b = 4$, so the period is $\dfrac{2\pi}{|4|}$ or $\dfrac{\pi}{2}$.

Answer: amplitude $= \dfrac{1}{2}$, period $= \dfrac{\pi}{2}$

7 What is the greatest element in the range of the function $y = 4\sin 2x + 3$?

(1) 8

(2) 7

(3) 3

(4) 4

SOLUTION

In this problem, the trigonometric equation of $y = 4\sin 2x$ has a constant value of 3 being added to the y-values. This equation is in the form $y = a\sin bx + d$, where d represents a vertical shift of the entire graph. (The line $y = d$ lies in the middle of the graph, so we call it the *midline* of the graph.) The amplitude of this function is 4. However, its maximum value is $4 + 3 = 7$, choice (2).

Answer: choice (2)

8 Using the graphing calculator, find all values of x for which $4\sin 2x = -\cos x$ in the interval $\{0 \le x \le 2\pi\}$. Approximate decimal values to the nearest hundredth.

SOLUTION

Enter the two equations in Y_1 and Y_2, set your window with x-values from 0 to 2π, and press (GRAPH).

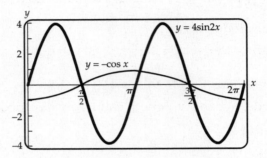

Notice that there are four points of intersection. Two occur at the quadrantal angles of $\dfrac{\pi}{2}$ and $\dfrac{3\pi}{2}$. The other two values you must find by using the intersect function of the calculator ((2nd) (TRACE) (5)). Remember to move your cursor close to the points whose value you want. The calculator will approximate the x-values in decimal form rather than in exact radian measure. The remaining x-values at the points of intersection are approximately 3.2669205 and 6.1578575.

Answer: $x = \dfrac{\pi}{2}, 3.27, \dfrac{3\pi}{2}, 6.16$

Phase Shift

Use your graphing calculator to graph the functions $f(x) = \sin x$ and $g(x) = \sin(x - \pi)$ on the interval $0 \le x \le 2\pi$. In the graph below, $f(x) = \sin x$ is drawn in bold, while $g(x) = \sin(x - \pi)$ is light. Observe that the shapes of the two curves are the same. The graph of $g(x) = \sin(x - \pi)$ is a horizontal shift of $f(x)$ a distance of π units to the right.

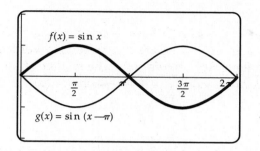

In general, the graph of $f(x + c)$ represents a horizontal shift or **phase shift** of $f(x)$ a distance of c units to the right if c is negative and c units to the left if c is positive.

MODEL PROBLEM

9 Without using a graphing calculator, sketch the graph of $y = 4\cos 2\left(x + \dfrac{\pi}{2}\right)$ in the interval $[-\pi, \pi]$.

SOLUTION

We first determine the amplitude, frequency, period, and horizontal (phase) shift.

This equation is in the form $y = a\cos b(x + c)$.

- The amplitude $|a|$ is 4.
- The frequency $|b|$ is 2.
- The period $\dfrac{2\pi}{|b|}$ is π.

- The cosine curve has been shifted $-c$ or $\dfrac{\pi}{2}$ units to the left.

Draw the x- and y-axes, with values of x from $-\pi$ to π and values of y from -4 to 4. Since a cosine function begins at its maximum value, we will first plot the maximum and minimum values of the function.

Since the function has been shifted $\dfrac{\pi}{2}$ units to the left, we begin our curve by plotting the point $\left(-\dfrac{\pi}{2}, 4\right)$

and end the curve by plotting the point $\left(\dfrac{\pi}{2}, 4\right)$. We then go halfway between these two points to plot the point $(0, -4)$, as shown below.

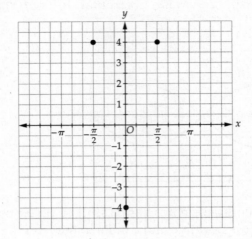

We then go halfway between the maximum and minimum values of the function to plot its zeros. These will occur at $\left(-\dfrac{\pi}{4}, 0\right)$ and $\left(\dfrac{\pi}{4}, 0\right)$, as shown below.

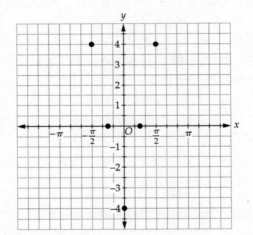

Connect the points to form a smooth cosine curve, as shown below.

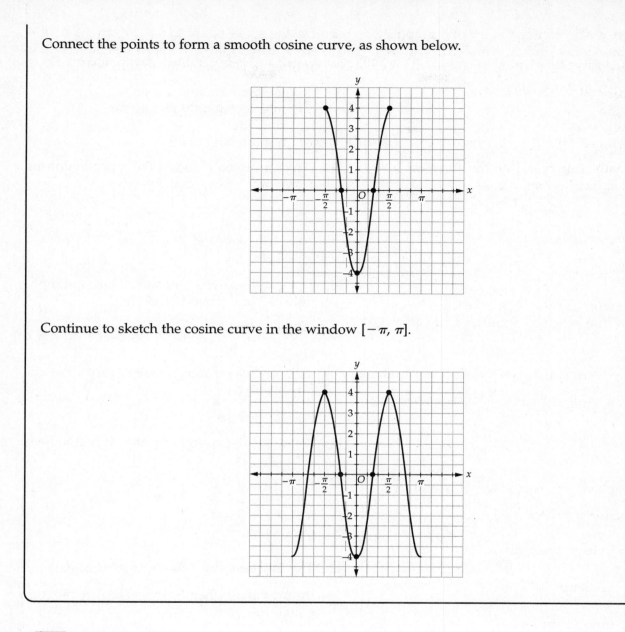

Continue to sketch the cosine curve in the window $[-\pi, \pi]$.

![Practice](pencil icon) **Practice**

Exercises 1–14: Select the numeral preceding the choice that best completes the statement or answers the question.

1. As angle x increases from $\dfrac{3\pi}{2}$ to 2π, which statement is true?

   (1) Sin x decreases from 0 to -1.
   (2) Cos x decreases from 0 to -1.
   (3) Cos x increases from 0 to 1.
   (4) Sin x increases from 0 to 1.

2. What is the minimum element in the range of the function $y = 5 + 2\sin\theta$?

   (1) -5
   (2) 2
   (3) 3
   (4) -7

3 Between $x = -2\pi$ and $x = 2\pi$, the graph of the equation $y = \sin x$ is symmetric with respect to the

(1) x-axis
(2) origin
(3) line $y = x$
(4) y-axis

4 How many full cycles of the function $y = 2\cos 3x$ appear in 2π radians?

(1) 1
(2) 2
(3) 3
(4) $\dfrac{3\pi}{2}$

5 The function $f(x) = -3\cos 2x$ reaches its minimum value when x, expressed in radians, equals

(1) -3
(2) $\dfrac{\pi}{4}$
(3) $\dfrac{\pi}{2}$
(4) π

6 The graph of $y = \sin\left(x + \dfrac{\pi}{3}\right)$ is a shift of the function $y = \sin x$

(1) $\dfrac{\pi}{3}$ units to the right
(2) $\dfrac{\pi}{3}$ units up
(3) $\dfrac{\pi}{3}$ units to the left
(4) $\dfrac{\pi}{3}$ units down

7 If the graphs of the equations $y = 2\cos x$ and $y = -1$ are drawn on the same set of axes, how many points of intersection will occur between 0 and 2π?

(1) 1
(2) 2
(3) 3
(4) 4

8 On the same set of axes, $y = \sin x$ and $y = \cos x$ are graphed. If the translation $T_{\frac{\pi}{2}, 0}$ is applied to $y = \cos x$, the graphs will

(1) intersect at only one point
(2) intersect at only two points
(3) coincide
(4) not intersect at all

9 Which is an equation of the reflection of the graph of $y = \sin x$ in the y-axis?

(1) $y = \sin(-x)$
(2) $y = \cos x$
(3) $y = -\sin(-x)$
(4) $y = -\cos x$

10 The graph of which equation has an amplitude of 2 and period of π?

(1) $y = 2\cos x$
(2) $y = \dfrac{1}{2}\sin 2x$
(3) $y = 2\cos\dfrac{1}{2}x$
(4) $y = -2\cos 2x$

11 What is the range of the function $y = 3\cos 2x + 1$?

(1) $-3 \le y \le 3$
(2) $-4 \le y \le 5$
(3) $-2 \le y \le 4$
(4) $-1 \le y \le 1$

12 The function $f(x) = 3\sin\dfrac{1}{2}x$ reaches its maximum value when x, expressed in radians, equals

(1) π
(2) $\dfrac{\pi}{2}$
(3) 3
(4) $\dfrac{3\pi}{2}$

13 How many cycles of the graph of $y = \dfrac{2}{3}\sin 4\theta$ appear in an interval of 2π radians?

(1) $\dfrac{2}{3}$
(2) 2
(3) π
(4) 4

14 The function $y = \cos\left(x + \dfrac{\pi}{2}\right)$ is equivalent to which of the following?

(1) $y = \sin x$
(2) $y = \sin(-x)$
(3) $y = \cos x$
(4) $y = \cos(-x)$

Exercises 15–18: Sketch each graph first by hand and then with your graphing calculator.

15 a On the same set of axes, sketch and label the graphs of the functions $y = -3\cos 2x$ and $y = \dfrac{3}{2}\sin x$ in the interval $0 \le x \le 2\pi$.

b Use the graphs drawn in part **a** to determine the value(s) of x where $-3\cos 2x + \dfrac{3}{2}\sin x = -3$ and x is a quadrantal angle.

16 a Sketch the graph of the function $y = 2\cos x$ in the interval $0 \le x \le 2\pi$.

b On the same axes, sketch the function $y = 3\sin \dfrac{1}{2}x$.

c Use the graphs drawn in part **a** and **b** to determine the value(s) of x where $2\cos x - 3\sin \dfrac{1}{2}x = -5$.

17 a On the same set of axes, sketch and label the graphs of the functions $y = -2\cos 2x$ and $y = \dfrac{3}{2}\sin 2x$ in the interval $-\dfrac{\pi}{2} \le x \le \dfrac{\pi}{2}$.

b Use the graphs drawn in part **a** to determine, to the *nearest hundredth*, the value(s) of x where $-2\cos 2x = \dfrac{3}{2}\sin 2x$.

18 a Sketch the graph of the function $y = 2\sin 2x$ in the interval $[-\pi, \pi]$.

b On the same axes, sketch the function $y = \dfrac{3}{2}\cos(x + \pi)$.

c How many points of intersection are there in the interval $[-\pi, \pi]$?

d Without using a calculator, determine the exact value of two of the intersection points of the graphs.

Exercises 19–22: Answer each question by graphing by hand or using a graphing calculator.

19 a Sketch the graph of the function $y = \cos(x + \pi)$ in the interval $[-2\pi, 2\pi]$.

b On the same axes, sketch the function $y = \cos x + \pi$.

c Describe the similarities and differences between the two graphs.

20 a Sketch the graph of the function $y = \sin(x - \pi)$ in the interval $[-2\pi, 2\pi]$.

b On the same axes, sketch the function $y = \sin x - \pi$.

c Describe the similarities and differences between the two graphs.

21 a Sketch the graph of the function $y = \sin(x + 2)$ in the interval $[-2\pi, 2\pi]$.

b On the same axes, sketch the function $y = \sin x + 2$.

c Describe the similarities and differences between the two graphs.

22 a Sketch the graph of the function $y = \cos(x - 1)$ in the interval $[-2\pi, 2\pi]$.

b On the same axes, sketch the function $y = \cos x - 1$.

c Describe the similarities and differences between the two graphs.

11.3 Writing the Equation of a Sine or Cosine Graph

In the first two sections of this chapter, we graphed functions of the form $y = a\sin b(x + c)$ or $y = a\cos b(x + c)$. We will now look at graphs and determine an equation that could be used to generate the graph.

Note: We will explore vertical shifts in Section 11.7.

MODEL PROBLEMS

1   Write an equation of the sine function shown in the graph below.

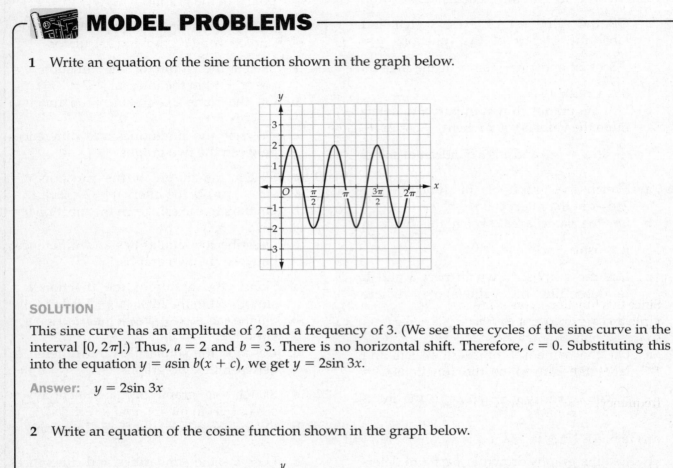

SOLUTION

This sine curve has an amplitude of 2 and a frequency of 3. (We see three cycles of the sine curve in the interval $[0, 2\pi]$.) Thus, $a = 2$ and $b = 3$. There is no horizontal shift. Therefore, $c = 0$. Substituting this into the equation $y = a\sin b(x + c)$, we get $y = 2\sin 3x$.

Answer: $y = 2\sin 3x$

2   Write an equation of the cosine function shown in the graph below.

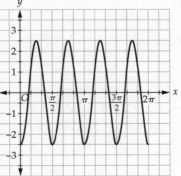

SOLUTION

This cosine curve has an amplitude of 2.5 and a frequency of 4. (We see four cycles of the cosine curve in the interval $[0, 2\pi]$.) Since the cosine curve starts its cycle at its minimum point, we set $a = -2.5$ and $b = 4$. Since $y = -2.5$ when $x = 0$, there is no horizontal shift. Therefore, $c = 0$. Substituting this into the equation $y = a\cos b(x + c)$, we get $y = -2.5\cos 4x$.

Answer: $y = -2.5\cos 4x$

3 Write an equation of the function shown in the graph below.

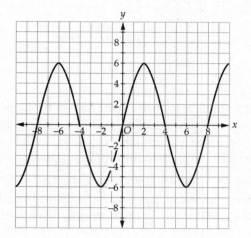

SOLUTION

Since this function curve starts its cycle at zero, ends at zero, and is zero halfway through the curve, we'll write an equation for a sine curve. The maximum value of the curve is 6 and the minimum value is −6, so the amplitude $= 6 = a$.

We have to calculate the frequency of the curve. We know that the period $= \dfrac{2\pi}{\text{frequency}}$, so frequency $= \dfrac{2\pi}{\text{period}}$. By looking at the curve, we can see that one cycle of the sine curve is completed in 8 radians. Thus, the period of this curve is 8 and frequency $= \dfrac{2\pi}{8} = \dfrac{\pi}{4} = b$.

There is no horizontal or vertical shift.

Substituting this into the equation $y = a\sin b(x + c)$, we get $y = 6\sin \dfrac{\pi}{4}x$.

ALTERNATIVE SOLUTION

We could have written the equation using a horizontal shift of a cosine curve. The cosine curve begins its cycle at the maximum of $(2, 6)$ and ends at the maximum of $(10, 6)$, so it is shifted 2 to the right. Using a shift of 2 to the right, we get $c = -2$. The amplitude and frequency are the same for the cosine and sine curves.

Substituting this into the equation $y = a\cos b(x + c)$, we get $y = 6\cos\left[\dfrac{\pi}{4}(x - 2)\right]$.

Answer: $y = 6\sin \dfrac{\pi}{4}x$ or $y = 6\cos\left[\dfrac{\pi}{4}(x - 2)\right]$

4 Write a sine equation and a cosine equation for the function shown in the graph below.

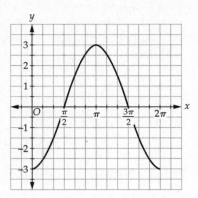

SOLUTION

When we look at the curve, we can decide to write an equation for a cosine or a sine curve. We can view it as an "upside-down" cosine curve or a horizontal shift of a sine curve. Either way, the amplitude is 3, since there is a distance of 6 units from the maximum point to the minimum point, or a distance of 3 points from the midline of the curve to its maximum (or minimum value). Thus, $|a| = 3$.

Since there is only one cycle of the curve in the interval $[0, 2\pi]$, we know that the frequency is 1, so $b = 1$.

We'll write the cosine function first. Since the curve starts at its minimum, ends at its minimum, and is at its maximum halfway through the curve, $a = -3$. Substituting this into the equation $y = a\cos b(x + c)$, we get $y = -3\cos x$.

If we view the sine function as a horizontal shift of $\dfrac{\pi}{2}$, we see that the curve starts its cycle at zero and ends at zero (if we continued the graph to the right), and is zero halfway through. Starting the graph at $x = \dfrac{\pi}{2}$, the curve begins its cycle by increasing. Thus, $a = 3$.

Substituting this into the equation $y = a\sin b(x + c)$, we get $y = 3\sin\left(x - \dfrac{\pi}{2}\right)$.

Answer: $y = -3\cos x$ or $y = 3\sin\left(x - \dfrac{\pi}{2}\right)$

 **Practice**

Exercises 1–5: Sketch the graph of the sine function described, and write an equation to fit the function.

1 amplitude = 4, period = $\dfrac{\pi}{3}$

2 amplitude = 1, zeros at $x = \dfrac{\pi}{3}$, $x = \dfrac{2\pi}{3}$, $x = \pi$

3 maximum at $(0, 4)$ and $(10, 4)$, minimum at $(5, -4)$

4 amplitude = 2, period = 4π, horizontal shift = 3

5 amplitude = 5, period = 3, horizontal shift = 1

Exercises 6 and 7: Select the numeral preceding the choice that best answers the question.

6 What is the equation of the graph sketched below?

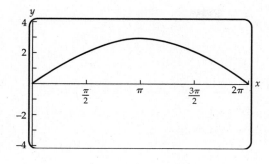

(1) $y = 3\sin x$

(2) $y = 3\sin \dfrac{1}{2} x$

(3) $y = 3\cos x$

(4) $y = 3\cos \dfrac{1}{2} x$

7 What is the equation of the graph sketched below?

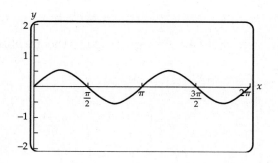

(1) $y = 2\sin \dfrac{1}{2} x$

(2) $y = \dfrac{1}{2}\cos x$

(3) $y = \dfrac{1}{2}\sin 2x$

(4) $y = \dfrac{1}{2}\sin \dfrac{1}{2} x$

Exercises 8–10: Determine the amplitude, period, and frequency for each function.

8

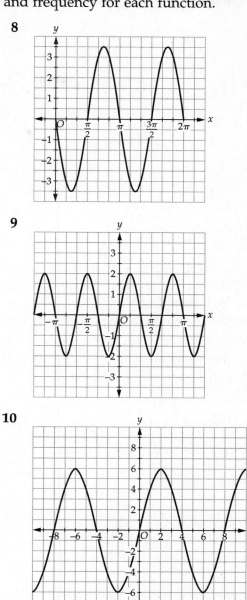

9

10

Exercises 11–13: Write an equation for each of the sine functions shown in Exercises 8–10.

Exercises 14–17: Match each graph with the appropriate function.

$$f(x) = 1.5\sin(x + \pi) \qquad g(x) = 1.5\sin\left(x - \frac{\pi}{2}\right)$$

$$h(x) = 1.5\cos\left(x - \frac{\pi}{2}\right) \qquad j(x) = -1.5\cos(x + \pi)$$

14

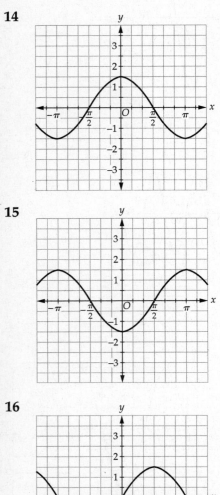

15

16

17

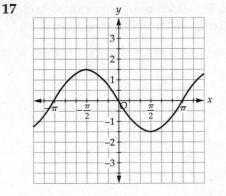

Exercises 18–20: Write an equation for the function shown in each graph.

18

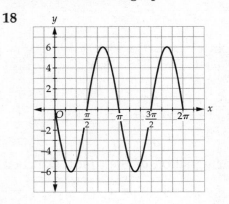

19

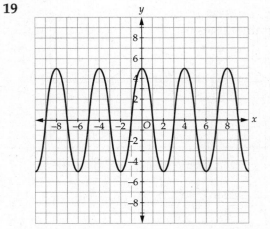

20

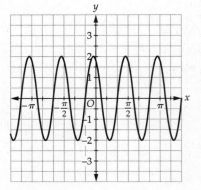

Exercises 21 and 22: Write both a sine and cosine function that could be used to represent each graph.

22

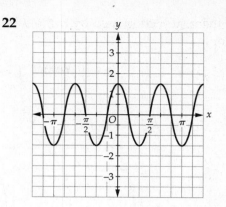

21

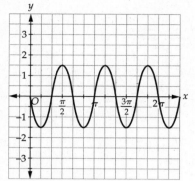

11.4 Graph of the Tangent Function

The graph of the tangent curve is very different from that of the sine and cosine curves because those curves are continuous. The tangent function, however, is undefined (U) when $x = \dfrac{\pi}{2}$, again at $x = \dfrac{3\pi}{2}$, and at every other odd multiple of $\dfrac{\pi}{2}$.

We know that $y = \tan x$ is positive in the first and third quadrants of the unit circle and negative in the second and fourth quadrants of the unit circle. We also know certain values of $y = \tan x$ as shown in the table below.

x	$-\dfrac{\pi}{2}$	$-\dfrac{\pi}{3}$	$-\dfrac{\pi}{4}$	$-\dfrac{\pi}{6}$	0	$\dfrac{\pi}{6}$	$\dfrac{\pi}{4}$	$\dfrac{\pi}{3}$
$\tan x$	U	$-\sqrt{3} \approx -1.7$	-1	$-\dfrac{\sqrt{3}}{3} \approx -0.58$	0	$\dfrac{\sqrt{3}}{3} \approx 0.58$	1	$\sqrt{3} \approx 1.7$

x	$\dfrac{\pi}{2}$	$\dfrac{2\pi}{3}$	$\dfrac{3\pi}{4}$	$\dfrac{5\pi}{6}$	π	$\dfrac{7\pi}{6}$	$\dfrac{5\pi}{4}$	$\dfrac{4\pi}{3}$
$\tan x$	U	$-\sqrt{3} \approx -1.7$	-1	$-\dfrac{\sqrt{3}}{3} \approx -0.58$	0	$\dfrac{\sqrt{3}}{3} \approx 0.58$	1	$\sqrt{3} \approx 1.7$

x	$\dfrac{3\pi}{2}$	$\dfrac{5\pi}{3}$	$\dfrac{7\pi}{4}$	$\dfrac{11\pi}{6}$	2π
$\tan x$	U	$-\sqrt{3} \approx -1.7$	-1	$-\dfrac{\sqrt{3}}{3} \approx -0.58$	0

Now look at the graph produced by this set of values.

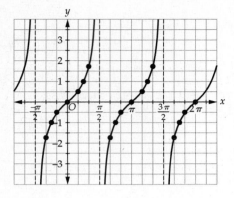

As x approaches $\dfrac{\pi}{2}$ from the left, the values of tan x continue to *increase* without bound, and as x approaches $\dfrac{\pi}{2}$ from the right, the values of tan x continue *decrease* without bound. To indicate this on the graph, we show a dashed vertical line at each undefined value of x to represent an *asymptote*. An **asymptote** is a line associated with a curve such that the points on the curve get closer and closer to the line but never touch it.

The lines $x = -\dfrac{\pi}{2}$, $x = \dfrac{\pi}{2}$, $x = \dfrac{3\pi}{2}$, $x = \dfrac{5\pi}{2}$, and so on, are all vertical asymptotes. The graph of the tangent function will approach these asymptotes, growing closer and closer to them but will never cross them.

Note that $y = \tan x$ has no maximum or minimum value; we can make the values of y as large or small as we want by choosing points sufficiently close to the odd multiples of $\dfrac{\pi}{2}$. Also note that the period of the function $y = \tan x$ is π. One complete cycle of the tangent curve is sketched in the interval $\left[-\dfrac{\pi}{2}, \dfrac{\pi}{2} \right]$.

Now that you've seen the process of graphing the tangent function by hand, let's graph it using the graphing calculator. Set Xmin = $-\dfrac{\pi}{2}$, Xmax = 2π, Ymin = -4, and Ymax = 4. The TI-83+ (left) shows vertical lines that are *not* part of the graph. The TI-84+ (right) shows only the tangent curve.

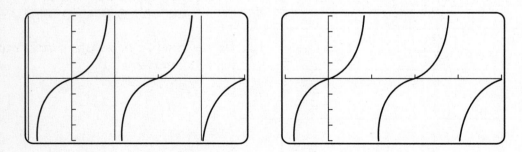

MODEL PROBLEM

Given the graph of $y = -\tan x$, determine:

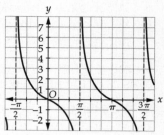

   a the period of the function

   b the domain of the function

   c what transformation was performed on $y = \tan x$ to produce this graph.

SOLUTION

   a One cycle of the function starts at $-\dfrac{\pi}{2}$ and ends at $\dfrac{\pi}{2}$, so the period is π.

Answer: period $= \pi$

   b The graph is undefined for $x =$ odd multiples of $\dfrac{\pi}{2}$. We can say that the domain is $\left\{ x : x \neq \dfrac{\pi}{2} + n\pi \text{ for } n \text{ an integer} \right\}$.

Answer: domain $= \left\{ x : x \neq \dfrac{\pi}{2} + n\pi \text{ for } n \text{ an integer} \right\}$

   c The function $y = \tan x$ was reflected either in the x-axis or in the y-axis.

Answer: $r_{x\text{-axis}}$ or $r_{y\text{-axis}}$

 Practice

1 Does the tangent function have an amplitude? Explain why or why not.

2 Using a domain of $-\dfrac{\pi}{2} \leq x \leq \dfrac{\pi}{2}$, graph the functions $y = \tan x$ and $y = \cos x$ on the same axes.

   a For how many values of x does $\tan x = \cos x$?

   b In what interval(s) do the graphs of both $y = \tan x$ and $y = \cos x$ increase?

3 Graph the functions $y = \tan x$ and $y = \sin x$ on the same axes over the interval $-2\pi \leq x \leq 2\pi$.

   a How many full cycles of the sine curve are present over this domain?

   b How many full cycles of the tangent curve are present over this domain?

   c For how many values of x does $\tan x = \sin x$?

   d In what interval(s) are both $y = \tan x$ and $y = \sin x$ increasing?

4 Graph $y = \tan x$ and $y = \tan 2x$ on the same axes over the interval $0 \le x \le \pi$.

  a What is the period of $y = \tan 2x$?
  b What are the similarities and differences between the two curves?

5 Graph $y = \tan x$ and $y = 2\tan x$ on the same axes over the interval $0 \le x \le \pi$.

  a What is the period of $y = 2\tan x$?
  b What are the similarities and differences between the two curves?

6 Graph $y = \tan \dfrac{1}{2}x$ and $y = \dfrac{1}{2}\tan x$ on the same axes over the interval $0 \le x \le 2\pi$. Describe the similarities and differences between the two curves.

7 Given the graph of $y = \tan\left(x + \dfrac{\pi}{2}\right)$, determine

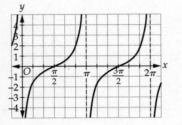

  a the period of the function
  b the domain of the function
  c what transformation was performed on $y = \tan x$ to produce this graph

8 In the interval $[-2\pi, 2\pi]$, give the equations of the asymptotes for the graphs of each of the following curves

  a $y = \tan x$
  b $y = \tan 2x$
  c $y = 2\tan x$
  d $y = \tan \dfrac{1}{2}x$
  e $y = \dfrac{1}{2}\tan x$

9 Based on your answers to Exercise 8, where would you expect to see the asymptotes for the graphs of

  a $y = 3\tan x$?
  b $y = \tan 3x$?
  c $y = \dfrac{1}{3}\tan x$?
  d $y = \tan \dfrac{1}{3}x$?

11.5 Graphs of the Reciprocal Functions

The Cosecant Function

We know that $\csc x = \dfrac{1}{\sin x}$. We will graph the cosecant function by using the reciprocals of the sine function values.

   We start with the values of $\sin x$ at the quadrantal angles and find their reciprocals.

x	0	$\dfrac{\pi}{2}$	π	$\dfrac{3\pi}{2}$	2π
$\sin x$	0	1	0	-1	0
$\csc x$	Undefined	1	Undefined	-1	Undefined

Notice that the cosecant function is undefined when the sine function is zero. Its graph will have vertical asymptotes at these values.

We will determine other values of csc x by using values of sin x that we know.

$$\csc \frac{\pi}{6} = \frac{1}{\sin \frac{\pi}{6}} = \frac{1}{\frac{1}{2}} = 2 \qquad \csc \frac{\pi}{3} = \frac{1}{\sin \frac{\pi}{3}} = \frac{1}{\frac{\sqrt{3}}{2}} \approx 1.15$$

$$\csc \frac{2\pi}{3} = \frac{1}{\sin \frac{2\pi}{3}} = \frac{1}{\frac{\sqrt{3}}{2}} \approx 1.15 \qquad \csc \frac{5\pi}{6} = \frac{1}{\sin \frac{5\pi}{6}} = \frac{1}{\frac{1}{2}} = 2$$

$$\csc \frac{7\pi}{6} = \frac{1}{\sin \frac{7\pi}{6}} = \frac{1}{-\frac{1}{2}} = -2 \qquad \csc \frac{4\pi}{3} = \frac{1}{\sin \frac{4\pi}{3}} = \frac{1}{-\frac{\sqrt{3}}{2}} \approx -1.15$$

$$\csc \frac{5\pi}{3} = \frac{1}{\sin \frac{5\pi}{3}} = \frac{1}{-\frac{\sqrt{3}}{2}} \approx -1.15 \qquad \csc \frac{11\pi}{6} = \frac{1}{\sin \frac{11\pi}{6}} = \frac{1}{-\frac{1}{2}} = -2$$

We see the graph beginning to take shape.

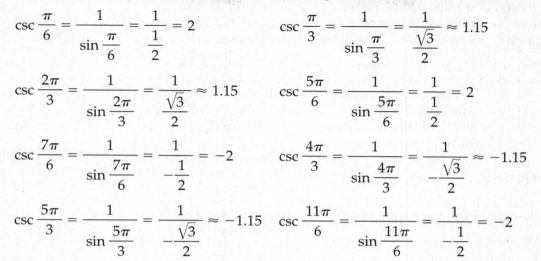

We add the asymptotes and begin to sketch the curve.

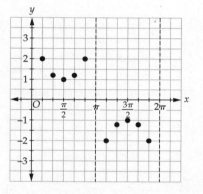

By graphing $y = \csc x$ on the same set of axes as $y = \sin x$, we can see how the two functions are related. For example, $\csc \frac{\pi}{2} = \sin \frac{\pi}{2} = 1$ and $\csc \frac{3\pi}{2} = \sin \frac{3\pi}{2} = -1$. Since $\sin 0 = \sin \pi = \sin 2\pi$ at all of these values, csc x is undefined. From $x = 0$ to $x = \frac{\pi}{2}$, the graph of $y = \sin x$ is increasing. Thus, in this same interval,

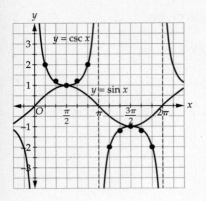

the graph of $y = \csc x$ is decreasing. From $x = \dfrac{\pi}{2}$ to $x = \pi$, the graph of $y = \sin x$ is decreasing. Thus, in this same interval, the graph of $y = \csc x$ is increasing.

As $\sin x$ gets closer and closer to zero, $\csc x = \dfrac{1}{\sin x}$ gets larger and larger ($\sin x > 0$), continuing to increase without bound, or smaller and smaller ($\sin x < 0$), continuing to decrease without bound. These same patterns continue throughout the graph.

The Secant Function

Since $\sec x = \dfrac{1}{\cos x}$, we can graph the secant function by following the same procedure that we used to graph the cosecant function. We start with the values of $\cos x$ at the quadrantal angles and find their reciprocals.

x	0	$\dfrac{\pi}{2}$	π	$\dfrac{3\pi}{2}$	2π
$\cos x$	1	0	-1	0	1
$\sec x$	1	Undefined	-1	Undefined	1

We determine additional values of $\sec x$ by using familiar values of $\cos x$.

$$\sec \frac{\pi}{6} = \frac{1}{\cos \dfrac{\pi}{6}} = \frac{1}{\dfrac{\sqrt{3}}{2}} \approx 1.15 \qquad \sec \frac{\pi}{3} = \frac{1}{\cos \dfrac{\pi}{3}} = \frac{1}{\dfrac{1}{2}} = 2$$

$$\sec \frac{2\pi}{3} = \frac{1}{\cos \dfrac{2\pi}{3}} = \frac{1}{-\dfrac{1}{2}} = -2 \qquad \sec \frac{5\pi}{6} = \frac{1}{\cos \dfrac{5\pi}{6}} = \frac{1}{-\dfrac{\sqrt{3}}{2}} \approx -1.15$$

$$\sec \frac{7\pi}{6} = \frac{1}{\cos \dfrac{7\pi}{6}} = \frac{1}{-\dfrac{\sqrt{3}}{2}} \approx -1.15 \qquad \sec \frac{4\pi}{3} = \frac{1}{\cos \dfrac{4\pi}{3}} = \frac{1}{-\dfrac{1}{2}} = -2$$

$$\sec \frac{5\pi}{3} = \frac{1}{\cos \dfrac{5\pi}{3}} = \frac{1}{\dfrac{1}{2}} = 2 \qquad \sec \frac{11\pi}{6} = \frac{1}{\cos \dfrac{11\pi}{6}} = \frac{1}{\dfrac{\sqrt{3}}{2}} \approx 1.15$$

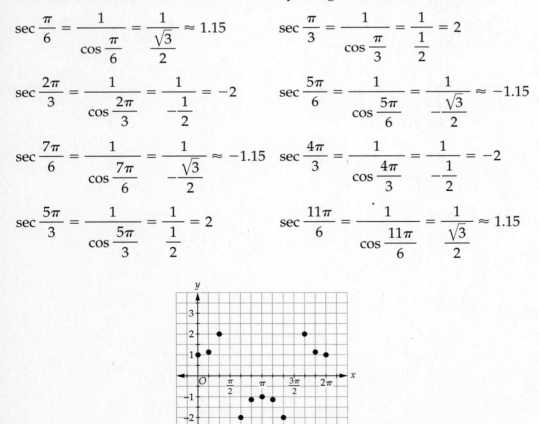

We add the asymptotes and sketch the curve.

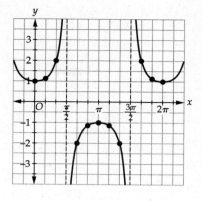

As before, we graph $y = \sec x$ on the same set of axes as $y = \cos x$ to see how the two functions are related. We can see that $\cos 0 = \cos 2\pi = 1$, $\sec 0 = \sec 2\pi = 1$, and $\sec \pi = \cos \pi = -1$. At $x = \dfrac{\pi}{2}$ and $x = \dfrac{3\pi}{2}$, $\cos x = 0$. Thus, at these values, $y = \sec x$ is undefined. Since $\sec x = \dfrac{1}{\cos x}$, as the graph of $y = \cos x$ increases, the graph of $y = \sec x$ decreases, and as the graph of $y = \cos x$ decreases, the graph of $y = \sec x$ increases.

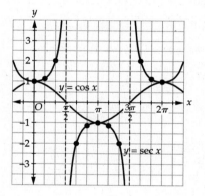

The Cotangent Function

Since $\cot x = \dfrac{1}{\tan x}$, we will graph the cotangent function in the same manner that we graphed the secant and cosecant functions. We begin by filling in values in the table below.

x	0	$\dfrac{\pi}{6}$	$\dfrac{\pi}{4}$	$\dfrac{\pi}{3}$	$\dfrac{\pi}{2}$	$\dfrac{2\pi}{3}$	$\dfrac{3\pi}{4}$	$\dfrac{5\pi}{6}$
$\tan x$	0	$\dfrac{\sqrt{3}}{3} \approx 0.58$	1	$\sqrt{3} \approx 1.7$	U	$-\sqrt{3} \approx -1.7$	-1	$-\dfrac{\sqrt{3}}{3} \approx -0.58$
$\cot x$	U	$\dfrac{3}{\sqrt{3}} = \sqrt{3} \approx 1.7$	1	$\dfrac{1}{\sqrt{3}} = \dfrac{\sqrt{3}}{3} \approx 0.58$	0	$\dfrac{1}{-\sqrt{3}} \approx -0.58$	-1	$\dfrac{-3}{\sqrt{3}} \approx -1.7$

x	π	$\dfrac{7\pi}{6}$	$\dfrac{5\pi}{4}$	$\dfrac{4\pi}{3}$	$\dfrac{3\pi}{2}$	$\dfrac{5\pi}{3}$	$\dfrac{7\pi}{4}$	$\dfrac{11\pi}{6}$	2π
$\tan x$	0	$\dfrac{\sqrt{3}}{3} \approx 0.58$	1	$\sqrt{3} \approx 1.7$	U	$-\sqrt{3} \approx -1.7$	-1	$-\dfrac{\sqrt{3}}{3} \approx -0.58$	0
$\cot x$	U	$\dfrac{3}{\sqrt{3}} \approx 1.7$	1	$\dfrac{1}{\sqrt{3}} \approx 0.58$	0	$\dfrac{1}{-\sqrt{3}} \approx -0.58$	-1	$\dfrac{-3}{\sqrt{3}} \approx -1.7$	U

We add the asymptotes and sketch the curve.

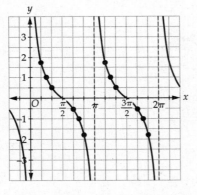

As before, we graph $y = \cot x$ on the same set of axes as $y = \tan x$ to see how the two functions are related. We see that when $y = \tan x = 0$, $y = \cot x$ is undefined. And, when $y = \tan x$ is undefined, $y = \cot x = 0$. As the graph of $y = \tan x$ increases, the graph of $y = \cot x$ decreases, and as the graph of $y = \tan x$ decreases, the graph of $y = \cot x$ increases.

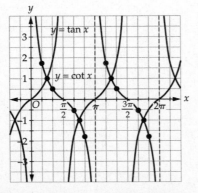

Note: Most calculators do not have the reciprocal functions built in. To graph the reciprocal functions, enter the functions in terms of sine, cosine, and tangent.

For example, to graph $y = \csc x$ in the calculator, go to the ⬚Y=⬚ screen and enter ⬚1⬚ ⬚÷⬚ ⬚SIN⬚ ⬚X,T,θ,n⬚ ⬚)⬚ as shown below.

```
Plot1  Plot2  Plot3
\Y1■1/sin(X)
\Y2=
\Y3=
\Y4=
\Y5=
\Y6=
\Y7=
```

To graph in the calculator's preset trigonometric window, press ⬚ZOOM⬚ ⬚7⬚. You will get the following graph.

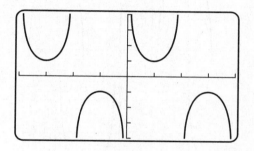

🖩 MODEL PROBLEM

On the same set of axes, graph $y = -\tan x$ and $y = \cot x$ in the interval $[-\pi, \pi]$. How do the functions relate to one another?

SOLUTION

We enter the two functions into the ⬚Y=⬚ screen of the calculator, making $y = \cot x$ or $y = \dfrac{1}{\tan x}$ bold.

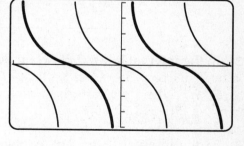

The graph of $y = -\tan x$ is the same as the graph of $y = \cot x$ shifted $\dfrac{\pi}{2}$ units left or right.

1 Without using your calculator, match each graph with its equation. Explain how you arrived at your conclusions.

$$y = \sec x \qquad y = \csc x \qquad y = \tan x \qquad y = \cot x$$

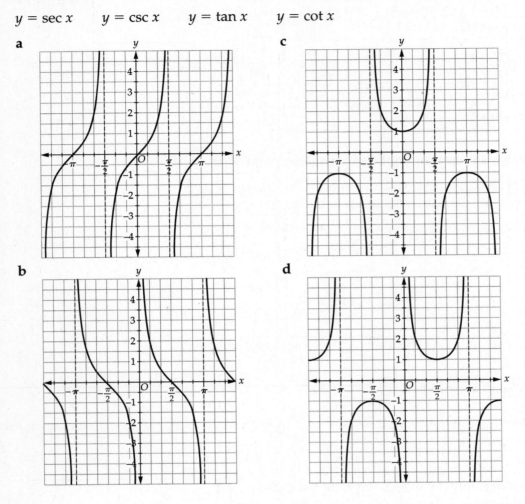

a

c

b

d

2 In the interval $[-2\pi, 2\pi]$, when does

  a $\sin x = \csc x$?

  b $\cos x = \sec x$?

  c $\tan x = \cot x$?

3 In the interval $[-2\pi, 2\pi]$, explain how you would know

  a when the secant, cosecant, and cotangent functions are undefined

  b when the secant, cosecant, and cotangent functions are equal to zero

  c where asymptotes occur for the graphs of the secant, cosecant, and cotangent functions

4 Explain the procedure you would follow to graph

  a $y = 2\sec x$

  b $y = -\csc x$

  c $y = \dfrac{1}{2}\cot x$

5 Name two functions that have asymptotes at

  a $x = \dfrac{\pi}{2}$

  b $x = \pi$

  c $x = \dfrac{3\pi}{2}$

  d $x = 2\pi$

6 a Fill in the blanks in the table, indicating the interval(s) in which the function is increasing and in which it is decreasing.

Interval	$\left(0, \dfrac{\pi}{2}\right)$	$\left(\dfrac{\pi}{2}, \pi\right)$	$\left(\pi, \dfrac{3\pi}{2}\right)$	$\left(\dfrac{3\pi}{2}, 2\pi\right)$
$y = \sin x$	Increasing			
$y = \cos x$				
$y = \tan x$				
$y = \csc x$				
$y = \sec x$				
$y = \cot x$				

b Explain any relationships you see with the various functions.

7 a What are the period, domain, and range of the function $y = \sec x$?
b What are the period, domain, and range of the function $y = \csc x$?

8 What are the period, domain, and range of the function $y = \cot x$?

11.6 Graphs of the Inverse Trigonometric Functions

Consider the function $y = \sin x$ over the interval $[-\pi, \pi]$ as shown below.

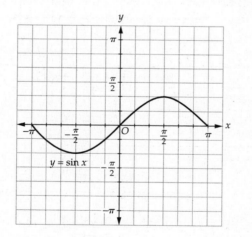

What happens if we reflect this graph in the line $y = x$? We know from our work with transformations that the equation becomes $x = \sin y$, meaning "y is the angle whose sine is x." Now consider the graph of $y = \sin x$ shown in bold below and its reflection in the line $y = x$.

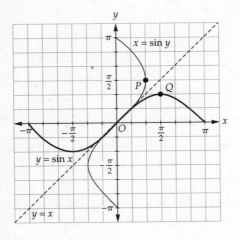

The coordinates of point P are $\left(1, \dfrac{\pi}{2}\right)$, the reflection of point $Q\left(\dfrac{\pi}{2}, 1\right)$ in the line $y = x$. We can say that $\dfrac{\pi}{2}$ is the angle whose sine is 1. This can also be written as $\dfrac{\pi}{2} = \arcsin 1$. The prefix *arc* before a function indicates that we are talking about the angle whose function value follows.

However, in the interval $[-\pi, \pi]$, the reflection of $y = \sin x$ is *not* a function. Remember that a relation is a function if, for each value of x, there is exactly one value of y.

Equation	Meaning	Values in the Interval $[-\pi, \pi]$
$y = \arcsin 0$	y is the angle whose sine is 0.	$y = -\pi, 0, \pi$
$y = \arcsin \dfrac{1}{2}$	y is the angle whose sine is $\dfrac{1}{2}$.	$y = \dfrac{\pi}{6}, \dfrac{5\pi}{6}$
$y = \arcsin \dfrac{\sqrt{2}}{2}$	y is the angle whose sine is $\dfrac{\sqrt{2}}{2}$.	$y = \dfrac{\pi}{4}, \dfrac{3\pi}{4}$

We see that the equation $y = \arcsin 0$ has three solutions: $-\pi$, 0, and π, while each of the other equations has two solutions. When we explore arcsine, arccosine, or arctangent equations, we must remember the rules for the unit circle quadrants in which the values are positive and negative and find those solutions in the appropriate quadrants. In solving the equation $y = \arcsin\left(-\dfrac{1}{2}\right)$, whose original function has the domain $[0, 2\pi]$, we must consider values of y in Quadrants III and IV of the unit circle, since the sine function is negative in both of those quadrants. So $y = \dfrac{7\pi}{6}$ or $\dfrac{11\pi}{6}$.

Now let's consider the graph of the function $y = \sin x$ over the interval $\left[-\dfrac{\pi}{2}, \dfrac{\pi}{2}\right]$, shown in bold in the graph below, and its reflection in the line $y = x$.

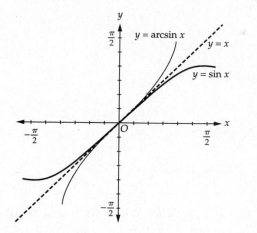

Both the original function and its reflection in the line $y = x$ are functions in this case. Recall the horizontal line test from Chapter 4 (page 130). A function's inverse will also be a function if any horizontal line drawn through the graph of the function intersects it at most once. When the domain is restricted to $\left[-\dfrac{\pi}{2}, \dfrac{\pi}{2}\right]$, $y = \sin x$ is positive in the first quadrant and negative in the third quadrant, and it passes the horizontal line test. Therefore, its inverse, $y = \arcsin x$, is a function in this interval as well. So when we use $\arcsin x$, it is with the understanding that the domain of $y = \sin x$ is restricted to create a one-to-one function. The equation of the inverse of $y = \sin x$ is therefore $y = \arcsin x$, which may also be symbolized $y = \sin^{-1} x$.

Note: $y = \arcsin x$ is a function since its graph would pass the vertical line test.

Below is a graph of $y = \arccos x$ over the interval $[-2\pi, 2\pi]$ and its reflection in $y = x$.

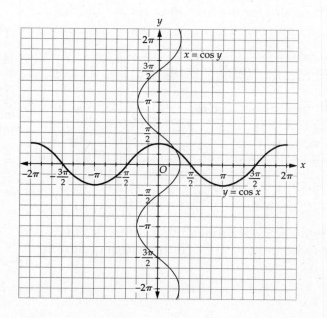

To create the inverse of $y = \cos x$, we limit the domain of the original function to $0 \le x \le \pi$, keeping the cosine function in the first and fourth quadrants where it is first positive and then negative, as shown on page 401. The inverse cosine function is written as $y = \arccos x$ or $y = \cos^{-1} x$.

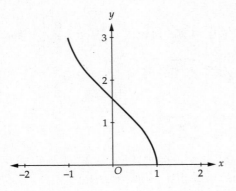

In a similar fashion, the domain of $y = \tan x$ is limited to the first and third quadrants to create an inverse function $y = \arctan x$ or $y = \tan^{-1} x$, as shown below.

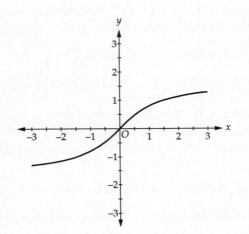

To help you remember the restricted domains for the functions, review the table below.

Function	Limited Domain	Equation of Inverse
$y = \sin x$	$-\dfrac{\pi}{2} \le x \le \dfrac{\pi}{2}$	$y = \arcsin x$ $y = \sin^{-1} x$
$y = \cos x$	$0 \le x \le \pi$	$y = \arccos x$ $y = \cos^{-1} x$
$y = \tan x$	$-\dfrac{\pi}{2} < x < \dfrac{\pi}{2}$	$y = \arctan x$ $y = \tan^{-1} x$

In some courses, capital letters are used to distinguish trigonometric functions with restricted domains. The inverse functions are symbolized

$y = $ Arcsin x or $y = $ Sin^{-1} x

$y = $ Arccos x or $y = $ Cos^{-1} x

$y = $ Arctan x or $y = $ Tan^{-1} x

Note the use of the capital A.

Remember: When solving an arcsine or arctangent problem that contains a negative value, measure the angle in a clockwise motion to reach the fourth-quadrant values.

1 Find the value of sin (arctan 1).

SOLUTION

We must work from inside the parentheses out. In the interval $\left[-\frac{\pi}{2}, \frac{\pi}{2}\right]$, "the angle whose tangent is 1" is $\frac{\pi}{4}$. Then we evaluate $\sin \frac{\pi}{4} = \frac{\sqrt{2}}{2}$.

Answer: $\frac{\sqrt{2}}{2}$

2 If $y = \arcsin\left(-\frac{1}{2}\right)$, then what is the value, in radian measure, of y?

SOLUTION

If $\sin y = -\frac{1}{2}$, we are restricted to Quadrant III, so $y = -\frac{\pi}{6}$.

Answer: $y = -\frac{\pi}{6}$

3 In order to create an inverse of the function $y = \cos x$, in which quadrants must the function fall?

(1) I, II, III, and IV
(2) I and II
(3) I and IV
(4) II and III

SOLUTION

To have only one positive and one negative quadrant for the inverse function, we restrict the domain to Quandrants I and IV, choice (3).

Answer: Choice (3)

Practice

Select the numeral preceding the choice that best completes the statement or answers the question.

1 When the function $y = \cos x$ is reflected in the line $y = x$, the new function is

(1) $y = \sin x$
(2) $y = \arcsin x$
(3) $y = \arccos x$
(4) $x = \arccos y$

2 In which quadrant would θ appear if $\theta = \arctan(-1)$?

(1) I
(2) II
(3) III
(4) IV

3 The value of $\tan^{-1}\left(-\dfrac{\sqrt{3}}{3}\right) - \sin^{-1}\left(\dfrac{\sqrt{2}}{2}\right)$ is

(1) $\dfrac{-2\sqrt{3} - 3\sqrt{2}}{6}$

(2) $-105°$

(3) $-75°$

(4) $255°$

4 Which of the following is a true statement with regard to the reflection of the graph of $y = \sin x$ in the line $y = x$?

(1) Unless the domain of $y = \sin x$ is restricted, the reflection is not a function.

(2) The graph of the reflection of $y = \sin x$ in the line $y = x$ is always a function.

(3) The equation of the graph of the reflection of $y = \sin x$ in the line $y = x$ is $y = \cos x$.

(4) The equation of the graph of the reflection of $y = \sin x$ in the line $y = x$ is $y = \sin(-x)$.

5 The value of $\cot\left(\arctan\left(-\dfrac{\sqrt{5}}{2}\right)\right)$ is which of the following?

(1) { }

(2) $-\dfrac{2\sqrt{5}}{5}$

(3) $\dfrac{2\sqrt{5}}{5}$

(4) $\dfrac{\sqrt{5}}{2}$

6 To obtain its inverse function, the domain of $y = \tan x$ must be restricted to which quadrants?

(1) I and II

(2) II and III

(3) III and IV

(4) I and III

7 The graph below shows which of the following?

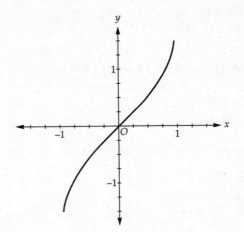

(1) $y = \arcsin x$

(2) $y = \arccos x$

(3) $y = \arctan x$

(4) $y = \arccos(-x)$

8 The value of $\arcsin\left(-\dfrac{\sqrt{3}}{2}\right) + \arcsin\dfrac{1}{2}$ is

(1) $-\dfrac{\pi}{6}$

(2) $\dfrac{\pi}{6}$

(3) $\dfrac{\pi}{3}$

(4) $\dfrac{3\pi}{2}$

9 Find the value of $\cos(\arctan(-1))$.

(1) 1

(2) $\dfrac{\sqrt{2}}{2}$

(3) $\dfrac{1}{2}$

(4) $-\dfrac{\sqrt{2}}{2}$

10 If $2\cos x = -1$, what is the equation of the inverse of this function?

(1) $\sin x = -\dfrac{1}{2}$

(2) $x = 2\arcsin(-1)$

(3) $-\dfrac{1}{2} = \arccos x$

(4) $x = \arccos\left(-\dfrac{1}{2}\right)$

11 Which expression has the same value as $\sin(\arccos(-1))$?

(1) $\cos \pi$

(2) $\csc \dfrac{3\pi}{2}$

(3) $\sec \dfrac{4\pi}{3}$

(4) $\sin 0$

12 If $\theta = \arctan\left(-\sqrt{3}\right)$, the value of θ is

(1) $-60°$
(2) $-30°$
(3) $120°$
(4) $150°$

13 Evaluate $\cos^{-1}(-1) + \sin^{-1}\dfrac{1}{2}$.

(1) $90°$
(2) $120°$
(3) $210°$
(4) $240°$

14 What is the inverse of the function shown below?

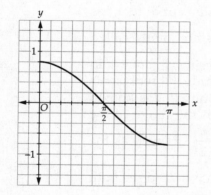

(1) $x = \arcsin y$
(2) $y = \arcsin x$
(3) $x = \arccos y$
(4) $y = \arccos x$

15 Which value does *not* appear in the range of $y = \arctan x$?

(1) $\dfrac{\pi}{2}$

(2) $\dfrac{\pi}{4}$

(3) $-\dfrac{1}{2}$

(4) $-\dfrac{\pi}{3}$

16 Given the function $y = \sin x$, which statement is true?

(1) An inverse will exist if the original function has a domain $-\dfrac{\pi}{2} \le x \le \dfrac{\pi}{2}$.

(2) An inverse will exist if the original function has a domain $-\pi \le x \le \pi$.

(3) An inverse will exist if the original function has a domain $0 \le x \le \pi$.

(4) The domain of the inverse will consist of $-1 \le x \le 2$.

11.7 Trigonometric Graphs and Real-World Applications

Display the graph of $y = \sin x$ in the interval $[0, 2\pi]$. Now consider the graph of $y = \cos x$ under a translation of $T_{\frac{\pi}{2},0}$. To do this on your graphing calculator rather than by hand, enter the equation $y = \cos\left(x - \dfrac{\pi}{2}\right)$ in Y_2. Then left arrow past Y_2

until the cursor is to the left of the equal sign. Press (ENTER) four times until your (Y=) screen looks like the one below. The graph of the second equation will create a path.

```
 Plot1  Plot2  Plot3
\Y1∎sin(X)
-□Y2∎cos(X-π/2)
\Y3=
\Y4=
\Y5=
\Y6=
\Y7=
```

Press (GRAPH) and look at the resulting graph:

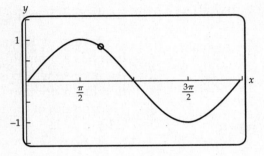

You see only one graph because a cosine curve is simply a sine curve that has been shifted $\dfrac{\pi}{2}$ to the right. Therefore, sine and cosine curves are jointly called **sinusoidal** functions. A **sinusoid** is a function in the form $y = a\sin b(x - c) + d$ in which a, b, c, and d are real numbers and $|a|$ represents amplitude, $|b|$ represents frequency, c is a horizontal shift, and d is a vertical shift. The line $y = d$ is known as the **midline** since this is a horizontal line midway through the range of the function. The graph below shows the function $y = \cos\left(x - \dfrac{\pi}{2}\right)$ as well as the function $y = \cos\left(x - \dfrac{\pi}{2}\right) + 1$. We made Ymin $= -2$ and Ymax $= 2$ to see both curves. Clearly the function $y = \cos\left(x - \dfrac{\pi}{2}\right) + 1$ is the original equation shifted upward one unit.

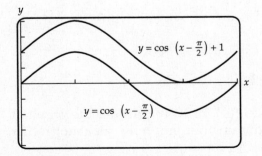

Real-life situations in which the rise and fall of values are periodic over a given interval are often modeled by sinusoidal functions.

MODEL PROBLEM

The occurrence of sunspots during the month of September 2001 can be approximated by the function $y = 148 + 44.2\sin\left(\dfrac{\pi}{7.83}(x - 2.9908)\right)$ in which x represents the day of the month.

a Graph this function for September. According to this model, what is the maximum and minimum number of sunspots that occurred?

b What is the average number of sunspots for the month? What element of the function indicates this average?

c How many cycles of sunspots occurred in September?

SOLUTION

a Enter the equation in Y_1. Graph in the window Xmin = 0, Xmax = 30 (30 days in September), Ymin = 0, and Ymax = 200 (greater than 148 + 44.2 = 192.2). Use the maximum and minimum functions of the CALC menu (2nd TRACE) to identify the highest and lowest values: 192.2 and 103.8.

b The average number of sunspots is 148, the value added to the sine function, the midline. Since our sine curve begins and ends on the midline, it represents the average value of the function.

c Look at the graph and you will see two cycles of the function (or divide 2π by the frequency, $\dfrac{\pi}{7.83}$, which equals a period of 15.66). This means that there were approximately two cycles in the 30 days of September.

Practice

Exercises 1–4: Select the numeral preceding the choice that best completes the statement or answers the question.

1 Liam's grandfather's clock has a pendulum that moves from its central position at rest according to the trigonometric function $P(t) = -3.5\sin\left(\dfrac{\pi}{2}t\right)$ where t represents the time in seconds. How many seconds does it take the pendulum to complete one full cycle from rest at the center to the left and then to the right and back to rest?

(1) 1 second
(2) 2 seconds
(3) 3.5 seconds
(4) 4 seconds

2 An oscilloscope is a machine that changes sound waves into electric impulses and shows their graph on a monitor. One such graph can be represented by the equation $A(t) = 12\sin\left(\dfrac{2\pi}{15}t\right)$ where t represents time in seconds. The period of this function is

(1) 12 seconds
(2) 15 seconds
(3) 18 seconds
(4) 30 seconds

3 Musical notes can be represented by the trigonometric function $y = \sin(2\pi qx)$ where q is the frequency of the note and x is the time in seconds that the note is played. The equation $y = 1.5\sin(524\pi t)$, where t represents time in seconds, represents a sound wave produced by the note middle C. What is the value of q, the musical frequency of middle C?

(1) 1.5
(2) 262
(3) 262π
(4) 524π

4 The voltage E of an alternating current electrical circuit can be represented by the sinusoidal function $E = 220\cos(\pi t)$ where E is measured in volts and t is measured in seconds. How long does it take the alternating current to complete one full cycle?

(1) 1 second
(2) 2 seconds
(3) π seconds
(4) 220 seconds

5 Sales of snow removal equipment approximate a trigonometric function. In fact, sales of snow blowers, in the hundreds of units, at one chain of hardware stores can be modeled by the function $j(x) = 4\cos\left(\dfrac{\pi}{6}x\right) + 4$ where x (an integer) represents time in months with $x = 0$ corresponding to January 1.

a When are sales the lowest? The highest?
b If the store's profit is \$79.00 for each snow blower, what is the income from snow blowers on February 1?
c Air conditioner sales at this chain of stores can be represented by the function
$$a(x) = -3\sin\left(\dfrac{\pi}{6}(x + 3.8197)\right) + 3.5$$
where $a(x)$ represents the number of air conditioners in hundreds sold and x represents the time in months with $x = 0$ corresponding to January 1. When are air conditioner sales the highest and lowest?
d When are an equal number of air conditioners and snow blowers sold?
e If the average profit on each air conditioner is \$49.00, what is the maximum profit?

6 Ethel Mermaid, the president of the South Hampton Swimming Pool Company, is studying the company's sales over the course of a year.

a If Ethel's company is located in Riverhead, New York, which equation would you expect to be a possible model for $S(t)$, the number of swimming pools sold, as a function of time, t (an integer), each month since December 31? Explain your answer.

(1) $S(t) = 200\cos\left(\dfrac{\pi}{6}t\right) + 300$

(2) $S(t) = -200\cos\left(\dfrac{\pi}{6}t\right) + 300$

(3) $S(t) = 200\sin\left(\dfrac{\pi}{6}t\right) + 300$

(4) $S(t) = -200\sin\left(\dfrac{\pi}{6}t\right) + 300$

b Using your answer from part **a**, what are the sales as of January 31?
c When does the company sell the most pools? How many pools do they sell that month?
d During which month(s) does the company sell 250 pools?

7 The number of hours of daylight in New York varies sinusoidally throughout the course of a year. The equation $y = -2.786\cos(0.017t) + 12.14$ could be used to model the number of hours of daylight in New York, where t (an integer) is the time in days since December 21.

a To the nearest tenth, approximately how many hours of daylight are there on February 22?
b On what day(s) are there approximately 12 hours of daylight?
c Based on the equation, when is there the least amount of daylight? What does this date represent? How many hours of daylight are there?

8 The depth of the water on the shore of a beach varies as the tide goes in and out. The equation $D(t) = 0.75\cos\left(\dfrac{\pi}{6}x\right) + 1.5$ could be used to model the depth of the water, $D(t)$, in feet, as a function of time, t, in hours for one day. Let $t = 0$ at midnight.

a What is the amplitude of the equation? What does that mean in terms of the tide?

b What is the period of the equation? What does that mean in terms of the tide?

c In how many hours after $t = 0$ will the tide be at its lowest?

d How deep will the water be 2 hours after the high tide?

e When will the water be 2 feet deep?

9 The temperature in Syracuse varies throughout the year. A sinusoidal equation provides a good model for the average temperature as a function of the month of the year. The equation $f(t) = -24.0321\cos(0.5030t) + 47.3635$ represents the average Fahrenheit temperature in Syracuse as a function of time, t (an integer), in months with $t = 0$ representing the month of January.

a To the *nearest degree*, what is the average temperature in January? In February?

b During which month does the temperature reach its highest point? What does the temperature average during that month?

c What is the "average" temperature, to the *nearest degree*, in Syracuse over the course of a year?

d During which month(s) is the temperature in Syracuse "average"?

e What is the amplitude of this equation? What does it represent in terms of the temperature in Syracuse?

10 Captain Freeze discovered that profits from his neighborhood ice cream truck business could be modeled by a periodic function that had greatest values during the warm months of the year. After studying his records for a four-year period, he found that his profits could be modeled by the function $P(t) = -720\cos\left(\dfrac{\pi}{26}(x - 103.45)\right) + 215$, where $P(t)$ is expressed in dollars and t (an integer) represents time in weeks with $t = 0$ corresponding the first week in January.

a What is the range of the function? What does that mean in practical terms to Captain Freeze?

b What is the period of the graph? What does this mean in practical terms?

c During what week of the year does Captain Freeze earn his maximum profit? What is this maximum profit?

d During what time period does Captain Freeze's business lose money?

e Compare the number of weeks Captain Freeze loses money and the number of weeks he makes money. Over the course of the full year, is the captain's business profitable? Defend your answer.

f Based on months of profit and loss, in what part of the U.S. might Captain Freeze live? Why do you think so?

Since the unit circle is not a function, we cannot graph it in function mode on our calculators. However, the TI-83/84+ calculators have a parametric mode that will enable us to graph the unit circle. Press (MODE) and you will obtain the following screen:

```
Normal  Sci  Eng
Float   0123456789
Radian  Degree
Func  Par  Pol  Seq
Connected  Dot
Sequential  Simul
Real  a+bi  re^θi
      Horiz  G-T
```

Scroll down and highlight Par as shown on the screen above. Now press (ENTER) (Y=) and the following screen will appear without the functions.

```
 Plot1  Plot2  Plot3
\X1T■cos(T)
 Y1T■sin(T)
\X2T=
 Y2T=
\X3T=
 Y3T=
\X4T=
```

Instead of expressing *y* as a function of *x*, in parametric mode both *x* and *y* are functions of another variable, *T*. Enter the information as shown in the screen above. To obtain the *T*, press (X,T,θ,n). Since we are in parametric mode, the *T* will appear on your screen. (The *x* appears only when you are in function mode.) To obtain the graph of this information, we need to set a suitable window. Press (WINDOW) and set your window as shown.

```
WINDOW
 Tmin=0
 Tmax=6.2831853...
 Tstep=.1308996...
 Xmin=-1.5
 Xmax=1.5
 Xscl=1
↓Ymin=-1.5■
```

```
WINDOW
↑Tstep=.1308996...
 Xmin=-1.5
 Xmax=1.5
 Xscl=1
 Ymin=-1.5
 Ymax=1.5
 Yscl=1■
```

410   Chapter 11: Graphs of Trigonometric Functions

Since x and y are both functions of T, to see a complete cycle we need to set the T-values to go from 0 to 2π. Although you should enter 2π for Tmax, the calculator will convert it to its decimal equivalent.

We want to plot points with increments of $\dfrac{\pi}{24}$, so we set Tstep $= \dfrac{\pi}{24}$. Again, the calculator will convert this to its decimal equivalent.

When you graph the equations you will obtain a graph that looks elliptical. This is because your screen is wider than it is high. To adjust for the differences, press (ZOOM) (5) and you will obtain the following graph.

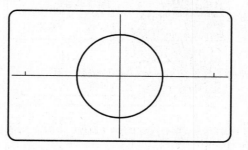

If you now check your window, you will see that the Xmin and Xmax have been adjusted to "square off" the window.

```
WINDOW
↑Tstep=.1308996...
 Xmin=-2.274193...
 Xmax=2.2741935...
 Xscl=1
 Ymin=-1.5
 Ymax=1.5
 Yscl=1
```

We can now see how the unit circle operates. Press (TRACE) and enter various values for T. If you enter $\dfrac{\pi}{6}$ for T, you will obtain the following screen.

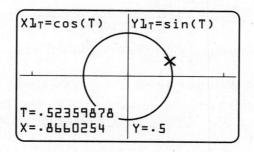

Notice that the calculator converted $\dfrac{\pi}{6}$ to its decimal equivalent. You should recall that $\cos\dfrac{\pi}{6} = \dfrac{\sqrt{3}}{2}$ and $\sin\dfrac{\pi}{6} = \dfrac{1}{2}$. Notice that these appear as the x- and y-values (written as their decimal equivalents). Continue moving around the unit circle, looking at the various values.

Let's "unwrap" the unit circle to show the graph of the sine and cosine curves as a function of the angle. Go back into (MODE) and change from Sequential graphing to Simultaneous graphing as shown below:

```
Normal  Sci  Eng
Float   0123456789
Radian  Degree
Func  Par  Pol  Seq
Connected  Dot
Sequential  Simul
Real  a+bi  re^θi
Full  Horiz  G-T
```

We want to graph y as a function of T. First, press (Y=) and set $X_{2T} = T$. Then, let $Y_{2T} = \cos T$.

```
 Plot1  Plot2  Plot3
\X1T=cos(T)
 Y1T=sin(T)
\X2T=T
 Y2T=cos(T)
\X3T=■
 Y3T=
\X4T=
```

Since $x = T$ and $x = \cos T$, to see the complete curve we have to adjust our window to include values of x up to 2π. Set Xmax = 2π. If we graph at this point, we will again get an elliptical shape. So we must press (ZOOM) (5). Now if we look at the window, we would see the following:

```
WINDOW
↑Tstep=.1308996...
 Xmin=-2.274193...
 Xmax=6.2831853...
 Xscl=1
 Ymin=-2.822114...
 Ymax=2.8221143...
 Yscl=1■
```

This enables you to see the graph with its proper proportions. Notice how the circle "unwraps" to show the cosine curve.

As you are graphing, press (ENTER) when the circle reaches the y-axis. (Pressing (ENTER) will pause the graph.) By looking at the cosine curve, you can see that $\cos T = 0$. Press (ENTER) and allow the graph to continue until the circle touches the x-axis. Continue along, pausing the graph to study it more closely. Notice how you can see that $\cos \pi = -1$.

When the unit circle completely unwraps, you should have the following graph:

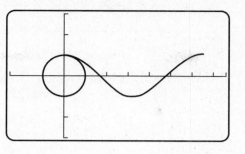

Now graph $y = \sin T$ and follow the same procedure.

CHAPTER REVIEW

Exercises 1–23: Write the numeral preceding the choice that best completes the statement or answers the question.

1 Find the value of $\cos\left(\arcsin \dfrac{1}{2}\right)$.

(1) $\dfrac{1}{2}$

(2) $\dfrac{\pi}{6}$

(3) $\dfrac{\sqrt{3}}{2}$

(4) $\dfrac{\pi}{3}$

2 Which is an equation of the graph shown below?

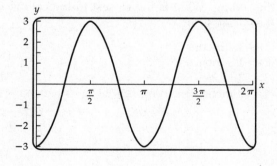

(1) $y = -3\cos \dfrac{1}{2}x$

(2) $y = 3\sin 2x$
(3) $y = -3\sin 2x$
(4) $y = -3\cos 2x$

3 Which graph is symmetric across the y-axis?

(1) $y = \sin x$
(2) $y = \cos x$
(3) $y = \tan x$
(4) $y = \cot x$

4 What is the minimum value of the function $f(x) = \csc x$?

(1) 1
(2) 0
(3) -1
(4) There is no minimum value.

5 What is the period of the graph whose equation is $y = 3\cos 2x$?

(1) π
(2) 2
(3) 3
(4) 2π

6 What is the amplitude of the graph whose equation is $y = -2\sin 4x$?

(1) π
(2) 2
(3) -2
(4) 4

7 $\arcsin \dfrac{1}{2} + \arccos \dfrac{\sqrt{3}}{2} =$

(1) $\arctan\left(\dfrac{1}{2} + \dfrac{\sqrt{3}}{2}\right)$

(2) 1.366
(3) $60°$
(4) $90°$

8 What is the range for $y = 5\sin x$?

(1) $0 \le x \le 2\pi$
(2) $0 \le y \le 2\pi$
(3) $-1 \le y \le 1$
(4) $-5 \le y \le 5$

9 The domain for $y = \arcsin x$ is

(1) $-1 \le x \le 1$
(2) $0 \le x \le \pi$
(3) $-\dfrac{\pi}{2} \le x \le \dfrac{\pi}{2}$
(4) $-\pi \le x \le \pi$

10 If the graph $y = \cos x$ is reflected in the x-axis, the equation of the image is

(1) $y = \sin x$
(2) $y = \tan x$
(3) $y = -\cos x$
(4) $y = \cos(-x)$

11 The transformation $T_{\frac{\pi}{2}, 0}$ maps $y = \sin x$ to

(1) $y = \cos x$
(2) $y = -\cos x$
(3) $y = -\sin x$
(4) $y = \dfrac{\pi}{2}\sin x$

12 What is the minimum value of the range of $y = 3 + 2\sin x$?

(1) 1
(2) 0
(3) -1
(4) -5

13 Which of the following is equivalent to $\sec x$?

(1) $\cos^{-1} x$
(2) $\dfrac{1}{\cos x}$
(3) both (1) and (2)
(4) None are true.

14 As θ increases from $\dfrac{\pi}{2}$ to $\dfrac{3\pi}{2}$, the value of $\sin \theta$

(1) increases only
(2) decreases only
(3) increases and then decreases
(4) decreases and then increases

15 For which value of θ is $\tan \theta$ undefined?

(1) 0
(2) $\dfrac{\pi}{2}$
(3) π
(4) It is never undefined.

16 Which function has the same period as $y = 4\cos 2x$?

(1) $y = 4\cos x$
(2) $y = 4\sin x$
(3) $y = \tan x$
(4) $y = \tan 2x$

17 What is the value of $\tan\left(\arccos \dfrac{\sqrt{2}}{2}\right)$?

(1) 1
(2) $\dfrac{\pi}{4}$
(3) $-\dfrac{\sqrt{2}}{2}$
(4) -1

18 If $f(x) = \sin x$ and $g(x) = \cos x$, for what value(s) of x is $f(x) = g(x)$?

(1) 0
(2) $\dfrac{\pi}{4}$ and $\dfrac{3\pi}{4}$
(3) $\dfrac{\pi}{4}$
(4) $\dfrac{3\pi}{4}$

19 The motion of a spring can be modeled by the equation $y = 1.6\cos(\pi x) + 3$, where x represents the number of seconds the spring is oscillating and y is the distance, in inches, of the spring from the ceiling. What is the closest to the ceiling that the spring gets?

(1) 1.4 inches
(2) 1.6 inches
(3) 3 inches
(4) 0 inches

20 In the graph of $y = a\sin bx$ with $a > 0$, as a increases,

    (1)   the period increases
    (2)   the period decreases
    (3)   the range increases
    (4)   the range decreases

21 Which function is undefined at $x = \dfrac{\pi}{2}$?

    (1) $y = \sin x$
    (2) $y = \sec x$
    (3) $y = \csc x$
    (4) $y = \cot x$

22 Which statement is true about the graph of $y = \sec \theta$?

    (1)   The y-intercept is $(0, 0)$.

    (2)   It is undefined at $\dfrac{\pi}{2}$.

    (3)   The range is all real numbers.
    (4)   The domain is all real numbers.

23 What is the maximum value of the function $f(x) = 12 - 3\sin\left(\dfrac{3\pi}{2}x\right)$?

    (1)   9
    (2)   12
    (3)   15
    (4) $12 - 3\pi$

24 **a** On the same set of axes, sketch the graphs of $y = 2\cos\dfrac{1}{2}x$ and $y = -\sin x$ in the interval $0 \le x \le 2\pi$.

    b Give the exact value(s) of the coordinates of the intersection point(s) of the two graphs.

    c From the graphs drawn in part **a**, find the exact value of x that satisfies the equation $2\cos\dfrac{1}{2}x + \sin(x) = 0$.

25 **a** What is the period of the graph $y = 3\cos 2x$?
    b Sketch the graph of $y = 3\cos 2x$ for one period.
    c What are the exact values of the x-intercept(s) of the graph drawn in part **b**?
    d On the same set of axes, sketch the image of the graph drawn in part **b** under $r_{x\text{-axis}}$ and label the graph **c**.
    e Write an equation for the graph drawn in part **d**.

26 **a** On the same set of axes, sketch the graphs of $y = -2\cos x$ and $y = \tan x$ in the interval $0 \le x \le \pi$.
    b From the graphs drawn in part **a**, find the exact value of x that satisfies the equation $\tan x + 2\cos x = 2$.
    c From the graphs drawn in part **a**, find the exact value of x that satisfies the equation $-2\cos x - \tan x = 2$.
    d For what value(s) of x in the interval $0 \le x \le \pi$ is $\tan x$ undefined?

27 **a** Sketch the graph of $y = \sin\dfrac{1}{2}x$ in the interval $-\pi \le x \le \pi$.
    b On the same set of axes, sketch graph of the transformation of the graph drawn in part **a** under $T_{\pi,0}$ and label it **b**.
    c Write an equation for the graph drawn in part **b**.

28 Stephanie has observed that the number of squirrels she sees varies sinusoidally over the course of a year. She found that the equation $S(t) = -30\cos\left(\dfrac{\pi}{6}x\right) + 50$ provided a good model for the number of squirrels, $S(t)$, Stephanie sees per month, where t (an integer) represents the number of months since December 1.

    a When did Stephanie see the most squirrels?
    b How many squirrels did she see then?
    c What is the number of squirrels that Stephanie saw on March 1? On May 1?

29 The graph below shows part of a track for a roller coaster.

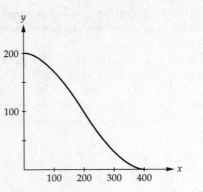

The roller coaster covers a horizontal distance of 400 feet as it descends a vertical distance of 200 feet.

a What kind of function does this appear to be?

b What is the period of the function? (Hint: Only half the curve is shown on this graph.)

c Since period $= \dfrac{2\pi}{\text{frequency}}$ and frequency $= \dfrac{2\pi}{\text{period}}$, what is the frequency of this curve?

d How high does the roller coaster go? Where is its midline (the line midway up the graph)?

e If we define amplitude as the distance from the midline to the highest point on the graph, what is the amplitude?

f To write an equation to model this graph, we use the equation $y = a\cos(bx) + d$, where a is the amplitude, b is the frequency, and d is the vertical shift (the midline). Write an equation of the curve that will model this graph.

30 The graph below represents the number of visitors, in hundreds of thousands, to Calculus Canyon each month for a year. If the equation is of the form $y = a\sin(bx) + d$, determine the values of a, b, and d and write an equation to model the function.

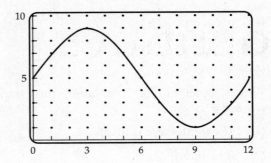

Trigonometric Identities

12.1 Proving Trigonometric Identities

As we said in Chapter 10, an identity is an equation that is true for all values of the variable for which the equation is defined. At that time we explored the reciprocal, quotient, and Pythagorean identities that we know to be true statements defining special relationships.

Reciprocal Identities	Quotient Identities	Pythagorean Identities
$\sec \theta = \dfrac{1}{\cos \theta}$	$\tan \theta = \dfrac{\sin \theta}{\cos \theta}$	$\sin^2 \theta + \cos^2 \theta = 1$
$\csc \theta = \dfrac{1}{\sin \theta}$	$\cot \theta = \dfrac{\cos \theta}{\sin \theta}$	$\tan^2 \theta + 1 = \sec^2 \theta$
$\cot \theta = \dfrac{1}{\tan \theta}$		$1 + \cot^2 \theta = \csc^2 \theta$

Now we will be deciding whether or not a given statement is an identity. As with evaluating trigonometric expressions, our primary tool will be substitution. Our goal in all cases is to make the left side of the statement exactly match the right. To do this, it is important to remember that *you are not solving an equation.* Rather, you are determining the validity of a trigonometric statement. Therefore, you cannot add, subtract, multiply, or divide terms on both sides of the equation as you would do if you were using algebra to solve an equation. When you prove an identity, you must work straight down on one or both sides of the equation, never crossing the equal sign for any purpose. To be clear: you are *not* solving an equation; you are simply checking that the identity is true.

The following are a few tips for proving identities:

- You want to make the left and right hand sides of the identities match by *substitution* and *cancellation*.
- Work with the more complicated side of the identity.
- Begin by writing all expressions in terms of $\sin \theta$ and/or $\cos \theta$.
- If there is a squared term, check to see if you can use one of the Pythagorean identities. If so, use it to replace the squared term.
- You are finished when the left side of the identity *exactly* matches the right side.

1 Prove that $\dfrac{\cos \theta + 1}{1 + \sec \theta} = \cos \theta$ is an identity.

SOLUTION

$$\dfrac{\cos \theta + 1}{1 + \sec \theta} \overset{?}{=} \cos \theta$$

$$\dfrac{\cos \theta + 1}{1 + \dfrac{1}{\cos \theta}} \overset{?}{=} \cos \theta \qquad \text{Write } \sec \theta \text{ in terms of } \cos \theta.$$

$$\dfrac{\cos \theta + 1}{\dfrac{\cos \theta + 1}{\cos \theta}} \overset{?}{=} \cos \theta \qquad \text{Simplify the complex fraction.}$$

$$\dfrac{\cancel{\cos \theta + 1}}{1} \cdot \dfrac{\cos \theta}{\cancel{\cos \theta + 1}} \overset{?}{=} \cos \theta \qquad \text{Multiply by the reciprocal of the denominator.}$$

$$\cos \theta = \cos \theta \; ✔ \qquad \text{Simplify.}$$

Since you have now simplified the entire left side of the identity to equal $\cos \theta$, you know that $\dfrac{\cos \theta + 1}{1 + \sec \theta} = \cos \theta$ is, indeed, an identity.

2 Prove that $\tan^2 \theta \,(1 - \sin^2 \theta) = 1 - \cos^2 \theta$ is an identity.

SOLUTION

In this case, notice that we have squared terms, so we can substitute the Pythagorean identities for $1 - \cos^2 \theta$ and $1 - \sin^2 \theta$.

$$\tan^2 \theta \,(1 - \sin^2 \theta) \overset{?}{=} 1 - \cos^2 \theta$$

$$\tan^2 \theta \cdot \cos^2 \theta \overset{?}{=} \sin^2 \theta \qquad \text{Substitute the Pythagorean identities.}$$

$$\dfrac{\sin^2 \theta}{\cancel{\cos^2 \theta}} \cdot \cancel{\cos^2 \theta} \overset{?}{=} \sin^2 \theta \qquad \text{Replace } \tan^2 \theta \text{ with its } \dfrac{\sin}{\cos} \text{ equivalent (quotient identity).}$$

$$\sin^2 \theta = \sin^2 \theta \; ✔ \qquad \text{Cancel common terms.}$$

3 Prove that the following is an identity: $\dfrac{\tan x \cdot \csc^2 x}{1 + \tan^2 x} = \cot x$

SOLUTION

There is often more than one approach to proving an identity.

Method 1

In this method, we will use the Pythagorean identities to replace the denominator.

$$\frac{\tan x \cdot \csc^2 x}{1 + \tan^2 x} \stackrel{?}{=} \cot x$$

$$\frac{\tan x \cdot \csc^2 x}{\sec^2 x} \stackrel{?}{=} \cot x$$

$$\frac{\dfrac{\sin x}{\cos x} \cdot \dfrac{1}{\sin^2 x}}{\dfrac{1}{\cos^2 x}} \stackrel{?}{=} \frac{\cos x}{\sin x} \qquad \text{Use reciprocal and quotient identities.}$$

$$\frac{\dfrac{1}{\cos x \sin x}}{\dfrac{1}{\cos^2 x}} \stackrel{?}{=} \frac{\cos x}{\sin x} \qquad \text{Cancel as appropriate.}$$

$$\frac{1}{\cos x \sin x} \cdot \frac{\cos^2 x}{1} \stackrel{?}{=} \frac{\cos x}{\sin x} \qquad \text{Multiply by the reciprocal of the denominator.}$$

$$\frac{\cos x}{\sin x} = \frac{\cos x}{\sin x} \checkmark \qquad \text{Cancel as appropriate.}$$

Method 2

In this case, we will replace all quotient and reciprocal identities at once.

$$\frac{\tan x \cdot \csc x^2}{1 + \tan^2 x} \stackrel{?}{=} \cot x$$

$$\frac{\dfrac{\sin x}{\cos x} \cdot \dfrac{1}{\sin^2 x}}{1 + \dfrac{\sin^2 x}{\cos^2 x}} \stackrel{?}{=} \frac{\cos x}{\sin x}$$

$$\frac{\dfrac{1}{\cos x \sin x}}{\dfrac{\cos^2 x + \sin^2 x}{\cos^2 x}} \stackrel{?}{=} \frac{\cos x}{\sin x} \qquad \text{Simplify the complex fraction.}$$

$$\frac{\dfrac{1}{\cos x \sin x}}{\dfrac{1}{\cos^2 x}} \stackrel{?}{=} \frac{\cos x}{\sin x} \qquad \text{Replace } \cos^2 x + \sin^2 x \text{ with 1.}$$

$$\frac{1}{\cos x \sin x} \cdot \frac{\cos^2 x}{1} \stackrel{?}{=} \frac{\cos x}{\sin x} \qquad \text{Simplify.}$$

$$\frac{\cos x}{\sin x} = \frac{\cos x}{\sin x} \checkmark$$

As long as you do not cross the equal sign or use incorrect substitutions, you may prove the identities in any way you choose.

Prove that each expression is an identity.

1 $\sin^2 \theta + \cot^2 \theta + \cos^2 \theta = \csc^2 \theta$

2 $\sec^2 \theta (1 - \cos^2 \theta) = \tan^2 \theta$

3 $\dfrac{1 - \sin^2 \theta}{\sin \theta} \cdot \sec \theta = \cot \theta$

4 $\dfrac{\sin^2 \theta - \cos^2 \theta + 1}{2\sin \theta \cos \theta} = \tan \theta$

5 $\dfrac{\sec \theta}{\sin \theta} - \dfrac{\sin \theta}{\cos \theta} = \cot \theta$

6 $(1 + \cos \theta)(1 - \cos \theta) = \sin^2 \theta$

7 $\cos^2 \theta (\tan^2 \theta + 1) + \cot^2 \theta = \csc^2 \theta$

8 $\dfrac{1}{\sin^2 \beta} + \dfrac{1}{\cos^2 \beta} = \sec^2 \beta \csc^2 \beta$

9 $\csc \theta - (\cos \theta)(\cot \theta) = \sin \theta$

10 $2 - \dfrac{1 - \cos^2 \theta}{\tan^2 \theta} = \sin^2 \theta + 1$

12.2 Sum and Difference of Angles

To find the sine of the sum of two angles, we cannot simply add the sines of the two angles. For example, $\sin (30° + 60°) = \sin (90°) = 1$ is very different from $\sin 30° + \sin 60° = \dfrac{1}{2} + \dfrac{\sqrt{3}}{2}$. We have a formula for the sine of the sum of two angles. We also have formulas for the cosine and tangent of the sum of two angles. Those formulas are found below.

Functions of the Sum of Two Angles

$\sin (A + B) = \sin A \cos B + \cos A \sin B$

$\cos (A + B) = \cos A \cos B - \sin A \sin B$

$\tan (A + B) = \dfrac{\tan A + \tan B}{1 - \tan A \tan B}$

We can check our example using our formula. We get

$$\sin (30° + 60°) = \sin 30° \cos 60° + \cos 30° \sin 60°$$

$$= \left(\frac{1}{2}\right)\left(\frac{1}{2}\right) + \left(\frac{\sqrt{3}}{2}\right)\left(\frac{\sqrt{3}}{2}\right)$$

$$= \frac{1}{4} + \frac{3}{4}$$

$$= 1$$

The following formulas are used to compute the functions of the difference of two angles.

Remember:
$\sin (A + B) \neq$
$\sin A + \sin B$
To compute sin
$(A + B)$, you must
use the formula
for the sine of the
sum of two angles.

Functions of the Difference of Two Angles

$$\sin (A - B) = \sin A \cos B - \cos A \sin B$$

$$\cos (A - B) = \cos A \cos B + \sin A \sin B$$

$$\tan (A - B) = \frac{\tan A - \tan B}{1 + \tan A \tan B}$$

MODEL PROBLEMS

1 $\cos 120° \cos 30° + \sin 120° \sin 30°$ is equivalent to which of the following?

(1) 1

(2) $\dfrac{1}{2}$

(3) 0

(4) $-\dfrac{\sqrt{3}}{2}$

SOLUTION

You are expected to recognize $\cos 120° \cos 30° + \sin 120° \sin 30°$ as the cosine of the difference of two angles. Therefore,

$$\cos 120° \cos 30° + \sin 120° \sin 30° = \cos (120° - 30°)$$
$$= \cos 90°$$
$$= 0$$

Answer: Choice (3)

2 If $\sin x = \dfrac{3}{5}$ and $\cos y = \dfrac{5}{13}$, and x and y are positive acute angles, find $\cos (x + y)$.

SOLUTION

Use the formula for the cosine of a sum:

$$\cos (x + y) = \cos x \cos y - \sin x \sin y$$

Since you must use the sine and cosine functions of each of the angles in the formula, you need to compute the missing functions: $\cos x$ and $\sin y$. You could either use a trigonometric identity or apply the Pythagorean theorem in a right triangle. We will use a trigonometric identity here and illustrate the second option in the next model problem.

We know that $\sin x = \dfrac{3}{5}$ and x is a positive acute angle.

$\sin^2 x + \cos^2 x = 1$

$\left(\dfrac{3}{5}\right)^2 + \cos^2 x = 1$ Use the Pythagorean identity.

$\cos^2 x = 1 - \left(\dfrac{3}{5}\right)^2$ Solve for $\cos x$.

$\cos^2 x = \dfrac{16}{25}$ Combine like terms.

$\cos x = \pm\dfrac{4}{5}$ Take the square root of both sides.

$\cos x = \dfrac{4}{5}$ Since x is a positive acute angle, choose the positive value.

Follow the same procedure to obtain $\sin y$.

We know that $\cos y = \dfrac{5}{13}$, and y is a positive acute angle.

$\sin^2 y + \cos^2 y = 1$

$\sin^2 y + \left(\dfrac{5}{13}\right)^2 = 1$ Use the Pythagorean identity.

$\sin^2 y = 1 - \left(\dfrac{5}{13}\right)^2$ Solve for $\sin y$.

$\sin^2 y = \dfrac{144}{169}$ Combine like terms.

$\sin y = \pm\dfrac{12}{13}$ Take the square root of both sides.

$\sin y = \dfrac{12}{13}$ Since y is a positive acute angle, choose the positive value.

Substitute the above information into the sum formula.

$\cos(x + y) = \cos x \cos y - \sin x \sin y$

$\qquad\qquad = \left(\dfrac{4}{5}\right)\left(\dfrac{5}{13}\right) - \left(\dfrac{3}{5}\right)\left(\dfrac{12}{13}\right)$

$\qquad\qquad = \dfrac{20 - 36}{65}$

$\qquad\qquad = -\dfrac{16}{65}$

Answer: $-\dfrac{16}{65}$

3 If $\cos \alpha = -\dfrac{2}{3}$, $\tan \beta = \dfrac{2}{3}$, and α and β both lie in Quadrant III, find $\sin (\alpha - \beta)$.

SOLUTION

The difference formula requires the sine and cosine of each of the angles, so you must compute the missing functions. You could either use a trigonometric identity or a right triangle. This time we'll use right triangle trigonometry.

Since α lies in Quadrant III, utilize the given information to sketch a triangle in the third quadrant with the reference angle. Use the Pythagorean theorem to fill in the missing side. You should obtain the following:

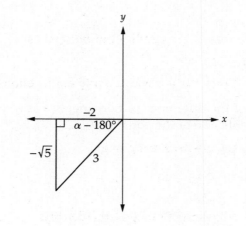

By looking at the triangle, we can see that $\sin \alpha = -\dfrac{\sqrt{5}}{3}$.

Since β lies in Quadrant III, utilize the given information to sketch a triangle in the third quadrant with the reference angle. Use the Pythagorean theorem to fill in the missing side. You should obtain the following:

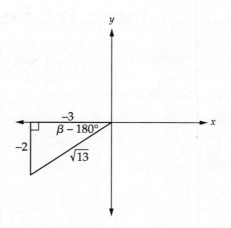

By looking at the triangle, we can see that $\sin \beta = -\dfrac{2}{\sqrt{13}} = -\dfrac{2\sqrt{13}}{13}$ and $\cos \beta = -\dfrac{3}{\sqrt{13}} = -\dfrac{3\sqrt{13}}{13}$.

Substitute the information into the difference formula.

$$\sin(\alpha - \beta) = \sin \alpha \cos \beta - \cos \alpha \sin \beta$$

$$= \left(-\frac{\sqrt{5}}{3}\right)\left(-\frac{3\sqrt{13}}{13}\right) - \left(-\frac{2}{3}\right)\left(-\frac{2\sqrt{13}}{13}\right)$$

$$= \frac{3\sqrt{65}}{39} - \frac{4\sqrt{13}}{39}$$

$$= \frac{3\sqrt{65} - 4\sqrt{13}}{39}$$

Answer: $\dfrac{3\sqrt{65} - 4\sqrt{13}}{39}$

4 Prove: $\cos(180° - x) = -\cos x$

SOLUTION

Use the formula for the cosine of the difference of two angles, $\cos(A - B) = \cos A \cos B + \sin A \sin B$, and work straight down on the left side of the equation.

$$\cos(180° - x) \overset{?}{=} -\cos x$$

$$\cos 180° \cos x + \sin 180° \sin x \overset{?}{=} -\cos x$$

$$(-1)\cos x + (0)\sin x \overset{?}{=} -\cos x$$

$$-\cos x + 0 \overset{?}{=} -\cos x$$

$$-\cos x = -\cos x \checkmark$$

 Practice

1 If $\sin x = \dfrac{7}{25}$ and $\cos y = \dfrac{3}{5}$, and x and y are positive acute angles, find

   a $\sin(x + y)$
   b $\cos(x - y)$
   c $\tan(x + y)$

2 Given $\sin \theta = 0.8$ and $\tan \varphi = 0.75$, $\dfrac{\pi}{2} < \theta < \pi$, and $\pi < \varphi < \dfrac{3\pi}{2}$, find $\cos(\theta + \varphi)$.

3 Carlos would like to determine the exact value of $\cos 15°$. Since he knows the exact values of $\cos 45°$ and $\cos 30°$, he can use the formula for the cosine of the difference of two angles. What is the *exact* value of $\cos 15°$?

4 Marietta will use her knowledge of trigonometry to compute the *exact* value of $\sin 105°$.

   a What combination of angles can she use?
   b What is the exact value of $\sin 105°$?

5 Prove: $\sin(\pi - \theta) = \sin \theta$

6 Prove: $\cos(360° - A) = \cos A$

7 Prove: $\sin(180° + x) = -\sin x$

8 Prove: $\cos\left(\dfrac{3\pi}{2} - \beta\right) = -\sin \beta$

Exercises 9–28: Write the numeral preceding the choice that best completes the statement or answers the question.

9 If A and B are both positive acute angles, and $\sin A = \dfrac{3}{5}$ and $\sin B = \dfrac{5}{13}$, then $\sin (A - B) =$

(1) $-\dfrac{33}{65}$

(2) $-\dfrac{16}{65}$

(3) $\dfrac{16}{65}$

(4) $\dfrac{33}{65}$

10 The expression $\tan (180° - y)$ is equivalent to

(1) $\tan y$
(2) $-\tan y$
(3) 0
(4) -1

11 $\sin 240° \cos 60° + \cos 240° \sin 60°$ is equivalent to

(1) $\sin 300°$
(2) $\cos 300°$
(3) $\sin 180°$
(4) $\cos 180°$

12 $\cos 300° \cos 30° + \sin 300° \sin 30°$ is equivalent to

(1) $\sin 330°$
(2) $\cos 330°$
(3) $\sin 270°$
(4) $\cos 270°$

13 $\sin 150° \cos 30° - \cos 150° \sin 30°$ is equivalent to which of the following?

(1) $\cos 180°$
(2) $\sin 180°$
(3) $\cos 120°$
(4) $\sin 120°$

14 The value of $\cos 26° \cos 154° - \sin 26° \sin 154°$ is

(1) -1
(2) $-\dfrac{1}{2}$
(3) 0
(4) $\dfrac{\sqrt{3}}{2}$

15 $\dfrac{\tan 25° + \tan 15°}{1 - \tan 25° \tan 15°}$ is equivalent to

(1) $\tan 10°$
(2) $\tan 30°$
(3) $\tan 40°$
(4) $\cot 40°$

16 If $f(x) = \cos (\pi + y)$, which of the following is equivalent to $f(x)$?

(1) $\cos y$
(2) $-\cos y$
(3) $\sin y$
(4) $-\sin y$

17 If $\tan x = 1$, $\sin y = \dfrac{\sqrt{2}}{2}$, and x and y are positive acute angles, find $\cos (x + y)$.

(1) 1
(2) -1
(3) 0
(4) $1 + \dfrac{\sqrt{2}}{2}$

18 If $\sin A = \dfrac{\sqrt{3}}{2}$, $\sin B = -\dfrac{1}{2}$, $\dfrac{\pi}{2} < A < \pi$, and $\pi < B < \dfrac{3\pi}{2}$, find $\sin (A + B)$.

(1) $-\dfrac{\sqrt{3}}{2}$

(2) $-\dfrac{1}{2}$

(3) $\dfrac{1}{2}$

(4) $\dfrac{\sqrt{3}}{2}$

19 If $\sin A = k$, find $\sin (A + 2\pi)$.

(1) $\sin k$
(2) $-\sin k$
(3) k
(4) $-k$

20 The expression $\sin (180° - x)$ is equivalent to

(1) $\sin x$
(2) $\cos x$
(3) $-\sin x$
(4) $-\cos x$

21 Which is equivalent to $\sin\left(\dfrac{\pi}{2} - y\right)$?

(1) $\cos y$
(2) $-\cos y$
(3) $\sin y$
(4) $-\sin y$

22 The exact value of $\sin 75°$ is

(1) $\dfrac{1}{2} + \dfrac{\sqrt{2}}{2}$
(2) $\dfrac{\sqrt{2} + \sqrt{6}}{2}$
(3) $\dfrac{\sqrt{2} + \sqrt{6}}{4}$
(4) $\dfrac{\sqrt{2} - \sqrt{6}}{4}$

23 The expression $\cos\left(\dfrac{\pi}{2} + \theta\right)$ is equivalent to

(1) $\sin \theta$
(2) $-\sin \theta$
(3) $\cos \theta$
(4) $-\cos \theta$

24 If angles A and B are both obtuse and $\sin A = \dfrac{6}{10}$ and $\sin B = \dfrac{8}{17}$, which represents $\cos(A - B)$?

(1) $\dfrac{84}{85}$
(2) $\dfrac{36}{85}$
(3) $-\dfrac{24}{85}$
(4) $-\dfrac{36}{85}$

25 $\sin\left(x + \dfrac{3\pi}{2}\right)$ is equivalent to

(1) $\sin x$
(2) $-\sin x$
(3) $\cos x$
(4) $-\cos x$

26 If $\sin x = -\dfrac{12}{13}$ and $\cos y = -\dfrac{6}{10}$, and x and y are in Quadrant III, the value of $\sin(x - y)$ is

(1) $-\dfrac{56}{65}$
(2) $-\dfrac{16}{65}$
(3) $\dfrac{16}{65}$
(4) $\dfrac{56}{65}$

27 The value of $\cos 60° \cos 30° + \sin 60° \sin 30°$ is

(1) 1
(2) $\dfrac{\sqrt{3}}{2}$
(3) $\dfrac{1}{2}$
(4) 0

28 The expression $\cos(A - B) - \cos(A + B)$ is equal to

(1) $-2\sin A \sin B$
(2) $-2\cos B$
(3) $2\cos A \cos B$
(4) $2\sin A \sin B$

12.3 Double-Angle Formulas

We know that $\sin 30° = \dfrac{1}{2}$. We also know that $\sin 60° = \dfrac{\sqrt{3}}{2} \neq 2\sin 30°$. Thus, to find $\sin 60°$ from $\sin 30°$, we need to use a formula. Since $60 = 30 + 30$, we can use the formula for the sine of the sum of two angles.

$$
\begin{aligned}
\sin 60° &= \sin (30° + 30°) \\
&= \sin 30° \cos 30° + \cos 30° \sin 30° \\
&= \left(\frac{1}{2}\right)\left(\frac{\sqrt{3}}{2}\right) + \left(\frac{\sqrt{3}}{2}\right)\left(\frac{1}{2}\right) \\
&= \frac{2\sqrt{3}}{4} \\
&= \frac{\sqrt{3}}{2}
\end{aligned}
$$

We can use this technique to derive the general formula for the sine of a double angle.

$$
\begin{aligned}
\sin 2A &= \sin (A + A) \\
&= \sin A \cos A + \cos A \sin A \\
&= 2\sin A \cos A
\end{aligned}
$$

The formulas for the cosine and tangent of a double angle can be derived using a similar approach. That will be left for you to do in a practice problem.

Functions of the Double Angle

$$\sin 2A = 2\sin A \cos A$$

$$\cos 2A = \cos^2 A - \sin^2 A$$

$$\cos 2A = 2\cos^2 A - 1$$

$$\cos 2A = 1 - 2\sin^2 A$$

$$\tan 2A = \frac{2\tan A}{1 - \tan^2 A}$$

Note: Three different formulas are given for $\cos 2A$. All three formulas are equivalent. Use whatever formula works best with the information that you are given.

MODEL PROBLEMS

1 Use the formula for sin 2A to show that sin 90° = 1.

SOLUTION

$\sin 90° = \sin(2 \cdot 45°)$ Copy the formula, replacing A with 45°.

$\qquad = 2\sin 45° \cos 45°$ $\sin 45° = \cos 45° = \dfrac{\sqrt{2}}{2}$

$\qquad = \cancel{2}\left(\dfrac{\sqrt{2}}{\cancel{2}}\right)\left(\dfrac{\sqrt{2}}{2}\right)$ Simplify.

$\qquad = \dfrac{2}{2}$

$\qquad = 1 ✔$

2 Which is equivalent to $2\cos^2 45° - 1$?

   (1)   1

   (2)   sin 90°

   (3) $\dfrac{1}{2}$

   (4)   cos 90°

SOLUTION

We are asked to evaluate $2\cos^2 45° - 1$, which is one of the double-angle cosine formulas:
$2\cos^2 45° - 1 = \cos 2(45°) = \cos 90°$.

Answer: Choice (4)

3 If $\cos \theta = \dfrac{7}{25}$, find $\cos 2\theta$.

SOLUTION

Since we are given $\cos \theta = \dfrac{7}{25}$, we will use the formula that contains cosine.

$\cos 2A = 2\cos^2 A - 1$

$\qquad = 2\left(\dfrac{7}{25}\right)^2 - 1$ Replace cos A with the value of cos θ.

$\qquad = 2\left(\dfrac{49}{625}\right) - 1$ Simplify.

$\qquad = \dfrac{98 - 625}{625}$

$\qquad = -\dfrac{527}{625}$

Answer: $\cos 2\theta = -\dfrac{527}{625}$

4 Show that $\tan 2\theta = \dfrac{\sin 2\theta}{\cos 2\theta}$.

SOLUTION

When we prove an identity, we work straight down one side of the equation. However, we may substitute for the variable.

$\tan 2\theta \overset{?}{=} \dfrac{\sin 2\theta}{\cos 2\theta}$

$\tan x \overset{?}{=} \dfrac{\sin x}{\cos x}$ Let $2\theta = x$.

$\dfrac{\sin x}{\cos x} \overset{?}{=} \dfrac{\sin x}{\cos x}$ Rewrite $\tan x$ using the quotient identity.

$\dfrac{\sin 2\theta}{\cos 2\theta} = \dfrac{\sin 2\theta}{\cos 2\theta}$ ✔   Sustitute 2θ back in for x.

Practice

1 If $\sin x = \dfrac{4}{5}$ and x is a positive acute angle, find $\sin 2x$.

2 If $\cos y = \dfrac{1}{2}$ and $\dfrac{3\pi}{2} < y < 2\pi$, find $\cos 2y$.

3 If $\sin \theta = 0.6$ and θ is in the second quadrant, find $\cos 2\theta$.

4 If $\tan \beta = \dfrac{1}{3}$ and β lies in Quadrant III, find $\sin 2\beta$.

5 Use the formula for sine of a double angle to find $\sin 120°$.

6 Use the formula for cosine of a double angle to find $\cos 180°$.

7 Prove the identity: $1 - \tan \theta \cdot \sin 2\theta = \cos 2\theta$

8 Prove the identity: $\dfrac{\cos 2\alpha}{\sin \alpha} + 2\sin \alpha = \csc \alpha$

9 Prove the identity: $\sin 2\theta = \dfrac{2\tan \theta}{1 + \tan^2 \theta}$

10 Prove the identity: $\cos 2\theta \left(1 + \tan^2 \theta \right) = 2 - \dfrac{1}{\cos^2 \theta}$

11 Prove the identity: $\sin 2\theta \sec \theta = 2\sin \theta$

12 **a** Use the fact that $\cos 2A = \cos (A + A)$ to derive the formula $\cos 2A = \cos^2 A - \sin^2 A$.

     b Use one of the Pythagorean identities to rewrite the formula from part **a** as $\cos 2A = 2\cos^2 A - 1$.

     c Use one of the Pythagorean identities to rewrite the formula from part **a** as $\cos 2A = 1 - 2\sin^2 A$.

Exercises 13–27: Write the numeral preceding the choice that best completes the statement or answers the question.

13 The expression $\dfrac{\sin 2\theta}{2\cos \theta}$ is equivalent to

     (1) $\sin \theta$
     (2) $\cos \theta$
     (3) $\tan \theta$
     (4) $\cot \theta$

14 Which is the range of $y = \cos 2x$?

(1) $-1 \le y \le 1$
(2) $-2 \le y \le 2$
(3) $-90° \le x \le 90°$
(4) $0° \le x \le 360°$

15 The expression $2\sin x \cos x$ is equivalent to

(1) $2\sin x$
(2) $\sin 2x$
(3) $\cos 2x$
(4) $\tan 2x$

16 If $\sin x = \cos x$, then $\sin 2x =$

(1) 1
(2) 2
(3) 0
(4) Cannot be determined

17 The expression $2\cos^2 (15°) - 1$ has the same value as

(1) $\sin 15°$
(2) $\cos 15°$
(3) $\sin 30°$
(4) $\cos 30°$

18 If $\sin y = -\dfrac{7}{25}$, find $\cos 2y$.

(1) $-\dfrac{48}{25}$

(2) $-\dfrac{14}{25}$

(3) $\dfrac{134}{625}$

(4) $\dfrac{527}{625}$

19 If A is a positive acute angle and $\sin A = \dfrac{\sqrt{5}}{3}$, what is $\cos 2A$?

(1) $-\dfrac{1}{3}$

(2) $-\dfrac{1}{9}$

(3) $\dfrac{1}{9}$

(4) $\dfrac{1}{3}$

20 The expression $\dfrac{2\sin \theta \cos \theta}{\cos^2 \theta - \sin^2 \theta}$ is equivalent to

(1) $\sin (2\theta)$
(2) $\cos (2\theta)$
(3) $\tan (2\theta)$
(4) $\cot (2\theta)$

21 If $\sin \beta = 0.6$, and β terminates in Quadrant II, find $\sin 2\beta$.

(1) -1.2
(2) -0.96
(3) 0.96
(4) 1.2

22 The maximum value of $3\sin 2\theta$ is

(1) 2π
(2) 2
(3) 3
(4) 6

23 If angle A is obtuse and $\tan A = -\dfrac{8}{6}$, which of the following represents $\cos 2A$?

(1) $-\dfrac{24}{25}$

(2) $-\dfrac{28}{100}$

(3) $\dfrac{28}{100}$

(4) $\dfrac{24}{25}$

24 Which statement is true for all values of x?

(1) $\cos x + \sin x = 1$
(2) $\cos 2x = 2\cos x$
(3) $\sin^2 x = \dfrac{1 - \cos 2x}{2}$
(4) $\cos^2 x - \sin^2 x = 1$

25 If $\cos 2\theta = -\dfrac{2}{3}$ and $\pi \le 2\theta \le \dfrac{3\pi}{2}$, what is the value of $\sin \theta$?

(1) $-\dfrac{\sqrt{30}}{6}$

(2) $-\dfrac{\sqrt{3}}{3}$

(3) $\dfrac{\sqrt{5}}{3}$

(4) $\dfrac{\sqrt{30}}{6}$

26 Given that $\dfrac{\pi}{2} \leq \beta \leq \pi$ and $\cos \beta = -\dfrac{\sqrt{2}}{2}$, find $\sin 2\beta$.

(1) -1

(2) $-\dfrac{1}{2}$

(3) $\dfrac{1}{2}$

(4) $\sqrt{2}$

27 Given that $\dfrac{3\pi}{2} \leq \alpha \leq 2\pi$ and $\cos \alpha = \dfrac{\sqrt{3}}{4}$, find $\cos 2\alpha$.

(1) $-\dfrac{3}{4}$

(2) $-\dfrac{5}{8}$

(3) $\dfrac{1}{8}$

(4) $\dfrac{5}{8}$

12.4 Half-Angle Formulas

We learned in the last section that $\cos 2\theta = 1 - 2\sin^2 \theta$. Since θ is half of 2θ, we can solve this identity for $\sin \theta$ to find the half-angle formula for sine.

$$\cos 2\theta = 1 - 2\sin^2 \theta$$

$$\cos 2\theta - 1 = -2\sin^2 \theta$$

$$\frac{\cos 2\theta - 1}{-2} = \sin^2 \theta$$

$$\sin^2 \theta = \frac{1 - \cos 2\theta}{2}$$

$$\sin \theta = \pm\sqrt{\frac{1 - \cos 2\theta}{2}}$$

Let $A = 2\theta$; then $\theta = \dfrac{1}{2}A$. Substituting, we have

$$\sin \frac{1}{2}A = \pm\sqrt{\frac{1 - \cos A}{2}}$$

If we look at a second version of the double-angle cosine formula, we can find the formula for the cosine of half of a given angle.

Let $2\theta = 2\cos^2 \theta - 1$. Now solve this identity for $\cos \theta$.

$$\cos 2\theta = 2\cos^2 \theta - 1$$

$$\cos 2\theta + 1 = 2\cos^2 \theta$$

$$\frac{\cos 2\theta + 1}{2} = \cos^2 \theta$$

$$\cos \theta = \pm\sqrt{\frac{\cos 2\theta + 1}{2}}$$

If we let $A = 2\theta$, then $\theta = \dfrac{1}{2}A$.

$$\cos \frac{1}{2}A = \pm\sqrt{\frac{1 + \cos A}{2}}$$

We can use the formulas for sine and cosine of $\frac{1}{2}A$ to find the formula for tangent of $\frac{1}{2}A$.

Using the quotient identity, $\tan \frac{1}{2}A = \dfrac{\sin \frac{1}{2}A}{\cos \frac{1}{2}A}$. Now solve this identity for $\tan \frac{1}{2}A$.

$$\tan \frac{1}{2}A = \dfrac{\sin \frac{1}{2}A}{\cos \frac{1}{2}A}$$

$$\tan \frac{1}{2}A = \dfrac{\pm \sqrt{\dfrac{1 - \cos A}{2}}}{\pm \sqrt{\dfrac{1 + \cos A}{2}}}$$

$$\tan \frac{1}{2}A = \pm \sqrt{\dfrac{1 - \cos A}{\cancel{2}} \cdot \dfrac{\cancel{2}}{1 + \cos A}}$$

$$\tan \frac{1}{2}A = \pm \sqrt{\dfrac{1 - \cos A}{1 + \cos A}}$$

When we work with functions of half angles we must use the following formulas.

Functions of the Half Angle

$$\sin \frac{1}{2}A = \pm \sqrt{\dfrac{1 - \cos A}{2}}$$

$$\cos \frac{1}{2}A = \pm \sqrt{\dfrac{1 + \cos A}{2}}$$

$$\tan \frac{1}{2}A = \pm \dfrac{\sqrt{1 - \cos A}}{\sqrt{1 + \cos A}}$$

In each case, we must use only the positive or negative value depending on the quadrant of the unit circle in which *half* of the original angle lies. For example, if we are talking about an angle A such that sine, cosine, and tangent are all positive, then $0 < A < \frac{\pi}{2}$. However, for $\frac{1}{2}A$, $0 < \frac{1}{2}A < \frac{\pi}{4}$. The following table will help you choose the positive or negative values.

Domain of Angle	Domain of Half Angle	Quadrant of Half Angle	Sign of Half-Angle Function
$0 < A < \dfrac{\pi}{2}$	$0 < \dfrac{1}{2}A < \dfrac{\pi}{4}$	I	$\sin \dfrac{1}{2}A > 0$ $\cos \dfrac{1}{2}A > 0$ $\tan \dfrac{1}{2}A > 0$
$\dfrac{\pi}{2} < A < \pi$	$\dfrac{\pi}{4} < \dfrac{1}{2}A < \dfrac{\pi}{2}$	I	$\sin \dfrac{1}{2}A > 0$ $\cos \dfrac{1}{2}A > 0$ $\tan \dfrac{1}{2}A > 0$
$\pi < A < \dfrac{3\pi}{2}$	$\dfrac{\pi}{2} < \dfrac{1}{2}A < \dfrac{3\pi}{4}$	II	$\sin \dfrac{1}{2}A > 0$ $\cos \dfrac{1}{2}A < 0$ $\tan \dfrac{1}{2}A < 0$
$\dfrac{3\pi}{2} < A < 2\pi$	$\dfrac{3\pi}{4} < \dfrac{1}{2}A < \pi$	II	$\sin \dfrac{1}{2}A > 0$ $\cos \dfrac{1}{2}A < 0$ $\tan \dfrac{1}{2}A < 0$

For $A > 2\pi$, follow a similar pattern.

MODEL PROBLEMS

1 Use the formula for $\sin \dfrac{1}{2}A$ to show that $\sin 45° = \dfrac{\sqrt{2}}{2}$.

SOLUTION

$$\sin \frac{1}{2}A = \pm\sqrt{\frac{1 - \cos A}{2}}$$

When we use this formula, we must decide whether to use the positive value or negative value. Since 45° is in the first quadrant, where sine is positive, we will choose the positive value.

$$\sin 45° = \sin \frac{1}{2}(90°)$$ Copy the formula, choosing the positive value, and substitute 90° for A.

$$= \sqrt{\frac{1 - \cos 90°}{2}}$$

$$= \sqrt{\frac{1 - 0}{2}}$$ $\cos 90° = 0$

$$= \sqrt{\frac{1}{2}}$$ Simplify.

$$= \frac{\sqrt{1}}{\sqrt{2}} \cdot \frac{\sqrt{2}}{\sqrt{2}}$$ Rationalize the denominator.

$$= \frac{\sqrt{2}}{2} \ ✔$$

2   If $\cos \alpha = \dfrac{3}{5}$, and $\dfrac{3\pi}{2} \le \alpha \le 2\pi$, find $\cos \dfrac{1}{2}\alpha$.

SOLUTION

If $\dfrac{3\pi}{2} \le \alpha \le 2\pi$, then $\dfrac{3\pi}{4} \le \dfrac{1}{2}\alpha \le \pi$. Because $\dfrac{1}{2}\alpha$ lies in Quadrant II, where cosine is negative, we choose the negative value of the square root.

$$\cos \frac{1}{2}\alpha = -\sqrt{\frac{1 + \cos \alpha}{2}}$$

$$= -\sqrt{\frac{1 + \dfrac{3}{5}}{2}}$$ Given: $\cos \alpha = \dfrac{3}{5}$.

$$= -\sqrt{\frac{\dfrac{8}{5}}{2}}$$ Simplify the numerator.

$$= -\sqrt{\frac{4}{5}}$$ Divide by 2.

$$= -\frac{2}{\sqrt{5}}$$ Simplify the radical.

$$= -\frac{2\sqrt{5}}{5}$$ Rationalize the denominator.

Answer: $\cos \dfrac{1}{2}\alpha = -\dfrac{2\sqrt{5}}{5}$

1 If $\sin x = \dfrac{4}{5}$ and x is a positive acute angle, find $\cos \dfrac{1}{2}x$.

2 If $\cos y = \dfrac{1}{2}$ and $\dfrac{3\pi}{2} < y < 2\pi$, find $\sin \dfrac{1}{2}y$.

3 If $\sin \theta = 0.6$, and θ is in the second quadrant, find $\cos \dfrac{\theta}{2}$.

4 If $\cos \beta = \dfrac{1}{3}$ and β lies in Quadrant IV, find $\sin \dfrac{\beta}{2}$.

5 Use the half-angle formula for cosine to find $\cos 30°$.

6 a Use the half-angle formula for sine to find the exact value of $\sin 15°$.
   b Use your answer to part **a** to approximate $\sin 15°$ to the *nearest thousandth*.
   c Use your calculator to find $\sin 15°$. Does your answer agree with part **a**?

7 a Use the formula for cosine of a half angle to find the exact value of $\cos 22.5°$.
   b Use your answer to part **a** to approximate $\cos 22.5°$ to the *nearest thousandth*.
   c Use your calculator to find $\cos 22.5°$. Does your answer agree with part **a**?

Exercises 8–15: Select the numeral preceding the choice that best completes the statement or answers the question.

8 If $\dfrac{3\pi}{2} < \alpha < 2\pi$, in what quadrant does $\dfrac{1}{2}\alpha$ lie?

(1) I
(2) II
(3) III
(4) IV

9 If $\cos \alpha = -\dfrac{5}{13}$, and $\pi < \alpha < \dfrac{3\pi}{2}$, then $\cos \dfrac{1}{2}\alpha =$

(1) $-\dfrac{10}{13}$

(2) $-\dfrac{2\sqrt{13}}{13}$

(3) $\dfrac{2\sqrt{13}}{13}$

(4) $\dfrac{10}{13}$

10 The exact value of $\sin 75°$ is

(1) $\dfrac{\sqrt{2 + \sqrt{3}}}{2}$

(2) $\dfrac{\sqrt{2 - \sqrt{3}}}{2}$

(3) $\dfrac{1}{2}\sin 150°$

(4) $-\dfrac{\sqrt{2 + \sqrt{2}}}{2}$

11 If θ is a positive angle and $\sin \dfrac{1}{2}\theta = 1$, what is the value of $\cos \theta$?

(1) 1
(2) -1
(3) $\dfrac{\sqrt{3}}{2}$
(4) $\dfrac{1}{2}$

12 If x is a positive acute angle and $\cos x = \dfrac{1}{9}$, then $\cos \dfrac{1}{2}x$ equals

(1) $\dfrac{1}{3}$

(2) $\dfrac{2}{3}$

(3) $\dfrac{\sqrt{5}}{3}$

(4) $\dfrac{2\sqrt{5}}{3}$

13 If angle A is obtuse and $\cos A = -\dfrac{6}{10}$,

$\cos \dfrac{1}{2} A$ is

(1) $-\dfrac{3}{5}$

(2) $-\dfrac{1}{5}$

(3) $\dfrac{\sqrt{5}}{5}$

(4) $\dfrac{2\sqrt{5}}{5}$

14 If θ is a positive acute angle and $\cos \theta = \dfrac{1}{8}$,

then $\sin \dfrac{1}{2} \theta$ equals

(1) $\dfrac{\sqrt{7}}{4}$

(2) $\dfrac{3}{4}$

(3) $\dfrac{\sqrt{7}}{2}$

(4) $\dfrac{3}{2}$

15 If θ is a positive acute angle and $\sin \dfrac{1}{2} \theta = \dfrac{1}{2}$,

what could be the value of θ?

(1) $30°$

(2) $45°$

(3) $60°$

(4) $75°$

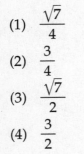 **FYI**

We can use a calculator to see trigonometric identities graphically.

Let's take the identity $\sin^2 \theta + \cos^2 \theta = 1$. On your calculator, enter $(\sin x)^2 + (\cos x)^2$ into Y_1 and 1 into Y_2. To the left of Y_2, press ⏎ENTER until you see the symbol -□. This Path option lets us watch the Y_2 function being graphed.

```
Plot1  Plot2  Plot3
\Y1=sin(X)²+cos(
X)²
-□Y2=1
\Y3=
\Y4=
\Y5=
\Y6=
```

Press ZOOM 7 to graph the two equations in the window. You will see that the second equation is identical to the first, as shown below.

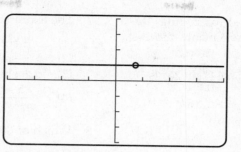

Although this does not prove the identity, it is a graphical illustration of the identity. Be aware that if two graphs *appear* identical, it does not guarantee that they *are* identical. However, the graphing calculator does provide a valuable illustration of identities.

Let's try another one:

$$\frac{\cos \theta + 1}{1 + \sec \theta} = \cos \theta$$

There is no key on your calculator for sec θ, so you have to enter sec θ as $\frac{1}{\cos \theta}$. Be careful to put parentheses where needed.

Enter the left side of the equation into Y_1 and the right side into Y_2 as follows:

```
Plot1  Plot2  Plot3
\Y1=(cos(X)+1)/(
1+1/cos(X))
-0Y2=cos(X)
\Y3=
\Y4=
\Y5=
\Y6=
```

Again select the Path option to the left of Y_2. When you graph the two functions, you can see that they are identical.

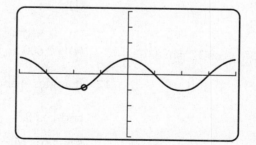

Try entering some of the other identities from Section 12.1 to illustrate the fact that they are identities.

Calculators can also be used to illustrate identities numerically. Look at the expression sin 12° cos 38° + cos 12° sin 38°. You may recognize this as the formula for sin $(A + B)$, that is, sin $(A + B) = \sin A \cos B + \cos A \sin B$. By letting $A = 12$ and $B = 38$, we can see that the expression sin 12° cos 38° + cos 12° sin 38° is equivalent to sin $(12° + 38°) = \sin 50°$. Verify this with your calculator. First, make sure that your calculator is in degree mode, and enter sin 12° cos 38° + cos 12° sin 38°. Now enter sin 50°. You can see that both expressions have an approximate value of 0.7660444431.

Exercises 1–15: Select the numeral preceding the choice that best completes the statement or answers the question.

1 The value of $\cos 64° \cos 26° - \sin 64° \sin 26°$ is

(1) 1
(2) 0.7880
(3) $\dfrac{1}{2}$
(4) 0

2 The expression $\cos (\pi - x)$ is equivalent to

(1) $\cos x$
(2) $\sin x$
(3) $-\sin x$
(4) $-\cos x$

3 The expression $\dfrac{\cos^2 \theta}{\sin \theta} + \sin \theta$ is equivalent to

(1) $1 + \cos^2 \theta$
(2) $\cos^2 \theta$
(3) $\sin \theta$
(4) $\csc \theta$

4 If θ is an acute angle and $\sin \theta = \dfrac{1}{2}$, the value of $\cos \left(\dfrac{\pi}{2} + \theta \right)$ is

(1) $\dfrac{\sqrt{3}}{2}$
(2) $\dfrac{1}{2}$
(3) $-\dfrac{1}{2}$
(4) $-\dfrac{\sqrt{3}}{2}$

5 The expression $\sin 37° \cos 83° + \cos 37° \sin 83°$ can also be written as

(1) $\cos 120°$
(2) $\sin 120°$
(3) $\cos 46°$
(4) $\sin 46°$

6 If $\tan x = -\dfrac{1}{4}$ and $\tan y = 2$, the value of $\tan (x + y)$ is

(1) $\dfrac{7}{6}$ (3) $\dfrac{7}{2}$
(2) $\dfrac{9}{6}$ (4) $\dfrac{9}{2}$

7 The expression $4 - \cos^2 A$ is equivalent to

(1) $5 - \sec^2 A$
(2) $5 - \sin^2 A$
(3) $5 + \sin^2 A$
(4) $\dfrac{5}{\sec^2 A}$

8 Which of the following is a valid identity?

(1) $\sin^2 4x + \cos^2 4x = 1$
(2) $\sin^4 x + \cos^4 x = 1$
(3) $\sin 4x = 4\sin x \cos x$
(4) $\cos^4 x = 1 - \sin^4 x$

9 If $\cos \theta = c$, then $\sin^2 \dfrac{\theta}{2}$ equals

(1) $\dfrac{1 - c}{2}$
(2) $\dfrac{1 + c}{2}$
(3) $\dfrac{1 - c}{c + c}$
(4) $\dfrac{1 - c}{4}$

10 If $f(x) = 2\sin x - \cos 2x$, the exact value of $f\left(\dfrac{\pi}{2} \right)$ is

(1) 1
(2) 2
(3) 3
(4) 0

11 If $f(\theta) = \sin^2 \theta + \cos^2 \theta$, evaluate $f(30°)$.

(1) 1
(2) 2
(3) 1,800
(4) 3,600

12 If angles A and B are both obtuse and $\sin A = \dfrac{6}{10}$ and $\cos B = -\dfrac{8}{17}$, which of the following represents $\cos (A + B)$?

(1) $\dfrac{36}{85}$
(2) $\dfrac{3}{17}$
(3) $-\dfrac{13}{85}$
(4) $-\dfrac{84}{85}$

13 The expression $\sin(2\pi - \theta)$ is equivalent to

(1) $\sin \theta$
(2) $-\sin \theta$
(3) $\cos \theta$
(4) $-\cos \theta$

14 The expression $1 - 2\sin^2 45°$ has the same value as which of the following?

(1) $\cos 22.5°$
(2) $\sin 22.5°$
(3) $\cos 90°$
(4) $\sin 90°$

15 If $\cos \gamma = -\dfrac{4}{5}$ when $90° \leq \gamma \leq 180°$, what is the value of $\cos 2\gamma$?

(1) $-\dfrac{57}{25}$

(2) $-\dfrac{9}{25}$

(3) $\dfrac{7}{25}$

(4) $\dfrac{16}{25}$

Exercises 16–20: Demonstrate the following identities to be true.

16 $\dfrac{\sin 2\theta}{1 + \cos 2\theta} = \tan \theta$

17 $\cot \theta = \dfrac{\sin 2\theta}{2\sin^2 \theta}$

18 $\dfrac{1 + \cos \theta + \cos 2\theta}{\sin \theta + \sin 2\theta} = \cot \theta$

19 $\dfrac{2\sin \beta}{\sin 2\beta \cos \beta} = \sec^2 \beta$

20 $\sec x - \sin x \tan x = \cos x$

13 Trigonometric Equations

13.1 First-Degree Trigonometric Equations

Reference Angles

In Section 9.5, we reviewed reference angles and how to find them. Recall that a reference angle is the positive acute angle formed by the terminal ray of an angle in standard position and the x-axis. The examples below show how to find the reference angle, R, of a given angle in each quadrant.

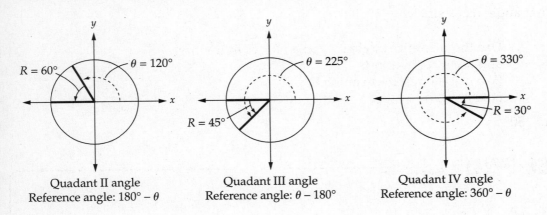

Quadant II angle
Reference angle: $180° - \theta$

Quadant III angle
Reference angle: $\theta - 180°$

Quadant IV angle
Reference angle: $360° - \theta$

Note: For additional review of reference angles, go to Section 9.5 on page 327.

First-Degree Trigonometric Equations

If you recall how to solve linear equations, you can solve first-degree trigonometric equations. A **trigonometric equation** is an equation with the variable expressed in terms of a trigonometric function value.

Solve for x: $4x + 3 = 5$ Subtract 3 from both sides.

$$\underline{\quad -3 \quad -3 \quad}$$

$$\frac{4x}{4} = \frac{2}{4}$$ Divide both sides by 4.

$$x = \frac{1}{2}$$

Solve for θ in the interval $0° \le \theta \le 360°$.

$4\sin \theta + 3 = 5$ Subtract 3 from both sides.

$$\underline{\quad -3 \quad -3 \quad}$$

$$\frac{4\sin \theta}{4} = \frac{2}{4}$$ Divide both sides by 4.

$$\sin \theta = \frac{1}{2}$$

Now we have found that $\sin \theta = \dfrac{1}{2}$. However, we were *not* asked to find $\sin \theta$.

We were asked to find θ. First, we need to find our reference angle. Then, we must recall that $\sin \theta$ is positive in Quadrants I and II, so we need to find values of θ in Quadrants I and II.

$\sin \theta = \dfrac{1}{2}$ What angle has a sine of $\dfrac{1}{2}$?

Reference angle: 30°   Use the reference angle to find answers in the first
                                and second quadrants.
  Quadrant I: 30°   (We use the reference angle.)
  Quadrant II: 150° $(180° - 30°)$

Answer: $\theta = 30°$ and $150°$

MODEL PROBLEMS

1 Solve for $\tan \theta$: $3\tan \theta - 4 = 5\tan \theta - 1$

SOLUTION

$3\tan \theta - 4 = 5\tan \theta - 1$ Subtract $5\tan \theta$ from both sides.

$-2\tan \theta - 4 = -1$ Add 4 to both sides.

$-2\tan \theta = 3$ Divide both sides by -2.

$$\tan \theta = -\frac{3}{2}$$

Answer: $\tan \theta = -\dfrac{3}{2}$

2 Solve for θ in the interval $0° \leq \theta \leq 360°$: $8\sec\theta - 2 = 10 + 2\sec\theta$

SOLUTION

$8\sec\theta - 2 = 10 + 2\sec\theta$	Subtract $2\sec\theta$ from both sides.
$6\sec\theta - 2 = 10$	Add 2 to both sides.
$6\sec\theta = 12$	Divide both sides by 6.
$\sec\theta = 2$	Since we are more familiar with cosine, we can take the reciprocal of both sides to get an equation containing cosine.
$\cos\theta = \dfrac{1}{2}$	Find the reference angle.

Reference angle = 60°; cosine $\theta > 0$ in Quadrants I and IV.

Find the appropriate angles in Quadrants I and IV.

Quadrant I: 60°   Quadrant IV: 300° (360° − 60°)

Answer: $\theta = 60°, 300°$

3 Solve for θ to the nearest degree in the interval $0° \leq \theta \leq 360°$: $3(\sin\theta - 1) = -4$

SOLUTION

$3(\sin\theta - 1) = -4$	Divide both sides by 3.
$\sin\theta - 1 = \dfrac{-4}{3}$	Add 1 to both sides.
$\sin\theta = -\dfrac{1}{3}$	Find the reference angle by pressing **2nd** **SIN** for $\sin^{-1}$ on your calculator.

Reference angle: $\approx 19°$

Sine $\theta < 0$ in Quadrants III and IV.

Quadrant III: 199° (180° + 19°)   Quadrant IV: 341° (360° − 19°)

Answer: $\theta = 199°, 341°$

4 Solve for exact values of θ in the interval $0 \leq \theta \leq 2\pi$: $2\cos\theta + 3\sqrt{2} = 2\sqrt{2}$

SOLUTION

$2\cos\theta + 3\sqrt{2} = 2\sqrt{2}$	Subtract $3\sqrt{2}$ from both sides.
$2\cos\theta = -\sqrt{2}$	Divide both sides by 2.
$\cos\theta = -\dfrac{\sqrt{2}}{2}$	Find the reference angle.

> **Note:** Make sure that your calculator is set in Degree mode if the question asks for an answer in degrees, and that it is set in Radian mode if the question asks for an answer in radians.

Reference angle: $\dfrac{\pi}{4}$

Cosine $\theta < 0$ in Quadrants II and III.

Quadrant II: $\dfrac{3\pi}{4} \left(\pi - \dfrac{\pi}{4} \right)$ Quadrant III: $\dfrac{5\pi}{4} \left(\pi + \dfrac{\pi}{4} \right)$

Answer: $\theta = \dfrac{3\pi}{4}, \dfrac{5\pi}{4}$

Use the table to help you obtain your answer after you find the reference angle.

To Find an Angle θ in Quadrant	Given Reference Angle R in Degrees	Given Reference Angle R in Radians
I	$\theta = R$	$\theta = R$
II	$\theta = 180° - R$	$\theta = \pi - R$
III	$\theta = 180° + R$	$\theta = \pi + R$
IV	$\theta = 360° - R$	$\theta = 2\pi - R$

 **Practice**

Exercises 1–6: Solve for exact values of θ in the interval $0° \le \theta \le 360°$.

1 $2\tan\theta - 3 = -5$

2 $4(\csc\theta + 2) = \csc\theta + 14$

3 $2\sin\theta + 3 = 3(\sin\theta + 1)$

4 $2\cos\theta + 5\sqrt{3} = 4\sqrt{3}$

5 $6\left(\cot\theta - \dfrac{\sqrt{3}}{2}\right) = 5\cot\theta - 2\sqrt{3}$

6 $3\sin\theta - 1 = 2$

Exercises 7–12: Solve for exact values of θ in the interval $0 \le \theta \le 2\pi$.

7 $3\tan\theta - 4 = 4\tan\theta - 5$

8 $3\sec\theta = \dfrac{2}{3}(3\sec\theta - 3)$

9 $2\left(\sin\theta + \sqrt{2}\right) = \sqrt{2}$

10 $6\cos\theta + \sqrt{3} = -4\left(\cos\theta + \sqrt{3}\right)$

11 $4\csc\theta + 5 = 3\csc\theta + 4$

12 $4\cos\theta + 3 = 3$

Exercises 13–17: Solve for β, to the *nearest tenth of a degree*, in the interval $0° \le \beta \le 360°$.

13 $9\sin\beta - 2 = 4\sin\beta - 1$

14 $-2(\tan\beta - 4) = 3(4 - \tan\beta)$

15 $3\sec\beta + 12 = \dfrac{3}{4}(8\sec\beta - 4)$

16 $\dfrac{1}{2}\csc\beta + 1 = \dfrac{1}{4}(\csc\beta + 8)$

17 $2\tan\beta - \sqrt{3} = 2\sqrt{3} - \tan\beta$

18 Find $m\angle B$ in the interval $180° \le B \le 270°$ that satisfies the equation $2\tan B - 3 = 3\tan B - 4$.

19 In the interval $90° \le x \le 180°$, find the value of x that satisfies the equation $3(\sin x - 2) = \sin x - 6$.

20 If $\dfrac{3\pi}{2} \le \theta \le 2\pi$, solve for θ: $5\cos\theta = 3\cos\theta + \sqrt{2}$

21 Find all values of x, to the *nearest tenth of a degree*, in the interval $0° \le x < 360°$: $|3\cos\theta + 1| = 2$

22 Solve for all values of θ in the interval $0° \le \theta < 360°$: $\sqrt{2\sin x + 7} + 1 = 4$

Exercises 23–30: Select the numeral preceding the choice that best completes the statement or answers the question.

23 If θ is a positive acute angle, and $2\tan\theta = 7$, what is the value of θ to the *nearest degree*?

(1) $\dfrac{7}{2}$

(2) $16°$

(3) $27°$

(4) $74°$

24 One root of the equation $3\sin\beta - 4 = 5\sin\beta - 3$ is

(1) $\dfrac{\pi}{6}$

(2) $\dfrac{\pi}{3}$

(3) $\dfrac{7\pi}{6}$

(4) $\dfrac{4\pi}{3}$

25 In which quadrants do the solutions of the equation $5\sin x - 3 = \sin x - 6$ lie?

(1) I and II
(2) II and III
(3) III and IV
(4) I and IV

26 Which is the solution set of $3\cos\alpha - \sqrt{2} = \cos\alpha - 2\sqrt{2}$ over the interval $0 \le \alpha \le 2\pi$?

(1) $\left\{\dfrac{\pi}{4}\right\}$

(2) $\left\{\dfrac{\pi}{4}, \dfrac{3\pi}{4}\right\}$

(3) $\left\{\dfrac{3\pi}{4}, \dfrac{5\pi}{4}\right\}$

(4) $\left\{\dfrac{5\pi}{4}, \dfrac{7\pi}{4}\right\}$

27 If x is an angle in Quadrant IV, which of the following is the solution of the equation $2\cos x - \sqrt{3} = 4\cos x$?

(1) $\dfrac{\pi}{6}$

(2) $\dfrac{5\pi}{6}$

(3) $\dfrac{7\pi}{6}$

(4) $\dfrac{5\pi}{6}$ and $\dfrac{7\pi}{6}$

28 Which equation does *not* have a solution?

(1) $3\sec\theta - 2 = 1$
(2) $4\csc\theta + 6 = 1$
(3) $5\csc\theta - 2 = 1$
(4) $2\sec\theta + 4 = 1$

29 Which value of x satisfies the equation $3\csc x - 4 = \csc x$?

(1) $-30°$
(2) $60°$
(3) $150°$
(4) $300°$

30 Which is the solution set of the equation $2\sin x - \sqrt{3} = 0$ over the interval $0 \le x \le 2\pi$?

(1) $\left\{\dfrac{\pi}{6}, \dfrac{5\pi}{6}\right\}$

(2) $\left\{\dfrac{\pi}{3}, \dfrac{2\pi}{3}\right\}$

(3) $\left\{\dfrac{7\pi}{6}, \dfrac{11\pi}{6}\right\}$

(4) $\left\{\dfrac{4\pi}{3}, \dfrac{5\pi}{3}\right\}$

13.2 Second-Degree Trigonometric Equations

We can solve second-degree trigonometric equations in the same way that we solve first-degree trigonometric equations: using the methods from algebra. Let us first review how to solve second-degree algebraic equations.

Solve for x: $x^2 - x - 1 = 1$

$x^2 - x - 2 = 0$	Set the equation equal to 0 and factor.
$(x + 1)(x - 2) = 0$	If the product of two factors is 0, one or both of the factors must equal 0.

$x + 1 = 0$	$x - 2 = 0$	Set each factor equal to 0 and solve.
$x = -1$	$x = 2$	

Let's solve a similar second-degree trigonometric equation.

Solve for θ in the interval $0° \leq \theta \leq 360°$: $\sin^2 \theta - \sin \theta - 1 = 1$

$\sin^2 \theta - \sin \theta - 2 = 0$	Set the equation equal to 0 and factor.
$(\sin \theta + 1)(\sin \theta - 2) = 0$	If the product of two factors is 0, one or both of the factors equals 0.

$\sin \theta + 1 = 0$	$\sin \theta - 2 = 0$	Set each factor equal to 0 and solve.
$\sin \theta = -1$	$\sin \theta = 2$	We need to find an angle whose sine is -1 and an angle whose sine is 2. There is no angle whose sine is 2. (The largest value in the range of $\sin \theta$ is 1.)
$\theta = 270°$	✘ Reject	

MODEL PROBLEMS

1 Solve for θ in the interval $0° \leq \theta \leq 360°$: $\tan^2 \theta = -\tan \theta$

SOLUTION

$$\tan^2 \theta = -\tan \theta$$

$\tan^2 \theta + \tan \theta = 0$	Set the equation equal to 0.
$\tan \theta(\tan \theta + 1) = 0$	Factor.

Set each factor equal to 0 and solve for θ:

$\tan \theta = 0$	$\tan \theta = -1$	First find the reference angle.
$\theta = 0°, 180°, 360°$	Reference angle = $45°$	Tangent is negative in Quadrants II and IV.
	Quadrant II: $135°$ $(180 - 45°)$	
	Quadrant IV: $315°$ $(360° - 45°)$	

Answer: $\theta = \{0°, 135°, 180°, 315°, 360°\}$

2 Solve for α in the interval $0 \le \alpha \le 2\pi$. $2\cos^2 \alpha + \cos \alpha + 2 = 3$

SOLUTION

$2\cos^2 \alpha + \cos \alpha + 2 = 3$

$2\cos^2 \alpha + \cos \alpha - 1 = 0$

$(2\cos \alpha - 1)(\cos \alpha + 1) = 0$

$2\cos \alpha - 1 = 0$	$\cos \alpha + 1 = 0$
$2\cos \alpha = 1$	$\cos \alpha = -1$
$\cos \alpha = \dfrac{1}{2}$	$\alpha = \pi$

Reference angle $= \dfrac{\pi}{3}$

Quadrant I: $\dfrac{\pi}{3}$

Quadrant IV: $\dfrac{5\pi}{3}$

Answer: $\alpha = \left\{ \dfrac{\pi}{3}, \pi, \dfrac{5\pi}{3} \right\}$

3 Solve for β in the interval $0 \le \beta \le 2\pi$. $\csc^2 \beta - \csc \beta + 3 = 5$

SOLUTION

$\csc^2 \beta - \csc \beta + 3 = 5$

$\csc^2 \beta - \csc \beta - 2 = 0$

$(\csc \beta - 2)(\csc \beta + 1) = 0$

$\csc \beta - 2 = 0$	$\csc \beta + 1 = 0$	
$\csc \beta = 2$	$\csc \beta = -1$	Convert $\csc \beta$ to $\sin \beta$.
$\sin \beta = \dfrac{1}{2}$	$\sin \beta = -1$	
	$\beta = \dfrac{3\pi}{2}$	

Reference angle $= \dfrac{\pi}{6}$

Quadrant I: $\dfrac{\pi}{6}$

Quadrant II: $\dfrac{5\pi}{6}$

Answer: $\beta = \left\{ \dfrac{\pi}{6}, \dfrac{5\pi}{6}, \dfrac{3\pi}{2} \right\}$

If a second-degree algebraic equation cannot be solved by factoring, we can use the quadratic formula, as shown below.

Solve for x: $x^2 + 2 = 4x$

$x^2 - 4x + 2 = 0$ Set the equation equal to 0.

Since the equation cannot be factored, use the quadratic formula with $a = 1$, $b = -4$, and $c = 2$.

$$x = \frac{4 \pm \sqrt{(-4)^2 - 4(1)(2)}}{2}$$

$$x = \frac{4 \pm \sqrt{8}}{2}$$

$$x = \frac{4 \pm 2\sqrt{2}}{2}$$

$$x = 2 \pm \sqrt{2}$$

We follow this same procedure for second-degree trigonometric equations.

MODEL PROBLEMS

4   To the nearest degree, solve for θ in the interval $0° \leq \theta \leq 360°$: $\sin^2 \theta + 2 = 4\sin \theta$

SOLUTION

Set the equation equal to 0: $\sin^2 \theta - 4\sin \theta + 2 = 0$

Since the equation cannot be factored, use the quadratic formula with $a = 1$, $b = -4$, and $c = 2$.

$$\sin \theta = \frac{4 \pm \sqrt{(-4)^2 - 4(1)(2)}}{2}$$

$$\sin \theta = \frac{4 \pm \sqrt{8}}{2}$$

$$\sin \theta = \frac{4 \pm 2\sqrt{2}}{2}$$

$\sin \theta = 2 \pm \sqrt{2}$ Break up into two separate equations.

$\sin \theta = 2 + \sqrt{2}$	$\sin \theta = 2 - \sqrt{2}$ Approximate $\sqrt{2}$.
$\sin \theta \approx 2 + 1.41421$	$\sin \theta \approx 2 - 1.41421$
$\sin \theta \approx 3.41421$	$\sin \theta \approx 0.58579$
✗ Reject	Reference angle $\approx 36°$
$(-1 \leq \sin \theta \leq 1)$	Quadrant I: $36°$
	Quadrant II: $144°$ ($180° - 36°$)

Answer: $\theta = \{36°, 144°\}$

5 To the nearest degree, solve for x in the interval $0° < x < 360°$: $\sin x - 3 = \dfrac{-1}{\sin x}$ ($\sin x \neq 0$)

SOLUTION

$$\sin x - 3 = \frac{-1}{\sin x}$$ Multiply both sides by $\sin x$.

$$\sin^2 x - 3\sin x = -1$$ Set the equation equal to 0.

$$\sin^2 x - 3\sin x + 1 = 0$$ Use the quadratic formula.

$$\sin x = \frac{3 \pm \sqrt{(-3)^2 - 4(1)(1)}}{2}$$

$$\sin x = \frac{3 \pm \sqrt{5}}{2}$$

$\sin x = \dfrac{3 + \sqrt{5}}{2}$	$\sin x = \dfrac{3 - \sqrt{5}}{2}$
$\sin x \approx 2.618034$	$\sin x \approx 0.381966$
✘ Reject	Reference angle $\approx 22°$
$(-1 \leq \sin x \leq 1)$	Quadrant I: 22°
	Quadrant II: 158°

Answer: $x = \{22°, 158°\}$

Practice

Exercises 1–5: Solve for *exact* values of θ in the interval $0° \leq \theta \leq 360°$.

1 $3\tan^2 \theta - 2 = 1$

2 $5\cos^2 \theta - 1 = 3(1 - \cos^2 \theta)$

3 $\sin^2 \theta - 2\sin \theta = 3$

4 $\csc^2 \theta - 1 = 3$

5 $2\cos^2 \theta = \cos \theta$

Exercises 6–10: Solve for *exact* values of θ in the interval $0 \leq \theta \leq 2\pi$.

6 $2\cos^2 \theta = \cos \theta + 1$

7 $\tan \theta(\tan \theta + 1) = \tan \theta + 3$

8 $2\sec^2 \theta = 3\sec \theta + 2$

9 $\cos \theta = \dfrac{1}{\cos \theta}$, $(\cos \theta \neq 0)$

10 $\sin \theta = \sqrt{\sin \theta}$

Exercises 11–16: Solve for β to the *nearest tenth of a degree* in the interval $0° \leq \beta \leq 360°$.

11 $5\tan^2 \beta + 3\tan \beta = 2$

12 $\sec^2 \beta = 6\sec \beta + 7$

13 $3\sin^2 \beta + \sin \beta + 5 = 4(1 - \sin \beta)$

14 $6\cos^2 \beta + 6\cos \beta + 2 = 1 + \cos \beta$

15 $3(1 - \sin^2 \beta) = \sin \beta$

16 $3\tan^2 \beta - 5\tan \beta = 2$

17 Find m$\angle B$ in the interval $180° \leq B \leq 270°$ that satisfies the equation $2\sin^2 B = 6\sin B$.

18 In the interval $90° \leq x \leq 180°$, find the value of x that satisfies the equation $2\cos^2 x = 1$.

19 If $\dfrac{3\pi}{2} \leq \theta \leq 2\pi$, solve for θ: $3\tan^2 \theta + 2 = 3$

Exercises 20–27: Select the numeral preceding the choice that best completes the statement or answers the question.

20 What is the total number of solutions for the equation $3\sin^2 x + \sin x = 2$ in the interval $0° \le x < 360°$?

(1) 1
(2) 2
(3) 3
(4) 4

21 The number of degrees in the smallest positive angle that satisfies the equation $2\cos^2 x - 3\cos x = 2$ is

(1) 30
(2) 60
(3) 120
(4) 210

22 Which of the following is *not* a solution of the equation $\tan^2 \beta = 3$?

(1) $-\dfrac{\pi}{3}$

(2) $\dfrac{2\pi}{3}$

(3) $\dfrac{5\pi}{6}$

(4) 120°

23 Which equation has roots of 0 and π?

(1) $\sin^2 x - 1 = 0$
(2) $\cos^2 x - 1 = 0$
(3) $\cos^2 x + \cos x = 0$
(4) $\cos^2 x + \cos x = 2$

24 Which third-quadrant angle satisfies the equation $2\cos^2 x - \cos x = 1$?

(1) 0

(2) $\dfrac{2\pi}{3}$

(3) $\dfrac{7\pi}{6}$

(4) $\dfrac{4\pi}{3}$

25 How many solutions does the equation $5\sin^2 x = 1 - 9\sin x$ have in the interval $0 \le x \le 2\pi$?

(1) 1
(2) 2
(3) 3
(4) 4

26 How many values of A in the interval $0° \le A < 360°$ satisfy the equation $2\sin^2 A + 3\sin A + 1 = 0$?

(1) 1
(2) 0
(3) 3
(4) 4

27 In the interval $0° \le A < 180°$, which value of x satisfies the equation $2\cos^2 x - 1 = 1$?

(1) 1
(2) 2
(3) 120°
(4) 180°

13.3 Trigonometric Equations That Use Identities

Sometimes a trigonometric equation contains different functions. In this form, it cannot be solved. However, you can use one or more of the trigonometric identities (see pages 417 and 427) to convert the equation into one that you can solve.

1 Solve for exact values of θ in the interval $0° \leq \theta \leq 360°$: $\cos^2 \theta + 2\sin \theta = 1$

SOLUTION

$\cos^2 \theta + 2\sin \theta = 1$ | Since $\sin^2 \theta + \cos^2 \theta = 1$, $\cos^2 \theta = 1 - \sin^2 \theta$.

$1 - \sin^2 \theta + 2\sin \theta = 1$ | Substitute for $\cos^2 \theta$ in the equation.

$-\sin^2 \theta + 2\sin \theta = 0$ | Factor.

$\sin \theta(-\sin \theta + 2) = 0$

$\sin \theta = 0$	$-\sin \theta + 2 = 0$
$\theta = 0°, 180°, 360°$	$\sin \theta = -2$ ✘ Reject

Answer: $\theta = 0°, 180°, 360°$

2 Solve for exact values of θ in the interval $0 \leq \theta \leq 2\pi$: $2\cos \theta = \sin 2\theta$

SOLUTION

$2\cos \theta = \sin 2\theta$ | Replace $\sin 2\theta$ with its double-angle formula.

$2\cos \theta = 2\sin \theta \cos \theta$ | Set the equation equal to 0.

$2\cos \theta - 2\sin \theta \cos \theta = 0$ | Factor out $2\cos \theta$.

$2\cos \theta(1 - \sin \theta) = 0$ | Set each factor equal to 0 and solve.

$2\cos \theta = 0$	$1 - \sin \theta = 0$
$\cos \theta = 0$	$\sin \theta = 1$
$\theta = \dfrac{\pi}{2}, \dfrac{3\pi}{2}$	$\theta = \dfrac{\pi}{2}$

Answer: $\theta = \dfrac{\pi}{2}, \dfrac{3\pi}{2}$

3 Solve for θ to the nearest tenth of a degree in the interval $0° \le \theta \le 360°$: $\cos 2\theta + 3\sin \theta = 0$

SOLUTION

$$\cos 2\theta + 3\sin \theta = 0$$

Since the equation contains $\sin \theta$, use the formula for $\cos 2\theta$ that contains $\sin \theta$: $\cos 2\theta = 1 - 2\sin^2 \theta$.

$$1 - 2\sin^2 \theta + 3\sin \theta = 0$$

Write the equation in the form $ax^2 + bx + c = 0$.

$$2\sin^2 \theta - 3\sin \theta - 1 = 0$$

Use the quadratic formula to solve for $\sin \theta$.

$$\sin \theta = \frac{3 \pm \sqrt{9 - 4(2)(-1)}}{2(2)}$$

$$\sin \theta = \frac{3 \pm \sqrt{17}}{4}$$

$\sin \theta = \dfrac{3 + \sqrt{17}}{4}$	$\sin \theta = \dfrac{3 - \sqrt{17}}{4}$
$\sin \theta \approx 1.780776$	$\sin \theta \approx -0.280776$
✗ Reject	Reference angle $\approx 16.3°$
	Quadrant III: $180° + 16.3° = 196.3°$
	Quadrant IV: $360° - 16.3° = 343.7°$

Answer: $\theta = 196.3°$ and $343.7°$

4 Solve for exact values of θ in the interval $0 \le \theta \le 2\pi$: $\sin \frac{1}{2}\theta = \sin \theta$

SOLUTION

$$\sin \frac{1}{2}\theta = \sin \theta$$

Use the half-angle sine formula.

$$\sqrt{\frac{1 - \cos \theta}{2}} = \sin \theta$$

Square both sides of the equation.

$$\frac{1 - \cos \theta}{2} = \sin^2 \theta$$

Replace $\sin^2 \theta$ with $1 - \cos^2 \theta$.

$$\frac{1 - \cos \theta}{2} = 1 - \cos^2 \theta$$

Multiply both sides of the equation by 2.

$$1 - \cos \theta = 2 - 2\cos^2 \theta$$

Set the equation equal to 0.

$$2\cos^2 \theta - \cos \theta - 1 = 0$$

Factor.

$$(2\cos \theta + 1)(\cos \theta - 1) = 0$$

Set each factor equal to 0 and solve.

$2\cos \theta + 1 = 0$	$\cos \theta - 1 = 0$
$\cos \theta = -\dfrac{1}{2}$	$\cos \theta = 1$
	$\theta = 0, 2\pi$
$\theta = \dfrac{2\pi}{3}, \dfrac{4\pi}{3}$	

Because we had a radical equation and squared both sides of the equation, we must check our solutions.

Check: $\sin \frac{1}{2}\theta = \sin \theta$

$$\theta = \frac{2\pi}{3} \qquad\qquad \theta = \frac{4\pi}{3} \qquad\qquad \theta = 0 \qquad\qquad \theta = 2\pi$$

$$\sin \frac{1}{2}\left(\frac{2\pi}{3}\right) \overset{?}{=} \sin \frac{2\pi}{3} \qquad \sin \frac{1}{2}\left(\frac{4\pi}{3}\right) \overset{?}{=} \sin \frac{4\pi}{3} \qquad \sin \frac{1}{2}(0) \overset{?}{=} \sin 0 \qquad \sin \frac{1}{2}(2\pi) \overset{?}{=} \sin 2\pi$$

$$\sin \frac{\pi}{3} \overset{?}{=} \sin \frac{2\pi}{3} \qquad\qquad \sin \frac{2\pi}{3} \overset{?}{=} \sin \frac{4\pi}{3} \qquad\qquad \sin 0 \overset{?}{=} \sin 0 \qquad\qquad \sin \pi \overset{?}{=} \sin 2\pi$$

$$\frac{\sqrt{3}}{2} = \frac{\sqrt{3}}{2} \; ✔ \qquad\qquad \frac{\sqrt{3}}{2} \neq \frac{-\sqrt{3}}{2} \; ✘ \qquad\qquad 0 = 0 \; ✔ \qquad\qquad 0 = 0 \; ✔$$

Answer: $\theta = 0, \dfrac{2\pi}{3}, 2\pi$

 **Practice**

Exercises 1–5: Solve for *exact* values of θ in the interval $0° \leq \theta \leq 360°$.

1 $\sin 2\theta = 0$

2 $\cos 2\theta = \cos \theta$

3 $2\cos^2 \theta + \sin \theta = 1$

4 $\sin \frac{1}{2}\theta = 1$

5 $\sin 2\theta + \cos \theta = 0$

Exercises 6–10: Solve for *exact* values of α in the interval $0 \leq \alpha \leq 2\pi$.

6 $\sin 2\alpha = -\sin \alpha$

7 $\cos 2\alpha + \cos \alpha = 0$

8 $\sin^2 \alpha + \cos^2 \alpha = \cos \alpha$

9 $\cos \frac{1}{2}\alpha = \cos \alpha$

10 $\tan \alpha = 2\sin \alpha$

Exercises 11–15: Find, to the *nearest tenth of a degree*, all values of θ in the interval $0° \leq \theta \leq 360°$ that satisfy each equation.

11 $3\cos^2 \theta - \sin \theta = 2$

12 $\tan \theta = \cos \theta$

13 $3\cos 2\theta + 2\cos \theta = 0$

14 $\cos 2\theta - \sin^2 \theta + \sin \theta + 1 = 0$

15 $\sin \frac{1}{2}\theta = \cos \theta + 1$

16 **a** On the same set of axes, graph $y = 2\sin x$ and $y = \cos 2x$ for values of x in the interval $0 \leq x \leq 2\pi$.

b Based on the graphs drawn in part **a**, what value(s) of x in the interval $0 \leq x \leq 2\pi$ satisfy the equation $2\sin x - \cos 2x = 3$?

c Using algebraic techniques, solve the equation $2\sin x - \cos 2x = 3$.

17 a On the same set of axes, graph $y = -\sin x$ and $y = 2\cos \frac{1}{2}x$ for values of x in the interval $0 \le x \le 2\pi$.

b Based on the graphs drawn in part **a**, find all values of x in the interval $0 \le x \le 2\pi$ that satisfy the equation $2\cos \frac{1}{2}x = -\sin x$.

c Using algebraic techniques, solve the equation $2\cos \frac{1}{2}x = -\sin x$.

18 a On the same set of axes, graph $y = -\cos x$ and $y = \sin 2x$ for values of x in the interval $0 \le x \le 2\pi$.

b Based on the graphs drawn in part **a**, what value(s) of x in the interval $0 \le x \le 2\pi$ satisfy the equation $-\cos x = \sin 2x$? Why is it difficult to get an exact value for some of the solutions using the graph?

c Using algebraic techniques, solve the equation $-\cos x = \sin 2x$.

19 a On the same set of axes, graph $y = -\cos x$ and $y = \sin \frac{1}{2}x$ for values of x in the interval $0 \le x \le 2\pi$.

b Based on the graphs drawn in part **a**, what value of x in the interval $0 \le x \le 2\pi$ satisfies the equation $-\cos x = \sin \frac{1}{2}x$?

c Using algebraic techniques, solve the equation $-\cos x = \sin \frac{1}{2}x$.

Exercises 20–23: Select the numeral preceding the choice that best answers the question.

20 What is the total number of solutions for the equation $5\sin^2 \theta = 7\cos \theta - 1$ in the interval $0° \le \theta \le 360°$?

(1) 1
(2) 2
(3) 3
(4) 4

21 Which is *not* a solution of the equation $\sin 2\theta = \cos \theta$?

(1) $\dfrac{\pi}{6}$

(2) $\dfrac{\pi}{2}$

(3) $\dfrac{5\pi}{6}$

(4) π

22 What is the measure, in degrees, of the smallest positive angle that satisfies the equation $3\cos 2x + 2\sin x + 1 = 0$?

(1) 1°
(2) 42°
(3) 90°
(4) 138°

23 What is the total number of solutions of the equation $\dfrac{\sin 2\theta}{\sin \theta} = \sec \theta$ in the interval $0 \le \theta \le 2\pi$?

(1) 1
(2) 2
(3) 3
(4) 4

Calculators are useful for solving and checking trigonometric equations. However, the calculator will give only approximate values. Therefore, when asked for exact values, you must use an algebraic method. Let us revisit Exercise 11 from Section 13.2: $5\tan^2 \beta + 3\tan \beta = 2$. To solve this equation using the calculator, enter the left side of the equation into Y_1 and the right side of the equation into Y_2, as shown below.

```
Plot1  Plot2  Plot3
\Y1■5(tan(X))²+3
tan(X)
\Y2■2
\Y3=
\Y4=
\Y5=
\Y6=
```

Make sure that your calculator is in Degree mode. Set Xmin = 0, Xmax = 360, Ymin = −1, and Ymax = 4, then graph the two equations. It's okay that we don't see the top of the Y_1 function because the graphs intersect at $y = 2$. The figure below shows the first intersection point, found by pressing (2nd) (TRACE) and choosing 5: intersect.

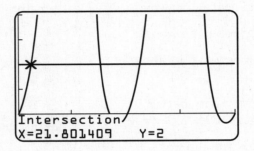

```
Intersection
X=21.801409    Y=2
```

The four solutions to this equation in the interval $0° \leq \theta \leq 360°$ are $\theta \approx 21.8°$, 135°, 201.8°, and 315°.

The calculator can also be used to solve equations containing two different functions.

Exercise 15 from Section 13.3 asks us to solve for θ: $\sin \frac{1}{2}\theta = \cos \theta + 1$. Input the left side of the equation into Y_1 and the right side of the equation into Y_2, as shown below.

```
Plot1  Plot2  Plot3
\Y1■sin(.5X)
\Y2■cos(X)+1
\Y3=
\Y4=
\Y5=
\Y6=
\Y7=
```

Graph these equations over the same domain as before, but with Ymin = −2 and Ymax = 2, and then find their points of intersection. The figure below shows one of the intersection points, again found using the Intersect feature.

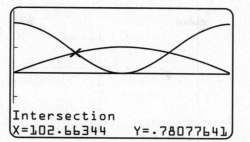

The two solutions in the interval $0° \leq \theta \leq 360°$ are $\theta \approx 102.7°$ and $\theta \approx 257.3°$.

CHAPTER REVIEW

Exercises 1–10: Select the numeral preceding the choice that best completes the statement or answers the question.

1 What value of x in the interval $90° \leq x \leq 180°$ satisfies the equation $\sin^2 x + \sin x = 0$?

(1) 90°
(2) 120°
(3) 135°
(4) 180°

2 The equation $\sqrt{4\sin\theta + 7} = 3$ has which of the following as a possible solution?

(1) $\dfrac{\pi}{2}$

(2) $\dfrac{\pi}{3}$

(3) $\dfrac{\pi}{4}$

(4) $\dfrac{\pi}{6}$

3 The equation $\sin^2\theta - 2\sin\theta + 1 = 0$ has how many possible solutions for θ if $0 \leq \theta \leq 2\pi$?

(1) 1
(2) 2
(3) 3
(4) 0

4 In the interval $0° \leq x \leq 360°$, how many values of x satisfy the equation $\cos^2 x - 5\cos x - 6 = 0$?

(1) 1
(2) 2
(3) 3
(4) 0

5 Which of the following is *not* a solution to the equation $2\cos\theta - 1 = \sec\theta$?

(1) 0°
(2) 120°
(3) 180°
(4) 240°

6 If $(\tan x - 2)(\tan x - 1) = 0$, then x may be an angle in

(1) Quadrant I, only
(2) Quadrant II or Quadrant IV
(3) Quadrant I or Quadrant III
(4) any of the four quadrants

7 Which value of x does *not* satisfy the equation $|2\tan\theta - 1| = 1$?

(1) 0°
(2) 90°
(3) 180°
(4) 225°

8 A value of x that satisfies the equation $2\cos^2 x - \cos x - 1 = 0$ is

(1) $\dfrac{\pi}{3}$

(2) $\dfrac{\pi}{2}$

(3) $\dfrac{3\pi}{4}$

(4) $\dfrac{4\pi}{3}$

9 In the interval $0° \leq A < 360°$, how many values of A satisfy the equation $\sin^3 A - 2\sin^2 A = 3\sin A$?

(1) 1

(2) 0

(3) 3

(4) 4

10 Which is *not* a solution to the equation $\sin^2 \theta + \sin \theta = 0$?

(1) $\dfrac{\pi}{2}$

(2) π

(3) $\dfrac{3\pi}{2}$

(4) 2π

Exercises 11–20: Solve each equation for all values of θ, to the *nearest tenth of a degree*, in the interval $0° \leq \theta < 360°$.

11 $\dfrac{2}{\cos \theta} = 5\cos \theta + 3$

12 $3\sin^2 \theta + 2 = 7\sin \theta$

13 $2\sin^2 \theta + 5\cos \theta = 4$

14 $3\sec^2 \theta - 5\tan \theta = 1$

15 $3\tan \theta - 2\cot \theta = 3$

16 $3\cos^2 \theta - 5 = 5\sin \theta$

17 $2\cos \theta - 3 = 5\sec \theta$

18 $2\cos 2\theta + 1 = \sin \theta$

19 $3\cos 2\theta = 2 - \sin \theta$

20 $4\sin \theta - 5 = \dfrac{6}{\sin \theta}, (\sin \theta \neq 0)$

Trigonometric Applications

14.1 Law of Cosines

If you are given the lengths of two sides of a right triangle, you would have no difficulty finding the length of the third side using the Pythagorean theorem. For example, the triangle below has legs of 7 and 24, so we can find the hypotenuse using the formula $c^2 = a^2 + b^2$.

$c^2 = a^2 + b^2$

$c^2 = 7^2 + 24^2$

$c^2 = 625$

$c = \pm\sqrt{625}$

$c = 25$

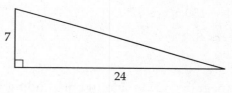

Note: Since we are finding the length of a side of a triangle, we use only the positive square root of 625, which is 25.

However, to solve triangles that do *not* contain right angles, we need other methods. One formula that is very useful, if you are provided information in a Side-Angle-Side or SAS pattern, is the Law of Cosines.

The **Law of Cosines** states:

$c^2 = a^2 + b^2 - 2ab\cos C$, where C is the angle opposite the side whose length you are trying to find.

MODEL PROBLEMS

1 In triangle *HAT*, $a = 6.4$, $t = 10.2$, and m∠*H* = 87. Find the length of side h to the nearest tenth.

SOLUTION

Always draw a diagram when you are doing trigonometric application problems. A helpful method is to label those sides and angles you are given with a large **S** or **A**. This visual cue can be key to deciding how to set up your formula and which variable corresponds to which side in the formula.

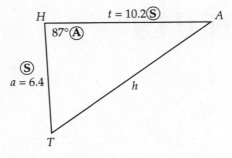

Since the diagram depicts an SAS pattern, we know to use the Law of Cosines, letting h replace the original c of the formula while a and t replace a and b.

$$h^2 = a^2 + t^2 - 2at\cos H$$

$$h^2 = 6.4^2 + 10.2^2 - 2(6.4)(10.2)\cos 87°$$

$$h^2 = 40.96 + 104.04 - 130.56\cos 87°$$

$$h = \sqrt{145 - 130.56\cos 87°}$$

$$h \approx 11.8$$

Again we reject the negative value since we are finding the side of a triangle. Be sure to follow the order of operations and multiply 130.56 by cos 87° before subtracting.

Answer: 11.8

2 In isosceles triangle *QRS*, $q = s = 4.7$ centimeters. If cos *R* = 0.1908, find the length of side r to the nearest hundredth of a centimeter.

SOLUTION

In this problem, we are not given the measure of the included angle but the value of its cosine instead. This means less work for us: we merely substitute that value in the Law of Cosines formula.

$$r^2 = q^2 + s^2 - 2qs\cos R$$

$$r^2 = 4.7^2 + 4.7^2 - 2(4.7)(4.7)(0.1908)$$

$$r^2 = 22.09 + 22.09 - 8.429544$$

$$r^2 = 35.750456$$

$$r \approx 5.979168504 \text{ centimeters}$$

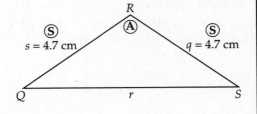

Answer: 5.98 centimeters

3 Mr. DeStefano wants to make his backyard garden unusual, so he decides to design it in the shape of an obtuse triangle with white alyssum acting as the border on the two shorter sides of the triangle and purple salvia along the length of the third side. The two shorter sides measure 8 feet and 9 feet, including an angle of 105°.

a To the nearest tenth of a foot, what is the measure of the third side of the triangle?

b If Mr. DeStefano needs 4 salvia plants for each foot of border, how many plants will he need?

SOLUTION

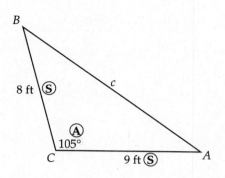

a Since we are looking for the side opposite the 105° angle, that side becomes c, but it really makes no difference which side we designate as a or b. Substitute the given values in the Law of Cosines formula and solve.

$c^2 = a^2 + b^2 - 2ab\cos C$

$c^2 = 8^2 + 9^2 - 2(8)(9)\cos 105°$

$c^2 = 64 + 81 - 144\cos 105°$

$c = \sqrt{145 - 144\cos 105°}$

$c \approx 13.5$ ft

Answer: 13.5 feet

b To find the number of plants needed, we multiply 13.5 by 4 and learn that Mr. DeStefano will need 54 salvia plants for his garden design.

Answer: 54 plants

Sometimes we are given the lengths of three sides of the triangle and asked to find an angle. In this case, it is often easier to manipulate the Law of Cosines so that the cosine value is isolated.

$$c^2 = a^2 + b^2 - 2ab\cos C$$

$$c^2 - a^2 - b^2 = -2ab\cos C$$

$$\frac{c^2 - a^2 - b^2}{-2ab} = \cos C \qquad \text{Divide both sides by } -2ab.$$

$$\cos C = \frac{a^2 + b^2 - c^2}{2ab} \qquad \begin{array}{l}\text{An alternate version of the}\\\text{Law of Cosines.}\end{array}$$

In this format, we always subtract the square of the side opposite the angle we are trying to find.

4 Jed is working on a stained-glass project and needs to form a triangle with sides of 8, 12, and 15 inches out of lead cane to enclose the glass. To the nearest tenth of a degree, what is the largest angle he needs to create using the lead caning?

SOLUTION

Since Jed needs to know the largest angle, we will represent the longest side as c. We substitute the values into the formula.

$$\cos C = \frac{a^2 + b^2 - c^2}{2ab}$$

$$\cos C = \frac{8^2 + 12^2 - 15^2}{2(8)(12)}$$

$$\cos C = -\frac{17}{192}$$

$$m\angle C \approx 95.1$$

Answer: 95.1°

Remember: When you are working with angles within a triangle, a negative cosine indicates an obtuse or second-quadrant angle.

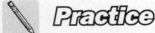

Practice

Exercises 1–10: Select the numeral preceding the choice that best completes the statement or answers the question.

1 An isosceles triangle has equal sides of 12.4 and an included angle of 93.4°. What is the length of the third side of the triangle to the *nearest tenth*?

(1) 4.9
(2) 18.0
(3) 18.5
(4) 48.9

2 In triangle *ABC*, $\cos A = -\dfrac{1}{2}$, $b = 6.5$, and $c = 7.2$. The length of a, to the *nearest hundredth*, is

(1) 11.87
(2) 8.87
(3) 7.87
(4) 6.78

3 In triangle *MNP*, $m\angle MNP = 120$, $NM = 5.8$ centimeters, and $NP = 8.3$ centimeters. The length of $\overline{MP}$, to the *nearest tenth*, is

(1) 7.4 centimeters
(2) 11.3 centimeters
(3) 12.3 centimeters
(4) 13.3 centimeters

4 Three sides of a triangle measure 5, 8, and 12. The triangle is

(1) isosceles
(2) right
(3) acute
(4) obtuse

5 A triangle has sides of lengths 7.1, 9.4 and 15.3. Which is the measure of the largest angle of the triangle?

(1) 135.6°
(2) 115.8°
(3) 103.6°
(4) 25.5°

6 In $\triangle XYZ$, $x = 11.7$ inches, $y = 9.6$ inches, and $z = 5.9$ inches. What is the cosine of the smallest angle of the triangle to the *nearest ten-thousandth*?

(1) -0.0876
(2) 0.0939
(3) 0.5761
(4) 0.8647

7 In $\triangle KLM$, $k = 9$ centimeters, $l = 40$ centimeters, and $m = 41$ centimeters. What is the measure of the largest angle of the triangle?

(1) $107°$
(2) $90°$
(3) $84°$
(4) $79°$

8 In $\triangle PQR$, m$\angle RPQ = 131$, $q = 10.8$ inches, and $r = 8.1$ inches. What is the length of side p to the *nearest tenth*?

(1) 17.2 inches
(2) 14.7 inches
(3) 12.9 inches
(4) 11.5 inches

9 The base angles of isosceles triangle GHI measure $57.4°$ while equal sides $\overline{GH}$ and $\overline{HI}$ measure 8.94 inches. The length of $\overline{GI}$, to the *nearest hundredth of an inch*, is

(1) 7.12 inches
(2) 8.26 inches
(3) 8.59 inches
(4) 9.63 inches

10 In parallelogram $ABCD$, $AB = 11$ inches and $BC = 17$ inches. If $\angle ABC = 102°36'$, then the length of diagonal $\overline{AC}$, to the *nearest tenth*, is

(1) 18.1 inches
(2) 21.2 inches
(3) 22.2 inches
(4) 28.0 inches

11 Emily and Jeff bought a beautiful slab of petrified wood that they would like to use as the top of a coffee table. Jeff is making a triangular base for the table as indicated in the diagram.

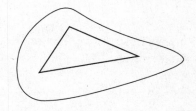

If the sides of the triangular base are 22 inches, 28.5 inches, and 30.7 inches, find the measures of the three angles, to the *nearest hundredth of a degree*, that Jeff must construct for the base.

12 Dimitri and Anna are in charge of setting the route for the Daffy Driver's Bike Race at the county fair. This is an event for children ages 8 to 14, in which each biker must complete the triangular course and collect souvenirs along the way.

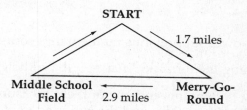

The distance from the start to the merry-go-round is 1.7 miles, the distance from the merry-go-round to the middle school field is 2.9 miles, and the angle included between these legs of the race is $51°24'$. Find the total distance, to the *nearest hundredth of a mile*, covered by the bikers in this event.

13 Two cabins are situated on Lake Happy Trails, at a distance of 800 feet apart. The owners of the cabins would like to put a wooden raft out in the lake so that it is 1,000 feet from each of the two cabins, labeled A and B.

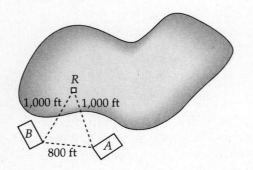

a What is the measure of ∠BAR, to the *nearest tenth of a degree* and to the *nearest ten minutes*?

b What is the measure of ∠ARB, to the *nearest tenth of a degree* and to the *nearest ten minutes*?

14 The lighthouse on Pine Island is visible from two boats off shore. Doug's sailboat is 4.2 miles from the lighthouse while Ralph's fishing trawler is 6.7 miles from the lighthouse. If the light from the lighthouse sweeps an angle of 66.5° between the two boats, how far apart are they, to the *nearest tenth of a mile*?

15 Bird watchers follow a prescribed path through the nature conservation park so they do not disturb mating or nesting birds. The bird watchers start at the pond, walk 2.1 miles east to a viewing platform, turn 124° southeast, and travel 4.7 miles until they reach the nesting area. After taking all the pictures they want, the bird watchers turn northwest and return to their starting point. How long, to the *nearest tenth of a mile*, is the path from the nesting area to the beginning of the trail?

14.2 Area of a Triangle

We know from previous mathematics courses that we can find the area of a triangle using the formula Area = $\frac{1}{2}$(base)(height), but in some triangles, like the one below, we are missing one of these measurements. In this case, we have only the lengths of two sides and the included angle of a triangle.

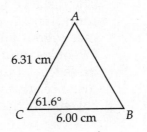

To find the area, we can set the triangle on a coordinate plane, placing one vertex at the origin and another vertex on the positive x-axis as shown below.

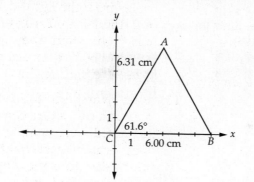

We can construct a line through point A perpendicular to $\overline{CB}$. The measure of the base $\overline{CB}$, is 6. The measure of the height is the length of $\overline{AP}$, which is the y-coordinate of point A. The coordinates of point A are

$$(b\cos C, b\sin C) = (6.31\cos 61.6°, 6.31\sin 61.6°) \approx (3, 5.55)$$

Thus, to the nearest hundredth, $AP = 5.55$ centimeters.

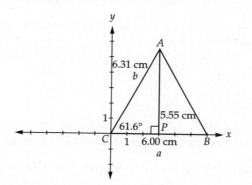

We can now use this information to find the area of $\triangle ABC$.

$$\text{Area} = \frac{1}{2}(\text{base})(\text{height})$$

$$= \frac{1}{2}(6)(6.31\sin 61.6°)$$

$$= \frac{1}{2}(6)(5.55)$$

$$\approx 16.65 \text{ square centimeters}$$

In general, we can find the area of a triangle when given two of its sides and the included angle by using the formula below. In triangle ABC,

$$\text{Area} = \frac{1}{2}(\text{base})(\text{height})$$

$$= \frac{1}{2}(a)(b\sin C)$$

$$= \frac{1}{2}ab\sin C$$

Remember: To utilize this formula to find the area of a triangle, we need the information in a Side-Angle-Side pattern.

MODEL PROBLEMS

1 In $\triangle ABC$, $a = 16$, $b = 12$, and $\sin C = \frac{1}{2}$. Find the area of $\triangle ABC$.

SOLUTION

We have the appropriate information, so we simply substitute into the formula:

$$\begin{aligned}\text{Area} &= \frac{1}{2}ab\sin C \\ &= \frac{1}{2}(16)(12)\left(\frac{1}{2}\right) \\ &= 48 \text{ square units}\end{aligned}$$

Answer: 48 square units

2 If the area of $\triangle DEF$ is 101 square centimeters, $d = 16$ centimeters, and $e = 14$ centimeters, find the measure of $\angle F$ to the nearest tenth of a degree.

SOLUTION

In this case, we know the area but are trying to find the measure of an angle. We use the same area formula but solve for $\angle F$.

$$\text{Area} = \frac{1}{2}de\sin F$$

$$101 = \frac{1}{2}(16)(14)\sin F$$

$$101 = 112\sin F$$

$$\frac{101}{112} = \sin F$$

$m\angle F \approx 64.4$ or $m\angle F \approx 180 - 64.4 = 115.6$

Note: Since $\sin \angle F$ is positive, there is both an acute angle and an obtuse angle with this sine value. Since we do not know the length of side f, we must list both angles as possible answers.

Answer: 64.4° or 115.6°

3 Find the area of the triangle to the nearest hundredth of a square meter.

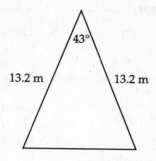

SOLUTION

In this case, we can simply substitute into the area formula.

Area $= \dfrac{1}{2}(13.2)(13.2)\sin 43°$

≈ 59.42 square meters

Answer: 59.42 square meters

4 In parallelogram *HOPE*, *HO* = 16.7 centimeters, *HE* = 20.1 centimeters, and m∠*OHE* = 108.3.

   a Find the length of $\overline{OE}$ to the nearest tenth of a centimeter.

   b Find the area of parallelogram *HOPE* to the nearest hundredth of a square centimeter.

SOLUTION

   a First we need to use the Law of Cosines to find the length of $\overline{OE}$.

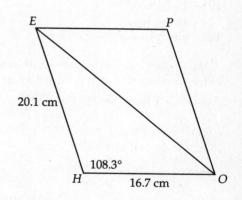

$c^2 = a^2 + b^2 - 2ab\cos c$

$h^2 = 16.7^2 + 20.1^2 - 2(16.7)(20.1)\cos 108.3°$

$h = \sqrt{682.9 - 671.34\cos 108.3°}$

$h \approx 29.9$ centimeters

Answer: 29.9 centimeters

   b To find the area of the parallelogram, we double the area of triangle *OHE*.

Area $= 2\left(\dfrac{1}{2}\right)oe\sin H$

Area $= 2\left(\dfrac{1}{2}\right)(20.1)(16.7)(\sin 108.3°)$

Area ≈ 318.69 square centimeters

Answer: 318.69 square centimeters

 **Practice**

Exercises 1–5: Find the area of each triangle to the *nearest hundredth of a unit.*

1 In △*KLM*, m∠*L* = 78.3, *k* = 12.8 inches, and *m* = 9.7 inches.

2 In △*ABC*, m∠*A* = 58.2, *b* = 8.6 centimeters, and *c* = 7.1 centimeters.

3 In △*DOG*, m∠*O* = 123, *d* = 17 centimeters, and *g* = 11.4 centimeters.

4 In isosceles △*LUV*, the measure of vertex angle *U* = 54° and *v* = 18 centimeters.

5 In isosceles △*CAT*, *CA* = *AT*, m∠*C* = 72, and *c* = 6.3 inches.

Exercises 6–15: Select the numeral preceding the choice that best completes the statement or answers the question.

6 If the area of △*END* is 24 square inches, m∠*E* = 150, and *d* measures 12 inches, what is the length of side *n*?

   (1) 8 inches
   (2) 12 inches
   (3) 16 inches
   (4) $24\sqrt{3}$ inches

7 If one side of an equilateral triangle measures 6 meters, what is number of square meters in the area of the triangle?

   (1) 9
   (2) $6\sqrt{3}$
   (3) $9\sqrt{3}$
   (4) 18

8 Find the area of a parallelogram to the *nearest tenth of a square inch* if its sides measure 14 and 17 inches and an angle of the parallelogram measures 74°.

   (1) 65.6
   (2) 114.4
   (3) 183.2
   (4) 228.8

9 The area of △*USA* is 74 square inches, side *u* measures 17 inches, and side *a* measures 13 inches. Which is an approximation of sin ∠*USA*?

   (1) 0.1629
   (2) 0.3258
   (3) 0.6697
   (4) 0.8319

10 In rhombus *LIFE*, each side measures 13.6 centimeters and m∠*LIF* = 112.5. The area of rhombus *LIFE* is approximately which of the following?

   (1) 70.8 square centimeters
   (2) 85.4 square centimeters
   (3) 170.9 square centimeters
   (4) 341.8 square centimeters

11 In △*JOG*, m∠*JOG* = 82, *j* = 8.4 centimeters, and *g* = 7.1 centimeters. Approximately how many square centimeters are in the area of △*JOG*?

   (1) 14.76
   (2) 29.53
   (3) 59.06
   (4) 59.64

12 Each base angle of an isosceles triangle measures 57.4° and the equal sides measure 10.8 inches. The area of the triangle is approximately which of the following, to the *nearest hundredth of a square inch*?

   (1) 24.46
   (2) 49.13
   (3) 52.94
   (4) 58.32

13 If the area of an isosceles triangle is 68 square feet and the vertex angle is 66°, what is the length of an equal side of the triangle?

   (1) 5.8 inches
   (2) 8.3 inches
   (3) 10.4 inches
   (4) 12.2 inches

14 In △QRS, m∠Q = 102.4, r = 15.3 miles, and s = 11.8 miles. To the *nearest hundredth of a square mile*, the area of △QRS is approximately

(1) 176.33
(2) 88.16
(3) 44.08
(4) 19.38

15 In parallelogram *JACK*, ∠JCK measures 61°15′, *JC* = 23.5, and *KC* = 18.7. The area of the parallelogram is approximately how many square units?

(1) 192.64
(2) 385.28
(3) 423.18
(4) 462.11

16 Given parallelogram *TIME* as shown in the diagram.

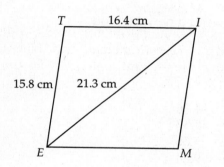

The lengths, in centimeters, of the sides of △TIE are *TI* = 16.4, *TE* = 15.8, and *EI* = 21.3.

a Find the measure of ∠TIE to the *nearest tenth of a degree*.
b Find the area of parallelogram *TIME* to the *nearest tenth of a square centimeter*.

17

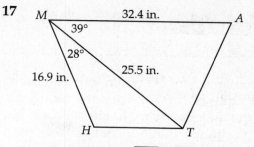

In the diagram, $\overline{MA} \parallel \overline{HT}$, *MA* = 32.4 inches, *MT* = 25.5 inches, *MH* = 16.9 inches, m∠AMT = 39, and m∠HMT = 28.

a Find the length of $\overline{HT}$ to the *nearest tenth of an inch*.
b Find the area of trapezoid *MATH* to the *nearest tenth of a square inch*.

14.3 Law of Sines and the Ambiguous Case

In some problems, you are given information for a triangle that does *not* include either the lengths of two sides and the included angle or the lengths of three sides, which are the data necessary to use the Law of Cosines. As shown below, the information provided about a triangle may be in an Angle-Side-Angle pattern (ASA), an Angle-Angle-Side pattern (AAS), or a Side-Side-Angle pattern (SSA).

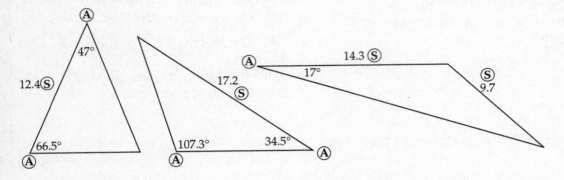

Since we cannot use the Law of Cosines in these cases, we need a new method to find the remaining sides.

As you recall from Section 14.2, we can find the area of triangle *ABC* by using the formula:

$$\text{Area of } \triangle ABC = \frac{1}{2}ab\sin C = \frac{1}{2}ac\sin B = \frac{1}{2}bc\sin A$$

We will divide each of the three terms of the equality by $\frac{1}{2}abc$.

$$\frac{\frac{1}{2}ab\sin C}{\frac{1}{2}abc} = \frac{\frac{1}{2}ac\sin B}{\frac{1}{2}abc} = \frac{\frac{1}{2}bc\sin A}{\frac{1}{2}abc}$$

$$\frac{\sin C}{c} = \frac{\sin B}{b} = \frac{\sin A}{a}$$

We call this formula the **Law of Sines**. Rearranging the terms, we have:

$$\frac{\sin A}{a} = \frac{\sin B}{b} = \frac{\sin C}{c}$$

The Law of Sines states that the sine of an angle is proportional to the side opposite that angle.

When applying this rule, it is helpful to draw a diagram to be certain you have the correct angle and side relationships. In writing Law of Sine equations, we use only two of the possible ratios, thus producing a proportion we can solve.

1 In triangle PQR, m$\angle PQR = 66.5$, m$\angle QRP = 47$, and $QR = 12.4$ inches. Find the length of $\overline{QP}$ to the nearest tenth of an inch.

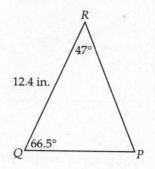

SOLUTION

Since the given information is in an ASA pattern, we need to use the Law of Sines. However, while we have the length of side $\overline{QR}$, we don't have the measure of $\angle QPR$ opposite that side. Since we do know the value of the other two angles of the triangle, we can subtract the sum of the two given angles from $180°$ to determine the measure of $\angle QPR$.

m$\angle QPR = 180 - ($m$\angle PQR + m\angle QRP)$

m$\angle QPR = 180 - (66.5 + 47)$

m$\angle QPR = 180 - 113.5$

m$\angle QPR = 66.5$

Because $\triangle PQR$ is isosceles, we could use the Law of Cosines to solve this problem. However, we have chosen to continue with the Law of Sines solution. Determine which ratios to use and write the equation. Then substitute the known values.

$$\frac{\sin R}{QP} = \frac{\sin P}{QR}$$

$$\frac{\sin 47°}{QP} = \frac{\sin 66.5°}{12.4}$$

Rewriting the problem to solve for QP, we find:

$$QP = \frac{12.4\sin 47°}{\sin 66.5°}$$

$$\approx 9.9 \text{ inches}$$

Answer: 9.9 inches

2 In triangle CTH, $m\angle T = 107.3$, $m\angle H = 34.5$, and $CH = 17.2$ centimeters. Find the length of $\overline{CT}$ to the nearest tenth of a centimeter.

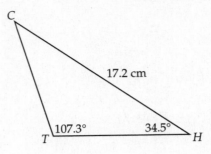

SOLUTION

Since the given information is in an AAS pattern, we use the Law of Sines.

$$\frac{\sin T}{t} = \frac{\sin H}{h}$$

$$\frac{\sin 107.3°}{17.2} = \frac{\sin 34.5°}{h}$$

$$h = \frac{17.2\sin 34.5°}{\sin 107.3°}$$

$$h \approx 10.2 \text{ cm}$$

Answer: $CT = 10.2$ cm

3 Given triangle JKL in which $JK = 14.3$, $KL = 5.8$, and $m\angle J = 17$, find the measure of $\angle L$ to the nearest tenth of a degree.

SOLUTION

In this case, the given information is in an SSA pattern, which means that we must take care to consider the possibility of two different triangles with the required measures. Since $JK > KL$, it follows that the measure of $\angle KLJ$ must be greater than the measure of $\angle KJL$, but whether the angle is acute or obtuse depends upon our solution. First, we set up the equation and find the value of $\sin L$.

$$\frac{\sin J}{j} = \frac{\sin L}{l}$$

$$\frac{\sin 17°}{5.8} = \frac{\sin L}{14.3}$$

$$\sin L = \frac{14.3\sin 17°}{5.8}$$

$$\sin L \approx 0.7208474789$$

$$\angle L \approx 46.1°$$

However, since the sine function is also positive in the second quadrant, it is possible that $\angle L$ is obtuse, measuring $180° - 46.1° = 133.9°$. It is certainly just as possible to have a triangle with $m\angle L = 46.1$, $m\angle J = 17$, and $m\angle K = 116.9$, as it is to have a triangle with $m\angle L = 133.9$, $m\angle J = 17$, and $m\angle K = 29.1$.

Answer: $\angle L = 46.1°$ or $\angle L = 133.9°$

The situation described in Model Problem 3 is often called the **ambiguous case** because we do not know which measure of ∠L is intended. We must give both possible measures of the angles. The two different possible triangles are shown below.

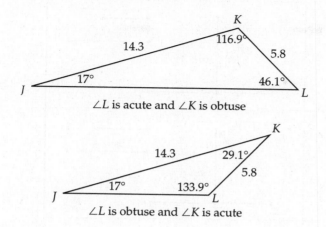

∠L is acute and ∠K is obtuse

∠L is obtuse and ∠K is acute

It may be helpful for you to remember the following information when you try to determine the number of possible triangles (0, 1, or 2) when given information in an SSA pattern. If you are given information about sides a and b and ∠A in △ABC, you can make a sketch to help you determine the number of possible triangles. First, fix side b and ∠A. Then sketch the possible positions of side a to determine the number of triangles that can be formed.

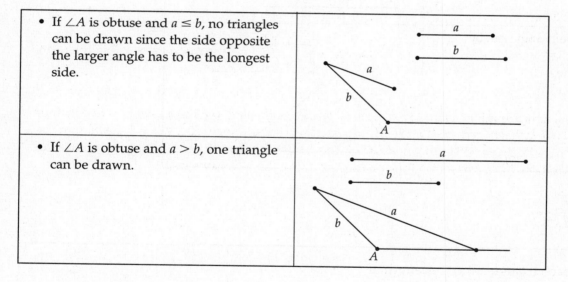

• If ∠A is obtuse and $a \leq b$, no triangles can be drawn since the side opposite the larger angle has to be the longest side.	
• If ∠A is obtuse and $a > b$, one triangle can be drawn.	

If ∠A is acute, we must drop an altitude to the base of the triangle. The length of the altitude is equal to $b\sin A$. The following four cases illustrate the number of triangles that can be drawn.

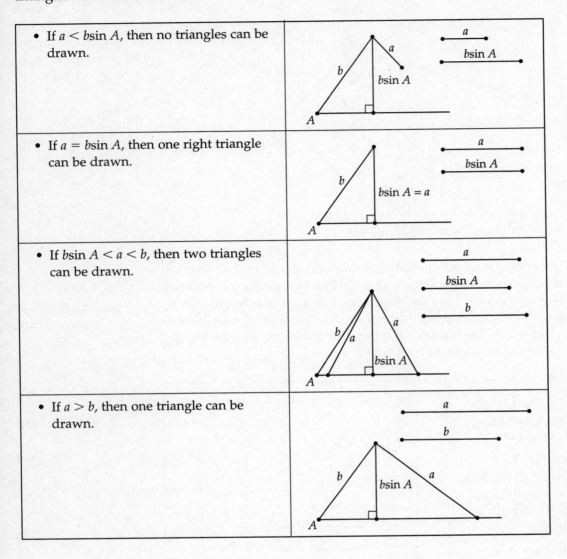

• If $a < b\sin A$, then no triangles can be drawn.	
• If $a = b\sin A$, then one right triangle can be drawn.	
• If $b\sin A < a < b$, then two triangles can be drawn.	
• If $a > b$, then one triangle can be drawn.	

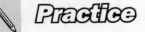

Practice

Exercises 1–5: For each triangle, find the length of the indicated side a to the *nearest tenth* or the measure of angle A to the *nearest tenth of a degree.*

1
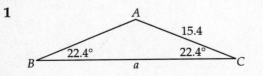

2
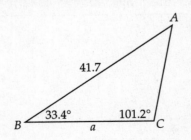

3

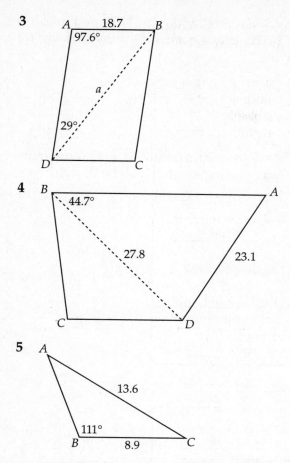

4

5

6 In △*MAN*, m∠*A* = 27.6, m∠*N* = 73.1, and *a* = 5.7 centimeters. Find the length of side *m* to the *nearest tenth of a centimeter*.

7 In isosceles triangle *YES*, the vertex angle *YES* measures 54.6°. If the base of the triangle measures 12.7 inches, find, to the *nearest tenth of an inch*, the length of the two equal sides of the triangle.

8 JoAnna and Ethel are designing a triangular hopscotch board similar to the one below. If the equal sides of their board are to be 8.5 feet in length, and the base angles measure 71°, find the length of the base to the *nearest tenth of a foot*.

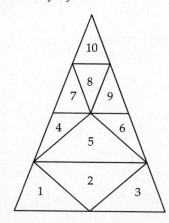

9 Kevin and Misha are going to make A-frame birdhouses as Mother's Day gifts. The basic design is shown below, but they need to know how long the base will be. If they want the sides of the A-frame to be 14.25 inches in length, with the crossbar placed 3 inches from the bottom, and the base angles to measure 65.3°, find the length of the crossbar to the *nearest hundredth of an inch*.

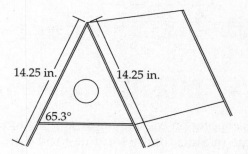

10 In parallelogram *MATH*, *MA* = 9, *MH* = 6.2, and m∠*HAM* = 38.2. Find the measure of ∠*AMH* to the *nearest tenth of a degree*. (Hint: Find m∠*AHM* first.)

11 In △*CTH*, m∠*C* = 17, *c* = 12, and *h* = 31.

  a How many distinct triangles *CTH* are possible?

  b Find all possible measures of ∠*H* to the *nearest degree*.

  c Find all possible lengths of $\overline{CH}$ to the *nearest integer*.

  d Sketch all possible triangles.

Exercises 12–16: Select the numeral preceding the choice that best completes the statement or answers the question.

12 In △*WXY*, *x* = 8.3 centimeters, *y* = 6.4 centimeters, and m∠*X* = 82.4. The measure of ∠*Y* is

  (1) 0.764°

  (2) 49.8°

  (3) 63.5°

  (4) 106.9°

13 In △*DAY*, sin *D* = 0.6437, sin *A* = 0.8134 and *a* = 13.2. The length of *d*, to the *nearest tenth*, is

  (1) 10.4

  (2) 18.6

  (3) 43.8

  (4) 67.7

14 In an isosceles triangle, the base angles measure 61° and the length of each congruent leg is 12.5. Which of the following can be used to find the length of the base?

(1) $\dfrac{\sin 52°}{12.5} = \dfrac{\sin 61°}{x}$

(2) $\dfrac{\sin 61°}{12.5} = \dfrac{\sin 58°}{x}$

(3) $\dfrac{\sin 122°}{12.5} = \dfrac{\sin 61°}{x}$

(4) $x^2 = 12.5^2 + 12.5^2 - 2(12.5)(12.5)\sin 61°$

15 In $\triangle VAL$, $v = 13.12$, $a = 11.3$, and $m\angle A = 44.5$. The triangle must be which of the following?

(1) cannot be determined
(2) obtuse
(3) isosceles
(4) right

16 If $m = 7$, $n = 10$, and $m\angle M = 85$, how many different triangles MNP can be drawn?

(1) 1   (3) 3
(2) 2   (4) 0

14.4 Mixed Trigonometric Applications

In this chapter on trigonometric applications, we have studied the Law of Cosines, the Law of Sines, and a formula for the area of a triangle. To help you remember which formula to use under which conditions, review the following table:

Given Information	Formula to Use
Two sides and the included angle (SAS)	Law of Cosines: $c^2 = a^2 + b^2 - 2ab\cos C$
Three sides (SSS)	Law of Cosines: $\cos C = \dfrac{a^2 + b^2 - c^2}{2ab}$
Two angles and the included side (ASA)	Law of Sines: $\dfrac{\sin A}{a} = \dfrac{\sin B}{b} = \dfrac{\sin C}{c}$
Two angles and a nonincluded side (AAS)	Law of Sines: $\dfrac{\sin A}{a} = \dfrac{\sin B}{b} = \dfrac{\sin C}{c}$
Two sides and a nonincluded angle (SSA) (the ambiguous case)	Law of Sines: $\dfrac{\sin A}{a} = \dfrac{\sin B}{b} = \dfrac{\sin C}{c}$
Area of a triangle (SAS)	Area $= \dfrac{1}{2} ab\sin C$
Area of a parallelogram	Area $= ab\sin C$

It is necessary to use these formulas only if you are not working with a right triangle. When given a right triangle, you can simply use the ratios:

$$\sin \theta = \frac{\text{opposite leg}}{\text{hypotenuse}} \qquad \cos \theta = \frac{\text{adjacent leg}}{\text{hypotenuse}} \qquad \tan \theta = \frac{\text{opposite leg}}{\text{adjacent leg}}$$

To solve any trigonometric application problem, first draw and label a diagram. Then determine the pattern of the given information and use the appropriate formula to solve.

MODEL PROBLEMS

1 An isosceles triangle has base angles of 53.4° and a base equal to 14.7 inches. Find, to the nearest tenth of an inch, the length of the equal sides of the triangle.

SOLUTION

First draw a diagram.

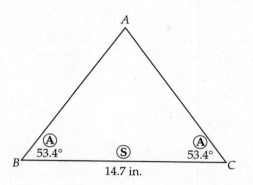

Since the information is in an angle-side-angle pattern, the problem is solved using the Law of Sines. First, however, we must find the vertex angle by subtracting the sum of the two base angles from 180°: $180° - 2(53.4°) = 180° - 106.8° = 73.2°$.

$$\frac{\sin A}{a} = \frac{\sin C}{c}$$

$$\frac{\sin 73.2°}{14.7} = \frac{\sin 53.4°}{c}$$

$$c = \frac{14.7\sin 53.4°}{\sin 73.2°}$$

$$c \approx 12.3 \text{ inches}$$

Answer: To the nearest tenth, each equal side of the triangle is 12.3 inches.

2 Dyana is working with stained glass, and she needs to cut an obtuse triangle with sides of 11.6 centimeters and 8.4 centimeters to fit into her design. If the area of the triangle must be 37.2 square centimeters, to the nearest tenth of a degree, what obtuse angle must she use to cut the glass?

SOLUTION

In this case we are given the area of the triangle and two sides and are asked for the angle between the two sides.

$$\text{Area} = \frac{1}{2}ab\sin C$$

$$37.2 = \frac{1}{2}(11.6)(8.4)\sin C$$

$$\frac{37.2}{48.72} = \sin C$$

$$49.8 \approx m\angle C$$

However, according to the problem, Dyana needs an obtuse triangle for her design, so we find the second-quadrant angle with the same sine: $180° - 49.8° = 130.2°$.

Answer: The angle Dyana needs is 130.2°.

3 Katie is out with her parents at the Long Island Fair when she sees a large balloon with her name on it. Her dad tells her the angle of elevation from where she is standing to the foot of the balloon is 32°, but Katie is in too much of a hurry to get closer to the balloon to listen. She runs 120 feet toward the spot where the balloon is hovering, before her dad, a mathematics teacher, catches up to tell her that the angle of elevation from where she is now standing to the foot of the balloon is 54°. But Katie wants to know only one thing. "I want to go up there. How high up is it?" she asks. Answer Katie's question to the nearest tenth of a foot.

SOLUTION

First we must find the length of the hypotenuse, a, between the two triangles using the Law of Sines. To do this, we must first realize that m∠ABK = 126 and m∠AKB = 22.

$$\frac{\sin 32°}{a} = \frac{\sin 22°}{120}$$

$$a = \frac{120\sin 32°}{\sin 22°}$$

$$a \approx 169.752249$$

Now we can use right triangle trigonometry to find the height of the right triangle.

$$\sin 54° = \frac{h}{169.752249}$$

$$h \approx 137.3 \text{ feet}$$

Answer: We can tell Katie that the balloon is 137.3 feet up in the air.

4   A land surveyor needs to determine the distance between two points, A and B, as shown in the figure.

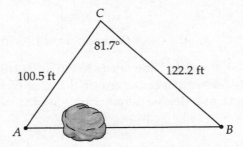

However, there is a large boulder in the way. Therefore, she has set a point C at a distance of 100.5 feet from A and 122.2 feet from B. She has also determined that m∠C = 81.7. To the nearest tenth of a foot, find the distance from A to B.

SOLUTION

Since we have two sides and the included angle, we can use the Law of Cosines.

$c^2 = a^2 + b^2 - 2ab\cos C$

$c^2 = 100.5^2 + 122.2^2 - 2(100.5)(122.2)\cos 81.7°$

$c = \sqrt{25{,}033.09 - 24{,}562.2\cos 81.7°}$

$c \approx 146.6 \text{ feet}$

Answer: 146.6 feet

Practice

Exercises 1–10: Select the numeral preceding the choice that best completes the statement or answers the question.

1 In triangle ABC, $a = 6$, $b = 4.8$, and $c = 8.1$. The value of $\cos C$ is

(1) -0.1141 (3) 0.6771
(2) 0.1141 (4) 0.8083

2 In $\triangle VAL$, $\sin V = 0.4525$, $\sin A = 0.3128$, and $v = 7.8$. The length of side a is

(1) 4.9 (3) 6.7
(2) 5.4 (4) 11.3

3 If the sides of a triangle measure 5, 9, and 11, to the *nearest tenth of a degree*, what is the measure of the largest angle in the triangle?

(1) $26.6°$ (3) $99.6°$
(2) $53.7°$ (4) $109.4°$

4 In $\triangle CTH$, $c = 12$, $h = 7$, and $m\angle T = 150$. The area of $\triangle CTH$, in square units, is

(1) 21
(2) $21\sqrt{3}$
(3) 42
(4) $42\sqrt{3}$

5 In $\triangle XYZ$, $m\angle X = 45$, $m\angle Y = 60$, and $XY = 8$. The measure of $\overline{XZ}$ is

(1) 7.2 (3) 9.8
(2) 8.9 (4) 10.3

6 The area of $\triangle JEN$ is 120 square centimeters. If $j = 12$ centimeters and $m\angle N = 30$, the length of side e is

(1) 20 centimeters (3) 40 centimeters
(2) 30 centimeters (4) 60 centimeters

7 If in $\triangle MAT$, $m\angle M = 30$, $m = 8$, and $t = 16$, which of the following must be true?

(1) $\triangle MAT$ is a right triangle.
(2) $\triangle MAT$ is an acute triangle.
(3) $\triangle MAT$ is an obtuse triangle.
(4) $\triangle MAT$ is an isosceles triangle.

8 If $m\angle A = 35$, $a = 7$, and $b = 10$, how many distinct triangles ABC can be formed?

(1) 1 (3) 3
(2) 2 (4) 0

9 In $\triangle AOK$, $a = 5$, $\sin A = 0.4$, and $k = 4$. Sin K equals

(1) 1 (3) 0.32
(2) 0.5 (4) 0.24

10 If the lengths of the sides of a triangle are 8, 15, and 17, the sine of the largest angle in the triangle is

(1) 1 (3) 0.4706
(2) 0.8824 (4) 0

Exercises 11–18: Show the diagrams and equations to solve each problem.

11 Ms. Donal's third-grade class is creating a food pyramid out of felt pieces. To fit on the bulletin board, the nutrition information will take the form of a triangle with sides of 24 inches, 24 inches, and 20 inches.

a Find the size of the vertex angle to the *nearest degree*.
b Find, to the *nearest square inch*, the area of the felt triangle.

12 A surveyor is reviewing a property deed to a triangular piece of land. According to the old deed, the property has sides that measure 112 feet, 120 feet, and 96 feet, with the largest angle of the property equal to 69.98° and the smallest angle between the sides of the property equal to 43.74°. If the surveyor finds the lengths of the sides of the property accurate, will she also find the angle measurements valid? Why or why not?

13 As Jackie and Beth bicycle to Jones Beach along the Wantagh Parkway, they take a sighting of the top of the Jones Beach Tower and find it to be 27.4°. After biking closer to the beach, they get an angle measurement of 41.2° to the top of the tower. Knowing that the Jones Beach Tower is 200 feet tall, how far, to the *nearest foot*, were they from the tower at each of the two locations where they took measurements?

14 Triangle *CTH* is inscribed in circle *O* as shown below.

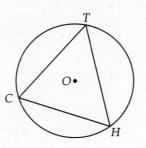

m∠*CHT* = 49, *TH* = 12.4 centimeters, and *CT* = 11.1 centimeters.

a Find the measure of ∠*TCH* to the *nearest tenth of a degree*.

b Find the measure of $\overline{CH}$ to the *nearest tenth of a centimeter*.

c Find the area of △*CTH* to the *nearest square centimeter*.

15 A parallelogram with sides of 15 and 18 centimeters contains an angle of 57.6°.

a Find the length of the shorter diagonal of the parallelogram to the *nearest centimeter*.

b Find the area of the parallelogram to the *nearest square centimeter*.

16 Mike and Marie want to build a triangular lean-to in their backyard. They'd like to use 12-foot sheets of wood for the sides of the lean-to, with a raised floor, one foot off the ground, measuring 13 feet.

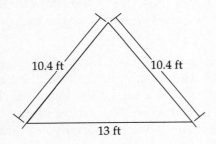

Note: Since the floor is raised, only 10.4 feet of the congruent sides will be in the lean-to.

a To the *nearest tenth of a degree*, what is the measure of the base angles for the design?

b What is the measure of the vertex angle, to the *nearest tenth of a degree*?

17 Janice, Molly, Ted, and Joe are hiking in the Catskills. They see a fire station high over the trees.

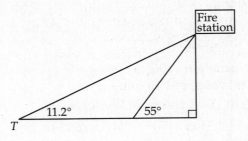

At point *T*, Ted takes a reading and finds the angle of elevation to the top of the fire station is 11.2°. They continue hiking for another half mile and decide to make camp. Molly takes a sighting on the fire station and discovers the angle of elevation to the top of the tower is now 55°.

a Find the height of the tower, to the *nearest foot*. (1 mile = 5,280 feet)

b Find the distance from point *T* to the fire tower, to the *nearest foot*.

18 The director of an amusement park wants to add a screening room to the Haunted House attraction, but he does not want the movie screen to be a rectangle. Instead, he has asked the designer to create a 22-foot by 12-foot screen in the shape of a parallelogram with the longer diagonal equal to 28 feet.

a Find the measure of the angles between the sides of the parallelogram, to the *nearest tenth of a degree*.

b Find, to the *nearest tenth of a square foot*, the area of the special screen.

14.5 Forces and Vectors

You know from your work with vectors and complex numbers that a **vector** has both direction and magnitude. Vectors are very useful in representing the properties of applied forces pushing or pulling an object in a given direction. For example, two children squabbling over ownership of a toy can be represented by vectors operating from the same given point, the toy, and moving in opposite—or differing—directions, as in the diagrams below. The length of each vector represents the strength or magnitude of the force, while the direction of the vector shows the movement of the force.

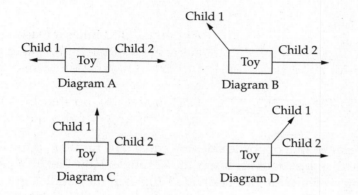

As the diagrams show, the force exerted by Child 1 is less than that exerted by Child 2, so in diagram A, Child 2 will win the toy. Starting in diagram B, however, Child 1 is now using some of Child 2's strength, and the force resulting from the children's actions is increasing in magnitude. This new force, created by the combination of the initial forces, is called the **resultant** and will appear between the two applied forces.

In force problems, each vector represents a force applied to an object at a specific point. These vectors are used to form two consecutive sides of a parallelogram with the resultant force of the vectors forming the diagonal of the parallelogram, as shown below.

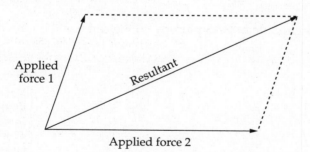

Note: The resultant does *not* bisect the angle between the two forces unless the forces are equal in magnitude.

Depending on what information is provided in a force problem, we will use either the Law of Cosines or the Law of Sines to solve the problem.

1 Two forces of 28 pounds and 41 pounds act on a body so that the angle between the two forces measures 72°. Find, to the nearest tenth of a pound, the magnitude of the resultant the forces produce.

SOLUTION

As with all trigonometric application problems, the first step is always to draw a diagram.

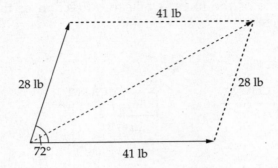

Since we have a parallelogram, we know that opposite sides are equal. The resultant is the diagonal, creating two congruent triangles. The diagonal does *not* bisect the 72° angle. However, in a parallelogram, consecutive angles are supplementary. Thus, the two undivided angles of the parallelogram must equal 180° − 72°, or 108°.

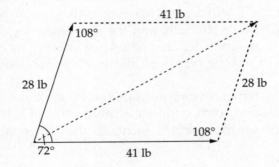

We now have information in a Side-Angle-Side or SAS pattern, so we can use the Law of Cosines.

$c^2 = a^2 + b^2 - 2ab\cos C$

$c^2 = 28^2 + 41^2 - 2(28)(41)\cos 108°$

$c = \sqrt{2{,}465 - 2{,}296\cos 108°}$

$c \approx 56.3$ pounds

Answer: To the nearest tenth, the magnitude of the resultant equals 56.3 pounds.

> Note: When the angle between the forces is acute, the strength (magnitude) or length of the diagonal between the forces is greater than either force alone.

2 Two applied forces produce a resultant force of 18.6 pounds. The smaller force measures 15.8 pounds, and the larger force is 24.3 pounds. Find the measure of the angle between the two forces, to the nearest tenth of a degree.

SOLUTION

The first step is to draw the diagram of the applied forces, using vectors to form a parallelogram.

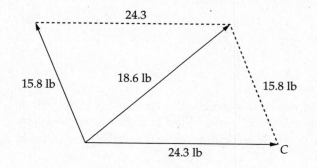

The given information forms triangles in a Side-Side-Side or SSS pattern so we can use the Law of Cosines to solve the triangle. Remember, though, that since the diagonal does not bisect the angles of a parallelogram, we must find the angle labeled C in the diagram and determine its supplement to find the angle between the two applied forces.

$$\cos C = \frac{a^2 + b^2 - c^2}{2ab}$$

$$\cos C = \frac{15.8^2 + 24.3^2 - 18.6^2}{2(15.8)(24.3)}$$

$$\cos C = \frac{494.17}{767.88}$$

$$C \approx 49.9°$$

Therefore, the angle between the forces must equal $180° - 49.9° = 130.1°$.

Answer: 130.1°

3 A resultant force of 162 pounds must be exerted to move a refrigerator. If the two applied forces act on the refrigerator at angles of 43.6° and 38.7°, respectively, find the magnitude of each of the two applied forces, to the nearest tenth of a pound.

SOLUTION

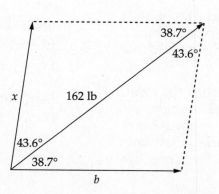

When the parallelogram is drawn, we see that the given information forms an Angle-Side-Angle or ASA pattern, meaning we need to use the Law of Sines twice to find the two applied forces. First, we'll find the angle opposite the force of 162 pounds, so we add the other two angles together and subtract from 180°. We have $180° - (43.6° + 38.7°) = 180° - 82.3° = 97.7°$ Now we'll find the force labeled b in the diagram.

$$\frac{\sin 43.6°}{b} = \frac{\sin 97.7°}{162}$$

$$b = \frac{162\sin 43.6°}{\sin 97.7°}$$

$$b \approx 112.7 \text{ pounds}$$

Having found one applied force, we could use the Law of Cosines to find the other applied force, but it is preferable to use only the information provided in the original problem to solve all parts of the problem unless otherwise instructed. So to find x, we will use the Law of Sines again:

$$\frac{\sin 38.7°}{x} = \frac{\sin 97.7°}{162}$$

$$x = \frac{162\sin 38.7°}{\sin 97.7}$$

$$x \approx 102.2 \text{ pounds}$$

Answer: The two applied forces are 112.7 pounds and 102.2 pounds.

Sometimes you will be asked to find the magnitude of the larger applied force or the smaller applied force. To determine which is the larger or smaller, remember that the largest side of a triangle is opposite the largest angle. In Model Problem 3, the larger applied force had to be opposite the larger angle, 43.6°. That force was 112.7 pounds versus the force of 102.2 pounds opposite the 38.7° angle.

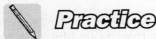 **Practice**

Show the diagrams and work necessary to solve each problem.

1   Two forces of 21.8 pounds and 34.2 pounds act on a body with an angle of 52.6° between them. Find, to the *nearest tenth of a pound*, the magnitude of the resultant.

2   Two forces act on a body such that the resultant is a force of 73.4 pounds. The angles between the resultant and the applied forces measure 56° and 47°. Find, to the *nearest tenth of a pound*, the magnitude of the larger applied force.

3   Find, to the *nearest tenth of a degree*, the angle between two applied forces of 37 newtons and 62 newtons if the resultant is 48.4 newtons. (The newton, N, is a unit of force in the metric system.)

4   If two forces of 21.8 pounds and 35.1 pounds act on a body with an angle of 110.6° between them, find the magnitude of the resultant to the *nearest tenth of a pound*.

5 Two forces of 37 pounds and 52 pounds act on a body, forming an acute angle between them. If the angle between the smaller force and the resultant is 29°15′, find, to the *nearest tenth of a pound*, the magnitude of the resultant. (Hint: Find the angle between the larger force and the resultant first.)

6 Find, to the *nearest minute*, the measure of the angle between two applied forces of 41.6 newtons and 64.8 newtons if the resultant formed has a magnitude of 83.4 newtons.

7 Two applied forces act on a body, forming angles of 18°25′ and 29°40′ between them and the resultant.

   a If the larger force is 48.3 newtons, what is the magnitude of the resultant to the *nearest tenth of a newton*?

   b What is the magnitude, to the *nearest tenth of a newton*, of the smaller force?

8 Two forces act on an object; the first force has a magnitude of 78 pounds and makes an angle of 31.5° with the resultant. The magnitude of the resultant is 124.7 pounds.

   a Find the magnitude of the second applied force to the *nearest tenth of a pound*.

   b Using the results from part **a**, find, to the *nearest tenth of a degree*, the angle the second applied force makes with the resultant.

9 A glider is moving forward at a speed of 12 miles per hour while air currents are working against the glider at a force of 8 miles per hour. The resultant speed of the glider is 10.2 miles per hour.

   a At what angle is the air current acting on the glider?

   b Find, to the *nearest hundredth of a degree*, the measure of the angle between the air current and the resultant.

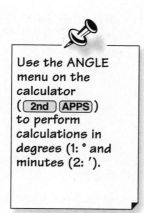

Use the ANGLE menu on the calculator (2nd APPS) to perform calculations in degrees (1: ° and minutes (2: ′).

CHAPTER REVIEW

1 In triangle *ABC*, $a = 12$, $b = 10$, and $\sin C = 0.6$. Find the area of triangle *ABC*.

2 In triangle *DEF*, $d = 20.5$, $f = 18.2$, and $\sin D = 0.345$. Find, to the *nearest thousandth*, $\sin F$.

3 In triangle *GHI*, $g = 4$, $h = 8$, and $m\angle G = 30$. Find $m\angle H$.

4 In triangle *JKL*, $j = 10$, $k = 6$, and $m\angle L = 60$. Find l to the *nearest tenth*.

5 Find the exact area of an equilateral triangle whose side is 8.

6 In triangle *MNO*, $m = 12$, $n = 18$, and $\cos O = \dfrac{1}{6}$. Find o to the *nearest tenth*.

7 In triangle *LAW*, $\sin A = \dfrac{1}{4}$ and $\sin W = \dfrac{3}{7}$. If $a = 28$, find w.

8 The largest angle of a parallelogram measures 120°. If the sides measure 14 inches and 12 inches, what is the exact area of the parallelogram?

9 Find, to the *nearest hundredth*, the length of the base of an isosceles triangle if the legs each measure 12.42 and the vertex angle measures 64°.

Exercises 10–18: Select the numeral preceding the choice that best completes the statement or answers the question.

10 Find the area of triangle *TRI* if $t = 8$, $r = 12$, and $m\angle I = 150$.

   (1) 24
   (2) $24\sqrt{3}$
   (3) 48
   (4) $48\sqrt{3}$

11 In triangle PQR, m$\angle P = 30$, $p = 18$, and $r = 22$. Find sin R.

(1) $\dfrac{9}{22}$

(2) $\dfrac{11}{18}$

(3) $\dfrac{18}{11}$

(4) 37

12 In triangle MAT, $m = 10$, $t = 4$, and m$\angle A = 60$. Find the length of side a.

(1) $2\sqrt{14}$
(2) $2\sqrt{19}$
(3) $4\sqrt{6}$
(4) $2\sqrt{39}$

13 In parallelogram $PARL$, $PA = 12$, $PL = 14$, and m$\angle P = 45$. What is the area of parallelogram $PARL$?

(1) $42\sqrt{2}$
(2) 84
(3) $84\sqrt{2}$
(4) 168

14 In triangle NED, $n = 6$, $e = 12$, and $d = 8$. What is the value of cos D?

(1) $-\dfrac{43}{48}$

(2) $-\dfrac{29}{36}$

(3) $\dfrac{29}{36}$

(4) $\dfrac{43}{48}$

15 An equilateral triangle has a side of length s. What is the area of the triangle?

(1) $\dfrac{s^2}{4}$

(2) $\dfrac{s^2}{4}\sqrt{3}$

(3) $\dfrac{s^2}{2}$

(4) $\dfrac{s^2}{2}\sqrt{3}$

16 What is the cosine of the largest angle of a triangle whose sides measure 6, 8, and 10?

(1) 1
(2) 0.8
(3) 0.6
(4) 0

17 In triangle ABC, $a = 20$, $b = 16$, and m$\angle A = 30$. Triangle ABC

(1) must be a right triangle
(2) must be an acute triangle
(3) must be an obtuse triangle
(4) could be an acute or an obtuse triangle

18 In triangle JON, side j is twice as long as side n. If m$\angle O = 30$, what is the area of triangle JON?

(1) $\dfrac{n^2}{4}$

(2) $\dfrac{n^2}{2}$

(3) n^2

(4) $2n^2$

19 Two forces of 57 pounds and 43 pounds act on an object at a 65.4° angle.

a Find the magnitude of the resultant force to the *nearest tenth of a pound*.

b Find the angle, to the *nearest tenth of a degree*, between the resultant and the larger force.

20 The Horticulture Club is designing a wildflower garden. They want to make it in the shape of a triangle whose sides have lengths 12 feet, 14 feet, and 18 feet.

a What is the measure of the largest angle in the triangle, to the *nearest tenth of a degree*?

b Using your answer to part **a**, find the area of the triangle to the *nearest tenth of a square foot*.

c If one package of wildflower seeds covers 25 square feet, how many packages must the Horticulture Club buy?

21 Two forces of 36 pounds and 52 pounds act on a body at an acute angle with each other. The angle between the resultant force and the 36-pound force is 41°. Find, to the *nearest degree*, the angle formed by the 36-pound force and the 52-pound force.

22 Marla plans to swim across the lake from point A to point B, as shown in the diagram. To determine the length of her swim, Marla set a point at C, which is 2.6 miles from A and 3.5 miles from B. She determined that $\angle ABC$ measures 78°18′. How long is Marla's swim, to the *nearest tenth of a mile*?

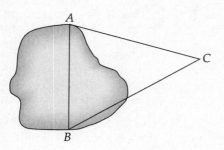

23 In triangle MAT, $a = 16$, m$\angle A = 34.6$, $t = 20$, and $\angle T$ is an obtuse angle. Find m$\angle M$ to the *nearest tenth of a degree*.

24 The field next to J. J. Smith High School is in the shape of a parallelogram. Two consecutive sides of the field measure 340 feet and 450 feet.

a If the largest angle of the parallelogram measures 112.3°, to the *nearest tenth of a foot*, what is the longest distance from one corner of the field to the opposite corner?

b The school wants to replace this field with blacktop. If the blacktop costs $4.29 per square foot, how much will it cost to lay the blacktop?

25 Eddie twisted together some pipe cleaners to make a square picture frame. However, he was not careful about making all of the sides perpendicular to each other, so it turned out to be a rhombus. The pipe cleaners are all 6 inches long, and he used $\dfrac{1}{4}$ inch of each end to twist them.

a If Eddie had made a square, exactly how long would the diagonal be?

b If the longer diagonal of Eddie's picture frame is 8.5 inches, to the *nearest degree*, how far off are the angles?

c Use your answer to part **b** to find the length of the shorter diagonal, to the *nearest tenth of an inch*.

CHAPTER 15

Statistics

15.1 Gathering Data: Univariate Statistics

Methods

Statistics is the study and interpretation of numerical data. If only one variable is being analyzed, we use the term **univariate** statistics. There are various ways that data can be gathered for statistical studies.

Surveys are often used to collect information from a group of people. A survey is an efficient way of obtaining a wide range of information from a large number of people. However, care must be taken to ensure that questions are asked in a neutral way. The validity of a survey also depends upon the honesty of the respondents. For example, if a teacher wants to determine the average amount of time students in her class studied for an exam, a survey of her students may not produce accurate results. Students may be hesitant to tell their teacher how little time they actually spent studying for a big mathematics test.

A **census** is a survey in which an attempt is made to reach every member of an entire **population**. This is different from a sampling, in which information is obtained only from a subset of a population. The term "census" dates backs to Roman times when the census was a list that kept track of all adult males fit for military service. In modern times, many countries take a census of their residents. The first United States census was conducted in 1790. That census, taken by U.S. marshals on horseback, counted 3.9 million inhabitants. Since that time, the decennial census has been conducted every ten years, generally on April 1, in years ending in a zero.

It is often not possible or not cost-effective to gather data from an entire population. In such cases, conclusions about the entire population may be based on results for a **sample** or subset of the population. For example, if a company were to report on the popularity of television shows, it could not take a census of every household in the United States. Instead, it selects a sample population of a cross-section of television-watching households from all over the United States. When conducting a survey by using a sample population, it is extremely important that the survey sample is representative of the entire population.

Another way of collecting data is by *simulating* an event. For example, to determine the amount of weight a bridge can hold, engineers may first simulate the effects statistically on a computer. Using the data they obtain, they can then draw conclusions about how the bridge should be constructed to bear the weight it will be holding.

A **controlled experiment** is another method of gathering data. The goal of a controlled experiment is to study the effect of some kind of intervention, such as a medicine or an exercise program. The results obtained from an experimental sample are compared to the results from a *control* sample, which is identical to the experimental sample except without the one aspect whose effect is being tested. For example, scientists may use this method to determine the effect of a new medicine. An experimental group would receive the medicine that the scientists are testing, while the control group would receive a placebo.

Another type of study is an **observational study**. As in a controlled experiment, individuals are observed or certain outcomes are measured. However, data are simply gathered without intervention. There is no attempt made to affect the outcome. For example, a researcher may track the effect that a smoking ban might have on the health of a community by comparing health statistics since the ban was instituted with health statistics before the institution of the ban.

Bias and Random Sample

Sometimes in statistics, the information presented is somewhat biased. That is, the data used in the sample have come from sources that have a particular interest in the impact of the statistics. Therefore, the sample is *not* representative of the general population, and it is said to be biased or skewed. For example, if dairy farmers were surveyed about the average number of ounces of milk every person in the United States should drink for better health, the results would be a **biased sample**. The sample would be biased since dairy farmers have an economic interest in increasing the amount of milk consumed by the average American. On the other hand, if the College of Pediatric Surgeons or the American Board of Nutritionists provided the information, it could be presumed to be relatively free of such bias.

Similarly, a sample of city residents chosen from only one neighborhood would probably not mirror the characteristics or concerns of the overall population of the entire city. It is important in interpreting any statistics that you explore the source of the data and the possibility of a biased sample.

MODEL PROBLEM

Car manufacturers want to explore the desirability of pre-installed infant seats in their new car designs. Which of the following groups would be most likely to provide an unbiased sample for a survey?

(1) adult shoppers at a supermarket with young children in the shopping carts
(2) couples signing up to win a honeymoon package at a bridal expo
(3) adults visiting a car show
(4) a group of teenagers playing ball at the park

SOLUTION

Choice 3 is the least biased group. Choice 1 contains people who already need car seats. Choice 2 involves young couples who might be planning to have children in the future. Choice 4 involves teenagers for whom parenthood is not relevant.

Answer: Choice (3)

Practice

Exercises 1–5: Select the numeral preceding the choice that best answers the question.

1   Which would be the most unbiased group of people to ask about methods of Social Security reform?

   (1)   adults at a senior citizen center
   (2)   college students in a sociology class
   (3)   members of a children's choir
   (4)   shoppers at a mall

2   The manufacturer of a new chocolate candy bar wants its ads to contain favorable comments from people who like their product. Which group would the manufacturer most likely choose to survey about its candy?

   (1)   people who received free samples of the candy
   (2)   dentists who specialize in children's teeth
   (3)   customers at a health food store
   (4)   nutritionists concerned with the American diet

3   Reporters on a news show want to survey adults about their exercise habits. Where should they go to find an unbiased sample?

   (1)   the boardwalk on the beach
   (2)   the post office
   (3)   an exercise gym
   (4)   a rock-climbing expo

4   The city board of directors is considering raising the cost of parking tickets. Which group of citizens would be least biased on this issue?

   (1)   fifty citizens who have never received a parking ticket
   (2)   fifty citizens who have had at least three parking tickets
   (3)   the first fifty people encountered on a city street
   (4)   fifty citizens who do not have driver's licenses

5   A radio station wants to conduct a survey to predict the winner of a city's mayoral election. Which method is most likely to provide an unbiased sampling?

   (1)   asking for callers and using the first fifty people who call in
   (2)   interviewing volunteers at a candidate's headquarters
   (3)   calling the tenth person listed on each page of the city telephone directory
   (4)   surveying the opinions of protestors at a rally

Exercises 6–12: Suggest a method (population survey, sample survey, simulation, observation, controlled experiment) that might be used to collect data for each study. Explain your reasoning.

6   effectiveness of a new patch to help smokers quit smoking

7   number of hours of sleep obtained by a lion living in an African jungle

8   popularity rating of the president of the United States among teenagers in New York State

9   number of hours spent watching television by members of your homeroom

10   amount of fertilizer to be used to produce prize-winning vegetables

11   amount of time for the red, green, and yellow lights to remain active in a busy intersection

12   effect of an advertising campaign on "name recognition" of a new product

Exercises 13–17: State whether a sample survey or a population survey would be more likely to be used to collect data for each of the following.

13   survey to determine the more likely winner in a national presidential election

14   survey to determine the more likely winner in a student government election in a school with 900 students

15   survey to determine the average number of siblings of each member of your mathematics class

16 survey to determine the average number of siblings of each citizen in the United States

17 survey to determine the amount of time people spend commuting to work on the Long Island Rail Road

18 Give an example of statistics that a researcher might gather from:

a a population survey
b a sample survey
c a controlled experiment
d an observational study

15.2 Measures of Central Tendency

Measures of central tendency are summary statistics that indicate where the *center* of a collection of data lies. Three common measures of central tendency are the *mean*, *median*, and *mode*. The **mean** is referred to as the arithmetic average of the data and is symbolized as $\bar{x}$, read "*x* bar."

Note: Two different symbols are used to represent the mean of a collection of data. When the mean of a sample population is being studied, $\bar{x}$ is commonly used. When the mean of an entire population is under investigation, the Greek letter mu, μ, is frequently used. However, in accord with current Regents practice, we will use only $\bar{x}$.

To find $\bar{x}$, we find the sum of all the given data and divide by the number of data values. Mathematically, $\bar{x} = \dfrac{\sum\limits_{i=1}^{n} x_i}{n}$, where n is the total number of terms.

For example, Priscilla has the following grades on her Algebra 2 quizzes this quarter: 74, 83, 79, 90, and 82. The mean of her grades so far is

$$\bar{x} = \frac{\sum\limits_{i=1}^{5} x_i}{5} = \frac{74 + 83 + 79 + 90 + 82}{5} = 81.6$$

The **median** of the given data is the positional middle when the data is placed in numerical order, either ascending or descending. To find out which position is the median, add 1 to the total number of data values and divide by 2. The value in that position, counting from the first or last term, is the median.

In the example above, the median of Priscilla's quiz grades is the third highest or lowest grade, which is 82.

We will discuss the mode after the following model problems.

MODEL PROBLEMS

1 Find the median of the following set of data: 11, 17, 31, 18, 25, 12, 29, 13, 15.

SOLUTION

First put the terms in order: 11, 12, 13, 15, 17, 18, 25, 29, 31

Since there are 9 terms, find $\dfrac{n + 1}{2} = \dfrac{9 + 1}{2} = 5$.

Answer: The fifth term, 17, is the median.

2 Find the median of the following set of data: 9, 11, 7, 10, 2, 17, 8, 13.

SOLUTION

In this problem, the number of terms, 8, is even. We find $\dfrac{n+1}{2} = \dfrac{8+1}{2} = 4.5$. The median will be halfway between the fourth and fifth terms once they are in order, that is, the *mean* of the fourth and fifth terms.

Given 2, 7, 8, 9, 10, 11, 13, 17, the median value is $\dfrac{9+10}{2} = 9.5$.

Answer: The median is 9.5.

3 Geoff stocked up on canned goods at the grocery store. The frequency table to the right shows the prices of the canned goods and the number of cans that Geoff bought at each price.

Price	Frequency
56¢	4
73¢	9
78¢	7
82¢	5
86¢	5

  a Find the mean price of the canned goods to the nearest cent.

  b Find the median price of the canned goods.

SOLUTION

  a To find the mean, multiply the frequency by the price of the item and find the sum of those products. Then divide by 30, since there is a total of 30 item values.

$$\text{mean} = \frac{4(56) + 9(73) + 7(78) + 5(82) + 5(86)}{30} = \frac{2{,}267}{30} = 75.56666\ldots$$

We must round to the nearest cent.

Answer: 76¢

  b The median is the middle term; we add 30 + 1 and divide by 2. The median value is in the 15.5th position. Since both the 15th and 16th terms are 78¢, the median is 78¢.

Answer: 78¢

The **mode** is the most commonly repeated data value in a set. Some collections of data, often referred to as *distributions*, will have no mode and others will have multiple modes.

4   Find the mode of the following data: 67, 54, 91, 67, 83, 46, 72, 54, 91, 81, 75, 67, 54, 88.

SOLUTION

Since 67 and 54 both appear three times, both of these serve as modes. This data set is said to be **bimodal**.

Answer: 67 and 54

5   Find the mode of the following data: 113, 154, 139, 112, 138, 129, 143, 170, 184, 206.

SOLUTION

In this set of data, there is no mode because none of the data values is repeated.

Answer: no mode

6   In May of 2008, the government predicted that gasoline prices would peak at a national average of $3.73 a gallon in June. However, this prediction turned out to be incorrect. The average weekly prices of gasoline in Rochester from May 7 to July 16, 2008, were: $3.85, $3.92, $4.02, $4.09, $4.12, $4.18, $4.20, $4.20, $4.23, $4.24. Find the mean, median, and mode for these data.

SOLUTION

Generally, you will not see data values in numerical order. However, since gasoline prices continued to increase each week during this period, this time our values are in ascending order. This problem can be done by hand, or by using the graphing calculator. Press (STAT) and choose 1: Edit. Then enter the prices in L_1. To find the mean and median, again press (STAT), then right arrow over to the CALC menu, as shown below.

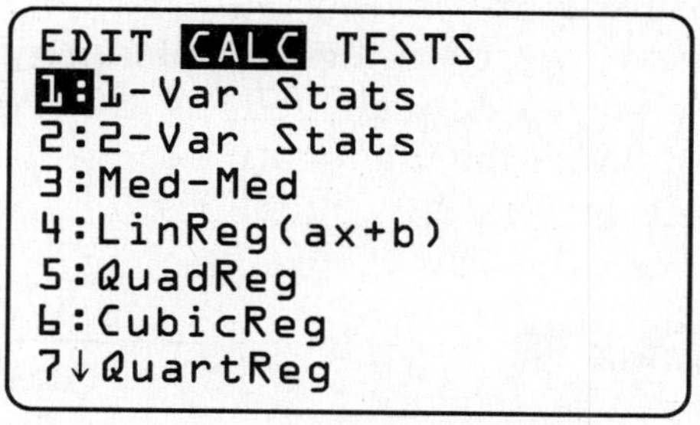

```
EDIT CALC TESTS
1:1-Var Stats
2:2-Var Stats
3:Med-Med
4:LinReg(ax+b)
5:QuadReg
6:CubicReg
7↓QuartReg
```

Choose 1: 1-Var Stats, which stands for one-variable statistics. The command 1-Var Stats is pasted onto the home screen. Tell the calculator which list to use, in this case, L_1 ((2nd) (1)).

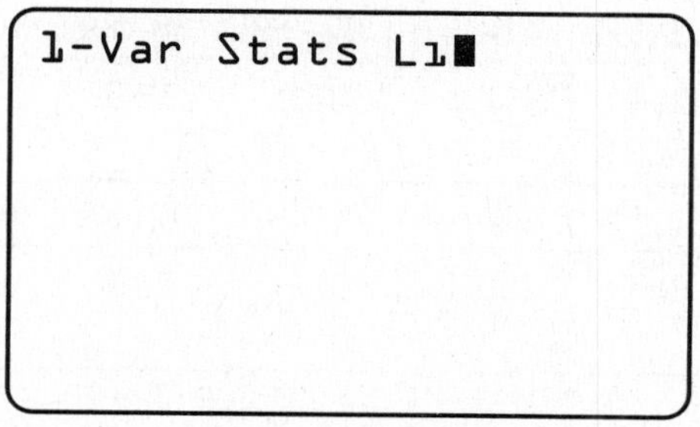

```
1-Var Stats L1█
```

Press (ENTER) again.

```
1-Var Stats
  x̄=4.105
  Σx=41.05
  Σx²=168.6747
  Sx=.135174784
  σx=.1282380599
 ↓n=10
```

```
1-Var Stats
 ↑n=10
  minX=3.85
  Q₁=4.02
  Med=4.15
  Q₃=4.2
  maxX=4.24
```

Note: When not specified, we round dollar values to the nearest cent.

We now have the statistical information for the data contained in L_1. We see that $\bar{x} = 4.105$ and the median = 4.15. To find the mode, you can visually examine the set of data values to find that $4.20 appears twice while no other terms are repeated.

Answer: mean = $4.11, median = $4.15, mode = $4.20

Notice that in the statistical information provided by the calculator in Model Problem 6, information is also given for the values of the first and third *quartiles*. The **first** or **lower quartile** is the median of the lower half of the data, not including the median. In the problem above, there are five data values in the lower half, thus the median is the third term, 4.02.

The **third** or **upper quartile** is the median of the upper half of the data, not including the median. There are five terms in the upper half, so the median is the middle term, 4.20.

The **interquartile range** is the difference between the third quartile and the first quartile. For the problem above, we compute the interquartile range as $4.20 - 4.02 = 0.18$. The interquartile range essentially tells us about the spread of the middle half of the data. We will revisit the interquartile range in Section 15.3 when we discuss measures of dispersion.

Remember: The median itself does not fall in either the lower or upper half of the data, so do not use it in computing the first and third quartiles.

MODEL PROBLEM

7   Among the numerous awards he received, Michael Jordan has been named one of the fifty greatest players in NBA history. The table below contains the average number of points scored per game by Michael Jordan during his NBA career.

Year	'84–'85	'85–'86	'86–'87	'87–'88	'88–'89	'89–'90	'90–'91	'91–'92
Points per Game	28.2	22.7	37.1	35.0	32.5	33.6	31.5	30.1
Year	'92–'93	'94–'95	'95–'96	'96–'97	'97–'98	'01–'02	'02–'03	
Points per Game	32.6	26.9	30.4	29.6	28.7	22.9	20.0	

Determine, to the nearest tenth, the mean, median, and mode of the data. Also, find the first quartile, the third quartile, and the interquartile range.

We will use the calculator to answer these questions. By entering the data into L_1 and choosing 1: 1-Var Stats for L_1, we get the following information.

```
1-Var Stats
  x̄=29.45333333
  Σx=441.8
  Σx²=13330.2
  Sx=4.763831991
  σx=4.602298942
↓n=15
```

```
1-Var Stats
↑n=15
  minX=20
  Q₁=26.9
  Med=30.1
  Q₃=32.6
  maxX=37.1
```

The mean, $\bar{x}$, is approximately 29.5, and the median is 30.1. The median of the lower half of the data, Q_1, is 26.9. The median of the upper half of the data, Q_3, is 32.6. To find the interquartile range, we subtract the first quartile from the third quartile:

$32.6 - 26.9 = 5.7$

When we inspect the data, we see that no data value is repeated. Thus, there is no mode.

Answer: The mean is 29.5, the median is 30.1, and the there is no mode. The first quartile is 26.9, the third quartile is 32.6, and the interquartile range is 5.7.

We can also use the calculator when we have a frequency table.

MODEL PROBLEM

8   The table below lists the scores for a multiple-choice test in Mrs. Santiago's class. Find the mean, median, and mode for the data to the nearest hundredth.

Test Grade	Frequency
100	1
95	2
90	2
85	7
80	6
75	5
70	3
60	2

On your calculator, press $\boxed{\text{STAT}}$, choose 1: Edit, and enter the test grades in L_1. Then enter the frequencies in L_2 as shown below.

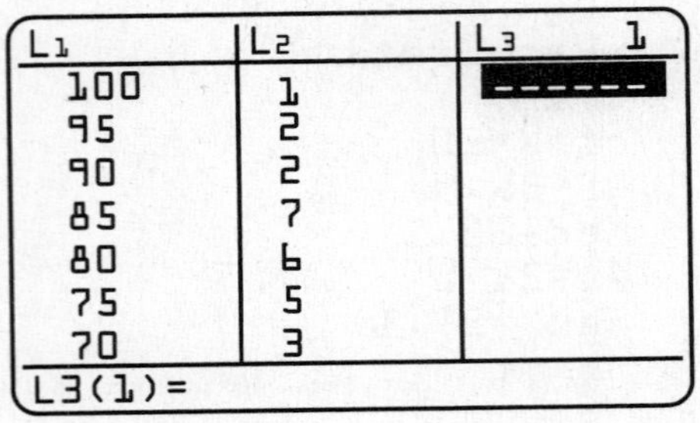

L1	L2	L3	1
100	1	------	
95	2		
90	2		
85	7		
80	6		
75	5		
70	3		
L3(1)=			

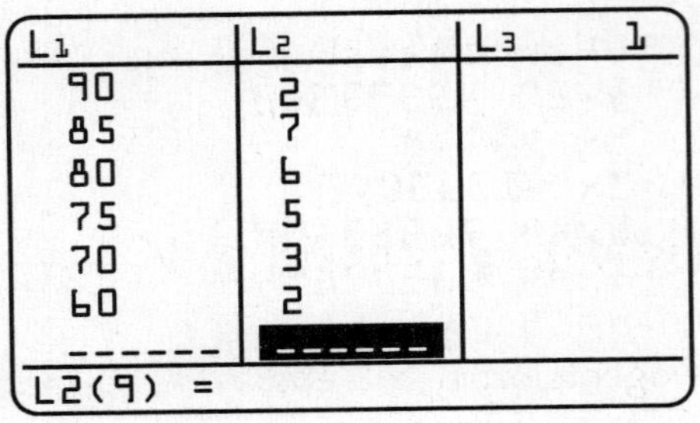

L1	L2	L3	1
90	2		
85	7		
80	6		
75	5		
70	3		
60	2		
------	------		
L2(9) =			

To find the mean and median, again press $\boxed{\text{STAT}}$, right arrow over to the CALC menu, and choose 1: 1-Var Stats. This time, we tell the calculator to look at the list with the scores, in this case, L_1. We also specify the frequencies of the scores, in this case, L_2.

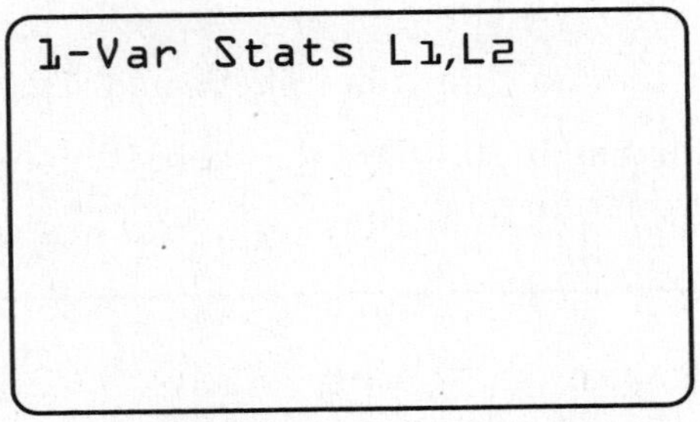

```
1-Var Stats L1,L2
```

Note: Although there are data in two lists, we still have univariate data, so we choose the command for one-variable statistics, 1-Var Stats.

Press $\boxed{\text{ENTER}}$ again.

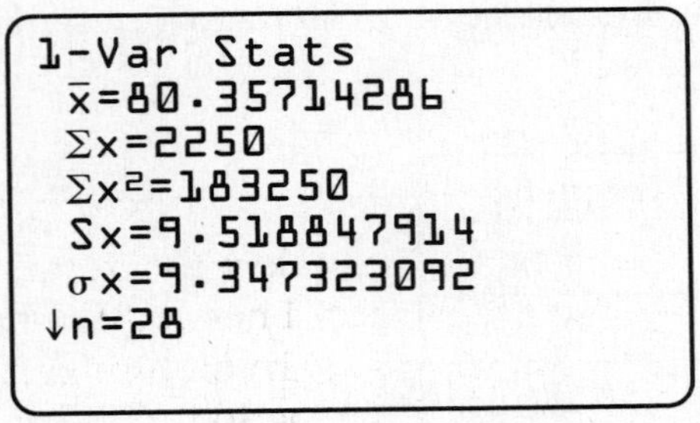

```
1-Var Stats
  x̄=80.35714286
  Σx=2250
  Σx²=183250
  Sx=9.518847914
  σx=9.347323092
↓n=28
```

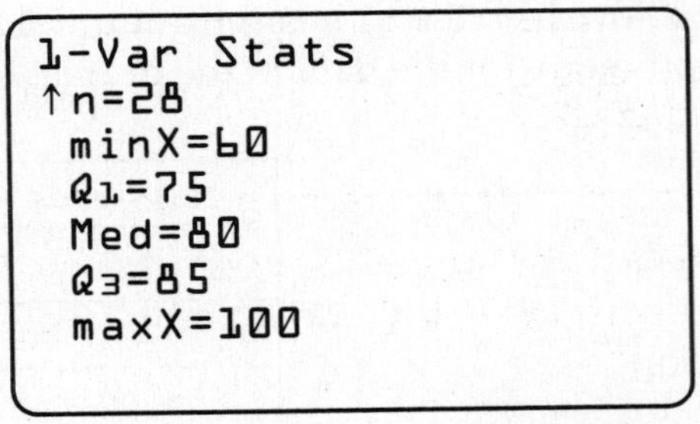

```
1-Var Stats
↑n=28
  minX=60
  Q1=75
  Med=80
  Q3=85
  maxX=100
```

Answer: We see that the mean is 80.36 and the median is 80. We can simply look at the frequency table to see that the mode is 85.

Choosing Appropriate Statistical Measures

While the mean, median, and mode all indicate an "average" value of a set of data, sometimes one is preferred over another. The mean, as a mathematical average, is affected by the *outliers*, or extreme values. The mode, a commonly used element, sometimes does not exist in a set of data, while at other times there could be more than one mode. In many cases, the median seems to be the most reliable as the middle term, the halfway piece of data in a group.

MODEL PROBLEM

9 Real estate agents often talk about the "average" house price in a neighborhood. Consider the following data, representing the prices of homes sold in a small community, and determine whether the mean, median, or mode would be most representative of the data at hand. Explain your answer.

Selling Prices of Homes						
$249,799	$258,239	$277,899	$274,599	$285,600	$295,299	$319,900
$252,599	$259,899	$274,599	$281,500	$293,799	$310,000	$435,000

SOLUTION

Enter data in L_1 and use 1: 1-Variable Stats to find the mean and median. Find the mode by observation.

mean: $290,623.64   median: $279,699.50   mode: $274,599

The mean is a bit higher than the median and mode because of the extremely high value of the last piece of data, $435,000. Though it is repeated, the mode represents only the prices of two houses out of 14 sold, so it is not a strongly representative value. In this case, the median would most accurately illustrate the "average" house price in this neighborhood, although an unscrupulous real estate company might prefer to use the mean price to impress some of its buyers with the higher "average" price.

 Practice

Exercises 1–8: Select the numeral preceding the choice that best completes the statement or answers the question.

1 The mean of 37, 54, 72, 89, 74, 83, 90, and 93 is

(1) 73
(2) 74
(3) 78
(4) 81.5

2 For the data 14, 18, 21, 19, 27, 23, 17, which statement is true?

(1) mean = median
(2) mean < median
(3) mean > median
(4) median = mode

3 Chantal has taken five tests so far this marking period and has an 88 average. What does she have to earn on her sixth and last test of the marking period to bring her average up to 90?

(1) 90
(2) 92
(3) 95
(4) 100

4 Given the data 6, 9, 3, 6, 10, 3, 9, 9, 12, 14, 7, what is the first quartile?

(1) 3.435
(2) 6
(3) 8
(4) 9

5 Consider the frequency table below. Which is a true statement?

x_i	f_i
62	6
71	5
80	5
89	4

(1) mean = median
(2) mean < median
(3) median < mode
(4) mean > mode

6 What is the interquartile range for the data 7, 4, 7, 2, 6, 9, 4, 3?

(1) 1.75
(2) 2
(3) 3.5
(4) 7

7 The mean of a set of data is 27, and the data includes 24, 34, 19, 22, 29, and x. The value of x is

(1) 27
(2) 29
(3) 34
(4) 37

8 The median height of the players on the basketball team is 6 feet 4 inches. This means

(1) the tallest player is 6 feet 4 inches
(2) no player is shorter than 6 feet 4 inches
(3) an equal number of players are taller than 6 feet 4 inches and shorter than 6 feet 4 inches
(4) most of the players are 6 feet 4 inches tall

9 The table below shows the 2008 PGA Tour Career Money Leaders. Find the mean, median, and mode of these data.

Golfer	Earnings
Tiger Woods	$82,354,376
Vijay Singh	$56,690,749
Phil Mickelson	$49,293,526
Jim Furyk	$37,268,879
Davis Love III	$35,921,309
Ernie Els	$32,621,832
David Toms	$28,423,857
Justin Leonard	$26,110,924
Kenny Perry	$25,107,999
Stewart Cink	$24,795,364

10 One hundred senior girls were interviewed about their price limit for the "perfect" prom dress. Their responses are summarized in the table below.

Maximum Price (prom dress)	Number of Girls
$100	23
$150	22
$200	26
$250	14
$300	15

a Determine the mean, median, and mode of the data.
b Which measure of central tendency should the buyer for a store at the mall use to place an order based on what price prom dresses will sell best?

11 The table below gives the speed of the fastest race lap at the Indianapolis 500 for the years from 1999 to 2008.

Year	1999	2000	2001	2002	2003
Speed (mph)	218.9	218.5	219.8	226.5	229.2
Year	2004	2005	2006	2007	2008
Speed (mph)	218.4	228.1	221.3	223.4	224.0

a Find the mean, median, and mode of these data.

b Which, in your opinion, is most representative of the data? Why?

c What is the interquartile range of the data?

12 Andrew wanted a raise in his allowance for doing yard work. His father said he should find out the "average" payment others in the neighborhood received. Andrew surveyed the other families on the block and discovered that they paid the following prices for having their lawns cut and raked: $18.00, $22.00, $17.50, $15.00, $25.00, $17.50, $20.00, $15.00, $26.00, $28.00.

a Which "average" should Andrew use to promote his increase in allowance?

b Which "average" might his father use to rebut Andrew's argument?

13 The data below represents the median age of Americans as per the U.S. census:

Year	1960	1970	1980	1990	2000
Age	29.4	27.9	32.8	33.0	35.3

Why would the United States Census Bureau report median ages rather than mean or modal ages? What makes the median most representative?

14 The following are the ten top grossing films of all times, adjusted for inflation, as of June 2008.

Movie Title and Year of Release	Money Earned (in millions)
Gone With the Wind, 1939	$1,362.5
Star Wars, 1977	$1,177.8
The Sound of Music, 1965	$945.3
E.T.: The Extra Terrestrial, 1982	$934.8
The Ten Commandments, 1956	$869.6
Titanic, 1997	$857.3
Jaws, 1975	$850.2
Doctor Zhivago, 1965	$803.8
The Jungle Book, 1967	$719.1
Snow White and the Seven Dwarfs, 1937	$705.7

a Find the mean and median of these data.

b Explain which measure you would use as the "average gross" of the mega-movies of the U.S. and why.

15 Give an example of the type of data set for which you would use the

a mean as the average
b median as the average
c mode as the average

16 Explain the procedure that you would follow to find the median, first quartile, and third quartile without using a calculator.

17 Explain how you can change one or more data values in a list and definitely not affect the median. Can you do the same for the mode? For the mean?

15.3 Measures of Dispersion: Range, Interquartile Range, Variance, and Standard Deviation

In the previous section, you studied where the center of a collection of data lies. In this section, you will study how the data are spread out, or **dispersed**, from the center.

For example, look at the following test grades for two students.

John: 85, 84, 83, 86, 87

Mike: 79, 98, 68, 94, 86

The mean score for both John and Mike is 85. Do you feel that the two boys are the same kind of student? Why?

Let us examine the scores of the two students. John's grades are all around 85. He is a very consistent student. Mike's grades show much more variability, going up and down from one test to the next. It would be difficult to predict Mike's next grade.

Range

A **measure of dispersion** is a number that indicates the spread, or variation, of data values about the mean. Perhaps the most basic measure of dispersion is the **range**. The range is the difference between the highest score and the lowest score. If we look at the test grades above, the range in John's scores is $87 - 83 = 4$, while the range in Mike's scores is $98 - 68 = 30$. The smaller the range, the more closely grouped are the data.

Interquartile Range

Recall from Section 15.2 that the interquartile range is the difference between the third quartile and the first quartile. In the example above, the interquartile range of John's scores is the difference $86.5 - 83.5 = 3$, while the interquartile range of Mike's scores is $96 - 73.5 = 22.5$. The interquartile range, like the range, points out the inconsistency of Mike's grades.

Outliers are values much lower or much higher than most of the other data. Outliers are often identified as values that fall more than 1.5 times the interquartile range from the quartiles.

Variance

There are several other measures of dispersion. If we look at John's scores, we find that the mean is 85. We see that he has an 84 and an 86; one score is 1 point below the mean, and one score is 1 point above the mean. His other two scores are 83 and 87; one score is 2 points below the mean, and one score is 2 points above the mean. If we add the differences between the mean and each of these scores, they sum to zero. Does that give us meaningful information? No. For *any* data set, the total number of points above the mean equals the total number of points below the mean. To more clearly indicate the dispersion of John's scores, we can square all of the numbers to avoid being misled by negative values.

The **variance** is the arithmetic average of the squares of the deviations from the mean. The formula for the variance is $v = \dfrac{\sum\limits_{i=1}^{n}(x_i - \bar{x})^2}{n}$.

MODEL PROBLEM

Find the variance for John's and Mike's scores.

SOLUTION

John's scores are 85, 84, 83, 86, and 87.

x_i	$\bar{x}$	$x_i - \bar{x}$	$(x_i - \bar{x})^2$
85	85	0	0
84	85	−1	1
83	85	−2	4
86	85	1	1
87	85	2	4
			$\dfrac{\sum\limits_{i=1}^{5}(x_i - \bar{x})^2}{5} = \dfrac{10}{5} = 2$

Mike's scores are 79, 98, 68, 94, and 86.

x_i	$\bar{x}$	$x_i - \bar{x}$	$(x_i - \bar{x})^2$
79	85	−6	36
98	85	13	169
68	85	−17	289
94	85	9	81
86	85	1	1
			$\dfrac{\sum\limits_{i=1}^{5}(x_i - \bar{x})^2}{5} = \dfrac{576}{5} = 115.2$

Answer: The variance for John's scores is 2 and the variance for Mike's scores is 115.2.

Standard Deviation

One problem with the variance is that we are now dealing with squares of scores, rather than the scores themselves. To get a measure comparable to the original deviations before they were squared, we can take the square root of the variance.

The square root of the variance is called the **standard deviation**, which is a widely used measure of dispersion that indicates the concentration of the scores around the mean. The formula for the standard deviation differs slightly depending on whether you are using an entire population or just a sample. The symbol for population standard deviation is a lowercase sigma, σ. You may also see the standard deviation written as σ_x.

The formula for the **population standard deviation** is $\sigma = \sqrt{\dfrac{\sum\limits_{i=1}^{n} (x_i - \bar{x})^2}{n}}$.

When we have sample data, we use the letter s to denote the standard deviation. For the **sample standard deviation**, we use the formula $s = \sqrt{\dfrac{\sum\limits_{i=1}^{n} (x_i - \bar{x})^2}{n - 1}}$.

Notice the formula for s is similar to the formula for the population standard deviation. However, the sum of the squared deviations is divided by $n - 1$ instead of n to compensate for the reduced variability in a sample as compared to a whole population.

In our example, John and Mike's scores are all listed, so we will use the population standard deviation. The standard deviation for John's scores is $\sqrt{2} \approx 1.414$. The standard deviation for Mike's scores is $\sqrt{115.2} \approx 10.733$.

Sometimes we need a frequency table to determine the standard deviation. Let's look at the scores in Ms. DiRocco's English class. If we have four scores of 80, three scores of 82, one score of 78, two scores of 81, and two scores of 83, a frequency table would make the calculations a bit simpler. We will use following table to find the mean, variance, and standard deviation.

x_i	f_i	$f_i x_i$	$\bar{x}$	$x_i - \bar{x}$	$(x_i - \bar{x})^2$	$f_i(x_i - \bar{x})^2$
78	1	78	81	-3	9	9
80	4	320	81	-1	1	4
81	2	162	81	0	0	0
82	3	246	81	1	1	3
83	2	166	81	2	4	8
	$n = 12$	$\sum\limits_{i=1}^{12} f_i x_i = 972$				$\sum\limits_{i=1}^{12} f_i(x_i - \bar{x})^2 = 24$

We used the sum of the third column, $x_i f_i$, to find the mean:

$$\bar{x} = \frac{\sum\limits_{i=1}^{12} f_i x_i}{12} = \frac{972}{12} = 81$$

To find the variance, we divide the sum of the last column ($9 + 4 + 0 + 3 + 8 = 24$) by the total number of scores ($n = 12$): $v = \dfrac{\sum\limits_{i=1}^{12} f_i(x_i - \bar{x})^2}{12} = \dfrac{24}{12} = 2$

To find the standard deviation, we take the square root of the variance:

$$\sigma = \sqrt{\dfrac{\displaystyle\sum_{i=1}^{12} f_i(x_i - \bar{x})^2}{12}} = \sqrt{2} \approx 1.414$$

The graphing calculator can calculate the standard deviation for you. First, press (STAT) (1) and enter the scores in L_1 and the frequencies in L_2.

Next, find the one-variable statistics for a frequency distribution, as we did in Section 15.2. Press (STAT) (▶) (1) and choose 1: 1-Var Stats from the CALC menu. Then specify the scores from L_1 and the frequencies from L_2 by pressing (2nd) (1) (,) (2nd) (2). Hit (ENTER) to view the statistics.

```
1-Var Stats L1,L2
```

```
1-Var Stats
 x̄=81
 Σx=972
 Σx²=78756
 Sx=1.477097892
 σx=1.414213562
↓n=12
```

You can see that the mean is 81, the sum of the x-values is 972, and the sum of the squares of the x-values is 78,756. We see that Sx, the sample standard deviation, is approximately 1.477 and the population standard deviation, σx, is approximately 1.414. If you scroll down, you'll also see the number of data values, the minimum x-value, the first quartile, the median, the third quartile, and the maximum x-value. If you need any of these values at a later time, you can press (VARS) (5), and then choose what you need.

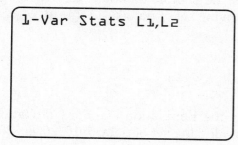

```
XY Σ EQ TEST PTS
1:n
2:x̄
3:Sx
4:σx
5:ȳ
6:Sy
7↓σy
```

When we calculated the standard deviation in this example, we assumed that the data represented the entire population, and calculated the population standard deviation. However, if these data were a sample to be used to estimate information for the scores in an entire population, the sample standard deviation would be used. To calculate the sample standard deviation ourselves, we would have followed the same procedure shown in the table on page 500, except instead of dividing by 12, the number of scores, we would have divided by 11, one less than the number of scores. Thus, $s = \sqrt{\dfrac{\displaystyle\sum_{i=1}^{12} (x_i - \bar{x})^2}{11}} = \sqrt{\dfrac{24}{11}} \approx 1.477$. This is the same answer we received from the statistical calculations of the calculator.

Exercises 1–10: Write the numeral preceding the choice that best completes the statement or answers the question.

1 If the range of a set of data is 40 and the highest score is 50, what is the lowest score?

(1) −10
(2) 1.2
(3) 10
(4) 90

2 If the variance of a set of data is 16, what is the standard deviation?

(1) 256
(2) 32
(3) 8
(4) 4

3 If the standard deviation of a set of data is 16, what is the variance?

(1) 256
(2) 32
(3) 8
(4) 4

4 Which of the following sets of data has the greatest range?

(1) {32, 65, 34, 43, 16}
(2) {14, 76, 56, 42, 86}
(3) {65, 54, 75, 45, 86}
(4) {21, 45, 90, 65, 54}

5 What is the variance for the following set of data: 4, 6, 8, 10, 12?

(1) 1.682
(2) 2.828
(3) 8
(4) 64

6 What is the interquartile range of the following set of data: 22, 48, 18, 34, 59, 47, 16, 82, 11, 39?

(1) 18.5
(2) 30
(3) 36.5
(4) 71

7 After giving a test to her class, Mrs. Statsrule decided to raise everyone's score by 5 points. How does this affect the standard deviation?

(1) increases it by 5 points
(2) increases it by $\sqrt{5}$ points
(3) there is no change
(4) the change cannot be determined

8 What is the sample standard deviation for the following set of data: 6, 12, 14, 19, 24, 26?

(1) 6.9
(2) 7.6
(3) 16.8
(4) 101

9 What is the population standard deviation for the following set of data: 5, 10, 20, 40, 80?

(1) 31
(2) 30.496
(3) 27.276
(4) 5

10 If each score in a set of data were multiplied by 2, the mean would

(1) be multiplied by 2
(2) be divided by 2
(3) not change
(4) the change cannot be determined

11 Mary stayed up late each night studying for her Algebra 2 and Trigonometry Regents examination. She kept track of the number of hours of sleep she received each night for the past week. If she slept 6 hours, 5 hours, 6 hours, 7 hours, 3 hours, 4 hours, and 4 hours, find

a the mean number of hours of sleep she received each night

b the range of the number of hours of sleep she received each night

c the interquartile range of the number of hours of sleep she received each night

12 The table below shows the temperature in various places in New York State on July 22, 2008.

Location	Temperature
Albany	85
Binghamton	81
Buffalo	77
Corning	81
Dunkirk	75
Elmira	81
Geneva	79
Glens Falls	81
Islip	85
Ithaca	81
Kingston	85
Massena	79
New York City	89
Niagara Falls	77
Oswego	77
Plattsburgh	80
Poughkeepsie	85
Rochester	79
Saranac Lake	75
Syracuse	81
Utica	81
Watertown	77
White Plains	89
Yonkers	89

a According to the data, to the *nearest tenth*, what was the mean temperature in New York State on July 21, 2008?

b What is the sample standard deviation of the temperatures, to the *nearest tenth*?

13 In Math 101 at a local college, the youngest member of the class is 18 and the oldest member is 43. What is the range in ages?

14 All of the students in Mr. Consistent's math class scored a 90 on a test.

a What is the mean score?
b What is the standard deviation?

15 Both of the following sets of data have the same mean. Without doing any computation, determine which one has the smaller standard deviation. Explain how you came to your conclusion.

A: 10, 90, 40, 5, 30, 5

B: 32, 30, 36, 28, 24, 30

16 The table below lists the heights of a possible 2008–2009 New York Knicks roster as of July 21, 2008.

Name	Height
Renaldo Balkman	6'8"
Wilson Chandler	6'8"
Mardy Collins	6'6"
Jamal Crawford	6'5"
Eddy Curry	6'11"
Chris Duhon	6'1"
Danilo Gallinari	6'10"
Jerome James	7'1"
Jared Jeffries	6'11"
Fred Jones	6'2"
David Lee	6'9"
Stephon Marbury	6'2"
Randolph Morris	6'11"
Zach Randolph	6'9"
Quentin Richardson	6'6"
Nate Robinson	5'9"
Malik Rose	6'7"

Use the data to find:

a the mean, to the *nearest tenth* of an inch
b the range
c the median, the first and third quartiles, and the interquartile range

17 The name, year of birth, and year of appointment for the 2008 Supreme Court justices are listed in the table below.

Name	Year of Birth	Year of Appointment
John G. Roberts (Chief Justice)	1955	2005
Samuel A. Alito, Jr.	1950	2006
Stephen Breyer	1938	1994
Ruth Bader Ginsburg	1933	1993
Anthony M. Kennedy	1936	1988
Antonin Scalia	1936	1986
David Souter	1939	1990
John Paul Stevens	1920	1975
Clarence Thomas	1948	1991

  a Find, to the *nearest tenth*, the mean, median, and first and third quartiles of the number of years the Supreme Court justices have served as of 2008.

  b Find the range of their years of service and the interquartile range of their years of service as of 2008.

  c What is the "average" age of a Supreme Court justice as of 2008? Explain why you chose the measure of central tendency that you did.

18 The PSAT scores of a group of students in Kennedy High School are given in the table below.

Score	Frequency
20	1
25	2
30	2
35	2
40	14
45	28
50	36
55	34
60	27
65	23
70	11
75	3
80	2

  a Based on the data given above, to the *nearest hundredth*, what is the mean PSAT score of these students?

  b To the *nearest hundredth*, what is the sample standard deviation of the students in Kennedy High School?

19 Monica and Maurice each have a 180 bowling average.

  a If the range of Monica's scores is 50 points, and her lowest score is a 140, what is her highest score?

  b If the interquartile range of Maurice's scores is 50 points, explain how Maurice's consistency compares to Monica's.

20 The names and finishing times of the ten top female finishers in the 2007 New York City Marathon are shown in the table below.

Name	Time
Paula Radcliffe	2:23:09
Gete Wami	2:23:32
Jelena Prokopcuka	2:26:13
Lidiya Grigoryeva	2:28:37
Catherine Ndereba	2:29:08
Elva Dryer	2:35:15
Robyn Friedman	2:39:19
Tegla Loroupe	2:41:48
Melisa Christian	2:41:57
Elena Meyer	2:42:36

a Find, to the *nearest tenth of a second*, the mean time for the top ten female finishers of the 2007 New York City Marathon.

b Find the range.

21 The highest temperature on record in New York State, 108°F, was recorded in Troy on July 22, 1926. The lowest temperature on record, −52°F, was recorded on February 18, 1979, at Old Forge. What is the range in temperatures?

22 The highest point in New York State is Mount Marcy, at 5,344 feet above sea level. The lowest point in New York State is where New York meets the Atlantic Ocean, at sea level. What is the range in altitudes?

23 The table below contains a lineup for the 2008 New York Jets offense, the position played by each player, and the weight of each player.

Name	Position	Weight
Chris Baker	Tight End	258
Laveranues Coles	Wide Receiver	193
Jerricho Cotchery	Wide Receiver	207
Alan Faneca	Guard	307
Brett Favre	Quarterback	222
D'Brickashaw Ferguson	Tackle	312
Thomas Jones	Running Back	215
Nick Mangold	Center	300
Brandon Moore	Guard	295
Tony Richardson	Fullback	238
Damien Woody	Tackle	335

a To the *nearest tenth of a pound*, what is the mean weight of the members of this New York Jets offense?

b What is the standard deviation, to the *nearest tenth of a pound*?

24 The table below contains a line up for the 2008 New York Jets defense, the position played by each player, and the weight of each player.

Name	Position	Weight
David Barrett	Cornerback	195
Eric Barton	Linebacker	245
Kenyon Coleman	Defensive End	295
Abram Elam	Safety	207
Shaun Ellis	Defensive End	285
David Harris	Linebacker	243
Kris Jenkins	Defensive Tackle	349
C.J. Mosley	Defensive Tackle	305
Darrelle Revis	Cornerback	204
Kerry Rhodes	Safety	220
Bryan Thomas	Linebacker	266

a To the *nearest tenth of a pound*, what is the mean weight of the members of this New York Jets defense?

b What is the standard deviation, to the *nearest tenth of a pound*?

25 The table below lists the ages of people who attended the Screaming Ghouls rock concert.

Age	Frequency	Age	Frequency
12	23	19	11
13	46	20	10
14	56	21	6
15	65	22	3
16	43	23	2
17	38	31	2
18	21	42	1

a What is the mean age of the rock concert attendees, to the *nearest hundredth*?

b What is the standard deviation, to the *nearest hundredth*?

c Who would be interested in this type of information?

26 The table below shows the hourly salaries of various employees in the Love to Eat Bakery.

Salary	Frequency
$5.15	2
$5.25	7
$5.50	8
$6.00	4
$10.00	2
$25.00	1

a To the *nearest cent*, what is the mean salary paid?

b To the *nearest cent*, what is the sample standard deviation?

27 The table below lists normal monthly precipitation, in inches, in Binghamton, New York.

Month	Precipitation (in inches)
January	2.40
February	2.33
March	2.82
April	3.13
May	3.36
June	3.60
July	3.50
August	3.36
September	3.32
October	2.89
November	3.28
December	3.00

a To the *nearest tenth of an inch*, what is the mean amount of monthly precipitation in Binghamton?

b What is the sample standard deviation, to the *nearest tenth of an inch*?

15.4 Normal Distribution

According to the U.S. Census Bureau, the average female in her twenties is 5 feet 4 inches tall. Certainly, a woman who is 5 feet 5 inches would not be considered tall, nor would a woman 5 feet 3 inches be considered short. There is a certain range of heights within which women would be considered "normal height."

If we took a large sample of twenty-year-old women and made a histogram of their heights, we could expect to see a graph similar to the one below.

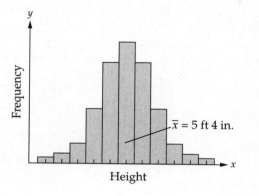

The mean height is 5 feet 4 inches. The middle bar of the histogram represents this height. If we connect the midpoints of the bars of the histogram, we obtain the frequency polygon shown below.

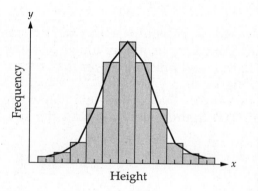

If we draw a smooth curve through the points that determine the frequency polygon, we get a curve that resembled a bell. In statistics, this curve is called a **normal curve**. Data that can be modeled by a normal curve is said to have a **normal distribution**. For example, people's heights, weights, temperatures, blood pressures, IQ scores, SAT scores, and ACT scores have a normal distribution. The amount of time a lightbulb burns also produces a normal distribution, as do the sizes of the bolts produced by a bolt manufacturer.

Note: All data are *not* modeled by a normal curve. For example, the test scores in your mathematics class would probably not be modeled by a normal curve since the grades are usually not equally distributed around the mean.

In a normal curve, the mean is the data value that occurs most frequently. (Thus, the mean is also the mode.) Half of the data values lie above the mean and half lie below the mean. (Thus, the mean is also the median.) Since the mean occurs at the center of the curve, it is the axis of symmetry for the curve.

In a normal curve:

- Approximately 68.2% of the data values occur within one standard deviation of the mean, 34.1% below the mean and 34.1% above the mean.
- Approximately 95.4% of the data values occur within two standard deviations of the mean, 47.7% above the mean and 47.7% below the mean.
- Approximately 99.8% of the data values occur within three standard deviations of the mean, 49.9% above the mean and 49.9% below the mean.

We can break up the normal curve into even smaller intervals. The graph below shows the percentage of high school students within 0.5, 1, 1.5, 2, 2.5, and 3 standard deviations of the mean for blood pressure.

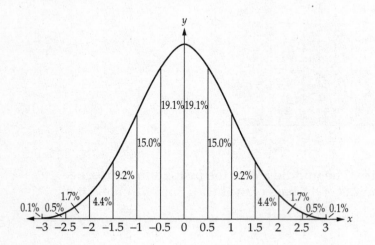

In statistics, the word *percentile* is often used. A **percentile** indicates a point below which a percentage of data values fall. For example, if your blood pressure is in the 75th percentile, 75% of the people have blood pressure lower than yours, and 25% of the people have blood pressure higher than yours.

In a normal curve, the mean is the 50th percentile—half of the data values are below the mean, half are above the mean. The figure below includes the percentiles for the normal curve.

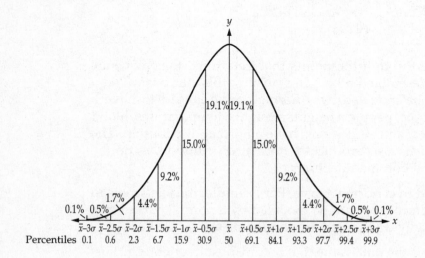

MODEL PROBLEMS

Use the following information to answer Problems 1–3.

Each year, the College Board publishes the mean SAT and the standard deviation for students taking the test. SAT scores are normally distributed. Assume for a group of students that the mean SAT score is 500 with a standard deviation of approximately 100 points.

1 Find the score that is:

   a one standard deviation above the mean

   b one standard deviation below the mean

SOLUTION

   a One standard deviation above the mean is $500 + 100 = 600$.

   b One standard deviation below the mean is $500 - 100 = 400$.

2 Approximately what percentile would a student be in if he or she scored

   a 500   **b** 600   **c** 450   **d** 750

SOLUTION

To determine the percentiles, we have to take our normal curve and include the SAT information. The mean is 500, so that goes in the center. Since the standard deviation is 100 points, 0.5 standard deviation is 50 points. Fill in the information as shown in the figure below.

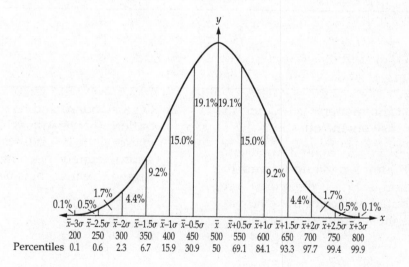

Look at the graph to answer the questions.

   a 500 is at the 50th percentile.

   b 600 is at the 84.1st percentile.

   c 450 is at the 30.9th percentile.

   d 750 is at the 99.4th percentile.

3 In 2007, approximately 1,500,000 students took the SAT. Approximately how many of them would be expected to score

 a between 400 and 450 **d** between 650 and 750

 b between 500 and 550 **e** above 750

 c between 300 and 400

SOLUTION

To answer this question we use the normal curve with the SAT information filled in. Refer to the figure in Problem 2 to answer the questions.

 a Between 400 and 450, 15.0% of the scores occur. 15% of 1,500,000 is 225,000 students.

 b Between 500 and 550, 19.1% of the scores occur. 19.1% of 1,500,000 is 286,500 students.

 c To find the number of scores between 300 and 400, we have to add the two percentages that are given: 4.4% and 9.2%. Thus, 13.6% of the scores occur between 300 and 400. 13.6% of 1,500,000 is 204,000 students.

 d To find the number of scores between 650 and 750, we have to add the two percentages that are given: 4.4% and 1.7%. Thus, 6.1% of the scores occur between 650 and 750, which is 91,500 students.

 e Since 750 is at the 99.4th percentile, we can see that 100% − 99.4% = 0.6% of the scores are above 750. Alternatively, we can take the two percentages that are above 750, 0.5% and 0.1%, and add them, which also gives us 0.6%. So, 0.6% of 1,500,000 is 9,000 students.

Practice

Exercises 1–10: Select the numeral preceding the expression that best answers the question.

1 The mean score in a national jump rope competition is 82.75 jumps per minute and the standard deviation is 2.25. If the scores were normally distributed, which of the following scores would be most likely to occur?

 (1) 90   (3) 80.5
 (2) 87.25 (4) 77

2 The Brite Lites R Us company manufactures lightbulbs. They advertise that the "average" lightbulb can burn for 1,000 hours. Tests have shown that this is the mean length of time. The times that the lights can burn are normally distributed with a standard deviation of 200 hours. What percent of the bulbs could be expected to last 600 or fewer hours?

 (1) 0.6   (3) 6.7
 (2) 2.3   (4) 30.9

3 On a standardized test with a normal distribution, the mean is 85 and the standard deviation is 5. If 1,200 students take the exam, approximately how many of them are expected to earn scores between 90 and 95?

 (1) 14
 (2) 98
 (3) 163
 (4) 1,172

4 If the mean of a set of normally distributed data is 14 and the standard deviation is 1.5, which of the following data values could be at the 17th percentile?

 (1) 15.6
 (2) 15.4
 (3) 12.6
 (4) 11.1

5 In a normal distribution, $\bar{x}$ is the mean, and σ is the standard deviation. If $\bar{x} + 0.5\sigma = 100$ and $\bar{x} - 0.5\sigma = 80$, what is the mean?

(1) 5
(2) 10
(3) 20
(4) 90

6 The We Go Farther Tire Company advertises a tire that last for 80,000 miles. The mileage for the tires is a normal distribution with a mean of 80,000 miles and a standard deviation of 10,000 miles. If the company produces 32,000 tires, how many of them would be expected to last between 65,000 and 100,000 miles?

(1) 27,212
(2) 29,120
(3) 30,528
(4) 31,264

7 In a national sit-up test with a normal distribution, the mean was 42 sit-ups per minute and the standard deviation was 2.6. Which score could be expected to occur less than 5% of the time?

(1) 50   (3) 39
(2) 45   (4) 37

8 The NuBolt Company manufactures nuts and bolts. The measures of the diameters of the bolts manufactured produce a normal distribution. The mean size of a certain bolt is 3 centimeters, with a standard deviation of 0.1 centimeter. Bolts that vary from the mean by more than 0.3 centimeter cannot be sold. If the company manufactures 150,000 of the 3-centimeter bolts, approximately how many of them cannot be sold?

(1) 150
(2) 300
(3) 15,000
(4) 30,000

9 On a standardized test with a standard deviation of 2, a score of 35 will occur less than 5% of the time. Which of the following could be the mean for this test?

(1) 32
(2) 34
(3) 38
(4) 40

10 In a normal distribution, $\bar{x}$ is the mean, and σ is the standard deviation. If $\bar{x} + 2\sigma = 60$, and $\bar{x} - 2\sigma = 40$, what is the standard deviation?

(1) 5
(2) 10
(3) 20
(4) 50

11 The incubation period for an outbreak of a disease similar to chicken pox is shown in the diagram below.

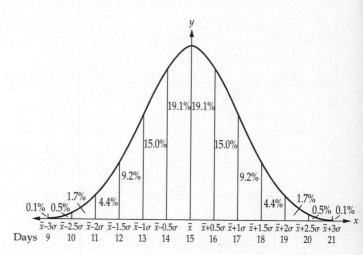

Based on the information in the diagram:

a What is the mean incubation period?
b What is the standard deviation?
c After being exposed to the disease, when can a person be 50% certain that he or she will not get the disease? 85% certain? 98% certain? (Assume that there was only one exposure to the disease.)
d When can a person be completely certain that he or she will not get the disease?

12 The mean age of the entering freshman class at a certain university is 18.5, with a standard deviation of 0.75 year. If the data produce a normal distribution, find:

a the percent of students who are between 19.25 and 17.75 years of age
b the percentile of a student who is 20 years old
c the number of students who could be expected to be younger than $\bar{x} - \sigma$ years of age, if the total number of incoming freshmen is 1,200 students

13 The average temperatures (degrees Fahrenheit) in Central Park in January are given in the table below.

Year	1875	1880	1885	1890	1895
Temp	23.8	39.6	29.4	37.6	29.8
Year	1900	1905	1910	1915	1920
Temp	31.8	29.3	31.1	34.5	23.4
Year	1925	1930	1935	1940	1945
Temp	28.4	33.3	28.9	25.0	25.1
Year	1950	1955	1960	1965	1970
Temp	41.4	31.0	33.9	29.7	25.1
Year	1975	1980	1985	1990	1995
Temp	37.3	33.7	28.8	41.4	37.5
Year	2000	2005	2006	2007	2008
Temp	31.3	31.3	40.9	37.5	36.5

a Determine the mean temperature in Central Park in January, to the *nearest tenth*.

b What is σ for these data, to the *nearest tenth*?

c Assume that, over a long period of time, the January Central Park temperature approximates a normal distribution. Based on your answers from parts **a** and **b**, answer the following questions.

  (1) What temperature is at the 50th percentile?

  (2) What is the range of temperatures that occur 95.4% of the time?

  (3) What is the likelihood of coming to Central Park in January and the temperature being above freezing?

  (4) What temperature is in the 6.7th percentile?

  (5) Between what two temperatures do 68.2% of the temperatures lie?

14 Scores on the ACT approximate a normal distribution. The following table contains the mean ACT score of students during several years.

Year	1987	1990	1997	2000	2007
Score	20.6	20.6	21.0	21.0	21.2

a Using the information from the table above, determine $\bar{x}$ and σ for students taking the ACT from 1987 to 2007.

b Based on your answer to part **a**, approximate the score needed for a student to be in the 97.7th percentile.

c Between what two scores do approximately 68.2% of the scores lie?

d In 2007, approximately 1,300,000 students took the ACT. Approximately how many of them would be expected to score between 20.8 and 21.04?

15.5 Bivariate Statistics, Correlation Coefficients, and the Line of Best Fit

We have been studying univariate statics, in which the data set being analyzed involves only one variable. For example, we looked at the heights of basketball players and the weights of football players. We will now look at how two variables change together as we study **bivariate statistics**, the analysis of a data set involving two variables. For instance, we will look at how the heights of some high school students compare to their shoe sizes and how the percentage of households with computers has increased over time.

If you are given two points on a coordinate graph and asked what line connects those two points, it is not a difficult job to determine the equation of the line. You know from previous courses that any two points form one and only line, so you could simply draw a line on the graph connecting the two points, calculate the slope and y-intercept, and determine the equation. Alternatively, you could calculate the slope and y-intercept algebraically. As an example, let us determine the equation of the line connecting the points $(-1, -2)$ and $(5, 6)$.

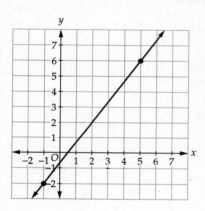

Connect the points $(-1, -2)$ and $(5, 6)$ and find the slope. In looking at the graph, we see that the y-intercept is not an integer. We will use an algebraic method to find the equation.

$$\frac{y - y_1}{x - x_1} = \frac{y_2 - y_1}{x_2 - x_1}$$

$$\frac{y - (-2)}{x - (-1)} = \frac{6 - (-2)}{5 - (-1)}$$

$$\frac{y + 2}{x + 1} = \frac{8}{6}$$

$$6y + 12 = 8x + 8$$

$$y = \frac{8}{6}x - \frac{4}{6} \qquad \text{or} \qquad y = \frac{4}{3}x - \frac{2}{3}$$

In some cases, however, you are given a set of points that do not lie on a unique line.

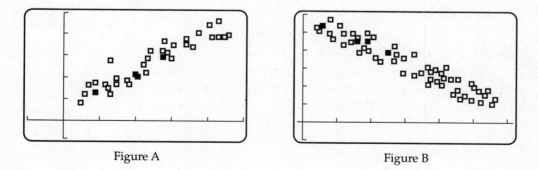

Figure A   Figure B

Figures A and B are graphs called **scatter plots**, basically a set of points scattered on the coordinate plane. In the two graphs shown above, no one line can be drawn to pass through all the points. Instead, we look for the **line of best fit**. To find this line, we utilize **linear regression**, which fits the data so that the sum of the squares of the vertical distances from the points to the line is as small as possible.

Formulas to find the line of best fit were developed by the mathematician Carl Friedrich in 1795. Today we are able to use software or calculators to find the line of best fit for our problems. Below, you can see the lines the graphing calculator created for each scatter plot.

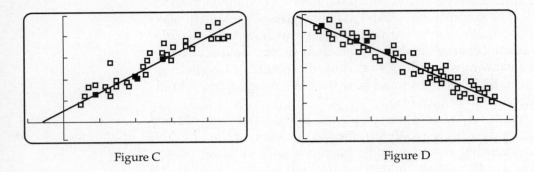

Figure C   Figure D

To determine how well the regression line fits the data, mathematicians use a **correlation coefficient** (denoted as r). If the y-coordinate of points is increasing as the x-coordinate increases, the correlation coefficient is positive, as in Figures A and C above. If the y-coordinate of the points is decreasing as the x-coordinate increases, the correlation coefficient is negative, as in Figures B and D. Notice that the sign of the correlation coefficient is the same as the sign of the slope of the line of best fit. If all of the points lie on the line of best fit, the correlation coefficient is +1 for an increasing linear function and −1 for a decreasing linear function. In Figure E below, the scatter plot has a correlation coefficient of +1. We can say that the elements of the pairs of data show a *strong positive* correlation. In Figure F, the correlation coefficient is −1. We can say that the elements of the pairs of data show a *strong negative* correlation.

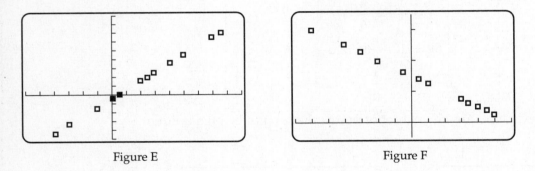

Figure E   Figure F

Figure G has a correlation coefficient of approximately 0.75, indicating that while the points form an approximately linear pattern, they do not form a line. We can say that the elements of the pairs of data show a *moderate positive* correlation. Since the points in Figure H do not nearly approximate a line, that graph has a correlation coefficient of practically zero, −0.05. There is *no linear correlation* between the elements of the pairs of data.

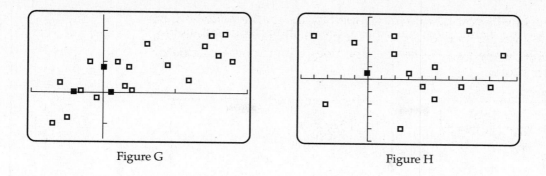

Figure G   Figure H

A correlation coefficient close to zero signifies no significant correlation while a correlation coefficient close to +1 or −1 indicates that the points in the scatter plot are close to the calculated line of best fit.

It is important to realize that just because there may be a strong correlation between dependent and independent data, there is not necessarily a cause-and-effect relationship. If we compare reading ability and age, it is probable that in most cases, reading ability will increase as an individual's age does, but only because as people grow older, they also gain more education and a higher reading level. To say that a person 16 years old reads better than a child 3 years old is probably accurate, but it is not valid to credit age as the cause of better reading.

MODEL PROBLEMS

1   The scatter plot below would most likely have which of the following correlation coefficients?

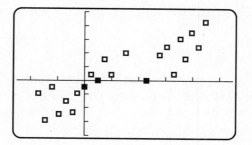

(1) 1
(2) 0.875
(3) −0.54
(4) −1

SOLUTION

The scatter plot shows a positive upward trend, so the correlation coefficient must be positive. This eliminates choices 3 and 4. The majority of points appear to be almost collinear, but there are some points outside the main cluster, so it is not a perfect line of best fit.

Answer: The correct answer is choice (2) 0.875.

2 Which of the following scatter plots could have a correlation coefficient of +1?

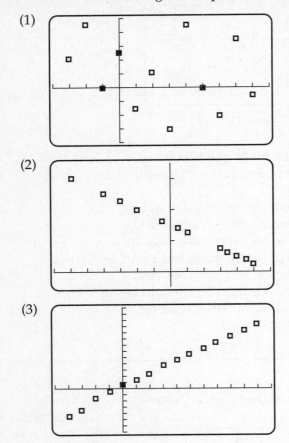

(1)

(2)

(3)

(4) none of these

SOLUTION

In choice 1, few of the points are collinear, so this would have a very poor correlation coefficient. Choice 2 has a negative correlation coefficient since the points trend downward from left to right. Choice 3 clearly has a positive correlation and all points appear collinear, so it would have a correlation coefficient of +1.

Answer: The correct answer is choice 3.

3 For each set of bivariate data, determine whether the correlation coefficient is positive, negative, or almost zero.

  a the size of a backyard pool and the amount of water it holds

  b the weight of a steak and the price it costs

  c the number of people in the audience and the cost of a movie ticket

SOLUTION

  a Positive correlation; the bigger the pool, the more water needed to fill it.

  b Positive correlation; meat is sold by weight, so the larger the steak, the more expensive it is.

  c A correlation of almost zero; movie prices are standard no matter how many people are in the theater.

Remember: Correlation coefficients of both +1 and −1 indicate excellent point alignment with the theoretical line of best fit. The negative is not a value judgment but an indication of slope of that line.

 **Practice**

Exercises 1–6: Match each scatter plot with the most appropriate correlation coefficient.

a +1	**b** +0.8	**c** +0.3
d +0.1	**e** −0.6	**f** −0.9

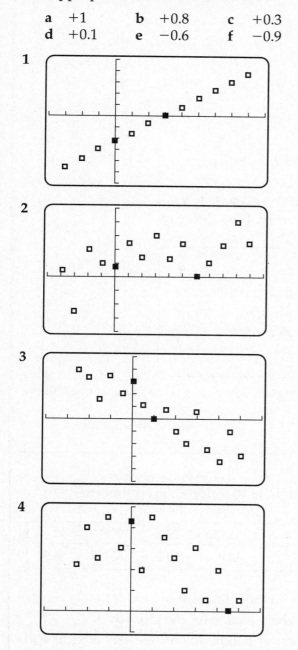

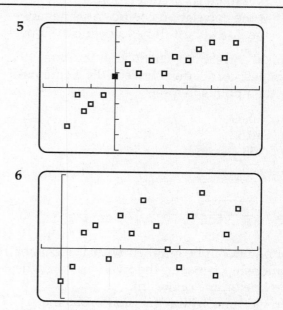

Exercises 7–10: Select the numeral preceding the choice that best completes the sentence or answers the question.

7 The scatter plot below could have a correlation coefficient of

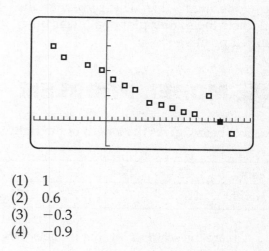

(1) 1
(2) 0.6
(3) −0.3
(4) −0.9

8 Which of the following is a *true* statement?

(1) The line of best fit always passes through each of the given data points.
(2) The line of best fit must have a correlation coefficient of +1 or −1.
(3) A correlation coefficient of −1 means that there is no correlation.
(4) If the correlation coefficient is negative, the line of best fit has a negative slope.

9 Which correlation coefficient indicates the strongest correlation between the elements of the data points in a set?

(1) −0.89
(2) −0.52
(3) 0.58
(4) 0.76

10 Which correlation coefficient would indicate little correlation between the data points and a line of best fit?

(1) −1
(2) −0.52
(3) 0.15
(4) 0.90

15.6 Linear Regression

A set of points can be graphed with a calculator. If the graph shows there is a linear relationship between the two variables, the calculator can find the linear regression line or line of best fit.

When working with regression problems, it is helpful to plot the given points and look at the scatter plot. It is useful to be able to recognize the graph of the scatter plot of various types of functions. A linear function is of the form $y = mx + b$. When you picture a linear regression, concentrate on the root of the word *linear, line*. The screen to the right depicts the scatter plot of a linear function with a positive slope.

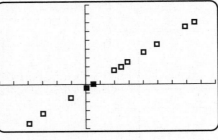

MODEL PROBLEM

The table below gives the length of the right foot and the height of 10 males, all in centimeters.

Foot	25.4	26.4	27.1	27.9	28	28.4	28.5	29.2	29.5	30
Height	165.1	170.2	175.3	179	181.2	182.9	183	184.2	185	186.9

a Create the scatter plot that models these data, using height as a function of foot size.
b To the nearest hundredth, determine the linear regression equation for the given data.
c What is the correlation coefficient, rounded to the nearest hundredth, for the size of right foot versus height?
d To the nearest tenth, predict the height of a male whose right foot measures 26 centimeters.
e Is it a logical premise that foot size and height are dependent measures? Why?

SOLUTION

a First, press (STAT) and enter the foot lengths in L_1 and the heights in L_2.

Second, press (2nd) (Y=) to access the Stat Plot menu. Turn on Plot 1. Be sure that the Type is set to scatter plot.

Third, press (ZOOM) (9) to graph the points on the home screen as shown below.

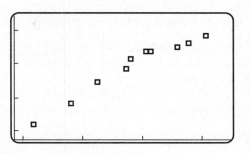

```
Plot1   Plot2   Plot3
On   Off
Type:  ⬛   ⬰   ⬛
      ⊞    ⊞    ⬕
Xlist:L1
Ylist:L2
Mark:  ⬛   +   .
```

This produces the scatter plot requested.

b The calculator has the points and we can find the equation now. Press (STAT) again, but this time use the right arrow to move over to the CALC menu. Since we want a linear regression equation, we select 4: LinReg(ax+b). The calculator now shows this statement on the home screen.

Assign the regression equation to Y_1 by typing L_1, L_2, Y_1. (To type Y_1, press (VARS) and right arrow over to the Y-VARS menu. Choose 1: Function followed by 1: Y_1.) Press (ENTER).

```
LinReg
 y=ax+b
 a=4.830882353
 b=43.82205882
 r²=.9556128231
 r=.9775545116
```

If we round our *a* and *b* values to the nearest hundredth and plug them into the standard linear equation, our answer is $y = 4.83x + 43.82$.

c The r indicates the correlation coefficient. To the nearest hundredth, $r = 0.98$. Notice that since *r* is close to 1, the data have a strong positive correlation.

Note: If *r*, the correlation coefficient, does not appear on your screen, go into the CATALOG ((2nd) (0)) and choose DiagnosticOn. Press (ENTER). Reenter the linear regression command and now you will see *r*.

d First, press (GRAPH) to graph the scatter plot and line of best fit.

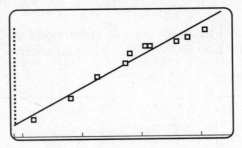

Now we use the regression line to predict the height.

Press (2nd) (TRACE) and choose 1: value from the CALC menu. Key in 26 and press (ENTER).

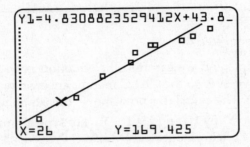

The calculator shows that the height of a male with a foot length of 26 centimeters can be expected to be 169.4 centimeters tall.

  e Yes. In addition to a strong positive correlation between a person's foot size and height, it makes sense that very tall individuals would need larger feet to support their weight.

Interpolation and Extrapolation

Regression models help us to predict data values based on known information.

In part **d** of the model problem, we used **interpolation**: we found the *y*-value that corresponds to an *x*-value that falls between other values supplied in the original data.

If we want to predict data values outside of the range of our original data, we use a process called **extrapolation**. For instance, let's predict the height of a male with a foot length of 32 centimeters. First change Xmax to 33. Again, press (2nd) (TRACE) and choose 1: value from the CALC menu. Key in 32 and press (ENTER).

We extrapolate that the height of a male with a foot length of 32 centimeters would be approximately 198.4 centimeters.

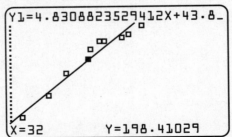

Exercises 1 and 2: Select the numeral preceding the choice that best completes the statement. Use the following data from a survey of eight female high school juniors comparing right foot size and height.

Right Foot (cm)	Height (cm)
22.1	157.1
22.9	160.8
23.1	161.4
23.4	161
24.1	162.8
24.6	164
25.4	164.7
26.1	164

1 The correlation coefficient of these data is

(1) 1
(2) 0.96711
(3) 0.9237
(4) 0.9017

2 The linear regression equation for these data is approximately

(1) $y = 122.4x - 1.65$
(2) $y = 122.4x + 1.65$
(3) $y = 1.65x + 122.4$
(4) $y = 1.65x - 122.4$

3 The number of sets of twins born in the United States has been increasing as per the data below.

Year	Sets of Twins
1990	93,865
1991	94,779
1992	95,372
1993	96,445
1994	97,064

(*Hint*: When years are given as part of the data, we sometimes set the first year as 0 in order to simplify the calculations. In this problem, enter 0, 1, 2, 3, and 4 as the independent variable, year, in L_1.)

a Find the line of best fit for the data.
b What is the correlation coefficient for these data?
c Based on the data, how many twin births might be expected in 1997?
d Actually in 1997, there were 104,137 sets of twins born. What does this mean about the line of best fit? What might explain this discrepancy?

4 Foreign adoptions have been growing in the United States. The data below show the number of adoptions from Russia in the period 1992–2004.

Year	Adoptions from Russia
1992	324
1993	746
1994	1,530
1995	1,896
1996	2,454
1997	3,816
1998	4,491
1999	4,348
2000	4,269
2001	4,279
2002	4,939
2003	5,209
2004	5,865

a Write the regression equation to represent the number of Russian adoptions as a function of the time in years since 1992. Round coefficients to the *nearest hundredth*.

b What is the correlation coefficient? What does this mean about the relationship between the year and the number of adoptions?

c Approximately how many more Russian children were adopted each year during this period? (What is the slope of the function?)

d Based on this mathematical model, how many Russian children would you expect to have been adopted in 2005?

e Actually, 4,639 Russian children were adopted in 2005. What might explain the discrepancy between this fact and your answer to part **d**?

f Find out the most recent Russian adoption statistics and see if the mathematical model holds true.

5 The following table represents the number of U.S. radio stations on the air since 1950.

Year	Radio Stations
1950	2,773
1955	3,211
1960	4,133
1965	5,249
1970	6,760
1975	8,844
1980	8,566
1985	10,359
1990	10,788
1995	11,834
1996	12,295
1997	12,482
1998	12,642
2001	13,058
2004	13,476
2005	15,559

a Create a scatter plot using these data. Let $x = 0$ represent the year 1950.

b Use linear regression to find the line of best fit for the number of radio stations on the air as a function of the year since 1950. Round coefficients to the *nearest hundredth*.

c To the *nearest thousandth*, what is the correlation coefficient for the line of best fit?

d According to this model, how many radio stations were there in 1982? In 2010? Are these values reasonable in terms of the other data?

6 The table below provides data about the percentage of females 25 or over who have completed four or more years of college over the time span 1970–2007, according to the U.S. Census Bureau.

Year	% of Females Completing Four or More Years of College
1970	8.2
1980	13.6
1991	18.8
1995	20.2
2000	23.6
2003	25.7
2005	26.5
2007	28.0

a Create a scatter plot using these data.

b Use linear regression to find the line of best fit for the percent of females who have completed four or more years of college in the years since 1970. Round coefficients to the *nearest thousandth.*

c Find the correlation coefficient for the information. What does it mean?

d Based on your equation, determine the percent of females, to the *nearest tenth,* who finished four or more years of college in 2002.

e What percent of females might be expected to have completed four or more years of college when the census is taken again in 2010? What about in 2020? Do you think these percents are reliable? Why or why not?

f In what year would approximately 12% of the female population first have completed four or more years of college?

7 The following data come from the U.S. Census Bureau, indicating the percent of households in the United States that have personal computers over the time span 1994–2006.

Year	% of Households with Computers
1994	24.1
1997	36.6
1998	42.1
1999	47.6
2000	51.0
2001	56.3
2002	60.0
2003	61.8
2005	65.0
2006	67.0

a Create a scatter plot using these data.

b Use linear regression to find the line of best fit for the percent of homes with personal computers in the years since 1994. Round the coefficients to the *nearest ten thousandth.*

c Use your equation to find the percent of homes with computers in 2004, to the *nearest tenth.*

d Based on this data, in what year will 85% of households in the United States first have personal computers?

15.7 Curve Fitting

If you look at the Statistics menu of your calculator, you will see that there are many possible types of regression equations. They are mainly types of equations that you've studied in this course.

Exponential Regression

Exponential functions are in the form $y = ab^x$, when neither a nor b equals 0, and $b > 0$. They grow (or decay) at a constant percent rate. The data shown in the scatter plot below can be approximated with an **exponential regression** model.

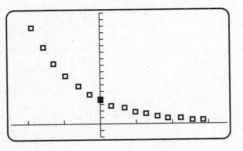

🗞 MODEL PROBLEM

If a cup of coffee is left on a countertop, it will cool off slowly. The following table shows the temperature variation of a cup of coffee left sitting for 50 minutes.

Time	0	5	10	15	20	25
Temp (°F)	176.81	162.91	146.34	135.18	126.28	118.8
Time	30	35	40	45	50	
Temp (°F)	112.53	107.11	102.72	99.1	96.44	

a What type of regression model is appropriate for these data?

b Use the regression capability of your calculator to obtain an equation for an exponential function that could model the data, rounding coefficients to the nearest hundredth.

c Based on the *data*, what was the initial temperature of the coffee?

d Based on the *equation*, what was the expected initial temperature of the coffee? Why is it different from your answer to part **c**?

e Use your equation to find $f(18)$ to the nearest hundredth, and explain its meaning.

f Use your equation to find x, to the nearest integer, such that $f(x) = 118$, and explain its meaning.

g Use your equation to find x, to the nearest integer, such that $f(x) = 18$. Does this make sense? Why?

a The graph of the data is shown below.

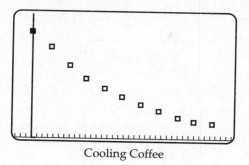

Cooling Coffee

The data approximates a decreasing exponential function, so an exponential regression model is appropriate.

b Follow the procedure for finding a linear regression equation, but instead of choosing 4: LinReg from the (STAT) CALC menu, choose 0: ExpReg. Assign the equation to Y_1 and press (ENTER). Rounding to the nearest hundredth, the regression equation is $y = 167.06(0.99)^x$.

c According to the table, the initial temperature of the coffee, at time 0 minutes, was 176.81°.

d According to the regression equation, the initial temperature, f(0), was approximately 167.06°. The regression model attempts to fit as much of the data as possible to the model and some points do not fit exactly.

e Graph the regression equation, which is in Y_1. Press (2nd) (TRACE) and choose 1: value from the CALC menu. Then enter 18 as the x-value. Rounded to the nearest hundredth, the y-value is 134.33. Eighteen minutes after the coffee was left on the counter, its temperature was approximately 134.33°.

f You must find the time when the temperature was 118°. Set $Y_2 = 118$ and see where the two graphs intersect. Press (2nd) (TRACE) (5) to find the point of intersection. The graphs show that approximately 29 minutes after the coffee was left on the counter, its temperature was 118°.

g You must find the time when the temperature was 18°. In Y_2, enter 18 and see where the two graphs intersect. (You will have to extend your graphing window to do so.) We see that approximately 184 minutes after the coffee is left on the countertop, its temperature would be 18°. Unless the temperature of the room is 18° or less, this is impossible. The lowest temperature the coffee could reach is room temperature. The mathematical model will work only until that point.

Logarithmic Regression

The inverse of an exponential equation is the logarithmic equation $y = \log_b x$. The scatter plot best modeled using **logarithmic regression** takes a shape similar to the one shown below.

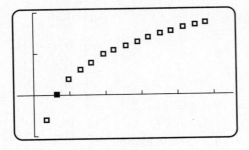

Just as every exponential equation of the form $y = b^x$ passes through the point $(0, 1)$, every logarithmic equation of the form $y = \log_b x$ passes through the point $(1, 0)$. An exponential equation of the form $y = ab^x$ passes through the point $(0, a)$.

A logarithmic equation of the form $y = \log_b\left(\dfrac{x}{a}\right)$ passes through the point $(a, 0)$,

and an equation of the form $y = c \log_b x$ passes through the point $(1, 0)$. Your calculator has the capability of performing logarithmic regression. In the (STAT) CALC menu, choose 9: LnReg.

Remember: Ln is the natural log.

For example, the Richter scale was developed in 1935 by Charles F. Richter to compare the size of earthquakes. If we graphed the magnitude of an earthquake as a function of its amplitude, we would obtain a graph similar to the one shown below. You can see that a logarithmic function would be a good model for the data.

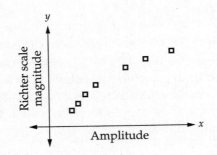

Exercises 1–8: Select the numeral preceding the choice that best answers the question.

1 Given the scatter plot below, which of the following equations could model the data?

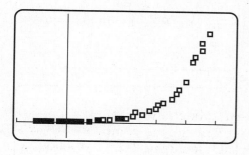

(1) $y = 1 + 1.7x$ (3) $y = 2(0.7)^x$
(2) $y = 2 + 0.7x$ (4) $y = 2(1.7)^x$

2 Given the scatter plot below, which of the following equations could model the data?

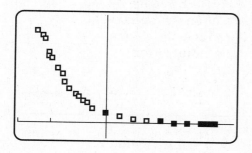

(1) $y = 5(0.4)^x$ (3) $y = -5(1.4)^x$
(2) $y = 5(1.4)^x$ (4) $y = 5 - 1.4^x$

3 Given the scatter plot below, which equation could best model the data?

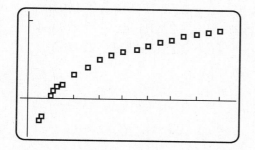

(1) $y = 20\log x$ (3) $y = 20(1.5)^x$
(2) $y = 20(0.5)^x$ (4) $y = 20 + \ln 3.4$

4 What type of function would best model the following data?

x	y
1	6
2	9.5
3	13
4	15
5	16.5
6	17.5
7	18.5
8	19
9	19.5
10	19.7
11	19.8

(1) linear
(2) exponential
(3) logarithmic
(4) none of the above

Exercises 5 and 6: Consider the following situation.

Charlie has been studying a colony of ants and has obtained the regression equation $A(t) = 23.12843(1.36840)^t$ to model the number of ants in the colony, where $A(t)$ is a function of time, t, in weeks since Charlie began studying the colony.

5 Approximately how many ants were there when Charlie first began to study them?

(1) 0   (3) 23
(2) 1.368   (4) 37

6 Approximately how many weeks did it take the ant colony to triple in size?

(1) 1.3   (3) 3
(2) 2.9   (4) 3.5

Exercises 7 and 8: Use the data $f(-1) = -8$, $f(0) = -6, f(0.8) = -4.4, f(1.5) = -3, f(2.7) = -0.6$.

7   What type of function would best model the given data?

(1) linear
(2) exponential
(3) logarithmic
(4) none of the above

8   Find $f(3)$.

(1) -0.5
(2) 0
(3) 0.6
(4) 1.6

9   Darren would like to be valedictorian of his graduating class. Each night he increases the time he spends studying. Darren has modeled the number of hours spent studying as a function of the number of weeks since school began. The equation that Darren uses is $S(t) = 3.6\log t$, where $S(t)$ is the number of hours spent studying each day, and t is the number of weeks since school began.

a   According to Darren's equation, how many hours will he spend studying around midterms (approximately 20 weeks after school began)?

b   How many hours will he spend studying for his final exams (approximately 40 weeks after school began)?

c   At what time of the year will Darren study for 5 hours a day?

10 Match each of the scatter plots below with one of the following equations that could be used to model it. Explain how you could do this without a calculator.

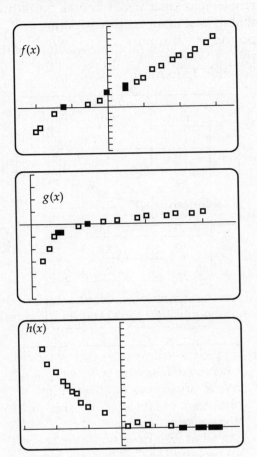

(i) $y = 2.731154\log x$
(ii) $y = -2.731154\log x$
(iii) $y = 2.731154\log(-x)$
(iv) $y = 2.76522(0.40359)^x$
(v) $y = 2.76522(1.40359)^x$
(vi) $y = -2.76522(0.40359)^x$
(vii) $y = 2.731154x + 2.214464$
(viii) $y = -2.731154x + 2.214464$
(ix) $y = 2.731154x - 2.214464$

11 When Janine was born, her grandparents invested $1,000 in a stock market fund for her. Now that she is 16 years old, Janine needs to decide whether to keep the money invested where it is or transfer it to a bank account where she can receive 4% interest, compounded annually. The following table shows how Janine's money has grown with her grandparents' investment.

Year	Amount ($)
0	1,000
2	1,200
4	1,300
6	1,555
8	1,660
10	2,000
12	2,100
14	2,600
16	3,000

a Enter the information in your calculator and make a scatter plot.

b Write an exponential equation to model the data, rounding to the *nearest ten-thousandth.*

c At what rate does the investment appear to be growing?

d Assuming that the investment continues to grow at the same rate, use your equation to determine the amount of money Janine will have in 10 more years.

e If Janine takes the $3,000 out now and puts it in the bank to grow at 4%, the equation $y = 3,000 \cdot 1.04^x$ will model the amount of money she would have x years from now. How much money would Janine have 10 years from now if she chooses this option?

f What advice would you give Janine about her investment? Explain your answer.

12 Kaitlyn is studying the decay of a radioactive substance. She has prepared the table below.

Days	Grams
0	10
2	7.01
4	5.29
5	4.50
8	2.70
10	1.99
14	0.92

a Make a scatter plot from the information above.

b Write an equation for an exponential function to fit the data.

c According to your equation, what was the initial amount of radioactive substance? Why is it not exactly 10 grams?

d How much of the radioactive substance remained after 6 days?

e When will the substance disappear entirely?

13 Elyssa needs $100 to make a deposit on a new bike. She has been working after school and saves as much as she can. However, Elyssa has a lot of other expenses, and she feels that she is not saving enough money. Each week, Elyssa records the total amount of money she has saved. The information appears in the table below.

Week	2	3	4	5	6	7	8	9
Money ($)	21	30	40	48	54	59	63	66

a Make a scatter plot using the information from the table above.

b By looking at your scatter plot, decide what type of function might model this data. What makes you think so?

c On the same set of axes, graph the function $y = 70\log x$. Use this equation to determine how long it will take Elyssa to save the $100 deposit she needs.

15.8 More Curve Fitting

Power Regression

Other functions to consider are power functions. We know that exponential functions are of the form $y = ab^x$ where the variable is in the exponent. Power functions are of the form $y = ax^n$, where a and n are constants. In other words, a power function consists of a monomial term in which the variable is in the base and the y-intercept is the origin. Graphs of some power functions are shown below. Notice that the graphs of all power functions pass through the point $(0, 0)$.

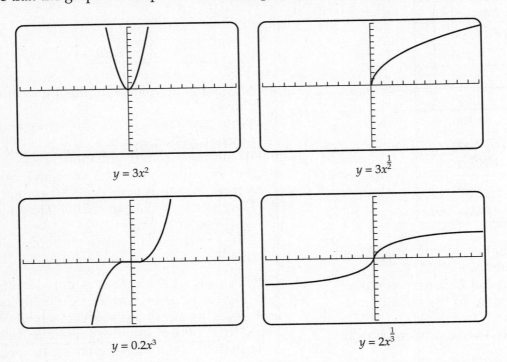

$y = 3x^2$

$y = 3x^{\frac{1}{2}}$

$y = 0.2x^3$

$y = 2x^{\frac{1}{3}}$

Your calculator has the capability of performing a **power regression**, as shown in the model problem. We use power regression when the data form a pattern like one of the graphs above.

1 If $f(x)$ is a power function with $f(1) = 0.2$, $f(2) = 3.2$, $f(3) = 16.2$, $f(4) = 51.2$, and $f(5) = 125$, find $f(6)$.

SOLUTION

Make a scatter plot of the information, as shown in the graph below.

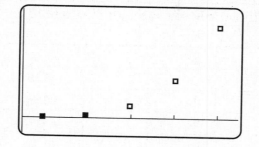

To generate an equation for $f(x)$ when your data is in L_1 and L_2, press (STAT) (▶) and choose A: PwrReg. Then press (ENTER).

$f(x) = 0.2x^4$.

We can solve $f(x)$ for $x = 6$ algebraically.

$f(6) = 0.2(6)^4$

$f(6) = 0.2(1,296)$

$f(6) = 259.2$

Answer: $f(6) = 259.2$

Two other types of regression are quadratic regression and cubic regression. We will now inspect them in closer detail.

Quadratic Regression

The graph of a quadratic function is a parabola. The standard form of a quadratic equation is $y = ax^2 + bx + c$, where a, b, and c are constants and $a \neq 0$. The following screen shows data that might be approximated with a **quadratic regression** model.

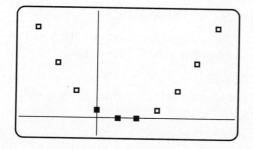

2   A kicker punts a football eleven times at the same velocity but at different angles. The table below shows the distance the football traveled, in yards, when kicked at each angle.

Angle of Kick (degrees)	Distance (yards)
30	57.74
33	60.83
36	63.21
39	65.07
42	66.19
45	66.56
48	66.20
51	65.11
54	63.32
57	60.85
60	57.73

   a Create a scatter plot for these data.

   b Find the quadratic regression equation that best fits this information. Round all coefficients to the nearest thousandth.

   c Based on the equation, how far would you expect a football to travel, to the nearest hundredth of a yard, if kicked at this same velocity but at a 47° angle?

   d Based on the equation, how far would you expect a football to travel, to the nearest hundredth of a yard, if kicked at this same velocity but at a 15° angle?

SOLUTION

   a

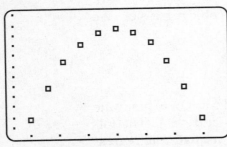

   b With the data entered into L_1 and L_2, press (STAT) (▶) and choose 5: QuadReg from the CALC menu. Assign the function to Y_1 and press (ENTER).

The quadratic regression equation is $y = -0.039x^2 + 3.528x - 12.902$.

   c We will interpolate the distance. First, graph the regression equation you found in part **b**. Then press (2nd) (TRACE) and choose 1: value from the CALC menu. Enter $x = 47$.

A football kicked at a 47° angle can be expected to travel 66.36 yards.

   d We extrapolate the distance. Change the Xmin value in the viewing window to 10. Again choose 1: value from the CALC menu, this time entering $x = 15$.

A football kicked at a 15° angle can be expected to travel 31.20 yards.

Cubic Regression

The standard equation of a cubic function is $y = ax^3 + bx^2 + cx + d$, where a, b, c, and d are constants and $a \neq 0$. Below is a scatter plot showing data that can be modeled using **cubic regression**.

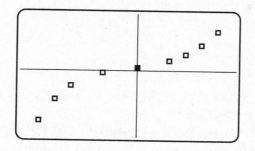

MODEL PROBLEM

3 Maya kept track of the number of visitors to her new Web site between December 2007 and November 2008. She recorded the data in a table as shown below.

Date	Web Site Visitors
Dec. 2007	794
Jan. 2008	1,203
Feb. 2008	1,674
Mar. 2008	1,834
Apr. 2008	1,916
May 2008	1,885
June 2008	1,977
July 2008	2,234
Aug. 2008	2,692
Sept. 2008	3,460
Oct. 2008	4,302
Nov. 2008	6,401

a Create a scatter plot for this data. Let $x = 0$ represent the month of December 2007.

b Find a cubic regression equation for this information, rounding coefficients to the nearest thousandth.

c Based on your equation, how many visitors do you expect that Maya's Web site received in January 2009?

a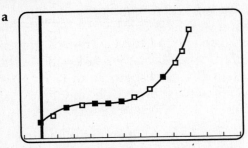

b With the data entered into L_1 and L_2, press (STAT) (▶) and choose 6: CubicReg from the CALC menu. Assign the function to Y_1 and press (ENTER).

The cubic regression equation is $y = 14.257x^3 - 183.785x^2 + 800.407x + 703.106$.

c Graph the scatter plot and regression curve using 9:ZoomStat. January 2009 corresponds to $x = 13$, which is outside the viewing window, so we must change Xmax to 14.

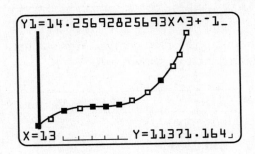

The number of visitors must be a whole number, so we expect that Maya's Web site received 11,371 visitors in January 2009.

Exercises 1 and 2: Select the numeral preceding the choice that best answers the question.

1 Given the scatter plot below, which equation could best model the data?

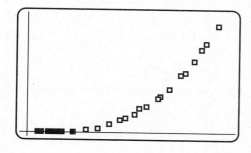

(1) $y = 2.969x^{0.73}$
(2) $y = 0.73x^{2.969}$
(3) $y = 0.73(2.969)^{-x}$
(4) $y = 0.73 + 2.929x$

2 What type of function would best model the following data?

x	−3	−2	−1	0	1	2	3
y	3	−8	−7	0	7	8	−3

(1) logarithmic
(2) exponential
(3) quadratic
(4) cubic

3 Write an equation for a power function that will model the data below:

x	1	1.1	1.7	2	2.5	3	4
y	4	5	15	30	50	90	165

4 Donnie wanted to determine if the length of a pendulum has any relationship to the time required for the pendulum to complete one oscillation (swing back and forth). He has placed the information in a table as shown below:

Length (ft)	Time (sec)
0.5	0.9
1	1.2
1.5	1.3
2	1.6
2.5	1.8
3	1.9
3.5	2
4	2.1

a Make a scatter plot of the information shown in the table, with time as a function of length.

b Write an equation for a power function to model the data.

c Use your equation to find the time required for a 5-foot pendulum to complete one oscillation.

d According to a physics formula, $T = \dfrac{2\pi}{\sqrt{32}}\sqrt{l}$, where T is the time (in seconds) for one complete oscillation and l is the length (in feet) of a pendulum. Use this formula to find the time for a 5-foot pendulum to complete one oscillation. How does that compare to the data given in the table above and the number obtained using the formula from part **c**?

5 In Section 15.6, we looked at a problem involving the number of sets of twins born in the U.S. between 1990 and 1994. Now consider the following data from more recent years.

Year	Sets of Twins
1996	100,750
1997	104,137
1998	110,670
2000	118,916
2001	121,246
2002	125,134
2003	125,665
2004	132,219
2005	133,122

a Create a scatter plot for these data, setting 1996 = year 1.

b Find both the power and exponential equations for the best fit curve, to the *nearest hundredth*.

c Use both regression equations to answer the following: If the number of sets of twins continues to grow according to these mathematical models, in what year will 150,000 sets of twins be born in the United States?

6 A reporter researching the history of Mountainview Hills found the following population data in the town hall.

Year	1920	1928	1947	1984
Population (in thousands)	8	32	72	128

a Create a scatter plot to model the above data, letting 1920 = year 1.

b Find the power regression equation that best fits these data.

c Based on your equation, what was the population in 1967?

d Based on your equation, in what year was the population first over 150,000?

7 The LeBeau method is used to calculate a dog's age in human years. The following table shows dog ages in normal years and their corresponding human ages.

Dog Age	Age in Human Years
0.5	7.5
1	15
2	24
4	32
6	40
8	48
10	56
12	64
14	72
16	77
20	87
24	97

a Create a scatter plot to model these data, with the age in human years a function of actual dog age.

b Find a logarithmic regression equation for these data. Round all coefficients to the *nearest thousandth*.

c Find a power regression equation for these data. Round all coefficients to the *nearest thousandth*.

d In your opinion, which of the regression equations is more appropriate to these data? Justify your answer.

e Based on the regression equation you chose in part **c**, what is the approximate age in human years of a 19-year-old dog.

8 Look at these data from *New York Newsday*, May 14, 2008, reporting the rising trading prices of long-grain rice futures in Chicago.

Date	Price per 100 Pounds
May 2007	10.21
June 2007	10.39
July 2007	10.43
Aug. 2007	10.85
Sept. 2007	11.73
Oct. 2007	11.85
Nov. 2007	12.87
Dec. 2007	13.55
Jan. 2008	14.82
Feb. 2008	18.00
Mar. 2008	19.69
Apr. 2008	21.48

a Create a scatter plot for these data. Let $x = 0$ represent the month of May 2007.

b Find an exponential regression equation for this information. Round to the *nearest thousandth*.

c Find a cubic regression equation for this information. Round to the *nearest thousandth*.

d Based on your equation from part **b**, find the price of rice in June 2008, to the *nearest cent*.

e Based on your equation from part **c**, find the price of rice in June 2008, to the *nearest cent*.

f According to each of your mathematical models, in what month and year will the price be $36.00? Which answer is more reasonable?

9 Although the first Olympics in 1896 did not permit women to participate, in recent years, the percent of athletes in the Summer Olympics who are female is increasing steadily, as shown by the data below.

Year	% Female Participants
1976	20.7
1980	21.5
1984	22.9
1988	26.1
1992	28.9
1996	34.0
2000	38.2
2004	40.7

a Create a scatter plot for these data. Let $x = 0$ represent the year 1976.

b Do you think an exponential or a logarithmic function might better model these data? Why?

c Find the equation from **b** that you think best fits this information.

d Determine the quadratic regression equation.

e Historically, we know the number of female participants did not start high and then fall to a minimum point before rising again, but sometimes a mathematical model does not mirror the cultural or historic issues surrounding the problem. Based on the two equations you have, what percent of the participants in 2012 might be female?

Another type of regression that your graphing calculator can perform is **sinusoidal regression**, in which a sine curve is fitted to the data.

The calculator requires a minimum of four points to do sinusoidal regression. It uses the equation $y = a\sin(bx + c) + d$, where a represents the amplitude, b the frequency, $\frac{c}{b}$ the horizontal shift, and d the vertical shift or midline. (Notice that the frequency value, b, is not distributed over the parentheses, unlike the equation $y = a\sin b(x + c) + d$ that we often use.)

The average temperature of a city often varies sinusoidally over the period of one year. We will use an example to illustrate how to perform a sinusoidal regression.

The following table lists the average monthly temperatures at Central Park in 2007.

Month	Jan.	Feb.	Mar.	Apr.	May	June	July	Aug.	Sept.	Oct.	Nov.	Dec.
Temp (°F)	37.5	28.2	42.2	50.3	65.2	71.4	75.0	74.0	70.3	63.6	45.4	37.0

Enter the months into L_1 and the temperatures into L_2. Let $x = 1$ represent the temperature in January. Press **ZOOM** **9** to see the following graph.

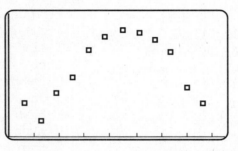

Notice that February's average temperature is colder than January's. Beginning in March, the average temperature increases until August, when the average temperature starts to decrease. If we continued entering data, we would see that, in January and February 2008, the average monthly temperatures continued to decrease, and then in March began to increase again.

This appears to be a sinusoidal function. Press **STAT** and then choose C:SinReg from the CALC menu. As with other regressions, when you press **ENTER**, the type of regression is pasted on the home screen, awaiting further information.

Assign the equation to Y_1 (**VARS** **▶** **1** **1**) and press **ENTER**. You should see the resulting coefficients and constants for your equation.

```
SinReg
 y=a*sin(bx+c)+d
 a=22.2212379
 b=.5349060934
 c=-2.368961781
 d=55.41652645
```

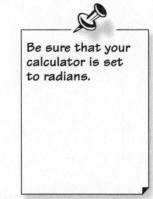

Be sure that your calculator is set to radians.

When you press (GRAPH), you should now get the sinusoidal graph you see below.

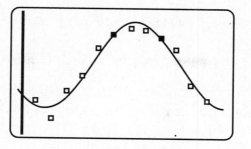

Notice that the graphed equation mirrors the data rather well but not perfectly. There is no correlation coefficient provided for sinusoidal regressions.

We can now answer the following questions:

a Write the equation of the sinusoidal regression equation that fits the data, rounding to the *nearest hundredth*.

b What is the midline of the function? What is its significance?

c What is the amplitude of the function? What is its significance?

CHAPTER REVIEW

Exercises 1–4: Match each scatter plot with one of the following descriptions.

(i) strong positive linear correlation
(ii) strong negative linear correlation
(iii) weak positive linear correlation
(iv) weak negative linear correlation
(v) linear correlation close to zero

1

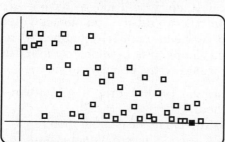

2

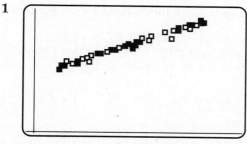

3

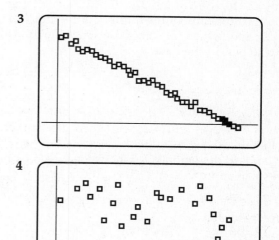

4

Exercises 5–20: Select the numeral preceding the choice that best completes the sentence or answers the question.

5 What is the median for the data in the table below?

Age	26	30	32	35	38
Frequency	8	5	6	3	3

(1) 26
(2) 30
(3) 32
(4) 38

6 A standardized test has a mean score of 86 and a standard deviation of 4.3. A student who is in the 41st percentile could have has a score of

(1) 41
(2) 80
(3) 83
(4) 90.3

7 Kelly Ann is on a traveling basketball team and has been working hard on improving her shooting average before the season starts. At the last nine practices she scored the following number of points: 2, 10, 17, 23, 28, 32, 35, 37, 38. Plot the points as a function of the number of the practice and decide which of the following functions seems to best fit the data.

(1) linear
(2) exponential
(3) logarithmic
(4) cubic

8 On a standardized test, the mean score is 79 and the standard deviation is 5.5. Between which two scores will approximately 15% of the scores fall?

(1) 73.5–79
(2) 76.25–79
(3) 79–81.75
(4) 81.75–84.5

9 In a normal distribution, $\bar{x} + 1.5\sigma = 73$ and $\bar{x} - 1.5\sigma = 58$ when $\bar{x}$ represents the mean and σ represents the standard deviation. The standard deviation is

(1) 5
(2) 10
(3) 12
(4) 15

10 If a set of SAT math scores has a normal distribution and its mean is 451, which score has the greatest probability of being chosen at random?

(1) 590
(2) 540
(3) 420
(4) 390

11 Scores on a calculus final examination at a local college were normally distributed and had a mean of 78.4 and a standard deviation of 8.4. If 240 students took the final exam, approximately how many students could expect a grade between 74.2 and 91?

(1) 91
(2) 120
(3) 150
(4) 163

12 If the variance of a set of data is 12.8, the standard deviation is approximately

(1) 3.58
(2) 6.4
(3) 25.2
(4) 163.84

13 Which equation best models the data in the table below?

x	0	1	2	3	4	5
y	0.9	3.2	8.97	28	85	247

(1) $y = 3x$
(2) $y = 3x + 3$
(3) $y = 3^x$
(4) $y = 3^{x+3}$

14 If the standard deviation is 5.7, the variance of the data is approximately

(1) 2.387
(2) 11.4
(3) 22.8
(4) 32.49

15 The local school would like to have a stoplight near the school crossing, but the town council decided it needs more information. To find an unbiased sampling of opinions, which of the following would be the best way to survey?

(1) question parents dropping children off at school
(2) ask drivers in the neighborhood
(3) hold a school meeting on this issue
(4) ask the students

16 Given the following set of data.

Measure (x_i)	20	32	45	51
Frequency (f_i)	4	3	3	6

Which of the following statements is true?

(1) mean > median
(2) median > mean
(3) mode < mean
(4) mode < median

17 The owner of a business proudly tells his employees that the median salary for the company is $41,000. He doesn't tell them that he is the only person receiving an annual salary of $150,000. He would like to increase his own salary to $200,000 per year. Which of the following statements is true?

(1) The median salary would not be affected.
(2) The median salary would be increased.
(3) The mean salary would not be affected.
(4) The mode salary would be increased.

18 If the variance of a set of data is doubled, the standard deviation is

(1) doubled
(2) halved
(3) multiplied by $\sqrt{2}$
(4) divided by $\sqrt{2}$

19 The population in Logtown increases logarithmically. Which scatter plot could be the population of Logtown?

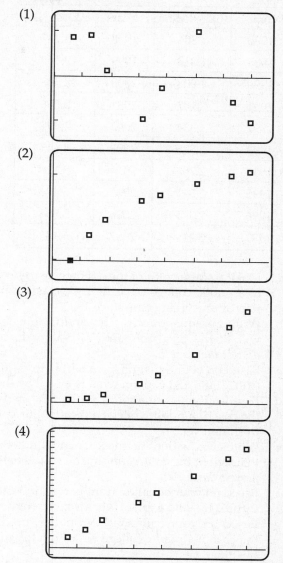

(1)

(2)

(3)

(4)

20 If the standard deviation of a set of data is halved, the variance is

(1) doubled
(2) halved
(3) divided by 4
(4) unchanged

21 Sketch a scatter plot for data showing a correlation coefficient close to 1.

22 Sketch a scatter plot for data showing a correlation coefficient close to −1.

23 The table below shows the average cost for annual tuition and fees in a public college.

Year	Cost ($)	Year	Cost ($)
1980	804	1998	3,247
1985	1,318	1999	3,362
1990	1,908	2000	3,508
1991	2,107	2001	3,766
1992	2,334	2002	4,098
1993	2,535	2003	4,645
1994	2,705	2004	5,126
1995	2,811	2005	5,492
1996	2,975	2006	5,804
1997	3,111	2007	6,185

a Make a scatter plot of the average yearly cost of a public college education, $C(t)$, as a function of time, t, in years since 1980.

b Write an equation for a linear function that will fit the data, rounding all values to the *nearest thousandth*.

c Based on your equation from part **b**, find $C(0)$, $C(8)$, $C(18)$, and explain what is meant by this.

d Based on your equation from part **b**, predict the cost of a public college education for your freshman year.

e Write an equation for an exponential function that will fit the data, rounding all values to the *nearest thousandth*.

f Based on your equation from part **e**, find $C(0)$, $C(8)$, $C(18)$, and explain what is meant by this.

g Based on your equation from part **e**, predict the cost of a public college education for your freshman year.

h Which function do you think fits the data better? Why?

i Which function do you hope is correct? Why?

24 The following table contains the average height (in inches) for girls and boys from 2 years to 13 years.

Age	Girls	Boys
2	35	36
3	38.5	39
4	41.75	42
5	44	44
6	46	46.75
7	48	49
8	50.75	51
9	53.25	53.25
10	55.5	55.25
11	58.5	57.25
12	60.5	59
13	61.25	61

a Make a scatter plot of the average girl's height (in inches) as a function of her age.

b Make a scatter plot of the average boy's height (in inches) as a function of his age.

c Write a linear equation for the average girl's height as a function of her age.

d Based on your equation, how tall is the average 10-year-old girl? How does this compare to the actual data?

e Based on your equation, how tall would you expect the average 14-year-old girl to be?

f Write a linear equation for the average boy's height as a function of his age.

g Based on your equations, who grows at a faster rate, boys or girls? Explain.

h Based on your equation, how tall is the average 7-year-old boy? How does this compare to the actual data?

i Based on your equation, how tall would you expect the average 21-year-old boy to be? Does this make sense? Why?

25 Alexander Borbely is a professor at the University of Zurich Medical School where he is the director of the sleep laboratory. The data below comes from the sleeping patterns of 100 random subjects over a twenty-four-hour period, documented in his book *Secrets of Sleep*.

Hours Slept	Frequency
3.5	1
4.5	1
5.5	2
6.5	11
7.5	32
8.5	45
9.5	7
10.5	1

a Find the mean of this data, to the *nearest tenth*.
b Find the variance of this data, to the *nearest tenth*.
c Find the standard deviation of this data, to the *nearest tenth*.
d Sketch the curve showing the distribution of this data.
e How many scores fall within $\pm 1\sigma$ of the mean?
f What percentage of the scores falls within $\pm 1\sigma$ of the mean?
g Compare the distribution curve for this data and the normal distribution. Is this set of data normally distributed? Why or why not?

26 The following table gives the orbital periods of the eight planets in relationship to Earth years, where one Earth year is the time required for Earth to orbit the sun. The average distance from each of the planets to the sun is given in astronomical units where 1 au is equal to the distance from Earth to the sun.

Planet	Period (in Earth years)	Average Distance to Sun (au)
Mercury	0.241	0.387
Venus	0.616	0.723
Earth	1	1
Mars	1.88	1.524
Jupiter	11.9	5.206
Saturn	29.5	9.539
Uranus	84	19.191
Neptune	165	30.071

a Make a scatter plot of the distance of the planets from the sun as a function of the planet's orbital period.
b Write the power regression equation for this set of data, rounding all values to the *nearest ten thousandth*.
c The dwarf planet, Pluto, has a period of 248 Earth years. Use your equation from part **b** to determine Pluto's distance from the sun, to the *nearest hundredth* au.
d Kepler's Third Law of Motion states that the square of the orbital period of a planet is proportional to the cube of the mean distance from the sun. Compare this statement to the equation you obtained in part **b**.

27 The grades in Mr. Bergersen's Algebra 2 class are

Grade	Frequency
60	1
65	2
70	2
75	3
80	5
85	7
90	5
95	2
100	1

a To the *nearest hundredth*, what are the mean, median, and mode for these scores?

b Without doing any further calculations, can you tell if these scores are normally distributed? Explain.

c Find the variance and standard deviation, to the *nearest hundredth*.

d How many scores lie within one standard deviation of the mean?

e Explain how your answer to **d** verifies your conclusion from **b**.

28 This table shows the time required to cook a turkey of various weights.

Weight (pounds)	8	11	15.5	19.5	23
Cooking Time (hours)	2.5	3	4	5	6

a Write an equation for a linear function to model these data.

b Use your equation to determine the cooking time of a 17-pound turkey.

c What size turkey would take 3.5 hours to cook?

d Find $C(20)$ and explain what is meant by this.

e Find w such that $C(w) = 20$ and explain what is meant by this.

f Do your answers to parts **d** and **e** make sense? Explain.

29 The following table gives statistics for the increasing number of Americans age 85 and over, in thousands, according to the U.S. Census Bureau.

Year	Population (thousands)
1900	122
1910	167
1920	210
1930	272
1940	365
1950	577
1960	929
1970	1,409
1980	2,240
1990	3,021
1995	3,685
2000	4,239
2004	4,859

a Create a scatter plot for these data.

b Would a linear, exponential, or logarithmic function best model these data in which the number of persons age 85 and over is dependent on the year since 1900?

c Use the calculator to find the regression equation for the function you think most appropriate. Use $x = 0$ to represent the year 1900 and round all values to the *nearest ten thousandth*.

d Use your equation from part **c** to predict the population over 85 years of age in the year 2010.

e Based on their data through 2004, the U.S. Census Bureau created a mathematical model that predicted that there would be 6,123 thousand people (or 6,123,000) over the age of 85 in 2010. Do you think their model used the same type of regression equation you chose? Explain.

f What explanation might there be for the increased longevity of seniors?

30 Because of environmental issues, the United States government has stepped in to monitor the fuel efficiency of new passenger cars. As part of the Energy Conservation Act of 1975, Congress established the U.S. Corporate Average Fuel Efficiency (CAFE) standards. Standards for new passenger cars' efficiency since 1975 are presented below.

Year of Car	Fuel Efficiency (miles per gallon)
1975	15.1
1980	22.6
1985	26.3
1990	26.9
1995	27.7
1997	27.8
1998	28.1
1999	28.3
2000	28.5
2004	29.1

a Create a scatter plot for these data.

b Consider which type of function might best represent these data. Justify your answer.

c To model the data, we can use the logarithmic function $f(x) = 15.3902 + 9.3602 \log x$, where $f(x)$ represents the miles per gallon and $x = 1$ represents the year 1975. What does the 15.3902 represent?

d Congress set a goal of increasing passenger car fuel economy average to 27.5 miles per gallon by 1985. According to the regression equation, in what year did passenger cars first surpass the CAFE of 27.5 miles per gallon?

e If the function holds true, what might you expect the average fuel efficiency of a passenger car to be in 2010?

f A power function might also be used to model these data. Write the equation for the power regression equation for the data where $g(x)$ represents the miles per gallon and $x = 1$ represents the year 1975, rounding all values to the *nearest ten-thousandth*.

g Use the power regression equation to estimate the year that passenger cars first surpassed the CAFE of 27.5 miles per gallon.

h If the power regression equation holds true, what might you expect the average fuel efficiency of a passenger car to be in 2010?

CHAPTER 16

Probability

16.1 The Counting Principle

Often in life we have to make choices. If you and your friend Angelo are going to the movies at the mall and then to the food court, you have to decide which movie to see and which type of food to eat. If the multiplex is showing 8 different movies and there are 7 food counters, you need to make two independent decisions. The choice of which movie is totally separate from which type of food, so to find the total number of possible ways to spend the evening, you multiply the number of options for each decision. For each of the 8 films, you could go to any of the 7 food places, so there are 8 • 7 or 56 different plans for your evening. In real life, you usually don't calculate the choices possible; you just make the decisions without thinking about them mathematically, but you are living a mathematical problem.

The **Counting Principle** is used when we need to make choices in two or more situations and we want to find the total number of different results possible. If there are m choices for the first situation and n choices for the second situation after the first occurs, then the total number of choices is $m • n$ or mn. If you have three selections to make and there are p choices for the third situation, then the total number of possible outcomes is $m • n • p$ or mnp.

📐 MODEL PROBLEMS

1   Nell has 8 different shirts and 6 pairs of pants that go together well. How many different outfits can she make from this group of clothes?

SOLUTION

Nell has 8 ways to choose a shirt and 6 ways to choose pants: 8 • 6 = 48 outfits

2   Garth is treating his little brother Mitch to an ice cream sundae. If Mitch has a choice of 12 flavors of ice cream and 5 different types of toppings, how many different sundaes could Mitch create, if he chose just one flavor of ice cream and one type of topping?

SOLUTION

Mitch has 12 flavors and 5 toppings to choose: 12 • 5 = 60 sundaes

3 Norah is going to the beach. She can choose from 5 different beach towels, 4 different pairs of flip-flops, and 2 different pairs of sunglasses. How many different choices of one towel, one pair of flip-flops, and one pair of sunglasses can she make?

SOLUTION

Norah has 5 towels, 4 pairs of flip-flops, and 2 pairs of sunglasses: $5 \cdot 4 \cdot 2 = 40$ choices

4 Raoul is going out for dinner. There is a choice of 6 appetizers, 4 soups, 12 entrees, and 3 desserts. How many different meals might he order, if he chooses one dish from each category?

SOLUTION

There are 4 courses in the meal, so we need to multiply the number of selections in each course: $6 \cdot 4 \cdot 12 \cdot 3 = 864$ different possible meals

Remember: Multiply the total number of selections in the first category times the total number of selections in the second category, and so on. You should have the same number of multipliers as you have decisions to be made.

 **Practice**

Exercises 1–10: Select the numeral preceding the choice that best answers the question.

1 Kavan and his friends are going to Jones Beach. They can take the bus, ride their bikes, or get a lift from Kavan's brother. When they get to the beach, they can go to any one of four areas. How many different options are there for their afternoon at Jones Beach?

(1) 1
(2) 5
(3) 7
(4) 12

2 Hannah is ordering a sandwich from the snack bar. She has a choice of 4 breads, 6 meats, and 3 cheeses. How many different sandwiches could Hannah order if she ordered one meat and one cheese?

(1) 13
(2) 36
(3) 72
(4) 96

3 The banquet committee is choosing the color scheme for the Senior Banquet. If the table-cloths come in white, yellow, green, burgundy, pink, ivory, or black while the napkins can be black, white, yellow, ivory, or pink, and the centerpieces are white, yellow, or pink, how many different table arrangements are possible?

(1) 120
(2) 105
(3) 70
(4) 15

4 The Book Nook is having a half-price sale on selected titles. Included in the sale are 4 biographies, 3 cookbooks, 3 art books, 5 novels, 2 pet-care books, and 2 travel guides. If a customer selects one title from each category, how many selections are possible?

(1) 19
(2) 34
(3) 720
(4) 1,020

5 A manufacturing company has been offered 8 different styles of cans, 4 different slogans, and 6 different advertising campaigns for their new lemon soft drink. How many different options do they have for launching their new product?

(1) 18
(2) 38
(3) 120
(4) 192

6 Dao-Ming is going to spend the afternoon at the gym. First, he wants to work on the weight machines, but he has to decide whether to work on his triceps, abs, deltoids, or biceps. Then he's going to do some cardio, but he has to decide whether to use the treadmill, the stationary bike, or the elliptical trainer. Next he will either swim laps, play basketball, or play handball. In how many different ways can Dao-Ming work out this afternoon?

(1) 36
(2) 27
(3) 24
(4) 12

7 Ethan's grandfather is paying for him to go to sports camp. In the mornings, Ethan can join wrestling, basketball, swimming, bowling, or fencing. In the afternoon, he can play baseball, lacrosse, tennis, or golf. How many different choices of sports are available to Ethan if he signs up for one sport in the morning and one after lunch?

(1) 1
(2) 2
(3) 16
(4) 20

8 Madison's friends gave her a gift certificate to Melody's Music Mart and she is trying to decide which songs to download to her MP3 player. There are 5 rock, 3 jazz, 2 R&B, 3 pop, 4 hip-hop, 2 classical, and 2 heavy metal songs that she likes, but she decides to choose 1 song from each genre. How many different choices of 7 songs can she download?

(1) 7
(2) 21
(3) 147
(4) 1,440

9 The Student Civic Club requires all students to donate time to one county activity, one community activity, and one school activity each year. Harmony can choose from the Special Olympics, the Emergency Evacuation drill, the McDonald House, or the Nutrition Network for her county hours. For the community hours, she can volunteer at the local hospital, do shopping for the homebound, rake leaves for senior citizens, shovel snow for senior citizens, help out at the local soup kitchen, or gather trash along the local roadway. Her school citizen hours can involve the Halloween Party, the Students Putting an End to Cancer program, the Relay for Life, the Walk of Dimes, the Senior Citizen Prom, tutoring elementary school students, helping with a blood drive, or collecting for the Shoe Drive. In how many different ways can Harmony donate her time?

(1) 120
(2) 192
(3) 216
(4) 720

10 The Create-a-Card computer program has 12 birthday card selections, 7 get-well cards, and 5 anniversary card options. If Jayne needs one of each type of card, how many different groupings are possible?

(1) 84
(2) 168
(3) 210
(4) 420

11 Joshua decides to get a bouquet of flowers for his mother. He has 4 colors of carnations, 3 types of roses, 4 categories of orchids, 2 kinds of lilies, and 5 varieties of daisies to choose from. If he wants to include one of each kind of flower, how many different bouquets can he put together?

12 Olivia's Perfect Pizza offers 2 free toppings on a 12-inch pizza. The choices of vegetable toppings are onions, broccoli, mushrooms, garlic, eggplant, zucchini, and peppers. The choices of meats are ham, pepperoni, sausage, meatballs, chicken, and salami.

   a If Craig requests one vegetable and one meat topping, how many different pizzas can he order?

   b Mei also orders a pizza with one vegetable and one meat topping, but she dislikes pepperoni. How many choices of pizza does she have?

13 Franklin is trying to decide what to take with him to his grandmother's house for the weekend. He has 6 trucks, 3 stuffed animals, 4 games, and 6 books, but his mother says he can take only one of each. How many different groups of items could he pack?

14 Ariel is visiting New York City on Saturday. She wants to go to the Empire State Building, the Statue of Liberty, the Hayden Planetarium, Central Park, the Wolman Ice-skating Rink, and the Museum of Modern Art. She wants to eat an authentic New York-style hot dog, pizza, cheese cake, and bagel. If her parents tell her she must choose one activity and one food to eat, how many different choices can she make?

15 Mr. DeStefano is preparing a still-life scene for his students to paint. He has an apple, a banana, an orange, and a kiwi, 4 different vases, 3 kinds of flowers, and 3 different tablecloths to use. If he chooses one piece of fruit, one vase, one kind of flower, and one tablecloth, how many different still lifes can he design?

16 Zainab promised to start supper for her family while she was baking for the French Club's dessert sale. She can prepare either pasta, chicken, or hamburgers for dinner, and she can bake brownies, chocolate chip cookies, sugar cookies, or cupcakes for the dessert sale. How many different combinations of a meal and a dessert can Zainab choose?

17 It is a rainy day at Camp Ukamela so the counselors have offered the 12-year-olds a choice of activities for the morning, afternoon, and evening. For the morning, the campers can paint a mural in the dining hall, design the brochure for next year's program, take pictures of various camp sites and activities for the brochure, play paint ball in the rain, or help groom the horses. After lunch, they can work on "found art" sculptures, help create a planetarium sky in the library, download music to make a Campers' Collection of favorite tunes, work on an act for the Ukamela talent show, or help design events for the upcoming Field Olympics. After dinner, the campers can watch a movie, read a book, play board games, make jewelry, learn to juggle, or write letters. How many different ways can a camper spend the day?

18 A company claims to offer 432 different choices for its sweaters. If the company offers its sweaters in 6 sizes, with 4 different necklines, and 2 different sleeve lengths, how many colors must be available for its claim to be true?

16.2 Permutations

There are two categories of problems involving the choice of elements from a group. The first, choosing one item from each of a number of different groups, we studied with the Counting Principle in Section 16.1. In the second category of problems, in which we want several items from one particular group, we must decide whether or not the order in which we make our selections is important.

For example, if 5 out of 8 finalists in a contest are to be chosen to receive prizes, and everyone chosen will receive a $100 gift certificate, it doesn't matter who is selected first or last. All 5 winners are equally rewarded. On the other hand, if the first person gets a $500 gift certificate, the second person a $250 gift certificate, the third person a $100 gift certificate, the fourth person a $75 gift certificate, and the fifth person a $50 gift certificate, you would care very much if you were selected for the first prize or the fifth. When the order of selection is important, we will use a *permutation*. By definition, a **permutation** is an arrangement of items in a specific order.

In the tiered gift certificate problem, we will select 5 out of 8 finalists. Make 5 lines on your paper to represent the number of positions, and then fill in the number of choices for each position. For the first spot, there is a choice of 8 people; for the second spot, a choice of only 7; the third spot, 6 people; followed by 5 and then 4 people to choose from. Since we want all of these positions filled, we use the Counting Principle to multiply these options together.

$$\underset{\text{(1st)}}{\underline{8}} \bullet \underset{\text{(2nd)}}{\underline{7}} \bullet \underset{\text{(3rd)}}{\underline{6}} \bullet \underset{\text{(4th)}}{\underline{5}} \bullet \underset{\text{(5th)}}{\underline{4}} = 6{,}720 \text{ possible ways 5 people can win}$$

The notation for a permutation of n items taken r at a time is $_nP_r$.

$$_nP_r = n \bullet (n-1) \bullet (n-2) \bullet (n-3) \bullet \cdots \bullet (n-r+1)$$

In this problem, we needed to choose 5 people out of a possible 8, so $n = 8$ and $r = 5$.

$$_8P_5 = 8 \bullet 7 \bullet 6 \bullet 5 \bullet 4 = 6{,}720$$

MODEL PROBLEMS

1 In how many different orders can the 8 students competing in the 200-meter race cross the finish line?

SOLUTION

We want to find the order of all 8 students finishes, so in our permutation, $n = r = 8$.

$$_8P_8 = \underline{8} \bullet \underline{7} \bullet \underline{6} \bullet \underline{5} \bullet \underline{4} \bullet \underline{3} \bullet \underline{2} \bullet \underline{1}$$

When we start with a value and multiply by each preceding digit down to 1, we have $n!$, read as "n factorial." To calculate 8! on your calculator, first enter the n value, 8. Then go to (MATH) and press ◀. You will see the following screen.

```
MATH NUM CPX PRB
1:rand
2:nPr
3:nCr
4:!
5:randInt(
6:randNorm(
7:randBin(
```

Choose 4:! for factorial and press (ENTER).

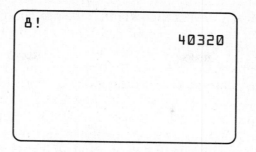

Answer: 40,320 ways

2   Disregarding skill, breeding, and training, in how many different ways can first, second, and third place be decided among the twelve horses running in the Kentucky Derby?

SOLUTION

First place can be won by 12 possible horses, second place can be won by 11 possible horses (we do not count the first-place winner), and third place can be won by 10 possible horses.

We evaluate: $_{12}P_3 = \underline{12} \cdot \underline{11} \cdot \underline{10} = 1{,}320$

To do this on your calculator, input the n value, 12, and then press (MATH) followed by (◄) to access the probability menu. This time choose 2:nPr for permutations. Input the r value, 3, and then press (ENTER). Your answer will appear as below.

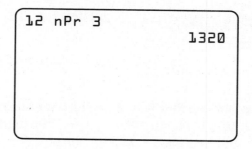

Answer: 1,320 ways

3   The Miss U.S.A. Pageant selects five finalists. If the choice of the winner was pure chance, in how many different ways could Miss U.S.A. and the first runner-up be chosen?

SOLUTION

There are 5 finalists and we need to find the top two: $_5P_2 = \underline{5} \cdot \underline{4} = 20$

Answer: 20 ways

Sometimes there are special conditions put on the choices to be made. These permutations set specific parameters for one or more of the items to be chosen; for example, numbers that are to be odd or even.

4 Given the set of numbers {1, 4, 5, 7, 8}, if each digit can be used only once, how many different

  a four-digit numbers can be formed?

  b four-digit odd numbers can be formed?

  c three-digit numbers larger than 700 can be formed?

  d even three-digit numbers greater than 800 can be formed?

SOLUTION

  a This is a straightforward permutation of five digits of which we will choose 4:

$_5P_4 = \underline{5} \cdot \underline{4} \cdot \underline{3} \cdot \underline{2} = 120$

Answer: 120 four-digit numbers

  b In this case there is a special condition. The last digit of a number determines whether it is odd or even, so rather than a line, draw a box for the fourth position.

$\underline{} \cdot \underline{} \cdot \underline{} \cdot \boxed{}$
  (odd)

Since the last position is the most important, we will fill in that box first. Given the original set of numbers {1, 4, 5, 7, 8}, three of them are odd; therefore, the fourth box has a choice of three digits.

$\underline{} \cdot \underline{} \cdot \underline{} \cdot \boxed{3}$

Since one of the digits for our choices has been eliminated, we have only 4 digits from which to choose 3, so we evaluate a permutation of $_4P_3$.

$\underline{4} \cdot \underline{3} \cdot \underline{2} \cdot \boxed{3} = 24 \cdot \boxed{3} = 72$

Answer: Of the 120 four-digit numbers created, 72 of them will be odd.

  c To find three-digit numbers greater than 700, we again have to consider the given set of numbers, {1, 4, 5, 7, 8}. If our number is to be greater than 700, the first digit must be 7 or 8, so this time the specified condition affects the first choice. Make your box, followed by two lines for the other digits.

$\boxed{2} \cdot \underline{} \cdot \underline{}$
(≥7)

Once you've fulfilled the special condition, you now need 2 more digits out of the remaining 4, or a permutation of $_4P_2$.

$\boxed{2} \cdot \underline{4} \cdot \underline{3} = \boxed{2} \cdot 12 = 24$

Answer: 24 three-digit numbers will be greater than 700.

d In the last part of this problem, we have two special conditions: the number must be even and greater than 800. Therefore, the first and last digits are special conditions to be indicated by boxes rather than lines. Given our choices of {1, 4, 5, 7, 8}, the number will be greater than 800 only if the first digit is 8, so the first box only has one choice.

$$\boxed{1} \bullet \underline{\ \ } \bullet \boxed{\ \ }$$
$$(\geq 8) \qquad\quad (\text{even})$$

Once we've chosen the 8, the only remaining digit that will create even numbers is 4. Therefore, our last box also has a choice of only one digit.

$$\boxed{1} \bullet \underline{\ \ } \bullet \boxed{1}$$

We have used 2 of our 5 original digits, so there are 3 remaining digits from which to select the middle digit, or a permutation of $_3P_1$.

$$\boxed{1} \bullet \underline{\ 3\ } \bullet \boxed{1} = 3$$

Answer: Only 3 even numbers greater than 800 can be formed. To prove this, let's list them: 814, 854, and 874.

Another type of permutation is one that contains repeated items in the given set.

MODEL PROBLEMS

5 How many different arrangements of the letters in the word TOMORROW can be made?

SOLUTION

The word TOMORROW has eight letters, but because there are multiple Os and Rs, we must eliminate the rearrangements in which the Os or the Rs are merely transposed. The formula for this type of problem is $\dfrac{n!}{r!}$, where n is the number of things taken n at a time when r are identical. In this example, since there are three Os and two Rs that are repeated, there will be two elements in the denominator.

$$\frac{8!}{2!3!}$$

To evaluate this by hand, we set up the numerator and denominator as below:

$$\frac{8!}{2!3!} = \frac{8 \bullet 7 \bullet 6 \bullet 5 \bullet 4 \bullet 3 \bullet 2 \bullet 1}{2 \bullet 1 \bullet 3 \bullet 2 \bullet 1} \qquad \text{We can cancel like terms.}$$

$$= \frac{8 \bullet 7 \bullet 6 \bullet 5 \bullet \overset{2}{\cancel{4}} \bullet \cancel{3} \bullet \cancel{2} \bullet \cancel{1}}{\cancel{2} \bullet 1 \bullet \cancel{3} \bullet \cancel{2} \bullet \cancel{1}}$$

$$= 3,360$$

If you wish to do the entire problem in one step on the calculator, use the factorial function. Be sure to put parentheses around the product 2!3! so that the calculator uses the correct order of operations.

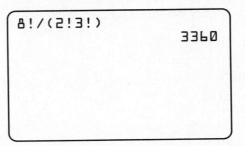

```
8!/(2!3!)
                    3360
```

You should get the same answer as we did above.

Answer: There are 3,360 different arrangements of the letters of TOMORROW.

6 The 12 cheerleaders from Hilldale High line up on the field, each carrying 2 pompoms. If there are 6 yellow, 12 blue, and 6 white pompoms, how many different arrangements of the pompoms can be made?

SOLUTION

There are three repeated colors, so while the numerator contains the total number of pompoms to be arranged, the denominator must contain the three factorial terms for the repeated items.

$$\frac{24!}{(6!12!6!)} = 2,498,640,144$$

Answer: There are 2,498,640,144 different ways to arrange the pompoms.

 Practice

1 Given the integers {2, 4, 6, 7}, if each digit can only be used once, how many different

   a four-digit numbers can be formed?
   b four-digit odd numbers can be formed?
   c four-digit even numbers can be formed?
   d four-digit numbers greater than 4,000 can be formed?
   e four-digit odd numbers greater than 4,000 can be formed? Identify them.

2 Cards, one with each of the following letters, are placed in a box: A, C, E, H, I, L, R, S, Y.

   a In how many different orders can the 9 letters be selected?
   b If only 5 letters are to be chosen, in how many different ways can this be done?
   c In how many different ways can 5 letters be chosen if the first letter must be C?
   d In how many different ways can 5 letters be chosen if the first letter must be C and the last letter must be S?

3 Tarit's school requires him to take 6 academic classes in an 8-period day in which 5th period must be lunch and 8th period must be gym. In how many different ways can his schedule be arranged?

4 The Bensen family is visiting all of the following New York State amusement parks for vacation: Adventureland, Rye Playland, Enchanted Forest Water Safari, the Great Escape, Martin's Fantasy Island, Midway Amusement Park, Seabreeze Amusement Park, Six Flags Darien Lake, Splish Splash, and Sylvan Beach Amusement Park.

a In how many different ways can the Bensens arrange their trip, disregarding mileage or nearness of parks?

b If they are saving Rye Playland for last, in how many different ways can they arrange their trip?

c If Rye Playland is to be last and the Great Escape is to be first, in how many different orders can they travel?

5 In Scrabble, each player has 7 tiles. If each of Melinda's tiles has a different letter, in how many different ways can those tiles be arranged if each arrangement of 7 letters is accepted as a word?

6 In how many different ways can president, vice president, secretary, and treasurer be chosen from

a a group of 7 nominees?

b a group of 8 nominees?

c a group of 8 nominees if Jacob must be treasurer?

7 In how many different ways can the letters of the following states be arranged?

a ALABAMA
b COLORADO
c HAWAII
d MISSISSIPPI
e TENNESSEE

Exercises 8–18: Write the numeral preceding the choice that best answers the question.

8 How many different 5-letter arrangements can be made from the letters of the word TOOTH?

(1) 12
(2) 24
(3) 30
(4) 60

9 A restaurant critic decides to sample 6 of the 9 desserts on the menu. In how many different orders can this be accomplished?

(1) 720
(2) 60,480
(3) 241,920
(4) 362,880

10 How many different four-digit odd numbers greater than 7,000 can be made from the digits {1, 3, 4, 6, 8} if each digit can be used only once?

(1) 12
(2) 24
(3) 48
(4) 120

11 The finalists in the 2008 Westminster Kennel Club Dog Show at Madison Square Garden included a 15-inch beagle, a toy poodle, a Sealyham terrier, an Akita, an Australian shepherd, a standard poodle, and a Weimaraner. Which answer below does *not* represent the number of different ways in which these dogs might have finished in the Best in Show judging?

(1) $_7P_1$
(2) $_7P_7$
(3) 7!
(4) 5,040

12 Knowing his huge appetite from training for football, Diego's mom gave him four different sandwiches for lunch: turkey, peanut butter and jelly, ham and cheese, and chicken. In how many different ways can Diego eat his lunch if he wants to save the peanut butter and jelly for last?

(1) 5
(2) 6
(3) 12
(4) 24

13 Kendra has homework in chemistry, trigonometry, Spanish, English AP, and history. In how many different ways can she choose to do her assignments?

(1) 12
(2) 24
(3) 120
(4) 720

14 In how many ways can the deejay at the school dance play 5 songs from the 8 songs the students requested?

(1) 120
(2) 720
(3) 6,720
(4) 40,320

15 Twenty-four students are entered into the Central Valley Singles Tennis Tournament. In how many different ways can the students take first and second place?

(1) 552
(2) 720
(3) 5,040
(4) 96,909,120

16 Audrey decides to buy a 3-scoop cone with each scoop a different flavor. If the ice cream stand has 7 flavors to choose from, in how many different ways can her scoops be stacked?

(1) 18
(2) 35
(3) 120
(4) 210

17 Thommi has arranged to take PSAT classes. The mathematics sessions meet on Mondays, Wednesdays, or Thursdays at 5:30 P.M. The writing sessions gather on Tuesdays at 5:30 P.M. or Thursdays at 8 P.M., and the English sessions meet on Mondays, Wednesdays, or Fridays at 8 P.M. or Saturdays at 9 A.M. All classes are 1 hour long. If Thommi plans to take all three kinds of classes, how many different schedules are available to her?

(1) 9
(2) 24
(3) 60
(4) 120

18 A manufacturing company puts a date code on their product using two digits from 0 to 9 followed by two letters from the English alphabet. If neither the digits nor the letters may be repeated, how many different codes are possible?

(1) 6,500
(2) 13,000
(3) 26,410
(4) 58,500

16.3 **Combinations**

A selection in which order is *not* important is called a **combination**. For example, if you are chosen for a team or a committee, the order in which you are chosen is not important. It only matters that you are chosen.

The mathematical notation for a combination of *n* items taken *r* at a time is $_nC_r$ or $\binom{n}{r}$. Mathematically,

$$_nC_r = \frac{_nP_r}{r!}.$$

This is equivalent to a permutation of *n* items taken *r* at a time, divided by the number of ways the *r* items can be arranged.

Fact: A combination lock does **not** use combinations. Number order matters: If you enter the numbers in the wrong order on a combination lock, your lock will not open. What we are really using to safeguard our property is a permutation lock!

You may wish to memorize two special combinations:

- A combination of n items taken 1 at a time is $_nC_1 = n$.
- A combination of n items taken n at a time is $_nC_n = 1$.

MODEL PROBLEM

1 Twelve students are trying out for the basketball team. If all students are equally skilled, in how many ways can the coach choose five starters?

SOLUTION

Order is not important here: only being chosen is. Therefore, this is a combination of 12 items taken 5 at a time.

$$_{12}C_5 = \frac{_{12}P_5}{5!} = \frac{\cancel{12} \cdot 11 \cdot \cancel{10} \cdot 9 \cdot 8}{\cancel{5} \cdot \cancel{4} \cdot \cancel{3} \cdot \cancel{2} \cdot 1} = 792$$

Answer: There are 792 ways the coach can choose the starting team.

Choosing 5 out of 12 is the same problem as deciding *not* to choose 7 out of 12.

$$_{12}C_7 = \frac{_{12}P_7}{7!} = \frac{\cancel{12} \cdot 11 \cdot \cancel{10} \cdot 9 \cdot 8 \cdot \cancel{7} \cdot \cancel{6}}{\cancel{7} \cdot \cancel{6} \cdot \cancel{5} \cdot \cancel{4} \cdot \cancel{3} \cdot \cancel{2} \cdot 1} = 792$$

We say that $_{12}C_5 = {}_{12}C_7$ or, more generally,

$$_nC_r = {}_nC_{n-r}$$

This rule can be very useful if we are asked to choose a large number of items from a group, as shown in the following problem.

MODEL PROBLEMS

2 The deejay at the dance realizes that he will have time to play only 15 of the 18 songs that the students requested. If order is not important, in how many different ways can he choose the 15 songs to play?

SOLUTION

Since the problem indicates that order is not significant, we will do this problem as a combination. To evaluate $_{18}C_{15}$ requires a great deal more computation than to find $_{18}C_3$. Because these values are equivalent, most students would prefer to find $_{18}C_3$. Both methods are demonstrated below.

Method 1

$$_{18}C_{15} = \frac{18 \cdot 17 \cdot 16 \cdot \cancel{15} \cdot \cancel{14} \cdot \cancel{13} \cdot \cancel{12} \cdot \cancel{11} \cdot \cancel{10} \cdot 9 \cdot 8 \cdot 7 \cdot 6 \cdot 5 \cdot 4}{\cancel{15} \cdot \cancel{14} \cdot \cancel{13} \cdot \cancel{12} \cdot \cancel{11} \cdot \cancel{10} \cdot 9 \cdot 8 \cdot 7 \cdot 6 \cdot 5 \cdot 4 \cdot 3 \cdot 2 \cdot 1}$$

$$= \frac{\cancel{18}^{3} \cdot 17 \cdot 16}{\cancel{3} \cdot \cancel{2} \cdot 1}$$

$$= 816$$

Method 2

$$_{18}C_3 = \frac{\overset{3}{\cancel{18}} \cdot 17 \cdot 16}{\cancel{3} \cdot \cancel{2} \cdot 1} = 816$$

The $_{18}C_3$ version is simpler to calculate by hand than $_{18}C_{15}$.

To use your calculator to solve a combination problem, enter the n value, then press (MATH) ◄ ☐ 3 and enter the r value.

Answer: There are 816 ways the songs can be played.

3 The local community board consists of 12 men and 9 women. If the county needs a representative committee of 3 people, how many

   a committees of 3 can be made?

   b committees of 2 men and 1 woman can be formed?

   c committees of only women can be selected?

SOLUTION

   a There are 21 board members in all and any 3 can be chosen, so we use:

$$_{21}C_3 = \frac{21 \cdot 20 \cdot 19}{3 \cdot 2 \cdot 1} = 1{,}330$$

Answer: 1,330 committees of 3 people

   b This problem requires a choice of 2 men out of 12 and a choice of 1 woman out of 9. Since both conditions must be met, you need to multiply the two combinations:

$$_{12}C_2 \cdot _9C_1 = 594$$

Answer: 594 committees of 2 men and 1 woman

   c If the choice is to be made from only the women, we disregard the 12 men and choose 3 from the 9 women: $_9C_3 = 84$

Answer: 84 committees of women

To determine whether to use a permutation or a combination, decide if the order is a significant factor in the choices being made. If the order of the selection matters, use a permutation. If the order would not affect the outcome, use a combination. The results of an election or a race, numbers, and words all depend on order so they would always be permutations.

Exercises 1–10: Write the numeral preceding the choice that best answers the question.

1 A committee of 7 is to be chosen from 15 sophomores to design their class ring. Which of the following is *not* a formula that could be used to determine in how many ways this committee could be chosen?

(1) $_{15}C_7$
(2) $_{15}C_8$
(3) $_{15}P_7$
(4) $\begin{pmatrix} 15 \\ 8 \end{pmatrix}$

2 The kindergarten teachers are decorating their bulletin boards with colorful pictures of baby animals and their names. If Ms. Yansick is selecting 4 animals from a group of 12, how many different groups of 4 animals could she choose?

(1) 330
(2) 495
(3) 7,920
(4) 11,880

3 Mrs. Wojikowski is planning goody bags for her son's birthday party. She wishes to include 6 different kinds of treats in each bag. If she has 14 types of candy and toys, how many different groups of goodies can be made?

(1) 1,001
(2) 2,002
(3) 3,003
(4) 40,320

4 Uri selects 7 video games to borrow from the Video Library, but his mother will let him take only 4. How many different selections of 4 games out of 7 can Uri make?

(1) 21
(2) 35
(3) 120
(4) 210

5 Mr. Titolo gave his students a picture of a circle with 12 points on it. How many line segments could the students make by connecting any 2 given points?

(1) 66
(2) 72
(3) 132
(4) 144

6 There are 16 certified referees available for PAL football games. If each game requires 3 referees, how many different assignments of refs are possible?

(1) 256
(2) 560
(3) 3,360
(4) 4,096

7 The Student Court needs 4 juniors and 5 seniors for its panel. If there are 9 juniors who volunteered and 11 seniors, how many different courts could be created?

(1) 2,002
(2) 5,040
(3) 11,088
(4) 58,212

8 Dr. Jenkins is purchasing magazine subscriptions for his waiting room. He wants to continue to receive 3 of his 5 sports magazines, 2 of 4 news magazines, and 3 of 5 entertainment magazines. In how many ways can he renew the 8 subscriptions?

(1) 336
(2) 360
(3) 540
(4) 600

9 The Society for Reformed Curmudgeons has agreed to support 3 food pantries and 2 homeless shelters this year. If there are 8 food pantries and 6 homeless shelters that requested assistance, in how many different ways can the Reformed Curmudgeons donate their money?

(1) 288
(2) 720
(3) 840
(4) 4,096

10 The school's summer reading list offers 8 biographies, 6 nonfiction commentaries on world events, and 12 novels to choose from. If students are required to read 2 biographies, 1 nonfiction commentary, and 2 novels, how many different selections of 5 books are possible?

(1) 720
(2) 3,003
(3) 5,040
(4) 11,088

11 Nicole has 7 assignments in her history class, 4 in her German class, and 5 in her Shakespeare class for the semester. If she is planning to complete 3 history, 1 German, and 2 Shakespeare assignments this weekend, how many different groups of assignments could she choose to do?

12 A Senate committee has 18 members, 11 of whom are Democrats and 7 of whom are Republicans. A subcommittee of 6 members is to be chosen to research and prepare a bill on subsidies for education. Show the formula to determine in how many ways the committee can be chosen if

a there must be an equal number of Democrats and Republicans
b there must be 4 Democrats and 2 Republicans
c all members of the subcommittee must be Democrats
d Eleanor, a Democrat, must be on the committee

Exercises 13–22: Determine if each situation involves a permutation or a combination. Then solve the problem.

13 Jack stopped at the store to buy sports drinks. The store had 11 flavors, and Jack will choose 4 of them. In how many ways could he

a buy different groups of 4 flavors?
b drink the 4 flavors he bought?

14 Glenbrook High's marching band is entered into a competition. If 9 schools are competing, in how many ways can first, second, and third place be awarded with the Glenbrook High band finishing first?

15 The meals at the space station come dehydrated in silver pouches. If there are 10 different choices available for dinner, in how many ways can an astronaut

a choose 7 dinners to consume this week?
b eat those meals over the week?

16 An animal shelter has these puppies to adopt: 4 Maltese, 3 Yorkshire terriers, 3 shih tzus, and 4 beagles. If the shelter wants to place 2 of each variety of dog in a puppy play area, how many different choices could be made?

17 A cable station is putting on a special Sci-Fi Day at the Movies. They have 11 different feature films to air. Because of the commentary and interviews related to each movie, there will be time to show only 9 films.

a How many selections of 9 films can be made?
b If the films *Alien* and *2001: A Space Odyssey* must be shown, how many different choices of films can be made?
c Once the films are chosen, in how many different orders can they be watched?

18 Given the digits {2, 3, 5, 8, 9}, if no digit is repeated, how many different

a five-digit numbers can be formed?
b five-digit odd numbers can be created?
c five-digit numbers greater than 30,000 can be formed?

19 The Key Club is holding a fund-raiser by raffling sports items at the Fall Fling Dance. First prize is two tickets to the Super Bowl, second prize is ten weeks of tennis lessons, and third prize is an autographed baseball glove. Two hundred people have entered the raffle.

a Write the formula to determine how many different ways the prizes could be awarded. Do *not* solve.
b If third prize is chosen first, write the formula to determine the number of ways that the second prize and first prize can then be awarded. Do *not* solve.

20 How many different 10-letter arrangements can be formed from the letters in the word BOOKKEEPER?

21 Wycliff Community Park is designing a new playground. The designers will choose 2 different swing sets out of 6 recommended, 3 different climb-and-slides out of 5, 2 different merry-go-rounds out of 5, and 1 wooden fort or castle out of 4 recommended. How many different selections of 8 items can be made for the park?

22 Every December, the Giannuzzi sisters get together to bake for the holidays. They make cookies from the family's recipes. This year they will make 2 of the 4 shortbread recipes, 3 of the 5 butter cookie recipes, 1 of the 3 oatmeal cookie recipes, 2 of the 6 chocolate chip cookie recipes, and 1 of the 2 spice cookie recipes.

a How many different selections of the 9 kinds of cookies are there?

b If Maria insists on making a particular kind of butter cookie and a specific spice cookie, how many cookie assortments are possible?

c If the Giannuzzi sisters bake one type of cookie at a time, in how many orders can those 9 kinds of cookies be baked?

16.4 Probability

Theoretical Probability

Probability is the likelihood that a given event will occur or the ratio of the number of equally likely outcomes that will produce a desired event to the total number of possible outcomes. In other words, Probability = $\dfrac{\text{Number of successes}}{\text{Total possible outcomes}}$.

As you will recall from Integrated Algebra,

- Probability is expressed as a fraction or a decimal between 0 and 1.
- Absolute certainty has a probability of 1.
- Total impossibility has a probability of 0.
- The sum of all probabilities in a situation equals 1.
- The probability of an event E occurring is written $P(E)$.

When we calculate the mathematical likelihood that an event will occur, we are finding the **theoretical probability**.

MODEL PROBLEM

1 A box of golf balls contains three yellow, four white, and one red. If Leroi chooses one golf ball from the box without looking, find the probability that the golf ball is:

a yellow **b** red **c** not red **d** green

SOLUTION

a There are 3 yellow golf balls out of 8 total golf balls, so the probability of choosing a yellow ball is $\dfrac{3}{8}$.

Answer: $\dfrac{3}{8}$

b There is only 1 red golf ball out of 8 total golf balls, so the probability of choosing a red ball is $\frac{1}{8}$.

Answer: $\frac{1}{8}$

c Since we know the probability of choosing a red ball is $\frac{1}{8}$, the probability of not choosing a red ball is $1 - \frac{1}{8} = \frac{7}{8}$.

Alternately, we could have counted the number of non-red balls, 3 yellow and 4 white, and used that as the numerator. The probability of not-red is still $\frac{7}{8}$.

Answer: $\frac{7}{8}$

> **Remember:** The sum of all probabilities in an event must always total 1.

d Since there are no green golf balls in Leroi's box, the probability of choosing green must be $\frac{0}{8}$ or 0.

Answer: 0

Probability of More than One Event

When we consider the probability of more than one event occurring simultaneously or sequentially, we take the probability of the first event and multiply it by the probability that the second event will also happen. Since *A and B* must happen, their probability is the product of each individual probability.

Probability (*A* and *B*) = Probability(*A*) • Probability(*B*)

If a die is rolled twice, the outcome of the first roll does *not* affect the outcome of the second roll. The two rolls are **independent events**.

For example, the probability of rolling a 5 first and then a number greater than 2 is

$$P(5 \text{ and number} > 2) = P(5) \cdot P(\text{number} > 2)$$
$$= \frac{1}{6} \cdot \frac{4}{6}$$
$$= \frac{4}{36} = \frac{1}{9}$$

Suppose a box contains 5 blue pens and 3 red pens. You randomly pick one pen, and then you pick another without replacing the first. In this case, the outcome of the first pick does affect the outcome of the second pick. The two picks are **dependent events**. You can still find the probability of two or more events by multiplying individual probabilities, but you must be sure to use the correct number of outcomes for each event.

For example. the probability of picking two blue pens is

$P(\text{blue and blue}) = P(\text{blue}) \cdot P(\text{blue following blue})$

$\qquad = \dfrac{5}{8} \cdot \dfrac{4}{7}$ After you pick the first blue, there are 7 pens left, only 4 of which are blue.

$\qquad = \dfrac{5}{14}$

MODEL PROBLEM

2 The spinner shown is spun twice. Find each probability.

a $P(\text{red and then green})$ **b** $P(\text{green and green})$

c $P(\text{blue and blue})$ **d** $P(\text{yellow and then blue})$

SOLUTION

First, it is necessary to examine the spinner. The colored sectors of the circle are not equal in area; the blue sectors account for $\dfrac{4}{8}$ or $\dfrac{1}{2}$ of the circle, the red is $\dfrac{3}{8}$, and the green is $\dfrac{1}{8}$. Since there is no yellow region, the probability of spinning a yellow is zero. The two spins are independent events.

a $P(\text{red and green}) = \dfrac{3}{8} \cdot \dfrac{1}{8} = \dfrac{3}{64}$

b $P(\text{green and green}) = \dfrac{1}{8} \cdot \dfrac{1}{8} = \dfrac{1}{64}$

c $P(\text{blue and blue}) = \dfrac{1}{2} \cdot \dfrac{1}{2} = \dfrac{1}{4}$

d $P(\text{yellow and blue}) = 0 \cdot \dfrac{1}{2} = 0$

Empirical Probability

Empirical probability deals with sets of possibilities based on experimentation or observation in the real world. In calculating empirical probability, we consider the ratio of the number of times a particular event occurred to the total number of observations:

$$P(E) = \frac{\text{Number of occurrences of } E}{\text{Total number of observations}}$$

For example, if Roger takes 50 shots from the free throw line of a basketball court and makes 28 baskets, then

$$P(\text{Roger makes basket}) = \frac{28}{50} = \frac{14}{25}$$

Probability of One *or* Another Event

When we are asked the probability of one *or* another event occurring, we must consider their joint probability, that is, the probability of the first or the second happening, assuming the two events are *mutually exclusive* or disjoint. Two events are **mutually exclusive** if they cannot happen at the same time. The probability of two mutually exclusive events is found by adding the individual probabilities.

Probability $(A$ or $B)$ = Probability(A) + Probability(B)

🖳 MODEL PROBLEM

3   A single card is randomly selected from a standard deck of 52 playing cards. Find the probability that the chosen card is

a an ace or a king
b a red card or a black card
c a black card or the 10 of diamonds

SOLUTION

A standard deck has 52 cards: 26 red cards and 26 black cards. It has four suits; the two red suits are diamonds and hearts and the two black suits are clubs and spades. Each suit has 13 cards, from 2 through 10 as well as jack, queen, king, and ace.

a $P(\text{ace or king}) = \dfrac{4}{52} + \dfrac{4}{52} = \dfrac{8}{52} = \dfrac{2}{13}$

b $P(\text{red card or black card}) = \dfrac{26}{52} + \dfrac{26}{52} = \dfrac{52}{52} = 1$

c $P(\text{black card or 10 of diamonds}) = \dfrac{26}{52} + \dfrac{1}{52} = \dfrac{27}{52}$

Notice that in each of the above problems, there was no duplication between the two events; that is, the events required were mutually exclusive. An ace could not be a king. A red card could not also be a black card; a black card could not be the 10 of diamonds. Sometimes, however, as in the model problems below, one element might meet both desired conditions and we do *not* want to count that element twice. In that situation, we must subtract the probability of meeting both requirements:

$P(A$ or $B) = P(A) + P(B) - P(A$ and $B)$

Note: When events are disjoint, $P(A$ and $B) = 0$ and the formula reduces to $P(A) + P(B)$.

4 A single card is randomly selected from standard deck of 52 playing cards. Find the probability that the chosen card is a

  a 3 or a heart

  b club or a black card

  c face card (jack, queen, king) or a diamond

SOLUTION

In each of these problems, it is possible for one or more cards to meet both conditions, so we will have to subtract the probability of that occurring.

a $P(\text{3 or heart}) = P(3) + P(\text{heart}) - P(\text{3 of hearts})$

$$= \frac{4}{52} + \frac{13}{52} - \frac{1}{52}$$

$$= \frac{16}{52}$$

$$= \frac{4}{13}$$

b $P(\text{club or black}) = P(\text{club}) + P(\text{black}) - P(\text{black club})$

$$= \frac{13}{52} + \frac{26}{52} - \frac{13}{52}$$

$$= \frac{26}{52}$$

$$= \frac{1}{2}$$

c $P(\text{face or diamond}) = P(\text{face}) + P(\text{diamond}) - P(\text{face diamond})$

$$= \frac{12}{52} + \frac{13}{52} - \frac{3}{52}$$

$$= \frac{22}{52}$$

$$= \frac{11}{26}$$

Sometimes the probability problems will require you to use permutations and combinations to find the solution.

5 Fiona and Tiffany are competing in the 200-meter breaststroke event. If all 8 swimmers have an equal chance of winning, what is the probability that Tiffany comes in first and Fiona comes in second?

SOLUTION

Order is significant in this situation since we are looking at a race. Hence, we must use permutations. There are 8 swimmers, so the total number of ways the 8 swimmers could finish is 8!. That becomes our denominator. The numerator of the probability fraction is the number of ways that Tiffany could be first and Fiona could be second. Since we have specific choices for first and second places, the only consideration is how the other 6 swimmers finish, which would be 6!.

$$P(\text{Tiffany 1st and Fiona 2nd}) = \frac{1 \cdot 1 \cdot 6!}{8!} = \frac{1 \cdot 1 \cdot \cancel{6} \cdot \cancel{5} \cdot \cancel{4} \cdot \cancel{3} \cdot \cancel{2} \cdot \cancel{1}}{8 \cdot 7 \cdot \cancel{6} \cdot \cancel{5} \cdot \cancel{4} \cdot \cancel{3} \cdot \cancel{2} \cdot \cancel{1}} = \frac{1}{56}$$

An alternate method of solving this problem is to use the Counting Principle: the probability of Tiffany finishing first is $\frac{1}{8}$ and, if Tiffany comes in first, the probability of Fiona finishing second is $\frac{1}{7}$.

Therefore, the probability of Tiffany finishing first and Fiona finishing second is $\frac{1}{8} \cdot \frac{1}{7} = \frac{1}{56}$.

Answer: $\frac{1}{56}$

6 Ms. Rito needs two seniors to head the November blood drive. If 12 students volunteer, 4 boys and 8 girls, what is the probability that one boy and one girl will be chosen to head the blood drive?

SOLUTION

In this problem, order is not significant. It does not matter if a girl or a boy is selected first, only that both are chosen, so we will be using combinations. First, we find the denominator; there are 12 volunteers and 2 are needed. That gives us $_{12}C_2$. For the numerator, we need two combinations, one to represent the number of ways a girl could be chosen and the other to represent the number of ways a boy could be chosen. Since there are 8 girls and 4 boys, the appropriate representations are $_8C_1$ and $_4C_1$. Because both conditions are required, we multiply these terms. The probability that one boy and one girl will be chosen is

$$\frac{_8C_1 \cdot {_4C_1}}{_{12}C_2} = \frac{8 \cdot 4}{\dfrac{12 \cdot 11}{2}}$$

$$= \frac{32}{66}$$

$$= \frac{16}{33}$$

Answer: The probability that one boy and one girl are chosen to head the blood drive is $\frac{16}{33}$.

Practice

Exercises 1–11: Select the numeral preceding the choice that best answers the question.

1   A fair coin is tossed and an unbiased die is thrown. What is the probability that the results are heads, 5?

(1) $\dfrac{1}{12}$

(2) $\dfrac{1}{10}$

(3) $\dfrac{1}{6}$

(4) $\dfrac{5}{12}$

2   In playing the game Yahtzee, 5 dice are tossed simultaneously. What is the probability that all 5 dice show the number 2?

(1) $\dfrac{5}{36}$

(2) $\dfrac{1}{36}$

(3) $\dfrac{1}{1,296}$

(4) $\dfrac{1}{7,776}$

3   Jake has eight crayons of different colors: pale blue, sky blue, navy blue, fire engine red, cherry red, forest green, lime green, and black. If he chooses two crayons without looking, what is the probability that both are blue?

(1) $\dfrac{3}{64}$

(2) $\dfrac{5}{56}$

(3) $\dfrac{3}{32}$

(4) $\dfrac{3}{28}$

4   Twelve students are in the Saturday morning Driver Education class, 7 boys and 5 girls. If there are 3 students assigned to each car, what is the probability that Maria, Grace, and Timothy are all assigned to Mr. Krieg's car?

(1) $\dfrac{1}{1,320}$

(2) $\dfrac{1}{220}$

(3) $\dfrac{7}{11}$

(4) $\dfrac{19}{22}$

5   There are eleven sections of Freshman Composition at Oneida Community College and three sections of International Diplomacy. If Kai has his classes scheduled first, what is the probability that Andrew is scheduled in the same sections?

(1) $\dfrac{1}{33}$

(2) $\dfrac{1}{14}$

(3) $\dfrac{1}{7}$

(4) $\dfrac{14}{33}$

6   If the probability of an event's occurring is $\dfrac{x^2}{y}$, what is the probability of the event *not* occurring?

(1) $-\dfrac{x^2}{y}$

(2) $\dfrac{y}{x^2}$

(3) $\dfrac{y - x^2}{y}$

(4) $\dfrac{x^2 - y}{y}$

7 From a group of 8 Democrats and 6 Republicans, a 5-member committee needs to be formed. Which of the following represents the probability that the committee contains 3 Democrats and 2 Republicans?

(1) $\dfrac{_8C_3 \bullet {}_6C_2}{_{14}C_5}$

(2) $\dfrac{_8C_3 + {}_6C_2}{_{14}C_5}$

(3) $\dfrac{_{14}C_3 \bullet {}_{13}C_2}{_{14}C_5}$

(4) $\dfrac{_{14}C_5}{_{14}C_8 \bullet {}_{13}C_6}$

8 The school musical next year will be *Grease*. After initial tryouts, seven girls are still in competition for the parts of Sandy, Frenchy, and Rizzo. If the selection is made by drawing names, what is the probability that Savannah, Loghan, and Kathleen are chosen for the roles of Sandy, Frenchy, and Rizzo in that order?

(1) $\dfrac{3}{7}$

(2) $\dfrac{1}{7}$

(3) $\dfrac{1}{70}$

(4) $\dfrac{1}{210}$

9 In horse racing, a trifecta is a bet in which the first, second, and third horses are predicted in that precise order. If George bets a trifecta in a race in which 9 horses are running, what is the probability he might win, assuming that all of the horses have equal talent?

(1) $\dfrac{1}{504}$

(2) $\dfrac{1}{168}$

(3) $\dfrac{1}{12}$

(4) $\dfrac{1}{3}$

10 A carton of books contains 5 different mysteries, 3 different horror novels, and 2 different romance novels. If Judith picks 3 books at random from the carton, what is the probability that she has selected one from each category?

(1) $\dfrac{1}{70}$

(2) $\dfrac{1}{12}$

(3) $\dfrac{1}{4}$

(4) $\dfrac{3}{10}$

11 In the diagram below, rectangle *MATH* has a length of 11 and a width of 4, while circles *O* and *P* have radii of 2.

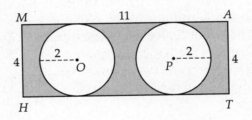

If a dart is thrown and lands in this figure, which expression below represents the probability that the dart will land in the shaded region?

(1) $\dfrac{11 - \pi}{11}$

(2) $\dfrac{11 - 2\pi}{11}$

(3) $\dfrac{\pi}{11}$

(4) $\dfrac{11 - 4\pi}{11}$

Exercises 12–14: Use the following information to answer each question.

After 3 P.M., Delilah's Donuts offers a daily special of eight donuts in a sack for $3.50. Two donuts are jelly-filled, two are custard-filled, three are chocolate, and one is plain.

12 If Jack grabs a donut from the sack without looking, find the probability that it is

   a custard-filled or chocolate
   b not jelly-filled

13 Ivan missed lunch and decides to eat two donuts at random from a new sack of eight. Find the probability he eats

   a a plain donut and a jelly donut, in that order
   b two jelly donuts
   c a filled donut and a chocolate donut, in either order

14 After Ivan has eaten the two custard donuts, he offers the bag to his friend Paco, who randomly chooses two donuts. What is the probability that Paco eats two chocolate donuts?

15 A box contains one each of the following shapes: parallelogram, rhombus, non-isosceles trapezoid, isosceles trapezoid, rectangle, square, isosceles triangle, equilateral triangle, scalene triangle, and regular hexagon. Find the probability that two figures chosen at random will both have

   a all equal angles
   b equal diagonals
   c at least two equal sides
   d at least two sides parallel

16 There is a strong school rivalry between the Generals and the Eagles football teams. If the probability that the Eagles win is $\frac{3}{4}$ and the teams play each other twice, what is the probability that the Eagles win both games?

17 Imelda planted new tulip bulbs in her front yard, but she confused the colors of the bulbs. If she had 8 yellow, 6 red, 5 pink, and 5 purple tulips, what is the probability that 6 bulbs planted around the maple tree will all be the same color?

18 Aimee empties her change purse and finds three quarters, four dimes, six nickels, and two pennies. If she chooses three coins at random, what is the probability that the coins she selects total fifty cents or more?

19 Anybody Airlines has overbooked a flight to Chicago. Volunteers are asked to accept a free flight to the destination of their choice and a rescheduled flight. If 16 people volunteer to give up their seats and only five seats are needed, what is the probability that Kelly is chosen to receive compensation?

20 Elena, Marta, and Aleida met on a trip to Mexico with 12 other people. At the end of the trip, three souvenir prizes were awarded in a random drawing. A person could win only one prize. What is the probability that Elena won the first souvenir, Marta won the second souvenir, and Aleida won the third souvenir?

16.5 The Binomial Theorem

From earlier work in algebra, we are familiar with the term *binomial*, an expression consisting of two terms, such as $x + y$, $2p + 5$, or $a^2 - 1$. These are binomials because they all show two monomial terms being combined by addition or subtraction. When n is a positive integer and $a + b$ represents the first and second terms of a binomial, then $(a + b)^n$ can be expressed as a polynomial called the **binomial expansion**.

$$(a + b)^0 = \qquad\qquad\qquad \mathbf{1}$$
$$(a + b)^1 = \qquad\qquad\qquad \mathbf{1}a + \mathbf{1}b$$
$$(a + b)^2 = \qquad\qquad \mathbf{1}a^2 + \mathbf{2}ab + \mathbf{1}b^2$$
$$(a + b)^3 = \qquad \mathbf{1}a^3 + \mathbf{3}a^2b^1 + \mathbf{3}a^1b^2 + \mathbf{1}b^3$$
$$(a + b)^4 = \quad \mathbf{1}a^4 + \mathbf{4}a^3b^1 + \mathbf{6}a^2b^2 + \mathbf{4}a^1b^3 + \mathbf{1}b^4$$
$$(a + b)^5 = \mathbf{1}a^5 + \mathbf{5}a^4b^1 + \mathbf{10}a^3b^2 + \mathbf{10}a^2b^3 + \mathbf{5}a^1b^4 + \mathbf{1}b^5$$

Look at the coefficients of each term in the expansion above and see if you notice a pattern.

```
            1
          1   1
        1   2   1
      1   3   3   1
    1   4   6   4   1
  1   5  10  10   5   1
```

This arrangement of numbers is known as **Pascal's triangle** after the French mathematician and physicist Blaise Pascal who developed the triangle in 1653. Among its interesting characteristics are:

- Every outer number on the left and right will always be 1.
- The triangle has a vertical axis of symmetry that can de drawn downward through the initial 1.
- Each row has one more number than the previous row.
- Each number not on the outer edge is the sum of the two numbers above it.
- The second number in each row indicates the power of the expansion being performed.

Using these facts, we can write the coefficients for the next two rows:

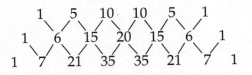

Pascal's triangle is based on the concept of combinations that we discussed in Section 16.3. Pascal's triangle can also be written as:

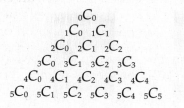

$$
\begin{array}{c}
{}_0C_0 \\
{}_1C_0 \quad {}_1C_1 \\
{}_2C_0 \quad {}_2C_1 \quad {}_2C_2 \\
{}_3C_0 \quad {}_3C_1 \quad {}_3C_2 \quad {}_3C_3 \\
{}_4C_0 \quad {}_4C_1 \quad {}_4C_2 \quad {}_4C_3 \quad {}_4C_4 \\
{}_5C_0 \quad {}_5C_1 \quad {}_5C_2 \quad {}_5C_3 \quad {}_5C_4 \quad {}_5C_5
\end{array}
$$

Each row represents the combinations of n things taken r at a time where n is the number of the row. The leftmost term in each row is ${}_nC_0$ while the rightmost term is ${}_nC_r$.

As we showed in Section 16.3, ${}_nC_r = {}_nC_{n-r}$, the triangle must be symmetric over its axis of symmetry.

In the binomial expansion of $(a + b)^n$, the exponents of the variables change with each successive term; in the first term, the exponent of a is n and the exponent of b is 0 (not usually written). In successive terms, the exponent of a decreases by 1 and the exponent of b increases by 1. The sum of the exponents in each term is n. The formula for a binomial expansion can be written as:

$$(a + b)^n = {}_nC_0a^nb^0 + {}_nC_1a^{n-1}b^1 + {}_nC_2a^{n-2}b^2 + {}_nC_3a^{n-3}b^3 + {}_nC_4a^{n-4}b^4 + \cdots + {}_nC_na^0b^n$$

Note: The number of terms in the complete expansion is $n + 1$. The formula above is known as the **binomial theorem**.

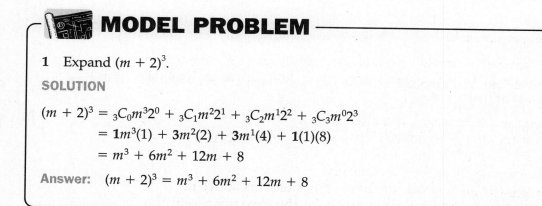

MODEL PROBLEM

1   Expand $(m + 2)^3$.

SOLUTION

$$
\begin{aligned}
(m + 2)^3 &= {}_3C_0m^32^0 + {}_3C_1m^22^1 + {}_3C_2m^12^2 + {}_3C_3m^02^3 \\
&= 1m^3(1) + 3m^2(2) + 3m^1(4) + 1(1)(8) \\
&= m^3 + 6m^2 + 12m + 8
\end{aligned}
$$

Answer: $(m + 2)^3 = m^3 + 6m^2 + 12m + 8$

Note that after simplifying the expression, the coefficients from Pascal's triangle are changed when they are multiplied by the other terms.

2 Expand $(a - 3)^4$.

SOLUTION

In this case, the second term is negative so we must be certain to keep track of the negative value as we set up the expansion. For that reason, it is best to keep the second term in its own parentheses.

$$(a - 3)^4 = {}_4C_0a^4(-3)^0 + {}_4C_1a^3(-3)^1 + {}_4C_2a^2(-3)^2 + {}_4C_3a^1(-3)^3 + {}_4C_4a^0(-3)^4$$
$$= 1a^4(1) + 4a^3(-3) + 6a^2(9) + 4a^1(-27) + 1(1)(81)$$
$$= a^4 - 12a^3 + 54a^2 - 108a + 81$$

Answer: $(a - 3)^4 = a^4 - 12a^3 + 54a^2 - 108a + 81$

3 Expand $(2x + 3y)^5$.

SOLUTION

In this example, you must take into account the coefficients of both the first and second terms when raising them to the appropriate powers.

$$(2x + 3y)^5 = {}_5C_0(2x)^5(3y)^0 + {}_5C_1(2x)^4(3y)^1 + {}_5C_2(2x)^3(3y)^2 + {}_5C_3(2x)^2(3y)^3 + {}_5C_4(2x)^1(3y)^4 + {}_5C_5(2x)^0(3y)^5$$
$$= 1(32x^5)(1) + 5(16x^4)(3y) + 10(8x^3)(9y^2) + 10(4x^2)(27y^3) + 5(2x)(81y^4) + 1(1)(243y^5)$$
$$= 32x^5 + 240x^4y + 720x^3y^2 + 1,080x^2y^3 + 810xy^4 + 243y^5$$

Answer: $(2x + 3y)^5 = 32x^5 + 240x^4y + 720x^3y^2 + 1,080x^2y^3 + 810xy^4 + 243y^5$

4 Write the binomial expansion of $(3 - 5i)^3$, where $i = \sqrt{-1}$, and simplify your answer.

SOLUTION

First do the binomial expansion. Then replace the various exponential i terms with their equivalents.

$$(3 - 5i)^3 = {}_3C_03^3(-5i)^0 + {}_3C_13^2(-5i)^1 + {}_3C_23^1(-5i)^2 + {}_3C_33^0(-5i)^3$$
$$= 1(27)(1) + 3(9)(-5i) + 3(3)(25i^2) + 1(1)(-125i^3)$$
$$= 27 - 135i + 225i^2 - 125i^3$$
$$= -198 - 10i$$

Answer: $(3 - 5i)^3 = -198 - 10i$

Sometimes you are asked for only one term of a binomial expansion. Certainly, you can expand the entire expression and use only the term you need, but there is a formula to help you find the specified term.

For example, if we wanted the third term of $(2x - 5)^5$, we could do the full expansion and simply choose the third term.

$$1(2x)^5(-5)^0 + 5(2x)^4(-5)^1 + 10(2x)^3(-5)^2 + 10(2x)^2(-5)^3 + 5(2x)^1(-5)^4 + 1(2x)^0(-5)^5$$

The third term is $10(2x)^3(-5)^2$ or $10 \cdot 8x^3 \cdot 25 = 2,000x^3$.

Alternately, if a represents the first term and b represents the second term, we can use the formula:

rth term of an n term expansion $= {}_nC_{r-1}(a \text{ term})^{n-(r-1)}(b \text{ term})^{r-1}$

Here, $r = 3$ so $r - 1 = 2$.

n is the power of the expansion: $n = 5$; a term $= 2x$; b term $= -5$.

$$ {}_5C_2(2x)^{5-2}(-5)^2 = 10(8x^3)(25) $$
$$ = 2{,}000x^3 $$

The third term of the expansion again equals $2{,}000x^3$. You may use either method to find the rth term of an n term expansion.

MODEL PROBLEMS

5 Find the fourth term of the expansion $(3x + 2)^5$.

SOLUTION

Always make a list of the values of the a term, the b term, n, r, and $r - 1$ before substituting into the formula.

a term $= 3x$ $\qquad$ b term $= 2$ $\qquad$ $n = 5$ $\qquad$ $r = 4$ $\qquad$ $r - 1 = 3$

Therefore, the formula becomes ${}_5C_3(3x)^2(2)^3 = 10(9x^2)(8) = 720x^2$.

Answer: The fourth term is $720x^2$.

6 Find the middle term of the expansion $(2m - 5)^6$.

SOLUTION

A binomial expansion always has one more term than its highest exponent. In this case, the expansion of $(2m - 5)^6$ has seven terms, so the middle term we want is the fourth.

a term $= 2m$ $\qquad$ b term $= -5$ $\qquad$ $n = 6$ $\qquad$ $r = 4$ $\qquad$ $r - 1 = 3$

$$ {}_6C_3(2m)^3(-5)^3 = 20(8m^3)(-125) $$
$$ = -20{,}000m^3 $$

Answer: The middle term is $-20{,}000m^3$.

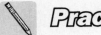

Exercises 1–6: Use the binomial theorem to write the binomial expansion for each expression. Simplify if possible.

1 $(z + 5)^3$

2 $(a - 3b)^4$

3 $(4p + 2)^5$

4 $(1 - 2i)^5$ if $i = \sqrt{-1}$

5 $(6x - 1)^4$

6 $\left(\dfrac{1}{2}z + 4\right)^6$

Exercises 7–10: Find the third term of each expansion.

7 $(4 - 2i)^7$ if $i = \sqrt{-1}$

8 $(3x + 2y)^6$

9 $\left(3 + \sqrt{2}\right)^5$

10 $(7d - 2c)^4$

Exercises 11–20: Select the numeral preceding the choice that best completes the statement or answers the question.

11 The third term of the expansion $(1 + \pi)^5$ is

    (1) $10\pi^2$
    (2) $15\pi^2$
    (3) $15\pi^3$
    (4) $20\pi^3$

12 The fourth term in the expansion of $(2 - \sin x)^4$ is

    (1) $-4\sin^4 x$
    (2) $4\sin^3 x$
    (3) $-8\sin^3 x$
    (4) $8\sin^3 x$

13 The third term of the expansion $(2 - 3i)^5$, if $i = \sqrt{-1}$, is

    (1) $720i$
    (2) -720
    (3) $-1{,}080i$
    (4) $-1{,}080$

14 The last term of the expansion $(3x - 2)^8$ is

    (1) 512
    (2) 256
    (3) -256
    (4) -512

15 The middle term of the expansion $(2\tan\theta - 3)^4$ is

    (1) $-216\tan^2\theta$
    (2) $-72\tan^2\theta$
    (3) $72\tan^2\theta$
    (4) $216\tan^2\theta$

16 The fifth term of $(1 + i)^7$, if $i = \sqrt{-1}$, is

    (1) -35
    (2) -21
    (3) 21
    (4) 35

17 The coefficient of the sixth term of $(4x + 3)^8$ can be found by which formula?

    (1) $_8C_6(4x)^2(3)^6$
    (2) $_8C_6(4x)^6(3)^2$
    (3) $_8C_5(4x)^5(3)^3$
    (4) $_8C_5(4x)^3(3)^5$

18 What is the numerical coefficient of the third term of the expansion $(1 - 2y)^7$?

    (1) 84
    (2) 21
    (3) -21
    (4) -84

19 $_{10}C_5(3a)^5(4)^5$ is a formula to find which term of the expansion $(3a + 4)^{10}$?

    (1) the last term
    (2) the tenth term
    (3) the middle term
    (4) the fifth term

20 What is the fourth term of $(1 - 2i)^6$ if $i = \sqrt{-1}$?

    (1) $-80i$
    (2) $80i$
    (3) $120i$
    (4) $160i$

16.6 Binomial Probability

If a fair coin is tossed 4 times, what is the probability of obtaining exactly 3 heads? We can list all the possibilities of our coin toss.

T T T T	T T H H	H H H H	H H T T
T T T H	T H H T	H H H T	H T T H
T T H T	T H T H	H H T H	H T H T
T H T T	T H H H	H T H H	H T T T

By looking at the list above, we obtain the following information:

- The probability of getting 0 heads $= \dfrac{1}{16}$.

  (T T T T)

- The probability of getting exactly 1 head $= \dfrac{4}{16}$ or $\dfrac{1}{4}$.

  (T T T H), (T T H T), (T H T T), (H T T T)

- The probability of getting exactly 2 heads $= \dfrac{6}{16}$ or $\dfrac{3}{8}$.

  (T T H H), (T H H T), (T H T H), (H H T T), (H T T H), (H T H T)

- The probability of getting exactly 3 heads $= \dfrac{4}{16}$ or $\dfrac{1}{4}$.

  (T H H H), (H H HT), (H H T H), (H T H H)

- The probability of getting 4 heads $= \dfrac{1}{16}$.

  (H H H H)

Thus, the probability of getting exactly 3 heads is $\dfrac{4}{16} = \dfrac{1}{4}$.

It seems unreasonable to always create a list of every possibility to determine the probability of our success. In creating our list, we took the two possible outcomes, tails and heads, and listed all of the possibilities for $(T + H)$ for 4 tosses of the coin: $(T + H)^4$.

If we expand $(T + H)^4$, we get $_4C_0T^4H^0 + _4C_1T^3H^1 + _4C_2T^2H^2 + _4C_3T^1H^3 + _4C_4T^0H^4$. After evaluating the combinations, we get $T^4 + 4T^3H + 6T^2H^2 + 4TH^3 + H^4$.

To obtain the probability of getting exactly 3 heads, we look for 3 heads in our list of possibilities, that is, $4TH^3$. Since the probability of obtaining a tail on any one toss of a fair coin is $\dfrac{1}{2}$ and the probability of obtaining a head on any one toss of a fair coin is $\dfrac{1}{2}$, the final step is to substitute that information in the term $4TH^3$.

$$4TH^3 = 4\left(\frac{1}{2}\right)\left(\frac{1}{2}\right)^3 = \frac{4}{16} = \frac{1}{4}$$

This is the same answer we obtained by listing all of the possibilities.

Suppose we were on a ski vacation and heard that there was a 25% chance of snow for each of the next 3 days. What is the probability of it snowing on exactly 2 of those 3 days? Again, there are two possibilities: either it snows or it does not snow. Let F represent failure of snow and S represent success of snow.

$$(F + S)^3 = {_3C_0}F^3S^0 + {_3C_1}F^2S^1 + {_3C_2}F^1S^2 + {_3C_3}F^0S^3$$

We want snow on 2 of those days: ${_3C_2}F^1S^2$.

The probability of snow on any one day is $25\% = \dfrac{1}{4}$, so the probability of it

not snowing on a day is $1 - \dfrac{1}{4} = \dfrac{3}{4}$. Thus, ${_3C_2}F^1S^2 = 3\left(\dfrac{3}{4}\right)\left(\dfrac{1}{4}\right)^2 = \dfrac{9}{64}$.

We do not have to write out the entire expansion each time we are interested in obtaining one piece of information. The probability of obtaining exactly r successes in n trials is:

$${_nC_r}(\text{failure})^{n-r}(\text{success})^r$$

In the given formula, "failure" and "success" are in alphabetical order. This corresponds to first term (a) and the second term (b) that we used in the binomial expansion. Instead of learning the formula in terms of "failure" and "success," you may have seen it written this way:

$${_nC_r}p^rq^{n-r}$$

This is the probability of obtaining exactly r successes in n trials when the probability of success is p and the probability of failure is q.

The two formulas are equivalent, so you may use either one of them.

📖 MODEL PROBLEMS

1   Instead of studying for his social studies quiz last night, Jared went to a rock concert. He needs to get a grade of 80 percent on the quiz to pass for the quarter, but he has no knowledge of the material that is on the quiz. If there are 5 questions on the quiz, and 5 answer choices for each question, what is the probability that Jason can completely guess on each question and get the 80 percent?

SOLUTION

To get an 80 percent on the quiz, Jared needs to get 4 of the 5 questions correct. Since there are 5 choices for each question, the probability of guessing correctly on any one question is $\dfrac{1}{5}$. The probability of

not guessing correctly is $\dfrac{4}{5}$. Use the formula for a binominal probability.

$$_{n\ \text{trials}}C_{r\ \text{successes}}(\text{failure})^{n-r}(\text{success})^r = {_5C_4}\left(\dfrac{4}{5}\right)^1\left(\dfrac{1}{5}\right)^4$$

$$= 5\left(\dfrac{4}{5}\right)^1\left(\dfrac{1}{5}\right)^4$$

$$= \dfrac{4}{625} = .0064$$

> Note: We write probability decimals without the leading zero.

Answer: The probability of scoring 80% by guessing is $\dfrac{4}{625}$ or .0064.

2 Marissa and Tyrone are playing a game of Yahtzee. To win the game, Marissa must get exactly 4 ones on the 5 dice that are thrown. What is the probability of Marissa winning the game?

SOLUTION

The probability of rolling a one on any die is $\frac{1}{6}$. So, the probability of not rolling a one on a die is $\frac{5}{6}$.

$$_nC_r(\text{failure})^{n-r}(\text{success})^r = {_5}C_4\left(\frac{5}{6}\right)^1\left(\frac{1}{6}\right)^4$$

$$= 5\left(\frac{5}{6}\right)^1\left(\frac{1}{6}\right)^4$$

$$= \frac{25}{7{,}776} \approx .0032150206$$

Answer: Marissa's chance of winning is $\frac{25}{7{,}776}$ or .003 to the nearest thousandth.

 **Practice**

1 A fair coin is tossed 3 times. Find the probability of getting

  a exactly 2 heads
  b exactly 3 heads
  c exactly 1 tail

2 Slugger McGraw has a .300 batting average. This means that Slugger hits 3 out of every 10 times at bat. What is the probability that Slugger will

  a get exactly 2 hits in his next 3 times at bat?
  b get exactly 4 hits in his next 5 times at bat?
  c get exactly 6 hits in his next 10 times at bat?
  d not get a single hit in his next 4 times at bat?

3 A fair die is rolled 4 times. What is the probability of getting

  a exactly 2 sixes?
  b exactly 3 threes?
  c exactly 1 two?
  d all fives?
  e no fives?

4 The spinner below is divided into 8 equal sectors. Find each probability.

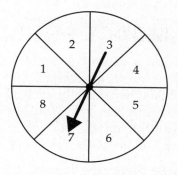

  a $P(4)$
  b $P(\text{even number})$
  c $P(\text{prime number})$
  d exactly 2 fours in 3 spins
  e exactly 3 even numbers in 5 spins
  f all prime numbers in 4 spins

5 A spinner is modeled from circle O shown below. $\overline{AD}$ is a diameter of circle O, $\overline{EO} \perp \overline{AD}$, $\overline{OF}$ bisects $\angle EOA$, and $\angle AOB \cong \angle BOC \cong \angle COD$.

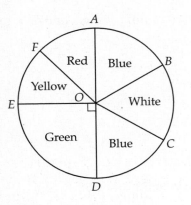

Find each probability.

a $P(red)$
b $P(white)$
c $P(blue)$
d $P(yellow)$
e $P(green)$
f exactly 2 reds in 3 spins
g exactly 1 blue in 3 spins
h exactly 4 greens in 5 spins
i exactly 2 whites in 4 spins
j all yellows in 4 spins

6 Which has a greater probability, answering 4 out of 5 questions correctly on a multiple-choice test where each question has 4 choices or answering 3 out of 5 questions correctly on a multiple-choice test where each question has 5 choices? Explain your answer.

Exercises 7–20: Select the numeral preceding the choice that best answers the question.

7 A fair die is rolled 3 times. What is the probability of getting no twos?

(1) $\dfrac{1}{216}$

(2) $\dfrac{1}{6}$

(3) $\dfrac{125}{216}$

(4) $\dfrac{5}{6}$

8 Marcus has a special weighted penny that he uses in his magic show. The probability of getting heads on this penny is $\dfrac{2}{3}$. What is the probability of getting exactly 2 heads on 3 tosses of this penny?

(1) $\dfrac{4}{27}$

(2) $\dfrac{4}{9}$

(3) $\dfrac{5}{8}$

(4) $\dfrac{3}{4}$

9 In a family of 4 children, what is the probability that *exactly* 2 of them are girls? (Assume that $P(boy) = P(girl)$.)

(1) $\dfrac{1}{8}$

(2) $\dfrac{1}{4}$

(3) $\dfrac{3}{8}$

(4) $\dfrac{1}{2}$

10 At the Bright Lites Manufacturing Company, the probability of a lightbulb being defective is 0.1%. In a sample of 10 lightbulbs, what is the probability of finding exactly one defective lightbulb?

(1) $_{10}C_9(.99)(.01)^9$
(2) $_{10}C_1(.99)^9(.01)$
(3) $_{10}C_1(.999)^9(.001)$
(4) $_{10}C_1(.9999)^9(.0001)$

11 In a true-false test of 10 questions, what is the probability of getting exactly 9 of them correct if you answer by guessing?

(1) $\left(\dfrac{1}{2}\right)^{10}$

(2) $\left(\dfrac{1}{2}\right)^{9}$

(3) $10\left(\dfrac{1}{2}\right)^{10}$

(4) $10\left(\dfrac{1}{2}\right)^{9}$

12 Edgar is a very consistent basketball player. When he shoots a foul shot, he is successful 2 out of 3 times. If he shoots 5 foul shots, what is the probability that he will make all 5 shots?

(1) $\dfrac{1}{243}$

(2) $\dfrac{32}{243}$

(3) $\dfrac{64}{243}$

(4) $\dfrac{128}{243}$

13 The figures below are drawn one to a card. Each of three students picks a card at random and replaces it before the next pick.

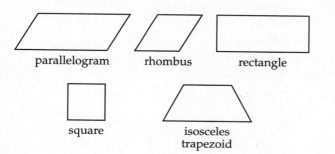

parallelogram   rhombus   rectangle

square   isosceles trapezoid

What is the probability that they all picked a card with a picture of a figure that is *not* a parallelogram?

(1) $\dfrac{1}{125}$ (3) $\dfrac{64}{125}$

(2) $\dfrac{1}{25}$ (4) $\dfrac{4}{5}$

14 In a car manufacturing plant, 2 out of every 10 cars manufactured are red. If 20 cars are randomly selected from the plant's production run, what is the probability that exactly 3 of them are red?

(1) $_{20}C_{17}\left(\dfrac{4}{5}\right)^3\left(\dfrac{1}{5}\right)^{17}$

(2) $_{20}C_{17}\left(\dfrac{3}{5}\right)^{17}\left(\dfrac{2}{5}\right)^3$

(3) $_{20}C_3\left(\dfrac{4}{5}\right)^3\left(\dfrac{1}{5}\right)^{17}$

(4) $_{20}C_3\left(\dfrac{4}{5}\right)^{17}\left(\dfrac{1}{5}\right)^3$

15 The four faces of a fair tetrahedron die are numbered 1, 2, 3, and 4. If the die is tossed 3 times, what is the probability of obtaining 2 twice?

(1) $\dfrac{9}{256}$

(2) $\dfrac{3}{64}$

(3) $\dfrac{27}{256}$

(4) $\dfrac{9}{64}$

16 A spinner is divided into five equal regions, numbered 1, 2, 3, 4, and 5. If the spinner is spun four times, what is the probability of obtaining exactly two odd numbers?

(1) $\dfrac{96}{625}$

(2) $\dfrac{144}{625}$

(3) $\dfrac{216}{625}$

(4) $\dfrac{432}{625}$

17 Each letter of the word ALGEBRA is written on a card and placed in a container. Then 3 letters are chosen at random. What is the probability that exactly 2 vowels are chosen?

(1) $\dfrac{27}{343}$

(2) $\dfrac{64}{343}$

(3) $\dfrac{108}{343}$

(4) $\dfrac{208}{343}$

18 Gordon tosses a fair die six times. Which of the following represents the probability that he will toss exactly two 5s?

(1) $_6C_5\left(\dfrac{5}{6}\right)^2\left(\dfrac{1}{6}\right)^4$

(2) $_6C_2\left(\dfrac{5}{6}\right)^2\left(\dfrac{1}{6}\right)^4$

(3) $_6C_2\left(\dfrac{1}{6}\right)^2\left(\dfrac{5}{6}\right)^4$

(4) $_6C_5\left(\dfrac{1}{6}\right)^5\left(\dfrac{5}{6}\right)^1$

19 The Sweet Dreams Candy Company is putting a coupon redeemable for a free box of candy in 1 out of every 100 boxes of candy. Which of the following represents the probability that Abby receives exactly 1 coupon if she buys 5 boxes of candy?

(1) $_5C_1(.99)^4(.01)^1$
(2) $_5C_1(.99)^5(.01)^1$
(3) $_{100}C_5(.99)^{95}(.01)^5$
(4) $_5C_1(.99)^1(.01)^4$

20 In a basketball game, the probability of the Eagles beating the Bears is $\frac{3}{5}$. The teams compete 4 times a season and each game has a winner. What is the probability that the Bears win all 4 contests?

(1) $\dfrac{16}{625}$ (3) $\dfrac{96}{625}$

(2) $\dfrac{81}{625}$ (4) $\dfrac{216}{625}$

16.7 At Least or at Most *r* Successes in *n* Trials

If a friend told you he could get *at least* two tickets for an upcoming concert you're eager to see and he gets only one ticket, you'd be really annoyed. *At least r* means the minimum number of successes is r. Other acceptable r values would be $r + 1$, $r + 2$, $r + 3$, and so on. In the case of your friend with the tickets, it would not have mattered to you if he had gotten 2, 3, 4, or 20 tickets as long as he had one for you. The probability of **at least *r* successes in *n* trials** is defined as:

$$P(\text{at least } r) = P(r) + P(r + 1) + P(r + 2) + P(r +) + \cdots + P(n) \text{ successes}$$

MODEL PROBLEM

1 Jack is tossing a fair penny and casually says he knows he can get at least 2 heads in 3 tosses. What is the probability of this happening?

SOLUTION

The probability of at least 2 successes out of 3 trials must include the probability of exactly 2 heads plus the probability of exactly 3 heads. Since Jack is using a fair penny, the probability of success and failure both equal $\frac{1}{2}$.

$$P(2 \text{ out of } 3 \text{ heads}) = {}_3C_2\left(\frac{1}{2}\right)^1\left(\frac{1}{2}\right)^2 + {}_3C_3\left(\frac{1}{2}\right)^0\left(\frac{1}{2}\right)^3$$

$$= 3\left(\frac{1}{2}\right)\left(\frac{1}{4}\right) + 1(1)\left(\frac{1}{8}\right)$$

$$= \frac{1}{2}$$

The probability of exactly two heads in three tosses is $\frac{3}{8}$ while the probability of all heads is $\frac{1}{8}$, so their sum is $\frac{4}{8}$ or $\frac{1}{2}$. Jack has an equal chance of winning as losing.

Answer: $\dfrac{1}{2}$

The expressions *at most r out of n* or *no more than r* provide the maximum allowed value and work downward from that point. That is, r is the maximum number permitted. If you receive a parking ticket and the back of the ticket says the fine will be at most $15 and you receive a bill for $35, you have a right to protest. We define the probability of **at most r successes out of n trials** as:

$$P(\text{at most } r) = P(r) + P(r-1) + P(r-2) + P(r-3) + \cdots + P(0) \text{ successes}$$

MODEL PROBLEM

2 The spinner shown to the right is divided into three equal areas. What is the probability that the spinner will land on a vowel at most twice in three spins?

SOLUTION

Since there is only one vowel among the three lettered areas, the probability of landing on a vowel is $\frac{1}{3}$ while the probability of *not* landing on a vowel is $\frac{2}{3}$. The probability of landing on a vowel at most two times is the sum of the probabilities of exactly 2 times, exactly 1 time, and exactly 0 times in three spins.

$P(\text{at most 2 vowels}) = P(2 \text{ vowels}) + P(1 \text{ vowel}) + P(0 \text{ vowels})$

$$= {}_3C_2\left(\frac{2}{3}\right)^1\left(\frac{1}{3}\right)^2 + {}_3C_1\left(\frac{2}{3}\right)^2\left(\frac{1}{3}\right)^1 + {}_3C_0\left(\frac{2}{3}\right)^3\left(\frac{1}{3}\right)^0$$

$$= 3\left(\frac{2}{3}\right)\left(\frac{1}{9}\right) + 3\left(\frac{4}{9}\right)\left(\frac{1}{3}\right) + 1\left(\frac{8}{27}\right)(1)$$

$$= \frac{26}{27}$$

This problem can also be done indirectly by figuring out the probability that the event *does not occur* and subtracting from 1. There is only one way to fail to get at most 2 vowels in 3 spins, which is to get 3 vowels in 3 spins.

$P(\text{at most 2 vowels}) = 1 - P(3 \text{ vowels})$

$$= 1 - {}_3C_3\left(\frac{2}{3}\right)^0\left(\frac{1}{3}\right)^3$$

$$= 1 - 1(1)\left(\frac{1}{27}\right)$$

$$= \frac{26}{27}$$

Answer: $\frac{26}{27}$

Exercises 1–5: A fair die is tossed 4 times. Find the probability of rolling

1 at least two 5s

2 at most three even numbers

3 no more than one odd number

4 at least one prime number

5 at most one number greater than 4

Exercises 6–14: Write the numeral preceding the choice that best answers the question.

6 If the probability of the Devils winning the game against the Angels is $2x$, what is the probability of the Angels winning?

(1) $-2x$
(2) $1 - 2x$
(3) $(2x)^2$
(4) $\dfrac{1}{2x}$

7 Dan has a biased coin for which the probability of tossing a head is $\dfrac{5}{8}$. What is the probability that Dan will get at least 4 heads in 5 tosses?

(1) 1
(2) $\dfrac{5}{8}$
(3) $\dfrac{3,125}{8,192}$
(4) $\dfrac{9,375}{32,768}$

8 Portia's Pinkettes, a dart team, and their opponent, Shaylala's Sisters, have tied the game for the championship. The probability that Portia will hit the bull's-eye is $\dfrac{5}{7}$. What is the probability she can do so at least 3 out of 5 times to win the trophy for the Pinkettes?

(1) $\dfrac{3,125}{16,807}$
(2) $\dfrac{1,625}{2,401}$
(3) $\dfrac{5}{7}$
(4) $\dfrac{14,375}{16,807}$

9 In the game of Monopoly, a player who rolls more than 2 consecutive sets of doubles goes to jail. What is the probability Eva will stay out of jail by rolling no more than 2 sets of doubles on 3 rolls? (*Hint:* First determine the probability of rolling a double.)

(1) $\dfrac{5}{216}$
(2) $\dfrac{1}{6}$
(3) $\dfrac{1}{3}$
(4) $\dfrac{215}{216}$

10 On Saturday mornings, Mrs. Elliott's children spin the chore wheel to determine their tasks for the week.

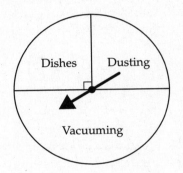

Assuming John always spins first, what is the probability that during a month with 4 Saturdays, John has to vacuum at least 3 times?

(1) $\dfrac{1}{4}$
(2) $\dfrac{5}{16}$
(3) $\dfrac{3}{8}$
(4) $\dfrac{1}{2}$

11 If a letter is selected at random from the word STATISTICS in three separate trials, what is the probability an S will be selected at most twice?

(1) .216
(2) .30
(3) .672
(4) .973

12 A standardized test has multiple-choice questions, each with 5 possible choices. Marc is tired of answering questions and decides to randomly guess on a reading comprehension section without reading the passage or the questions. Approximately what is the probability he will get no more than 3 of the 8 questions on this section correct?

    (1) .94
    (2) .85
    (3) .50
    (4) .20

13 Gary Yansick's career batting average is .293. In a game where he comes to bat 5 times, approximately what is the probability that he gets at least 2 hits?

    (1) .293
    (2) .376
    (3) .457
    (4) .570

14 Danny assembles the following jigsaw puzzle while blindfolded. All of the lettered triangular pieces are the same size and fit into each location.

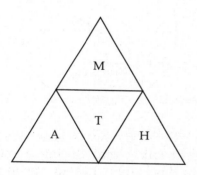

If Danny assembles the puzzle 4 times, what is the probability that a vowel piece will be in the top position no more than once?

    (1) $\dfrac{81}{256}$

    (2) $\dfrac{93}{256}$

    (3) $\dfrac{189}{256}$

    (4) $\dfrac{201}{256}$

15 Mr. Bernardo decides to give his first-period class a multiple-choice quiz with 4 choices per question and his fifth-period class a true-false quiz. Each quiz has 5 questions. The grades of the students in the fifth-period class are significantly higher than the grades of the students in the first-period class. Using probability, explain why this does not necessarily mean that the fifth-period students knew the material better than the students in the first-period class.

16 Snow Angel Ski Resort promises that the probability of snow, man-made or natural, on each day in February is $\dfrac{2}{3}$. In fact, their brochure says, "If it doesn't snow at least 2 days out of the 3 days you are here, we will refund half the cost of your stay." If reservations increase from 120 to 135 for the month of February, is this a wise marketing strategy or will the resort lose money? Explain your answer.

17 A spinner is made from circle O with diameter $\overline{AOB}$ and radii $\overline{OC}$ and $\overline{OD}$, $m\angle AOC = 60$ and $m\angle BOD = 45$.

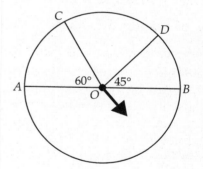

Find the probability that a spinner lands in

  a region AOC at least twice in 3 spins
  b region BOD no more than once in 4 spins
  c the lower semicircle at least twice in 5 spins

18 Ms. Weikman's badminton team is going to play Mr. DeStefano's team for the school intramural championship. The probability that Ms. Weikman's team will win a game is $\dfrac{2}{3}$.

In a three-game series, find the probability that

  a Ms. Weikman's team wins at least 2 games
  b Mr. DeStefano's team does *not* lose all 3 games

19 A children's game Hugs & Kisses is played on a regular hexagonal board like the one shown below.

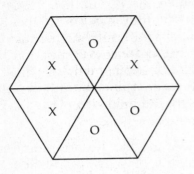

Katie and Mavis take turns tossing X or O markers over their shoulders onto the board. Whoever gets three markers on her letter first wins. Assuming that all of the markers hit the board, what is the probability that

a Katie can score at least three Xs in four tosses of her X markers?

b Mavis scores no more than one O in 3 tosses of her O markers?

20 Mark is starting his college search. He has chosen 8 schools that he would like to visit. His parents have said they will visit 5 of the farthest schools over the summer and then take weekend trips to visit the closest schools.

a Disregarding location, in how many ways can Mark choose 5 out of 8 schools to visit during the summer?

b In how many different orders can Mark and his parents visit those schools?

c If only one of the schools offers competitive diving, and Mark wants to see that school first, in how many ways can the family see the 5 schools over the summer?

16.8 Normal Approximation to the Binomial Distribution

When n is large or there are a great many cases of success to be found, binomial probabilities can be quite tedious to calculate. However, when n is large, the binomial distribution resembles a normal distribution. Even if success p and failure q are not quite equal and the binomial distribution is not symmetrical, as n increases, the binomial distribution changes to look more and more like the normal distribution. The figure below shows the shape of a binomial distribution with $n = 20$, $p = \frac{1}{4}$, and $q = \frac{3}{4}$ with a bell curve drawn in.

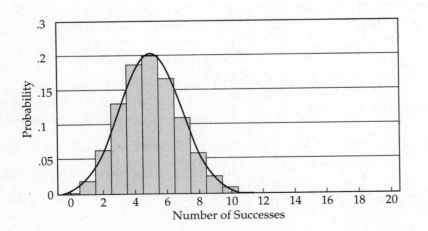

On a normal curve, we can determine what percent of the data lie within a specific standard deviation from the mean. This makes it possible to calculate probabilities. If we find the **normal approximation to the binomial distribution**, we can estimate the probabilities easier than with the binomial theorem.

Binomial probabilities are calculated only for integral values of n. (We would never look for the probability of a coin landing on heads 3.5 out of 5 tosses.) The normal distribution is continuous with probabilities corresponding to areas over intervals. The problem below shows the method for approximating a binomial distribution with a normal distribution. To apply this method, we first find the mean and standard deviation of the normal approximation using the following formulas:

$$\text{mean} = np \qquad \text{standard deviation} = \sqrt{np(1 - p)}$$

where n is the number of trials of the binomial distribution and p is the probability of success. (Since $1 - p$ is the probability of failure, or q, the standard deviation can be expressed as $\sqrt{npq}$.)

Then we adjust the endpoints of the interval by 0.5 and use the normalcdf(command on the calculator to find the probability of the adjusted interval. The following model problem will illustrate this procedure.

The normal distribution is considered a good approximation to the binomial when $np \geq 10$ and $n(1 - p) \geq 10$.

📓 MODEL PROBLEM

A department store has determined that the probability of a customer making a purchase is approximately .6. Find the probability, to the nearest thousandth, that at least 70 of the next 100 customers will make a purchase.

SOLUTION

The mean is $np = (100)(.6) = 60$ and the standard deviation is:

$$\sqrt{np(1 - p)} = \sqrt{(100)(.6)(.4)} = \sqrt{24} \approx 4.899$$

The normal distribution with a mean of 60 and a standard deviation of 4.899 is considered to be a good approximation to the binomial distribution.

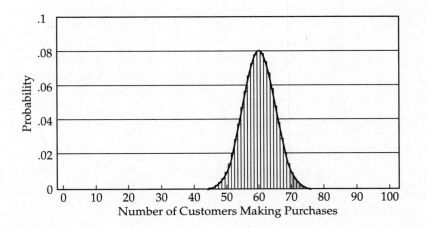

The probability of at least 70 out of 100 customers making a purchase is approximately equal to the area under this normal curve from 69.5 (the boundary value between 69 and 70) and 100.5 (the boundary value for the largest value).

The desired probability can be found using the normalcdf(command on the calculator. Press (2nd) (VARS) to access the DISTR (Distribution) menu, and select option 2. This pastes the normalcdf(command onto the home screen. You must then enter the lower and upper limits, the mean, and the standard deviation with commas between them. Press (ENTER).

```
normalcdf(69.5,1
00.5,60,√(24))
            .0262396804
```

Answer: The probability that at least 70 customers out of 100 will make a purchase is about .026.

Practice

Exercises 1–5: Use the normal approximation to estimate each probability. Round your answer to the *nearest thousandth*.

1 P(exactly 36 successes); $p = .8$, $n = 50$

2 P(at least 60 successes); $p = \dfrac{1}{2}$, $n = 100$

3 P(at least 55 successes); $p = .75$, $n = 80$

4 P(no more than 50 success); $p = \dfrac{3}{5}$, $n = 100$

5 P(between 10 and 20 successes); $p = .3$, $n = 40$

6 A weighted coin has a probability of .4 of landing on tails.

a Use the binomial theorem to calculate the probability that the coin will land on tails on exactly 3 of the next 10 tosses.

b Use the normal approximation to calculate the probability that the coin will land on tails on exactly 3 of the next 10 tosses.

c Compare your results from above.

d Use the normal approximation to calculate the probability that the coin will land on tails at least 25 times in the next 60 tosses.

→ FYI

The graphing calculator can help you determine the probabilities of binomial experiments. For a single probability (exactly r successes in n trials), we use the binomial probability distribution function command. Press (2nd) (VARS) to access the DIST (Distribution) menu. Scroll down to the binompdf(command and press (ENTER). This pastes the command on the home screen. You must now enter three pieces of information: n, the number of trials; p, the probability of success; r, the number of desired successes. For example, when you enter binompdf(4, .25, 3), as shown below, you are asking for the probability of exactly 3 successes out of 4 trials in a situation in which the probability of success is .25 or $\dfrac{1}{4}$.

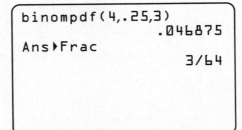

```
binompdf(4,.25,3)
            .046875
Ans▶Frac
            3/64
```

The calculator gives you the probability of .046875 or $\frac{3}{64}$.

If you omit the third parameter, the calculator will give all probabilities from 0 successes to 4 successes in 4 trials. The probabilities are listed horizontally, as shown below. You must use the right arrow to see them all.

```
binompdf(4,.25)
{.31640625 .421...
```

For your convenience, those probabilities are printed below in a table as decimals and fractions.

Number of Successes	Probability as a Decimal	Probability as a Fraction
0	.31640625	$\frac{81}{256}$
1	.421875	$\frac{108}{256} = \frac{27}{64}$
2	.2109375	$\frac{54}{256} = \frac{27}{128}$
3	.046875	$\frac{12}{256} = \frac{3}{64}$
4	.00390625	$\frac{1}{256}$

If we want to find the probability of at most 3 out of 4 successes in a situation where the success is .25 or $\frac{1}{4}$, we could add those values shown above, or we can use the binomcdf(command for binomial cumulative distributive frequency. This is found on the Distribution menu just below binompdf(. Again, there are three inputs after the command: n, p, and r.

```
binomcdf(4,.25,3)
              .99609375
Ans▶Frac
              255/256
```

The probability of at most 3 out of 4 successes is .99609375 or $\frac{255}{256}$.

Practice

Find the probability of obtaining

a 3 successes in 5 trials if the probability of success is $\frac{2}{3}$

b 2 successes in 3 trials if the probability of success is $\frac{3}{4}$

c 1 success in 4 trials if the probability of success is .45

d at most 4 successes in 5 trials if the probability of success is .2

e at least 3 successes in 5 trials if the probability of success is .2

CHAPTER REVIEW

Exercises 1–23: Write the numeral preceding the choice that best completes the statement or answers the question.

1 Marta is going to plant tulip bulbs around her patio. She has 6 varieties. In how many different arrangements can she plant 6 different types of tulips?

(1) 36
(2) 120
(3) 240
(4) 720

2 Hank and Marlee are going to dinner at the local Italian restaurant. Their meal includes soup, pasta, entrée, and dessert. If there are 6 soups, 5 pastas, 8 entrées, and 4 desserts to choose from, how many different complete meals could they order?

(1) 23
(2) 24
(3) 960
(4) 1,001

3 What is the third term in the expansion $(x + 2y)^4$?

(1) $6x^2y^2$
(2) $4x^2y^2$
(3) $12x^2y^2$
(4) $24x^2y^2$

4 If a fair coin is tossed 3 times, what is the probability of getting at least 2 heads?

(1) $\dfrac{1}{2}$

(2) $\dfrac{3}{8}$

(3) $\dfrac{1}{4}$

(4) $\dfrac{1}{8}$

5 The weather forecaster has predicted that there is a 25 percent probability of rain on any of the next 4 days. What is the probability that it will rain at least twice?

(1) $\dfrac{66}{256}$

(2) $\dfrac{67}{256}$

(3) $\dfrac{68}{256}$

(4) $\dfrac{175}{256}$

6 Freida's Fruit Shop prepares fruit baskets that contain green vegetable leaves and 6 pieces of fruit. If the shop stocks 8 kinds of fruit, how many different selections can be made for a fruit basket?

(1) 28
(2) 48
(3) 56
(4) 120

7 If the probability that an event will occur is $\dfrac{1}{2x + 1}$, then the probability that the event will *not* occur is

(1) $\dfrac{2x + 2}{2x + 1}$

(2) $\dfrac{2x}{2x + 1}$

(3) $\dfrac{1}{2x + 1}$

(4) $-\dfrac{1}{2x + 1}$

8 What is the fourth term in the expansion $(a + bi)^6$?

(1) $15a^2b^2$
(2) $20a^3b^3$
(3) $20a^3b^3i$
(4) $-20a^3b^3i$

9 Twelve divers have qualified for the Empire State Games. In how many ways can first, second, and third place be awarded?

(1) 12
(2) 220
(3) 1,001
(4) 1,320

10 Nicole is taking a 5-question multiple-choice test. If she guesses every answer, and each question has 4 choices, what is the probability that she gets at most one wrong answer?

(1) .85234
(2) .694528
(3) .6328125
(4) .015625

11 What is the last term in the expansion $(\sin \theta + \cos \theta)^3$?

(1) 1
(2) $\cos^3 \theta$
(3) $\sin^3 \theta$
(4) $\sin^3 \theta + \cos^3 \theta$

12 A spinner is divided into five equal sectors labeled 1 through 5. What is the probability of getting at most two prime numbers in three spins?

(1) $\dfrac{98}{125}$

(2) $\dfrac{64}{125}$

(3) $\dfrac{61}{625}$

(4) $\dfrac{27}{625}$

13 How many four-digit even numbers can be formed from the digits {2, 4, 6, 7, 9} if no digit is used more than once?

(1) 24
(2) 72
(3) 120
(4) 720

14 What is the numerical coefficient of the fourth term in the expansion $(2x - y)^5$?

(1) -40
(2) -20
(3) -10
(4) 40

15 A coin is biased so that the probability of obtaining heads is $\dfrac{3}{5}$. What is the probability of obtaining at least three heads in four tosses of the coin?

(1) $\dfrac{81}{625}$

(2) $\dfrac{135}{625}$

(3) $\dfrac{216}{625}$

(4) $\dfrac{297}{625}$

16 What is the middle term in the expansion $(a - 3b)^4$?

(1) $-54a^2b^2$
(2) $-6a^2b^2$
(3) $6a^2b^2$
(4) $54a^2b^2$

17 The probability of the Mets winning a game against the Diamondbacks is $\dfrac{3}{4}$. If they are playing a three-game series this weekend, what is the probability that the Mets will win at least 2 out of 3 games?

(1) $\dfrac{9}{64}$

(2) $\dfrac{27}{64}$

(3) $\dfrac{27}{32}$

(4) $\dfrac{63}{64}$

18 If one letter is selected at random from the word PARALLEL and then replaced in four random trials, what is the probability that no more than one L is chosen?

(1) $\dfrac{1,695}{4,096}$

(2) $\dfrac{1}{2}$

(3) $\dfrac{2,125}{4,096}$

(4) $\dfrac{5}{6}$

19 The expansion $(3 - 2i)^6$ equals

(1) $729 - 64i$
(2) $729 + 64i$
(3) $-2,035 + 828i$
(4) $2,035 - 828i$

20 The president's press conference is being shown nationally on channels 2, 4, 7, and 8. Of the six television sets randomly tuned in to this news program at Ella's Electronic Expo, what is the probability that at least half are tuned to channel 8?

(1) $\dfrac{81}{1,024}$

(2) $\dfrac{347}{2,048}$

(3) $\dfrac{1}{2}$

(4) $\dfrac{1,701}{2,048}$

21 A survey of coffee drinkers found that given a choice, 5 out of 7 coffee drinkers prefer regular coffee to decaffeinated coffee. What is the probability that of the next 5 coffee drinkers who enter the Coffee Bean, none of them will want decaf?

(1) $\dfrac{3,125}{16,807}$

(2) $\dfrac{6,250}{16,807}$

(3) $\dfrac{13,682}{16,807}$

(4) $\dfrac{15,625}{16,807}$

22 A traffic light on Hempstead Turnpike is green for 40 seconds, yellow for 5 seconds, and red for 15 seconds out of every minute. What is the probability that at least four of the next 5 cars get a green light?

(1) $\dfrac{32}{243}$

(2) $\dfrac{80}{243}$

(3) $\dfrac{112}{243}$

(4) $\dfrac{67}{81}$

23 Arati and Linda are planning a surprise party for their boss. They have 8 different colors of balloons and 4 different colors of crepe paper streamers to use for decorating. If they use only 3 colors of balloons and 2 colors of crepe paper streamers, how many different decorating schemes are possible?

(1) 112
(2) 120
(3) 336
(4) 672

24 The Boy Scouts and Girl Scouts are sponsoring a Youth Volunteer Festival, but they need a committee to organize the program. If there are 8 Boy Scout leaders and 11 Girl Scout leaders to choose from, show the formulas needed to solve each of the following questions. (Do *not* solve.)

a How many committees of 5 can be formed from the scout leaders?

b How many committees of 5 can be formed of 2 Boy Scout leaders and 3 Girl Scout leaders?

c What is the probability that a committee of 5 chosen at random consists of 2 Boy Scout leaders and 3 Girl Scout leaders?

d What is the probability that a randomly chosen committee of 5 consists of 2 Boy Scout leaders and 3 Girl Scout leaders, one of which is Mary.

25 Write the binomial expansion for $(a - 2b)^3$.

26 Rosa has a reputation for being late. Her family has decided that there is a 90% probability of Rosa being late for any 1 event. If there are 4 family events coming up, what is the probability that

a Rosa is late for all 4 of them?
b Rosa is on time for all 4 of them?
c Rosa is late for at most one of them?
d Rosa is late for at least one of them?

27 What is the sum of the coefficients for the expansion of $(x + y)^4$?

28 The figure below shows a spinner in the shape of regular pentagon divided into 5 equal sections.

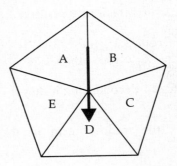

Find

a $P(B)$
b $P(\text{vowel})$
c the probability of obtaining exactly two Bs on three spins
d the probability of obtaining at least one vowel on three spins

29 Mrs. Superteacher has 15 students in her math class. Each time a student does something special, she writes the student's name on a piece of paper and puts it in a container. At the end of the week, she randomly selects the name of one or more students to receive a "no homework night." If more than one selection is to be made, Mrs. Superteacher replaces the slip in the box before picking an additional slip. Jason has 4 slips in the box; Mandy and Mya each have 3 slips; Frank, Juanita, Kaitlyn, and Steve each have 2 slips; and all the other students have one slip each. What is the probability of

a a student with 1 slip being selected if only 1 selection is made?

b Juanita or Kaitlyn being selected if only 1 selection is made?

Set up, but do not calculate, the probability of each of the following situations:

c Mya being selected exactly twice if 3 selections are made

d Jason being selected at least once if 3 selections are made

e Steve being selected at least twice if 3 selections are made

30 Write the binomial expansion for $(2 + i)^4$ if $i = \sqrt{-1}$.

31 A cereal company puts a secret decoder ring in 1 out of every 100 boxes of cereal they manufacture. Set up, but do not calculate, the probability of Danny and Jimmy receiving

a exactly 1 decoder ring if they buy 6 boxes of cereal

b no decoder ring if they buy 10 boxes of cereal

c at least 2 decoder rings if they buy 8 boxes of cereal

d at most 1 decoder ring if they buy 10 boxes of cereal

32 The American Red Cross collects approximately half of all blood needed in the United States. Different blood types occur in the U.S. population with varying probabilities.

a Approximately 34 percent of the population has type A^+ blood. To the *nearest thousandth*, what is the probability that of the first 5 donors, at least 2 have type A^+ blood?

b The universal donor is the person with type O blood. If 45 percent of the U.S. population has type O blood, what is the probability that exactly 4 out of 6 donors waiting to donate will have type O? Round to the *nearest thousandth*.

c Type B blood occurs in 11 percent of the population. If one of the players on the YMCA softball team of 18 players needs a transfusion of type B blood, what is the probability that none of the players on the team have type B blood to donate to him? Round to the *nearest thousandth*.

d Four-day-old Baby Jones needs a transfusion of AB^+ blood, found in only 3 percent of the population. If the blood drive collected 152 units of blood, what is the probability that at least one unit of AB^+ was collected? Round to the *nearest thousandth*.

33 At a university, the probability that an incoming freshman will graduate within four years is .553. Use the normal approximation to estimate, to the *nearest thousandth*, the probability that

a at least 50 out of a group of 100 incoming freshman will graduate in four years

b at least 60 out of a group of 100 incoming freshman will graduate in four years

c no more than 80 out of a group of 150 incoming freshman will graduate in four years

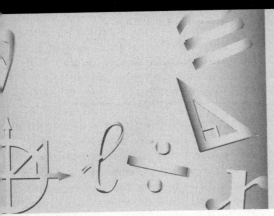

Cumulative Reviews

CUMULATIVE REVIEW
CHAPTERS 1–2

Part I

Answer all questions in this part. Each correct answer will receive 2 credits. No partial credit will be allowed.

1 Solve for x: $|10 - 2x| = 2$

(1) $\{\ \}$

(2) $\{4, 6\}$

(3) $\{6\}$

(4) $\{4\}$

2 The graph shown below is the solution to which inequality?

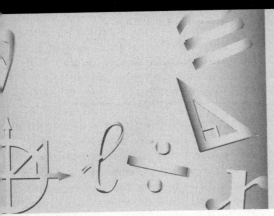

(1) $x^2 + 2x < 8$

(2) $x^2 + 2x \geq 8$

(3) $x^2 + 2x \leq 8$

(4) $x^2 + 2x > 8$

3 The solution set for the equation $\dfrac{x + 1}{x - 1} + \dfrac{1}{x - 1} = x - 2$ is

(1) $\{0\}$

(2) $\{2\}$

(3) $\{0, 4\}$

(4) $\{4\}$

4 Which of the following value(s) would make $\dfrac{2x - 8}{x^2 - 1}$ undefined?

(1) 1

(2) -1 or 1

(3) -1

(4) 1 or 4

5 Abby, Frank, and Kimberly went shopping for the class picnic. If Abby spent $2x^2 - 7x + 13$, Frank spent $x^2 + 10x - 4$, and Kimberly spent $x^3 - 8$, find the polynomial that represents the total amount of money the three spent.

(1) $x^3 + 3x^2 - 3x + 9$

(2) $x^3 + x^2 + 3x - 1$

(3) $-x^3 + 3x^2 + 3x + 5$

(4) $x^3 + 3x^2 + 3x + 1$

6 When reduced to lowest terms, $\dfrac{6x^2 - 5x - 4}{8 - 2x - 3x^2}$ is

(1) -1

(2) 2

(3) $-\dfrac{2x + 1}{2 + x}$

(4) $\dfrac{2x + 1}{2 + x}$

7 The solution set of $\dfrac{2}{2x + 1} + \dfrac{3x + 1}{x + 2} = 2$ is

(1) $\{1\}$

(2) $\left\{\dfrac{1}{2}\right\}$

(3) $\left\{\dfrac{1}{2}, 1\right\}$

(4) $\{\ \}$

8 Given isosceles triangle CTH with $\overline{CT} \cong \overline{TH}$. If the perimeter of the figure is $5a + 5b + 2c$ and the measure of $CH = a - b + 2c$, the measure of CT is

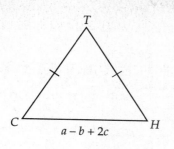

(1) $4a + 6b$ (3) $3a + 2b$

(2) $6a + 4b$ (4) $2a + 3b$

9 Which statement regarding the expression $2x^3 + 3x^2 - 8x - 12$ is true?

(1) Its factors are $2(x - 3)(x^2 + 2)$.

(2) Its factors are $(2x + 3)(x + 2)(x - 2)$.

(3) Its factors are $(2x^2 - 3)(x - 4)$.

(4) Its factors are $(2x - 3)(x + 2)(x - 2)$.

10 Expressed as a single fraction, $\dfrac{5}{x - 3} - \dfrac{1}{x}$ is equivalent to

(1) $\dfrac{6x - 3}{x^2 - 3x}$ (3) $\dfrac{4x + 3}{2x - 3}$

(2) $\dfrac{4x + 3}{x^2 - 3x}$ (4) $\dfrac{4}{x^2 - 3x}$

11 Which graph represents the solution to $2x^2 - x - 3 < 0$?

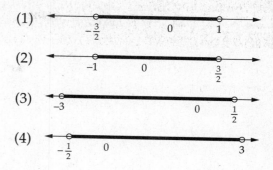

12 Noah and Alanna collected money for a homeless shelter. The total amount of money they collected can be represented by the expression $4x^2 + 11x + 5$. If Noah's collections totaled $3x^2 - 4x - 12$, how much money did Alanna collect?

(1) $7x^2 + 7x + 17$ (3) $x^2 + 15x + 17$

(2) $-x^2 - 15x - 17$ (4) $7x^2 + 15x - 17$

13 In simplest form, $\dfrac{x^2 + x - 20}{4x + 20} \div \dfrac{x^2 - 16}{2x^2 + 6x - 8}$ is equivalent to

(1) 1 (3) $\dfrac{x + 1}{2}$

(2) $\dfrac{x - 1}{2}$ (4) $x - 1$

Part II

Answer all questions in this part. Each correct answer will receive 2 credits. Clearly indicate the necessary steps, including appropriate formula substitutions, diagrams, graphs, charts, etc. For all questions in this part, a correct numerical answer with no work shown will receive only 1 credit.

14 Ilana tells Mateo that the fraction $\dfrac{2x^2 - 3x + 1}{x^2 + 3}$ is never undefined, but he does not believe her. Explain to Mateo why Ilana is correct.

15 Cody and Efrim were competing in a road rally. If $x > 2$ and Cody traveled $\dfrac{x^2 - 4}{3x - 6}$ miles in the first hour and Efrim traveled $\dfrac{2x^2 + 3x - 2}{8x - 4}$ miles, who traveled farther during the first hour? Explain your reasoning.

16 Solve for x: $\dfrac{x - 1}{x + 3} = \dfrac{x - 2}{x + 1}$

17 Find all values of x for which $x + |3 - 2x| = 4$.

Answer all questions in this part. Each correct answer will receive 4 credits. Clearly indicate the necessary steps, including appropriate formula substitutions, diagrams, graphs, charts, etc. For all questions in this part, a correct numerical answer with no work shown will receive only 1 credit.

18 Solve for x: $\frac{1}{2}x^2 - 4x + 8 = 2$

19 If the length of a rectangle is represented by $\frac{x^2 - 5x - 14}{2x^2 + 5x + 2}$ and its width is represented by $\frac{2x^2 + 9x + 4}{x^2 - 7x}$, express the area of the rectangle in simplest form.

Part IV

Answer this question. A correct answer will receive 6 credits. Clearly indicate the necessary steps, including appropriate formula substitutions, diagrams, graphs, charts, etc. A correct numerical answer with no work shown will receive only 1 credit.

20 Solve for x: $\frac{x-1}{x} - \frac{1}{x-1} = \frac{5}{x^2 - x}$

CUMULATIVE REVIEW
CHAPTERS 1–3

Part I

Answer all questions in this part. Each correct answer will receive 2 credits. No partial credit will be allowed.

1 The expression $\dfrac{1 + \sqrt{5}}{2 + \sqrt{5}}$ is equivalent to

(1) $\sqrt{5} - 3$ (3) $3 - \sqrt{5}$

(2) $\dfrac{1}{2}$ (4) $3 + \sqrt{5}$

2 Simplify: $\dfrac{\dfrac{1}{x} - \dfrac{1}{y}}{\dfrac{y}{x} - \dfrac{x}{y}}$

(1) $\dfrac{1}{x + y}$ (3) $-\dfrac{1}{x + y}$

(2) $\dfrac{1}{x - y}$ (4) $-\dfrac{1}{x - y}$

3 Solve: $|2x - 3| = 5$

(1) $\{1, 4\}$ (3) $\{-1, 4\}$

(2) $\{-1, -4\}$ (4) $\{1, -4\}$

4 Written in simplest form, the expression $\dfrac{a^3b^2 - 5}{5 - a^3b^2}$ is

(1) 1 (3) $\dfrac{a^3b^2 - 5}{5 - a^3b^2}$

(2) 0 (4) -1

5 The expression $\sqrt{48}$ can be rewritten in simplest form as $a\sqrt{b}$ where a and b are integers. Which of the following represents a?

(1) 16 (3) 3

(2) 12 (4) 4

6 The product of $\dfrac{x^2 - 3x}{x^2 - 9}$ and $\dfrac{x^3 - x^2 - 12x}{x^3 - 4x^2}$ is

(1) 1 (3) $\dfrac{x - 4}{x^2}$

(2) $\dfrac{1}{3}$ (4) $\dfrac{x^2}{(x - 3)(x - 4)}$

7 In simplest form, the expression $\sqrt{18a^8b^9}$ is equivalent to

(1) $2a^4b^3\sqrt{3}$ (3) $3b^3\sqrt{2a^8}$

(2) $3a^4b^3\sqrt{2}$ (4) $3a^4b^4\sqrt{2b}$

8 The solution set of $|x + 2| < 5$ is

(1) $-7 < x < 3$

(2) $-3 < x < 7$

(3) $x < -7$ or $x > 3$

(4) $x < -3$ or $x > 7$

9 Solve for x: $4x - \sqrt{32} = 8\sqrt{18}$

(1) $10\sqrt{5}$ (3) $7\sqrt{2}$

(2) $2\sqrt{50}$ (4) $5\sqrt{2}$

10 For what value(s) of x is the fraction $\dfrac{x^2 - 9}{x - 7}$ undefined?

(1) 9 only   (3) ± 3

(2) 7 only   (4) ± 3 and 7

11 Perform the indicated addition: $\dfrac{1}{\sqrt{5}} + \dfrac{1}{\sqrt{2}}$

(1) $\dfrac{1}{\sqrt{10}}$ (3) $\dfrac{\sqrt{5} + \sqrt{2}}{10}$

(2) $\dfrac{\sqrt{5} + \sqrt{2}}{\sqrt{10}}$ (4) $\dfrac{2\sqrt{5} + 5\sqrt{2}}{10}$

12 The solution of $x^2 < 6x$ is

(1) $0 < x < 6$ (3) $x < 0$ or $x > 6$

(2) $x < 6$ (4) $x < 0$

13 Solve for x: $\sqrt[4]{5x + 1} = 2$

(1) $\dfrac{7}{5}$ (3) 3

(2) $\dfrac{9}{5}$ (4) $\dfrac{17}{5}$

Part II

Answer all questions in this part. Each correct answer will receive 2 credits. Clearly indicate the necessary steps, including appropriate formula substitutions, diagrams, graphs, charts, etc. For all questions in this part, a correct numerical answer with no work shown will receive only 1 credit.

14 Mrs. Sheehan's math class is designing a game. They have decided to make the game board in the shape of a regular pentagon. If the length of each side is $\dfrac{x}{x+1}$, what is the perimeter of the game board?

15 Solve for y: $|y + 4| = 3y + 6$

16 Solve for the positive value of x: $\dfrac{x}{5} - \dfrac{4}{x} = \dfrac{8}{5}$

17 Solve the inequality: $2x^2 - 7x \le 15$

Part III

Answer all questions in this part. Each correct answer will receive 4 credits. Clearly indicate the necessary steps, including appropriate formula substitutions, diagrams, graphs, charts, etc. For all questions in this part, a correct numerical answer with no work shown will receive only 1 credit.

18 Solve for x: $\sqrt{x + 14} = x + 2$

19 Frank and Nora are driving from Huntington Station to Valley Cottage, a trip that takes approximately 110 minutes. Depending on traffic, their traveling time, t, could differ from the 110 minutes by less than 20 minutes.

   a Write an inequality involving absolute value that could be used to express this information.

   b Solve the inequality from part **a** to find t.

Part IV

Answer this question. A correct answer will receive 6 credits. Clearly indicate the necessary steps, including appropriate formula substitutions, diagrams, graphs, charts, etc. A correct numerical answer with no work shown will receive only 1 credit.

20 Solve for x: $\dfrac{x}{x + 3} - \dfrac{1}{x + 2} = \dfrac{x}{2x + 4}$

CUMULATIVE REVIEW
CHAPTERS 1–4

Part I

Answer all questions in this part. Each correct answer will receive 2 credits. No partial credit will be allowed.

1 When simplified, the expression $\frac{1}{2}\sqrt{80} + 2\sqrt{45} - 10\sqrt{\frac{1}{5}}$ equals

   (1) $10\sqrt{5}$ (3) $5\sqrt{6}$

   (2) $6\sqrt{5}$ (4) $\frac{\sqrt{5}}{10}$

2 Solve for x: $\sqrt{2x^2 + 1} = x + 1$

   (1) $\{0\}$ (3) $\{0, 2\}$

   (2) $\{2\}$ (4) $\{\ \}$

3 Which of the following is *not* a function?

   (1) $3x + 4y = 20$ (3) $\{(1, 1), (2, 1), (3, 1)\}$

   (2) $x^2 + 5x = y$ (4) $y^2 - 3y - 2 = x$

4 Which inequality states that the temperature of rare roast beef, t, is less than 5° from 140°?

   (1) $|5 - t| < 140$ (3) $|5 + t| < 140$

   (2) $|140 - t| < 5$ (4) $|140 + t| < 5$

5 The cost of renting a ski chalet varies inversely as the number of renters. If 6 renters pay \$350 each for the week, what would be the individual price for each of 10 renters?

   (1) \$135   (3) \$210

   (2) \$185   (4) \$350

6 The domain of $y = \dfrac{x^2 - 3x + 2}{x^2 - 9}$ is

   (1) all real numbers

   (2) ± 3

   (3) $-3 < x < 3$

   (4) all real numbers except ± 3

7 If $f(x) = 2x^2 + 6x + 1$, evaluate $f(-3)$.

   (1) 1   (3) 21

   (2) 9   (4) 37

8 The inverse of the function $f(x) = 3x^2 - 1$ is

   (1) $f^{-1}(x) = \sqrt{\dfrac{x - 1}{3}}$

   (2) $f^{-1}(x) = 1 - 3x^2$

   (3) $f^{-1}(x) = \sqrt{\dfrac{x + 1}{3}}$

   (4) $f^{-1}(x) = 3x^2 + 1$

9 The multiplicative inverse of $\dfrac{2 + \sqrt{3}}{5}$ is written as

   (1) $\dfrac{5}{2 - \sqrt{3}}$ (3) $10 + 5\sqrt{3}$

   (2) $\dfrac{2 - \sqrt{3}}{5}$ (4) $10 - 5\sqrt{3}$

10 The freshman class is selling popcorn as a fundraiser. Each can of gourmet popcorn provides a profit of $8 + x\sqrt{3}$. If the class sold $15 + 2x\sqrt{3}$ cans of popcorn, express their total profit in simplest radical form.

   (1) $120 + 31x\sqrt{3} + 6x^2$

   (2) $120 + 31x\sqrt{3} + 18x^2$

   (3) $23 + 3x\sqrt{3}$

   (4) $120 - 31x\sqrt{3} + 2x^2\sqrt{3}$

11 Factor completely: $2x^3 + 7x^2 - 2x - 7$

   (1) $(x^2 + 1)(2x - 7)$

   (2) $(x - 1)(x + 1)(2x + 7)$

   (3) $(x - 1)(2x^2 + 7)$

   (4) $(x - 1)(x + 1)(2x - 7)$

12 Solve for x: $\dfrac{x}{x + 2} = \dfrac{2x}{3x + 1}$

   (1) $\{1\}$ (3) $\{3\}$

   (2) $\{0\}$ (4) $\{0, 3\}$

13 Which of the following is a one-to-one function?

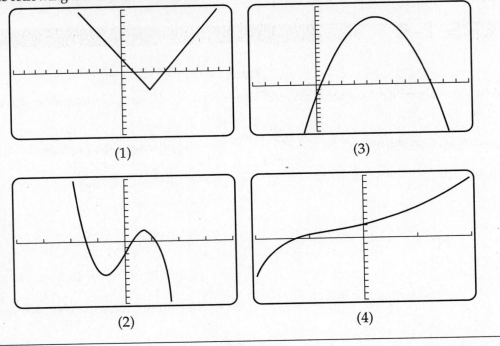

(1)

(3)

(2)

(4)

Part II

Answer all questions in this part. Each correct answer will receive 2 credits. Clearly indicate the necessary steps, including appropriate formula substitutions, diagrams, graphs, charts, etc. For all questions in this part, a correct numerical answer with no work shown will receive only 1 credit.

14 Simplify $2\sqrt{54} - \dfrac{3}{2}\sqrt{24} + \sqrt{96}$.

15 Kyle cannot remember how to rationalize the denominator of the expression $\dfrac{15}{2 - \sqrt{7}}$. In a few sentences, explain the process to be used, and demonstrate the correct answer.

16 Write the equation of a circle with a radius of 5 and a center at $(-3, 8)$.

17 Given the function $g(x) = \dfrac{5x + 12}{\sqrt{x^2 - 4}}$, determine its domain and explain why those values are the domain.

Part III

Answer all questions in this part. Each correct answer will receive 4 credits. Clearly indicate the necessary steps, including appropriate formula substitutions, diagrams, graphs, charts, etc. For all questions in this part, a correct numerical answer with no work shown will receive only 1 credit.

18 Rectangle *MATH* has a length of $\dfrac{x^2 - 16}{2x^2 + 11x + 12}$ and a width of $\dfrac{3 - 7x - 6x^2}{2 - 6x}$. Express the area of rectangle *MATH* in simplest form.

19 If $f(x) = x^2 - 2x - 11$ and $g(x) = 3x - 2$, find the rule that represents the expression $(f \circ g)(x)$.

Part IV

Answer this question. A correct answer will receive 6 credits. Clearly indicate the necessary steps, including appropriate formula substitutions, diagrams, graphs, charts, etc. A correct numerical answer with no work shown will receive only 1 credit.

20 Simplify $\dfrac{20 + 7x - 3x^2}{x^2 - 16} \div \dfrac{6x + 10}{2x^2 + 5x - 12}$.

CUMULATIVE REVIEW
CHAPTERS 1–5

Part I

Answer all questions in this part. Each correct answer will receive 2 credits. No partial credit will be allowed.

1 Which expression is equivalent to $\dfrac{\sqrt{5} + \sqrt{3}}{\sqrt{5} - \sqrt{3}}$?

   (1) $\dfrac{8}{5}$ (3) $4 + \sqrt{15}$

   (2) -1 (4) $\dfrac{10\sqrt{15}}{2}$

2 The value of $(2 + 3i)^2$ is

   (1) -5 (3) $-5 + 12i$

   (2) $-5 + 6i$ (4) 5

3 What is the product of the roots of the equation $x^2 - 3x + 7 = 0$?

   (1) -7 (3) 3

   (2) -3 (4) 7

4 If $f(x) = x + 2$ and $g(x) = x^2$, find $(f \circ g)(3)$.

   (1) 11 (3) 25

   (2) 14 (4) 45

5 What is the solution set for $|2x - 4| < 6$?

   (1) $\{x : -1 < x < 5\}$

   (2) $\{x : -5 < x < 1\}$

   (3) $\{x : x < -1 \text{ or } x > 5\}$

   (4) $\{x : x < -5 \text{ or } x > 1\}$

6 If -2 and 3 are the roots of the quadratic equation $x^2 + kx - 6 = 0$, then k must be

   (1) 1 (3) -5

   (2) -1 (4) 5

7 The fraction $\dfrac{1 - \dfrac{1}{a}}{1 - \dfrac{1}{a^2}}$ is equivalent to

   (1) 1 (3) $\dfrac{1}{a}$

   (2) $-\dfrac{1}{a}$ (4) $\dfrac{a}{a + 1}$

8 What is the domain of $f(x) = \dfrac{1}{\sqrt{9 - x^2}}$?

   (1) All real numbers

   (2) $x < 3$

   (3) $x > 3$

   (4) $-3 < x < 3$

9 What is the vertex of the parabola $y = (x - 2)^2 + 7$?

   (1) $(-2, 7)$ (3) $(2, -7)$

   (2) $(-2, -7)$ (4) $(2, 7)$

10 If $g(x) = 3x + 2$, what is $g^{-1}(x)$?

   (1) $-3x - 2$

   (2) $\dfrac{1}{3x + 2}$

   (3) $\dfrac{2 + x}{3}$

   (4) $\dfrac{1}{3}x - \dfrac{2}{3}$

11 Simplify: $3i^2 - 2i^4 + 5i^{23}$

   (1) $1 - 5i$ (3) $5 - 5i$

   (2) $-5 - 5i$ (4) $5 + 5i$

12 The roots of the equation $y^2 + 4y = 8$ are

   (1) real, rational, and equal

   (2) real, rational, and unequal

   (3) real, irrational, and unequal

   (4) imaginary

13 Which relation is a function?

   (1) $x = 3$ (3) $x = y^2$

   (2) $y = 3$ (4) $x^2 + y^2 = 9$

Part II

Answer all questions in this part. Each correct answer will receive 2 credits. Clearly indicate the necessary steps, including appropriate formula substitutions, diagrams, graphs, charts, etc. For all questions in this part, a correct numerical answer with no work shown will receive only 1 credit.

14 Simplify and express in $a + bi$ form:
$(2 - 6i)(8 + 3i)$

15 Solve for x: $\sqrt{x + 2} = x$

16 In the accompanying table, r varies inversely as s. What is the value of x?

r	4	12	x
s	6	2	3

17 Mary Lu is 4 years younger than her sister, Jane. Their mother, who is a mathematics teacher, noticed that the product of the ages of the two sisters is 32. How old are the girls? (Only an algebraic solution will be accepted.)

Part III

Answer all questions in this part. Each correct answer will receive 4 credits. Clearly indicate the necessary steps, including appropriate formula substitutions, diagrams, graphs, charts, etc. For all questions in this part, a correct numerical answer with no work shown will receive only 1 credit.

18 Given: $Z_1 = 2 + 5i$ and $Z_2 = 5 + 3i$.

  a Graph each number: Z_1 and Z_2.

  b Graph the sum of Z_1 and Z_2.

  c Express the sum of Z_1 and Z_2 as a complex number.

19 Solve for x: $\dfrac{3}{x - 2} + \dfrac{8}{x^2 - 4} = 1$

Part IV

Answer this question. A correct answer will receive 6 credits. Clearly indicate the necessary steps, including appropriate formula substitutions, diagrams, graphs, charts, etc. A correct numerical answer with no work shown will receive only 1 credit.

20 Solve the system of equations algebraically.
$$y = 3x - 4$$
$$y = x^2 + 5x - 39$$

CUMULATIVE REVIEW
CHAPTERS 1–6

Part I

Answer all questions in this part. Each correct answer will receive 2 credits. No partial credit will be allowed.

1 Given the sequence 22, 13, 4, −5, . . . , what is the next term?

   (1) −22   (3) 4

   (2) −14   (4) 13

2 Which graph shows a quadratic function with imaginary roots?

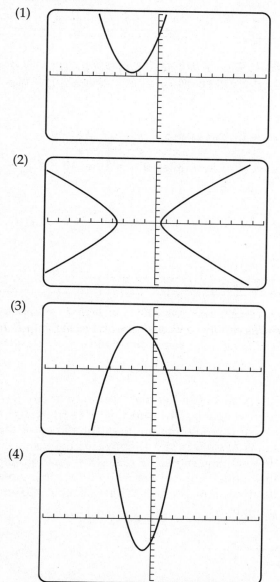

   (1)

   (2)

   (3)

   (4)

3 The height Rima's model rocket attains can be represented by the equation $y = -16x^2 + 70x + 37$, where x represents the time in seconds since the rocket was launched and the height is expressed in feet. To the *nearest tenth of a foot*, what was the maximum height Rima's rocket achieved?

   (1) 243.6   (3) 113.6

   (2) 143.4   (4) 39.4

4 If the 4th term of an arithmetic sequence is 31 and the 8th term of the sequence is 59, find the 1st term of the sequence.

   (1) 10   (3) 3

   (2) 7   (4) 28

5 Which of these discriminants would indicate that a quadratic equation has two roots that are rational, real, and unequal?

   (1) −43   (3) 17

   (2) 0   (4) 36

6 Evaluate: $\displaystyle\sum_{j=4}^{7} j^2 - 2j$

   (1) 170   (3) 122

   (2) 144   (4) 82

7 Which of the following is true of the product of $(3 + 4i)(3 - 4i)$?

   (1)   The product is a real, rational number.

   (2)   The product is $0 + 0i$.

   (3)   The product is an imaginary number.

   (4)   The product is an irrational number.

8 The nth term of the geometric sequence 2, 8, 32, 128, 512, . . . , is represented by

   (1) $4\left(\dfrac{1}{2}\right)^n$ (3) $2(2)^n$

   (2) $\dfrac{1}{2}(4)^n$ (4) $\dfrac{1}{4}(8)^n$

9 The smallest integral value of c that will produce imaginary roots in the equation $4x^2 - 7x + c = 0$ is

(1) 0 (3) 3

(2) 2 (4) 4

10 Find the value of r in the geometric sequence whose 2nd term is 81 and whose 4th term is $\dfrac{729}{16}$.

(1) $\dfrac{16}{9}$ (3) $\pm\dfrac{3}{4}$

(2) $\pm\dfrac{9}{16}$ (4) $\dfrac{11}{4}$

11 Simplify: $\dfrac{6 + 3i}{2 - 3i}$

(1) $-\dfrac{3 + 24i}{5}$ (3) $\dfrac{8 + 6i}{13}$

(2) $\dfrac{3 + 24i}{13}$ (4) $\dfrac{3 - 2i}{12}$

12 Solve for x: $x^2 + 5 = 2x$

(1) $1 \pm 2i$ (3) $-1 \pm 2i$

(2) $2 \pm i$ (4) $-2 \pm i$

13 If $f(x) = |10 - 4x - x^2|$, the value of $f(2)$ is

(1) -2 (3) 6

(2) 2 (4) 22

Part II

Answer all questions in this part. Each correct answer will receive 2 credits. Clearly indicate the necessary steps, including appropriate formula substitutions, diagrams, graphs, charts, etc. For all questions in this part, a correct numerical answer with no work shown will receive only 1 credit.

14 One root of a quadratic equation is $3 + 2i$. Determine the other root and write the equation that has these values as its roots.

15 Michael says that he can describe the roots of a quadratic equation without actually solving the equation. Jillian challenges him to describe the roots of the equation $y = 3x^2 - 4x - 2$. What does Michael tell her and how does he know?

16 Solve for x: $\sqrt{4x + 8} - 1 = x - 2$

17 Solve for x in simplest $a + bi$ form: $4x - 4 = -\dfrac{17}{x}$

Part III

Answer all questions in this part. Each correct answer will receive 4 credits. Clearly indicate the necessary steps, including appropriate formula substitutions, diagrams, graphs, charts, etc. For all questions in this part, a correct numerical answer with no work shown will receive only 1 credit.

18 Find the sum of the first six terms of the series: $-96, 144, -216, 324, \ldots$

19 The profits of an Internet auction company can be represented by the function $P = -t^2 + 8t + 12$, where P represents profits in hundreds of thousands of dollars and t represents the years since the company started. If 2005 is $t = 0$, according to this model, in what year will the company reach its maximum profits? What will the maximum profit be?

Answer this question. A correct answer will receive 6 credits. Clearly indicate the necessary steps, including appropriate formula substitutions, diagrams, graphs, charts, etc. A correct numerical answer with no work shown will receive only 1 credit.

20 The scenery for the ballet *The Nutcracker* contains a large grandfather clock. The pendulum of the clock swings a total distance of 96 inches on its first swing and decreases the distance traveled by 0.4 percent on each swing.

a Write a rule to find a_n in this geometric sequence.

b If the clock needs to be rewound when the pendulum travels less than 8 inches, after how many swings will the stagehand have to tend to the clock?

CUMULATIVE REVIEW
CHAPTERS 1–7

Part I

Answer all questions in this part. Each correct answer will receive 2 credits. No partial credit will be allowed.

1 In what quadrant does the sum of $6 - 5i$ and $4 + 6i$ lie?

(1) I

(2) II

(3) III

(4) IV

2 If $f(x) = 2x^0$, find $f(4)$.

(1) 1

(2) 2

(3) 8

(4) 0

3 Evaluate: $\displaystyle\sum_{j=3}^{10} (2j^2)$

(1) 208

(2) 380

(3) 760

(4) 1,028

4 If x varies inversely as y and $x = 4$ when $y = 12$, when $y = 3$, $x =$

(1) 1

(2) 9

(3) 13

(4) 16

5 Simplify: $\dfrac{6a^{2b}}{3a^2}$

(1) a^{b-1}

(2) $2a^{2b-2}$

(3) $3a^{2b-2}$

(4) $3a^b$

6 Which point is *not* part of the solution set of $y \le 12 + x - x^2$?

(1) $(1, 12)$

(2) $(0, 11)$

(3) $(3, 5)$

(4) $(-4, -1)$

7 When a new video game is first introduced, the number of people who have the game grows slowly. As the game catches on, more and more people buy it, and the rate of growth increases. Which of the following graphs could be used to model the number of people who own the game as a function of time since the game was introduced?

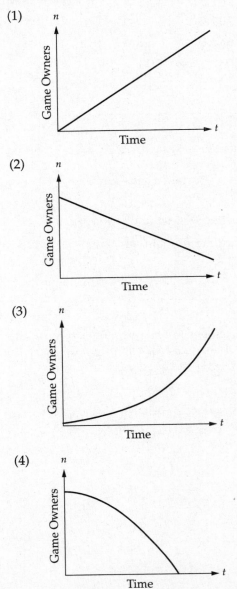

8 Given a geometric sequence with $a_6 = 27$ and $a_9 = 1$, find a_{10}.

(1) $-\dfrac{17}{3}$ (3) $\dfrac{1}{3}$

(2) $-\dfrac{14}{3}$ (4) 3

9 Which is an equation of a circle whose center is $(3, -6)$ and whose radius is 5?

(1) $(x + 3)^2 + (y - 6)^2 = 5$

(2) $(x + 3)^2 + (y - 6)^2 = 25$

(3) $(x - 3)^2 + (y + 6)^2 = 5$

(4) $(x - 3)^2 + (y + 6)^2 = 25$

10 The graph of a function $y = b^x$ lies in quadrants

(1) I and II (3) II and III

(2) I and IV (4) III and IV

11 The graph shows the solution to which inequality?

(1) $x^2 - 2x - 24 \le 0$

(2) $x^2 + 2x - 24 \le 0$

(3) $x^2 - 2x - 24 \ge 0$

(4) $x^2 + 2x - 24 \ge 0$

12 If $g(x) = 4^x$, find x such that $g(x) = 2$.

(1) -2 (3) 0

(2) $-\dfrac{1}{2}$ (4) $\dfrac{1}{2}$

13 What is the solution set of the equation $x = \sqrt{5x + 24}$?

(1) $\{-3, 8\}$ (3) $\{-3\}$

(2) $\{-8\}$ (4) $\{8\}$

Part II

Answer all questions in this part. Each correct answer will receive 2 credits. Clearly indicate the necessary steps, including appropriate formula substitutions, diagrams, graphs, charts, etc. For all questions in this part, a correct numerical answer with no work shown will receive only 1 credit.

14 What is the product of $(5 + 2i)$ and its conjugate?

15 What are the domain and range of the function $y = x^2 + 3$?

16 Solve for x: $3^{2x} = 27^{x-1}$

17 Solve for all values of x: $|3x - 4| = 5$

Part III

Answer all questions in this part. Each correct answer will receive 4 credits. Clearly indicate the necessary steps, including appropriate formula substitutions, diagrams, graphs, charts, etc. For all questions in this part, a correct numerical answer with no work shown will receive only 1 credit.

18 Find all solutions to the equation $2x^3 + 12x^2 + 50x = 0$. Express any complex roots in simplest $a + bi$ form.

19 Using the function $f(x) = 3^x$ in the interval $-2 \le x \le 2$, write an equation for a new function such that

a $f(x)$ is shifted up 2 units

b $f(x)$ is shifted to the right 3 units

Answer this question. A correct answer will receive 6 credits. Clearly indicate the necessary steps, including appropriate formula substitutions, diagrams, graphs, charts, etc. A correct numerical answer with no work shown will receive only 1 credit.

20 A new television show, *The World of Mathematics*, has just premiered. The number of people who watch the show can be modeled by the function $N(t) = 3(1.15)^t$, where $N(t)$ is the number of millions of viewers and t is the time, in months, since the show was first introduced.

a Evaluate $N(4)$ to the *nearest thousand* and explain what this means in terms of the show.

b Find t, to the *nearest thousandth*, such that $N(t) = 4$ and explain what this means in terms of the show.

CUMULATIVE REVIEW
CHAPTERS 1–8

Part I

Answer all questions in this part. Each correct answer will receive 2 credits. No partial credit will be allowed.

1 Given $f(x) = 2x^2 - 4x + 5$, we know its roots are

  (1) real, rational, and equal

  (2) real, rational, and unequal

  (3) real, irrational, and unequal

  (4) imaginary

2 Given $f(x) = \log_4 x$, then $f(8)$ equals

  (1) $\dfrac{3}{2}$ (3) 3

  (2) 2   (4) 4

3 When simplified, $\dfrac{\dfrac{c}{2} - \dfrac{2}{c}}{1 + \dfrac{c}{2}}$ equals

  (1) c (3) $\dfrac{c-2}{c}$

  (2) $\dfrac{c+2}{2}$ (4) $\dfrac{c-2}{2}$

4 The graphs of $y = \log_2 x$ and $2^y = x$

  (1) intersect in only one point

  (2) intersect in two points

  (3) are the same graph

  (4) do not intersect at all

5 The value of x in the expression $4^{3x} = 16^{x+1}$ is

  (1) -2 (3) 3

  (2) 2   (4) 4

6 Which statement is true for the product $(7 + 4i)(1 - 4i)$?

  (1) It is a real, rational number.

  (2) It is $7 - 16i^2$.

  (3) It is an irrational number.

  (4) It is a complex number.

7 The solution set for the equation $1 + \sqrt{3x + 1} = x$ is

  (1) $\{0\}$ (3) $\{0, 5\}$

  (2) $\{5\}$ (4) $\{\ \}$

8 If $\log_a 3 = m$ and $\log_a 5 = p$, which of the following represents $\log_a 75$?

  (1) $m + p^2$ (3) $m + 2p$

  (2) $2mp$ (4) mp^2

9 If the product of the roots of a quadratic equation is $-\dfrac{1}{4}$ and the sum of the roots of the equation is $\dfrac{5}{2}$, the equation may be which of the following?

  (1) $2x^2 - 5x = \dfrac{1}{2}$ (3) $4x^2 - 1 = 0$

  (2) $5x = 1 + 2x^2$ (4) $4x^2 = 5x + 1$

10 If $f(x) = \dfrac{1}{2}x^2 - x^{\frac{1}{2}} - 3x^0$, $f(4)$ equals

  (1) 1   (3) 3

  (2) 2   (4) 4

11 The fifth term of the geometric sequence $-\dfrac{1}{4}, \dfrac{1}{3}, -\dfrac{4}{9}, \ldots$, is

  (1) $-\dfrac{4}{3}$ (3) $-\dfrac{64}{81}$

  (2) $-\dfrac{2}{9}$ (4) $-\dfrac{256}{729}$

12 The value of x in the equation $\log_{(x-1)} 9 = 2$ is

(1) 1

(2) 2

(3) 3

(4) 4

13 When David was born, his grandparents deposited \$1,000 in a college account that promised 4% interest compounded annually for 18 years. Which equation represents the worth of the account when David is 18?

(1) $y = 18(4)(1{,}000)$

(2) $y = 18(0.04)(1{,}000)$

(3) $y = 1{,}000(0.04)^{18}$

(4) $y = 1{,}000(1.04)^{18}$

Part II

Answer all questions in this part. Each correct answer will receive 2 credits. Clearly indicate the necessary steps, including appropriate formula substitutions, diagrams, graphs, charts, etc. For all questions in this part, a correct numerical answer with no work shown will receive only 1 credit.

14 If $f(x) = x^2 - 4x$ and $g(x) = 2x + 3$, express $(f \circ g)(x)$ in simplest form.

15 The function $P(t) = 17{,}432(0.7882)^t$ represents the population of Elvesville, North Pole, where $t = 0$ represents the year 2009. Explain whether or not the population is increasing or decreasing as well as the significance of the 17,432 and 0.7882 in the equation.

16 Simplify: $\dfrac{9x^2}{3x^2 - 6x} \cdot \dfrac{2x^2 - 5x + 2}{6x - 3}$

17 Solve for x in simplest $a + bi$ form: $9x^2 - 6x + 2 = 0$

Part III

Answer all questions in this part. Each correct answer will receive 4 credits. Clearly indicate the necessary steps, including appropriate formula substitutions, diagrams, graphs, charts, etc. For all questions in this part, a correct numerical answer with no work shown will receive only 1 credit.

18 **a** Graph the function $f(x) = \log_2 x$ over the interval $-3 \le x \le 3$.

b Graph the inverse of the function $f(x) = \log_2 x$.

19 Given $\log_c 3 = 1.857$ and $\log_c 2 = 1.214$, evaluate

a $\log_c \sqrt{12}$

b $\log_c \dfrac{3}{2}$

Part IV

Answer this question. A correct answer will receive 6 credits. Clearly indicate the necessary steps, including appropriate formula substitutions, diagrams, graphs, charts, etc. A correct numerical answer with no work shown will receive only 1 credit.

20 The amount a of a medication, in milligrams, active in a patient's bloodstream t hours after it has been administered is given by the formula $a = 8(6.85)^{-0.36t}$. Find, to the *nearest tenth of an hour*, how long it will take until only 0.1 milligram of the drug remains in the patient's bloodstream.

CUMULATIVE REVIEW
CHAPTERS 1–9

Part I

Answer all questions in this part. Each correct answer will receive 2 credits. No partial credit will be allowed.

1 For which value of θ is the fraction $\dfrac{3}{1 - \cos \theta}$ undefined?

  (1) 0°   (3) 60°

  (2) 45°   (4) 90°

2 If $f(x) = 3x - 2$ and $g(x) = x^2$, find $(f \circ g)(5)$.

  (1) 26   (3) 73

  (2) 28   (4) 169

3 Write as a monomial in terms of i:
$2\sqrt{-9} + 7\sqrt{-36} - 4\sqrt{-25}$

  (1) $-62i$ (3) $28i$

  (2) $-28i$ (4) $62i$

4 The roots of the equation $x^2 - x + 10 = 0$ are

  (1) real, rational, and equal

  (2) real, rational, and unequal

  (3) real, irrational, and unequal

  (4) imaginary

5 Find the sum of the first 10 terms of the geometric series $2, 10, 50, 250, \ldots$.

  1) 2,555   (3) 976,562

  (2) 5,115   (4) 4,882,812

6 Which element is *not* in the range of the function $f(x) = -x^2 + 10$?

  (1) 1   (3) 10

  (2) 5   (4) 15

7 If $\sin \theta < 0$ and $\cos \theta > 0$, which of the following might be the measure of θ?

  (1) 450°   (3) 225°

  (2) 330°   (4) 120°

8 Members of the Drama Club are going to paint the scenery for their play. They calculated that it would take 4 of them 6 days to paint the scenery. If they need the scenery in 3 days, and they work at the same rate, how many members do they need to help paint?

  (1) 1   (3) 8

  (2) 2   (4) 12

9 Which of the following might be the value of the discriminant of a parabola that lies entirely above the x-axis?

  (1) -6 (3) 3

  (2) 0   (4) 50

10 The coordinates of a point on the unit circle are $\left(-\dfrac{\sqrt{3}}{2}, -\dfrac{1}{2}\right)$. If the terminal side of angle θ in standard position passes through the given point, find $m\angle \theta$.

  (1) 120°   (3) 210°

  (2) 150°   (4) 300°

11 Solve for x: $|x - 3| = 2x$

  (1) $\{1\}$ (3) $\{-3\}$

  (2) $\{1, 3\}$ (4) $\{1, -3\}$

12 When the graph of $y = 2^x$ is reflected over the line $y = x$, what is the equation of the resulting graph?

  (1) $y = 2^{-x}$ (3) $y = \log_x 2$

  (2) $y = -2^x$ (4) $y = \log_2 x$

13 If $\log_4 x = 3$, which of the following could be $\sqrt{x}$?

  (1) 64   (3) 8

  (2) 16   (4) 4

Part II

Answer all questions in this part. Each correct answer will receive 2 credits. Clearly indicate the necessary steps, including appropriate formula substitutions, diagrams, graphs, charts, etc. For all questions in this part, a correct numerical answer with no work shown will receive only 1 credit.

14 The length of a rectangle is $\dfrac{2x + 4}{x^2 - 9}$ and its width is $\dfrac{3}{x - 3}$. Express the perimeter of the rectangle as a single fraction in simplest form.

15 For what value of k are the roots of $3x^2 - 6x + k = 0$ equal?

16 Write as the log of a single function: $\log x + 2\log y - \log z$

17 Solve for x: $5e^x = 5$

Part III

Answer all questions in this part. Each correct answer will receive 4 credits. Clearly indicate the necessary steps, including appropriate formula substitutions, diagrams, graphs, charts, etc. For all questions in this part, a correct numerical answer with no work shown will receive only 1 credit.

18 Tina can paint a room in 8 hours, but when she and her friend Emily work together, they can complete the job in 3 hours. How long would it take Emily to paint the room alone?

19 Express in simplest form:
$$\frac{3x - 9}{9 - x^2} \cdot \frac{x^2 + 7x + 12}{3x + 12}$$

Part IV

Answer this question. A correct answer will receive 6 credits. Clearly indicate the necessary steps, including appropriate formula substitutions, diagrams, graphs, charts, etc. A correct numerical answer with no work shown will receive only 1 credit.

20 A radioactive substance decays at the rate of 2 percent per year.

  a Write an equation to model the amount of material left after t years, if there were initially 500 grams.

  b Use your equation to determine the amount of material that would remain after 50 years. (Round your answer to the *nearest hundredth*.)

  c How long would it take until there were only 250 grams remaining?

CUMULATIVE REVIEW
CHAPTERS 1–10

Part I

Answer all questions in this part. Each correct answer will receive 2 credits. No partial credit will be allowed.

1 The domain of which function is $-1 \leq x \leq 1$?

(1) $y = \dfrac{3x + 7}{x^2 - 1}$ (3) $y = \sqrt{1 - x^2}$

(2) $y = \dfrac{x^2 - 1}{3x + 7}$ (4) $y = \dfrac{1}{\sqrt{1 - x^2}}$

2 Find the fifth term of the geometric sequence $\dfrac{16}{5}, 4, 5, \ldots$.

(1) $\dfrac{5}{4}$ (3) 25

(2) $\dfrac{125}{16}$ (4) $\dfrac{625}{16}$

3 If $f(x) = 3\sin x + 2\cos 2x$, evaluate $f\left(\dfrac{\pi}{2}\right)$.

(1) 1 (3) 3

(2) 2 (4) 5

4 In February, the price charged by Friendly Flowers for roses is inversely proportional to the number of days before Valentine's Day the order is placed. A dozen roses ordered ten days before February 14 cost $12.00 while the same order placed five days before Valentine's Day costs $24.00. What is the cost of a dozen roses ordered one day before Valentine's Day?

(1) $36.00   (3) $72.00

(2) $54.00   (4) $120.00

5 If $\sin \theta = -\dfrac{\sqrt{2}}{2}$ and $\tan \theta = -1$, θ measures

(1) $45°$ (3) $225°$

(2) $135°$ (4) $315°$

6 Coach Willful believes that the best sixth-grade soccer players are 58 inches tall, and he will accept only students whose heights are within 4 inches of his ideal as players on his team. Which equation expresses the height, h, of Coach Willful's team players?

(1) $|h - 4| > 58$ (3) $|h + 4| > 58$

(2) $|58 - h| < 4$ (4) $|h - 58| > 4$

7 Express $330°$ in radian measure.

(1) $\dfrac{5\pi}{6}$ (3) $\dfrac{11\pi}{6}$

(2) $\dfrac{5\pi}{3}$ (4) $\dfrac{11\pi}{4}$

8 If $4x^2 + 9 = kx$, what value of k will produce equal roots?

(1) -3 (3) 9

(2) 5 (4) 12

9 If $\log_n 3 = a$ and $\log_n 2 = b$, what is the value of $\log_n 24$?

(1) $a + b^3$ (3) $3ab$

(2) $a + 3b$ (4) $4ab$

10 If one root of a quadratic equation is $\dfrac{1}{2} - 2i$, what is the equation?

(1) $4x^2 - 4x + 17 = 0$

(2) $4x^2 - 4x + 4 = 0$

(3) $x^2 - x + 17 = 0$

(4) $4x^2 + 4x + 17 = 0$

11 If $\sin (2\theta + 18)° = \cos (5\theta - 12)°$, which pair of angles is represented in this equation?

(1) $42°, 48°$ (3) $12°, 68°$

(2) $38°, 52°$ (4) $45°, 45°$

12 If $4.5^x = 97$, an approximate value of x is

(1) 2.15 (3) 3.16

(2) 3.04 (4) 3.47

13 Crossing a wooden bridge at Letchworth Park, Melissa dropped a penny in the water for good luck. If the height of the dropped penny is modeled by the function $h(t) = 64 - 16t^2$, where t represents time in seconds and $h(t)$ is the height of the penny in feet, how many seconds did it take the penny to hit the water?

(1) 1 (3) 3

(2) 2 (4) 4

Part II

Answer all questions in this part. Each correct answer will receive 2 credits. Clearly indicate the necessary steps, including appropriate formula substitutions, diagrams, graphs, charts, etc. For all questions in this part, a correct numerical answer with no work shown will receive only 1 credit.

14 Oscar is having trouble remembering in which quadrants the sine function is positive. Sammy tells him not to worry about it, he will explain. After Sammy explains his reasoning, Oscar understands. Explain where the sine function is positive and why.

15 Damon won a charity raffle with a prize of $7,500. If he invests the money at an interest rate of 4.3% compounded continuously, determine the number of years, to the *nearest tenth*, that it will take for the money to double. (The formula for continuous interest is $P = Ae^{rt}$, where A is the initial amount invested, r is the rate of interest, and t is the time invested.)

16 Kelly Ann has been offered a job that promises a salary package represented by the function $S(t) = 42{,}500(1.038)t$, where t is the number of years worked. Evaluate $S(3)$ and explain its meaning.

17 Graph the solution to the inequality $y > -5x^2 - 6x + 8$ on the coordinate plane.

Part III

Answer all questions in this part. Each correct answer will receive 4 credits. Clearly indicate the necessary steps, including appropriate formula substitutions, diagrams, graphs, charts, etc. For all questions in this part, a correct numerical answer with no work shown will receive only 1 credit.

18 If the third term of an arithmetic sequence is 34 and the sixth term is 55, find the first term of the sequence and the common difference.

19 Solve for x: $\log_4 (2x + 3) - \log_4 (x + 1) = 1$

Part IV

Answer this question. A correct answer will receive 6 credits. Clearly indicate the necessary steps, including appropriate formula substitutions, diagrams, graphs, charts, etc. A correct numerical answer with no work shown will receive only 1 credit.

20° The Edisons are deciding whether or not to sell their 6-year-old SUV. Its original price was $39,289 and its annual rate of depreciation is 17%. A smaller, new car with better gas mileage will cost $33,757.

    a How much is their old car worth today?

    b If the dealer will credit the Edisons with the dollar value of the car after 6 years' depreciation, how much additional money must they pay for the new vehicle?

CUMULATIVE REVIEW
CHAPTERS 1–11

Part I

Answer all questions in this part. Each correct answer will receive 2 credits. No partial credit will be allowed.

1 If $5 - 6i$ is one root of a quadratic equation, what is another root?

  (1) $-5 - 6i$

  (2) $-5 + 6i$

  (3) $5 + 6i$

  (4) Cannot be determined

2 The origin of a coordinate grid is labeled O. Line segment OP forms an angle of $30°$ with the x-axis. If $OP = 1$, what are the coordinates of point P?

  (1) $(1, 1)$ (3) $\left(\dfrac{\sqrt{3}}{2}, \dfrac{1}{2}\right)$

  (2) $\left(\dfrac{\sqrt{2}}{2}, \dfrac{\sqrt{2}}{2}\right)$ (4) $\left(\dfrac{1}{2}, \dfrac{\sqrt{3}}{2}\right)$

3 The temperature, t, in Frigidland is always within 2 degrees of freezing (32°F). Which equation could represent the temperature in Frigidland?

  (1) $|2 + t| < 32$ (3) $|32 + t| < 2$

  (2) $|2 - t| < 32$ (4) $|32 - t| < 2$

4 If $f(x) = 2x + 3$ and $g(x) = x^2 - x - 4$, what is $(f \circ g)(2)$?

  (1) -38 (3) 18

  (2) -1 (4) 38

5 David leaves his house to visit his friend Mark, who lives 3 miles away. On the way, he stops to have lunch and then continues to Mark's house. Which graph could be used to model David's distance from home as a function of time?

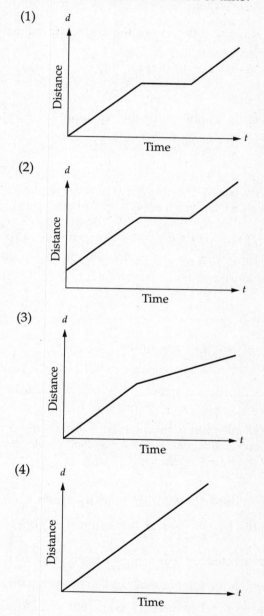

6 Evaluate $\sin\left(\arccos\dfrac{\sqrt{2}}{2}\right)$.

(1) 1

(3) $\dfrac{\sqrt{3}}{2}$

(2) $\dfrac{\sqrt{2}}{2}$

(4) $\sqrt{2}$

7 Solve for y: $y(y-2)<8$

(1) $y<0$ or $y<2$

(2) $y<0$ or $y>2$

(3) $y<-2$ or $y>4$

(4) $-2<y<4$

8 What is the 10th term of the arithmetic sequence $7, 8.5, 10, \ldots$?

(1) 20.5

(3) 23.5

(2) 22

(4) 25

9 Which is a solution of the equation $2x^3 + 3x^2 + 4x + 6 = 0$?

(1) $-\dfrac{3}{2}$

(3) $\dfrac{2}{3}$

(2) $-\dfrac{2}{3}$

(4) $\dfrac{3}{2}$

10 If $f(x) = a\sin bx$ for $a > 0$, the maximum value in the range is

(1) a

(2) b

(3) $a+b$

(4) There is no maximum.

11 If $\log_3(x^2-3) = \log_3 22$, then the solution set for x is

(1) $\{-5, 5\}$

(3) $\{5\}$

(2) $\{-5\}$

(4) $\{\ \}$

12 If $\sin\beta = \dfrac{3}{5}$ and $\tan\beta < 0$, what is the value of $\sec\beta$?

(1) $-\dfrac{5}{3}$

(3) $\dfrac{5}{4}$

(2) $-\dfrac{5}{4}$

(4) $\dfrac{5}{3}$

13 What is a possible equation for the graph shown below?

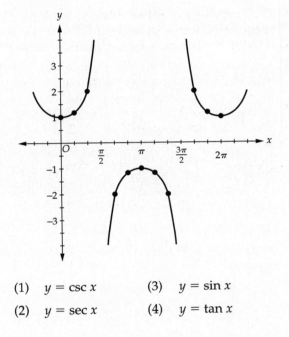

(1) $y = \csc x$

(3) $y = \sin x$

(2) $y = \sec x$

(4) $y = \tan x$

Part II

Answer all questions in this part. Each correct answer will receive 2 credits. Clearly indicate the necessary steps, including appropriate formula substitutions, diagrams, graphs, charts, etc. For all questions in this part, a correct numerical answer with no work shown will receive only 1 credit.

14 The number of goldfish in an aquarium is represented by $\dfrac{x}{x+2}$ and the number of guppies is represented by $\dfrac{2}{x^2-x-6}$. Express as a single fraction the total number of fish in the aquarium.

15 The senior class has decided to rent a hall for their prom. If only 75 members of the class come to the prom, it will cost them $50 each. However, they want to keep the cost to only $25 each. How many people would have to come to the prom for this to happen?

16 Solve for x: $\dfrac{x}{2} - \dfrac{9}{x} = \dfrac{3}{2}$

17 Name the smallest positive acute angle that is coterminal with a $-310°$ angle.

Answer all questions in this part. Each correct answer will receive 4 credits. Clearly indicate the necessary steps, including appropriate formula substitutions, diagrams, graphs, charts, etc. For all questions in this part, a correct numerical answer with no work shown will receive only 1 credit.

18 The doorway of a new office building is in the shape of a parabolic arch. The equation that models the doorway is $y = -x^2 + 8x$. Partytime Caterers have been asked to plan a grand opening celebration. They want to hang a banner across the doorway, 8 feet above the ground. To the *nearest tenth of a foot*, how wide can the banner be?

19 The population of Mathland can be modeled by the equation $P(t) = 25(1.03)^t$, where $P(t)$ is the population, in thousands, and t is the number of years since Mathland was founded. What is the meaning of the 25 and the 1.03 in the equation? To the *nearest tenth of a year*, how long will it take until there are 100,000 people in Mathland?

Part IV

Answer this question. A correct answer will receive 6 credits. Clearly indicate the necessary steps, including appropriate formula substitutions, diagrams, graphs, charts, etc. A correct numerical answer with no work shown will receive only 1 credit.

20 On a summer day in Long Beach, NY, the tides varied from a high of approximately 3.6 feet to a low of 0.6 foot and back up to approximately 3.6 feet again. The time from one high tide to another high tide is approximately 12 hours. If $t = 0$ represents the time of the first high tide, write an equation to model this function. Approximately how long after the first high tide was the water one foot deep? (Round your answer to the *nearest tenth*.)

CUMULATIVE REVIEW
CHAPTERS 1–12

Part I

Answer all questions in this part. Each correct answer will receive 2 credits. No partial credit will be allowed.

1 The graph of the function shown can best be represented by which equation?

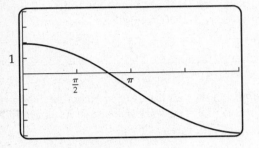

(1) $y = 4\sin\frac{1}{2}x - 2$

(2) $y = 3\cos\frac{1}{2}x - 1$

(3) $y = 2\cos\frac{1}{2}x - 3$

(4) $y = 3\sin\frac{1}{2}x - 1$

2 If $\sin\theta < 0$ and $\cos\theta < 0$, which angle might be θ?

(1) $\dfrac{\pi}{2}$

(2) $\dfrac{3\pi}{4}$

(3) $\dfrac{7\pi}{6}$

(4) $\dfrac{5\pi}{3}$

3 If $4^x = 2^y$ and $9^{x-1} = 3^{x+1}$, which are the values of x and y?

(1) $x = 2, y = 4$

(2) $x = 3, y = 6$

(3) $x = 4, y = 2$

(4) $x = 6, y = 3$

4 If the roots of a quadratic equation are real, irrational, and unequal, which might be the value of $b^2 - 4ac$ for the equation?

(1) –9

(2) 0

(3) 14

(4) 25

5 Krieg's Kaleidoscopes' yearly profits are modeled by the function $P(x) = -5x^2 + 18x - 2$ where x represents the number of units sold in thousands and $P(x)$ represents the profit earned in hundreds of thousands of dollars. What is the maximum profit Krieg's Kaleidoscopes can anticipate?

(1) 1.8 hundred thousand dollars

(2) 7.4 hundred thousand dollars

(3) 14.2 hundred thousand dollars

(4) 21.0 hundred thousand dollars

6 If $f(x) = 2\sin^2\theta + 2\cos^2\theta$, evaluate $f(45°)$.

(1) 1

(2) 2

(3) 3

(4) 4

7 Alvin of the Squirrels invested his royalties in a mutual fund whose annual performance can be represented by the function $P(t) = A(1.068)^t$. What is the annual rate of interest on Alvin's royalties?

(1) 0.068%

(2) 0.68%

(3) 1.068%

(4) 6.8%

8 Simplify: $\dfrac{1 + \dfrac{\sin^2\theta}{\cos^2\theta}}{\sec^2\theta}$

(1) 1

(2) $\sin^2\theta - \cos^2\theta$

(3) $\cos^4\theta$

(4) $\cos 2\theta$

9 Solve for x: $1 + \sqrt{x + 3} = x - 2$

(1) $\{1\}$

(2) $\{6\}$

(3) $\{1, 6\}$

(4) $\{\ \}$

10 If $\theta = \dfrac{5\pi}{4}$ and $\beta = \dfrac{3\pi}{4}$, evaluate $\cos(\theta + \beta)$.

(1) 1

(2) –1

(3) $\sqrt{2}$

(4) $2\sqrt{2}$

11 Find the sum of the infinite series 250, 125, 64.5, 32.25, ...

(1) 400 (3) 500

(2) 475 (4) 575

12 If $f(x) = \log_2 x$ and $g(x) = x^2 + 3$, evaluate $g(f(128))$.

(1) 16,387 (3) 52

(2) 67 (4) 14

13 In the diagram of the unit circle shown, point P has coordinates $\left(\dfrac{\sqrt{3}}{2}, -\dfrac{1}{2}\right)$. What is the measure of central angle AOP?

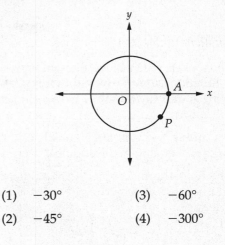

(1) $-30°$ (3) $-60°$

(2) $-45°$ (4) $-300°$

Part II

Answer all questions in this part. Each correct answer will receive 2 credits. Clearly indicate the necessary steps, including appropriate formula substitutions, diagrams, graphs, charts, etc. For all questions in this part, a correct numerical answer with no work shown will receive only 1 credit.

14 Find two arithmetic means between 64 and 118.

15 Convert the equation $2x^2 - 8x + 13 = y$ to vertex form.

16 The number of electric blankets sold at Jenkins' Home Furnishings from January 1 through December 31 can be modeled by the function $y = 680\cos\left(\dfrac{\pi}{6}t\right) + 708$, in which t (an integer) is time in months and $t = 0$ corresponds to January 1. Determine when the fewest electric blankets were sold and how many were sold at that time.

17 If $\cos\theta = \dfrac{1}{9}$ and θ is an obtuse angle, find $\sin\dfrac{1}{2}\theta$.

Answer all questions in this part. Each correct answer will receive 4 credits. Clearly indicate the necessary steps, including appropriate formula substitutions, diagrams, graphs, charts, etc. For all questions in this part, a correct numerical answer with no work shown will receive only 1 credit.

18 For Independence Day, the village of Treetop is planning to launch fireworks from a barge on the lake. The rockets will achieve a height represented by the function $H(t) = -16t^2 + 104t + 12$, where $H(t)$ is measured in feet and t is time in seconds after the launch.

a How many seconds after launch is the fireworks rocket at its highest point?

b If the rockets are designed to explode at their highest point, at what height will the rockets explode?

19 Using logarithms, solve for x, to the *nearest thousandth*: $8^{0.2x} = 787$

Part IV

Answer this question. A correct answer will receive 6 credits. Clearly indicate the necessary steps, including appropriate formula substitutions, diagrams, graphs, charts, etc. A correct numerical answer with no work shown will receive only 1 credit.

20 Given the sequence 324, 216, 144, 96, . . .

a Explain whether this sequence is arithmetic or geometric and why.

b Find a formula for the nth term of the sequence.

c Find the sum of the first 6 terms of this sequence.

CUMULATIVE REVIEW
CHAPTERS 1–13

Part I

Answer all questions in this part. Each correct answer will receive 2 credits. No partial credit will be allowed.

1 The amplitude of the graph of the equation $y = 2\sin 3x$ is

(1) π (3) 3

(2) 2 (4) $\dfrac{2\pi}{3}$

2 The expression $(3 + 4i)^2$ is equivalent to

(1) $-7 - 24i$ (3) 25

(2) $-7 + 24i$ (4) $9 + 16i$

3 Which is a solution of the equation $\sin^2 \alpha - \sin \alpha = 0$?

(1) $\dfrac{2\pi}{3}$ (3) $\dfrac{\pi}{3}$

(2) $\dfrac{\pi}{2}$ (4) $\dfrac{\pi}{4}$

4 If the length of a rectangle is $\dfrac{a}{2}$ and its width is $\dfrac{1}{a + 2}$, its perimeter is

(1) $\dfrac{a^2 + 2a + 1}{a + 2}$ (3) $\dfrac{a^2 + 2a + 1}{2(a + 2)}$

(2) $\dfrac{a^2 + 2a + 2}{a + 2}$ (4) $\dfrac{a^2 + 2a + 2}{2(a + 2)}$

5 The expression $\dfrac{\sin 2\theta}{\sin \theta}$ is equivalent to

(1) $\cos \theta$ (3) $2\sin \theta$

(2) 2 (4) $2\cos \theta$

6 If $f(x) = x^{\frac{5}{2}} + x^{-1} - \dfrac{1}{4}x^0$, find $f(4)$.

(1) 32 (3) 10

(2) $27\dfrac{3}{4}$ (4) $5\dfrac{3}{4}$

7 Express $135°$ in radian measure.

(1) $\dfrac{\pi}{4}$ (3) $\dfrac{3\pi}{4}$

(2) $\dfrac{2\pi}{3}$ (4) $\dfrac{5\pi}{4}$

8 In 1998, a cell phone company had 5 thousand customers. Each year, the number of customers has increased by 8 percent. Which equation could be used to express the number of customers, in thousands, that the cell phone company has if t represents the number of years since 1998?

(1) $N(t) = 5(0.8)^t$

(2) $N(t) = 5(1.8)^t$

(3) $N(t) = 5(1.08)^t$

(4) $N(t) = 8(1.05)^t$

9 Jill drove at 50 miles per hour for 4 hours to visit her brother Jack. Jill hit traffic on her way home and could drive only at 40 miles per hour for the entire trip. What was Jill's average speed, in miles per hour, for the entire trip?

(1) 42.346 (3) 45

(2) 44.444 (4) 47.263

10 Solve for x: $2x^{\frac{2}{3}} + 1 = 129$

(1) 512 (3) 64

(2) 96 (4) 16

11 For what value of θ is the fraction $\dfrac{1 - \cos \theta}{1 + \sin \theta}$ undefined?

(1) 1 (3) π

(2) -1 (4) $\dfrac{3\pi}{2}$

12 A population increases from 250 at a continuous rate of 3 percent per year. Which of the following functions would model this?

(1) $P(t) = 250e^{0.3t}$

(2) $P(t) = 250e^{0.03t}$

(3) $P(t) = 250e^{1.3t}$

(4) $P(t) = 15{,}000e^{1.03t}$

13 Simplify: $\log 10^{x+3} - \log 10^x$

(1) x (3) 3

(2) $\dfrac{x + 3}{x}$ (4) $1{,}000$

Part II

Answer all questions in this part. Each correct answer will receive 2 credits. Clearly indicate the necessary steps, including appropriate formula substitutions, diagrams, graphs, charts, etc. For all questions in this part, a correct numerical answer with no work shown will receive only 1 credit.

14 Solve for x and express the roots in simplest $a + bi$ form: $x^2 - 2x + 10 = 0$

15 Solve: $|2n - 4| < 8$

16 Moisha says that the roots of the equation $y = 2x^2 - x - 3$ are real, rational, and unequal. Abdul says that the roots are real, irrational, and unequal. Explain who is correct, and why.

17 Is the graph of a circle an example of a function? Explain.

Part III

Answer all questions in this part. Each correct answer will receive 4 credits. Clearly indicate the necessary steps, including appropriate formula substitutions, diagrams, graphs, charts, etc. For all questions in this part, a correct numerical answer with no work shown will receive only 1 credit.

18 a Juliet is standing on a balcony and mistakenly knocks over the flowerpot that is sitting on the ledge. If the height above the ground, in feet, of the flowerpot is represented by the equation $h(t) = -16t^2 + 64$, where t is the time measured in seconds, in how many seconds will the flowerpot hit the ground?

   b If 6-foot-tall Romeo were standing directly under the flowerpot, to the *nearest tenth of a second*, how long would he have to get out of the way before the flowerpot hit him on the head?

19 The graph of $y = 2\sin 3x$ is reflected in the x-axis.

   a Sketch a graph of one period of the original curve and a graph of the curve after the reflection.

   b Write an equation for the new curve.

   c How would your equation in part **b** differ if the curve were reflected in the y-axis instead of the x-axis? Explain.

Part IV

Answer this question. A correct answer will receive 6 credits. Clearly indicate the necessary steps, including appropriate formula substitutions, diagrams, graphs, charts, etc. A correct numerical answer with no work shown will receive only 1 credit.

20 Find all positive values of θ less than 360° that satisfy the equation $2\cos^2 \theta + \sin \theta = 1$.

CUMULATIVE REVIEW
CHAPTERS 1–14

Part I

Answer all questions in this part. Each correct answer will receive 2 credits. No partial credit will be allowed.

1 If $f(x) = \dfrac{6x - x^2}{x^{\frac{3}{2}}}$, evaluate $f(16)$.

(1) $\dfrac{2}{3}$ (3) $-\dfrac{5}{2}$

(2) 2 (4) $\dfrac{5}{2}$

2 If $\sin \theta = -\dfrac{\sqrt{2}}{2}$ and $\tan \theta = -1$, what is the value of θ?

(1) $-45°$ (3) $135°$

(2) $45°$ (4) $225°$

3 Given the geometric sequence $192, -144, 108, -81, \ldots$, find the common ratio.

(1) $-\dfrac{3}{4}$ (3) $-\dfrac{1}{2}$

(2) $-\dfrac{2}{3}$ (4) $-\dfrac{3}{8}$

4 Which statement is *not* true about the quadratic function $f(x) = 2x^2 - 8x + 7$?

(1) Its vertex is $(2, -1)$.

(2) Its axis of symmetry is $x = -2$.

(3) It is equivalent to $f(x) = 2(x - 2)^2 - 1$.

(4) Its y-intercept is $(0, 7)$.

5 The number of hours of daylight in North Reindeer Falls can be modeled by the sinusoidal function $H(d) = -7\cos\left(\dfrac{2\pi}{365}(d + 10)\right) + 12.4$, where d is the day of the year and $d = 0$ is January 1. What is the fewest number of hours of daylight experienced by this northern village?

(1) 12.4 (3) 5.6

(2) 8.2 (4) 5.4

6 Express $\sin(-113°)$ as the function of a positive acute angle less than $45°$.

(1) $\sin 57°$ (3) $-\cos 23°$

(2) $\cos 23°$ (4) $\csc 23°$

7 Simplify: $\dfrac{2x^2 + x - 3}{4x + 6}$

(1) $\dfrac{2x + 2}{2}$ (3) $x - 1$

(2) $\dfrac{x - 1}{2}$ (4) $\dfrac{x + 1}{2}$

8 In $\triangle CTH$, $c = h$, $m\angle T = 30$, and $c = 10$. Find the area of $\triangle CTH$.

(1) 25 (3) 50

(2) $25\sqrt{3}$ (4) $50\sqrt{3}$

9 The number of visitors to Westwoods Butterfly Habitat after May 31 can be represented by the function $V(t) = 693(1.026)^t$, where t is the number of days since May 31. Approximately how many visitors will enjoy the butterflies on June 20?

(1) 723 (3) $1{,}158$

(2) 896 (4) $1{,}317$

10 Solve for x: $3x^{\frac{1}{2}} - 11 = 7$

(1) 6 (3) 24

(2) 12 (4) 36

11 If $\log_a 3 = 5.926$, find the value of $\log_a \sqrt{3}$.

(1) 1.5 (3) 2.713

(2) 2.434 (4) 2.963

12 Which statement is true of the inequality $3x^2 - 6x < 0$?

(1) The solution includes all values of (x, y) that lie within the parabola, including those values on the parabola.

(2) The solution includes all values of (x, y) that lie outside the parabola, including those values on the parabola.

(3) The solution is a portion of the number line including 0 and 2 and all the numbers between them.

(4) The solution is a portion of the number line between 0 and 2 but excluding 0 and 2.

13 Solve for θ in the interval $0° \le \theta < 360°$: $3\sin^2 \theta - \sin \theta = 4$

(1) $\left\{ -1, \dfrac{4}{3} \right\}$ (3) $\{90°\}$

(2) $\{90°, 270°\}$ (4) $\{270°\}$

Part II

Answer all questions in this part. Each correct answer will receive 2 credits. Clearly indicate the necessary steps, including appropriate formula substitutions, diagrams, graphs, charts, etc. For all questions in this part, a correct numerical answer with no work shown will receive only 1 credit.

14 Find the sum of the first 30 terms of this arithmetic series: 60, 41, 22, 3, . . .

15 Solve and express the answer in simplest $a + bi$ form: $x^2 + 20 = 8x$

16 The graph below depicts the attendance at one movie theater for the first eight weeks following the release of the megahit *The Dark Knight*. Explain what type of function this is and what it means.

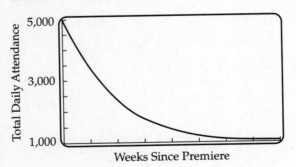

17 If $\cos \beta = -\dfrac{4}{5}$ when $90° < \beta < 180°$, find the value of $\sin 2\beta$.

Answer all questions in this part. Each correct answer will receive 4 credits. Clearly indicate the necessary steps, including appropriate formula substitutions, diagrams, graphs, charts, etc. For all questions in this part, a correct numerical answer with no work shown will receive only 1 credit.

18 Solve the following system of equations algebraically.

$$y = x^2 - 5x - 14$$
$$y = -x^2 - 2x$$

19 Jack and Brandon have found an old property deed in their grandfather's desk. The property is described as a triangular parcel with two sides of lengths 27.8 feet and 34.7 feet, respectively. The angle opposite the 27.8-foot length measures 42.4°. The third side of the parcel measures 18.82 feet. Brandon doesn't believe the figures in the deed are accurate and talks Jack into taking their own measurements. Using trigonometry rather than measuring tools, determine if Brandon is correct or not and explain why.

Part IV

Answer this question. A correct answer will receive 6 credits. Clearly indicate the necessary steps, including appropriate formula substitutions, diagrams, graphs, charts, etc. A correct numerical answer with no work shown will receive only 1 credit.

20 Carbon-14 is a radioactive isotope used to date objects. The element's decay can be modeled by the function $A(t) = A_0 (0.999879)^t$, where $A(t)$ is the amount of carbon-14 currently present in an artifact, A_0 is the initial amount of carbon-14, and t is the time in years. An oil painting supposedly painted by Picasso is presented for examination and found to contain 92.4 percent of its original carbon.

a Write an equation that can be used to determine the age of the painting.

b Using logarithms, solve the equation.

c Comment on the likelihood that Pablo Picasso (1881–1973) painted this work.

CUMULATIVE REVIEW

CHAPTERS 1–15

Part I

Answer all questions in this part. Each correct answer will receive 2 credits. No partial credit will be allowed.

1 In triangle ABC, $b = 6$, $c = 10$, and $m\angle A = 30$. Find the area of triangle ABC.

(1) 15   (3) 30

(2) 25.98   (4) 51.96

2 What are the real numbers a and b that make the statement $a + bi = 3 + 6i - 2 + i$ true?

(1) $a = 1, b = 6$ (3) $a = 5, b = 6$

(2) $a = 1, b = 7$ (4) $a = 5, b = 7$

3 Keisha and her friends have started a business designing web pages. They charge clients a \$100 initial fee and \$20 per hour for the time spent designing the web page. What type of function could be used to model their business?

(1) exponential   (3) logarithmic

(2) linear   (4) power

4 If $f(\theta) = \sin 2\theta - \cos \theta$, find $f(\pi)$.

(1) 1   (3) -1

(2) 0   (4) -2

5 Find x if $\log_x 9 = \dfrac{2}{3}$.

(1) 1   (3) 27

(2) 9   (4) 81

6 The frequency table below contains the test scores of Ms. Newfield's first-period class. What is the interquartile range?

x_i	100	90	80	70	60	50
f_i	2	4	10	9	3	1

(1) 10   (3) 50

(2) 20   (4) 80

7 What is *not* an element in the range of the function $y = 2\sin x$?

(1) 1   (3) 3

(2) 2   (4) 0

8 The linear correlation coefficient for the data shown below would be closest to

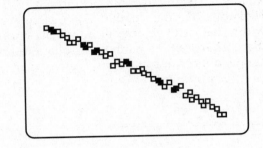

(1) 0.9   (3) -0.5

(2) 0.5   (4) -0.9

9 Angles A and B are positive acute angles. If $\sin A = \dfrac{3}{5}$ and $\cos B = \dfrac{5}{13}$, find $\sin (A + B)$.

(1) $\dfrac{33}{65}$ (3) $\dfrac{64}{65}$

(2) $\dfrac{63}{65}$ (4) $\dfrac{99}{65}$

10 For what value of k are the roots of the equation $2x^2 + 8x + k = 0$ real, rational, and equal?

(1) 1   (3) 16

(2) 8   (4) 64

11 If $\cos \theta < 0$ and $\tan \theta < 0$, in what quadrant does θ terminate?

(1) I   (3) III

(2) II   (4) IV

12 The test scores in Mrs. Kaste's mathematics class are normally distributed with a mean of 85 and a standard deviation of 5. Between what two scores would approximately 95 percent of the scores fall?

(1) 85–90   (3) 75–95

(2) 80–90   (4) 70–100

13 Solve for b: $\log_b 16 = 4$

(1) $\dfrac{1}{4}$ (3) $\dfrac{7}{2}$

(2) 2   (4) 4

Part II

Answer all questions in this part. Each correct answer will receive 2 credits. Clearly indicate the necessary steps, including appropriate formula substitutions, diagrams, graphs, charts, etc. For all questions in this part, a correct numerical answer with no work shown will receive only 1 credit.

14   Express in simplest form: $\dfrac{1 - \dfrac{1}{9x^2}}{1 - \dfrac{1}{3x}}$

15   Miguel wants to buy a new rug for his bedroom. He knows that the length is 2 feet more than the width, but can't remember either dimension. If the total area of the room is 90 square feet, what are the dimensions of Miguel's room, to the *nearest tenth of a foot*?

16   Mrs. Tightenup, the gym teacher, has listed the heights and weights of the students in her gym class as a set of ordered pairs. For example, (60, 110) would represent a person whose height is 60 inches and weight is 110 pounds. Are the weights of the members of the class a function of the heights? Explain.

17   Solve for values of θ where $0° \le \theta \le 90°$: $2\cos^2 \theta - \cos \theta = 0$

Part III

Answer all questions in this part. Each correct answer will receive 4 credits. Clearly indicate the necessary steps, including appropriate formula substitutions, diagrams, graphs, charts, etc. For all questions in this part, a correct numerical answer with no work shown will receive only 1 credit.

18   The members of the Delta Delta Delta Sorority want to take a picture of themselves standing in the shape of a triangle. They determined that the three sides of the triangle must measure 20 feet, 22 feet, and 24 feet. To the *nearest hundredth of a degree*, what is the measure of the largest angle of the triangle?

19   The Bugs R Us exterminating company specializes in ridding homes of all types of insects. The company's monthly income, given in thousands of dollars, as shown in the diagram below, over a twelve-month period can be modeled by the equation $y = A\cos Bx + D$. Determine the values of A, B, and D and explain how you arrived at your values.

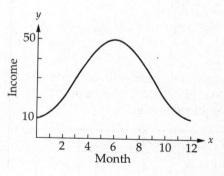

Answer this question. A correct answer will receive 6 credits. Clearly indicate the necessary steps, including appropriate formula substitutions, diagrams, graphs, charts, etc. A correct numerical answer with no work shown will receive only 1 credit.

20 The following table shows the number of students from Tidewater High School working part-time jobs.

Year	1996	1998	2000	2002	2004	2006	2008
Number of Students	200	239	280	322	359	400	442

a Using the data in the table, create a scatter plot and state the linear regression equation with the slope and *y*-intercept rounded to the *nearest thousandth*. Let 0 represent 1996.

b Based on your equation, determine the number of students who are expected to have part-time jobs in 2011.

c If the trend continues, when will 848 students at the school be holding part-time jobs? Does this answer make sense? Why?

CUMULATIVE REVIEW
CHAPTERS 1–16

Part I

Answer all questions in this part. Each correct answer will receive 2 credits. No partial credit will be allowed.

1 The solution set to $\dfrac{x-2}{x} + \dfrac{x}{x+1} = \dfrac{4x+1}{x^2+x}$ is

(1) $\left\{-\dfrac{1}{2}\right\}$

(3) $\{3\}$

(2) $\left\{-\dfrac{1}{2}, 3\right\}$

(4) $\{\ \}$

2 If the area of isosceles triangle *DOG* is 32.49 and vertex angle *O* measures 30°, what are the lengths of equal sides *DO* and *OG*?

(1) 16.245

(3) 9.6

(2) 11.4

(4) 8.06

3 There were seven decorated floats in the Bethpage Homecoming Parade. If the junior class took the gold medal for their float, in how many ways could the silver and bronze medals be awarded?

(1) 12

(3) 42

(2) 30

(4) 210

4 Evaluate: $\arccos\left(-\dfrac{\sqrt{3}}{2}\right) + \arctan 1$

(1) 75°

(3) 165°

(2) 105°

(4) 195°

5 When expanded, $(1-3i)^3$ equals

(1) $-26 + 18i$

(3) $-8 + 18i$

(2) $-18 + 26i$

(4) $10 - 18i$

6 A linear regression equation of best fit between the time studied for an exam and the grade on the exam is $h = 0.72x + 18.5$. The correlation coefficient, *r*, for these data would be

(1) $0 < r \le 1$

(3) $-1 \le r < 0$

(2) $r = -1$

(4) $r = 0$

7 Which statement about $y = 38(1.083)^x$ is *not* true?

(1) The initial value of the function is 38.

(2) This is an increasing function.

(3) The rate of change is 83 percent.

(4) The graph of this function never crosses the *x*-axis.

8 In the trigonometric equation $y = 3\cos\left(\dfrac{2\pi}{12}x\right) - 2$, what is the period?

(1) $\dfrac{2\pi}{12}$

(3) 12

(2) 2π

(4) $-5 \le y \le 1$

9 The school board has launched a study into the possibility of closing the high school campus for lunch. From which group might they obtain the least biased opinions?

(1) people who live at the retirement housing complex in town

(2) juniors and seniors who attend the school

(3) parents who attend an informational meeting on the situation

(4) every fifth person who enters the local mall

10 Solve for *x* to the *nearest hundredth*: $5^x = 401$

(1) 3.13

(3) 3.81

(2) 3.72

(4) 3.93

11 When simplified, $i^{37} + i^{27}$ equals

(1) 0

(3) $-i$

(2) i

(4) -1

12 How many different 6-letter arrangements can be made with the letters in the word TATTOO?

(1) 720

(3) 60

(2) 120

(4) 24

13 The Games Institute has designed floral beds to commemorate various classic games.

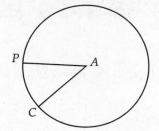

In circle A, the sector PAC is to be filled with blue flowers while the rest of the bed shown in the figure is to be yellow. If radius $PA = 8$ ft and $m\angle PAC = 30$, what is the measure of $\overarc{PC}$?

(1) $\dfrac{3}{4}\pi$

(3) $30°$

(2) $\dfrac{4}{3}\pi$

(4) $42°$

Part II

Answer all questions in this part. Each correct answer will receive 2 credits. Clearly indicate the necessary steps, including appropriate formula substitutions, diagrams, graphs, charts, etc. For all questions in this part, a correct numerical answer with no work shown will receive only 1 credit.

14 If $z_1 = 4 - 5i$ and $z_2 = 1 + 3i$, show the sum of $z_1 + z_2$ graphically.

15 In ten of the season's games, Jerry had the following point scores: 7, 10, 9, 14, 18, 21, 18, 10, 12, and 17. Find the mean to the *nearest tenth* and the sample standard deviation of his scores to the *nearest thousandth*.

16 Write the trigonometric equation of the sine function that has a midline of -3, an amplitude of 4.2, and a period of π.

17 Find the third term of the binomial expansion $(2a + 3b)^5$.

Part III

Answer all questions in this part. Each correct answer will receive 4 credits. Clearly indicate the necessary steps, including appropriate formula substitutions, diagrams, graphs, charts, etc. For all questions in this part, a correct numerical answer with no work shown will receive only 1 credit.

18 Solve for all values of θ to the *nearest tenth of a degree*: $3\tan^2 \theta - 2\tan \theta - 8 = 0$, over the interval $0° \le \theta < 360°$

19 Preston will win the All County Billiards Championship if he sinks the last ball. Analyzing the position of the balls, he is going to try a bank shot, as shown in the diagram.

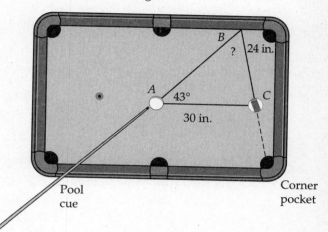

a To the *nearest degree*, at what angle must the cue ball (*A*) hit the side of the table to sink the last ball (*C*)?

b How far, to the *nearest tenth of an inch*, will the cue ball travel in its path from *A* to *B* to *C*?

Part IV

Answer this question. A correct answer will receive 6 credits. Clearly indicate the necessary steps, including appropriate formula substitutions, diagrams, graphs, charts, etc. A correct numerical answer with no work shown will receive only 1 credit.

20 The table gives the percentage of the U.S. population with 4 years of college or more between 1970 and 2007.

Year	Percent with Degrees
1970	10.7
1980	16.2
1985	19.4
1990	21.3
1997	23.9
2000	25.6
2003	27.2
2005	27.7
2007	28.7

a Find the line of best fit for these data with the number of degrees as a function of *t* with *t* = 0 representing 1970. (Round to the *nearest thousandth*.)

b If the trend continues as indicated in these data, what percent of the U.S. population will have college or postgraduate degrees in 2010? (Round to the *nearest hundredth*.)

c How many years after 1970 will 50 percent of the U.S. population have at least a college degree? Explain why you think this is a reasonable or unreasonable conclusion.

Algebra 2
and Trigonometry
Regents Examinations

Part I

Answer all 27 questions in this part. Each correct answer will receive 2 credits. No partial credit will be allowed. For each question, record your answer, using a No. 2 pencil, on the separate sheet provided to you. [54]

1. What is the common difference of the arithmetic sequence 5, 8, 11, 14?

   (1) $\dfrac{8}{5}$ (2) −3   (3) 3   (4) 9

2. What is the number of degrees in an angle whose radian measure is $\dfrac{11\pi}{12}$?

   (1) 150   (2) 165   (3) 330   (4) 518

3. If $a = 3$ and $b = -2$, what is the value of the expression $\dfrac{a^{-2}}{b^{-3}}$?

   (1) $-\dfrac{9}{8}$ (2) −1   (3) $-\dfrac{8}{9}$ (4) $\dfrac{8}{9}$

4. Four points on the graph of the function f(x) are shown below.

   $$\{(0, 1), (1, 2), (2, 4), (3, 8)\}$$

   Which equation represents f(x)?
   (1) $f(x) = 2^x$ (2) $f(x) = 2x$ (3) $f(x) = x + 1$ (4) $f(x) = \log_2 x$

5. The graph of $y = f(x)$ is shown below.

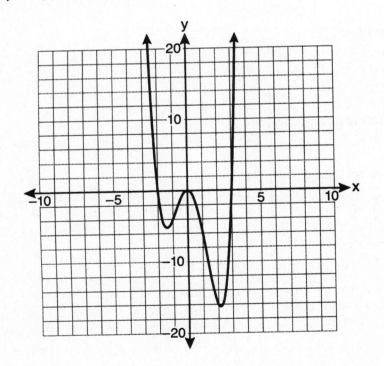

   Which set lists all the real solutions of f(x) = 0?
   (1) {−3, 2}   (2) {−2, 3}   (3) {−3, 0, 2}   (4) {−2, 0, 3}

6. In simplest form, $\sqrt{-300}$ is equivalent to

    (1) $3i\sqrt{10}$ (2) $5i\sqrt{12}$ (3) $10i\sqrt{3}$ (4) $12i\sqrt{5}$

7. Twenty different cameras will be assigned to several boxes. Three cameras will be randomly selected and assigned to box A. Which expression can be used to calculate the number of ways that three cameras can be assigned to box A?

    (1) $20!$ (2) $\dfrac{20!}{3!}$ (3) $_{20}C_3$ (4) $_{20}P_3$

8. Factored completely, the expression $12x^4 + 10x^3 - 12x^2$ is equivalent to
    (1) $x^2(4x + 6)(3x - 2)$ (3) $2x^2(2x - 3)(3x + 2)$
    (2) $2(2x^2 + 3x)(3x^2 - 2x)$ (4) $2x^2(2x + 3)(3x - 2)$

9. The solutions of the equation $y^2 - 3y = 9$ are

    (1) $\dfrac{3 \pm 3i\sqrt{3}}{2}$ (2) $\dfrac{3 \pm 3i\sqrt{5}}{2}$ (3) $\dfrac{-3 \pm 3i\sqrt{5}}{2}$ (4) $\dfrac{3 \pm 3\sqrt{5}}{2}$

10. The expression $2 \log x - (3 \log y + \log z)$ is equivalent to

    (1) $\log \dfrac{x^2}{y^3 z}$ (2) $\log \dfrac{x^2 z}{y^3}$ (3) $\log \dfrac{2x}{3yz}$ (4) $\log \dfrac{2xz}{3y}$

11. The expression $(x^2 - 1)^{-\frac{2}{3}}$ is equivalent to

    (1) $\sqrt[3]{(x^2 - 1)^2}$ (2) $\dfrac{1}{\sqrt[3]{(x^2 - 1)^2}}$ (3) $\sqrt{(x^2 - 1)^3}$ (4) $\dfrac{1}{\sqrt{(x^2 - 1)^3}}$

12. Which expression is equivalent to $\dfrac{\sqrt{3} + 5}{\sqrt{3} - 5}$?

    (1) $-\dfrac{14 + 5\sqrt{3}}{11}$ (2) $-\dfrac{17 + 5\sqrt{3}}{11}$ (3) $\dfrac{14 + 5\sqrt{3}}{14}$ (4) $\dfrac{17 + 5\sqrt{3}}{14}$

13. Which relation is *not* a function?
    (1) $(x - 2)^2 + y^2 = 4$ (2) $x^2 + 4x + y = 4$ (3) $x + y = 4$ (4) $xy = 4$

14. If $\angle A$ is acute and $\tan A = \dfrac{2}{3}$, then

    (1) $\cot A = \dfrac{2}{3}$ (2) $\cot A = \dfrac{1}{3}$ (3) $\cot(90° - A) = \dfrac{2}{3}$ (4) $\cot(90° - A) = \dfrac{1}{3}$

15. The solution set of $4^{x^2 + 4x} = 2^{-6}$ is
    (1) $\{1, 3\}$ (2) $\{-1, 3\}$ (3) $\{-1, -3\}$ (4) $\{1, -3\}$

16. The equation $x^2 + y^2 - 2x + 6y + 3 = 0$ is equivalent to
    (1) $(x - 1)^2 + (y + 3)^2 = -3$ (3) $(x + 1)^2 + (y + 3)^2 = 7$
    (2) $(x - 1)^2 + (y + 3)^2 = 7$ (4) $(x + 1)^2 + (y + 3)^2 = 10$

17. Which graph best represents the inequality $y + 6 \geq x^2 - x$?

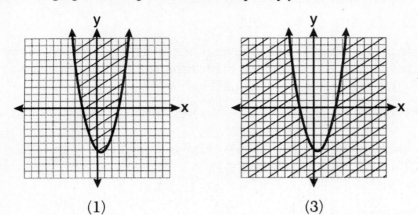

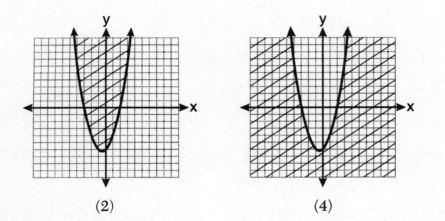

(1)   (3)

(2)   (4)

18. The solution set of the equation $\sqrt{x + 3} = 3 - x$ is
   (1) $\{1\}$ (2) $\{0\}$ (3) $\{1, 6\}$ (4) $\{2, 3\}$

19. The product of i^7 and i^5 is equivalent to
   (1) 1   (2) -1 (3) i (4) $-i$

20. Which equation is represented by the graph below?

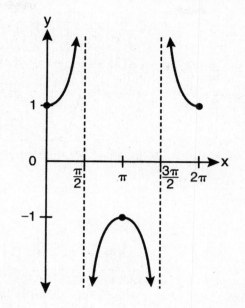

    (1) $y = \cot x$ (2) $y = \csc x$ (3) $y = \sec x$ (4) $y = \tan x$

21. Which value of r represents data with a strong negative linear correlation between two variables?
    (1) -1.07 (2) -0.89 (3) -0.14 (4) 0.92

22. The function $f(x) = \tan x$ is defined in such a way that $f^{-1}(x)$ is a function. What can be the domain of $f(x)$?

    (1) $\{x \mid 0 \le x \le \pi\}$ (3) $\left\{x \mid -\dfrac{\pi}{2} < x < \dfrac{\pi}{2}\right\}$

    (2) $\{x \mid 0 \le x \le 2\pi\}$ (4) $\left\{x \mid -\dfrac{\pi}{2} < x < \dfrac{3\pi}{2}\right\}$

23. In the diagram below of right triangle KTW, $KW = 6$, $KT = 5$, and $m\angle KTW = 90$.

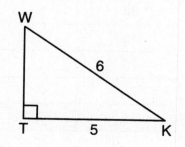

    What is the measure of $\angle K$, to the *nearest minute*?
    (1) $33°33'$ (2) $33°34'$ (3) $33°55'$ (4) $33°56'$

24. The expression $\cos^2\theta - \cos 2\theta$ is equivalent to
    (1) $\sin^2 \theta$ (2) $-\sin^2 \theta$ (3) $\cos^2 \theta + 1$ (4) $-\cos^2 \theta - 1$

25. Mrs. Hill asked her students to express the sum $1 + 3 + 5 + 7 + 9 + \ldots + 39$ using sigma notation. Four different student answers were given. Which student answer is correct?

(1) $\displaystyle\sum_{k=1}^{20} (2k - 1)$ (2) $\displaystyle\sum_{k=2}^{40} (k - 1)$ (3) $\displaystyle\sum_{k=-1}^{37} (k + 2)$ (4) $\displaystyle\sum_{k=1}^{39} (2k - 1)$

26. What is the formula for the nth term of the sequence 54, 18, 6, . . .?

(1) $a_n = 6\left(\dfrac{1}{3}\right)^n$ (2) $a_n = 6\left(\dfrac{1}{3}\right)^{n-1}$ (3) $a_n = 54\left(\dfrac{1}{3}\right)^n$ (4) $a_n = 54\left(\dfrac{1}{3}\right)^{n-1}$

27. What is the period of the function $y = \dfrac{1}{2} \sin\left(\dfrac{x}{3} - \pi\right)$?

(1) $\dfrac{1}{2}$ (2) $\dfrac{1}{3}$ (3) $\dfrac{2}{3}\pi$ (4) 6π

Part II

Answer all 8 questions in this part. Each correct answer will receive 2 credits. Clearly indicate the necessary steps, including appropriate formula substitutions, diagrams, graphs, charts, etc. For all questions in this part, a correct numerical answer with no work shown will receive only 1 credit. All answers should be written in pen, except for graphs and drawings, which should be done in pencil. [16]

28. Use the discriminant to determine all values of k that would result in the equation $x^2 - kx + 4 = 0$ having equal roots.

29. The scores of one class on the Unit 2 mathematics test are shown in the table below.

Unit 2 Mathematics Test

Test Score	Frequency
96	1
92	2
84	5
80	3
76	6
72	3
68	2

Find the population standard deviation of these scores, to the *nearest tenth*.

30. Find the sum and product of the roots of the equation $5x^2 + 11x - 3 = 0$.

31. The graph of the equation $y = \left(\dfrac{1}{2}\right)^x$ has an asymptote. On the grid below, sketch the graph of $y = \left(\dfrac{1}{2}\right)^x$ and write the equation of this asymptote.

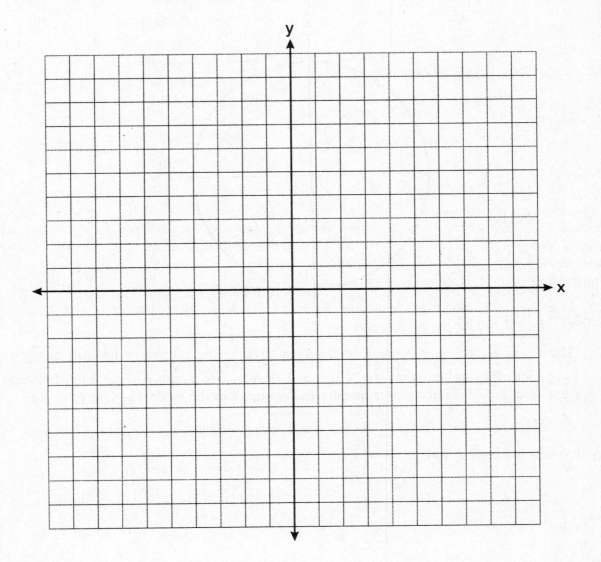

32. Express $5\sqrt{3x^3} - 2\sqrt{27x^3}$ in simplest radical form.

33. On the unit circle shown in the diagram below, sketch an angle, in standard position, whose degree measure is 240 and find the exact value of sin 240°.

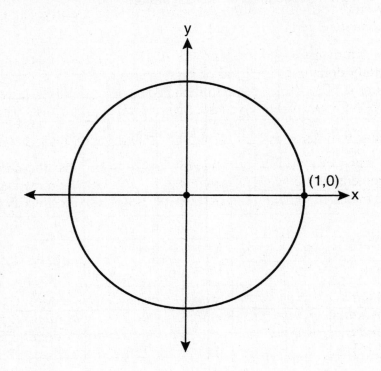

34. Two sides of a parallelogram are 24 feet and 30 feet. The measure of the angle between these sides is 57°. Find the area of the parallelogram, to the *nearest square foot*.

35. Express in simplest form: $\dfrac{\dfrac{1}{2} - \dfrac{4}{d}}{\dfrac{1}{d} + \dfrac{3}{2d}}$

Part III

Answer all 3 questions in this part. Each correct answer will receive 4 credits. Clearly indicate the necessary steps, including appropriate formula substitutions, diagrams, graphs, charts, etc. For all questions in this part, a correct numerical answer with no work shown will receive only 1 credit. All answers should be written in pen, except for graphs and drawings, which should be done in pencil. [12]

36. The members of a men's club have a choice of wearing black or red vests to their club meetings. A study done over a period of many years determined that the percentage of black vests worn is 60%. If there are 10 men at a club meeting on a given night, what is the probability, to the *nearest thousandth*, that *at least* 8 of the vests worn will be black?

37. Find all values of θ in the interval $0° \leq \theta < 360°$ that satisfy the equation $\sin 2\theta = \sin \theta$.

38. The letters of any word can be rearranged. Carol believes that the number of different 9-letter arrangements of the word "TENNESSEE" is greater than the number of different 7-letter arrangements of the word "VERMONT." Is she correct? Justify your answer.

Part IV

Answer the question in this part. A correct answer will receive 6 credits. Clearly indicate the necessary steps, including appropriate formula substitutions, diagrams, graphs, charts, etc. A correct numerical answer with no work shown will receive only 1 credit. The answer should be written in pen. [6]

39. In a triangle, two sides that measure 6 cm and 10 cm form an angle that measures 80°. Find, to the *nearest degree*, the measure of the smallest angle in the triangle.

Part I

Answer all 27 questions in this part. Each correct answer will receive 2 credits. No partial credit will be allowed. For each question, write on the separate answer sheet the numeral preceding the word or expression that best completes the statement or answers the question. [54]

1. The product of $(3 + \sqrt{5})$ and $(3 - \sqrt{5})$ is
   (1) $4 - 6\sqrt{5}$ (2) $14 - 6\sqrt{5}$ (3) 14 (4) 4

2. What is the radian measure of an angle whose measure is $-420°$?

   (1) $-\dfrac{7\pi}{3}$ (2) $-\dfrac{7\pi}{6}$ (3) $\dfrac{7\pi}{6}$ (4) $-\dfrac{7\pi}{3}$

3. What are the domain and the range of the function shown in the graph below?

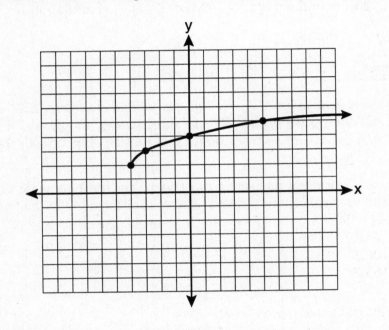

   (1) $\{x|x > -4\}$; $\{y|y > 2\}$ (3) $\{x|x > 2\}$; $\{y|y > -4\}$

   (2) $\{x|x \geq -4\}$; $\{y|y \geq 2\}$ (4) $\{x|x \geq 2\}$; $\{y|y \geq -4\}$

4. The expression $2i^2 + 3i^3$ is equivalent to
   (1) $-2 - 3i$ (2) $2 - 3i$ (3) $-2 + 3i$ (4) $2 + 3i$

5. In which graph is θ coterminal with an angle of −70°?

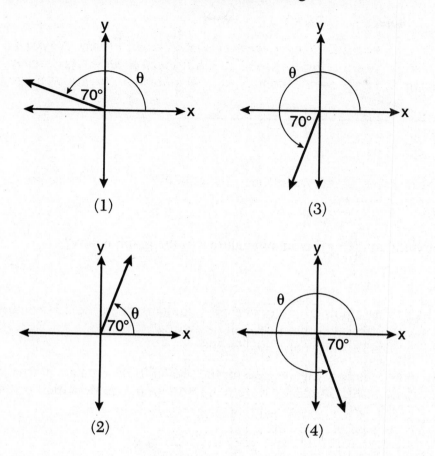

6. In $\triangle ABC$, m$\angle A = 74$, $a = 59.2$, and $c = 60.3$. What are the two possible values for m$\angle C$, to the *nearest tenth*?
(1) 73.7 and 106.3   (3) 78.3 and 101.7
(2) 73.7 and 163.7   (4) 78.3 and 168.3

7. What is the principal value of $\cos^{-1}\left(-\dfrac{\sqrt{3}}{2}\right)$?

(1) −30°   (2) 60°   (3) 150°   (4) 240°

8. What is the value of x in the equation $9^{3x+1} = 27^{x+2}$?

(1) 1   (2) $\dfrac{1}{3}$ (3) $\dfrac{1}{2}$ (4) $\dfrac{4}{3}$

9. The roots of the equation $2x^2 + 7x − 3 = 0$ are

(1) $-\dfrac{1}{2}$ and -3 (3) $\dfrac{-7 \pm \sqrt{73}}{4}$

(2) $\dfrac{1}{2}$ and 3 (4) $\dfrac{7 \pm \sqrt{73}}{4}$

10. Which ratio represents csc A in the diagram below?

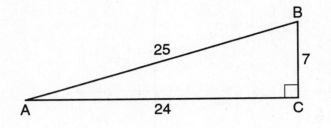

(1) $\frac{25}{24}$ (2) $\frac{25}{7}$ (3) $\frac{24}{7}$ (4) $\frac{7}{24}$

11. When simplified, the expression $\left(\dfrac{w^{-5}}{w^{-9}}\right)^{\frac{1}{2}}$ is equivalent to

(1) w^{-7} (2) w^2 (3) w^7 (4) w^{14}

12. The principal would like to assemble a committee of 8 students from the 15-member student council. How many different committees can be chosen?
(1) 120   (2) 6,435   (3) 32,432,400   (4) 259,459,200

13. An amateur bowler calculated his bowling average for the season. If the data are normally distributed, about how many of his 50 games were within one standard deviation of the mean?
(1) 14   (2) 17   (3) 34   (4) 48

14. What is a formula for the nth term of sequence B shown below?

$$B = 10, 12, 14, 16, \ldots$$

(1) $b_n = 8 + 2n$ (3) $b_n = 10(2)^n$

(2) $b_n = 10 + 2n$ (4) $b_n = 10(2)^{n-1}$

15. Which values of x are in the solution set of the following system of equations?

$$y = 3x - 6$$
$$y = x^2 - x - 6$$

(1) 0, −4   (2) 0, 4   (3) 6, −2   (4) −6, 2

16. The roots of the equation $9x^2 + 3x - 4 = 0$ are
(1) imaginary   (3) real, rational, and unequal
(2) real, rational, and equal   (4) real, irrational, and unequal

17. In $\triangle ABC$, $a = 3$, $b = 5$, and $c = 7$. What is m$\angle C$?
(1) 22   (2) 38   (3) 60   (4) 120

18. When $x^{-1} - 1$ is divided by $x - 1$, the quotient is

(1) −1   (2) $-\dfrac{1}{x}$ (3) $\dfrac{1}{x^2}$ (4) $\dfrac{1}{(x-1)^2}$

19. The fraction $\dfrac{3}{\sqrt{3a^2b}}$ is equivalent to

(1) $\dfrac{1}{a\sqrt{b}}$ (2) $\dfrac{\sqrt{b}}{ab}$ (3) $\dfrac{\sqrt{3b}}{ab}$ (4) $\dfrac{\sqrt{3}}{a}$

20. Which graph represents a one-to-one function?

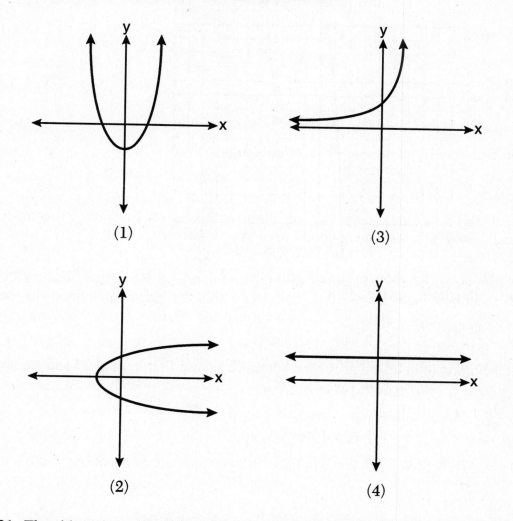

(1)

(3)

(2)

(4)

21. The sides of a parallelogram measure 10 cm and 18 cm. One angle of the parallelogram measures 46 degrees. What is the area of the parallelogram, to the *nearest square centimeter*?
   (1) 65   (2) 125   (3) 129   (4) 162

22. The minimum point on the graph of the equation $y = f(x)$ is $(-1, -3)$. What is the minimum point on the graph of the equation $y = f(x) + 5$?
   (1) $(-1, 2)$ (2) $(-1, -8)$ (3) $(4, -3)$ (4) $(-6, -3)$

23. The graph of $y = x^3 - 4x^2 + x + 6$ is shown below.

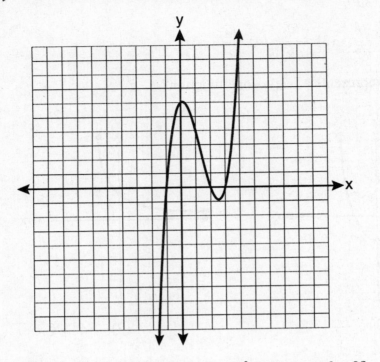

What is the product of the roots of the equation $x^3 - 4x + x + 6 = 0$?
(1) –36   (2) –6   (3) 6   (4) 4

24. What is the conjugate of $-2 + 3i$?
(1) $-3 + 2i$ (2) $-2 - 3i$ (3) $2 - 3i$ (4) $3 + 2i$

25. What is the common ratio of the geometric sequence whose first term is 27 and fourth term is 64?
(1) $\frac{3}{4}$ (2) $\frac{64}{81}$ (3) $\frac{4}{3}$ (4) $\frac{37}{3}$

26. Which graph represents one complete cycle of the equation $y = \sin 3\pi x$?

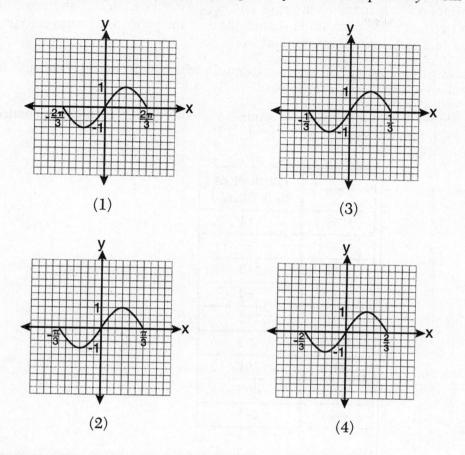

(1)

(3)

(2)

(4)

27. Which two functions are inverse functions of each other?
    (1) $f(x) = \sin x$ and $g(x) = \cos x$
    (2) $f(x) = 3 + 8x$ and $g(x) = 3 - 8x$
    (3) $f(x) = e^x$ and $g(x) = \ln x$
    (4) $f(x) = 2x - 4$ and $g(x) = -\frac{1}{2}x + 4$

Part II

Answer all 8 questions in this part. Each correct answer will receive 2 credits. Clearly indicate the necessary steps, including appropriate formula substitutions, diagrams, graphs, charts, etc. For all questions in this part, a correct numerical answer with no work shown will receive only 1 credit. All answers should be written in pen, except for graphs and drawings, which should be done in pencil. [16]

28. Factor completely: $10ax^2 - 23ax - 5a$

29. Express the sum $7 + 14 + 21 + 28 + \ldots + 105$ using sigma notation.

30. Howard collected fish eggs from a pond behind his house so he could determine whether sunlight had an effect on how many of the eggs hatched. After he collected the eggs, he divided them into two tanks. He put both tanks outside near the pond, and he covered one of the tanks with a box to block out all sunlight.

    State whether Howard's investigation was an example of a controlled experiment, an observation, or a survey. Justify your response.

31. The table below shows the number of new stores in a coffee shop chain that opened during the years 1986 through 1994.

Year	Number of New Stores
1986	14
1987	27
1988	48
1989	80
1990	110
1991	153
1992	261
1993	403
1994	681

    Using $x = 1$ to represent the year 1986 and y to represent the number of new stores, write the exponential regression equation for these data. Round all values to the *nearest thousandth*.

32. Solve the equation $2 \tan C - 3 = 3 \tan C - 4$ algebraically for all values of C in the interval $0° \le C < 360°$.

33. A circle shown in the diagram below has a center of (–5, 3) and passes through point (–1, 7).

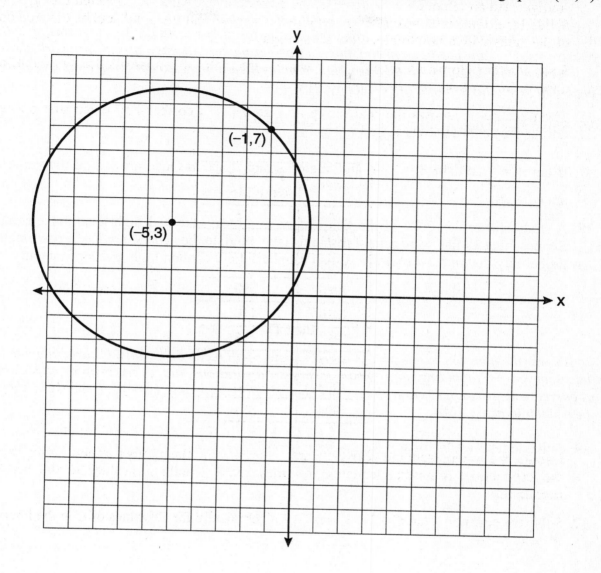

Write an equation that represents the circle.

34. Express $\left(\dfrac{2}{3}x - 1\right)^2$ as a trinomial.

35. Find the total number of different twelve-letter arrangements that can be formed using the letters in the word *PENNSYLVANIA*.

Part III

Answer all 3 questions in this part. Each correct answer will receive 4 credits. Clearly indicate the necessary steps, including appropriate formula substitutions, diagrams, graphs, charts, etc. For all questions in this part, a correct numerical answer with no work shown will receive only 1 credit. All answers should be written in pen, except for graphs and drawings, which should be done in pencil. [12]

36. Solve algebraically for x: $\dfrac{1}{x+3} - \dfrac{2}{3-x} = \dfrac{4}{x^2-9}$

37. If $\tan A = \dfrac{2}{3}$ and $\sin B = \dfrac{5}{\sqrt{41}}$ and angles A and B are in Quadrant I, find the value of $\tan(A+B)$.

38. A study shows that 35% of the fish caught in a local lake had high levels of mercury. Suppose that 10 fish were caught from this lake. Find, to the *nearest tenth of a percent*, the probability that *at least* 8 of the 10 fish caught did *not* contain high levels of mercury.

Part IV

Answer the question in this part. A correct answer will receive 6 credits. Clearly indicate the necessary steps, including appropriate formula substitutions, diagrams, graphs, charts, etc. A correct numerical answers with no work shown will receive only 1 credit. The answer should be written in pen. [6]

39. Solve algebraically for x: $\log_{x+3}\dfrac{x^3+x-2}{x} = 2$

Sources

Throughout *Preparing for the Regents Examination: Algebra 2 and Trigonometry*, we have tried to create problems using real-world data. The following list shows the sources of data for the problems indicated. Teachers and students can use these sources to create additional projects and practice problems.

Chapter/Section	Page(s)	Problem	Source
2.4	50	Text	http://www.laborlawcenter.com/federal-minimum-wage.asp?gclid=CPrT-N_H1I0CFRPdPgodJW9onQ
	52	MP 3	http://www.x-rates.com/calculator.html
	52	MP 4	http://www.infoplease.com/ipa/A0933563.htm; http://www.etymonline.com/index.php?term=percent
	53	23	http://www.northeastrehab.com/Articles/ramps.htm
	53	24	http://www.americanresearchgroup.com/
	53	25	http://www.fueleconomy.gov/feg/hybrid_sbs.shtml
	54	27	http://www.mcs.surrey.ac.uk/Personal/R.Knott/Fibonacci/fib.html; http://goldennumber.net/fibonser.htm
4.4	127	22	http://www.xe.com/ucc/convert.cgi
4.8	148		http://www.mta.info/mnr/index.html
	150	4	http://www.dietbites.com/CalorieIndexTreats.html
	152	16	http://www.eia.doe.gov/oil_gas/petroleum/data_publications/wrgp/mogas_home_page.html
	152	18	http://home.sc.rr.com/nurdosagecal/Dose%20by%20Weight.htm
6.1	218	21	http://www.geom.uiuc.edu/~demo5337/s97b/fibonacci.html
6.2, 6.3	218, 222	Text	http://www.playbill.com/reference/theatre_info/seating/2184.html
6.4	226	Text	http://en.wikipedia.org/wiki/Carl_Friedrich_Gauss#Early_years
6.5	229	Text	http://wiki.answers.com/Q/How_thick_is_one_sheet_of_paper http://mathworld.wolfram.com/Folding.html; http://en.wikipedia.org/wiki/Britney_Gallivan; http://mathforum.org/library/drmath/view/60675.html
	232	19	http://www.cadillac.com/cadillacjsp/model/landing.jsp?model=escalade&year=2008
7.5	269	MP 1	http://www.collegeboard.com/student/pay/add-it-up/4494.html
	275	16	http://www.presidency.ucsb.edu/ws/index.php?pid=29503; http://www.census.gov/main/www/popclock.html
Ch. 7, Review	278	31	*Newsday*, August 31, 1997
8.5	300	18	*The World Almanac and Book of Facts 2008*, p 597
	300	20	http://www.collegeboard.com/student/pay/add-it-up/4494.html
11.7	407	MP 1	www.nasa.gov/soho/
	409	9	http://205.156.206/er/bgm/cli/syrcli.htm
15.1	486	Text	http://factfinder.census.gov/jsp/saff/SAFFInfo.jsp?_pageId=sp4_decennial http://www.nielsenmedia.com/nc/portal/site/Public/menuitem.3437240b94 3437240b94cacebc3a81e810d8a062a0/?vgnextoid=130547f8b5264010Vgn VCM100000880a260aRCRD
15.2	491	MP 3	http://www.nytimes.com/2008/05/07/business/07oil.html http://www.newyorkgasprices.com/retail_price_chart.aspx
	492	MP 7	http://www.nba.com/history/players/jordan_stats.html
	496	9	http://www.pgatour.com/r/stats/info/?014
	497	11	http://www.indy500.com/images/stats/pdfs/fastest_race_lap_1951-present_.pdf
		13	http://www.census.gov/prod/2007pubs/08abstract/pop.pdf; *The New York Times 2008 Almanac*, page 283
		14	http://www.the-movie-times.com/thrsdir/alltime.mv?adjusted+ByAG

Chapter/Section	Page(s)	Problem	Source
15.3	503	12	http://www.weathercentral.com/weather/us/states/NY/index.html
		16	http://www.nba.com/knicks/roster
	504	17	http://usgovinfo.about.com/blctjustices.htm http://www.cbsnews.com/elements/2006/09/29/in_depth_us/frameset2053025.shtml
	505	20	http://www.nycmarathon.org/results/index.php
		21	http://ggweather.com/climate/extremes_us.htm
		22	http://www.netstate.com/states/geography/ny_geography.htm
		23	http://www.newyorkjets.com/team/roster
	506	24	http://www.newyorkjets.com/team/roster
		27	http://www.met.utah.edu/jhorel/html/wx/climate/normrain.html
15.4	507	Text	U.S. Census Bureau, *Statistical Abstract of the United States: 2000* (120th edition) Washington, DC, 2000, Table 230.
	509	MP 1	http://www.collegeboard.com/prod_downloads/highered/ra/sat/SAT_CR_mathematics_writing_percentile_ranks_gender_ethnic_groups.pdf
	510	MP 3	http://www.collegeboard.com/prod_downloads/highered/ra/sat/SAT_CR_mathematics_writing_percentile_ranks_gender_ethnic_groups.pdf
	511	11	http://virology-online.com/viruses/VZV.htm http://en.wikipedia.org/wiki/Lag_time http://dermatology.about.com/cs/infectionvirus/g/incubation.htm
	512	13	http://www.erh.noaa.gov/okx/climate/records/monthannualtemp.html
		14	*The New York Times 2008 Almanac*, p. 363
15.6	521	3	http://www.cdc.gov/nchs/births.htm
	522	4	http://www.internationaladoptionstories.com/adoption-statistics.htm
		7	*The New York Times 2008 Almanac*, p. 402
	523	6	http://www.census.gov/population/socdemo/education/cps2003/tab01a-04.pdf
		7	http://www.census.gov/population/www/socdemo/computer.html
15.7	526	Text	http://pubs.usgs.gov/gip/earthq4/severitygip.html
		1	http://pubs.usgs.gov/gip/earthq4/severitygip.html
		5	http://www.cdc.gov/nchs/births.htm
15.8	537	9	http://www.mapsofworld.com/olympic-trivia/number-of-participants.html
Ch. 15, Review	542	23	http://www.collegeboard.com/student/pay/add-it-up/4494.html; *The New York Times 2008Almanac*, p 364.
	543	25	Alexander Borbely, *Secrets of Sleep*, Perseus Books, 1988
	543	26	http://www.iki.rssi.ru/mirrors/stern/stargaze/Kep3laws.htm
	544	29	http://www.census.gov/compendia/statab/tables/08s0010.xls; www.census.gov/Press-Releases/www/releases/archives/facts_for_features_special_editions/004210
	545	30	*The New York Times 2008 Almanac*, p 417; http://www.nhtsa.dot.gov/CARS/rules/CAFE/overview.htm
Ch. 15, FYI	538	Text	http://www.erh.noaa.gov/okx/climate/records/monthannualtemp.html
Cumulative Review 1–11	615	20	http://coops.nos.noaa.gov/get_predictions.shtml?year=2004&stn=2812+Sandy+Hook&secstn=Hempstead+Bay,+Long+Beach&thh=%2b0&thm=18&tlh=%2b0&tlm=2&hh=*0.84&hl=*0.85

Index